The Official CompTIA IT Fundamentals+ Study Guide (Exam FC0-U61)

Acknowledgements

The Official CompTIA IT Fundamentals+ Study Guide (Exam FC0-U61)

PROJECT TEAM

Thomas Reilly, Vice President Learning

Katie Hoenicke, Director of Product Management

James Chesterfield, Manager, Learning Content and Design

Becky Mann, Senior Manager, Product Development

James Pengelly, Senior Manager, Product Development

Rob Winchester, Senior Manager, Technical Operations

Table of Contents

Course Introduction i

Table of Contents ... iii
About This Course ... viii

Module 1 / Using Computers 1

Module 1 / Unit 1
Common Computing Devices *3*

Information Technology ... 4
Personal Computers (PC) ... 6
Mobile Devices ... 10
Internet of Things (IoT) Devices ... 11

Module 1 / Unit 2
Using a Workstation *14*

Setting up a PC System ... 15
Ergonomic Concepts ... 17
Navigating an OS ... 18
Using Input Devices ... 26
Recognizing Desktop Icons ... 30
Working with Windows ... 31

Module 1 / Unit 3
Using an OS *39*

Functions of an Operating System ... 40
Types of Operating System ... 42
Virtualization ... 44
Microsoft Windows ... 46
Apple macOS and iOS ... 49
Linux, Chrome, and Android ... 51
File Explorer ... 53
Windows Settings and Control Panel ... 55
Using a Web Browser ... 58

Module 1 / Unit 4
Managing an OS *65*

Management Interfaces ... 66
Process and Service Management ... 67
Memory and Disk Management ... 70
Command Line Interfaces ... 73
Access Control and Protection ... 74

Module 1 / Unit 5
Troubleshooting and Support *85*

Support and Troubleshooting ... 86
Identifying the Problem ... 87
Understanding the Problem ... 89
Resolving and Documenting the Problem ... 91

Troubleshooting PC Issues 94
Getting Support 95
Using a Search Engine 98

Module 1 / Summary
Using Computers 105

Module 2 / Using Apps and Databases **107**

Module 2 / Unit 1
Using Data Types and Units 109

Notational Systems 110
Units of Measure 112
Data Types 114
Data Representation 115
The Value of Data 117
Intellectual Property 118
Data-driven Business Decisions 121

Module 2 / Unit 2
Using Apps 124

Installing Applications 125
Application Management 127
Managing Software Licensing 130
Productivity Software 132
Collaboration Software 134
Business Software 137

Module 2 / Unit 3
Programming and App Development 144

Programming Logic 145
Programming Languages 148
Programming Concepts 151
Object-Oriented Programming 155
Scripting Languages 156
Application Platforms and Delivery 158

Module 2 / Unit 4
Using Databases 178

Database Concepts 179
Database Structures 181
Relational Methods 185
Database Access Methods 187
Application Architecture Models 188

Module 2 / Summary
Using Apps and Databases 205

Module 3 / Using Computer Hardware **207**

Module 3 / Unit 1
System Components 209

Selecting a Computer 210
Motherboard Components 212
Processors 213
Features of Processors 214
System and Expansion Bus Technologies 216
System Cooling 218
BIOS and UEFI System Firmware 220

Module 3 / Unit 2
Using Device Interfaces 225

Computer Port and Connector Types 226
USB and Firewire 227
Graphics Devices 229
Graphic Device Interfaces 230
Input Devices 233
Configuring Peripherals 236
Bluetooth 239
RF and Near Field Communications (NFC) 241
Networking Interfaces 241

Module 3 / Unit 3
Using Peripheral Devices 249

Installing and Uninstalling Peripherals 250
Display Devices 254
Display Settings 257
Multimedia Ports and Devices 261
Printer Types 264
Installing and Configuring a Printer 265
Scanners and Cameras 268

Module 3 / Unit 4
Using Storage Devices 276

System Memory 277
Mass Storage Devices 279
Optical Discs and Drives 281
Removable Flash Memory Devices 284

Module 3 / Unit 5
Using File Systems 289

Managing the File System 290
Folders and Directories 293
File Explorer 295
Files 298
File Attributes and Permissions 304
Searching for Folders and Files 307
File Types and Extensions 310

Module 3 / Summary
Using Computer Hardware 325

Module 4 / Using Networks **327**

Module 4 / Unit 1
Networking Concepts 329

Network Components 330
TCP/IP 332
Internet Protocol 335
Packet Delivery and Forwarding 337
DNS and URLs 338
Internet Application Services 341

Module 4 / Unit 2
Connecting to a Network 346

Internet Service Types 347
Wireless Internet Services 349
Setting Up a Wireless Network 351
Configuring a Wireless Client 355
Connecting to an Enterprise Network 356

Module 4 / Unit 3
Secure Web Browsing 365

Safe Browsing Practices 366
Configuring Browser Security 368
Managing Cookies and PII 372
Digital Certificates and Anti-phishing 377
Enabling a Firewall 378

Module 4 / Unit 4
Using Shared Storage 386

Local Network Sharing and Storage 387
Windows File Sharing 389
Hosted Sharing and Storage 393
Backups 397
Windows Backup 400

Module 4 / Unit 5
Using Mobile Devices 410

Using a Mobile Device 411
Mobile Applications and App Stores 414
Network Connectivity 415
Email Configuration 417
Synchronization and Data Transfer 418

Module 4 / Summary
Using Networks 421

Module 5 / Security Concepts **423**

Module 5 / Unit 1
Security Concerns 425

Computer Security Basics 426
Social Engineering 429
Business Continuity 432
Disaster Recovery 435

Module 5 / Unit 2
Using Best Practices 437

Securing Devices 438
Malware 439
Preventing Malware Infections 443
Spam 448
Software Sources and Patch Management 452

Module 5 / Unit 3
Using Access Controls *461*

Access Controls 462
User Account Types 464
Authentication Factors 465
Uses of Encryption 470
Password Cracking and Management 473

Module 5 / Unit 4
Behavioral Security Concepts *477*

Policies and Procedures 478
Handling Confidential Information 479
Acceptable Use Policies 480
Expectations of Privacy 482

Module 5 / Summary
Managing Security *485*

Taking the Exam **487**

Career Advice **497**

Answers to Review Questions **507**

Glossary **531**

Index **555**

About This Course

CompTIA Information Technology Fundamentals+ (ITF+) Certification is the essential qualification for beginning a career in IT Support. CompTIA (comptia.org) is a not-for-profit trade association set up in 1982 to advance the interests of IT professionals and companies. It is most well-known for its vendor-neutral IT certifications.

> *The CompTIA IT Fundamentals+ exam will certify the successful candidate has the knowledge and skills required to identify and explain the basics of computing, IT infrastructure, software development and database use. In addition, candidates will demonstrate their knowledge to install software, establish basic network connectivity and identify/prevent basic security risks. Further, this exam will assess the candidate's knowledge in the areas of troubleshooting theory and preventative maintenance of devices. This exam is intended for candidates who are advanced end users, are considering a career in IT, and are interested in pursuing professional-level certifications, such as A+.*
>
> *CompTIA IT Fundamentals+ Exam Objectives Blueprint*

This course will prepare you to take the FC0-U61 exam to obtain the IT Fundamentals+ certification and help you to learn some of the basic principles and techniques of providing PC, mobile, applications, and network support.

Course Outcomes

This course and the IT Fundamentals+ certification are designed as the starting point for a career in IT support. Obtaining ITF+ certification will show that you have the aptitude to pursue a professional-level certification, such as CompTIA A+.

Completing this course will also help you acquire the knowledge and skills to set up and use a computer at home securely and keep it in good working order and to provide informal support for PCs and simple computer networks to your colleagues in a small business.

On course completion, you will be able to:

- Set up a computer workstation and use basic software applications.
- Explain the functions and types of devices used within a computer system.
- Apply basic computer maintenance and support principles.
- Describe some principles of software and database development.
- Configure computers and mobile devices to connect to home networks and to the Internet.
- Identify security issues affecting the use of computers and networks.

Target Audience and Course Prerequisites

CompTIA IT Fundamentals+ is aimed at those considering a career in IT and computer-related fields. Consequently, there are no special prerequisites to start this course. We have made the assumption that you don't know much about how computers or software work, or even how to use them. Some experience with using a keyboard and mouse will be helpful but is not essential.

About the Course Material

The CompTIA IT Fundamentals+ exam contains assessment items based on objectives and example content listed in the exam blueprint, published by CompTIA. The objectives are divided into six **domains**, as listed below:

CompTIA ITF+ Certification Domains	Weighting
1.0 IT Concepts and Terminology	17%
2.0 Infrastructure	22%
3.0 Applications and Software	18%
4.0 Software Development	12%
5.0 Database Fundamentals	11%
6.0 Security	20%

This course is divided into five **modules**, each covering a different subject area. Each module is organized into several **units**, containing related topics for study.

- Module 1 / Using Computers
- Module 2 / Using Apps and Databases
- Module 3 / Using Computer Hardware
- Module 4 / Using Networks
- Module 5 / Security Concepts

As you can see, the course modules do not map directly to the CompTIA exam domains. Instead, we try to present topics and technologies in the order that will make it easiest for you to understand them. Each module and each unit starts with a list of the CompTIA domain objectives and content examples that will be covered so that you can track what you are learning against the original CompTIA syllabus. Each unit in a module is focused on explaining the exam objectives and content examples. Each unit has a set of **review questions** designed to test your knowledge of the topics covered in the unit. Answers to the review questions are provided at the end of the book.

In addition, the back of the book contains an **index** to help you look up key terms and concepts from the course and a **glossary** of terms and concepts used.

The following symbols are used to indicate different features in the course book:

Icon	Meaning
	A tip or warning about a feature or topic.
	A reference to another unit or to a website where more information on a topic can be found.
	Review questions to help test what you have learned.
	A hands-on lab exercise for you to practice skills learned during the lesson.

Completing the Labs

The practical lab exercises in this book are designed to be completed on a typical home computer running Microsoft Windows 10 Spring Creators Update (1803).

You should note some conventions used in the lab instructions:

- Text in **bold** refers to a command or part of a dialog.
- Text in **`Bold, Courier font`** represents something you should type.
- Text in **`COURIER FONT CAPITALS`** represents a key or key combo. For example, **`CTRL+C`** means press the **`CTRL`** and **`C`** keys at the same time.

Finding a Job

The CompTIA IT Fundamentals+ certification is a great thing to have to prove to employers that you know the basics of Information Technology and support, but it is not a golden ticket into employment. To get a job, you need to know where to look, how to write an effective resume and application letter, how to prepare for an interview, and generally how to impress potential employers.

Knowing where to start when looking for a job can be daunting, so the last section of the course contains a guide to help you research the local job market, write a resume and application letter, and prepare for an interview.

There's also advice on the next steps you might take in your career in IT support.

Four Steps to Getting Certified

This training material can help you prepare for and pass a related CompTIA certification exam or exams. In order to achieve CompTIA certification, you must register for and pass a CompTIA certification exam or exams. In order to become CompTIA certified, you must:

1) Review the certification objectives at certification.comptia.org/certifications/it-fundamentals to make sure you know what is covered in the exam.

2) After you have studied for the certification, use the "Taking the Exam" chapter to find tips on booking the test, the format of the exam, and what to expect. You can also take a free assessment and sample test from CompTIA at certification.comptia.org/training/practice-questions to get an idea what type of questions might be on the exam.

3) Purchase an exam voucher on the CompTIA Marketplace, which is located at store.comptia.org.

4) Select a certification exam provider and schedule a time to take your exam. You can find exam providers at www.pearsonvue.com/comptia/.

Visit CompTIA online at comptia.org to learn more about getting CompTIA certified.

CompTIA Career Pathway

This course will particularly benefit you in pursuing a career in supporting desktop personal computer users, in job roles such as Support Engineer, Maintenance Engineer, Desktop Engineer, Computer Administrator, or PC Support Analyst.

CompTIA offers a number of credentials that form a foundation for your career in technology and allow you to pursue specific areas of concentration. Depending on the path you choose to take, CompTIA certifications help you build upon your skills and knowledge, supporting learning throughout your entire career.

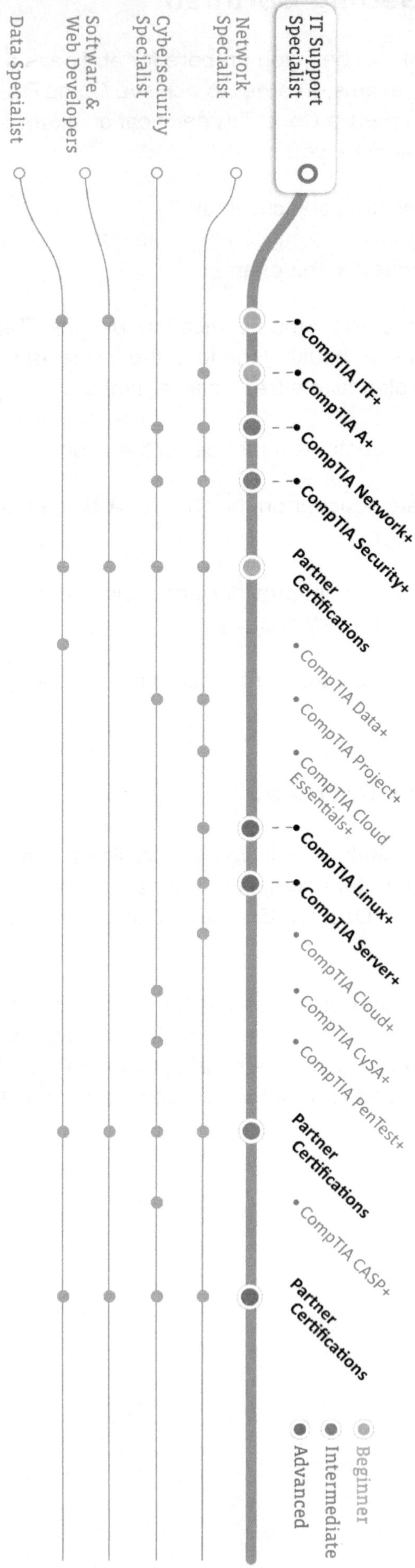

View the CompTIA career pathway at comptia.org/content/it-careers-path-roadmap/it-support-specialist.

Module 1 / Using Computers

The following CompTIA IT Fundamentals+ domain objectives and examples are covered in this module:

CompTIA ITF+ Certification Domains	Weighting
1.0 IT Concepts and Terminology	17%
2.0 Infrastructure	22%
3.0 Applications and Software	18%
4.0 Software Development	12%
5.0 Database Fundamentals	11%
6.0 Security	20%

Refer To	Domain Objectives/Examples
Unit 1.1 / Common Computing Devices	**1.3 Illustrate the basics of computing and processing.** *Input • Processing • Output • Storage*
	2.6 Compare and contrast common computing devices and their purposes. *Mobile phones • Tablets • Laptops • Workstations • Servers • Gaming consoles • IoT (Home appliances, Home automation devices, Thermostats, Security systems, Modern cars, IP cameras, Streaming media devices, Medical devices)*
Unit 1.2 / Using a Workstation	**This unit does not cover specific exam domain objectives or content examples.**
Unit 1.3 / Using an OS	**3.1 Explain the purpose of operating systems.** *Interface between applications and hardware • Types of OS (Mobile device OS, Workstation OS, Server OS, Embedded OS, Firmware, Hypervisor [Type 1])*
Unit 1.4 / Managing an OS	**3.1 Manage applications and software.** *Disk management • Process management/scheduling (Kill process/end task) • Memory management • Access control/protection*
	3.2 Compare and contrast components of an operating system. *Services • Processes • Utilities (Task scheduling) • Interfaces (Console/command line, GUI)*

Refer To	Domain Objectives/Examples
Unit 1.5 / Troubleshooting and Support	**1.6 Explain the troubleshooting methodology.** *Identify the problem (Gather information, Duplicate the problem, if possible, Question users, Identify symptoms, Determine if anything has changed, Approach multiple problems individually) • Research knowledge base/Internet, if applicable • Establish a theory of probable cause (Question the obvious, Consider multiple approaches, Divide and conquer) • Test the theory to determine the cause (Once the theory is confirmed [confirmed root cause], determine the next steps to resolve the problem, If the theory is not confirmed, establish a new theory or escalate) • Establish a plan of action to resolve the problem and identify potential effects • Implement the solution or escalate as necessary • Verify full system functionality and, if applicable, implement preventive measures • Document findings/lessons learned, actions and outcomes*

Module 1 / Unit 1
Common Computing Devices

Objectives

On completion of this unit, you will be able to:

- Describe the basics of how a computer processes data.
- Describe the functions and capabilities of types of computing devices, such as PCs, servers, mobiles, and home automation.

Syllabus Objectives and Content Examples

This unit covers the following exam domain objectives and content examples:

- 1.3 Illustrate the basics of computing and processing.
  Input • Processing • Output • Storage
- 2.6 Compare and contrast common computing devices and their purposes.
  Mobile phones • Tablets • Laptops • Workstations • Servers • Gaming consoles • IoT (Home appliances, Home automation devices, Thermostats, Security systems, Modern cars, IP cameras, Streaming media devices, Medical devices)

Information Technology

An **Information Technology (IT)** system is one that processes, stores, and transfers information. *Information* can take many different forms including words, numbers, pictures, sound, or video. These can all be represented in an IT system using nothing more complicated than the binary digits one and zero. When information is stored and processed like this, it is often referred to as **data**. An IT system could use computers, the telecommunications network, and other programmable electronic devices. In fact, because of the importance of communications in IT, the term ICT (Information and Communications Technology) is often used in preference to IT.

We live in an "Information Age." The effective use of information is regarded as the defining element of the 21st century, as important as the industrial revolution before it. Computers and software programs enable us to process data and perform certain tasks much more quickly than we could ourselves. IT systems are very flexible and can be made to perform a variety of different tasks. IT networks, such as the global Internet, allow us to distribute and share information quickly.

Computer Hardware and Software

A **computer** is a system that manipulates data according to a set of instructions. Three elements are required for a computer to perform useful tasks: **hardware**, **software**, and the computer's **user**.

- The devices and components that make up a computer system are called hardware. Many parts are contained within the computer's case. Other parts are connected to the computer and are referred to as **peripheral devices**. Most peripherals allow information to be entered (input) and retrieved (output).
- The instructions that a computer follows come from software (computer programs). A basic software environment is established by the computer's **Operating System (OS)**. Software **applications**, such as word processors, spreadsheet programs, and payroll programs, can be installed within the OS to extend the range of things that the computer can be used to do. Having different software applications means that the same hardware can be put to a variety of uses.
- Software provides an **interface** for the user to control the computer system. The user creates data files by inputting information and selecting commands from the interface.

Basics of Computing and Processing

A good way to understand the functions of the different components of the PC is to think of them working as *interfaces*. Input and output hardware devices, such as a mouse and a monitor, provide an interface between the user and the computer; the operating system provides an interface between hardware components and software applications. In general terms, this works as follows:

- When a user selects a **command** (perhaps using a mouse to click an icon on the application toolbar), the **software application** receives the command and, using the functions of the **operating system**, converts it into a series of **instructions**, which are stored in **system memory**, commonly referred to as **Random Access Memory (RAM)**. Similarly, when a user types using the keyboard or scans a picture, the input is converted to digital data and stored in memory.

- The **Central Processing Unit (CPU)** retrieves each instruction or data file from memory and processes it.

- The CPU then writes the result back to memory and directs other components to perform actions. For example, it may instruct the display subsystem to update the image shown to the user or the storage subsystem to save data to a disk.

We'll discuss the types and features of system components such as the CPU and RAM in detail in Unit 3.1.

All the instructions and data processed by a computer are ultimately represented as strings of 1s and 0s. These 1s and 0s are represented as on or off states in the **transistors** that make up CPU and RAM components. A CPU can process billions of these **binary** instructions per second, which gives it the illusion of being able to "think."

Input, Output, Processing, and Storage

The four functions listed above represent most of the ways that data moves through a computer system:

- **Input**—the computer receives data entered by the user through peripheral devices, such as mice, keyboards, scanners, cameras, and microphones.

- **Processing**—the data is written to memory and manipulated by the CPU, acting on instructions from the operating system and applications software.

- **Output**—the processed data is shown or played to the user through an output device, such as a monitor or loudspeaker system.

- **Storage**—the data may be written to different types of storage devices, such as hard disks or optical discs, because data stored in most types of system memory is only preserved while the computer is powered on.

Additionally, most computers are configured in **networks**, allowing them to exchange data. You can think of networking as a special class of input and output, but it is probably more helpful to conceive of it as a separate function.

Personal Computers (PC)

There are many different types of computer. Some of the first types of **mainframe** computers created in the 1960s and 1970s are unrecognizable from the sorts of desktop and laptop computers you may be familiar with. The term "Personal Computer" is generally understood to apply to versions of the **IBM PC**, developed in 1981. The IBM PC was based on a microprocessor or Central Processing Unit (CPU) designed by **Intel**. This is also called the x86 architecture or platform. This type of computer was fundamentally different to mainframes as it was operated directly by the end user.

While technologies and performance have completely transformed what we know as PCs from the boxes available in 1981, most **workstation** and **laptop** personal computers designed for home and office use are still based on the IBM PC design and x86 platform. As this PC platform matured, it came to be associated with use of Microsoft's Windows operating system software. Hardware and software development for PCs is often (but not exclusively) undertaken with Windows compatibility in mind.

In the last couple of decades however, personal computers have become available as much smaller, more portable devices such as **tablets** and **smartphones**. These devices can use different hardware platforms and operating systems. This has been coupled with the growth of the **Internet** as a global data communications network. As the miniaturization of electronics continues, many "ordinary" appliances and systems are being designed with processing and communications capabilities, creating an **Internet of Things (IoT)**.

Desktop and Workstation Computers

A **workstation** type of PC is housed in a case that can sit on or under a desk. Consequently, they are often referred to as **desktop** PCs or just as **desktops**. A desktop computer can be used independently by a single user to run powerful software applications with many functions. It can also be used as a **network client** to access shared resources.

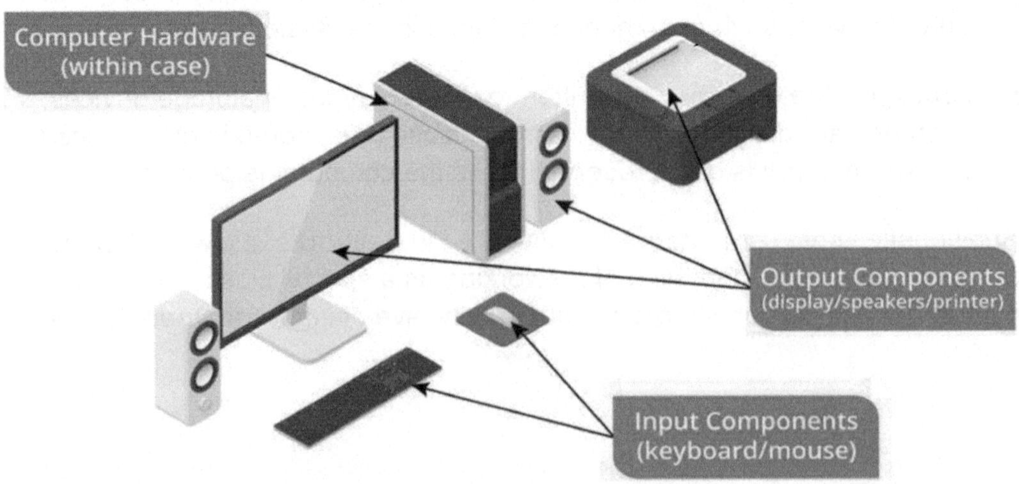

PC system showing processing and storage components (within case), input components (keyboard and mouse), and output components (display, speakers, printer). Image © 123rf.com.

Sometimes the terms PC, desktop computer, and workstation are used interchangeably. Quite often however, the term workstation is used to mean a particularly powerful type of desktop computer.

Some of a PC's components are attached to a **motherboard** contained within the computer's case. However, a desktop PC also requires the use of **peripheral devices**, connected to the motherboard via ports aligned to holes in the case. Some peripheral devices, such as a mouse and keyboard for input and a monitor for output, are essential. Others, such as speakers and microphone or a printer, are optional.

The advantage of desktops is that the basic design can be modified with higher or lower specified components and optional features, making a particular model better suited to different tasks. A workstation-class computer with higher specification components, such as CPU and system memory, will cost more but be able to process data faster. The computer's performance is largely determined by the following factors:

- The **speed** of the CPU determines the basic speed of the computer.
- More **system memory** makes it possible to run more applications simultaneously and process large amounts of data more quickly.
- The **capacity** of the main storage drive determines how much data can be stored on the computer when it is switched off.
- Optional components extend the range of things the computer can do (for example, a sound card makes it possible to play audio while a webcam allows sound and video recording).
- The quality of peripherals such as the display, mouse, and keyboard make the computer more comfortable to use (this is referred to as **ergonomics**).

We are simplifying a bit here. In fact, the type and speed of the main storage drive also has a big impact on system speed. Legacy hard drives were a serious performance bottleneck, but these are being replaced by solid state drives, which can work much more quickly. Storage devices are discussed in more detail in Unit 3.4. The graphics subsystem is also an important performance factor.

Desktop PCs can also be purchased as "all-in-one" units. All-in-one means that the computer components (except the keyboard and mouse) are contained within the monitor case.

All-in-One PC—the system components are all contained within the monitor case. Image © 123rf.com.

Servers

A **server** is any computer providing services to other computers, but usually the term server implies a powerful computer that supports a number of users *simultaneously* in a computer **network**. Most servers use the same type of components as a desktop. The main difference is that the components are more powerful and more reliable, and consequently more expensive. If a desktop PC stops working, a single user may be unable to do their job; if a server computer stops working, *tens* or even *hundreds* of users may not be able to do their jobs. Consequently, servers need to be very reliable. This is achieved by specifying high quality components and also by using extra copies of components for redundancy. This makes a server system **fault tolerant**.

Server systems are also, usually designed to be easy to expand and upgrade with additional or improved components. Very often, server computers use a special type of case designed to fit into a steel **rack** shelving system.

You should also understand that the term server can refer either to hardware or software. A hardware server may be running many software servers and sometimes different types of software servers. Examples of types of software servers include web servers, email servers, database servers, authentication servers, and so on.

Laptops

A **laptop** computer is one that integrates the display, system components, and input/output devices within a single, portable case (or chassis).

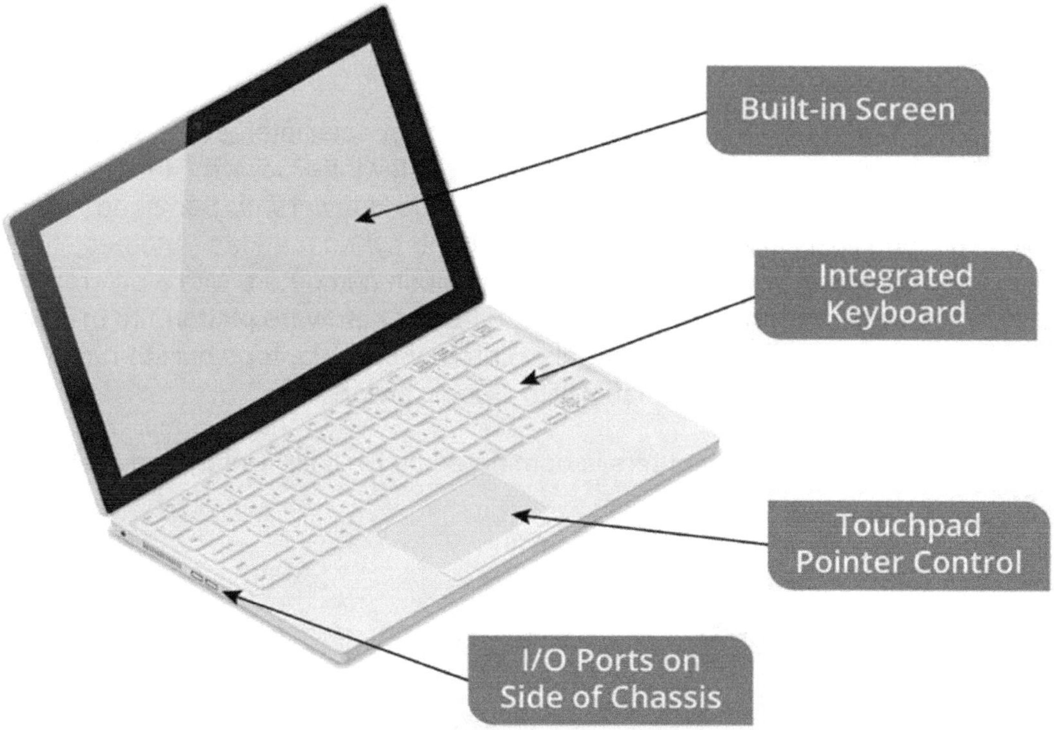

Distinctive features of a laptop computer, including the built-in screen, Integrated keyboard, touchpad pointer control, and I/O ports (on both sides and rear of chassis). Image © 123rf.com.

The main features distinguishing laptops from desktop PCs are:

- **Size and weight**—laptops weigh between 1 and 4 kg (2–9 lbs).
- **Display type**—laptops use flat-panel display technologies to provide lightweight, slimline screens that are built into the case. Laptop screen sizes come in the ranges 11–14", 15–16", and 17"+.
- **Input devices**—the main input devices are integrated into the case, such as a built-in keyboard, a touchpad instead of mouse, and/or a touchscreen.
- **Power source**—portable computers can be run from internal battery packs as well as from building power.
- **Components**—laptops often use different system components (CPU, RAM, and graphics) that are smaller, lighter, and draw less power than desktop versions.
- **Networking**—portable computers use wireless radio technologies to connect to networks rather than cabled connections.

Small laptops can also be described as notebooks and subnotebooks, while bigger models are often called "desktop replacements." The term Ultrabook is used for laptops meeting a particular Intel specification for performance, size/weight, and battery life. There are also hybrid laptops that can be used like a tablet (see below) as well as like a traditional laptop.

PC and Laptop Vendors

Most companies producing PCs and laptops are referred to as **Original Equipment Manufacturers (OEM)**. This is because rather than making each component that goes into a PC, they source components such as CPUs and RAM modules from manufacturers and put them together as a branded PC system.

While there are many vendors serving local and special interest markets, global PC manufacturing is dominated by Dell, Hewlett-Packard (HP)/Compaq, Lenovo (previously IBM's PC division), Acer, and Huawei with Samsung, Sony, Toshiba, and Asus also strong in the laptop and hybrid markets. Another personal computer vendor, Apple, ship Macintosh computers with a different operating system (Apple Mac OS) and a different hardware platform to the IBM PC-compatible vendors. There are also chromebooks, laptops built to run Chrome OS and interface primarily with Google's web apps.

The market for server computers is dominated by Dell, HP Enterprise (HPE), and Lenovo.

Mobile Devices

Many of the uses of PCs and laptops have been superseded by smaller personal devices or by specialized devices.

Smartphones and Tablets

A **smartphone** is a device with roughly the same functionality as a personal computer that can be held in one hand. Previous handheld computers, known as Personal Digital Assistants (PDA), and earlier types of mobile phones with some software functionality (feature phones), were hampered by clumsy user interfaces. Modern smartphones use touchscreen displays, making them much easier to operate. Most smartphones have a screen size between 4.5" and 5.7".

Typical smartphone form factor. Image © 123rf.com.

Prior to the Apple iPad, **tablet** PCs were usually laptops with touchscreens. The iPad defined a new form factor; smaller than a laptop and with no keyboard. Tablet screens tend to be sized between 7" and 10".

Smartphones sized between the 5" and 7" form factors are often called phablets.

Many Windows mobile devices adopt a hybrid approach where a laptop can be converted into a tablet by flipping the screen. Microsoft's Surface Pro tablet is available with a detachable keyboard, which can also function as a cover for the screen. Other vendors are also producing "two-in-one" devices that can function as both a laptop and a tablet.

The main smartphone and tablet vendors are Apple and Samsung. Other vendors include LG, HTC, Huawei, Motorola/Lenovo, Microsoft, Nokia, Sony, and Amazon.

Internet of Things (IoT) Devices

Aside from devices easily recognizable as "computers," your home and office are quite likely populated by other consumer electronics devices connected to each other and to the Internet. The **Internet of Things (IoT)** refers to a world in which many different types of things are embedded with processing and networking functionality. Processing and networking functionality can be provisioned by very small chips, so the "things" can range from motor vehicles and washing machines to clothing and birthday cards.

Home Automation

Pretty much anything from a clock to an alarm system or a refrigerator can be controlled over the Internet by **home automation** software, if the appliance or device is "smart." Often, sitting at the heart of this automation, is a **hub** to which other devices connect. Hubs are usually controlled using voice recognition systems and smartphone apps. Some of the major vendors include Amazon (Alexa voice recognition), Samsung (S Voice), Apple (Siri), and Logitech (working with either Alexa or Google Assistant), but there are many others.

One of the critical points in building a "smart" or "digital" home or office solution is ensuring compatibility between the networking or communications standards supported by the hub and the appliances. Most devices support ordinary Wi-Fi standards-based wireless networking, but some may require connectivity standards designed for low power use, such as Z-Wave, ZigBee, or Bluetooth LE.

Some of the specific home automation product categories include:

- **Thermostats**—monitor and adjust your home or office Heating, Ventilation, and Air Conditioning (HVAC) controls from an app installed on your phone.
- **Security systems**—monitor and control alarms, locks, lighting, and videophone entry systems remotely.
- **IP cameras**—often used for security, these devices connect to Internet Protocol (IP)-based networks such as the Internet and support direct upload and sync to cloud storage for remote monitoring.

- **Home appliances**—check the contents of your refrigerator from your smartphone while out shopping or start the washing machine cycle so that it has finished just as you get back to your house.
- **Streaming media**—play content stored on a storage device through any smart speaker or TV connected to the home network.

Modern Cars and Drones

Modern motor vehicles use a substantial amount of electronics. As well as computer systems to control the vehicle's engine and brakes, there may be embedded systems for in-vehicle entertainment and for navigation (sat-nav) using Global Positioning Systems (GPS) to identify the vehicle's precise location. Some vehicles are now, also fitted with a "black box," or event data recorder, that can log the car's telemetry (acceleration, braking, and position).

There are also sophisticated systems to control the vehicle on behalf of the driver, including automatic collision detection and avoidance, and parking assist. Companies are experimenting with fully-automated self-driving or autonomous vehicles.

Another rapidly developing sector is that of **Unmanned Aerial Vehicles (UAV)**. This sector ranges from full-size fixed wing aircraft to much smaller multi-rotor hover drones.

Medical Devices

Medical devices represent another class of devices where use of electronics to remotely monitor and configure the appliance is expanding rapidly. It is important to recognize that use of these devices is not confined to hospitals and clinics but includes portable devices such as cardiac monitors/defibrillators and insulin pumps. These allow doctors and nurses to remotely monitor a patient and potentially to adjust dosage levels or other settings without the patient having to visit the care provider.

Gaming Consoles

A **gaming console** contains many of the same components as a workstation. Gaming consoles have powerful CPUs and graphics processors, plus Ethernet and Wi-Fi for wired and wireless home networking and Internet connectivity. Web cameras and microphones are also available as peripherals. The main difference to a workstation is that a console is designed to be operated by a gaming pad rather than a keyboard and mouse, though these are often also available as options. A gaming console would use an HD (High Definition) TV for a display.

The market for consoles is dominated by Sony (PlayStation), Microsoft (Xbox), and Nintendo (Wii and Switch).

There are also handheld game consoles, such as Nintendo's 3DS and Switch, and Sony's Vita. These come with Wi-Fi to connect to the Internet or to other consoles.

Review Questions / Module 1 / Unit 1 / Common Computing Devices

Answer these questions to test what you have learned in this unit. You can review the model answers at the end of the book.

1) True or false? All types of computers use CPU and system memory.
2) What type of computer is most likely to need peripheral devices?
3) What type of computer is best suited for using in a job where you have to make notes and be able to move around easily?
4) Why don't laptops make good servers?
5) Why isn't a smartphone a good tool for writing a report?
6) What type(s) of IoT appliance are less likely to be controlled via a home automation hub?

Module 1 / Unit 2

Using a Workstation

Objectives

On completion of this unit, you will be able to:

- Set up a computer system with regard for safety and healthy working practices.
- Navigate an OS and use input devices effectively.

Syllabus Objectives and Content Examples

This unit does not cover specific exam domain objectives or content examples.

Setting up a PC System

When you install a computer system, you need to consider the following:

- Is the environment suitable for the computer? Dust, dirt, heat (or extreme cold), and dampness can be very damaging to computers.
- Is the installation safe for yourself and passers-by? The main risks associated with computer equipment are electrical and trip hazards.
- Is the installation healthy to use? Improper use of computers, notably the mouse and keyboard, is associated with a number of health risks.

Setting up a Personal Computer

Given the above, you should perform the following basic steps when setting up a computer.

1) If the computer has just been delivered, check the contents of the box, read the instruction manual, and allow at least 30–60 minutes for the components to adjust to room temperature. There is a slight risk from condensation if you unpack a computer and start it immediately.
2) Read the manufacturer's setup and safety guidelines and plan the installation of the computer to comply with them.
3) Position the monitor and system unit so that cables can be tucked away neatly and do not cross any walkways. When lifting a heavy object such as a monitor, take care to protect your back. Ensure that any object placed on a desk is not at risk of toppling.
4) Ensure there is adequate air flow around the monitor, system unit, and larger peripherals, such as a printer or scanner.
5) Check that the screen is not exposed to excessive glare from windows or lighting and that equipment is not in direct sunlight.
6) Adjust the monitor, chair, and position of the mouse and keyboard so that the user can sit and type comfortably.
7) Connect each peripheral to the computer using an appropriate cable. Inspect each cable and connector for any sign of visible damage before plugging it in. Use any available cable management features to keep wiring tidy and ensure it does not pose a trip hazard.

Built-in cable management such as on this flat-panel monitor make it less likely trailing wires will cause an accident.

You will learn how to identify ports and connectors in Unit 3.2.

8) Connect the power cables from the monitor, system unit, and any peripherals to electrical outlets, again checking that the cables are undamaged and the plugs are fitted with fuses of the correct rating. Ensure that the electrical outlets are not overloaded.

9) Switch on any peripherals connected to the computer that you want to use then switch on the system unit.

You start a computer by pressing the power switch, which will be marked by the following symbol: ⏻. If the computer does not start, check that a power cable connects the back of the computer to a wall socket and that the socket is switched on.

Setting up a Laptop

You should follow the same basic principles when using a laptop for the first time. Read the instruction manual and let the system acclimatize if it has just been delivered. You will probably have to insert the battery pack, which should clip into a slot on the underside of the laptop. When you use the laptop for the first time, you will probably have to connect it to the building power supply using the supplied AC adapter to charge the battery.

Obviously, you can use a laptop without connecting any peripherals, unlike a desktop computer, but there may be some optional components to plug in. When you have set up the laptop as explained in the documentation, use the catch on the lid to open it. Press the power switch or key with the symbol ⏻ and wait for the laptop to start.

Ergonomic Concepts

Ergonomics is the study of factors affecting the performance of people at work. It is well established that a poor working environment can cause certain health problems and decrease productivity.

Proper Keyboard and Mouse Placement

Repetitive Strain Injury (RSI) is a condition that occurs when the same task is carried out repeatedly for a long period, making use of the same muscles continuously. Symptoms can include muscle pain, numbness, tingling, prickly heat, and loss of strength.

RSI has been linked with the use of keyboards and mice. When you use a mouse, keep your wrist straight and rest your palm on the body of the mouse. When using a keyboard, keep your forearms parallel with the keyboard. It will help if you learn to touch-type. With both devices, avoid working with your wrists bent, do not hunch your shoulders or bend forward, and take frequent breaks, to stretch or walk around for instance.

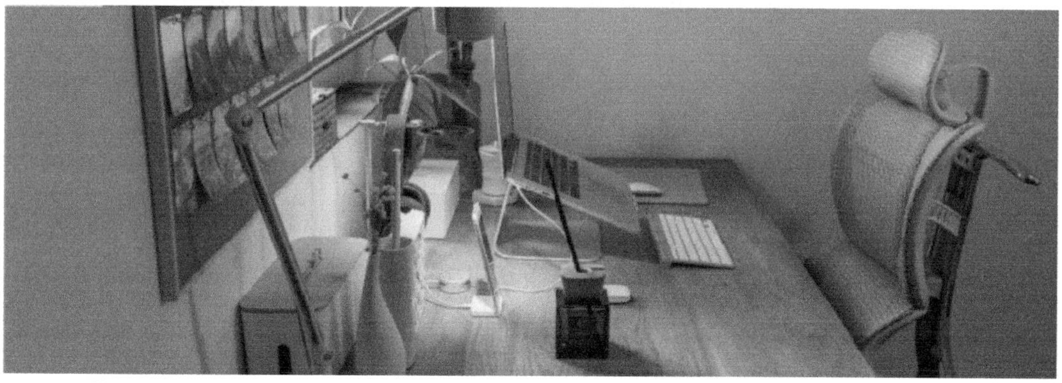

Ergonomically-designed work area. Photo by Glenn Carstens-Peters on Unsplash.

Ergonomically designed, angled keyboards and molded mice are designed to reduce the risk of strain injury. Using a mouse mat makes the action of the mouse smoother and is therefore less straining.

Sitting Position and Monitor Placement

Sitting at a desk in a poor position can cause back pain. This is especially true if you sit for a long period without getting up and stretching. To help prevent back pain, monitors should be adjustable so that they can be positioned at the correct height and chairs should provide support for the back and neck.

You should be able to sit up straight with the top of the monitor at or slightly below eye level. You should be able to rest your feet flat on the floor comfortably and your thighs should be parallel with the floor. You should be able to hold your forearms level with the desk.

As you work, try to avoid hunching your shoulders forward and remember to take frequent breaks to stretch your arms and legs.

Position the monitor so that you can sit up straight. Photo by Samule Sun on Unsplash.

If you need to type a lot of text from a source document, use a copyholder to position the source text at eye-level rather than flat on the desk.

For more detailed advice, read HP's Safety & Comfort Guide at hp.com/ergo.

Navigating an OS

The main function of an operating system such as Microsoft Windows is to provide a stable environment for different software applications to work together. The operating system controls access to the computer hardware; applications software can only access the computer hardware via functions of the OS. An OS provides tools for configuring the hardware, such as the Settings app in Windows. The OS also provides file management tools and can include a number of utilities. For example, Windows includes a text editor (Notepad), picture editor (Paint), a word processor (WordPad), a calculator, some games, and so on.

CompTIA IT Fundamentals+ is a vendor-neutral exam, so you will not be asked detailed questions on how Windows works. The practical elements in this course are to help you learn to use an operating system and use Microsoft Windows 10 as an example. If you use a different version of Windows at home (or even a different operating system), you should find that many of the skills you learn are transferable, with a bit of effort.

One of the first set of tasks to master is to be able to sign in to Windows, start applications, and use the features of the desktop.

Signing in to Windows

Some text or a logo may be displayed on-screen while the computer starts up ("boots"). The computer performs a **Power-On Self-Test (POST)** to check that the main components work and then loads Windows. After a minute or so, a screen prompting you to **sign in** to the computer is displayed.

A sign in means that changes you make to the desktop are saved as your own personal settings. It may also give you access to resources on a computer network. At work, you will be given a **sign in ID** (a **user name** and **password**) by your IT Department. At home you will create user accounts for yourself and your family. Signing in using a password that only you know means that you are **authenticated** as the valid owner of the computer account.

See Unit 1.3 for more details on creating accounts.

1) When Windows 10 has loaded, the **Lock Screen** is displayed. Press a key, click the mouse, or (if you have a touchscreen) swipe to open the sign in prompt.

Windows 10 lock screen—press a key or click with the mouse to start sign in. Screenshot used with permission from Microsoft.

On an enterprise network or earlier version of Windows, you may need to press **CTRL+ALT+DEL** *to access the sign in prompt.*

2) The sign in prompt displays the last user account that accessed the machine. If necessary, click the icon representing your account on the left of the display.

Windows sign in screen. Enter a password or click the appropriate user icon to sign in with a different account. Each account is represented by its own name and, optionally, a picture. Screenshot used with permission from Microsoft.

3) With your user name shown, type your password into the box.

   What you type will be shown as black dots so that no one else can see your password. Note that the password is *case-sensitive.*

4) Point to the arrow button then click once (or press **`ENTER`**).

   Windows will start and, after a few seconds, the **desktop** is shown.

Windows 10 uses a feature called Windows Hello to provide support for sign in by using a PIN or by using biometrics, such as fingerprint scanning or facial recognition. You can configure Windows Hello in Settings, provided that you have appropriate hardware installed for supporting the biometric authentication mechanisms you want to use. See Unit 5.3 for more information about different authentication methods.

Using the Desktop and Taskbar

The **desktop** contains several tools to help you start and switch between software applications. The desktop itself can contain **shortcut icons** used to open applications, folders, and files.

Windows 10 desktop showing 1) Shortcut icon; 2) Start button; 3) Start Screen with apps and tiles; 4) Programs pinned to the taskbar; 5) Notification area. Screenshot used with permission from Microsoft.

The **taskbar** is principally used to manage open windows (applications and files). It is usually positioned at the bottom of the desktop and may only appear when you point the mouse at the bottom of the screen.

If the taskbar is not locked (using taskbar settings), it can be dragged to different sides of the screen and resized using the mouse. The ***Automatically hide the taskbar in desktop mode*** *setting makes the taskbar disappear unless the cursor is pointing at it.*

When you run applications, each program appears as an icon on the taskbar. You can click the icons to switch between windows. Alternatively, hold the **ALT** key then press **TAB** to cycle through the windows or on a touch-enabled screen, swipe from the left edge. You can also click the **Task View** button  to list running programs. This is located to the right of the search box on the taskbar.

Each icon has a shortcut menu, allowing you to close the program or access recently used documents. Pointing at an icon shows a preview of any open windows, which you can select by clicking. Right-clicking an icon exposes a context menu which you can use to perform functions that relate to that icon. For example, right-clicking the icon for Microsoft Word exposes pinned and recently opened document files.

The taskbar also contains "pinned" icons for frequently used programs, such as email and web browser. Pinned items *always* remain on the taskbar. A program with open windows is shown with a highlight. You can add, remove, or reposition pinned items by dragging and dropping.

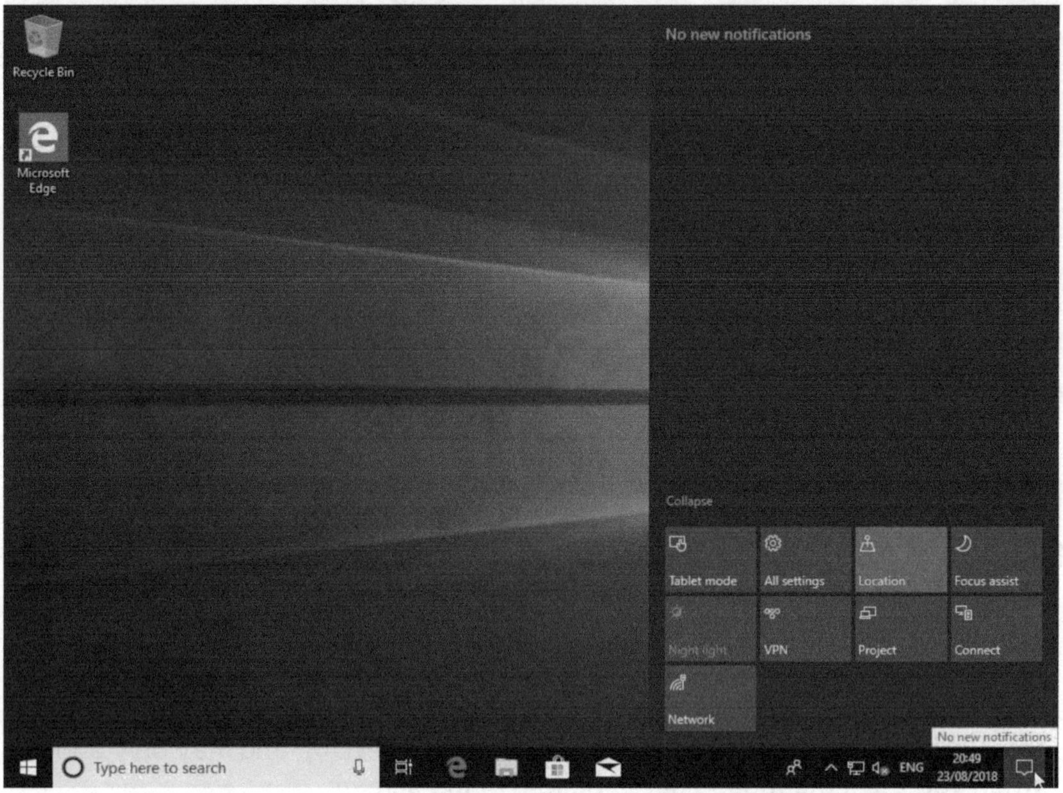

Notification area in Windows 10. Screenshot used with permission from Microsoft.

The **Notification Area** on the right-hand side of the taskbar displays the current time and icons for programs that run without a window, such as anti-virus software, the volume control, battery meter, network status, and so on. These icons have shortcut menus for enabling, disabling, and configuring the related application or setting. You can configure what displays in the notification area and also control application notification settings.

On a touchscreen, swiping in from the right of the screen is another way of showing notifications.

Using the Start Screen

The **Start Screen** in Windows 10, or **Start Menu** in earlier versions, is used to manage apps and PC settings and launch desktop software applications. It is accessed by clicking the **Start** button on the left-hand side of the taskbar or by pressing the `START` key.

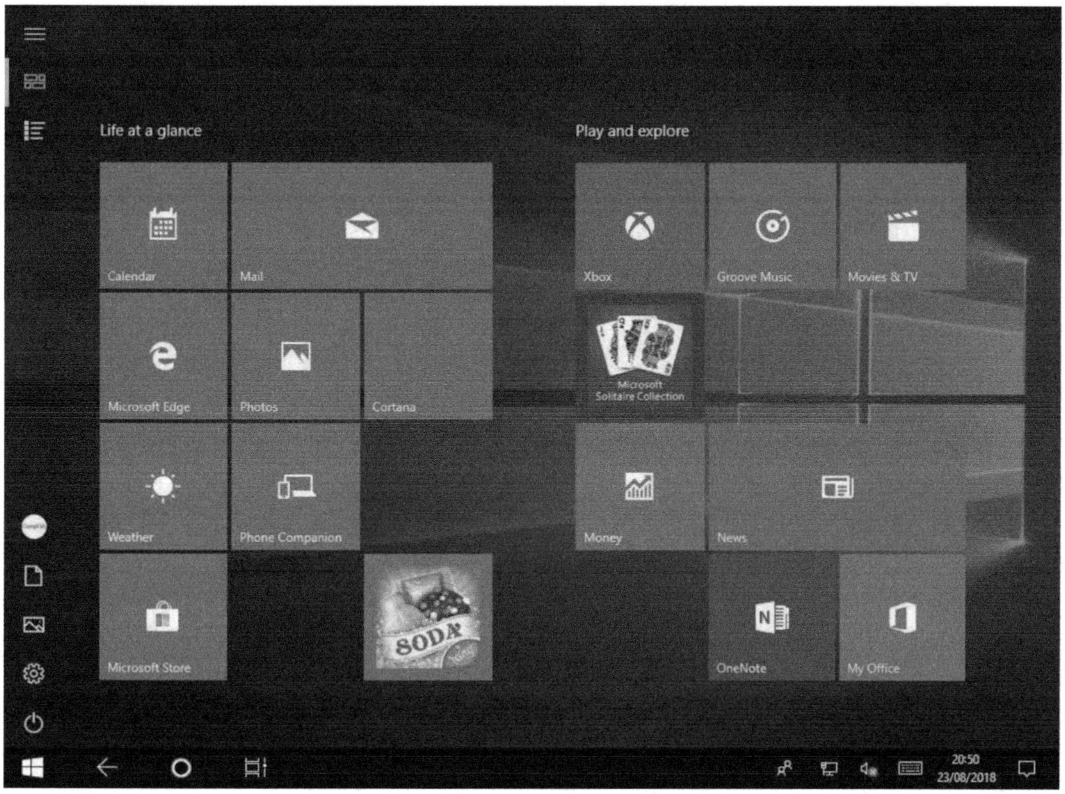

Windows 10 Start Screen in Tablet mode. Screenshot used with permission from Microsoft.

The Start screen displays in full screen mode if your computer is in tablet mode, otherwise, it displays as a menu. Tablet mode is selected automatically (by default) on hybrid laptop/tablet devices. For example, removing the keyboard from a Microsoft Surface tablet or folding the screen of an HP X360 device over through 360 degrees puts Windows 10 into tablet mode. You can use Windows 10 settings to manually select tablet mode and to configure these automatic behaviors.

To display all applications in tablet mode, click the **All apps** icon on the upper left of the display. In desktop mode, all applications are displayed in Start on the left side without intervention by the user.

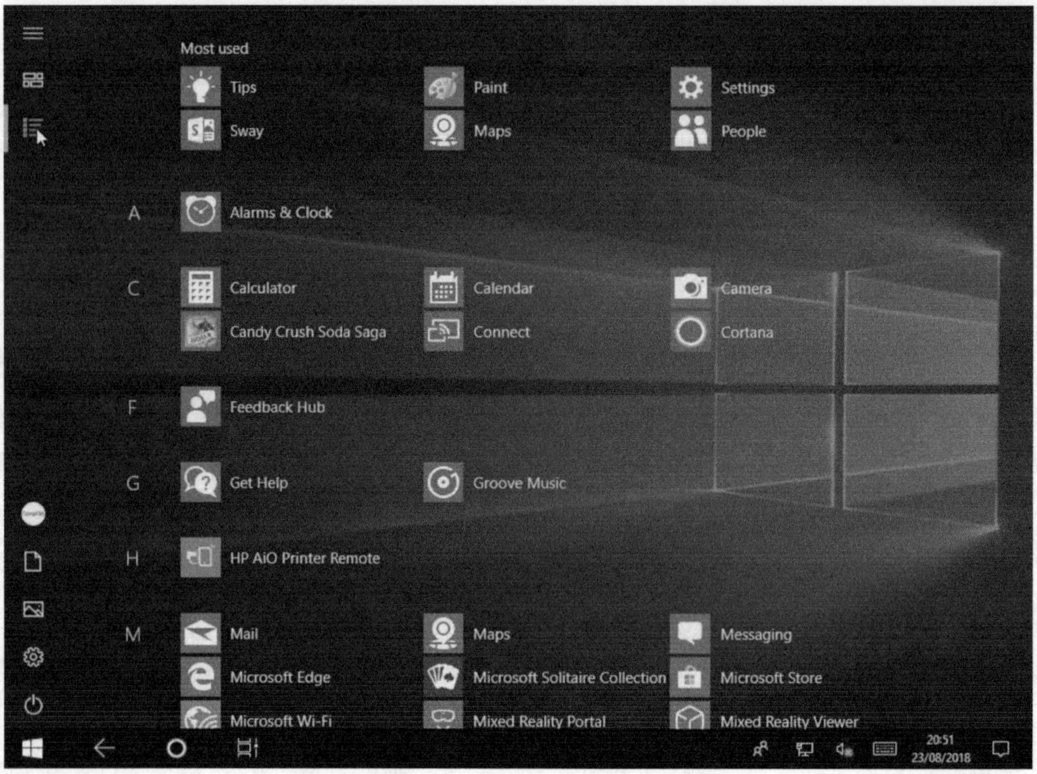

Viewing installed apps from the Start Screen in Windows 10 in tablet mode. Screenshot used with permission from Microsoft.

Apps are installed and managed by using the Microsoft Store app. Desktop software programs are managed with Control Panel. See Unit 2.2 for more information about different types of software.

Any app, program, or file can be launched from the Start Screen by typing its name and selecting the icon from the list of search results. The **Search** box is on the taskbar next to Start.

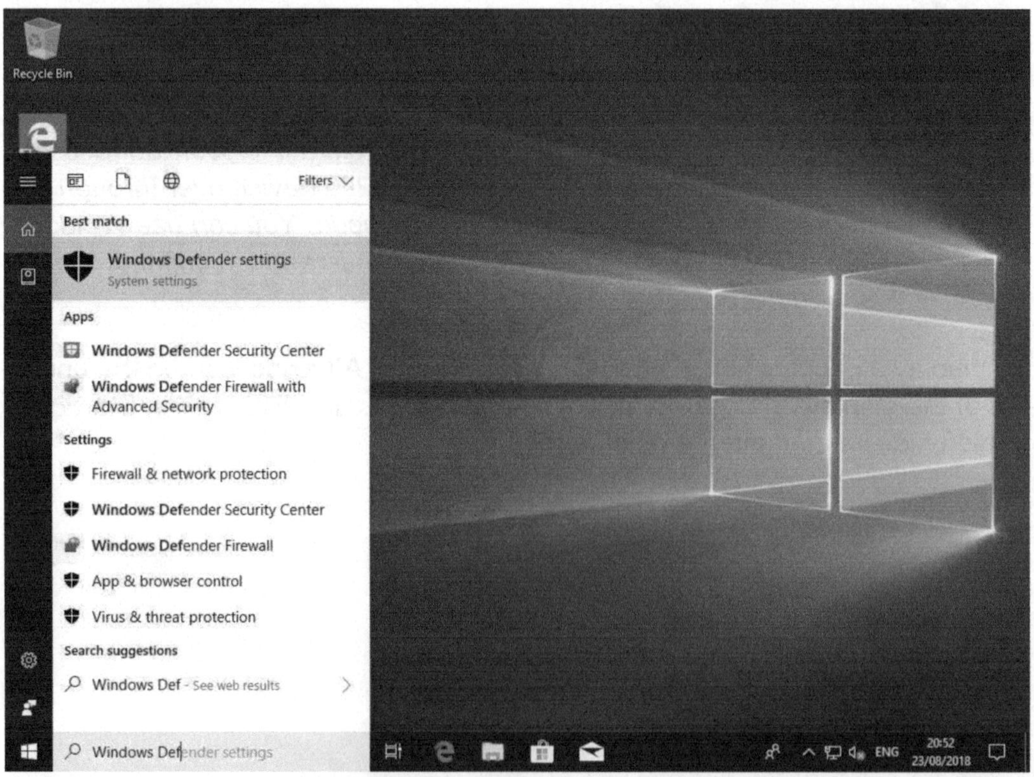

Launching applications by using search. Screenshot used with permission from Microsoft.

Customizing the Start Screen and Taskbar

You can configure the look and behavior of the tiles showing in Start. Select **Start > All Apps**, right-click the application you want to configure, and select **Pin to Start**. After a tile is pinned, you can configure it. Right-click the tile and then choose from the following options:

- Unpin from Start.
- Resize (Select from Small, Medium, Large, and Wide).
- Uninstall.
- More (for Microsoft Store apps)—select from Turn Live Tile Off, Pin to taskbar, Rate and review, Share.
- More (for desktop applications)—select from Pin to taskbar, Run as administrator, Open file location.

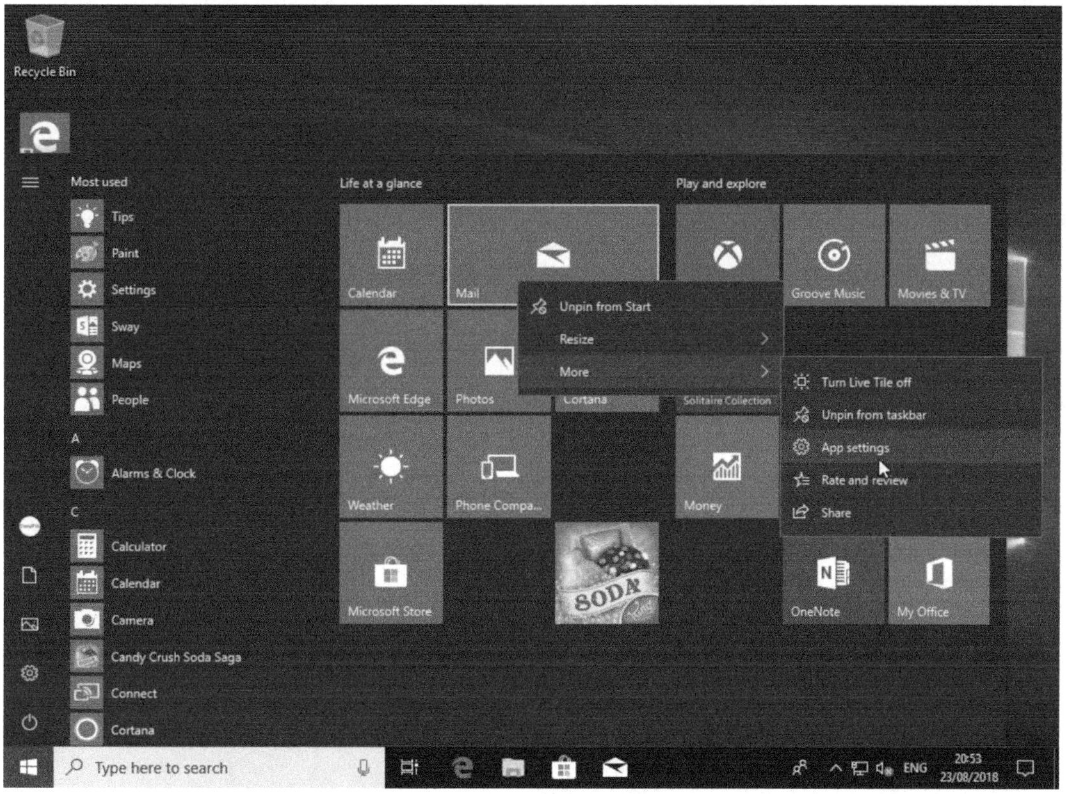

Configuring tiles. Screenshot used with permission from Microsoft.

Once you have pinned and configured your tiles on Start, you can group the tiles. If you want to create a new group for your tiles, drag one of the tiles to an unused area. Drag additional tiles to the new group. You can drag tiles between groups if you want to move them. Hover your mouse above the new group of tiles and type a name for your group.

You can set options for how the taskbar and Start Menu are displayed. Select **Start > Settings > Personalization**, and click **Start** or **Taskbar** as required.

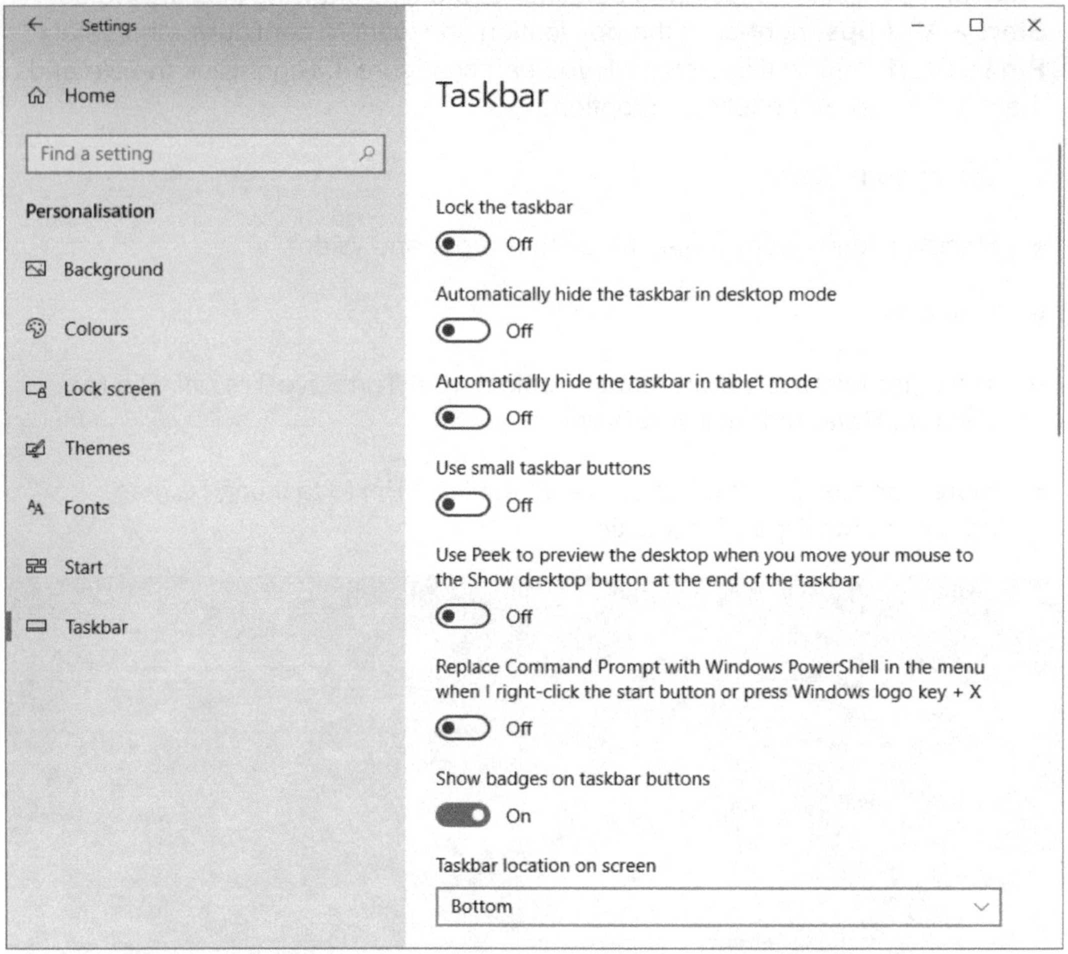

Configuring taskbar settings. Screenshot used with permission from Microsoft.

Using Input Devices

To operate a PC, you need to be familiar with the operation of input devices, such as a mouse, keyboard, and touchscreen.

Using a Mouse or Touchpad

The **mouse** or **touchpad** is used to select and move objects on the desktop and in windows. Moving the mouse (or moving your finger on a pad) moves the cursor.

- To select an object such as an **icon**, point to it with the cursor then click the main mouse button once. To open an object, *double-click* it with the main mouse button.

You can configure the main mouse button as either the left or right button depending on whether you are right- or left-handed. See Unit 3.2 for notes on configuring mouse properties.

A touchpad will come with buttons and may also support tapping the surface of the pad to perform a mouse click.

- To select commands in **menus** and **dialogs**, point to the command or button and click the main mouse button *once*.

- To select the **shortcut menu** for an object, point the cursor at it then click with the second mouse button (right-click).

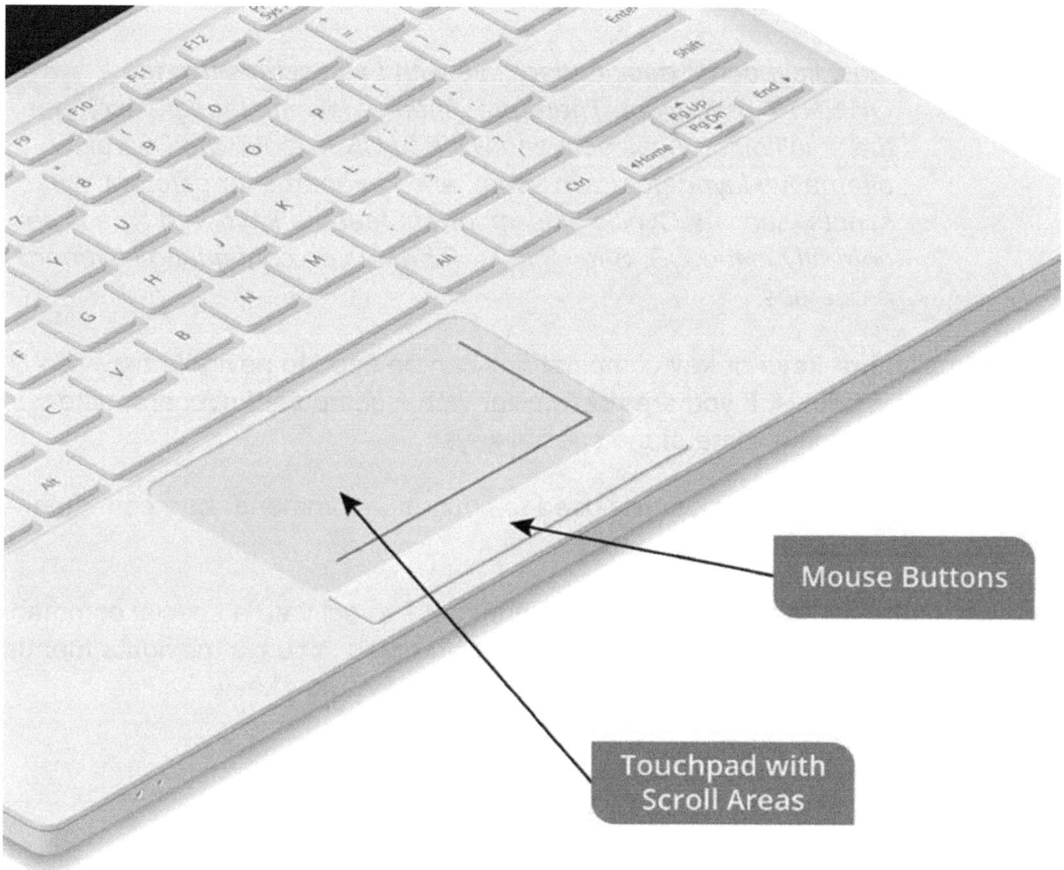

Laptop touchpad—note the scroll areas and left and right buttons. Image © 123rf.com.

- To **move** an icon or window, point to it and hold down the main mouse button. Move the mouse to the target then release the button. This process is called **Drag and Drop**.

- To **scroll** within a window, rotate the scroll wheel or drag your finger in the marked scroll area of the touchpad.

Using a Keyboard

The keyboard is used for simple typing and also to issue commands.

Ideally, you should learn to **touch type**. This will make operating the computer more comfortable and efficient. To touch type, you use the `A` to `F` and `J` to `;` keys as a "base" for your fingers. Once you have learned the position of the other keys, you can reach for them without looking. For example, you use the little finger on your left hand to press `Q` then return it to rest on `A`.

Most keyboards designed for use with Latin scripts use the QWERTY key layout. There are different layouts though, such as the small differences between US and UK layouts, the Dvorak alternative layout for Latin script, and keyboards for different scripts, such as Cyrillic. It is important that the keyboard type is set correctly in the OS. See Unit 3.2 for notes on configuring keyboard properties.

Additionally, **hot keys** or key combinations can be used to navigate between and around windows. If you are not familiar with a computer keyboard, take some time to identify some of the special keys:

- `ENTER` (or `RETURN`) is usually used to confirm a command. `ESC` can often be used to cancel a command.
- `CTRL` and `ALT` are often used with other keys to activate a special command. The `ALT` key also activates an application's menu. You can navigate menus using the underlined **access keys** or using the `ARROW` keys.

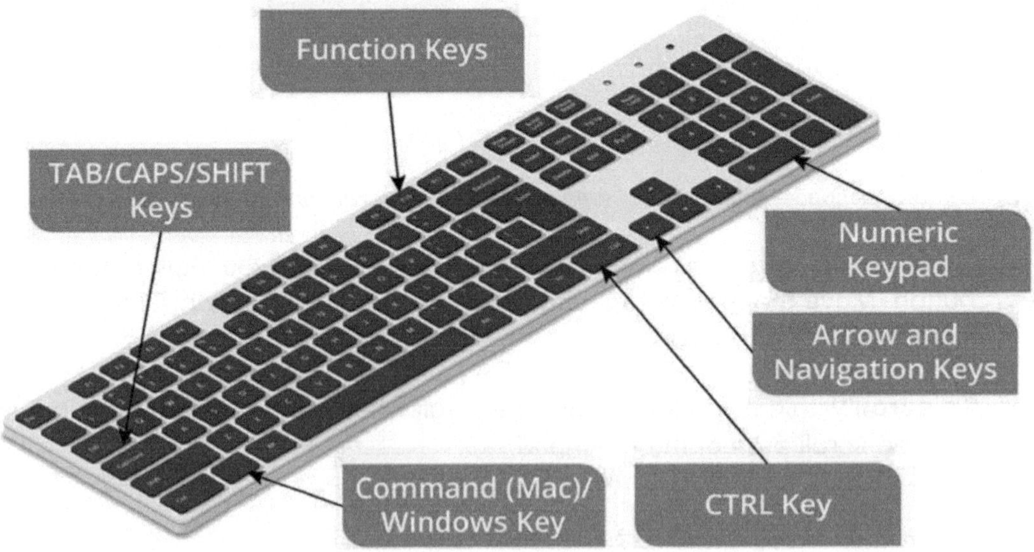

Special keys on a PC keyboard. Image © 123rf.com.

Menus in Windows 10 are not shown until you press the `ALT` key. Most other software applications show the menu all the time.

- **TAB** can be used in a window to move to the next pane. **SHIFT+TAB** moves back. Use the **ARROW** keys and the **PAGE UP** / **DOWN**, **HOME**, and **END** to navigate between icons or within a text file.

- The **SHIFT** key is used to type capitals or the superscript symbol shown on the key. You can toggle **CAPS LOCK** on and off to type in capitals without holding down **SHIFT**. You can also use the **SHIFT** key with the **ARROW** keys to select multiple icons.

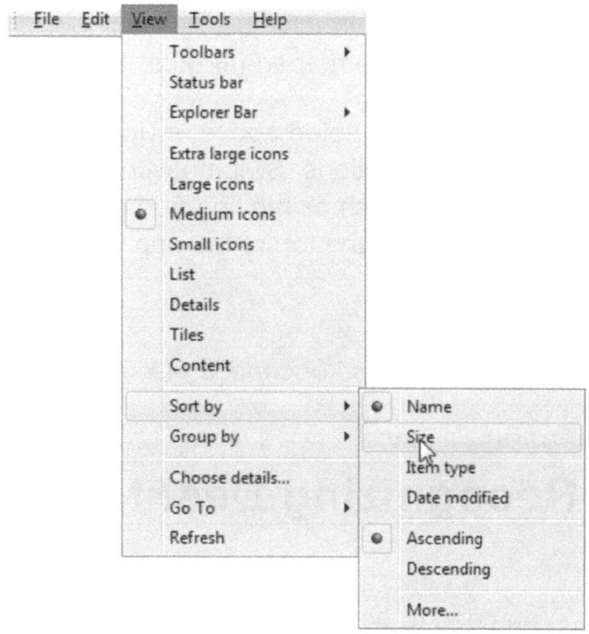

Press ALT to show menus and use the underlined access keys or arrow keys to navigate and ENTER to select an item. Screenshot used with permission from Microsoft.

- When **NUM LOCK** is off, the keypad works like the **ARROW** keys; when it is on, the keypad works like a calculator keypad.

On a laptop keyboard, there might not be a separate numeric keypad. In this case, keypad functions marked on normal keys can be toggled on or off.

- Press **START** to display the Start Screen or Start Menu and enable Instant Search. Press **SHORTCUT** to display a context menu for the selected object.

- The function keys (**F1**, **F2**, and so on) perform special actions (for example, **F1** always activates the help file for an application).

- **BACKSPACE** deletes the character to the left in a document or returns to the previous window. **DELETE** erases the character to the right or deletes an icon when working within a window.

- On a laptop, use the **FN** key to operate commands marked on other keys in a color accent. These perform laptop-specific functions, such as toggling the display or switching the wireless radio on or off.

Using a Touchscreen

Most portable devices can be operated using a **touchscreen**. Touchscreen input is made by performing **gestures** or using the **on-screen keyboard**. Some of the basic Windows 10 gestures are as follows:

- Tap—pressing once is the same as a left mouse click.

- Tap and hold—this is equivalent to a right-mouse click. For example, you might swipe to select some content then tap and hold the selection to open a "copy" command. This might also be implemented as a two-finger tap.

- Pinch and stretch—using two fingers, either pinch them together to zoom in or move them apart (stretch) to zoom out.
- Swipe—as noted above, swiping from a particular screen edge performs different actions. Swiping within an app window can also perform custom actions, such as moving from page to page or screen to screen. Swiping down from the top of the app window usually refreshes the content.

Most touchpads also have gesture support.

Recognizing Desktop Icons

You need to be familiar with some of the standard types of objects and interface controls you see on-screen.

Icons are the pictures used in an operating system to represent folders, files, and other system objects. The main types of icons are as follows:

- 

File (or document) icons—data files have the picture of the application used to edit the file on them. There are hundreds of different types but the icon shows what type of data is in the file (text, pictures, or music for instance) and which application is used to open it.
- 

Shortcut icons—links to a file have an arrow icon superimposed. Do not confuse a shortcut for the file itself. You can delete the shortcut at any time without losing the information in the file itself.

  In Windows, shortcuts to all your programs are located in the Start Menu or Start Screen. Programs may also put shortcuts on the desktop, and you can add desktop shortcuts to files or folders that you use often.
- 

Folder icons—folders are used to store and organize files. The type of icon also indicates what the folder contains (documents, pictures, subfolders, and so on).

- 

Application icons—these are the files that contain the program itself. Contrast Word's **program** file shown here with the icon for a Word **document** file shown above.
- **Device** icons—hard disk drives store data saved or installed on the computer. Removable drives have different icons, such as an optical drive or USB thumb drive. You may also see an icon for printers and other devices connected to the computer.

Hard Disk, Blu-Ray/DVD Drive, and Printer icons. Screenshot used with permission from Microsoft.

If you allow it, Windows can display vendor-specific icons for compatible devices by downloading the image from the Internet.

Working with Windows

Every desktop application runs in a window. You can open multiple windows and switch between them. All windows share some basic features in common.

Some windows are split into multiple panes; click or press **TAB** and **SHIFT+TAB** to navigate between them. If the window is not large enough to display its contents, a scroll bar is shown. Click the arrows or click the button on the scroll bar to move it (or use the scroll wheel on the mouse).

The application controls are displayed as toolbars and/or a menu bar at the top of the window.

Microsoft prefers the use of buttons or tools on a "ribbon" that combines the functions of a menu bar and toolbar. A menu bar may only be shown if you press the **ALT** *key.*

The **Status** bar shows useful information about whatever is selected in the rest of the window. When selecting files, you can enter information about the file here.

A window can either fill the whole desktop or occupy a part of it. This is done by clicking the **Maximize** /**Restore** button. To *resize* a window, you can click-and-drag on the window's **border**. To *move* a window, click-and-drag the **title** bar. *Right*-clicking the taskbar gives you options for arranging windows in a single pattern.

The **Minimize** button hides the window from the desktop. You can re-activate it by clicking its taskbar icon. You can also use the taskbar to switch between windows.

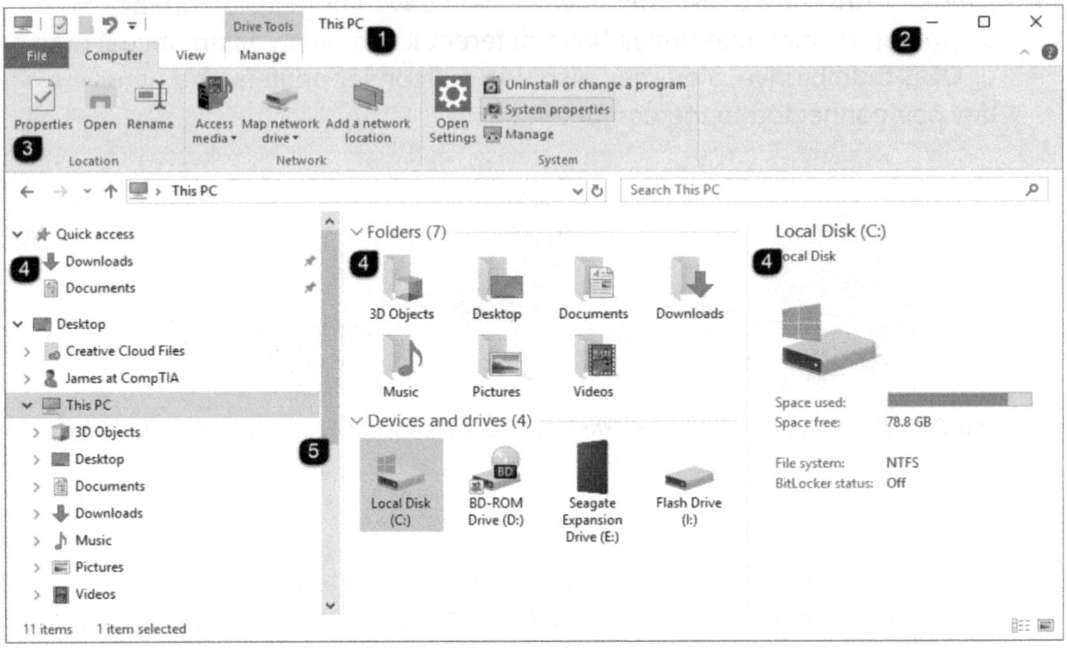

Typical window layout with 1) Title bar; 2) Control icons; 3) Menu bar and toolbars; 4) Panes; 5) Scroll bars. Screenshot used with permission from Microsoft.

*Right-click an **empty** part of the taskbar. If you right-click a window button, you will get a different shortcut menu.*

When working with a window, you can "shake" it to clear the desktop of other windows or drag it to the edge of the screen to "snap" it to an appropriate size relative to other windows.

You can work with several programs at the same time, but you should note that each program takes up memory. If you open too many windows, your computer will slow down. If you have finished using a program, close the window to free up resources.

To close a window, either select **Close** or **Exit** from the **File** menu, click the **Close** button , or press `ALT+F4`.

Review Questions / Module 1 / Unit 2 / Using a Workstation

Answer these questions to test what you have learned in this unit. You can review the model answers at the end of the book.

1) What should you do before attempting to set up a new computer system?
2) When setting up a desktop computer, what factor should you consider when deciding on the location of the system case?
3) What factors should you consider when positioning input and output devices?
4) You have to sign in to Windows—does it matter if the CAPS LOCK light on the keyboard is activated?
5) You have to open a word processing application but you cannot see an icon on the desktop. What should you do?
6) Your colleague has to run many applications at the same time and finds it difficult to know which icon to choose when switching between them. What alternative method could you suggest?
7) Your colleague is using a laptop and you notice that he laboriously clicks the mouse repeatedly to scroll through the document you are co-editing. What technique could he use to be more productive?

Lab 1 / Setting up the Computer

If you happen to have a new computer, complete this lab to set it up correctly. If you are already using a computer, run through the steps to check that it is set up safely.

1) Read the PC's instruction manual and make sure the contents listed on the box are all present.
2) Put the system unit on the desk or floor—remember the following points:
    - Close enough to an electrical outlet.
    - Close enough to your desk so that cables for the mouse and keyboard are not stretched.
    - 6" space around the unit for air to circulate freely.
    - Not positioned close to a radiator and ideally not exposed to direct sunlight.
3) Position the monitor on your desk and adjust it and your chair so that the top of the screen is level with your eyes.
4) Connect the monitor to the port on the system unit, using the connector as shown in your system documentation.
5) Connect the mouse and keyboard to the ports on the system unit, using the connector as shown in your system documentation.
6) Try to keep the cables tidy so that they do not trail under your desk or cross walkways.
7) Plug the monitor into a building power outlet or into the power socket on the system unit (check the system documentation to find out how the monitor is powered).
8) Plug the power cable into the back of the system unit and then into the building power. Turn on the building power wall switch.
9) Press the power switch on the monitor then the power switch on the PC.
10) Wait for the computer to start ("boot"). As the PC powers up, listen and look for the following signs that the computer is operating normally:
    - Power LED comes on
    - Fans start spinning
    - Single short beep (most computers these days do not beep though)
    - Hard disk activity (LED flickers and there may be some soft noise [grinding or clicking indicates a problem])

Lab 2 / Navigating the Windows User Interface

In this lab, you will sign in to your computer and explore the features of the Start Screen, desktop, and taskbar. If you are using a new computer, a wizard may run to help you set up your computer (choose a user name and password and so on). Refer to the computer's setup guide to complete this, then continue with the lab. It is assumed you are using Windows 10 Spring Creators Update (1803). If you are not, steps might vary slightly.

Exercise 1 / Exploring the Start Screen

In this exercise, you will learn to navigate around the Start Screen.

1) Press a key to open the privacy shade then, if necessary, click the icon representing your computer account.
2) With your account name and picture showing, type your password. Remember that this is case-sensitive, so upper and lower case characters are treated as different.
3) Press `ENTER` or click the arrow button. Wait for the desktop to load.
4) Point to the **Start** button and click once to show the **Start Screen** menu.
5) On the right-hand side of the taskbar, click **Notifications** and then click **Tablet mode**. Notice that Start is now displayed as a full screen.
6) At the top of the Start Screen on the left-hand side, click **All Apps** then locate and click the **Tips** tile.
7) Take a few minutes to read the various articles.
8) Press the `START` key to switch to the Start Screen again.
9) Back on the main part of the Start Screen practice customizing the tile layout:
    - Drag tiles to new positions.
    - Right-click or long finger-press to resize a tile.
10) From the Start Screen, if you have a touchscreen, swipe from the right edge to view **Notifications**. Otherwise, click **Notifications** on the taskbar.
11) Click **Tablet mode** to switch back to desktop mode.
12) Click the Tips window icon on the taskbar.

13) Click the **Close** button on the top-right corner of the window to exit the app.

14) Click **Start**, click **Settings** and then click **Personalization**. You can make any changes you want to the pictures and colors used on the desktop.

15) Close the Settings app when you have finished.

Exercise 2 / Exploring the Desktop and Taskbar

In this exercise, you will explore the features of the desktop and taskbar.

1) Press the `START` key to switch to the Start Screen.

2) Open the **Photos** tile. If prompted to add a Microsoft account, click the **Close** button to cancel the dialog.

   Photos is an example of a Microsoft Store app. In Windows 10 (1709 and later), all apps, even those downloaded from the Microsoft Store display in a window on the desktop.

3) Click **Start** and then type `paint`, then click the icon that appears in the search results. This loads the Paint application. This is an example of a desktop application.

4) In Paint, create a picture; perhaps of a boat sailing on the sea.

5) When you have created a picture, click the **File** menu on the ribbon once. Move the mouse down the menu to point to the **Save** command and click once.

6) Enter a file name of `The Sea`, double-click the **Pictures** folder, and then click the **Save** button.

7) Press the keys `START+E` together (hold down `START` and press `E` then release both at the same time). This should open a File Explorer window.

   Note the file you created is listed under "Recent files."

8) Double-click the **Pictures** folder to view the file where you saved it.

   There are various ways to switch between windows when you have more than one open. We'll take a look at each of these methods.

9) Look at the taskbar—you should see underlined icons for the three windows you have open. Note the difference between open windows and icons that have been "pinned" to the taskbar but that aren't currently running. Also, the active (currently selected) window is shown with a highlight.

10) Click the icons to switch between the windows. Right-click the icons to observe their shortcut menus (do not select anything from the menus though).

11) Try using the **ALT+TAB** keyboard shortcut. Hold down the **ALT** key then press-and-release **TAB**. This shows a list of open desktop windows and Start Screen apps. Still holding **ALT**, press **TAB** again and keep pressing it to cycle through the icons until you have found one you want to look at. Release the **ALT** key to open the selected app or window.

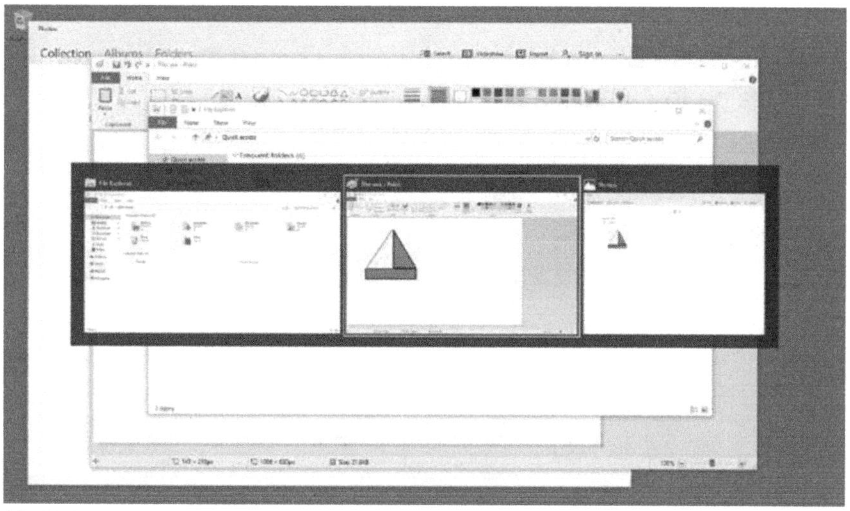

Using Alt+Tab to switch between windows. Screenshot used with permission from Microsoft.

Finally, you can use Task View to switch between windows.

12) Press **START+TAB** or click the taskbar icon  to open Task View. Alternatively, if you have a touchscreen, you can swipe from the left edge.

    Task View shows previews of all open windows, whether they are minimized or not. You can also use Task View to configure multiple desktops, but we won't explore that feature here. In Windows 10 (1803), you'll also see a timeline of previously used apps. You can choose to sync this with other devices, via a Microsoft account.

13) Click the **Photos** app to select it.

14) Press **START+D** or click the empty space on the taskbar to the right of the date and time to minimize all windows. You can also use **START+D** to return to the desktop from the Start Screen quickly.

15) Press **START+D** to show all the windows again then practice using the window control icons to maximize, restore, and minimize them.

16) Practice arranging windows on the desktop:

    - Using its title bar, drag the File Explorer window to the left edge. Select the Paint window to display alongside it.
    - Drag the Paint window out of its current position and then to the top of the screen to maximize it.
    - Drag the Paint window back to the middle of the screen to restore the window size then use the window borders to resize it manually.
    - Drag the title bar on the Paint window then shake the window to minimize all other windows. Shake again to restore them.

17) Close all the open windows using either the button or by pressing **`ALT+F4`**. You can close minimized windows from the taskbar by right-clicking and selecting **Close window**.

18) Point to each of the icons in the Notification Area in turn. A ScreenTip will be displayed to identify each one.

19) Right-click an empty part of the taskbar and select **Taskbar settings**. This opens a dialog to configure the taskbar.

20) Browse the options on the **Taskbar** tab.

21) Click the **Start** tab.

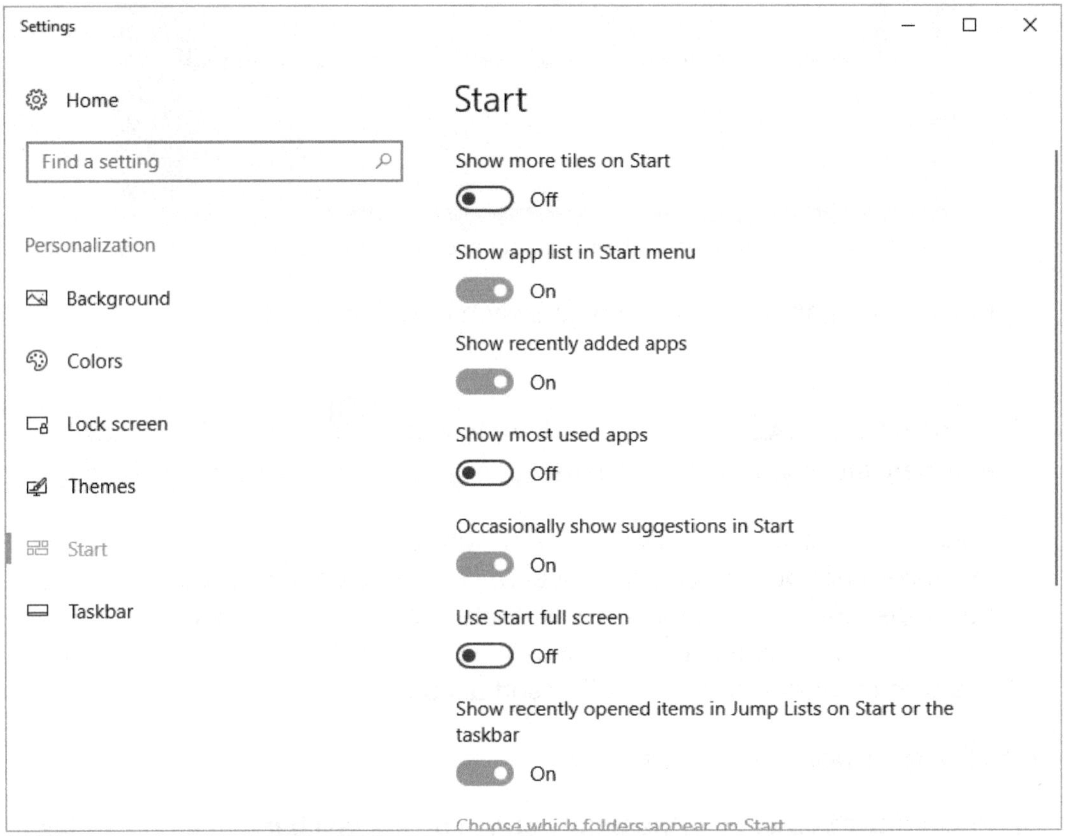

Start settings. Screenshot used with permission from Microsoft.

22) Browse the options.

When you have finished using the computer, you should shut it down.

23) Open the **Start Screen**, click the **Power** icon  in the bottom-left. Select **Shut down** from the submenu.

Module 1 / Unit 3
Using an OS

Objectives

On completion of this unit, you will be able to:

- Distinguish between different types of operating systems designed for workstations, servers, mobiles, embedded systems, and virtualization.
- Identify commonly used commercial and open source operating systems, such as Windows, macOS, iOS, Linux, Chrome, and Android.
- Use a browser to view websites.

Syllabus Objectives and Content Examples

This unit covers the following exam domain objectives and content examples:

- 3.1 Explain the purpose of operating systems.
  Interface between applications and hardware • Types of OS (Mobile device OS, Workstation OS, Server OS, Embedded OS, Firmware, Hypervisor [Type 1])

Functions of an Operating System

A computer requires an **Operating System (OS)** in order to function. The operating system provides interfaces between the **hardware**, **application programs**, and the **user**. The OS handles many of the basic system functions, such as interaction with the system hardware and input/output.

Interface Between User and Computer

One of the basic functions of an OS is to provide an interface between the user and the computer. This type of interface is referred to as a **shell**. The earliest operating systems for PCs, such as Microsoft's Disk Operating System (DOS), used a command-line interface or simple menu systems. Windows and later applications were marked by the use of a **Graphical User Interface (GUI)**. This helped to make computers easier to use by non-technical staff and home users.

Actually, some DOS applications presented a GUI (of a kind). Windows is sometimes described as a WIMP (Window, Icon, Menu, Pointing device) interface.

Consequently, an OS may have more than one shell. For example, it might have a graphical shell, allowing users to select commands via icons and menus, *and* it might have a command line shell, allowing the user to access functions by typing commands.

A shell will allow the user to configure the computer hardware, install and manage software applications, and access programs and files.

Interface Between Applications and Hardware

Another function of an OS is to "drive" the computer hardware. OS software is built from a **kernel** of core functions with additional **driver** software and system **utility** applications. Each hardware component requires a driver to work. The OS is responsible for identifying the components installed on the PC and loading drivers to enable the user to configure and use them.

One fundamental difference between computer systems is the "size" of the instructions that the Central Processing Unit (CPU) can process. Through the 1990s and early 2000s, most computers and software were based around processing 32-bit instructions. Most CPUs released in the last few years can work in either 32-bit or 64-bit mode. 64-bit mode is not necessarily that much faster, but it can address more memory.

A computer with a 64-bit CPU can run *either* 64-bit operating systems and 64-bit and/or 32-bit applications *or* a 32-bit operating system and 32-bit applications. A computer with a 32-bit CPU *cannot* run 64-bit OS or applications software at all.

An OS provides a common environment within which different software applications can run. Application software is the programs that allow users to perform different tasks, such as web browsing, email, and word processing. With an OS, application software developers do not need to worry about writing routines to access the hard disk or send a document to a printer; they simply "call" functions of the OS that allow them to do these things.

This allows application software designers to concentrate on application functions and makes the computer more reliable. One consequence of this is that there are relatively few operating systems, as it takes a lot of work to produce software applications that will work with different systems. Application vendors have to decide which operating systems they will support.

Changes to an operating system have to be made very carefully in order to remain compatible with previous generations of software and hardware. Eventually though, the OS may change so much that legacy software will no longer work.

System Health and Functionality

As mentioned above, an OS comes with a kernel and driver files that provide the core functionality of interacting with the hardware. Operating systems also ship with additional utility software that allows the user to configure and monitor the computer. One class of utility software is that which allows the user to monitor system health and performance.

An OS might provide logs to record system events or trigger alerts. Performance monitoring tools would allow the user to find out if a component is "overworked" and might require upgrading or if a software application or driver is faulty.

Data Management

Another class of utility software provides an interface between the user and the storage devices and mechanisms available to the computer. In a computer, information is stored as **files**. There are many different types of files. The OS and software applications are made up of executable and configuration files. Users can also create data files in different formats using different software applications.

Files must be **saved** to some sort of persistent storage, such as a hard disk. To organize files on a storage device, the OS creates a directory (or folder) structure. Files are saved to the storage device within a particular directory.

Operating systems may also provide tools for the user to manage directories, allowing them to create directories and move or copy files between them.

Types of Operating System

While they share the same basic functions, there are many different types of operating systems. These support different commercial models and types of devices.

Workstation, Server, and Mobile Device OS

A **workstation OS** is one that runs a traditional desktop PC or laptop. Examples include Microsoft Windows, Apple OS X/macOS, Linux, and Chrome OS. The market for workstation operating systems is divided into three main sections:

- Enterprise client—designed to work as a client in business networks.
- Network Operating System (NOS) or server OS—designed to run on servers in business networks.
- Home client—designed to work on standalone or workgroup PCs and laptops in a home or small office. This will also allow each client to run some basic *peer-to-peer* network services, such as file sharing.

A **mobile device OS** is one designed for handheld devices, such as smartphones and tablets. The principal mobile operating systems are Apple iOS and Android.

A workstation OS can normally be uninstalled and replaced with a different kind of OS. For example, you could remove Microsoft Windows from a PC and install Linux instead. This is not typically possible with a mobile device OS. A smartphone or tablet can only run the OS it was designed for.

A **server OS**, such as Windows Server, Linux, or UNIX, is often based on similar code to its workstation OS equivalent. For example, Windows 10 and Windows Server 2016 are very similar in terms of the OS kernel. A server OS is likely to include software packages (or roles) to run network services and use different licensing to support more users. A server OS is also likely to have a simpler command-line interface, rather than a GUI, to make it more secure and reliable.

Open Source versus Commercial

A **commercial OS** means that the user must purchase a license to install and use the OS software on a particular device. The programming code used to design the operating system is kept a secret by the developer. Microsoft Windows, Apple macOS, and Apple iOS are examples of commercial operating systems.

Open source means that the programming code used to design the software is freely available. Open source doesn't necessarily mean available for free (although many distributions are); it means that developers are free to make changes to the way the operating system works, so long as they make the changes they have made available in turn. Some software vendors are reluctant to make their source code available to third parties fearing piracy, infringement of copyright, and loss of market position. This means that users of these systems must wait for the vendor to make the modifications they need, if they make them at all. The open source model claims to make improvements to software available more quickly and cost-effectively.

UNIX, Linux, and Android are examples of open source operating systems.

Embedded OS

With a workstation, laptop, or server, you can delete the operating system and install a different one. These are general purpose types of computer systems capable of running software to perform a variety of different tasks. An **embedded system** by contrast is a computer or appliance designed for a very specific function. These systems can be as contained as a microcontroller in an intravenous drip-rate meter or as large and complex as an industrial control system managing a water treatment plant.

You could also think of home automation hubs, smart TVs, and gaming consoles as running an embedded OS in that the OS that ships with the device cannot usually be changed. These devices do have more scope for modification than the more industrial embedded systems though. You can install apps and games, add peripheral devices, and configure network connectivity for instance.

Embedded systems are typically **static environments**. A PC is a dynamic environment. The user can add or remove programs and data files, install new hardware components, and upgrade the operating system. The static environment provided by an embedded OS does not allow or require such frequent changes.

Many embedded systems operate devices, such as drip meters or flow valves, that perform acutely time-sensitive tasks. The kernels or operating systems that run these devices must be much more stable and reliable than the OS that runs a desktop computer or server. Embedded systems typically cannot tolerate reboots or crashes and must have response times that are predictable to within microsecond tolerances. Consequently, these systems often use differently engineered platforms called **Real Time Operating Systems (RTOS)**.

Firmware

In an embedded system, the embedded OS acts as **firmware**. It provides all the functions for interacting with the device hardware. The term "firmware" is used because unlike regular software, the firmware is not designed to be continually changed. Firmware can support updates, but such updates or configuration changes are supposed to be infrequent.

Workstations, laptops, and servers also use a type of firmware. Such PC firmware provides a low-level interface to allow the OS to load and take control of the PC's components. There are two types of PC firmware:

- The **Basic Input/Output System (BIOS)** provides industry standard firmware that operates the essential components of the PC and ensures that the design of each manufacturer's motherboard is PC compatible.
- Newer motherboards may use a different kind of firmware called **Unified Extensible Firmware Interface (UEFI)**. UEFI provides support for 64-bit CPU operation at boot, a full GUI and mouse operation at boot, and better boot security. A computer with UEFI may also support booting in a legacy BIOS mode.

Additionally, some of the PC system components, notably graphics adapters, storage devices, and network controllers, will have their own firmware. Most peripheral devices also contain firmware. Lastly, network devices, such as Internet routers and wireless access points, also run from firmware.

Virtualization

For most of the history of the microcomputer, a single computer has been able to run a single operating system at any one time. This makes multiple applications available on that computer (whether it be a workstation or server), but the applications must all share a common environment. **Virtualization** means that multiple operating systems can be installed and run simultaneously on a single computer.

A virtual platform requires at least three components:

- Computer(s)—the physical machine (or host) that provides the resources, such as CPU and memory, for the virtual environment.
- Hypervisor (or Virtual Machine Monitor [VMM])—manages the virtual machine environment and facilitates interaction with the host hardware and network. There are two main classes of hypervisor:
    - A Type I (or "bare metal") hypervisor is installed directly on the computer and interacts directly with its hardware.
    - A Type II hypervisor runs as a software application within a host operating system. The host operating system retains direct control of the hardware and the hypervisor must request use of it through the host OS.

- Guest operating systems (or Virtual Machines [VM])—operating systems installed under the virtual environment. The number of operating systems is generally only restricted by hardware capacity. The hypervisor may also restrict the type of operating systems that can be installed.

The presence of other guest operating systems can be completely transparent to any single OS. Each OS "thinks" it is working with a normal CPU, memory, hard disk, and network link. The guest operating systems can be networked together or they may be able to share data directly through the hypervisor (though this is not commonly done for security reasons).

Virtualization is used on network servers to utilize the hardware more efficiently. Virtualization software can also be used on desktop computers for various purposes. Some typical uses of desktop virtualization are:

- Virtual labs—create a research lab to analyze viruses, worms, and Trojans. As the malware is contained within the guest OS, it cannot infect the researcher's computer or network.
- Support legacy software applications—if the host computers have been upgraded, software may not work well with the new operating system. In this scenario, the old OS can be installed as a VM and the application software accessed using the VM.
- Development environment—test software applications under different operating systems and resource constraints.
- Training—lab environments can be set up so that students can practice using a live operating system and software without impacting the production environment. At the end of the lab, changes to the VM can be discarded so the original environment is available again for the next student to use.

Windows 10 Professional and Enterprise editions are bundled with virtualization software (Hyper-V). Third-party products include VMware and VirtualBox.

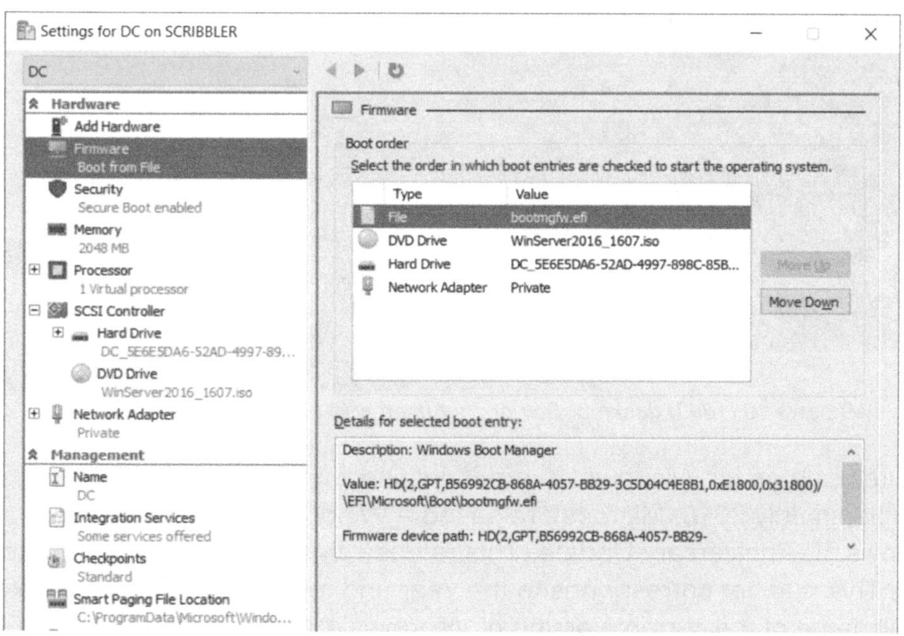

The hypervisor determines the resources allocated to a virtual machine. Screenshot used with permission from Microsoft.

Microsoft Windows

Microsoft Windows is the dominant commercial workstation OS, estimated to be installed on 90% of the world's desktop and laptop computers. The **Windows Server** OS is also widely used on PC servers.

Like most software, Windows and Windows Server have been released in a number of **versions** over the years. Historically, a new version would have to be purchased, though upgrade discounts are usually available. A new version may introduce significant changes in the look of Windows and add new features and support for new types of hardware. On the downside, a new version may not be compatible with hardware and software applications designed for earlier versions.

Windows 10

Windows 10, first released in 2015, is the current version. In fact, Microsoft indicated that they would no longer release new *versions* of Windows, but would instead maintain Windows 10 with *feature updates* on a periodic basis. Thus, the current version of Windows (at the time of writing) is still Windows 10. This approach is known as "Windows as a service" and promises continued updates to the operating system.

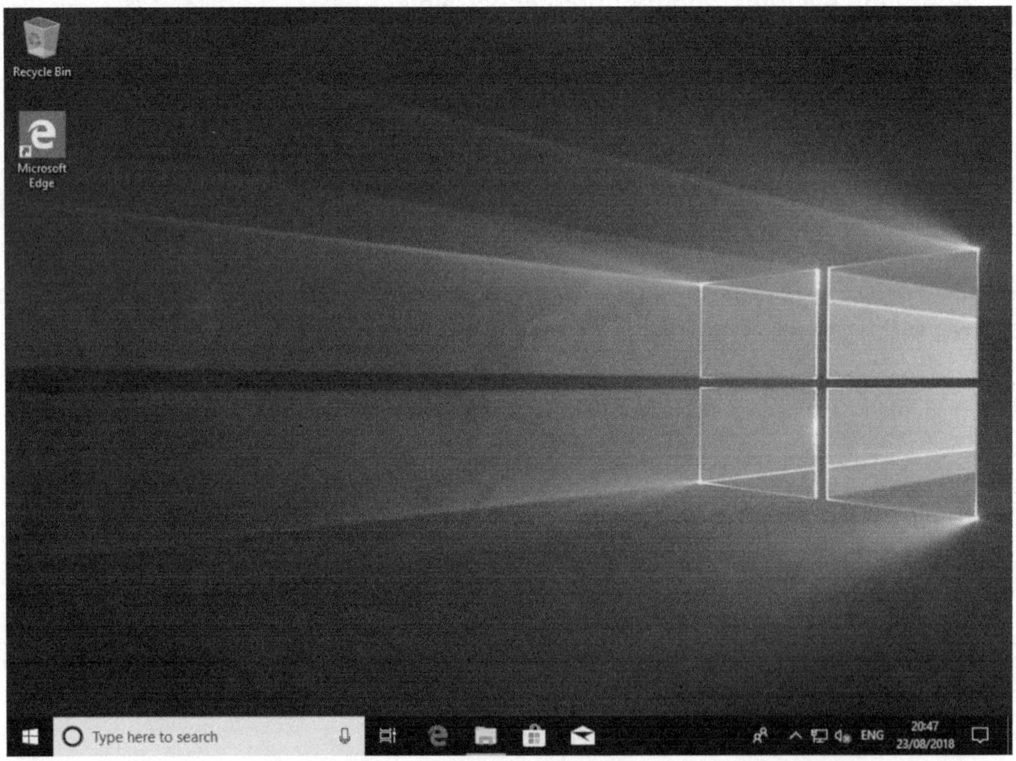

Windows 10 (1803) desktop. Screenshot used with permission from Microsoft.

Feature updates for Windows 10 are identified with a name and number. For example, in July 2016, Microsoft released a Windows 10 feature update called Windows 10 Anniversary Update. This release was identified with a number: 1607. This number corresponds to the year and month of release. Therefore, the full name of the current version of Windows 10 at the time of writing (June 2018) is Windows 10 Spring Creators Update (1803), replacing the Fall Creators Update (1709).

In addition to feature updates, Windows is updated periodically with *quality updates*. Quality updates do not usually make radical changes to Windows, though some do include new features. Quality updates might sometimes cause compatibility problems with some hardware devices and software applications, but this is less likely than with feature updates.

Windows 10 aims to provide a consistent user experience across different types of devices, including desktop PCs, laptops, tablets, and smartphones.

Older Windows Versions

Windows 10 is the successor to Windows 8 (2012) and Windows 8.1 (2013). Windows 8 and Windows 8.1 imposed significant user interface changes to provide better support for touchscreens, but not all of these changes were popular with users familiar with Windows 7. Windows 10 addressed this feedback and was also made available as a free upgrade to Windows 8. Consequently, Windows 10 very quickly replaced Windows 8 and Windows 8 is not that widely used, having about 7% market share at the time of writing.

Windows 8 was swiftly updated to Windows 8.1 to address some issues with the interface. Any reference to Windows 8 in this course can be taken to mean Windows 8.1. There was never a Windows 9.

Prior to Windows 8 there were **Windows 7 (2009)**, **Windows Vista (2007)**, and **Windows XP (2001)**. Windows 7 is still widely used, with an estimated installation base of around 45% of all PCs. Despite no longer being officially supported by Microsoft, Windows XP is still installed on about 5% of devices. Windows Vista never achieved a significant market share.

Windows 7 desktop. Screenshot used with permission from Microsoft.

Windows Editions

Each version of Windows is available in different **editions**. Editions are used by Microsoft to create different markets for Windows. Windows 7 editions included Home Basic, Home Premium, Professional, Enterprise, and Ultimate. Windows 10 is available in the following editions:

- Windows 10 Home—designed for domestic consumers and Small Office Home Office (SOHO) business use. The home edition cannot be used to join a corporate Windows domain network.
- Windows 10 Pro—designed for small and medium-sized businesses. The Professional edition comes with networking and management features designed to allow network administrators more control over each client device.
- Windows 10 Enterprise/Windows 10 Enterprise (Long Term Servicing Channel)—similar to the Pro edition but designed for licensing by medium and large enterprises.
- Windows 10 Education/Pro Education—variants of the Enterprise and Pro editions designed for licensing by schools and colleges.

64-bit Windows

Each version and edition of Windows is available as 32-bit or 64-bit (x64) software. 64-bit editions of Windows can run most 32-bit applications software, though there may be some exceptions (you should check with the software vendor). The reverse is not true however; a 32-bit version of Windows *cannot* run 64-bit applications software.

64-bit editions of Windows also require 64-bit hardware device drivers authorized ("signed") by Microsoft. If the vendor has not produced a 64-bit driver, the hardware device will not be usable.

Windows 10 Mobile

Microsoft has developed versions of Windows for mobile devices, including Windows CE, Windows Phone 7, and Windows Phone 8. None of these have enjoyed the same sort of success as Windows has in the PC market.

With Windows 10 Mobile, Microsoft has adopted a consistent user interface and code base across all types of device. Windows 10 Mobile has a very small smartphone market share compared to Android and iOS. Microsoft develops and sells Windows 10 Mobile smartphones and Surface tablets.

Apple macOS and iOS

In 1984, when the IBM PC was the dominant desktop standard, Steve Jobs and Steve Wozniak created a new type of personal computer—the Apple Macintosh (or Mac). It was revolutionary because it came with a graphical user interface at a time when IBM's PC used the command-line DOS operating system. The Mac has never matched Windows' huge user base, although its current incarnation does have a truly devoted following.

Apple Mac OS/OS X/macOS

The main difference between Mac OS and other operating systems is that the OS is only supplied with Apple-built computers. You cannot purchase Mac OS and install it on an ordinary PC. This helps to make Mac OS stable but does mean that there is far less choice in terms of buying extra hardware.

macOS desktop.

The current lines—OS X and more recently macOS—were re-developed from the kernel of another type of operating system called UNIX. This kernel is supplemented with additional code to implement the Mac's graphical interface and system utilities and to maintain compatibility with older Mac OS applications. macOS gets periodic "dot" version updates. At the time of writing, the current version is 10.13 or "High Sierra" and updates are being released to existing customers free-of-charge.

Apple iOS

iOS is the operating system for Apple's iPhone smartphone and iPad tablet. New versions are released approximately every year with various .x updates. Version 11 is current at time of writing with version 12 due for release shortly. Apple makes new versions freely available, though older hardware devices may not support all the features of a new version, or may not be supported at all. While also derived from UNIX (through macOS), iOS is a closed source operating system. This means that the code used to design the software is kept confidential and can only be modified by Apple.

The popularity of iOS is primarily because it is so easy to navigate. Apart from volume and power, the only external button is the **Home** key, which returns the user to the Home Screen "Desktop."

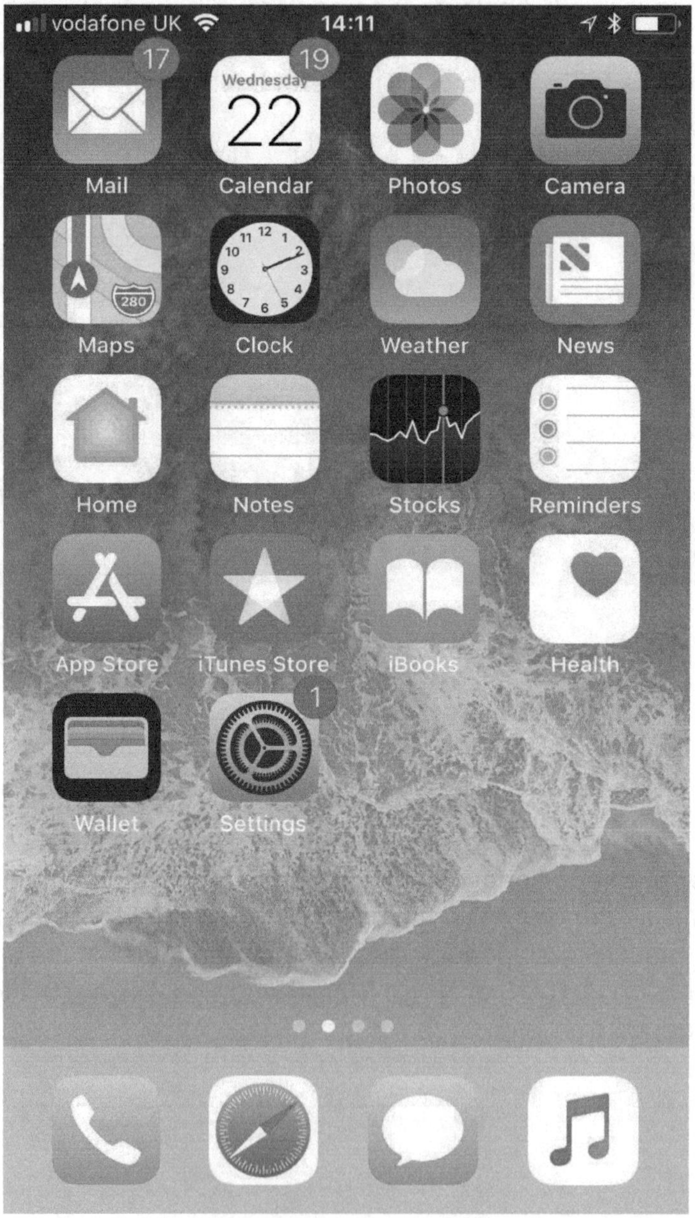

iOS 11 running on an iPhone 7.

The interface is then entirely controlled via touch. Point to icons to open apps, swipe or flick from left-to-right to access the keyboard and search, or flick right-to-left to view more icons. Re-arrange icons by tapping and holding for a few seconds. The icons will then "wobble" and can be dragged to a different page or into the dock taskbar at the bottom. Press the Home key to save.

To view and manage open apps, double-click the Home key to open the Multitasking bar.

Touch can be operated either with your fingers or with a special soft-touch stylus. There are many more gestures in addition to those listed above. For example, shaking the device is often used to activate undo. There are also external keyboards available and most Apple devices support Siri, a voice recognition system and personal assistant.

Linux, Chrome, and Android

Originally developed by Linus Torvalds, **Linux** is based on the UNIX operating system. UNIX was developed over 30 years by various commercial, academic, and not-for-profit organizations. This resulted in several versions, not all of which are compatible, and many of which are proprietary or contain copyrighted or patented code or features. Linux was developed as a fully open source alternative to UNIX (and for that matter, to Windows and macOS and iOS).

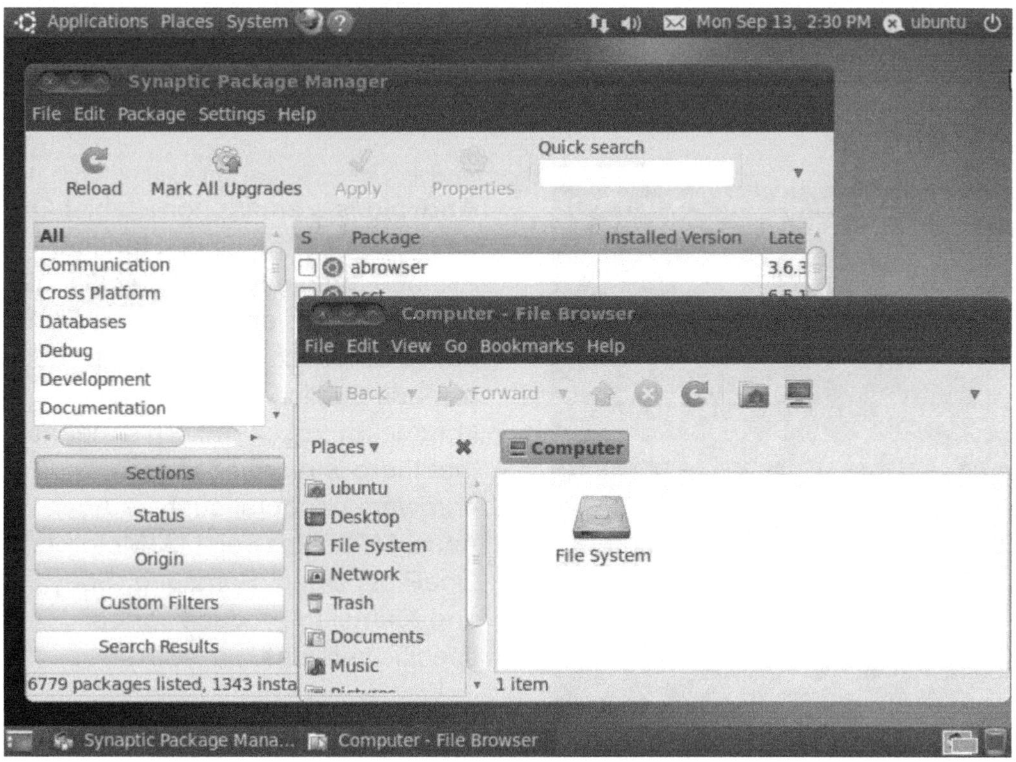

Ubuntu Linux.

Linux can be used as a desktop or server OS. There are many **distributions** or **distros**, notably SUSE, Red Hat, Fedora, Debian, Ubuntu, and Mint. Each distro adds specific packages and interfaces to the generic Linux Kernel and provides different support options. Linux does not require a graphical interface, though most distributions provide one.

IBM, Sun/Oracle, and Novell are among the vendors producing end-user applications for Linux. As a desktop OS it tends to be used in schools and universities more than in business or in the home. As a server OS, it is very widely deployed on web servers.

Chrome OS

Chrome OS is derived from Linux, via an open source OS called Chromium. Chrome OS itself is proprietary. Chrome OS is developed by Google to run on specific laptop (Chromebook) and PC (Chromebox) hardware. This hardware is designed for the budget market.

Chrome OS was primarily developed to use web applications. In a web application, the software is hosted on a server on the Internet and the client connects to it using a browser. The client computer does not need to be particularly powerful as the server does most of the processing. Chrome OS provides a minimal environment compared to Windows. This means that there is less chance of some other software application or hardware device driver interfering with the function of the browser.

There are also "packaged" apps available for use offline and Chrome OS can run apps developed for Android.

Android

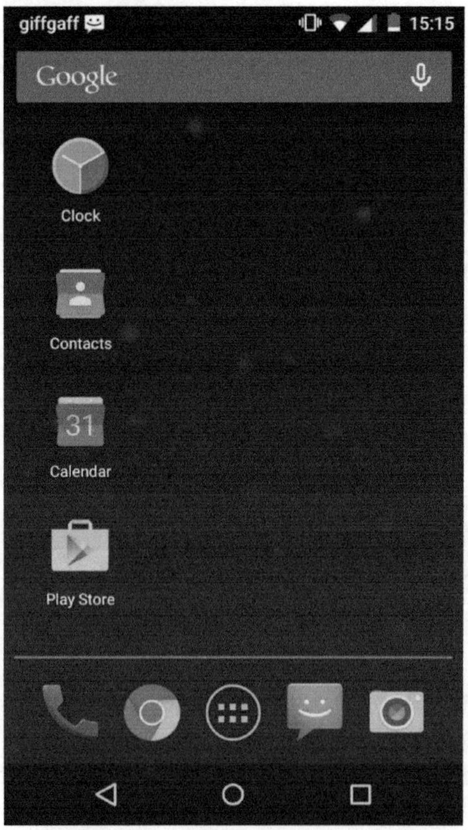

Android lollipop home screen.

Android is a smartphone/tablet OS developed by the Open Handset Alliance, primarily driven by Google. Unlike iOS it is an open-source OS, based on Linux. The software code is made publicly available (source.android.com). This means that there is more scope for hardware vendors, such as Acer, Asus, HTC, Huawei, LG, Motorola, OnePlus, Oppo, Samsung, Sony, and Xiamoi to produce vendor-specific versions.

Like iOS, Android is updated with new major (1.x) and minor (x.1) versions, each of which is named after some kind of sweet stuff. At the time of writing, current versions include 7.1 (Nougat) and 8.1 (Oreo). Because handset vendors produce their own editions of Android, device compatibility for new versions is more mixed compared with iOS.

File Explorer

Once you have learned how to use icons and windows, another crucial step in learning to use an operating system is being able to navigate around the file system.

File Explorer/Windows Explorer

File Explorer (formerly known as **Windows Explorer** and often just called "Explorer") is the file management interface for Microsoft Windows. You use it to view, create, rename, and delete folders and files on local disks, removable drives, and the network.

You can open an Explorer window by selecting its taskbar icon . You can also right-click any folder object and select **Explore** or you can press **START+E**.

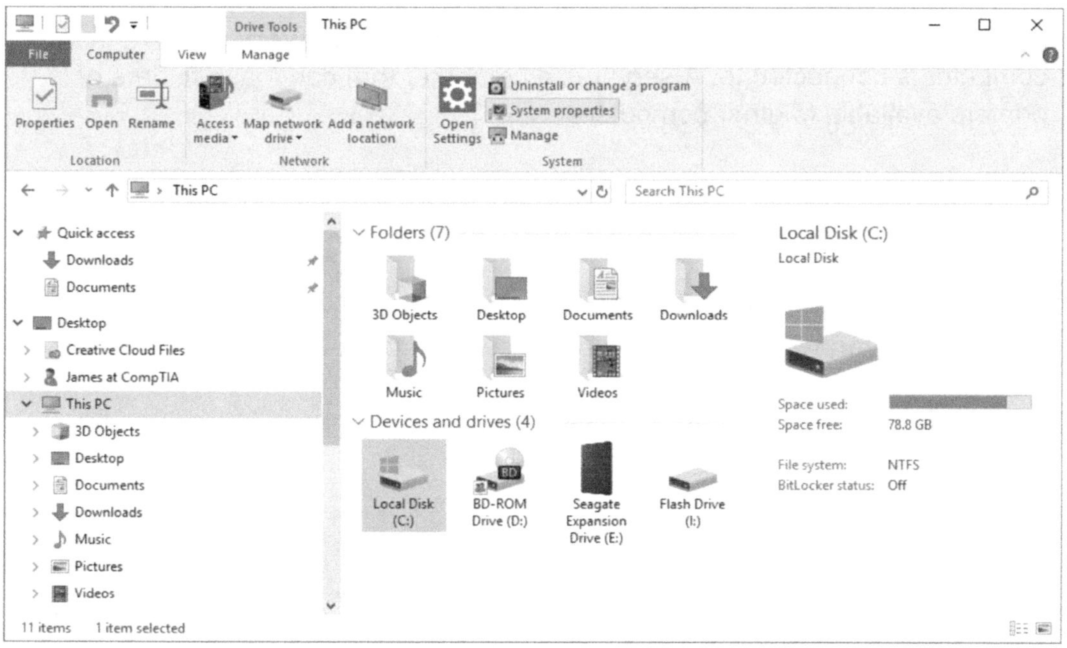

File Explorer in Windows 10. Screenshot used with permission from Microsoft.

This PC

The **This PC**  represents the local PC. When you open This PC, you get an Explorer window showing the local, removable, and network drives available to the PC.

The **This PC** object also allows you to change configuration settings by right-clicking it and selecting **Properties** (to access System properties) or **Manage** (to access the default Computer Management console).

In previous versions, the "ThIs PC" object is called "Computer" or "My Computer".

Network

The **Network** object  is a container for any **network servers** that the computer is connected to. A server is a computer that can make folders or printers available to other computers.

Sharing files is discussed in Unit 4.4.

The **Properties** shortcut menu option for Network opens the **Network and Sharing Center**, which you can use to view the status of network links and configure options for sharing folders.

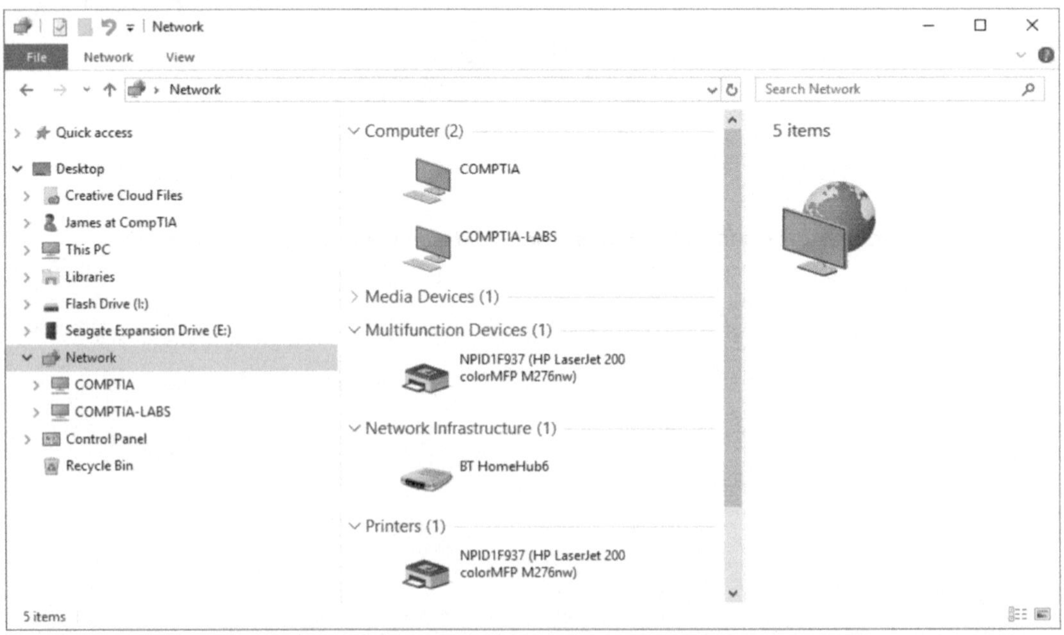

Browsing the network using File Explorer—you can see other computers plus a networked printer/scanner and a router (network infrastructure). Screenshot used with permission from Microsoft.

Windows Settings and Control Panel

As well as navigating the file system, you should also understand the tools used to configure settings and features in an operating system.

Windows Settings

Windows Settings is a touchscreen-enabled "app" interface for managing the computer. *Most* of the standard Windows 10 configuration settings can be located within Windows Settings but not all of them.

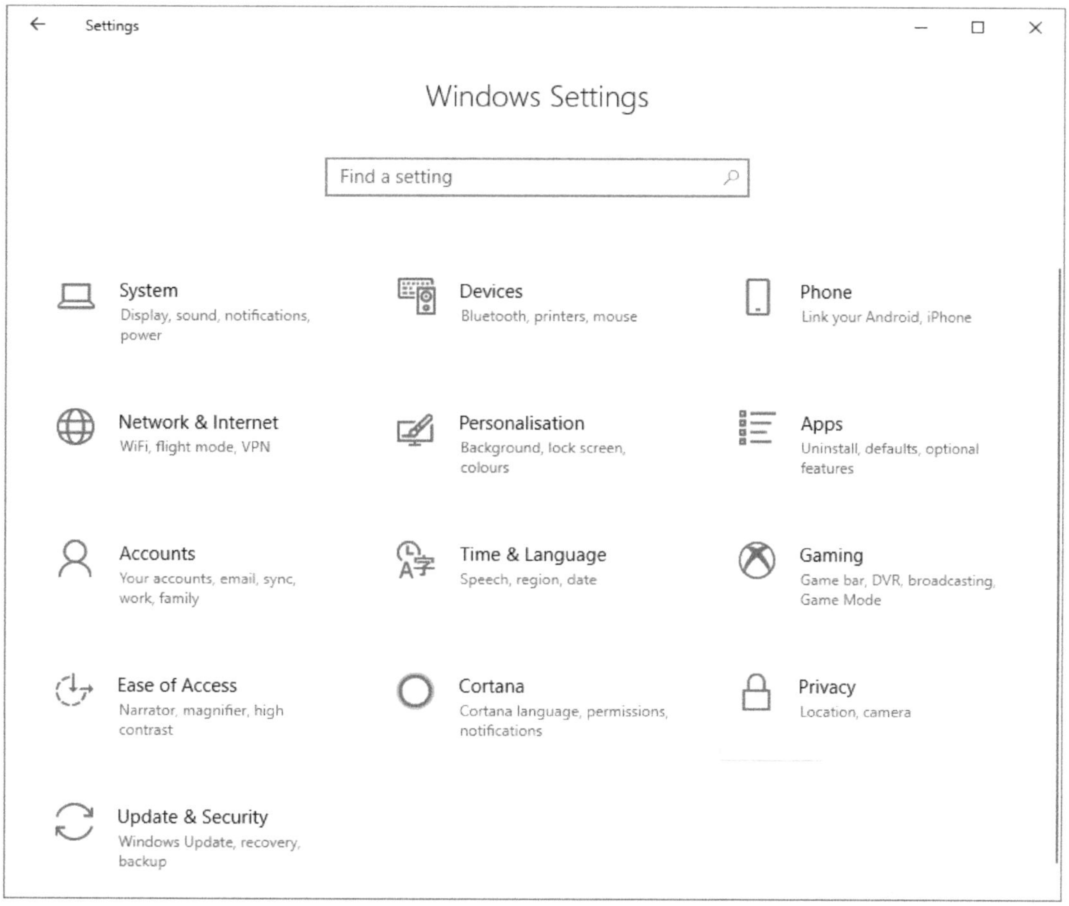

Windows Settings app. Screenshot used with permission from Microsoft.

In earlier versions, this app is referred to as the "PC Settings" app.

Control Panel

Control Panel  is the location for the basic user-configurable settings for Windows and some applications (such as anti-virus or email software) via **applets**. Control Panel is the default interface in Windows XP and Windows 7. In Windows 10, as noted above, a number of settings are now changed via Windows Settings, but Control Panel still hosts some of the configuration options. Each Windows 10 feature update tends to move more configuration options from Control Panel to Windows Settings.

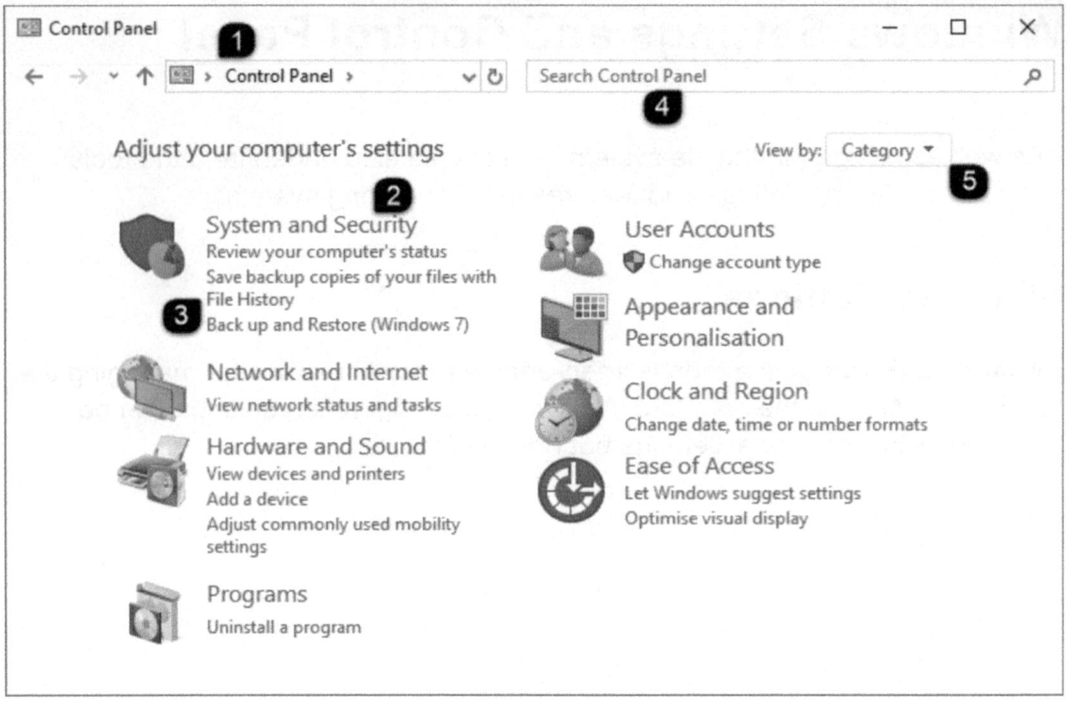

Control Panel in Windows 10 version 1803 showing 1) Navigation breadcrumb; 2) Task groups; 3) Configuration applets; 4) Search box; 5) View options. Screenshot used with permission from Microsoft.

In Control Panel, the default view displays a task-based list of the most commonly-used Control Panel options. You can also display all Control Panel applets by clicking the arrow in the navigation breadcrumb, changing the **View by** option, or by using the **Search** box to find a particular item.

Ease of Access Options

Ease of Access settings help people with a physical impairment to use the computer effectively. Some of the main options that can be configured are:

- Touchscreen—allows the use of touch to control the desktop, rather than a keyboard or pointing device. This requires a touch-enabled display device.
- Voice control and narration—use voice commands to operate the desktop and speech to input text and get audio narration describing available features in application windows and text in documents.
- Visual alternatives for sounds—replace alert and notifications with text alerts or visual effects.
- On-screen keyboard—use a virtual keyboard, operated by touch or using a pointing device.
- Magnifier—zoom in to a particular feature.
- Display settings—make the display more readable by using larger font sizes or a high contrast color scheme.

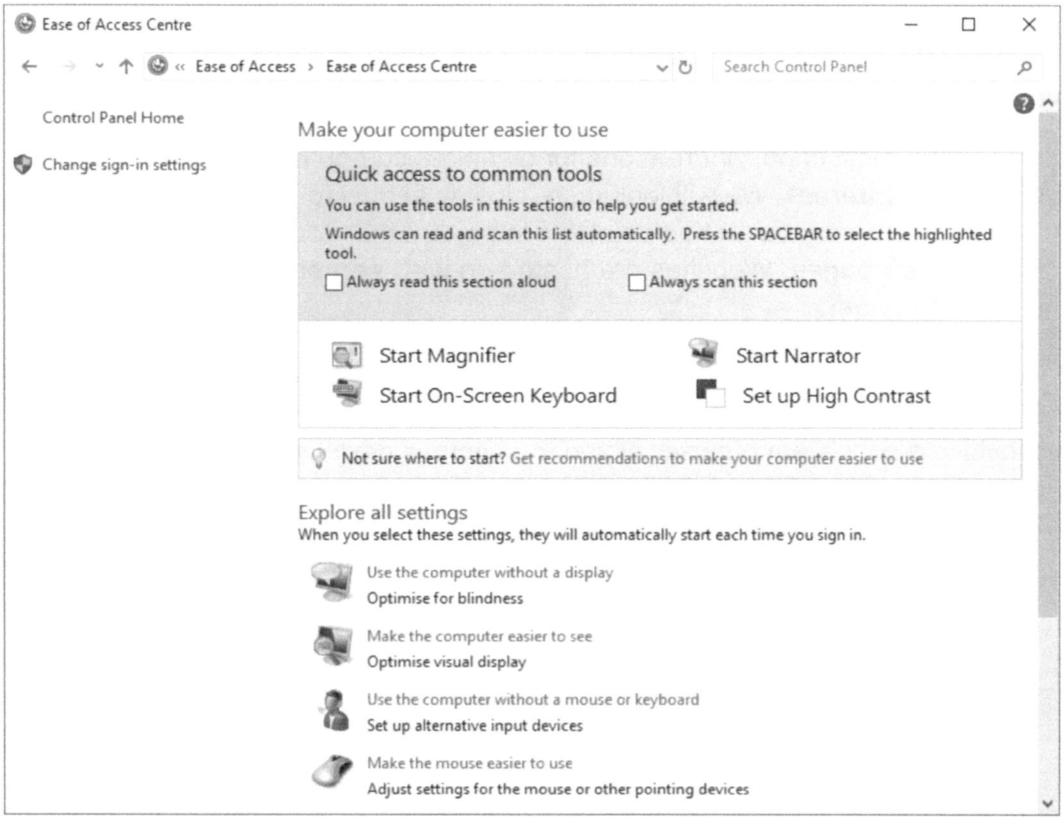

Use the Ease of Access Center in Windows to set up accessibility options. Screenshot used with permission from Microsoft.

Advanced Management Utilities

There are other utilities for configuring more advanced or technical aspects of the way Windows work. Pressing **START+X** or right-clicking the **Start** button shows a shortcut menu including Control Panel, Windows Settings, and File Explorer but also management utilities such as Device Manager, Computer Management, Command Prompt, and Windows PowerShell. These are used for advanced configuration of OS settings.

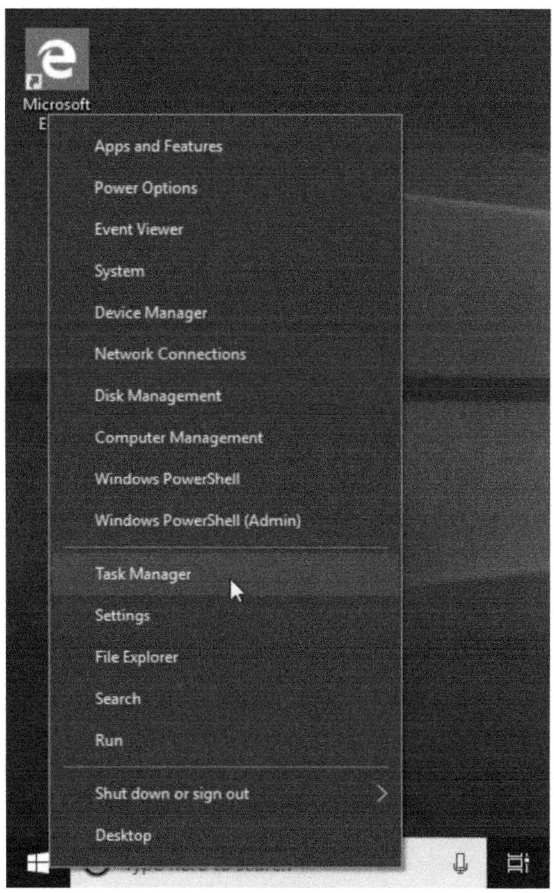

Windows 10 START+X menu (right-click the Start button). Screenshot used with permission from Microsoft.

Using a Web Browser

One of the most important reasons for owning a computer is to be able to access the **Internet**. We will look more closely at how to connect to the Internet later in the course, but at this point it is important that you understand how to browse **web pages**. Websites are hosted on **web servers** and are viewed using a **browser**.

Two browsers are shipped with Windows 10: Microsoft Edge and Internet Explorer. Generally, it is recommended that you use Microsoft Edge; this provides a consistent browser experience across devices because Microsoft provides Microsoft Edge for other platforms, including Android and iOS. Internet Explorer is provided for backwards compatibility for certain website functions important for users in large, enterprise networks.

You can also install and use a third-party browser. Mozilla Firefox (www.mozilla.org/en-US/firefox/new/) and Google Chrome (www.google.com/chrome/) are popular, but there are many others. Apple iOS and macOS ship with the Safari browser.

Opening a Web Page

To open a page, you just open the browser icon located on the taskbar then enter the page's address into the **address bar**. You can open several pages at the same time by clicking the tab icon. Alternatively, press **`CTRL+T`** to open a new tab. You can press **`CTRL+TAB`** to cycle through open tabs.

Edge browser window showing 1) Navigation buttons and address bar; 2) Tabs; 3) Site navigation menu. Screenshot used with permission from Microsoft.

URLs, Websites, and Hyperlinks

Resources on the Internet are accessed using an address known as a **Uniform Resource Locator (URL)**. The URL contains the information necessary to open a page on the web. For example, the URL `http://www.comptia.org/index.htm` instructs the browser to use the HTTP protocol to display the file `index.htm` from the server identified as `www.comptia.org`.

You do not need to type the `http://` *part of the URL, but when the page opens, the full URL is shown in the address bar. A web browser will always interpret the http:// bit for you. In fact, you can often leave off "www" as well. For example, entering* `comptia.org` *would get you to the same place as* `www.comptia.org`.

A **website** is a collection of web pages published by a particular organization.

A website features **hyperlinks** to allow you to navigate between the pages without having to know the specific address of each page. Often these hyperlinks are organized as **navigation bars**.

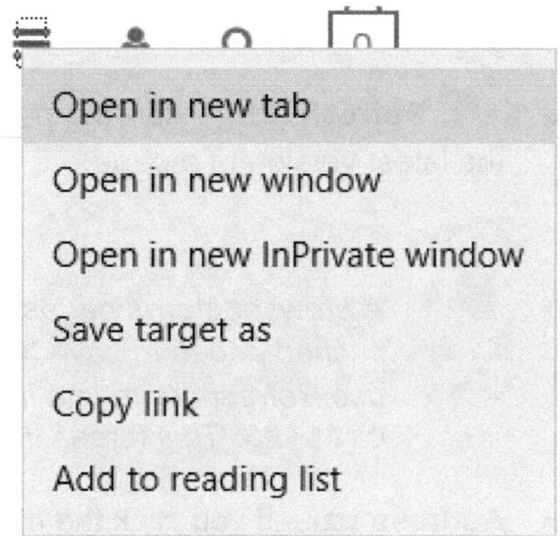

Shortcut menu for a hyperlink. Screenshot used with permission from Microsoft.

A hyperlink appears either as *text* or as a *picture*. When you point the cursor at a hyperlink, it appears as a pointing finger.

When you open a link, it may open in the same tab, in a different tab, or in a new browser window. The web designer sets the default action, but you can choose how to open any link by right-clicking it then selecting from the shortcut menu.

Using Browser Controls

A web browser has a number of tools to help you visit pages you have been to previously.

- **Back** (`BACKSPACE`)—visit the page you just left. If you click the arrow on the button, you can select from a list of pages you have visited before.
- **Forward** (`ALT+RIGHT ARROW`)—this can be used after using the Back button to return to the page you left. Again, you can click the arrow to skip ahead by a number of pages.
- **Stop** (`ESC`)—halt the download of a page. You may want to do this if you have a slow Internet connection and the page is taking a long time.
- **Refresh** (`F5`)—start the page downloading again. This also displays the latest version of a page.

A browser stores pages you have visited in its ***cache*** *and uses the cached pages to save time. If you suspect a page is out of date, use Refresh to update it. If it still seems out-of-date, press* `CTRL+F5`*. This* forces *the browser to ignore the cached files.*

- **Address bar**—if you click the arrow on the address bar, you can select from the **AutoComplete** list of sites you have entered previously.

AutoComplete only remembers addresses you have ***typed*** *into the address bar. Also, when you type an address, the list is displayed automatically, and you can select a link from it if you wish. You can view any pages you have visited before by opening* ***History*** *(*`CTRL+SHIFT+H`*).*

Setting the Home Page

The home page of a *website* is the default page that opens when you enter the site's simplest URL: comptia.com or microsoft.com for example. It acts like a front door for the site. *Your* home page is the page that Microsoft Edge displays when it is started. You can choose any address you like for your home page (or choose more than one home page and open multiple tabs by default when the browser starts).

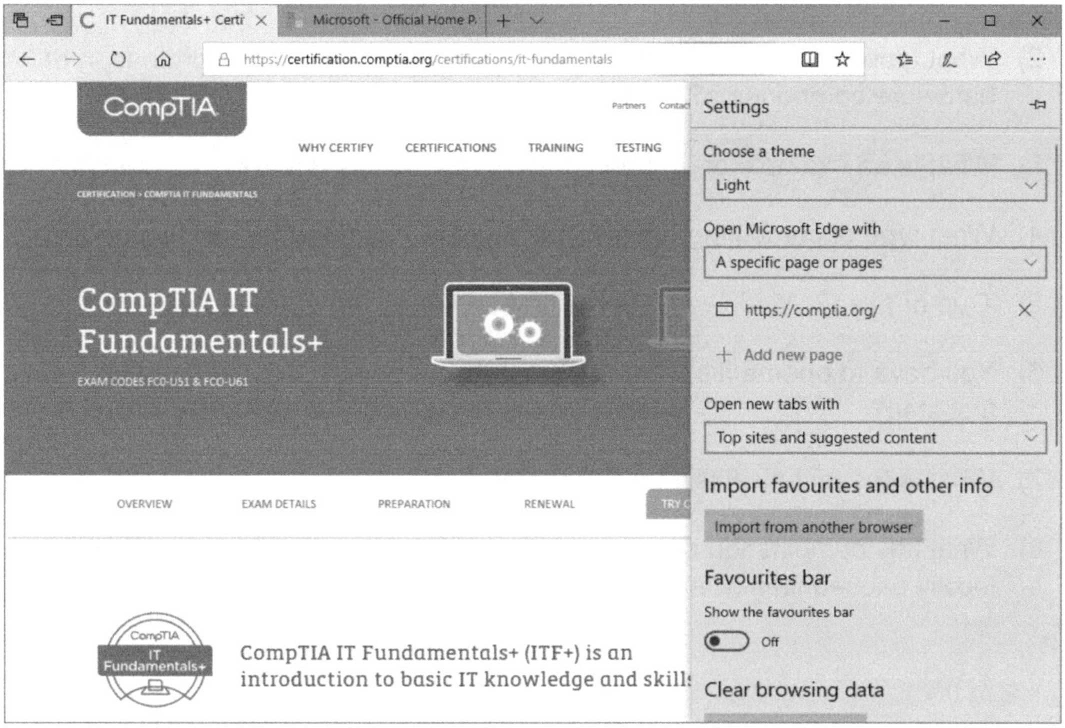

Setting the home page through the Settings menu. Screenshot used with permission from Microsoft.

To set the home page, click the ellipse button and select **Settings**. From the **Open Microsoft Edge with** list box, select **A specific page or pages**. In the "Enter a URL" box, type the URL to your homepage, and then click **Save**.

Open your home page by clicking the **Home** button  (or press **ALT+HOME**).

Review Questions / Module 1 / Unit 3 / Using an OS

Answer these questions to test what you have learned in this unit. You can review the model answers at the end of the book.

1) What function of an operating system is performed by the "shell?"
2) What type of file in an OS is the main means of providing coordination of hardware components?
3) What is an example of an open source operating system?
4) What type of computing device(s) is macOS designed for installation on?
5) True or false? Windows 10 is the first 64-bit edition of Windows.
6) You have to open a file located on a network server. What should be your first step?
7) What is the technical term for a web address?
8) What key combination can you use to force the browser to ignore any locally cached files when refreshing a page?

Lab 3 / Browsing a Website

In this lab, you will practice using some of the features of the web browser Microsoft Edge.

If you do not have an Internet connection set up already, you may want to refer to Unit 3.1.

Windows 10 provides two web browsers: Microsoft Edge and Microsoft Internet Explorer.

1) Start the computer and sign in. Then, if necessary, show the desktop (**START+D**).

2) Click the **Microsoft Edge** icon on the taskbar to start the browser.

3) Your browser home page is loaded. Navigate to comptia.org by typing in the address bar and pressing **ENTER**.

   Notice that when you open the page the full URL **https://www.comptia.org/** is displayed in the address bar.

4) Spend a couple of minutes browsing the site. Try all of the following:

   - Using the scroll bar or mouse scroll wheel to view a page.
   - Following text and picture hyperlinks to other pages within the same site.
   - Using the **Back** button or **BACKSPACE** to return to a previous page.
   - Following hyperlinks to pages on other sites.

5) Point to the new tab icon and click it. This opens a new tab. Tabbed browsing makes it easier to view multiple pages at the same time. In the address bar, type msn.com and press **ENTER**.

6) Click the **Hub** button. This displays a number of options:

   - **Favorites**—a list of web pages that you have bookmarked. You can bookmark a page by visiting it then clicking the Add To icon in the address bar.

- **Reading list** —adding a page to the reading list rather than favorites saves a copy of the page to your device, meaning that you can view it later, even if you not connected to the Internet.
- **History** —a browser keeps a record of the pages you have visited, unless you choose to browse in "private" mode.
- **Downloads** —some web pages include files that you can download, such as documents or apps. The downloads icon lets you see which files you have chosen to save to your computer.

7) Click **History** and then click **comptia.org**.
8) Close the **comptia** tab.
9) Click the **More Actions** ellipse icon and then click **Settings**.
10) Click **View advanced settings**. You can configure a number of options and control the way Microsoft Edge handles new tabs and website browsing and security options.
11) Close Microsoft Edge and when prompted, click **Close all**.
12) Click **Start**, scroll down and click **Windows Accessories**.
13) Right-click **Internet Explorer**, point to **More**, and then click **Pin to taskbar**.
14) On the taskbar, click the **Internet Explorer** icon.
15) Click the **Tools** icon and then click **Internet Options**.
16) In the **Internet Options** dialog box, click through the available tabs (General, Security, Privacy, Content, Connections, Programs, and Advanced). View the available options and then click **Cancel**.
17) To configure a preferred browser, click **Start** and then click **Settings**.
18) Click **Apps**, and then, on the **Default apps** tab, under the Web browser heading, click and select **Internet Explorer**. If prompted, click **Switch anyway**.
19) To default to Microsoft Edge, under **Web browser**, click and select **Microsoft Edge**. Close Settings.
20) Optionally, shut down your computer if you are not continuing to use it after this lab.

Module 1 / Unit 4

Managing an OS

Objectives

On completion of this unit, you will be able to:

- Use GUI and command-line management interfaces to configure an operating system.
- Explain the importance of access control features and configure user accounts.

Syllabus Objectives and Content Examples

This unit covers the following exam domain objectives and content examples:

- 3.1 Manage applications and software.
  Disk management • Process management/scheduling (Kill process/end task) • Memory management • Access control/protection
- 3.2 Compare and contrast components of an operating system.
  Services • Processes • Utilities (Task scheduling) • Interfaces (Console/command line, GUI)

Management Interfaces

A **management interface** is a graphical or command-line tool used to perform some aspect of system configuration. A number of administrative tools are used to manage Windows:

- Control Panel/Windows Settings—individual applets to configure various aspects of Windows. The Control Panel is a legacy interface; increasingly, configuration options are being moved to the touchscreen-friendly Settings app.

- Management Consoles—these represent more technical system configuration options. The default **Computer Management** console contains a number of different administrative **snap-ins**. Each snap-in configures the settings for a different OS sub-system, such as disk management or user management. There are various other consoles, and you can also create custom ones with **mmc.exe**.

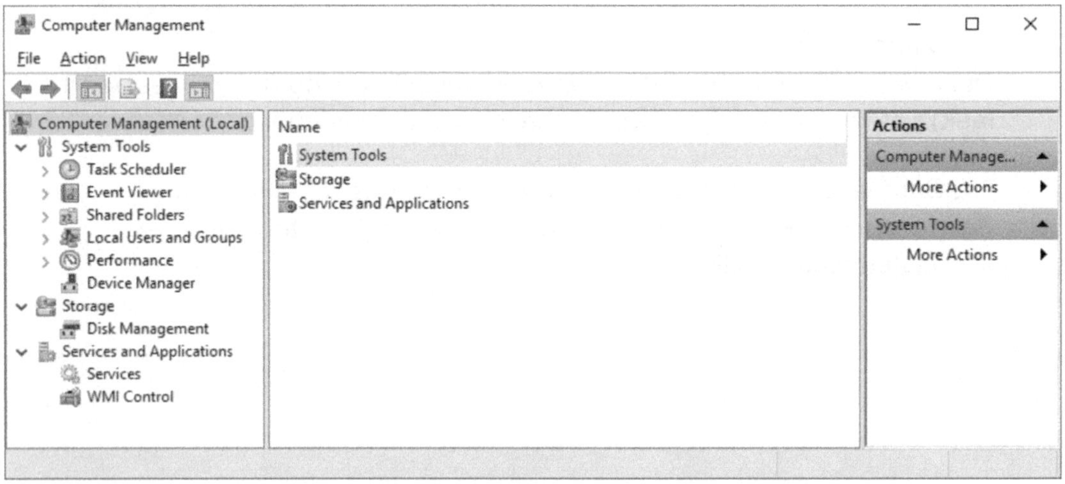

The default Computer Management console with the configuration snap-ins shown on the left. Screenshot used with permission from Microsoft.

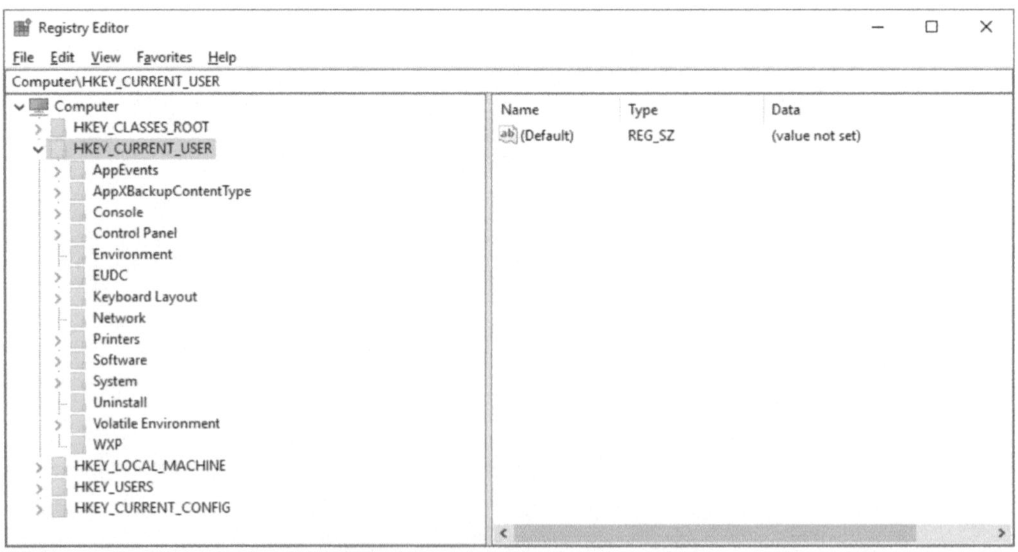

Registry Editor—most configuration changes are stored as values in the Registry database. Screenshot used with permission from Microsoft.

- Registry Editor (`regedit`)—when you change a setting via a management interface, you are usually changing something stored in the Windows Registry configuration database. The Registry Editor is a means of directly editing this database.

- Command prompt/PowerShell—settings can also be changed by typing native Windows commands or the PowerShell scripting language.

*In Windows 10, the most useful system administration tools can be accessed by right-clicking the **Start** button or by pressing* **START+X**.

We will not go into detail in this course, but in Linux all configuration is performed by modifying text files. This can be done directly in a text editor, such as `vi` or `nano`, but many Linux distributions include graphical tools and system commands to assist with the process of making the underlying changes.

Process and Service Management

When a program starts (either because it has been scheduled to do so by the OS or opened by a user), the application code executes in memory as a **process**.

*A process is the main unit governing a program and managing the memory resources allocated to it by the OS. A process may contain one or more **threads**, which are parts of the program scheduled for execution by the CPU.*

Task Manager

The **Task Manager** utility (`taskmgr`) allows the user to shut down processes that are not responding. An ordinary user can end unresponsive applications, but administrative rights are required to end processes that were started by the system rather than the signed in user. This protects the system as things like malware cannot disable anti-virus software. In addition to this functionality, Task Manager can be used to monitor the PC's key resources.

There are various ways to run Task Manager, including pressing **CTRL+SHIFT+ESC**, right-clicking the taskbar, or right-clicking the Start button (**START+X**).

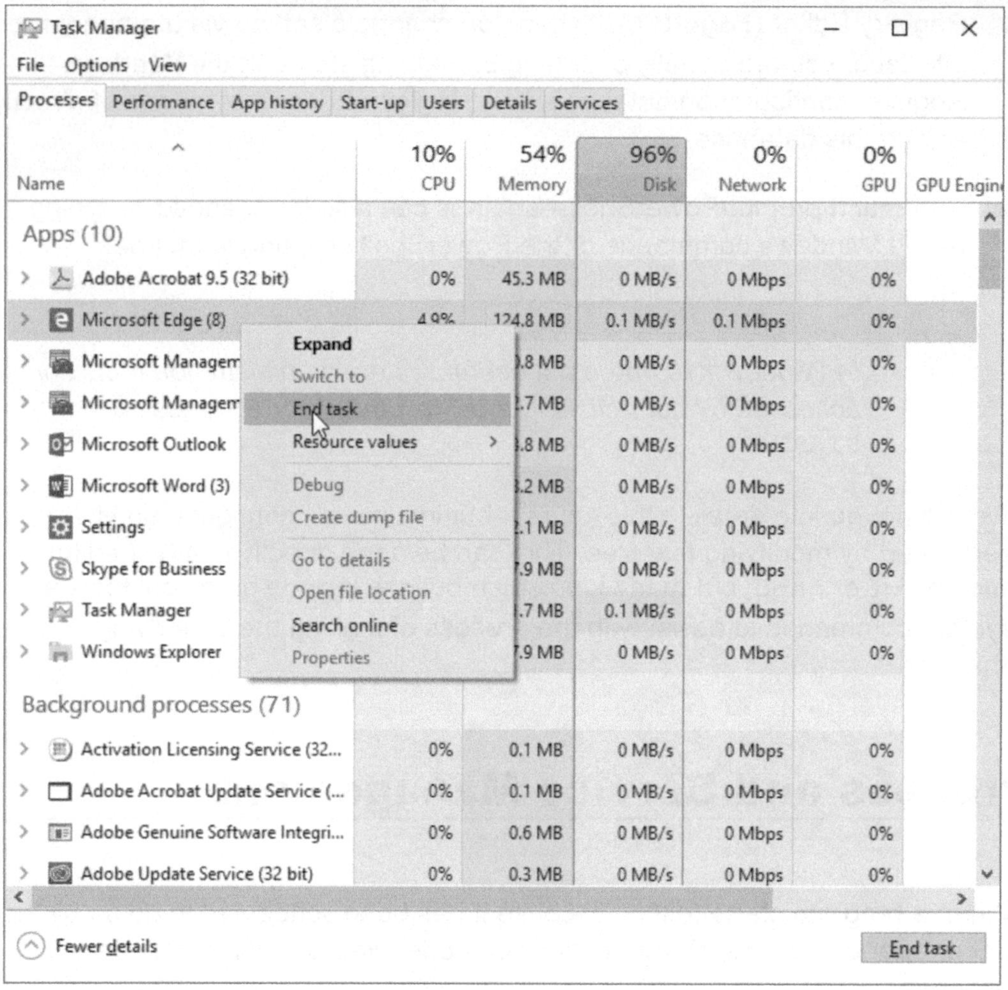

Using Task Manger to end a process. Screenshot used with permission from Microsoft.

Terminating a process like this (rather than using the application's Close or Exit function) is often called "killing" the process. The command line option for doing this in Windows is indeed called `taskkill`*. Always try to close or end a task normally before attempting to "kill" it.*

Service Management

A **service** is a Windows process that does not require any sort of user interaction and thus runs in the background (without a window). Services provide functionality for many parts of the Windows OS, such as allowing sign in, browsing the network, or indexing file details to optimize searches. Services may be installed by Windows and by other applications, such as anti-virus, database, or backup software.

You can use the **Services** snap-in to check which services are running and to start and stop each service or configure its properties, such as whether it starts automatically at system boot time.

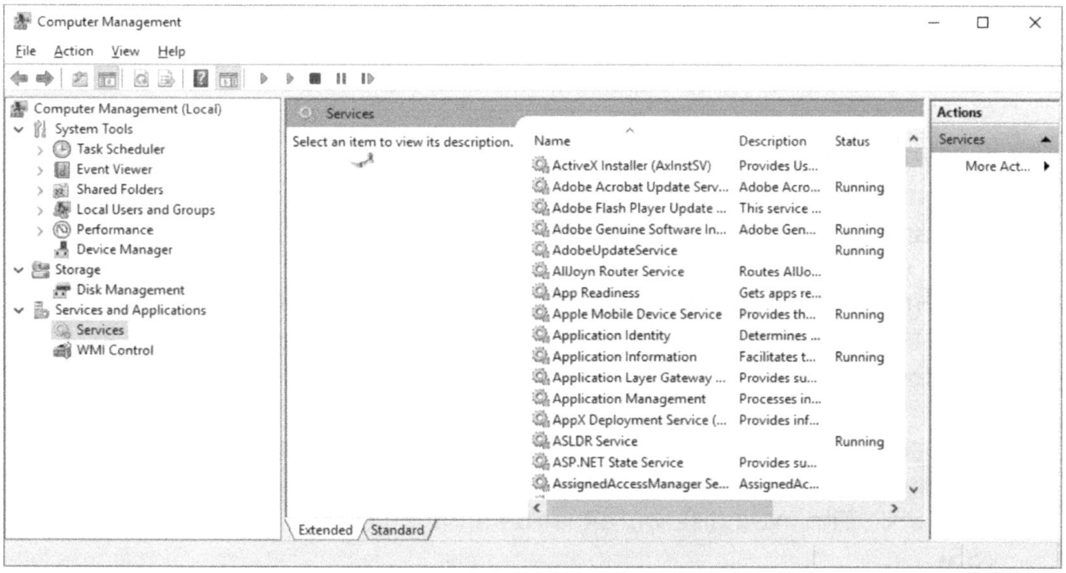

Managing services using the Computer Management console. Screenshot used with permission from Microsoft.

Task Scheduler

As noted above, a process (whether it is interactive or a background service) can be started either manually by the user or automatically by the operating system. In Windows, **Task Scheduler**, as its name suggests, sets tasks to run at a particular time. Tasks can be run once at a future date or time or according to a recurring schedule. A task can be a simple application process (including switches if necessary) or a batch file or script. Task Scheduler is accessed via its own console and can also be found in the Computer Management console.

Many of Windows' processes come with predefined task schedules (Disk Defragmenter, for instance, is configured to run automatically by default).

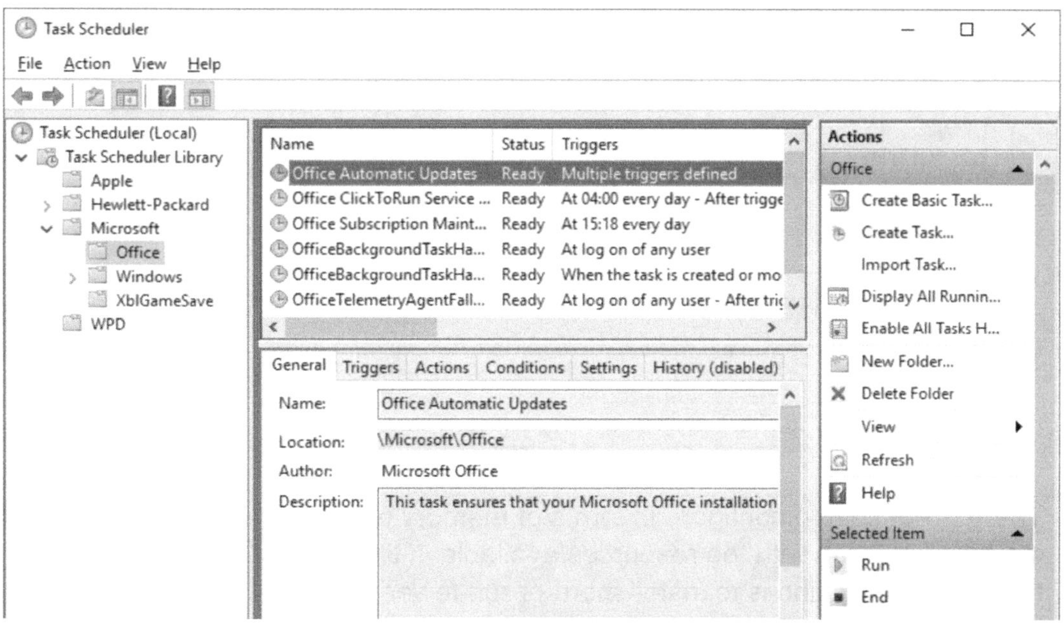

Task Scheduler. Screenshot used with permission from Microsoft.

In Linux, the **`cron`** *utility is often used to run tasks or scripts at a particular time.*

Memory and Disk Management

As the CPU only has a limited amount of storage space in which to store instructions, it has to work with other storage components. The two main types of these are system memory and mass storage (or fixed disk storage).

- System memory—this type of memory is volatile, meaning that it is only preserved while the system is powered up. System memory is provided by Random Access Memory (RAM) modules.
- Mass storage—to preserve data when the system is turned off, it is written as files to a mass storage device. Every PC comes with at least one such fixed disk. The fixed disk will either be a hard disk or a Solid-State Drive (SSD).

Memory Management

When a process executes, it takes up space in system memory. If the system runs out of memory, then processes will be unable to start, and running processes may crash because they cannot load the data they need.

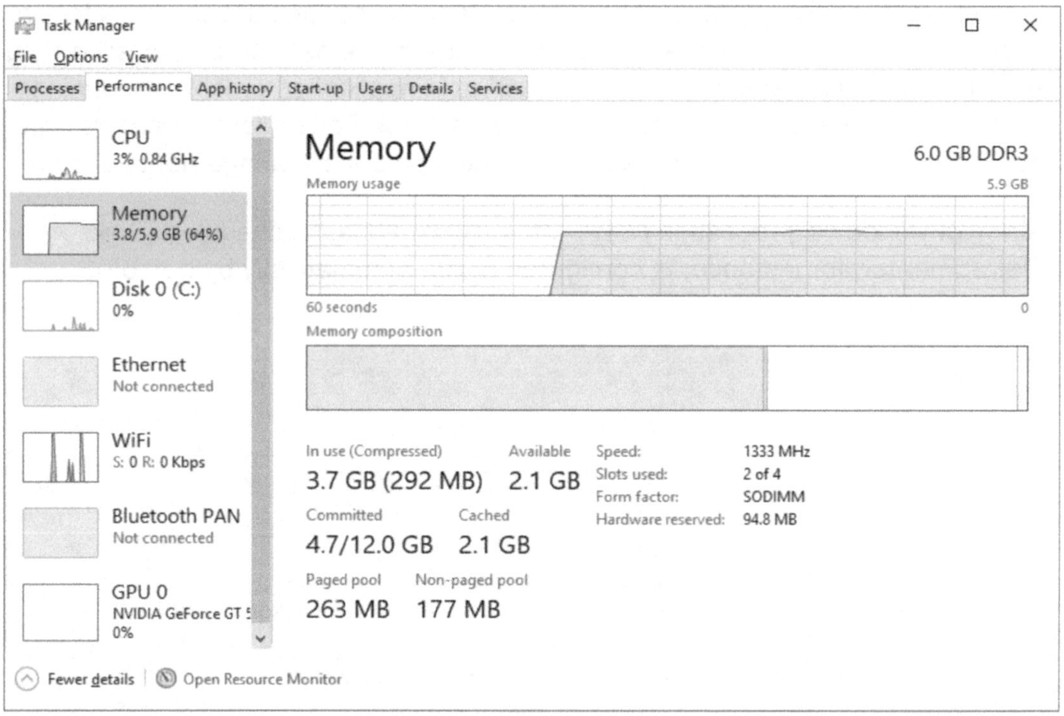

Using Task Manager to check system memory usage. Screenshot used with permission from Microsoft.

There is not a lot to configure in terms of memory management. The OS will do the best job it can with the resources available; if there is not enough memory the only real solution is to install more or run fewer programs simultaneously. Badly written programs and malware can cause a memory leak, where the process keeps claiming memory addresses without releasing them. If the system keeps running out of memory, you would use Task Manager or another monitoring program to find the offending process and disable it from running.

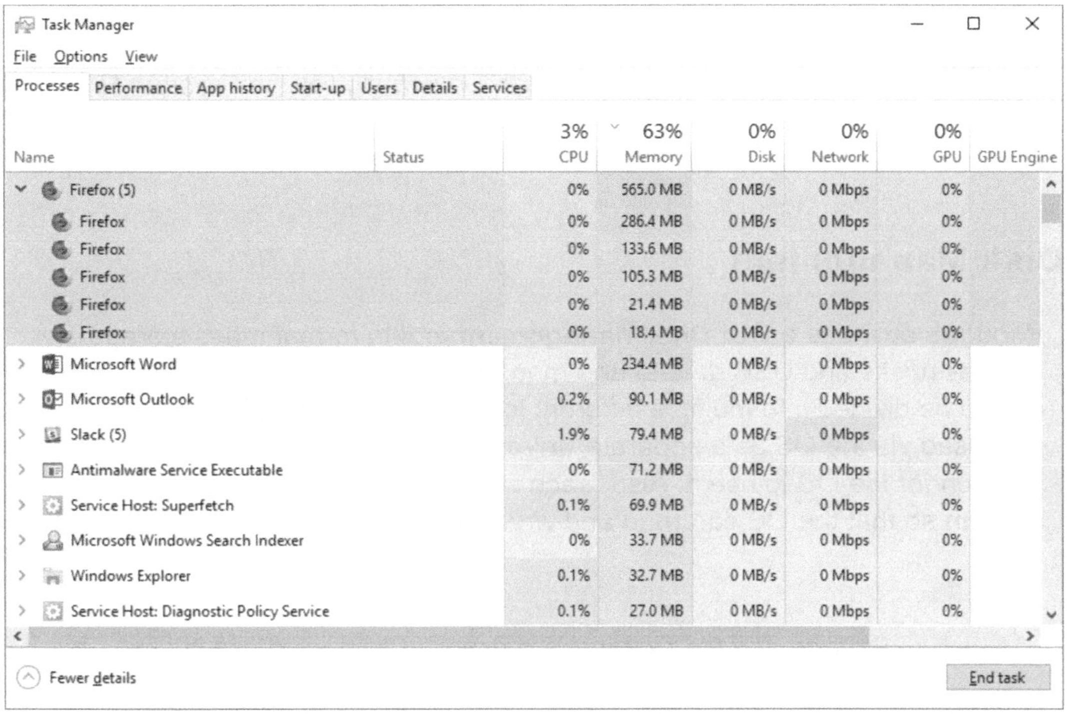

Using Task Manager to check how much memory a process is using. In this example each browser (Firefox) tab has its own memory space—you can see that some web pages use more memory than others! Screenshot used with permission from Microsoft.

Virtual Memory/Pagefile

There are situations where the OS loads more data than can fit within the amount of system memory modules installed. The OS can use the fixed disk to supplement RAM by paging it to the disk. This is called a **pagefile** or **virtual memory**. The pagefile is usually user configurable (in Windows via the **Advanced system settings** link in the **System** control panel applet), but in most circumstances you would leave the OS to manage it.

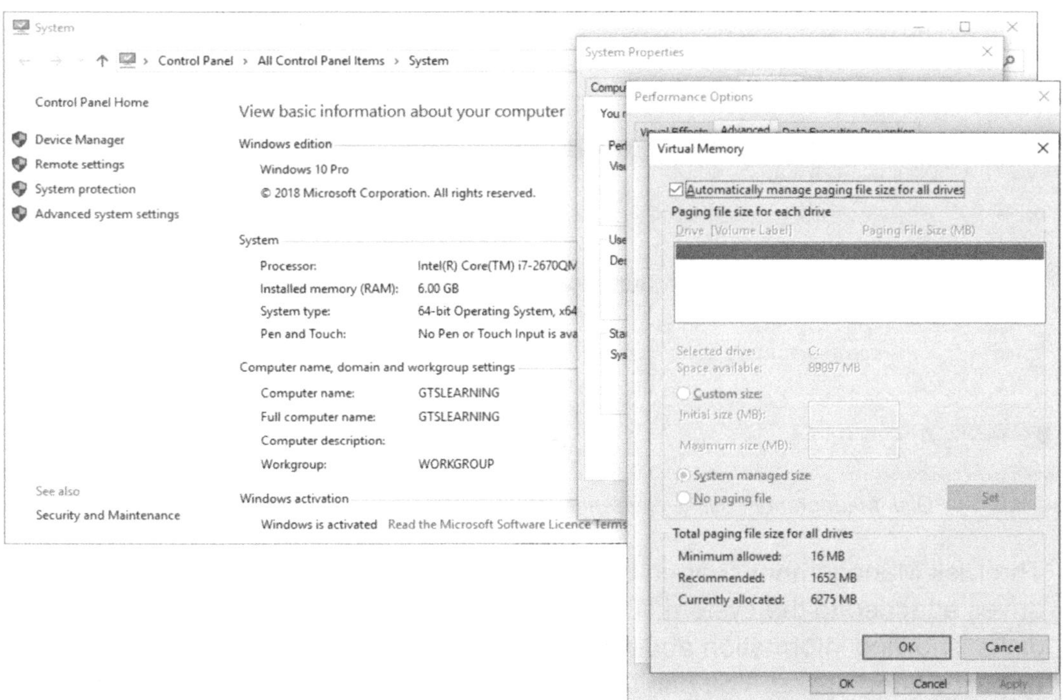

Viewing virtual memory (or pagefile) settings via the System applet. The PC has 6 GB of system RAM and Windows has automatically allocated the same amount of space to the pagefile. Screenshot used with permission from Microsoft.

A traditional hard drive is much, much slower than system RAM and is often a performance bottleneck. Using an SSD as the main fixed disk will greatly improve performance.

Disk Management

Windows provides a GUI **Disk Management** tool to format mass storage devices (disks and USB drives) and manage partitions. Partitions allow a single disk to be divided into multiple different logical areas, each of which can be accessed via the OS as a separate **drive**. A disk must have at least one partition for the OS to use it. Also, each partition must be formatted with a **file system** so that the OS can read and write files to the drive.

Storage and file systems are covered in more detail in Unit 3.4.

Disk Management is one of the snap-ins included with the default Computer Management console, or you can open the tool directly from the **`START+X`** menu (or run **`diskmgr.msc`**).

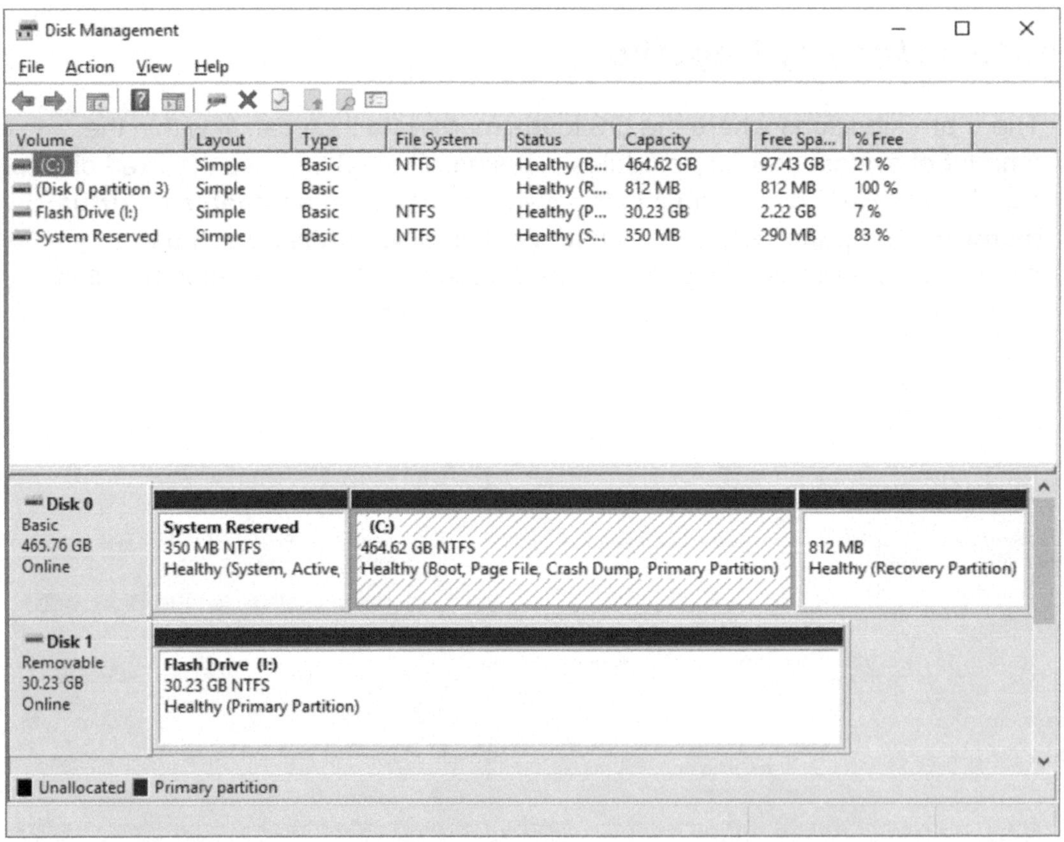

Disk Management utility. Screenshot used with permission from Microsoft.

The Disk Management snap-in displays a summary of any fixed and removable drives attached to the system. The top pane lists drives; the bottom pane lists disks, showing information about the partitions created on each disk plus any **unpartitioned** space. You can use the tool to create and modify partitions, reformat a partition, assign a different drive letter, and so on.

Reformatting or deleting a partition deletes any data stored on it. Always back up data before using Disk Management.

Command Line Interfaces

As you have seen, most operating systems can be operated using a **Graphical User Interface (GUI)** controlled via a mouse, keyboard, and/or touchscreen, but a GUI is only one type of interface or **shell**. A **Command Line Interface (CLI)** shell represents an alternative means of configuring an OS or application. Some operating systems only present a CLI and have no GUI. A CLI displays a prompt, showing that it is ready to accept a command. When you type the command plus any switches and press **`ENTER`**, the shell executes the command, displays any output associated with the execution, and then returns to the prompt.

The term "console" is often used interchangeably with "command line" or "command prompt" but has different technical meanings in Windows and UNIX/Linux.

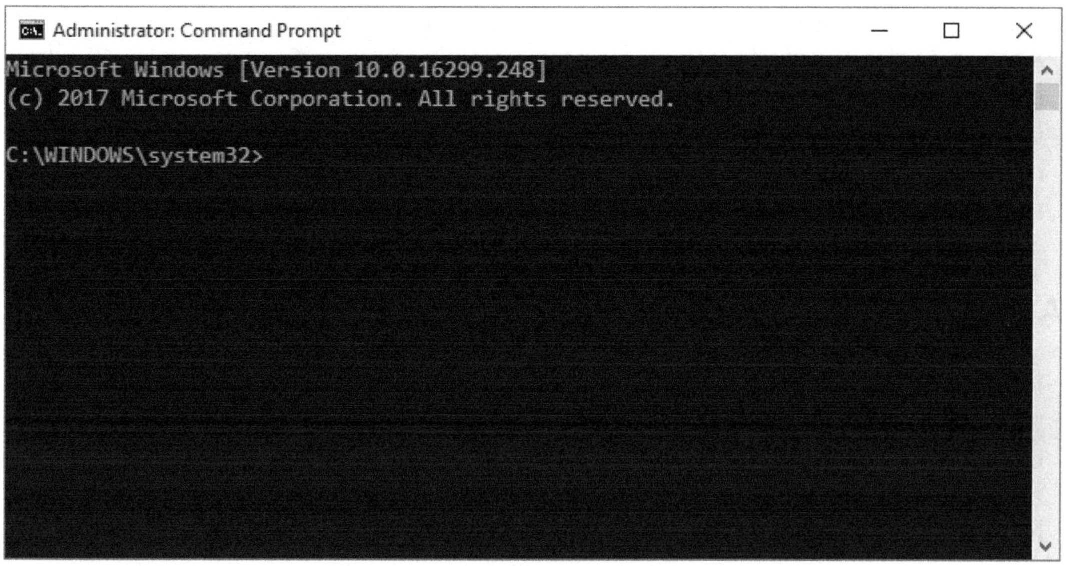

Windows command prompt (cmd.exe). Screenshot used with permission from Microsoft.

Note that there may be more than one CLI environment included with an operating system. For example, Windows provides both the Windows Command Prompt (cmd.exe) and PowerShell CLIs. Linux usually presents the Bash (Bourne Again SHell) but there are alternatives.

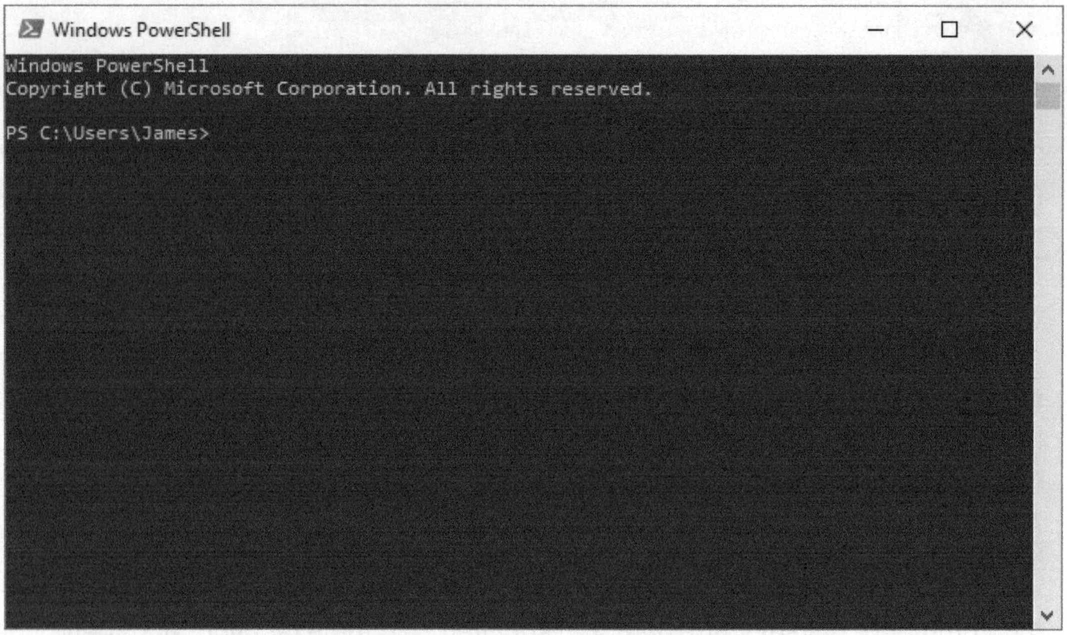

Windows PowerShell command prompt. Screenshot used with permission from Microsoft.

Access Control and Protection

Access control means that a computing device (or any information stored on the device) can only be used by an authorized person, such as its owner. Access control on workstation operating systems is usually enforced by the concept of user accounts. Each user of the device is allocated an account and uses a password (or other credential) to **authenticate** to that account. The OS can restrict the **privileges** allocated to an account so that it is not able to reconfigure settings or access certain data areas.

Administrator and Standard User Accounts

When the OS is first installed, the account created or used during setup is a powerful local administrator account. The account is assigned membership of the local Administrators group. Generally speaking, you should only use this account to manage the computer (install applications and devices, perform troubleshooting, and so on).

You should create ordinary user accounts for day-to-day access to the computer. This is done by putting additional users of the computer in the **Standard users** group. Standard users cannot change the system configuration and are restricted to saving data files within their own user profile folder or the Public profile. For example, a user named David could only save files within **C:\Users\David** or **C:\Users\Public**. Administrators can access any folder on the computer.

Least Privilege and User Account Control

The principle of **least privilege** is that users should have only sufficient permissions required to perform tasks and no more.

User Account Control (UAC) is Windows' solution to the problem of **elevated privileges**. In order to change important settings on the computer (such as installing drivers or software), administrative privileges are required. Early versions of Windows make dealing with typical administrative tasks as an ordinary user very difficult, meaning that most users were given administrative privileges as a matter of course. This makes the OS more usable, but it also makes it much more vulnerable, as any malicious software infecting the computer would run with the same administrative privileges.

UAC counters this by running accounts in a protected **sandbox**. When users need to exercise administrative rights, they must explicitly confirm use of those rights by entering the administrator's credentials or by clicking through an authorization dialog. The desktop darkens into a special secure mode to prevent third-party software from imitating the authorization dialog.

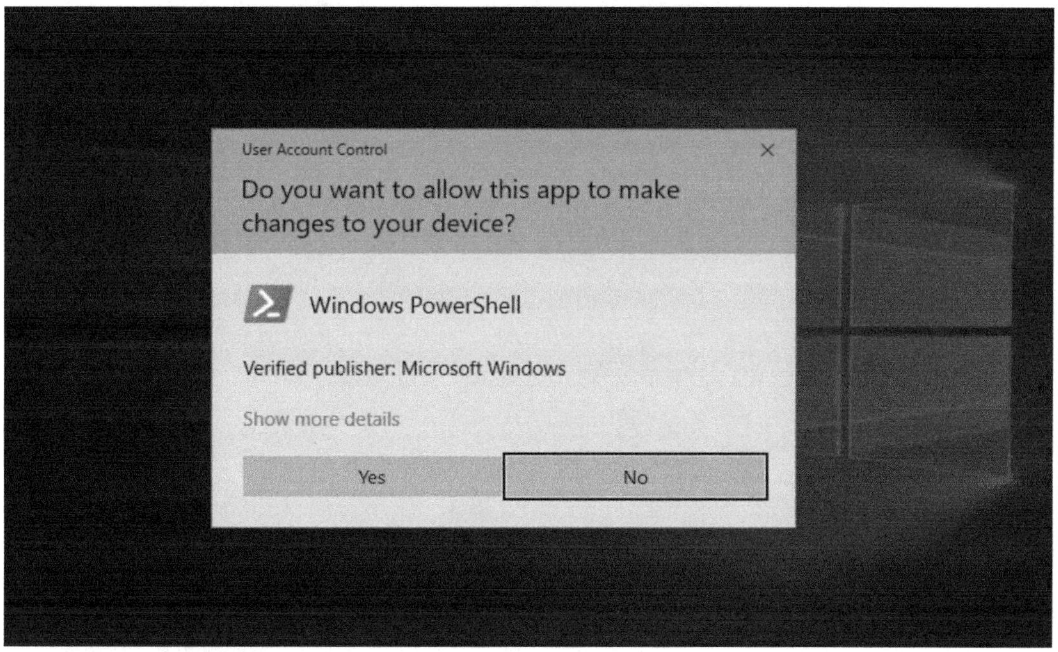

UAC requiring confirmation of the use of administrator privileges. Screenshot used with permission from Microsoft.

Note that options in Control Panel and menus and dialogs with the icon on or next to them may require you to authorize use of the command through UAC.

Creating Other User Accounts

Windows supports two types of user accounts:

- Local accounts—these are defined on one computer only.
- Microsoft accounts—these are connected to Microsoft's cloud services. A Microsoft account can be used to sign in on multiple devices and synchronize settings, apps, and data between them.

To create a new account, open **Settings** then click **Accounts**. Select **Family & other people** then click **Add someone else to this PC**.

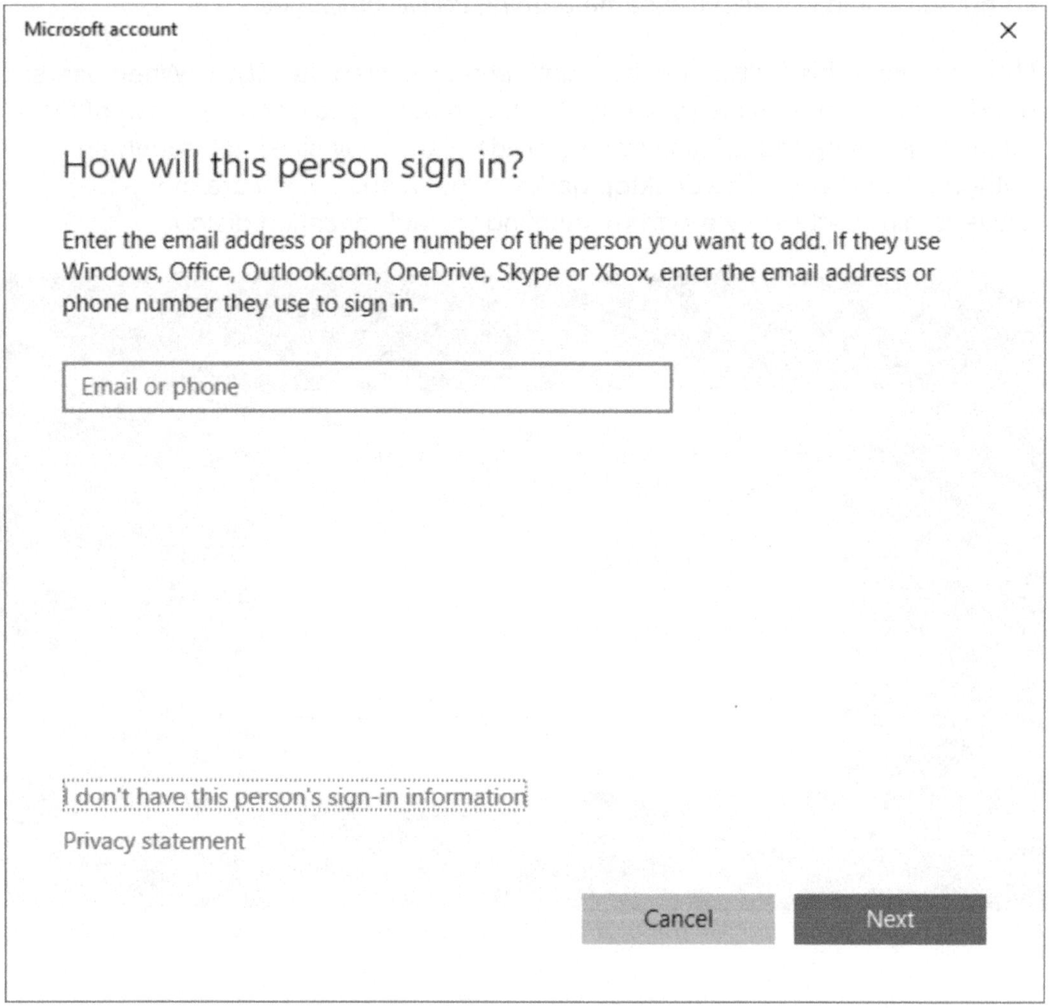

Creating a new account. Screenshot used with permission from Microsoft.

Enter the user's email address for their Microsoft account, click **Next** and click **Finish**. The user must complete the process of signing in themselves.

*To create a local account, you would click the **I don't have this person's sign-in information** link.*

Managing User Accounts

Users can manage their own account from **Settings**. In the **Accounts** node, they can select and configure options on the following tabs:

- **Your info**—enables you to configure options such as a picture for your account.
- **Email & app accounts**—allows you to associate accounts with email and other apps on the local computer, such as a Microsoft Outlook or Gmail account.
- **Sign-in options**—allows you to enable and configure advanced sign in options, such as Windows Hello (biometrics), Picture password, and PIN sign in.
- **Access work or school**—from here, you can define additional accounts that you use to access other networks, such as a work account or an account used for accessing school resources.

In professional/enterprise Windows editions, administrators can use the **Local Users and Groups** snap-in within the Computer Management console to configure accounts. Options include setting a user's password, disabling/enabling an account, unlocking an account after too many bad passwords, configuring group membership, or specifying login scripts and profile paths.

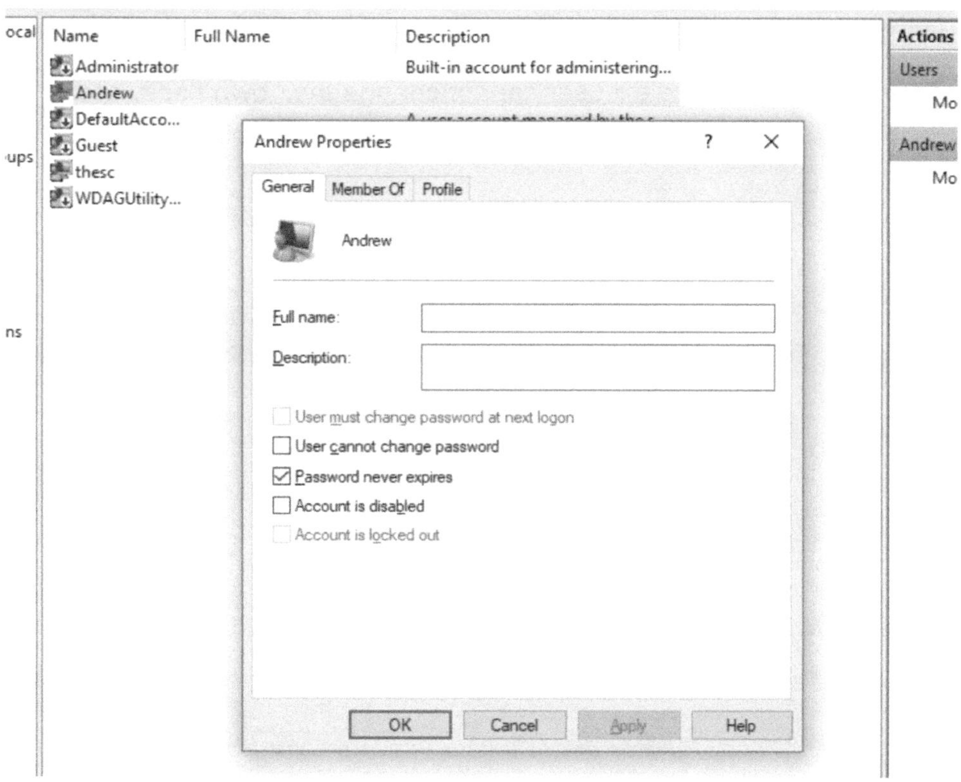

Configuring local user accounts. Screenshot used with permission from Microsoft.

This describes managing accounts on a standalone computer. On a corporate network, such as a Windows domain, accounts, privileges, and permissions are managed on a centralized server rather than on each workstation.

Review Questions / Module 1 / Unit 4 / Managing an OS

Answer these questions to test what you have learned in this unit. You can review the model answers at the end of the book.

1) What is the registry and how does it distinguish Windows and Linux?
2) What term is used to describe terminating a process that is not responding to user input?
3) Why might you use the Services snap-in to manage background processes rather than Task Manager?
4) The Task Scheduler allows you to run a process automatically in Windows. What is a widely-used Linux equivalent?
5) What part of the system memory setup is most user-configurable?
6) What two things are configured on a disk to make storage space on the disk available to the Windows OS?
7) What is a CLI?
8) What protection feature in Windows is designed to prevent a script or software from making unauthorized changes to the OS configuration?
9) True or false? A standard user cannot change their own password.

Lab 4 / Using Management Interfaces

In this lab, you will learn how to access the principal management interfaces in Windows 10.

1) If necessary, start your computer and sign in.

2) Right-click the **Start** button or press **`START+X`**.

   This opens the Quick Access menu. This contains shortcuts to most of the tools required by "power users."

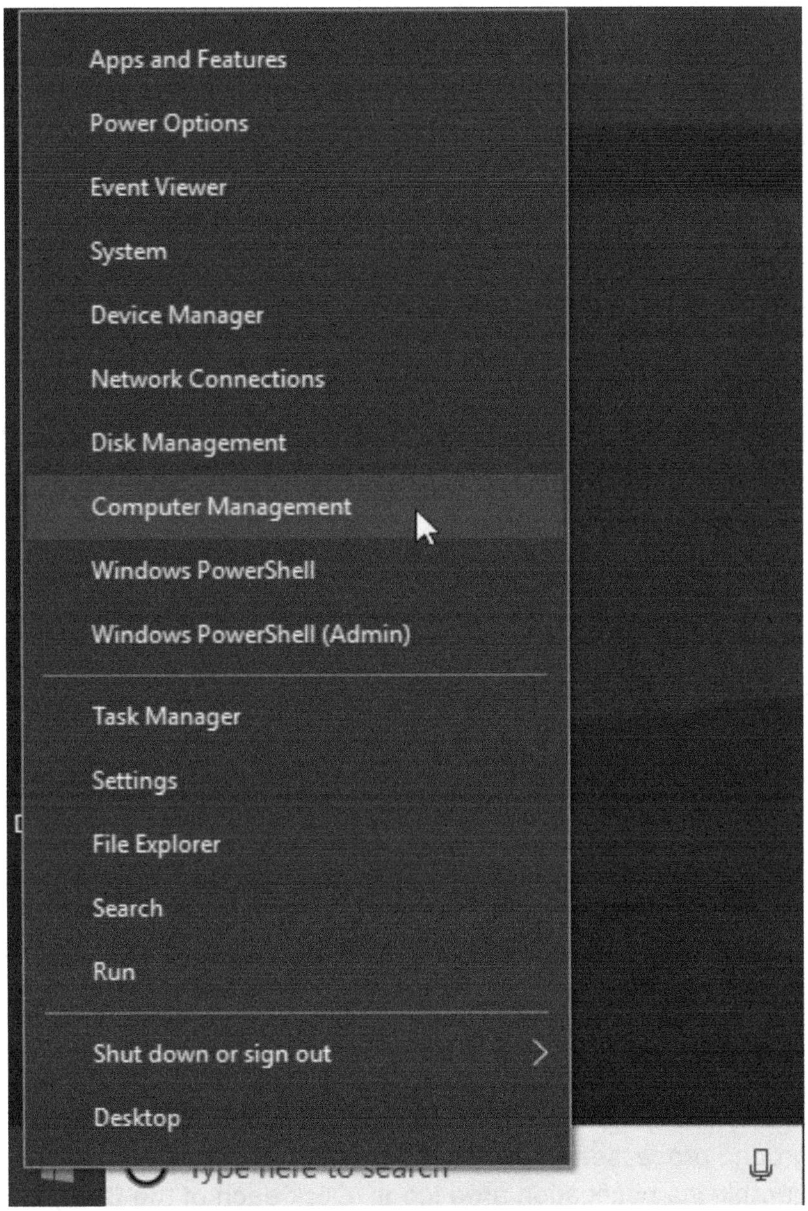

Quick Access menu. Screenshot used with permission from Microsoft.

3) From the Quick Access menu, select **System**.

   This settings page provides information about the PC status and the version of Windows currently installed.

4) Take some time to browse other pages in the Settings app.

5) Press **CTRL+SHIFT+ESC** to open Task Manager. Alternatively, use the Quick Access menu or right-click the taskbar. If necessary, click **More details** at the bottom of the window to show the tabs.

6) On the **Processes** tab, right-click **Settings** and select **End Task**.

   You can "kill" this task without risk of data loss but note that if you end a task that is processing unsaved data, the information will be lost.

7) Start **Paint** and draw a picture in the window. Do not save the file.

8) In Task Manager, right-click **Paint** and select **End Task**.

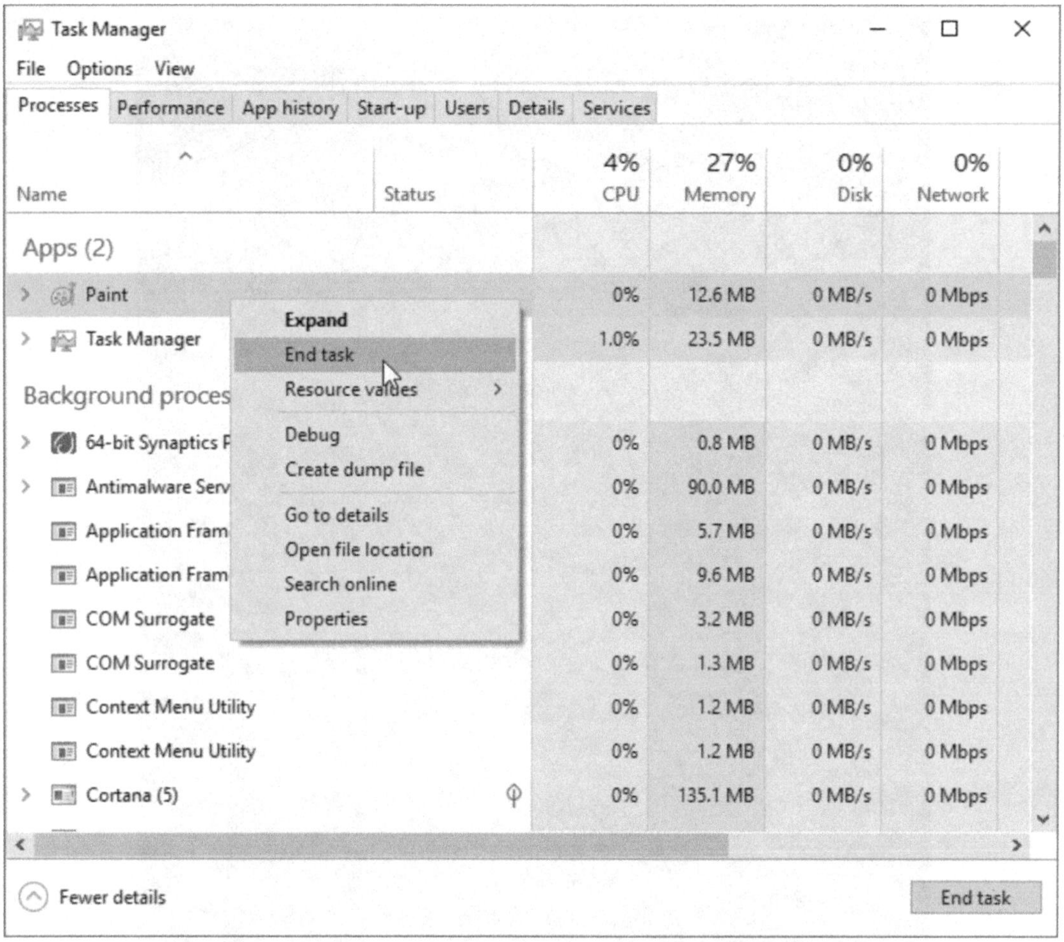

"Killing" a process using Task Manager. Screenshot used with permission from Microsoft.

   The Paint window closes without prompting you to save the image you created.

9) Note the division of processes into apps and background processes. The background processes run without a window, though some may be configurable via notification area icons. Click each of the **CPU**, **Memory**, **Disk**, and **Network** headings in turn to sort processes by how much of the computer's resources each is consuming.

10) Close Task Manager.

11) Press **START+X** and select **Computer Management**.

Computer Management is the default management console. Management consoles can be configured with snap-ins to control most of the "power" configuration options in Windows.

12) Select each of the following snap-ins to view them:

   - **Task Scheduler**—expand the node to view items in the task scheduler library. You can see that Windows runs many processes automatically.
   - **Disk Management**—this shows you a summary of the disks attached to the computer and the drives (partitions and file systems) configured on them.
   - **Services** (expand Services and Applications)—the shortcut menu for each service allows you to stop and start it or configure its properties.

13) Close Computer Management.

14) Press the `START` key and type `control panel`. Open the **Control Panel** icon that appears in the search results.

   Microsoft has removed Control Panel (and the legacy command prompt) from the Quick Access menu in recent updates. You have to directly edit the registry to recreate the shortcut.

   With the latest feature update, there are relatively few configuration options left in Control Panel.

15) Optionally, browse some of the applets then close the Control Panel window.

16) Right-click **Start** and select **Windows PowerShell**.

   Windows PowerShell is an example of a Command Line Interface (CLI).

17) Type the following command then execute it by pressing `ENTER`.

```
Get-NetIPConfiguration
```

   This PowerShell commandlet displays configuration information for the computer's network adapters.

   You do not actually have to match the case of the command when using PowerShell. The command environment is typically case-insensitive. Using case makes the command easier to read and typing mistakes less common however. In Linux, the command environment is case-sensitive.

18) Type the following command then execute it by pressing `ENTER`.

```
ipconfig
```

   This is an older command that displays similar information. PowerShell can run both Windows command prompt commands and native commandlets.

19) Press the **START** key and type **cmd**. Open the **Command Prompt** icon that appears in the search results.

20) Type the following command then execute it by pressing **ENTER**.

```
ipconfig
```

Note that this executes in the same way as in the PowerShell CLI.

21) Type the following command then execute it by pressing **ENTER**.

```
Get-NetIPConfiguration
```

This produces an error message. The command prompt environment cannot understand (parse) PowerShell commandlets. When using a CLI, you need to understand which commands it can run as they are not all the same.

22) Close any open windows.

Lab 5 / Managing User Accounts

In this lab, you will practice using some of the account features of Windows 10.

1) Click **Start** and then click the **Settings** icon .
2) Click **Accounts**.
3) In the left-hand pane, click **Sign-in options**.
4) Under "PIN," click **Add**.
5) If prompted, enter your user account password and click **OK**.
6) In the **Set up a PIN** window, in the **New PIN** and **Confirm PIN** boxes, enter a four-digit PIN and click **OK**.
7) Right-click the **Start** button and select **Shut down or sign out > Sign out**.
8) Press a key to dismiss the privacy shade then in the **PIN** box, type your four-digit PIN. You are signed in.
9) Open **Settings** and then click **Accounts**.
10) In the left-hand pane, click **Family & other people**.
11) Click **Add someone else to this PC**.
12) In the "How will this person sign in?" window, click **I don't have this person's sign-in information**.
13) On the "Let's create your account" page, click **Add a user without a Microsoft account**.
14) On the "Create an account for this PC" page, in the "Username" box, type `User1`.
15) In the "Password" and "Re-enter password" boxes, type `Pa$$w0rd`
16) For the "Security question" boxes, just enter `Pa$$w0rd` each time.

We're just doing this to make the lab simpler. In a real scenario, get the user to input the responses properly.

17) On the "Family & other people" page, click **User1**, and then click **Change account type**. Notice that the user is a standard user. Click **Cancel**.

Remember that a standard user is able to launch apps and install apps from the Windows Store but is not able to change the system settings or install desktop applications. It is always safer to sign in with a standard user account for day-to-day computer use than it is to sign in with administrator privileges.

18) Click **Start**, and then click the "head and shoulders" default user icon  that represents your account.

19) Click **User1**.

20) Enter `Pa$$w0rd` and press `ENTER`. Wait while the account's profile is built.

21) When the account has been signed in, open **Settings** and then select **Accounts**.

    Note that there is no option to manage Family & other accounts.

22) Click the **Sign-in options** tab. You can configure an account password from here (or use a different means of authenticating).

23) Open Microsoft Edge and view a few websites then open some apps or desktop programs.

24) Right-click the **Start** button and select **Shut down or sign out > Sign out**.

25) Sign back into your own account by entering the PIN.

    To complete this lab, we will reverse the changes you made.

26) Open **Settings** and then select **Accounts**.

27) In the left-hand pane, click **Sign-in options**. Under "PIN," click the **Remove** button then confirm by clicking the **Remove** button. Enter your password when prompted.

28) In the left-hand pane, click **Family & other people**.

29) Click the **User1** account then click the **Remove** button. In the "Delete account and data?" dialog, read the warning then click the **Delete account and data** button.

    When configuring a computer, it is important to take your time and read the warnings displayed on notifications and dialogs.

30) Optionally, shut down your computer if you are not continuing to use it after this lab.

Module 1 / Unit 5
Troubleshooting and Support

Objectives

On completion of this unit, you will be able to:

- Describe basic support and troubleshooting procedures.
- Use websites and tools to obtain support and search for advice and help.

Syllabus Objectives and Content Examples

This unit covers the following exam domain objectives and content examples:

- 1.6 Explain the troubleshooting methodology.
  Identify the problem (Gather information, Duplicate the problem, if possible, Question users, Identify symptoms, Determine if anything has changed, Approach multiple problems individually) • Research knowledge base/Internet, if applicable • Establish a theory of probable cause (Question the obvious, Consider multiple approaches, Divide and conquer) • Test the theory to determine the cause (Once the theory is confirmed [confirmed root cause], determine the next steps to resolve the problem, If the theory is not confirmed, establish a new theory or escalate) • Establish a plan of action to resolve the problem and identify potential effects • Implement the solution or escalate as necessary • Verify full system functionality and, if applicable, implement preventive measures • Document findings/lessons learned, actions and outcomes

Support and Troubleshooting

To some extent, being an effective troubleshooter simply involves having a detailed knowledge of how something is supposed to work and of the sort of things that typically go wrong. However, the more complex a system is, the less likely it is that this sort of information will be at hand, so it is important to develop general troubleshooting skills to approach new and unexpected situations confidently.

Troubleshooting is a process of problem solving. It is important to realize that problems have *causes*, *symptoms*, and *consequences*. For example:

- A computer system has a fault in the hard disk drive (cause).
- Because the disk drive is faulty, the computer is displaying a "bluescreen" (symptom).
- Because of the loss of service, the user cannot do any work (consequence).

From a business point-of-view, resolving the consequences of the problem is often more important than solving the original cause. For example, the most effective solution might be to provide the user with another workstation, *then* get the drive replaced.

CompTIA Troubleshooting Model

Make sure that you know the order of the steps in CompTIA's troubleshooting model:

1) Identify the problem.
    - Gather information.
    - Duplicate the problem, if possible.
    - Question users.
    - Identify symptoms.
    - Determine if anything has changed.
    - Approach multiple problems individually.
2) Research knowledge base/Internet, if applicable.
3) Establish a theory of probable cause.
    - Question the obvious.
    - Consider multiple approaches.
    - Divide and conquer.

4) Test the theory to determine cause.
    - Once the theory is confirmed (confirmed root cause), determine the next steps to resolve the problem.
    - If the theory is not confirmed, establish a new theory or escalate.
5) Establish a plan of action to resolve the problem and identify potential effects.
6) Implement the solution or escalate as necessary.
7) Verify full system functionality and, if applicable, implement preventive measures.
8) Document findings/lessons learned, actions and outcomes.

These steps and the approach and attitude you should apply when troubleshooting are explained in a bit more detail below.

A methodical process is the ideal, but troubleshooting in help desk and IT support departments is often a time-critical process. In the real world, you often have to balance being methodical with being efficient.

Identifying the Problem

It is important that when you encounter a troubleshooting situation, you approach it logically. The first stage in the troubleshooting process is to identify the problem. This stage involves a number of techniques.

Information gathering is the first step in troubleshooting. Image by rawpixel © 123rf.com.

Question Users and Determine Changes

When a user first discovers a problem and reports it to the help desk, you will attempt to classify the problem in terms of the problem's nature and scope. Most of your troubleshooting information will have to be obtained by questioning the user. You must be patient and address your questions and any test actions you ask them to perform to the user's level of expertise and knowledge. Be polite, avoid blaming the user for causing the problem, and help them to help you.

You will probably start by asking the user to describe the symptoms of the problem and the status of the computer, including any error messages or unusual conditions. During a discussion with the user, you should also ask:

- How many people are affected by the problem? This helps determine the severity of a problem. Clearly, if all users are affected, that is more serious than if only one user is experiencing the problem.
- When did the problem first occur? This could help you identify possible causes of the problem. For example, if the problem occurred on Monday morning during sign in, then that might indicate that the user's password expired over the weekend. The user might tell you that the problem has been intermittent for the last three weeks, but that it suddenly got worse. Either of these responses might help you focus your troubleshooting.
- What might have changed? This is a crucial question because often, problems occur after something changed. Sometimes, the thing that changed might seem totally unrelated. For example, someone experiences a problem right after some desks were moved. This might indicate a cabling problem that has arisen after a cable was broken or unplugged. The change might be a configuration change on your network or on the specific user's computer. Rolling back that change might resolve the issue.

Duplicate the Problem and Identify Symptoms

It is very helpful to be able to observe the issue as it occurs. You might be able to do this via remote desktop or by visiting the user, but if these are not practical you could test whether the problem can be repeated on a lab system or virtual machine. If the problem cannot be duplicated on a reference system, this points to some issue with the user's local environment.

You can also ask the user to describe symptoms, such as error messages appearing on the screen, or ask them to navigate to the relevant log file and report on its contents.

Approach Multiple Problems Individually

When you start to investigate symptoms, you might discover symptoms of more than one problem. Perhaps a user has reported that a machine has lost Internet connectivity, and you discover that it has also not been receiving maintenance updates. The issues could be related, or one might be incidental to the other.

If the problems do not seem to be related, treat each issue as a separate case. If they seem to be related, check for outstanding support or maintenance tickets that might indicate existing problems.

It may also be the case that a user reports two different problems at the same time (often preceded by, "While you're on the line..." sort of statements). Treat each problem as a separate case. In most cases you should advise the user to initiate a separate support ticket.

Gather Information and Research Symptoms

Your main source of information about a problem is likely to be the user reporting it, but if this is insufficient to successfully troubleshoot, you may have to consider other sources.

- Use a remote desktop tool to access the system or travel to the user to observe it in operation.
- View system, application, or network log files.
- Monitor other support requests to identify similar problems.

Once you have gathered sufficient information it is possible that you are able to learn enough to resolve the problem. This is likely with simple issues, such as password lockouts. If not, during this classification stage, you will document the problem in your ticket system and provide as much background information as you are able to determine. This will help you, or a colleague to whom you might escalate the issue, resolve the problem.

If you do not recognize the problem, use a product Knowledge Base or a web/Internet search tool to research the symptoms you have identified. Using support resources and web searches is discussed in more detail later in this unit.

Understanding the Problem

After you have gathered sufficient information about a reported problem, you must start to determine a **theory of probable cause** from analysis of the symptoms. This is a process of thinking about possible causes then eliminating those possible causes through testing to arrive at the root cause. Ultimately, the purpose is to complete the testing stage with a single probable cause, enabling you to search for and implement a resolution.

Question the Obvious

If you can prove that there is no inherent fault (perhaps by failing to duplicate the problem on a reference system), make sure that the system is set up and being operated in the correct way. Step through the process of using the system or application making sure that you verify even the simplest steps by **questioning the obvious**, best illustrated by the age-old "Is it switched on?" question.

Divide and Conquer

Often, a testing process might consist of a **divide and conquer** approach. This means that you try to envisage different problem areas. In computing, this might be like making the distinction between a workstation problem, a server problem, a storage problem, or a network problem. You then devise a testing routine to eliminate one or more categories of problem. This helps you more quickly identify probable causes. For example, if you suspect a physical cabling problem, try plugging the device into a different wall socket. If that makes no difference, the problem lies elsewhere.

If you think about a typical automotive problem – your car won't start – you might go through a testing process yourself. You might start by listing possible causes, and then eliminating them one by one. You check that there's fuel in the tank, so you move on. You verify, by turning the ignition, that the starter motor turns, so the battery is good and so is the starter. You progress through a series of tests to eliminate those possibilities that are not the cause of the symptoms you have recorded. With luck, you end up with a single possibility which you can then seek to resolve. Bear in mind that although there is fuel in your tank, it might be contaminated or unable to flow to the engine. So, you might need to perform several tests for a given possible cause.

This process also works with computer-related problems. Think back to the cabling example. You plugged the computer into a different socket, but perhaps the cabling issue lies at the wiring closet end?

Don't jump to conclusions. Sometimes, reported symptoms can be identical for several different causes. If you jump to a conclusion, you might waste valuable time attempting to resolve the wrong issue. You will also frustrate your users by taking longer to fix their problem. For example, if the light in your kitchen does not come on, you could assume it's a problem with the bulb when the cause could also lie with the light fitting, the fuse box, or even the electrical supply to your house. They all have the same symptom of your kitchen light not coming on when you flick the switch. Before you head out to the store to buy a new bulb, run simple tests to eliminate those other possible causes, by flicking on another light or running an appliance for instance.

Consider Multiple Approaches

If one troubleshooting method does not yield results, be prepared to try something different. For example, you might start by a process of questioning the obvious and step through the operating procedure but switch to a divide and conquer approach of testing each component in the process in isolation.

You might also suggest workarounds. A workaround doesn't actually solve the reported problem but provides a way for the user to continue to work with the system. That way you can deal with the consequences of the problem quickly and give yourself more time to investigate the underlying issue.

Test the Theory and Escalate the Problem

As you devise different theories of cause, you will naturally also be testing them to see if they fit the facts. While "testing" follows "establishing" in the methodology, the process is iterative (establish a theory, test it, if it doesn't work, establish another theory). You might discover that the immediate cause of a problem is itself just the symptom of a wider problem with a different cause. The end result of this process, therefore, is to establish a **root cause** for the problem.

If you are unable to resolve a problem during the initial phases, you might need to **escalate** the problem. This largely depends on how your help desk organization is structured.

Most help desks use a tiered system, with Tier 1 staff performing the classification and some of the testing stages. If a problem cannot be resolved quickly, then the problem is recorded and escalated to Tier 2. Staff at this level have more experience and are allocated more time to work on these more complex problems.

However, for even more difficult problems, Tier 2 staff can escalate to Tier 3. These are IT specialists who have many years of experience in troubleshooting. They might also be skilled in specific technologies, such as email, networking, cloud platforms, and so on. In the unlikely situation where a Tier 3 specialist is unable to resolve an issue, it can be escalated outside your organization to a manufacturer.

When testing your theory of probable cause, it is important not to make actual changes to the production system. If you make uncontrolled changes, reversing what you've done might be very difficult and you could cause worse problems than were originally reported.

Resolving and Documenting the Problem

The result of the identifying and understanding phases of troubleshooting is a diagnosis of the root cause of the reported problem. The final phase of troubleshooting is to establish a **plan of action** to eliminate the root cause *without destabilizing some other part of the system.*

Establish a Plan of Action

There are typically three solutions to any problem.

- **Repair**—you need to determine whether the cost of repair/time taken to reconfigure something makes this the best option.

- **Replace**—often more expensive and may be time-consuming if a part is not available. There may also be an opportunity to **upgrade** the device or software.

A basic technique when troubleshooting a cable, connector, or device is to have a "known good" duplicate on hand (that is, another copy of the same cable or device that you know works) and to test by substitution.

- **Ignore**—as any software developer will tell you, not all problems are critical. If neither repair nor replace is cost-effective, it may be best either to find a workaround or just to document the issue and move on.

When you consider solutions, you have to assess the cost and time required. Another consideration is potential effects on the rest of the system. A typical example is applying a software patch, which might fix a given problem in one piece of software but cause other programs not to work. This is where an effective configuration management system comes into play, as it should help you to understand how different systems are interconnected and cause you to seek the proper authorization for your plan.

Implement the Solution

Your plan of action should contain the detailed steps and resources required to implement the solution. As well as these practical steps, you have to consider the issue of authorization. If you do not have the authority to implement a solution, you will need to escalate the problem to more senior personnel. If applying the solution is disruptive to the wider network, you also need to consider the most appropriate time to schedule the reconfiguration work and plan how to notify other network users.

When you make a change to the system as part of implementing a solution, test after each change. If the change does not fix the problem, reverse it and then try something else. If you make a series of changes without recording what you have done, you could find yourself in a tricky position.

Verify Full System Functionality and Implement Preventive Measures

When you apply a solution, validate that it fixes the reported problem *and* that the system as a whole continues to function normally (that is, identify the results and effects of the solution). Ensure that you were right and that the problem is resolved. Can the user now log in properly? Is there any way you can induce the problem again?

Before you can consider a problem closed, you should both be satisfied in your own mind that you have resolved it *and* get the customer's acceptance that it has been fixed. Restate what the problem was and how it was resolved then confirm with the customer that the incident log can be closed.

To fully solve the root cause of a problem, you should try to eliminate any factors that may cause the problem to recur. For example, if a user plugs their laptop into the wrong network jack, ensure that the jacks are clearly labeled to help users in the future. If a faulty server induces hours of network downtime, consider implementing failover services to minimize the impact of the next incident.

Document Findings, Actions, and Outcomes

All the way through the preceding steps, it is important that information about the problem, tests performed, and attempted resolutions are recorded. That way, when a problem is resolved, a complete record exists documenting the symptoms, possible causes investigated, and the ultimate resolution. This information can be very helpful when troubleshooting similar symptoms on subsequently reported problems and provides the foundation of a knowledge base for your help desk.

Most troubleshooting takes place within the context of a ticket system. This shows who is responsible for any particular problem and what its status is. This gives you the opportunity to add a complete description of the problem and its solution (findings, actions, and outcomes).

This is massively useful for future troubleshooting, as problems fitting into the same category can be reviewed to see if the same solution applies. It also helps to analyze IT infrastructure by gathering statistics on what type of problems occur and how frequently.

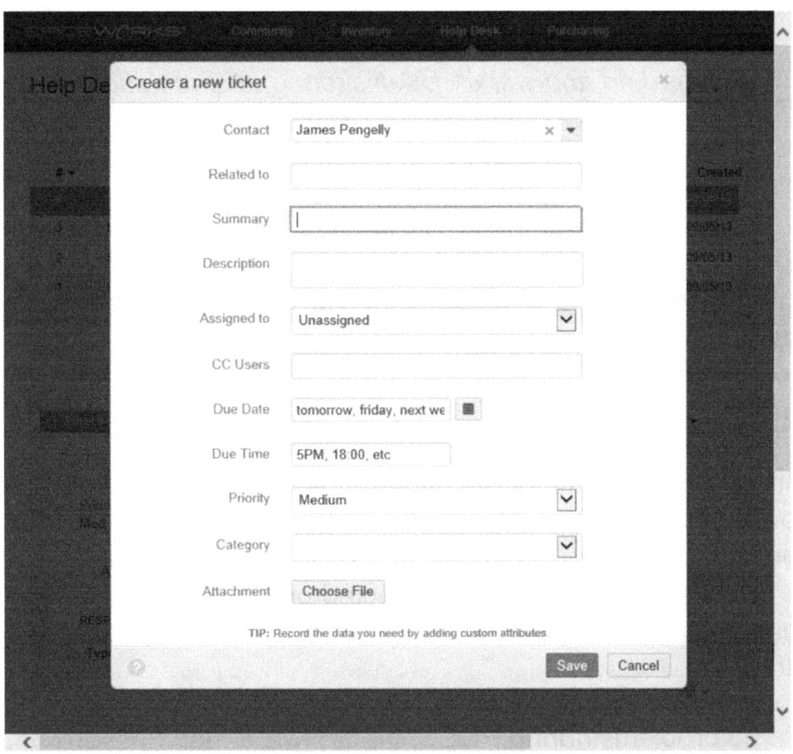

Creating a ticket in the Spiceworks IT Support management tool.

When you complete a problem log, remember that people other than you may come to rely on it. Also, logs may be presented to customers as proof of troubleshooting activity. Write clearly and concisely, checking for spelling and grammar errors.

Troubleshooting PC Issues

If you are troubleshooting a computer that will not start or a peripheral device that will not work, first inspect the component for physical damage. Look for dents, scratches, or cracks that might show a device has been dropped or banged. This might have caused damage to the internal components. Inspect cables and connectors for signs of wear and dirt. Inspect the ports on the computer case for dirt and damage.

When you start a computer, it automatically runs a program stored in firmware called the **Power-On Self-Test (POST)**. The POST routine ensures that all the components required to start the computer are present. If the tests complete successfully, the computer may issue a single beep. Not many computers beep these days, so do not be worried if the computer boots silently. You should also be able to see images on the screen. Otherwise, try to isolate the issue using the following tests:

- No beep—check whether the power light has come on and whether the disk light is flickering and whether there is an image on the screen. You should also be able to hear some disk activity and the whir of fans inside the PC. If you can detect none of these things, there is a power problem. Check the power cable and fuse. If these are OK, then the problem is either with the computer's internal power supply or the electrical outlet (try plugging in a lamp to test).

  Solid green lights (LEDs) generally show that something is switched on and working. A flickering LED is usually a sign that something is working too (for example, a disk or network activity LED). A flashing or blinking LED or an LED colored other than green can be a sign that there is a problem. Check the manual to understand what the LED signifies.

- More than one beep—the beeps specify where the problem is (and there may be an error message on the screen), but you will probably need to get help to diagnose and fix it. Do check that nothing is resting on the keyboard; if a key is pushed down it can cause this type of error.

- Screen is dark—check that the monitor is plugged in and switched on, that the power cable and fuse are good, and that the cable from the monitor to the computer is properly connected. If you see a message such as "No sync," the cable is probably disconnected or damaged. If you can see a very dim image, check that the brightness control hasn't been turned all the way down.

If there are no problems during POST, the firmware then passes control of the computer to the operating system, which finishes loading before displaying the logon prompt. If the operating system fails to load, there should be an error message. The error message should help to diagnose the cause of the boot failure.

If the system boots but a peripheral device does not work, first check for loose connections between the device and the computer. If you can discount physical problems, the device's driver might need updating or replacing.

If a computer crashes during operation and stops responding to any mouse clicks or keyboard presses, there could be a fault in either hardware or software. These issues can be difficult to diagnose, but do check that the computer is not becoming too hot. If the computer overheats, it can stop working suddenly, and overheating can be a relatively common occurrence.

Getting Support

When troubleshooting a system, it is important not to attempt solutions that may be beyond your experience or expertise. You could easily cause more damage by "experimenting." In the first instance, follow the basic guidelines for troubleshooting specific problems in the manufacturer's documentation. The setup or maintenance guide should be included with a new PC system, though often it is available as a PDF rather than printed copy.

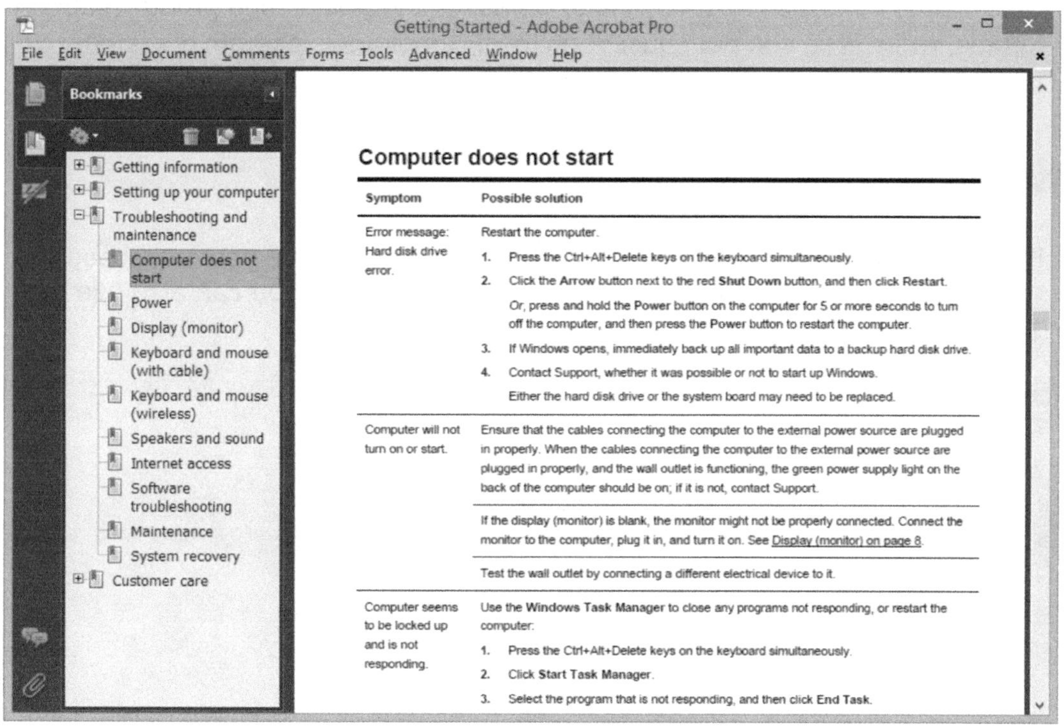

The system's "Setup" or "Getting Started" guide will usually include troubleshooting advice.

You can also use the vendor's website to look for the documentation; typically, you will need to use the product code to find this. For example, on HP's website, click the link for "Support" then choose the "Drivers and Downloads" option. Enter the product name or code to view the available files. This will include drivers for hardware components and system guides and manuals.

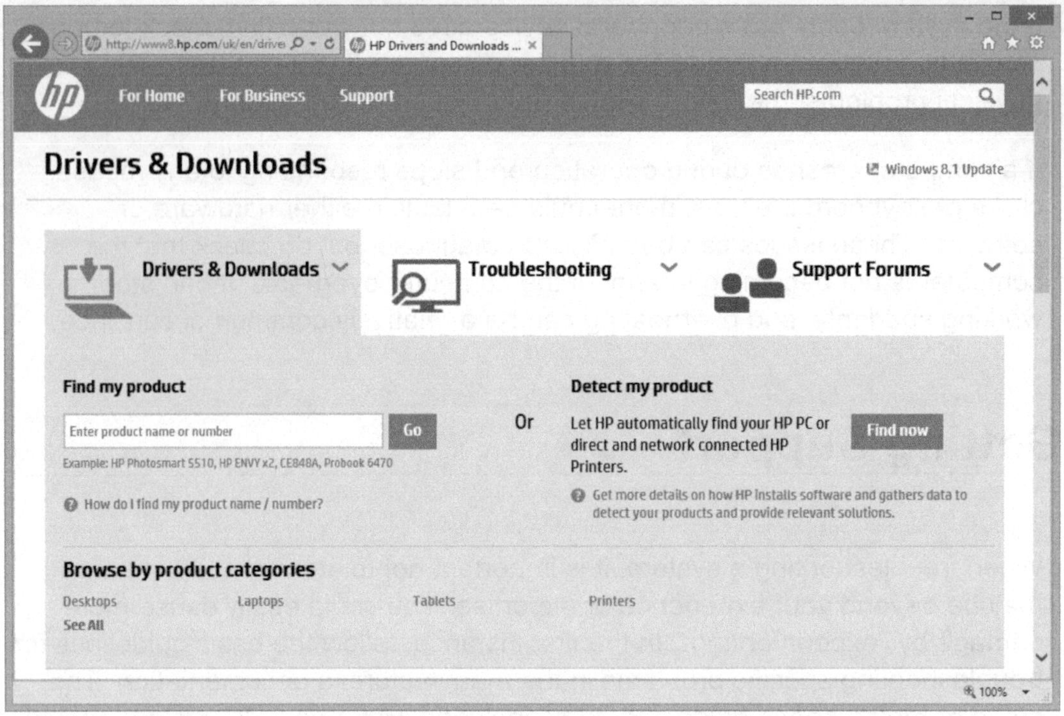

Use a vendor support site to obtain the documentation, drivers, and advice.

Note that the site also hosts online troubleshooting guides and product support forums, where you can post questions to HP employees and other system owners.

Windows Help and Tips

If you have a software problem rather than a computer one, you can access online help for Windows by pressing **F1**. In Windows 10, you can also use the **Tips** app from Start.

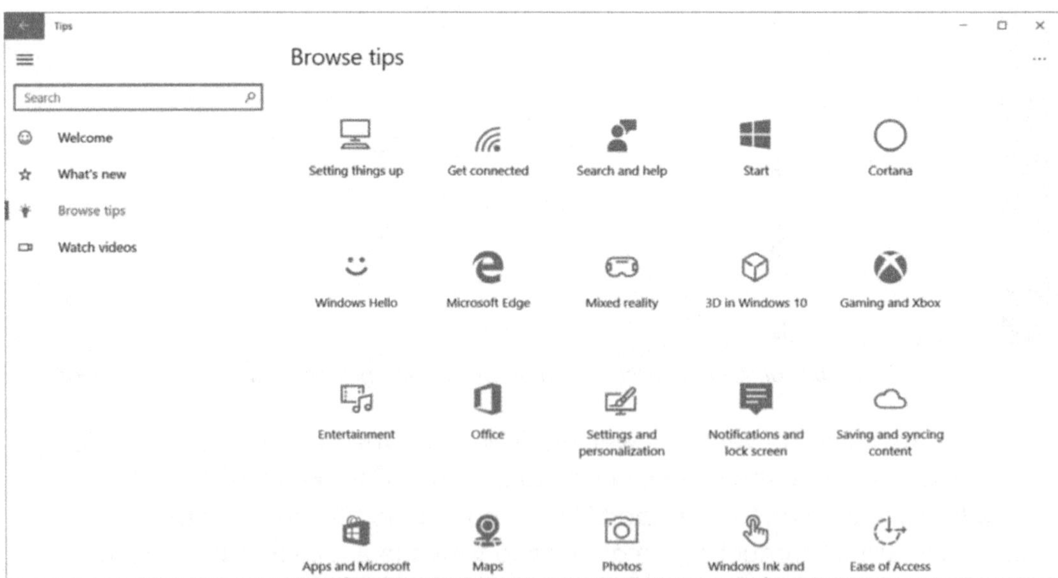

Windows 10 Tips app. Screenshot used with permission from Microsoft.

Contacting Technical Support

If there is a problem with your computer or with a software application, it is likely that you will need help to fix it. You may be able to get help from your business's help desk, from the computer manufacturer, or from the software vendor. You may be able to access support services by phone, by email, or through a website.

A lot of support is now done remotely. This means that the operator takes control of your computer to try to diagnose and fix the problem.

Most IT support works on the basis of a job ticket. When you contact a support operator, they will open the ticket and ask you to provide a description of the problem. You should provide the following information:

- Your name and contact information.
- The software or device you are having trouble with (including its version number, which can usually be found through the Help > About command, or model and serial number).
- The date you purchased the system (if applicable).
- A description of the problem, including any error message or number.

Be polite and calm when reporting problems. You may feel frustrated or be a bit fearful that you will lose important work, but if you are rude or cannot provide clear information it will just make the problem harder to resolve.

The operator should then work with you to try to resolve the problem. If the operator asks you to perform troubleshooting actions, listen carefully to the steps and confirm when you have completed each one. If the operator has to call you back, make sure you get their name and your job ticket number.

When you agree that the problem has been solved, the ticket can be closed.

Technical Community Groups

Formal technical support may not be available to you or a user. A product might be out of warranty and support may be expensive for instance. In this case, you might want to use alternative support methods. Do be aware that these may not be as reliable. If warranty support is available to you, use that in the first instance.

As mentioned above, PC and hardware vendors all operate forums to support their products. There are also many community forums not tied to particular vendors but hosting reviews, advice, support, and discussions about laptops, or phones (or pretty much anything else). If you use an Internet search engine to look for the symptoms of the problem you are having, the results are certain to include posts in forums such as these.

When posting a problem to a newsgroup or forum, remember that people are responding to you out of goodwill. Pick the appropriate forum and check the Frequently Asked Questions (FAQ) before posting. The FAQ is usually the first post in the forum. Do not "cross-post" problems to multiple forums. Describe the problem accurately, and be patient.

Software vendors also maintain forums and support websites. For example, Microsoft's support website support.microsoft.com hosts solution centers for each product. You can access troubleshooting articles and (if applicable) assisted support via phone, email, or chat. More advanced articles plus product documentation and some online books can be found at technet.microsoft.com.

The communities site (answers.microsoft.com) features newsgroups, blogs, webcasts, and forums dedicated to different Microsoft products. These resources are generally monitored by **Microsoft Most Valued Professional (MVP)** volunteers. mvps.org contains links to useful sites maintained by MVPs. There are also numerous other technical community groups, some of which are subscription-based. Some well-known ones include experts-exchange.com, petri.com, and tomshardware.com.

Using a Search Engine

A **search engine** is a tool to help locate web pages. A search engine may be designed to search the entire web for pages or to locate pages within a particular site.

A search engine usually works by compiling a database of information about web pages. This is often done automatically by software agents called robots or spiders. When users want to perform a search, they enter keywords on the topic they want to read about. The search engine checks these keywords against its database and returns a list of links that are relevant. The user can then click one or more links to go to the web page.

The most widely used search engines are **Google** and Microsoft's **Bing**, though there are many more. Also, search engines have different sites for different countries. For example, you can access Google at google.co.uk, google.com, google.co.za, google.com.au, and so on.

In most browsers, if you type text into the address bar, the browser will convert the text into a search using the default search provider if it does not match an actual web address. You can use browser settings or preferences to change the default search provider.

When you construct a search phrase, it helps to use as many words as possible. Do not use common words such as "and" or "the." Using more unusual words will help to limit the number of matches.

Search Selection Criteria

As you start to build more complex search phrases, you can use special syntax and search engine tools to combine keywords and perform advanced searches.

Syntax	Usage	Example
"	Use double quotation marks (") to specify a match to the exact phrase as you typed it.	`"Monty Python"`
+	Put a plus sign (+) in front of a word that must be found in the documents exactly as you typed it.	`+snake +Python`
-	Put a minus sign (-) in front of a word to exclude it.	`python -Monty`
OR	Find either of the words. The pipe (|) can also be used to mean the same thing.	`snake | python`
*	The wildcard * represents unknown words between known ones.	`genius * python`
Fields	Some engines may allow you to search for words within a particular field (for example, the document's URL or its TITLE).	`inurl:monty python`

As an alternative to using syntax, you can usually access the search engine's **Advanced Search** page to specify criteria using a form.

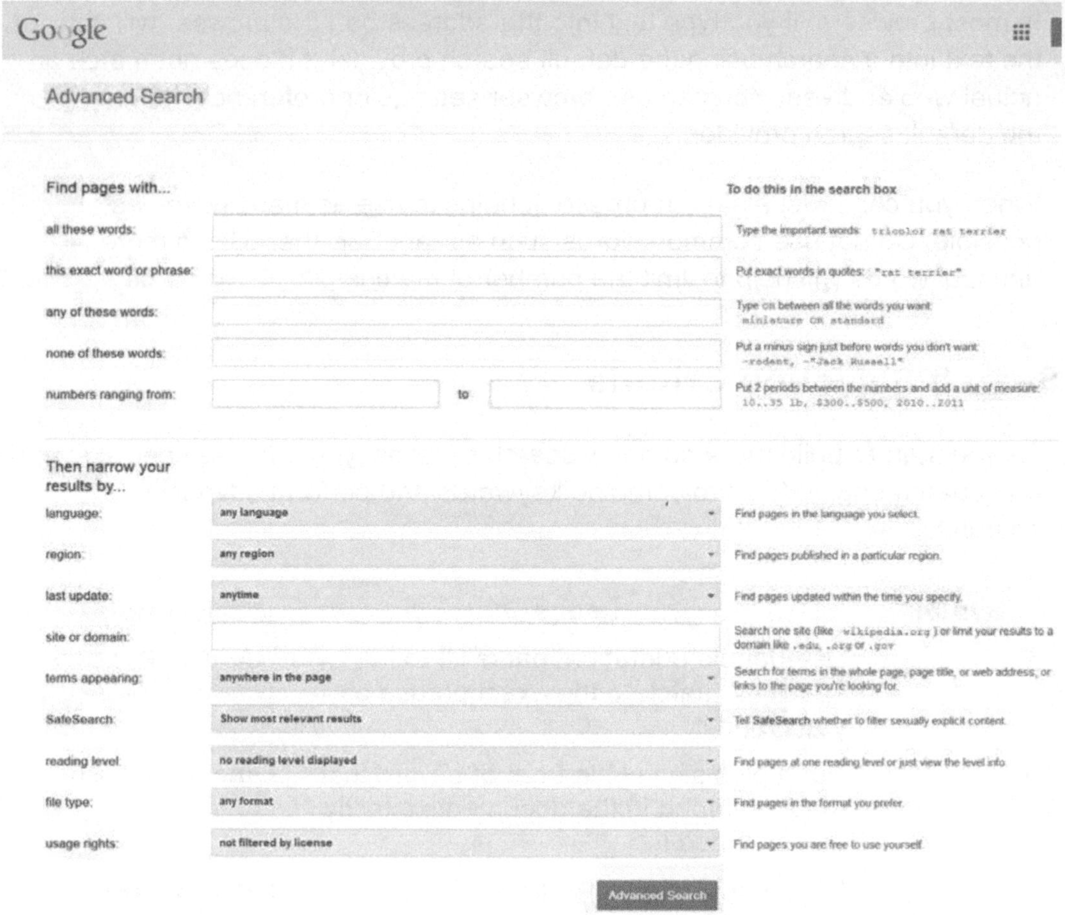

Google advanced search form.

Note that this syntax is not always supported by all search engines. Also, there may be additional requirements (for example in Google you have to enter an advanced query within square brackets).

Review Questions / Module 1 / Unit 5 / Troubleshooting and Support

Answer these questions to test what you have learned in this unit. You can review the model answers at the end of the book.

1) You are advising a colleague about best practices when troubleshooting. You have identified the following techniques to use to identify a problem: gather information, duplicate the problem, question users, identify symptoms, and approach multiple problems individually. If you are following CompTIA's troubleshooting model, what other piece of advice should you give?

2) You have asked a senior manager to authorize your plan of action for resolving a fault in a software application. What name is given to the process you are following?

3) You are setting up a new computer, but it doesn't seem to be working. Should you check anything or contact the manufacturer?

4) Your computer locks up periodically and feels hot to the touch. Could these things be related?

5) What crucial piece of information would you need when trying to locate support information about a computer system on the manufacturer's website?

6) If you do not have a support contract, what is likely to be the best option for obtaining advice about a problem with an application?

7) You are looking for content on a topic but your search is returning millions of matches that are not particularly helpful. What two methods could you use to get better search results?

8) You want to find something on a particular website, but the site does not have a search tool. Could you use a general search engine, and if so, how?

Lab 6 / Using a Search Engine

Using a search engine effectively is one of the most important skills you can learn in terms of Internet use. In this lab, imagine you are troubleshooting an issue where several users have reported that the cursor keeps jumping around when they type on their laptops.

1) If necessary, start your computer and sign in then open the Edge browser from the taskbar.

   When you buy a computer from an OEM, you may want to change the default search provider. For Edge, the engine must support OpenSearch (opensearch.org) and you must have visited the search engine home page.

2) Open google.com (you will be redirected to the home page for your country). If prompted, complete the wizard explaining Google's privacy and data collection policies.
3) Click the **More Actions** ellipse icon and then click **Settings**.
4) Click **View advanced settings**. Scroll down to the "Privacy and services" section then click **Change search engine**.
5) If you want to change the search provider (you do not have to), select **Google Search** then click the **Set as default** button.
6) Click in the address box and type `laptop cursor jumps` then press `ENTER`.
7) Browse through the results—you should find a mix of ad-supported sites explaining the issue and forums with multiple posts relating to similar issues. Take some time to explore some of these, using the **Back** button to return to your search results.

   Alternatively, right-click to open links in a new tab, then close the tab when you have finished.

   You might find a number of solutions, including an option in Windows 8 to delay click events. As the user is running Windows 7 though, you determine that a more specific search might yield better results.

8) Click in the address box and type `hp laptop cursor jumps "windows 7"` then press `ENTER`.
9) In a new tab, search for `hp notebook cursor jumps "windows 7"` and compare the results.

As you can see, the more specific you make the search, the fewer results are returned and the more likely they are to address the same issue that you are researching.

10) Pick one of the HP forum pages ("h30434.www3.hp.com"), and read the posts.

11) Click in the forum's search box and type `dm4 cursor jumps "windows 7,"` change the list box option to **Entire Forum** and click **Go**.

12) Read some of the posts and their replies—note that the frequent request to specify the exact model number when posting.

    You decide to locate the latest touchpad driver version as the configuration settings for palm rest do not seem to be present in the version you have.

13) Point to the forum's **Support** menu link and select **Download drivers**.

14) In the product box, type `dm4-2070` then click **Go**. Open the link for the matched product.

15) Note the option to use a software tool to identify missing drivers but use the **Go** link under option 2.

16) Choose the OS option as **Windows 7** then click **Update**.

17) Expand **Driver-Keyboard, Mouse and Input Devices** and you will see the link for the touchpad driver.

    We will not continue from here, but the next steps would be to ensure the user's computer is backed up then download and install the driver. It can be difficult to test whether a problem like this has really been solved so you would encourage the user to report back after a day or two to confirm whether the cursor problem was still present.

18) Optionally, shut down your computer if you are not continuing to use it after this lab.

This page left blank intentionally.

Module 1 / Summary
Using Computers

In this module you learned the basics of using a computer, operating system, and software applications. You also learned some best practices to follow when troubleshooting a problem or obtaining technical support.

- Computer functions can be described as belonging to one of input, output, processing, and storage. Make sure you can identify the type of function performed by PC components.
- Different types of computing devices include desktops/workstations, laptops, servers, smartphones, and tablets. Computing and networking functions are also being incorporated into "Internet of Things" appliances and objects.

Module 1 / Unit 2 / Using a Workstation

- When installing computer equipment, work methodically and refer carefully to system documentation and installation guides.
- You learned about the main Windows user interfaces and how to navigate around the Windows desktop and Start Screen or Start Menu using a keyboard and mouse or touchpad.

Module 1 / Unit 3 / Using an OS

- The main functions of an operating system are to act as a user interface, provide a common platform for applications, and provide system and file maintenance tools.
- There are different types of operating systems for different devices and commercial models. Windows is a commercial operating system, available in a number of editions with different features. Alternative desktop operating systems include Apple Mac OS and the various types of Linux (open source) plus Google Chrome, while mobile devices are supported by Windows Mobile, iOS, and Android.
- Virtualization allows a single host computer to run multiple guest operating systems or Virtual Machines (VM). The VMs are managed by a hypervisor.
- You also learned how to use File Explorer to browse the file system and network locations, Settings/Control Panel to adjust settings in Windows, and a web browser to view websites.

Module 1 / Unit 4 / Managing an OS

- As well as user interfaces for navigating the software and files stored on the OS, there are management interfaces for performing configuration.
- You learned how to use tools to perform different management tasks, such as for processes, memory, disks, and scheduling.
- A Command Line Interface (CLI) allows control of the OS without a GUI. There may be more than one CLI included with an OS and the commands supported will vary.
- The user who installs an OS typically becomes the administrator account with complete control over system settings. Use standard accounts for day-to-day use of the computer.

Module 1 / Unit 5 / Troubleshooting and Support

- You should try to learn the steps and sequence of the CompTIA troubleshooting model.
- Make sure you can recognize common external issues. Be aware of the consequences of problems, such as risk of data loss or loss of service, and measures that can be taken to reduce them.
- If there is a problem with hardware or software, you should be aware of the various sources of assistance and information that you can use to try to resolve it.
- Make sure you can use a search engine effectively, including use of advanced search tools or query syntax.

Module 2 / Using Apps and Databases

The following CompTIA IT Fundamentals+ domain objectives and examples are covered in this module:

CompTIA ITF+ Certification Domains	Weighting
1.0 IT Concepts and Terminology	17%
2.0 Infrastructure	22%
3.0 Applications and Software	18%
4.0 Software Development	12%
5.0 Database Fundamentals	11%
6.0 Security	20%

Refer To	Domain Objectives/Examples
Unit 2.1 / Using Data Types and Units	**1.1 Compare and contrast notational systems.** *Binary • Hexadecimal • Decimal • Data representation (ASCII, Unicode)*
	1.2 Compare and contrast fundamental data types and their characteristics. *Char • Strings • Numbers (Integers, Floats) • Boolean*
	1.4 Explain the value of data and information. *Data and information as assets • Importance of investing in security • Relationship of data to creating information • Intellectual property (Trademarks, Copyright, Patents) • Digital products • Data-driven business decisions (Data capture and collection, Data correlation, Meaningful reporting)*
	1.5 Compare and contrast common units of measure. *Storage unit (Bit, Byte, KB, MB, GB, TB, PB) • Throughput unit (bps, Kbps, Mbps, Gbps, Tbps) • Processing speed (MHz, GHz)*
Unit 2.2 / Using Apps	**3.1 Manage applications and software.** *Application management*
	3.3 Explain the purpose and proper use of software. *Productivity software (Word processing software, Spreadsheet software, Presentation software, Web browser, Visual diagramming software) • Collaboration software (Email client, Conferencing software, Instant messaging software, Online workspace, Document sharing) • Business software (Database software, Project management software, Business-specific applications, Accounting software)*
	3.6 Compare and contrast general application concepts and uses. *Licensing (Single use, Group use/site license, Concurrent license, Open source vs. proprietary, Subscription vs. one-time purchase, Product keys and serial numbers) • Software installation best practices (Reading instructions, Reading agreements, Advanced options)*

Refer To	Domain Objectives/Examples
Unit 2.3 / Programming and App Development	**3.4 Explain methods of application architecture and delivery models.** *Application delivery methods—locally installed (Network not required, Application exists locally, Files saved locally) • Application delivery methods—Local network hosted (Network required, Internet access not required) • Application delivery methods—Cloud hosted (Internet access required, Service required, Files saved in the cloud)*
	3.6 Compare and contrast general application concepts and uses. *Single-platform software • Cross-platform software (Compatibility concerns)*
	4.1 Compare and contrast programming language categories. *Interpreted (Scripting languages, Scripted languages, Markup languages) • Compiled programming languages • Query languages • Assembly language*
	4.2 Given a scenario, use programming organizational techniques and interpret logic. *Organizational techniques (Pseudocode concepts, Flow chart concepts, Sequence) • Logic components (Branching, Looping)*
	4.3 Explain the purpose and use of programming concepts. *Identifiers (Variables, Constants) • Containers (Arrays, Vectors) • Functions • Objects (Properties, Attributes, Methods)*
Unit 2.4 / Using Databases	**3.4 Explain methods of application architecture and delivery models.** *Application architecture models (One tier, Two tier, Three tier, n-tier)*
	5.1 Explain database concepts and the purpose of a database. *Usage of database (Create, Import/input, Query, Reports) • Flat file vs. database (Multiple concurrent users, Scalability, Speed, Variety of data) • Records • Storage (Data persistence)*
	5.2 Compare and contrast various database structures. *Structured vs. semi-structured vs. non-structured • Relational databases (Schema, Tables, Rows/records, Fields/columns, Primary key, Foreign key, Constraints) • Non-relational databases (Key/value databases, Document databases)*
	5.3 Summarize methods used to interface with databases. *Relational methods (Data manipulation [Select, Insert, Delete, Update], Data definition [Create, Alter, Drop, Permissions]) • Database access methods (Direct/manual access, Programmatic access • User interface/utility access, Query/report builders) • Export/import (Database dump, Backup)*

Module 2 / Unit 1
Using Data Types and Units

Objectives

On completion of this unit, you will be able to:

- Recognize and use different notational systems, data types, and units of measure.
- Compare and contrast fundamental data types and their characteristics.
- Discuss the importance of data and ways that a company can use it to make business decisions.

Syllabus Objectives and Content Examples

This unit covers the following exam domain objectives and content examples:

- 1.1 Compare and contrast notational systems.
  Binary • Hexadecimal • Decimal • Data representation (ASCII, Unicode)
- 1.2 Compare and contrast fundamental data types and their characteristics.
  Char • Strings • Numbers (Integers, Floats) • Boolean
- 1.4 Explain the value of data and information.
  Data and information as assets • Importance of investing in security • Relationship of data to creating information • Intellectual property (Trademarks, Copyright, Patents) • Digital products • Data-driven business decisions (Data capture and collection, Data correlation, Meaningful reporting)
- 1.5 Compare and contrast common units of measure.
  Storage unit (Bit, Byte, KB, MB, GB, TB, PB) • Throughput unit (bps, Kbps, Mbps, Gbps, Tbps) • Processing speed (MHz, GHz)

Notational Systems

In computing, a **notational system** is one used to represent different quantities or characters. Notational systems used to represent values and quantities include decimal, binary, and hexadecimal.

Decimal Notation

For most people around the world, when they want to count something, they use a numbering system based on **decimal**. The decimal system (or **base 10**) is so well understood, it's actually quite easy to overlook how it actually works. Decimal is based on the principle of expressing ten different numbers using a single digit in the range 0 to 9. Once you have a value of more than ten, then you require two digits of decimal to express it. Thus, when twelve is expressed numerically in decimal as `12` that means `1*10` plus `2*1`.

```
1000      100      10       1
   0        0       1       2
1000*0   100*0    10*1     1*2
   0   +    0  +   10  +    2
= 12
```

You will notice that the rightmost column is worth one, while the second column is worth ten times that (10). The third column is worth ten times the second column (100), and so on. In other words, each digit as we move from right to left (from least to most significant) is worth the base number (ten) times more than the preceding digit. This is referred to as **place value**.

Binary Notation

While people find decimal easy to use, computers use **binary** to calculate and process information. Binary is a numbering system where each single digit can express only two values, in the range 0 to 1. The reason binary works well with computers is that these two values can represent the off/on states of the transistors that make up computer memory. Binary can also be referred to as **base 2**.

As with decimal, to express a value of more than one, you must use multiple binary digits in a place value system. For example, the number `51` in decimal can be expressed in binary as `110011`. As with decimal, when you write the number down, and assign the digit values, you can see that each column is worth the base number (two) times more than the preceding column as we move from least to most significant (right to left). Thus, the second column is worth twice the first, the third column is two times the second, and so on.

128	64	32	16	8	4	2	1
0	0	1	1	0	0	1	1
128*0	64*0	32*1	16*1	8*0	4*0	2*1	1*1
0 +	0 +	32 +	16 +	0 +	0 +	2 +	1

= 51

Hexadecimal Notation

When handling large values, expressing them in binary can consume many digits. For example, `1234` in decimal uses four digits, whereas the same number in binary is `100 1101 0010`, which requires 11 digits. You can express large numbers more efficiently by using **hexadecimal**, often shortened to "hex." The hex notation system enables you to express 16 different numbers using a single digit in the range 0 to F. For example, the number `1234` (in decimal) can be expressed in hex as `4D2`, using one fewer digit. In this notation, the letters A through F are used to express numbers larger than nine (which require two digits of decimal to express). Thus, A is 10, B is 11, C is 12, D is 13, E is 14 and F is 15.

4096	256	16	1
0	4	D	2
4096*0	256*4	16*13	1*2
0 +	1024 +	208 +	2

= 1234

Hex is used in programming. You will also encounter this numbering system when you plan and implement Internet Protocol (IP) networks. IPv6 network and host addresses are expressed using a hexadecimal notation system.

Conversion

If you are going to get involved in computing, it's worth the effort of learning how to convert numbers from binary to decimal and back. You can do so manually using the place value columns shown above. You can also use a programming calculator to achieve this conversion. Windows 10 provides one, as shown below.

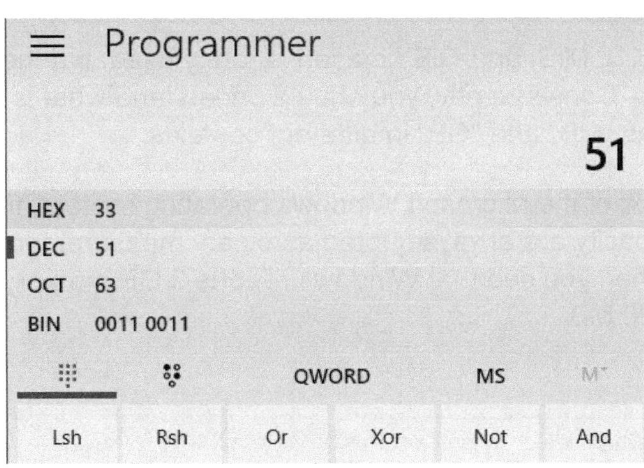

Windows 10 Calculator app in Programmer mode. Screenshot used with permission from Microsoft.

Units of Measure

You need to understand the units used to describe computer storage and data transfer technologies.

Bits and Bytes

The basic unit of computer data is the **binary digit** or **bit**, which can represent two values (zero or one). Computer memory and file sizes in Windows are measured in multiples of bits. The first multiple is the **byte**, which is eight bits. A **double byte** is 16 bits. As a byte represents very little information in terms of file sizes and storage capacity, the following multiples are used:

- KiloByte (KB)—1000 bytes (or 10^3 or 10*10*10 bytes). Small files are often measured in KB.
- MegaByte (MB)—1000*1000 bytes (or 1,000,000 bytes). Many files would be measured in megabytes.
- GigaByte (GB)—1000*1000*1000 bytes (1,000,000,000 bytes). Gigabytes are usually used to talk about disk capacity.
- TeraByte (TB)—1000 GB (1,000,000,000,000 bytes). Some individual disk units might be 1 or 2 terabytes but these units are usually used to describe large storage networks.
- PetaByte (PB)—1000 TB or 10^{15} bytes (1,000,000,000,000,000 bytes). The largest storage networks and cloud systems would have petabytes of capacity.

You should also be aware that a different system of notation is available to describe these multiples in binary terms (base 2), where the multiples express powers of two rather than powers of 10:

- KibiByte (KiB)—1024 bytes (2^{10} bytes).
- MebiByte (MiB)—1024*1024 bytes (or 1,048,576 bytes).
- GibiByte (GiB)—1024*1024*1024 bytes (1,073,741,824 bytes).

In practice the KiB, MiB, and GiB notation is rarely used, but the binary measurement is. Consequently, you should understand what is generally meant by terms such as "MB" and "GB" in different contexts.

- In the context of the Microsoft Windows operating system, file sizes and memory capacity are always quoted as binary measurements (base 2). For example, when you see that Windows reports 2 GB memory, this means 2048 MB, not 2000 MB.

- Storage capacity is typically quoted by vendors in decimal measurements (base 10). For example, a hard disk advertised with a capacity of 300 GB has an "actual" capacity of 286 GiB. Some operating systems, such as Ubuntu Linux and macOS, also use the decimal notation for system memory, disk capacity, and file sizes.

Throughput Units

When data is transferred between components in the computer or between computers over a network, the **throughput rate** that a particular connection can sustain is measured in bits per second (bps). As with storage, the basic unit of bits per second would result in writing out very long values, so throughput can be expressed more efficiently using the following multiples:

- Kbps (or Kb/s)—1000 bits per second. Older computer peripheral interfaces (or buses) and slow network links would be measured in Kbps.
- Mbps (or Mb/s)—1,000,000 bits per second. Many internal computer interfaces have throughputs measured in Mbps. Wireless networks and residential Internet links also typically have this sort of throughput.
- Gbps (or Gb/s)—1,000,000,000 bits per second. The latest PC bus standards and networks can support this higher level of throughput.
- Tbps (or Tb/s)—1,000,000,000,000 bits per second. This sort of capacity is found in major telecommunications links between data centers, cities, and countries.

Throughput units are *always* base 10.

Also note that transfer rates can be expressed as Bytes per second, in which case the "B" is capitalized (KBps, MBps, GBps, and TBps).

Processing Speed Units

While throughput rates describe how much data is transferred over a link, the speed at which a computer works can also be described independently of how much data is involved in each operation. A computer's internal clock and the speed at which its processors work is measured in units of time called Hertz (Hz). 1 Hz represents one cycle per second.

- Megahertz (MHz)—1 million (1,000,000) cycles per second. Older PC bus interfaces and many types of network interface work at this slower signaling speed.
- Gigahertz (GHz)—1000 million (1,000,000,000) cycles per second. Modern CPUs and bus types plus fiber optic network equipment work at these much faster speeds.

Throughput is not always the same as the signaling rate. System memory and network technologies can transmit more than one bit per cycle for instance.

Data Types

It is important to understand the different **data types** that a computer program can use. This is especially important when you start to write your own programs (coding) or work with database systems.

The CPU and storage devices in a computer only process data as ones and zeros. These hardware components have no conception of what the data mean. When it comes to programming software applications though, data types are very important because they determine what sort of operations can be performed. For example, the characters `51` can be treated as a number value, in which case you can use the data in additions and subtractions, or it can be treated as a text string (representing a house number for instance). If `51` is stored as a string, it must be converted before it can be used in a mathematical operation.

There are different types of number values and a variety of text forms. These include:

- **Integers**—these are whole numbers. For example: `5`, `21`, or `65536`. An integer data type consumes 1 to 8 bytes of computer storage.
- **Floating-point numbers**—this type can support decimal fractions such as `4.1`, `26.4`, or `5.62`. A floating-point number (or just "float") consumes between 4 and 8 bytes of storage. Note that the floating-point type could store a whole number too (`4.0` for instance).
- **Boolean values**—these are a special numeric data type indicating that something is either **`TRUE`** or **`FALSE`** (with a `1` or `0`). They consume a single bit of storage.
- **Characters**—a character (or **char**) is a single textual character, and can be a letter of the alphabet, a symbol, or, indeed, a numerical character. For example: **`a`**, `D`, `7`, **`$`**, `@`, **`#`**. These consume one byte of storage. Note that when a number is entered as a character data type, you cannot perform any mathematical operations on it.
- **Strings**—a string is a collection of text characters. For example: **`XYZ`**, **`Hello world`**. There is no real limit on the amount of storage that can be used by a string. Generally, you define the string length when you define the data type.

When single or double quotes can be used to delimit a string ("Hello World"), the quotes are NOT part of the string itself. If you want to represent a quote character (or other delimiter) within a string, you have to use an escape character. For example, the string "John said \'Hello World\' then left again." contains two single quotes, escaped using the backslash character (\).

Data Representation

When binary values (1s and 0s) are used for char and string data types, there must be some means of data representation by which different value bytes map to letters, numbers, and symbols in a **character set**. There are two common ways of presenting character set data: **ASCII** and **Unicode**.

ASCII Data Representation

In **ASCII (American Standard Code for Information Interchange)**, each number or character in a text file or string variable is represented by a seven-bit binary number. With seven bits of binary, you can express 128 different values (0 through 127).

Binary	Dec	Character	Binary	Dec	Character	Binary	Dec	Character
010 0000	32	space	011 0000	48	0	100 0000	64	@
010 0001	33	!	011 0001	49	1	100 0001	65	A
010 0010	34	"	011 0010	50	2	100 0010	66	B
010 0011	35	#	011 0011	51	3	100 0011	67	C
010 0100	36	$	011 0100	52	4	100 0100	68	D
010 0101	37	%	011 0101	53	5	100 0101	69	E
010 0110	38	&	011 0110	54	6	100 0110	70	F
010 0111	39	'	011 0111	55	7	100 0111	71	G
010 1000	40	(	011 1000	56	8	100 1000	72	H
010 1001	41	)	011 1001	57	9	100 1001	73	I
010 1010	42	*	011 1010	58	:	100 1010	74	J
010 1011	43	+	011 1011	59	;	100 1011	75	K
010 1100	44	,	011 1100	60	<	100 1100	76	L
010 1101	45	-	011 1101	61	=	100 1101	77	M
010 1110	46	.	011 1110	62	>	100 1110	78	N
010 1111	47	/	011 1111	63	?	100 1111	79	O

Binary	Dec	Character	Binary	Dec	Character	Binary	Dec	Character
101 0000	80	P	110 0000	96	@	111 0000	112	p
101 0001	81	Q	110 0001	97	a	111 0001	113	q
101 0010	82	R	110 0010	98	b	111 0010	114	r
101 0011	83	S	110 0011	99	c	111 0011	115	s
101 0100	84	T	110 0100	100	d	111 0100	116	t
101 0101	85	U	110 0101	101	e	111 0101	117	u
101 0110	86	V	110 0110	102	f	111 0110	118	v
101 0111	87	W	110 0111	103	g	111 0111	119	w
101 1000	88	X	110 1000	104	h	111 1000	120	x
101 1001	89	Y	110 1001	105	i	111 1001	121	y
101 1010	90	Z	110 1010	106	j	111 1010	122	z
101 1011	91	[	110 1011	107	k	111 1011	123	{
101 1100	92	\	110 1100	108	l	111 1100	124	¬
101 1101	93	]	110 1101	109	m	111 1101	125	}
101 1110	94	↑	110 1110	110	n	111 1110	126	|
101 1111	95	←	110 1111	111	o			

ASCII table.

ASCII was designed a long time ago (1963) when using seven bits rather than eight represented a significant cost saving. As most systems now use byte-based storage (eight bits), various ways of using extended ASCII to encode 256 values have been developed.

Unicode

ASCII, although widely adopted, is a very old standard (devised in early 1960s). More recently, **Unicode** has become more prevalent. Unicode enables you to handle character data and express that data across platforms in a uniform way.

Unicode comprises:

- A set of code charts that handle visual reference.
- A data encoding method.
- A set of standard character encodings.
- A set of reference data files.
- Additional properties, including:
    - Character properties.
    - Rules to handle normalization, rendering, display order (for languages that display right to left instead of left to right).

There are a number of different Unicode character encoding standards, including UTF-8, UTF-16, and UTF-32. UTF-8 is used by many websites.

The Value of Data

When you think about data, it is important that you understand that it represents more than just encoded numbers and letters. For organizations, and even for individuals, computer data can be considered an **asset**. An asset is something of commercial value. Therefore, it is important that you take steps necessary to protect this asset.

Investing in Security

A mechanism designed to protect an information asset or processing system is called a **security control**. There are many types of security controls, and they can be classed in different ways. Typically they are designed to prevent, deter, detect, and/or recover from attempts to view or modify data without authorization. Security controls can be costly, both in terms of purchasing hardware and software and in terms of more complex procedures and staff training. The business case for investing in security is made by a calculation called **Return on Security Investment (ROSI)**. To calculate ROSI, you perform **risk assessments** to work out how much the loss of data would cost your organization and how likely it is that data loss might occur. The use of security controls should reduce both the impact and likelihood of losses, justifying the investment made.

When an attacker removes data from your network without authorization, this can be called data exfiltration. Data breach is a similar circumstance but can occur whenever your network exposes private data publicly, whether the data is actively stolen or not.

Security Controls

As mentioned above, a security control is something designed to ensure that data is contained within the information processing system and is only accessible with authorization. Some typical examples of security controls to help protect your data might include:

- Backup—ensure that you maintain copies of your data and that these copies can be quickly and easily accessed when necessary.
- Access control—your data might have a value to your business competitors. Therefore, it makes sense to try to control access to stored data. You can use the following technologies to control access:
    - Permissions—most operating systems provide a number of methods with which you can assign permissions on data files to users and groups of users.
    - Usage restrictions—you can use rights management software to control what users can do with data files. For example, you can allow specified users to read a file but not to copy or print a file.

- Data encryption—this means that data is encoded in some way that only a person with the correct key can read it. Even if someone obtained a copy of encrypted data, they would not be able to read it without the key. This means that rather than try to protect the data, the security system only has to protect the key, which is smaller and easier to defend. Some operating systems offer the ability to encrypt data while it is at rest (when stored on a disk). You can also use technologies to encrypt data when it is in transit between the nodes on a network.

Make sure you understand the difference between permissions and encryption. Permissions only work when the data is stored within an OS or network that "respects" the access control system. If the data were transferred to a different computer, the permissions could be overridden. Encryption prevents this possibility (unless the key is transferred with the data). Most security systems use both permissions and encryption.

- Firewalls—on a network, a firewall can control how hosts and network applications are accessible to one another.

- High availability—it is often the case that temporary loss of access to data can lead to high costs for an organization. Consider a situation when financial transactions are not available to a banking institution. You can implement technologies that enable you to ensure your data is available in the event of one or several failures of hardware or software components within your infrastructure. These technologies are referred to as fault tolerance.

Any organization that does not take some, or all, of the preceding steps stands to lose data and in all probability, suffer financial loss as a result.

Intellectual Property

Intellectual Property (IP) is often the most valuable information asset that an organization owns. There are various different types of IP and different ways to protect them from theft.

Copyright

Copyright is automatic legal protection granted to certain types of work indicating that the copyright holder owns the right to control the use of the work, including rights of publication, distribution, or sale.

There is no need to apply for copyright or display any copyright notice in order to be protected by it. The creation of the work ensures copyright protection automatically. Nonetheless, in case of a dispute, you might need to prove when the work was created in order to defend yourself against charges of plagiarism. Plagiarism is the unacknowledged or unauthorized use of someone else's work.

Most authors and publishers demonstrate that they hold copyright over a work by displaying the copyright symbol © with the date and their name. While copyright laws vary throughout the world, demonstrating copyright in this way is likely to protect the owner in most circumstances. In the USA, proof of authorship can be demonstrated by registering the work with the Copyright Office (copyright.gov).

Copyright does not apply to an idea that is not actualized, nor does it apply to names, phrases, or titles. Copyright applies to both the original content of the work and to original features of its layout, format, and appearance.

Copyright lasts for a number of years after the owner's death. The exact length of time varies between 15 and 70 years depending on the nature of the work. After this time, provided the copyright has not been extended for some reason, the work becomes public domain and may be used freely. Also, in some circumstances, a copyright holder may have waived their rights and designated the work as public domain.

Even though copyright is not granted to an idea, the ownership of copyright is not transferred if you purchase an edition of the copyrighted work. So, for example, ownership of this book does not give you ownership of the copyright in this book, and you are forbidden to copy or distribute it to others. In a similar way, purchasing a software application does not give you the right to use it in any way you want. Take another example: you download a song recording from an Internet website. There is no copyright symbol displayed, but in fact the copyright in the recording is held by Widget Music, who has not given permission for the recording to be distributed in this way. You have broken the law by downloading the song, and the website owner has broken the law by making the song available for download.

Copyright can be transferred however. For example, if you create a piece of work as an employee of a company, you will hold the copyright to the work, unless your terms and conditions of employment contain a clause saying otherwise (which they probably will). Ownership of copyright can also be sold, as is common with the rights to music recordings.

Most types of original, created work are covered by copyright whether the work is printed, broadcast, distributed on a CD, CD-ROM, DVD, or other type of computer disk, exhibited in a gallery or theatre, or published on the Internet. Examples include books, films, plays, computer software, games, and artwork.

Note that a work does not have to be "artistic" to secure copyright; technical subject matter (such as an automobile's driver's handbook) is protected too. Also, if material is stored electronically, the type of file has no bearing on copyright; text, graphic, audio, and video files are protected equally.

Trademarks

As copyright is not given to the selection of a name, if a company wants to promote its goods it will normally **trademark** its name and/or logo. A trademark must be distinctive within the industry in which the company is selling goods and services. An ordinary trademark is indicated by the ™ symbol. A registered trademark is indicated by ®.

If you re-use or imitate an existing trademark, you are liable to legal action from the owner.

Patents

A **patent** is legal protection for some kind of invention. Unlike copyright, a patent *can* apply to an idea so long as the idea is original (or novel), useful, and distinctive or non-trivial. If you have registered the patent, you do not actually have to have made a copy of the invention or put it into practice. A patent must be applied for and registered; however, there is no automatic protection, as there is for copyright. In a lot of cases the registration must be international, or you have no basis for action against people in other countries infringing upon your patent. This can be complex as different countries have different standards for accepting patents. Patents are registered for a limited time only.

A patent infringement is where someone uses, makes, sells, or imports your invention without your permission. It does not matter whether the use was intentional or not.

It is important that any organization is able to protect its intellectual property. This might extend to making sure that you register appropriate product trademarks, protect your intellectual property, and ensure that for products, you take out patents.

Digital Products

A **digital product** is one that is sold or distributed as binary computer data. Examples of digital products include software, computer games, ebooks, music tracks, streaming video, video downloads, and so on. Digital products typically have low manufacturing and distribution costs, though hosted products can have substantial infrastructure costs. The downside is that digital products are quite easy to copy and steal.

Various copy protection or **Digital Rights Management (DRM)** systems have been invented to try to enforce "pay-per-use" for digital products. When you purchase a digital product, the vendor may license the file for use on a restricted number of devices. You generally need to use your account with the vendor to authorize and deauthorize devices when they change.

Data-driven Business Decisions

As well as having importance and value as an asset, data and information are critical in driving **business decisions and strategies**. For example, data can help a company become more efficient and develop better products and services:

- Production and fulfilment—analysis of things such as process flows, manufacturing and assembly, delivery and transportation networks, and ordering and billing systems provides the opportunity to make them more productive (efficient). Better productivity reduces costs and can improve customer satisfaction.
- Sales and marketing—information about individual consumers gleaned from web search and social media histories allows for personalized advertising. Large data sets of the same information aggregating the activity of millions of consumers can be used to identify trends and develop products and services to meet changing demands and interests.

Data Analytics (Relationship of Data to Information)

The process of using data in this way is usually called **analytics**. In an analytics process, you can think of **data being used to create information** in the following way:

- **Data** is the raw values collected by the system. The system must have some way of tagging or normalizing these values, similar to the way that data is defined with different types, so that they can be used for comparisons. For example, a web server might log whenever a page is visited and record information about the visitor, such as the time, the location, the type of browser, how long they spent viewing the page, or any link from the page that was clicked. All these things are data points with distinct types and formats.
- **Information** is some level of summarization of the individual data points. For example, you could use the logs of page visits to work out how many unique visitors there were (as opposed to the same visitor viewing the page more than once).
- **Insights** are things that inform meaningful business decisions. For example, from the information provided by the analysis of unique visitors, you may devise a plan to increase unique visitor numbers through better marketing or page design.

Facilitating Data-driven Business Decisions

Following the definitions of data, information, and insights set out above, it follows that you need systems to support these processing, analyzing, and reporting functions.

- **Data capture and collection**—data points can be collected from many different sources. In the previous example, most of the data points come from web server log files. The Internet of Things facilitates the use of sensors attached to all kinds of components, packages, and appliances to capture huge amounts of raw data. As well as collecting the data, it must be stored and secured. A traditional way of storing data is a relational database, but such structured data stores are being replaced (or supplemented) by semi-structured data warehouses.
- **Data correlation**—the information layer requires software to perform data correlation. This means analyzing the whole data set and finding connections and links between data points. For example, software may find a correlation between page visitors and the color schemes used on pages, with pages that are predominantly blue attracting more visitors than pages that make more use of yellow. The ability of software to perform data correlation without much human intervention is being greatly boosted by the development of Artificial Intelligence (AI) and machine learning systems.
- **Meaningful reporting**—to inform human decision making at the insights layer, the information identified by the analytics system must be presented in ways that humans can analyze and interpret. The system must support search and query tools plus charts and graphs and other ways to present information pictorially. There is also the security requirement; only authorized users should be able to query the information store.

Review Questions / Module 2 / Unit 1 / Using Data Types and Units

Answer these questions to test what you have learned in this unit. You can review the model answers at the end of the book.

1) Which notation system supports presenting the largest numbers using the fewest digits: Binary, Decimal, or Hexadecimal?
2) What is the decimal number 75 in binary and hexadecimal?
3) Which data type provides for whole numbers only?
4) What is the difference between the char and string data types?
5) Which data representation format can encode the widest range of characters?
6) What type of legal protection could be obtained for a novel software algorithm?
7) What data protection technology could you implement in order to restrict the type of activity that users could employ on digital products that they have purchased or rented?
8) What part of the process of data analytics is most closely supported by meaningful reporting?

Module 2 / Unit 2

Using Apps

Objectives

On completion of this unit, you will be able to:

- Install and uninstall software applications and configure compatibility settings.
- Explain the importance of software licensing and the types of license available.
- Describe the key features of different types of application and associated file formats.

Syllabus Objectives and Content Examples

This unit covers the following exam domain objectives and content examples:

- 3.1 Manage applications and software.
  Application management
- 3.3 Explain the purpose and proper use of software.
  Productivity software (Word processing software, Spreadsheet software, Presentation software, Web browser, Visual diagramming software) • Collaboration software (Email client, Conferencing software, Instant messaging software, Online workspace, Document sharing) • Business software (Database software, Project management software, Business-specific applications, Accounting software)
- 3.6 Compare and contrast general application concepts and uses.
  Licensing (Single use, Group use/site license, Concurrent license, Open source vs. proprietary, Subscription vs. one-time purchase, Product keys and serial numbers) • Software installation best practices (Reading instructions, Reading agreements, Advanced options)

Installing Applications

Applications (or **apps**) are the software programs that let users do useful things with their computer, such as create and edit documents, browse websites, send email, watch videos, or play games. When you have installed an operating system such as Windows, you are also likely to want to install and manage software applications and perhaps enable or disable OS features and components.

The term "app" originally referred specifically to software written for mobile devices, such as smartphones and tablets, while "application" came to mean software written for a desktop PC or laptop. The distinction has since broken down, and the terms are now somewhat interchangeable.

Reading Instructions and Documentation

Before you try to install an application, make sure you are following **software installation best practices**. Read the accompanying documentation to verify:

- That the software is compatible with your operating system.
- That your computer hardware meets the application's recommended system requirements.
- Any special installation instructions or known issues.
- That you have a valid agreement or license to install and use the product.

Installing a Desktop Application

Windows creates special folders for storing system and application files called "Windows" and "Program Files." The contents of these folders should not be changed manually. Moving or deleting files in these folders could cause Windows or software applications not to start properly. Access to these folders and files is restricted to administrative users in any case.

Applications should be installed using the supplied setup program. To install a program, the user account must be a Computer Administrator. An application's setup files are usually either provided on a setup disc or downloaded from the Internet.

- Put the program disc in the drive and choose the option to install the software.
- Download the setup program from a website then locate and open the setup program through Explorer.

In order to install a program successfully, you should exit any other applications or files. You may also need to disable anti-virus software.

When you try to install a program, you will see another example of Windows' User Account Control (UAC) security feature in action. UAC prompts you to confirm any important change to the system, such as installing a program or hardware device or changing a security setting. In the case of programs, Windows also checks whether the program has a **digital certificate** proving it has been created by a trustworthy software publisher; if a certificate is not there or not valid, Windows displays another warning.

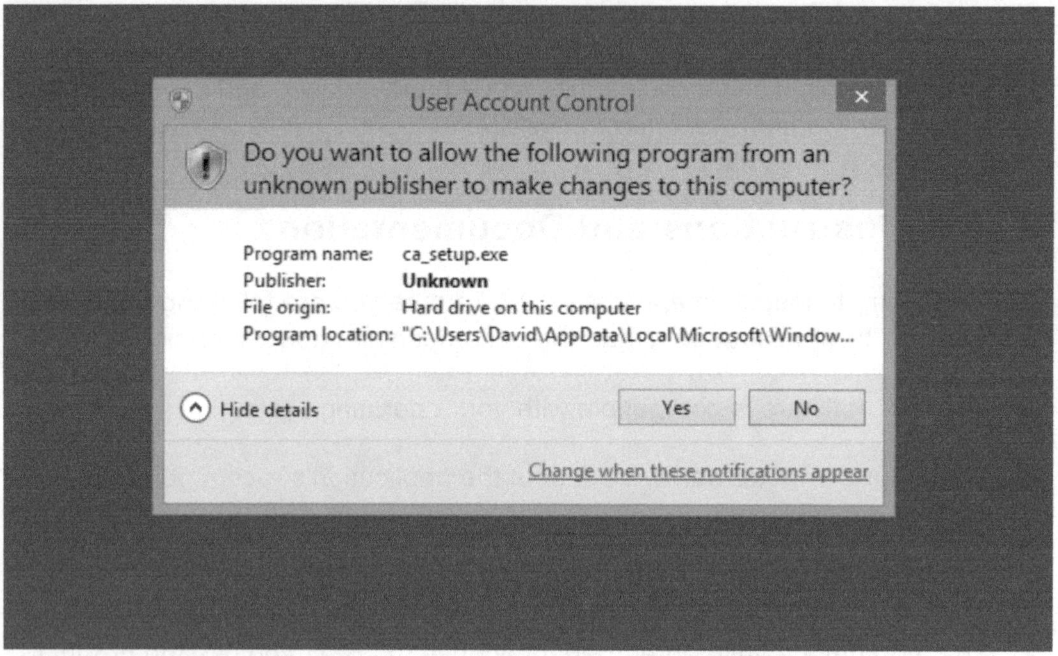

Untrusted publisher warning—this does not necessarily mean that the program is harmful as not all publishers obtain valid certificates but do not run it if you do not know that it is from a reputable source. Screenshot used with permission from Microsoft.

Confirm the UAC prompt if you are happy to proceed. The setup program will then provide a wizard for you to choose the appropriate options, such as choosing program components, selecting the install location (always choose "Program Files" unless you have a good reason not to), and creating shortcuts.

Advanced Options

Most software installer packages offer a choice between a default installation and a custom (or advanced options) installation. A custom installation allows you to choose specific settings, such as where to install the software and what icons or startup/autorun options to configure. A custom installation may also involve the selection of specific feature sets or modules within the software package.

Microsoft Store Apps

In recent versions of Windows, you can install two types of software. Desktop applications are installed and managed using Programs and Features, as described above. Apps are installed and managed via the **Microsoft Store**.

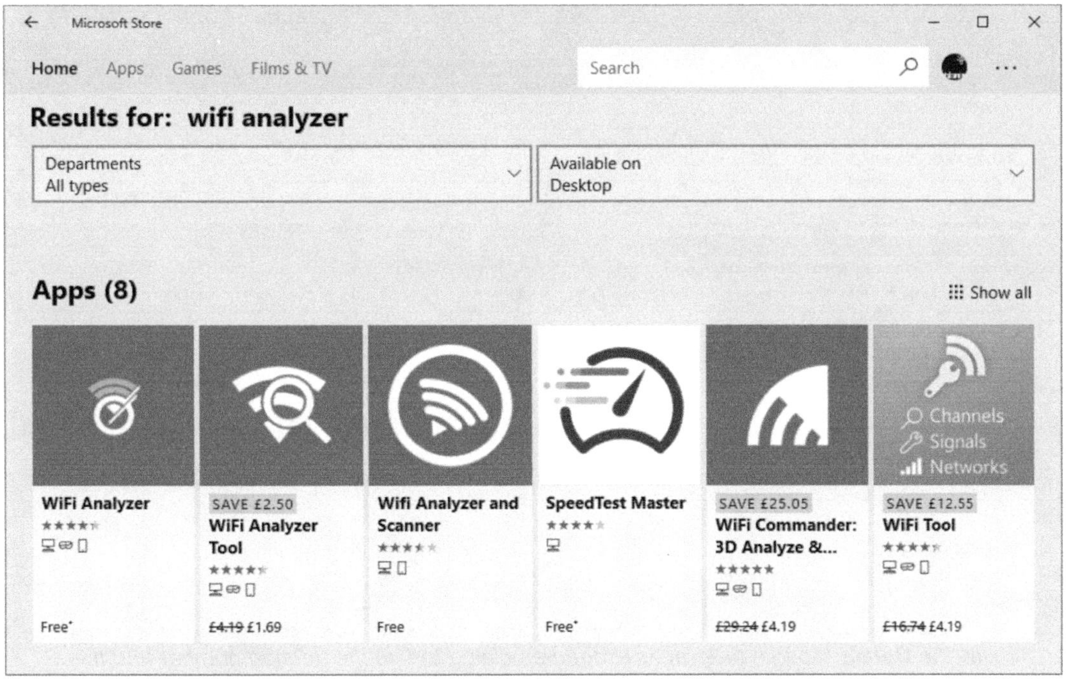

Microsoft Store. Screenshot used with permission from Microsoft.

Unlike desktop applications, store apps run in a restrictive **sandbox**. This sandbox is designed to prevent a store app from making system-wide changes and prevent a faulty store app from "crashing" the whole OS or interfering with other apps and applications. This extra level of protection means that users with only standard permissions are allowed to install store apps. Installing a store app does not require confirmation with UAC or computer administrator-level privileges.

Application Management

Once the application has been installed, there are various ways to perform additional configuration and application management.

Configuring Application Compatibility

After an application has been installed, you may experience difficulties getting it to run. If this is the case, you can inspect the properties of the executable file (or a shortcut to the executable). The **Details** tab is useful for troubleshooting, as it will let you know whether you are running a version with the latest patches. The **Compatibility** tab can be used to run the program in a compatibility mode (for Windows 98 for instance) and adjust the display settings.

Windows features such as UAC and its greater protection for system folders (Program Files and the system root) plus the redesigned desktop compositing engine have made application compatibility more challenging. UAC problems can be solved by running the program as an administrator, and there is an option to turn off advanced desktop compositing effects.

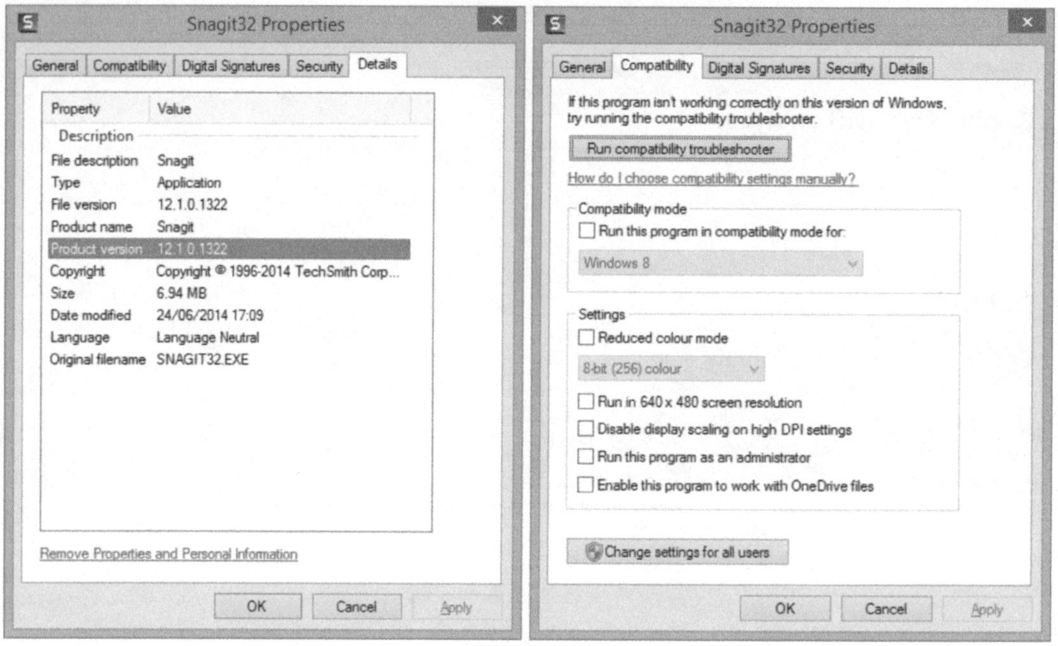

Use the Details tab in a program's Properties dialog to find the version number and the Compatibility tab to configure settings for legacy applications. Screenshot used with permission from Microsoft.

If you need a user to tell you the version number, it is usually listed by selecting the "About" menu option in the software. The "About" option may be accessed via a "Help" menu.

Repairing and Uninstalling Software

If a software program stops working, the best solution is usually to uninstall then reinstall it. Some programs may also support a **Repair** option, which can be a bit quicker and preserve your custom settings. Some programs may have optional components, which you can add or remove using the **Change** option. You will also want to **uninstall** unneeded programs. A new PC or laptop may come with bundled software programs and trial versions (sometimes unkindly referred to as "bloatware"). There may also be programs you no longer use. To use any of these options, open **Programs and Features** in **Control Panel**, click the program icon, then choose the appropriate option.

In order to uninstall a program successfully, you should close any applications or files that might lock files installed by the application or the PC will need to be restarted. You might also need to disable anti-virus software (although not Windows Defender). If the uninstall program cannot remove locked files, it will normally prompt you to check its log file for details. The files and directories can then be deleted manually.

If uninstalling and reinstalling does not work, you may need to perform a **clean uninstall**. Essentially this means removing files and settings manually, following the instructions on the vendor's website.

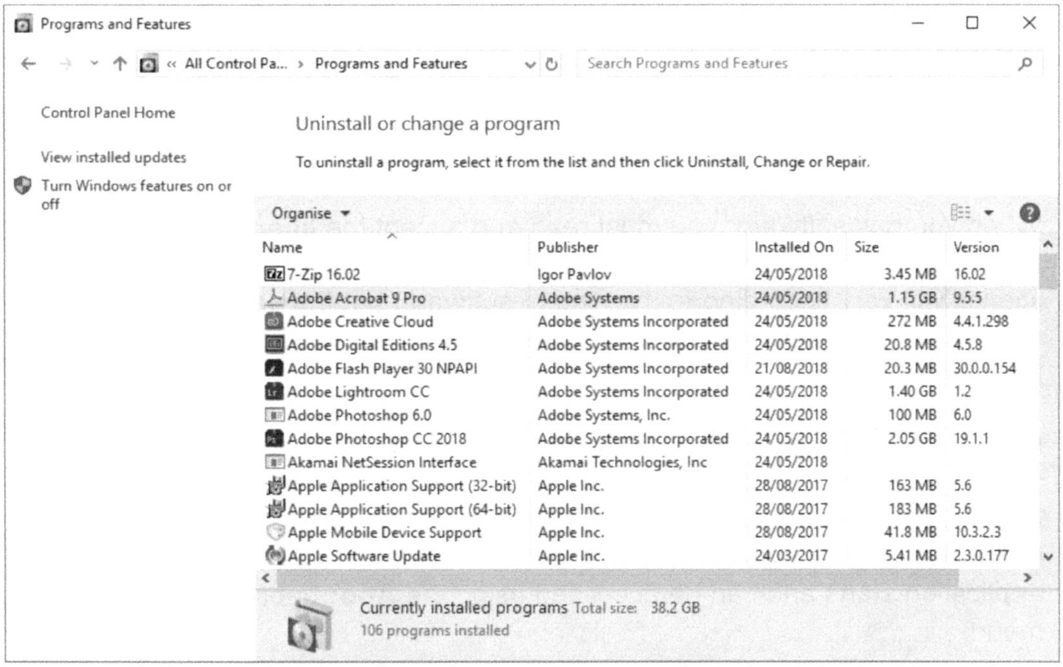

Programs and Features—select a program then choose an option from the toolbar. Screenshot used with permission from Microsoft.

If you click **View installed updates**, the list will display patches or hotfixes installed for Windows. You can use the wizard to uninstall a patch.

Enabling and Disabling Windows Features

Windows comes with a number of components and add-ons that may be enabled or disabled by default. You can control these by clicking the **Turn Windows features on or off** link in Programs and Features.

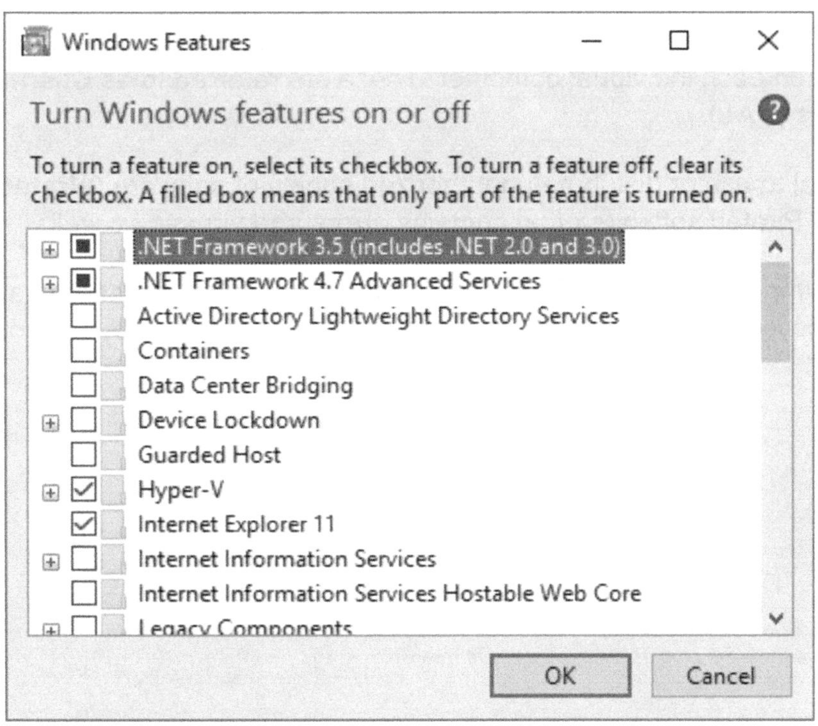

Turning Windows features on or off. Screenshot used with permission from Microsoft.

Managing Software Licensing

When installing an app, you need to ensure that the software is properly licensed for use.

Software Licensing and Agreements

When you buy software, you must read and accept the **license** governing its use, often called the **End User License Agreement (EULA)**. The terms of the license will vary according to the type of software, but the basic restriction is usually that the software may only be installed on *one* computer (**single use license**).

Usually, the software is activated using a **product key**, which will be a long string of characters and numbers printed on the box or disk case. The product key will generate a different **product ID** or **serial number**, which is often used to obtain technical support. The product ID is usually displayed when the application starts and can be accessed using the **About** option on the **Help** menu.

A company may have hundreds of employees who need the same software on their computers. Software manufacturers do not expect such companies to buy individual copies of the software for each employee. Instead, they will issue either a **group use/site license**, which means that the company can install the software on an agreed number of computers for an unlimited number of employees to use at the same time, or a **concurrent license**, which means that the company can allow only a set number of users access to it at any one time. It is important to monitor usage of the software to ensure that the permitted number of host-installs or concurrent users is not exceeded.

If a site has a large number of computers, these computers are often networked. This means that software bought under license can be installed onto a network server so that all authorized users can access it without it being installed on each individual computer. These are referred to as **Client Access Licenses (CAL)**.

It is illegal to use or distribute unauthorized copies of software (**pirated copies**). Pirated software often contains errors and viruses as well.

Another important aspect of a software agreement is how any data gathered and processed by the software is used, stored, and retained by the software vendor.

Registration

The software setup program will often prompt you to register the application, either using an online form or the card supplied with the setup disc. Registering is usually optional but may be required to obtain product support and updates and validate the warranty.

Subscription versus One-time Purchase

Historically, software licensing tended toward **one-time purchases** of licenses for a given number of devices or user seats. The one-time purchase price would give perpetual use of the software, though subsequent upgrades would normally involve a new license fee. This model is being replaced by **subscription-based licensing**, where organizations pay a per-user monthly fee to get access to the software. In this model, upgrades are provided as part of the subscription. Examples of subscription pricing include Adobe Creative Cloud and Microsoft Office 365.

Shareware, Freeware, and Open Source Applications

Not all software is distributed using the commercial licensing or subscription models described above. Shareware, freeware, and open source licenses represent some different ways of making applications available.

- **Shareware** is software that you can install free of charge so that you can evaluate it for a limited period. If you decide to continue using the software after this period, you must register it, usually for a fee. When you register the software you often become entitled to extra features and support.
- **Freeware** is software that is available free of charge.

  Even if software is distributed as shareware or freeware, the copyright is still held by the publisher or designer. Both shareware and freeware may still be governed by a license, which may restrict its use (for example, to prevent commercial use of the product or unauthorized redistribution or resale).

- **Open source** is software that also makes the **program code** used to design it available. The idea is that other programmers can investigate the program and make it more stable and useful. An open source license does not forbid commercial use of applications derived from the original, but it is likely to impose the same conditions on further redistributions.

Productivity Software

Productivity software refers to applications that help users complete typical office tasks. Such tasks might include writing a letter or report, making a sales presentation, or processing orders.

Most productivity software is sold or distributed in **suites**, such as Microsoft Office or Open Office. Each application within the suite shares a common look and feel with other applications, helping users to switch between them more easily. Using an integrated software suite means that users can learn to use the basic layout and commands of an application more quickly (for example, to access file commands, run a spell check, and so on). It is easier to share data between the different applications (for example, to embed a spreadsheet in a word-processed report).

Web Browser Software

While there is some risk that an employee with access to a **web browser** will waste a certain percentage of the work day, web access is important to many professions and organizations, not only for information and research but also to contact customers, suppliers, and business partners through social media.

Spreadsheet Software

A **spreadsheet** consists of a table containing rows, columns, and cells. When values are entered into the cells, formulas can be applied to them, enabling complex calculations to be carried out. Spreadsheet packages can be used for many tasks including tracking and analyzing sales data and working on company accounts.

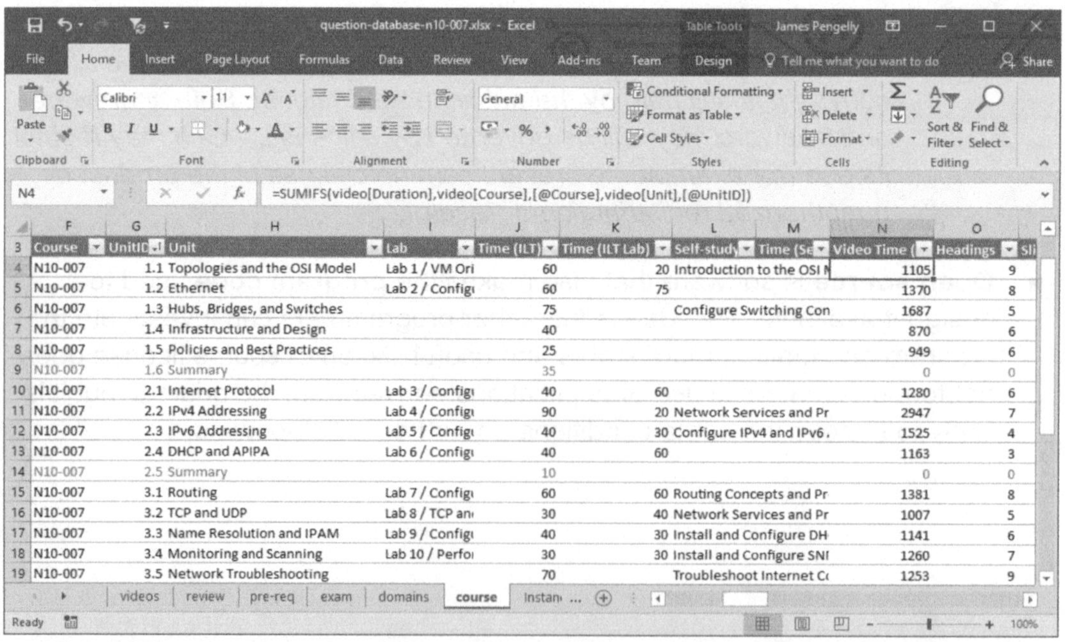

Microsoft Excel spreadsheet software. Note the lettered columns and numbered rows. Each intersection is a cell that can contain data or a formula. Screenshot used with permission from Microsoft.

Word Processing Software

Word processing means applications that help users to write and edit **documents**. A word processor will come with features enabling the user to edit and review text quickly, using an automated spell checker for instance. Most word processors also provide formatting and layout tools, allowing the use of pictures and tables in a document for instance. They are also likely to allow output to different formats, such as print or online web page.

Presentation Software

Presentation software enables users to create sophisticated **slide shows**. Pictures, company logos, graphs, and text can be added to the slides, together with a variety of animations.

Visual Diagramming Software

Diagrams are an important means of communicating or recording ideas or configurations clearly. **Visual diagramming** software assists the creation of these by providing templates and shapes for different kinds of diagram. The user does not have to worry about creating icons or shapes; they can just drag shapes from the template (or stencil) into the diagram and use the software tools to connect them appropriately.

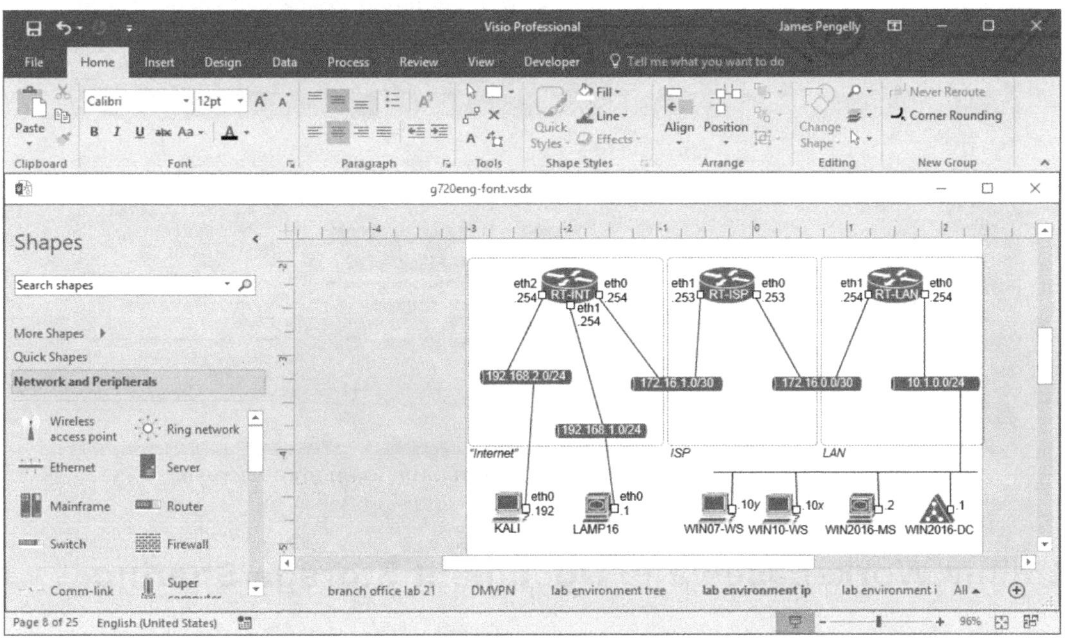

Microsoft Visio diagramming software with a network diagram document open. In this sort of diagram, you can add shapes from the stencil collections shown on the left of the window and then draw connectors to link the shapes. Screenshot used with permission from Microsoft.

Collaboration Software

Collaboration software means that multiple users can work together on the same file or project.

Email Software and Personal Information Managers

Email software is an application that allows the user to compose and send messages and then receive messages from others. The **email client** software works in conjunction with an **email server**, which handles the business of actually transmitting the messages over the network.

Email software is very often coupled with a **Personal Information Manager (PIM)**. PIM software provides features for storing and organizing information, such as contacts and calendar events and appointments.

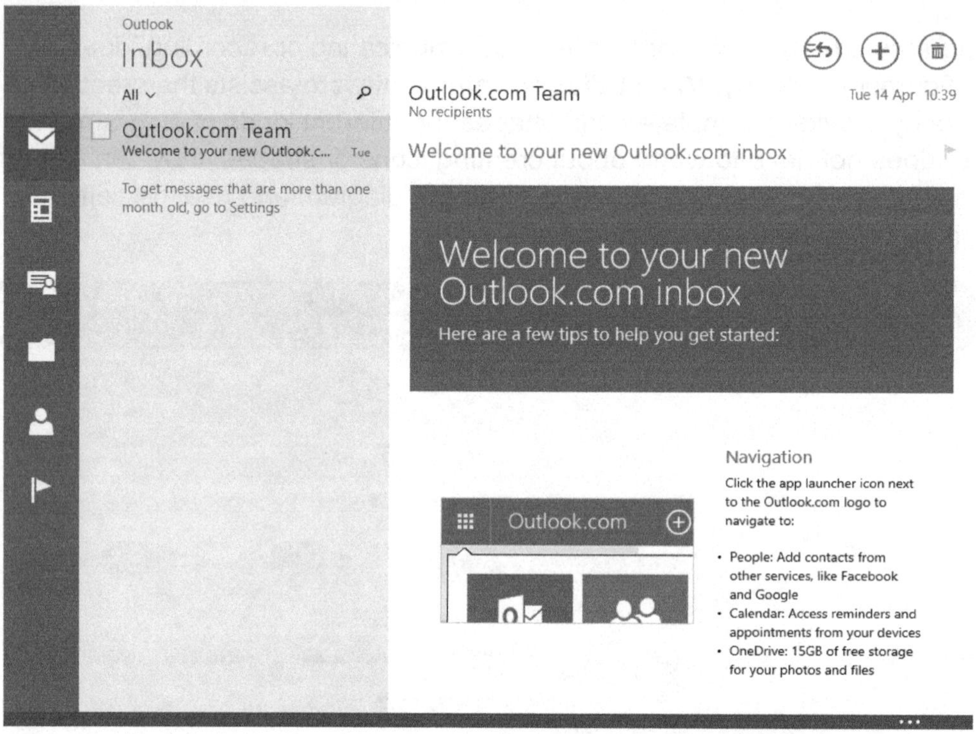

Windows Mail client. Screenshot used with permission from Microsoft.

Online Workspaces and Document Storage/Sharing

An **online workspace** is one where a file is hosted on a network, and users can sign in to get access to it. Different users might be assigned different permissions over the document. For example, some users may be able to view or print the document or add comments to it; others may be able to edit it.

As with email, this type of application uses servers and clients. The server software, such as Microsoft's SharePoint Server, or cloud-based services, such as Google Drive or Smartsheet, provide the storage and sharing features. The workspace server hosts the document and contains the accounts and permissions of the users allowed to access it.

The client software provides the user with the tools to view and edit the document. The client software might be a productivity suite (such as Microsoft Office) or might be provided with the workspace (Google Docs and Smartsheet tools for instance).

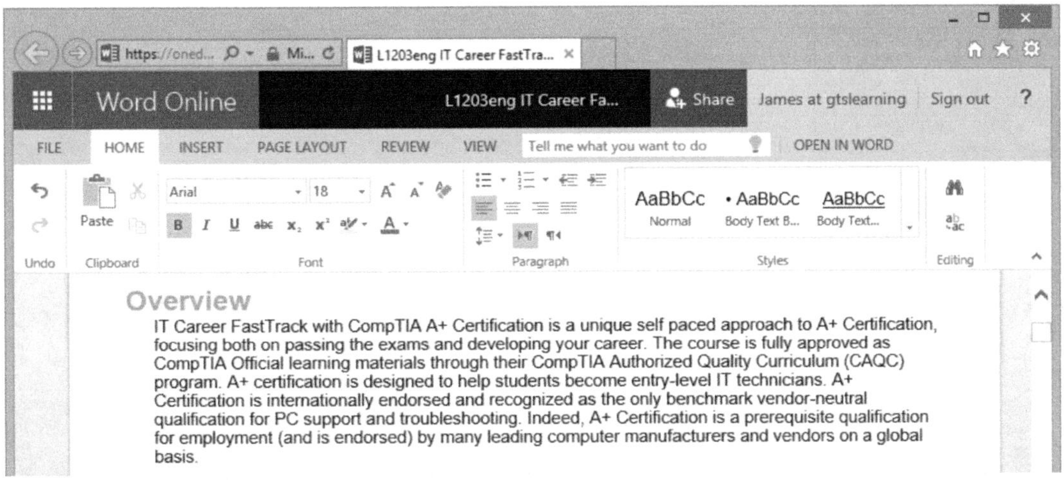

Editing a document stored in Microsoft's OneDrive cloud storage solution with a cloud-based version of Microsoft Word. Screenshot used with permission from Microsoft.

When multiple users are editing a document, there has to be a process for managing changes. One option is to provide a "check out" feature, where a user checks a document out for editing, and it becomes locked for other users. Another option is to allow a master editor to view multiple revisions and approve and merge or reject changes to a single published version.

Remote Desktop and Screen Sharing Software

Remote Desktop allows a user to connect to a computer over a network. The remote desktop server runs on the target computer. The user starts a remote desktop client application and enters the connection information. When the connection is established, the user can operate the remote computer's desktop via a window on their local computer.

An ordinary user might use remote desktop to connect from a field laptop to a machine in the office. Remote desktop is also used by IT support staff to login to a user's computer to provide support and assistance without having to travel to the user's location.

Remote connection utilities can also be used in a "read-only" type of mode to facilitate **screen sharing**. This means that the remote user can view the host's desktop but cannot interact with it. This mode is often used for software demonstrations and for product support.

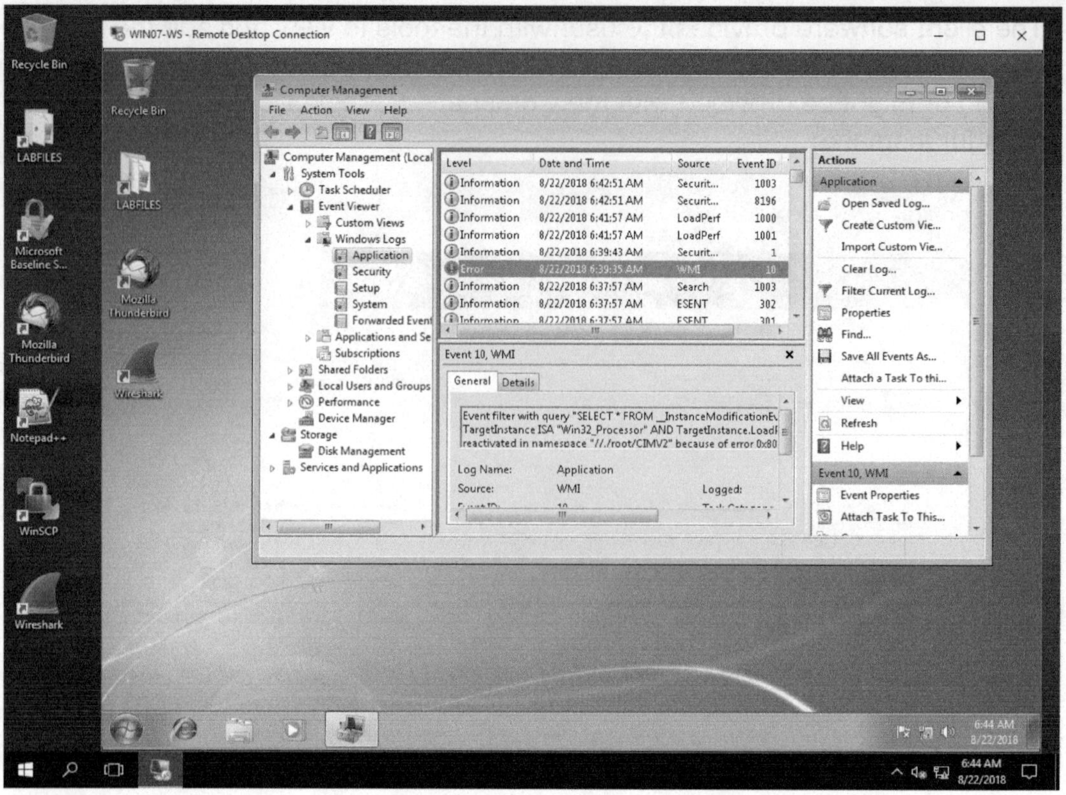

Operating a Windows 7 host from a Windows 10 client using Remote Desktop. Screenshot used with permission from Microsoft.

Instant Messaging and VoIP Software

Instant Messaging (IM) software allows users to communicate in real time. Unlike with email, there is (virtually) no delay between sending and receiving a message. Basic IM software allows for the transfer of text messages and can also be used for file attachments. These days, all IM applications facilitate voice and video calls too.

Voice over Internet Protocol (VoIP) packages voice communications as data packets, transmits them over the network, then reassembles the packets to provide two-way, real-time voice communication.

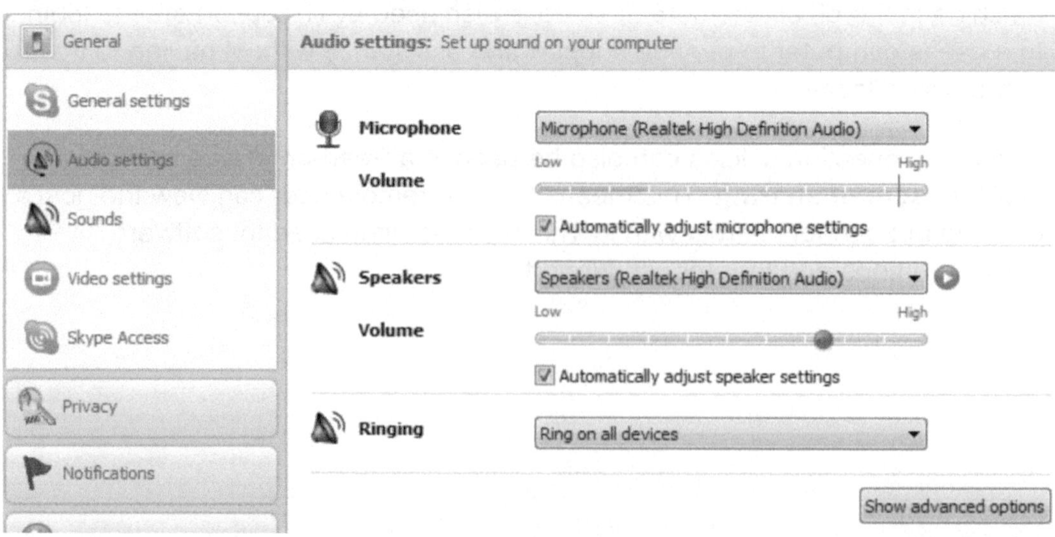

Configuring audio devices in Skype. Screenshot used with permission from Microsoft.

There are numerous different ways of implementing VoIP, each with different protocols which are often proprietary to a particular VoIP software vendor. To implement VoIP to make calls from a computer in a typical Peer-to-Peer configuration, you need software (such as Skype or Slack), an Internet connection, and usually a headset (more convenient than using PC microphone and speakers).

IM software requires a good quality network link between the participants. "Real-time" applications such as IM are sensitive to **latency**, which is the delay in seconds that a packet of data takes to travel over a network. IM voice and video calling also requires sufficient **bandwidth**. These factors might be controllable on a private network, but on the Internet, where a packet might traverse many different networks to reach its final destination, link quality is more difficult to guarantee.

Video Conferencing Software and Telepresence

Video conferencing or **Video Teleconferencing (VTC)** software allows users to configure virtual meeting rooms, with options for voice, video, and instant messaging. Other features often include screen sharing, presentation/whiteboard, file sharing, and polls and voting options. Most conferencing suites also provide a fallback teleconference option, to be used in conjunction with the presentation features, in case some participants cannot get a good enough connection for an IP voice or video call.

Telepresence is a term used to refer to particularly sophisticated video conferencing solutions. The idea is that the participants have a real sense of being in the same room. This can be achieved by a number of video technologies, including HD or 4K resolutions, large and/or curved flat-screens, and 3D. Emerging technologies might make use of virtual reality headsets, holograms, and robotics.

Business Software

Productivity software covers general office functions and tasks. Applications such as spreadsheets and databases can be developed to perform a wide range of tasks, covering operations from accounting and sales to production and distribution. However, a company or individual will often want to use **specialized business software** designed to assist with a particular business process or consumer demand.

Desktop Publishing Software

Desktop Publishing (DTP) is similar to word processing but with more emphasis on the formatting and layout of documents than on editing the text. DTP software also contains better tools for preparing a document to be printed professionally. DTP software combines text and images in the best possible layout for a wide variety of media, including books, magazines, posters, ebooks, and web pages.

Graphic Design

DTP and web design software is often used in conjunction with **graphic design** applications. There are many types of graphic design applications, which can be broadly categorized as follows:

- Digital darkroom products such as Adobe Photoshop assist with the correction and manipulation of photographic images.
- Digital paint products such as Corel Painter allow the creation of bitmap artwork on a computer.
- Digital drawing products such as Adobe Illustrator allow the creation of vector-based line art.

Bitmap artwork means that the file records the color value of each pixel in the image. Vector artwork records the plot points and color values of the lines and shapes used. Vector artwork can be resized without loss of quality whereas resizing a bitmap will require some pixels to be lost or added, using some dithering process to determine the color values of the remaining pixels.

- 3D and animation packages allow the creation of digital films or creation of effects in motion pictures.

Computer Aided Design (CAD)

Computer Aided Design (CAD) software makes technical drawings and schematics easier to produce and revise. Drawings can be rotated or viewed in 3D and easily transmitted to a client for feedback. CAD is often linked to Computer Aided Manufacturing (CAM) which enables the data produced in CAD drawings to be loaded into a machine which then manufactures the part.

Project Management

Project management involves breaking a project into a number of tasks and assigning responsibilities, resources, and timescales to ensure the completion of those tasks. Project management also involves identifying dependencies between tasks. Software such as Microsoft Project or Smartsheet assists with this process by visualizing task timelines and dependencies and recording information about task properties and progress.

Accounting and Commercial

There are many software applications designed to support **financial** and **commercial** functions, such as order processing, accountancy, and payroll. For corporates and Small and Medium Sized Enterprises (SME), these packages allow companies to input orders and create invoices and profit and loss reports. There are also consumer versions designed to help with household budgets and financial planning.

Another important class of commercial software is Customer Relationship Management (CRM). These are applications for organizing sales leads and contacts. There are also any number of programs designed to assist with marketing, including optimizing use of the web and social media.

Database Software

Database packages enable the user to store, organize, and retrieve information. Databases can search through thousands of records very quickly and display data in a format specified by the user. They can be used to store many different types of information, such as timetables, customer details, and patient records. The database application in Microsoft Office is called Microsoft Access. This is suitable for creating databases with tens of users.

Databases are also used at every level of IT infrastructure. Fast and reliable database products are as important as operating systems for large organizations. Examples of enterprise-level database products include SQL Server and Oracle. The **XML (eXtensible Markup Language)** format is also increasingly important for data storage, as it allows for a high level of integration between different types of systems.

Business-specific

A company may also commission custom-made software to implement specific **Line of Business (LOB)** functions. LOB applications would cover functions that cannot be performed by "off-the-shelf" software. This might include product design and manufacturing, fulfilment and inventory control, plus marketing and sales.

Review Questions / Module 2 / Unit 2 / Using Apps

Answer these questions to test what you have learned in this unit. You can review the model answers at the end of the book.

1) What compatibility information should you confirm before installing a software application?
2) Following installation of a program written for an older version of Windows, you receive an alert that it might not have installed correctly. What feature could you use to make the program run correctly?
3) Why would Windows prompt you to enter a password if you try to install a software application?
4) Windows comes with web server software but it is not enabled by default. How would you install this software?
5) Following installation of an application, another program on your computer has stopped working. What could you do to try to fix it?
6) Why might one of your first tasks on receiving a new computer be to remove software applications?
7) In order to obtain support, the software vendor wants to know the application's product ID. How would you locate this information?
8) What is the difference between freeware and open source software?
9) What type of software would you use to configure a server by connecting to it over the network?
10) What type of software manages tasks, dependencies, and timelines?

Lab 7 / Managing Software Applications

In this lab, you will install and uninstall a software application and examine Windows Update settings.

The software application you will install displays technical information about the system components installed on your computer. It is published by CPUID. Optionally, browse CPUID's website (cpuid.com) before proceeding to learn about the company and its products.

This lab involves downloading and installing a program from a third-party website. The authors and publisher believe the website and program to be reputable and pose no risk to your computer or personal information but cannot be held responsible for any loss or damage that may occur as a result of following the steps in this lab. If you have any concerns we recommend that you do NOT proceed.

1) If necessary, start your computer and sign in.
2) Open Microsoft Edge (or your preferred browser), and type the following URL into the address bar:

   `http://download.cpuid.com/cpu-z/cpu-z_1.85-en.exe`

3) In the prompt box displayed at the bottom of the window, click **Run**.

   In the "Open File—Security Warning" dialog, note that the publisher is identified as CPUID. When you allow a software program to install itself, you need to be confident that it is a legitimate application (not a Trojan Horse that might be installing some malware). If the setup program is digitally signed and comes with a trusted certificate, then that is some evidence that the software is trustworthy.

4) Optionally, click the **CPUID** link then inspect the publisher's digital certificate. If you are happy to proceed, click **Run**.

The fact that the certificate is issued by a company that Windows trusts (DigiCert) is a fair indication that the publisher is legitimate. You should always take care when installing software from unknown sources.

5) Complete the application's Setup wizard by making the following choices:

    - Select **I accept the agreement** and click **Next**.
    - Accept the default installation folder and click **Next**.
    - Accept the default start menu folder and click **Next**.
    - Accept the option to create a desktop shortcut and click **Next**.
    - Select **Install**.
    - When installation is complete, uncheck the **View readme** box and click **Finish**.

6) Show the desktop and open the **CPUID CPU-Z** icon.

    The User Account Control dialog is displayed. CPU-Z obtains detailed information about system components by installing a special device driver each time it runs. This requires administrator-level access to perform.

    If you were not sure of the provenance of the software, you might be suspicious of software that requests this level of access.

7) If you are happy to proceed, click **Yes**.

    The program will execute and display a dialog showing detailed information about the CPU, memory modules, motherboard, and graphics adapter installed in your computer.

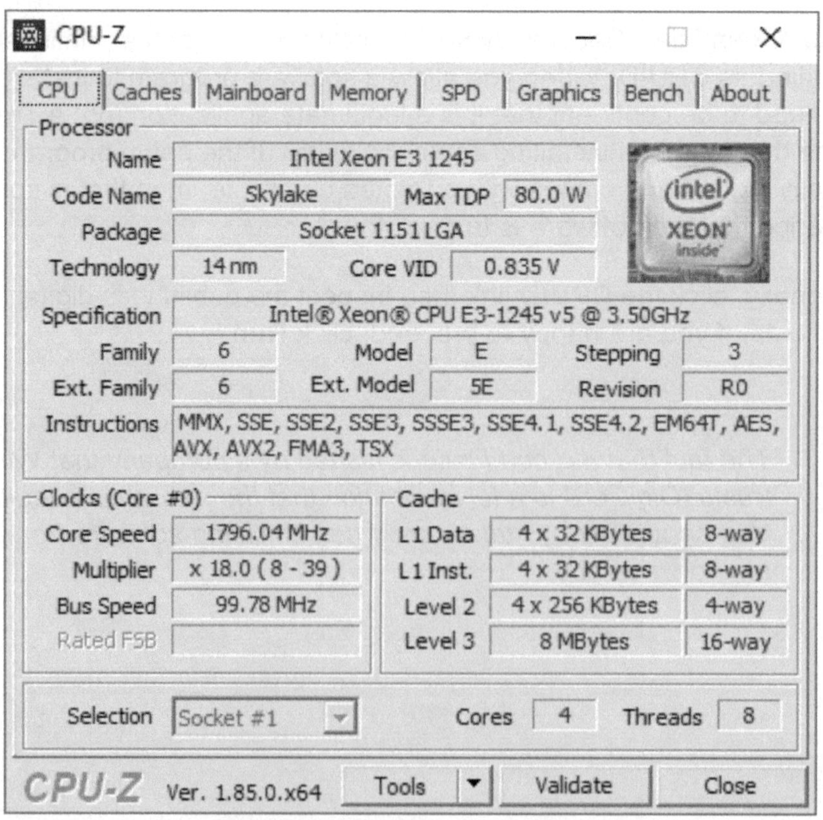

CPU-Z utility from CPUID (cpuid.com).

8) Browse the information reported by selecting the tab headings for a few minutes, then click **Close**.

We recommend that you do NOT select options from the **Tools** *menu, as these link to ad-supported software programs.*

9) Press `START+X` then select **Apps and Features**.

You can also display this shortcut menu by right-clicking the Start button. It contains most of the "power" tools for configuring Windows.

10) Select the **CPUID CPU-Z** icon and click the **Uninstall** button. Click **Uninstall** to confirm.

11) Click **Yes** to confirm (again) then **OK** when the process is complete.

12) Take a moment to browse the programs installed on your computer. This view shows you when a program was installed, its size, and (in some cases) its version number.

13) Press `START` then type `appwiz.cpl` and click the icon for the Control Panel applet returned in the search results.

    Programs and Features is the older program management interface. This only lists desktop applications (not Windows Store apps).

14) In the left-hand pane of "Programs and Features," click **Turn Windows features on or off**.

15) Browse the features already installed and available then click **Cancel**.

16) In the left pane of "Programs and Features," click **View installed updates**.

    You can use this view to check whether a particular update is installed.

17) Close any open windows.

18) Optionally, shut down your computer if you are not continuing to use it after this lab.

Module 2 / Unit 3

Programming and App Development

Objectives

On completion of this unit, you will be able to:

- Describe programming organizational techniques and logic.
- Categorize types of programming languages and list the advantages and disadvantages of each type.
- Describe some of the main features of application code and Object-Oriented Programming.
- Describe the ways that an application can be deployed.

Syllabus Objectives and Content Examples

This unit covers the following exam domain objectives and content examples:

- 3.4 Explain methods of application architecture and delivery models.
  Application delivery methods—locally installed (Network not required, Application exists locally, Files saved locally) • Application delivery methods—Local network hosted (Network required, Internet access not required) • Application delivery methods—Cloud hosted (Internet access required, Service required, Files saved in the cloud)
- 3.6 Compare and contrast general application concepts and uses.
  Single-platform software • Cross-platform software (Compatibility concerns)
- 4.1 Compare and contrast programming language categories.
  Interpreted (Scripting languages, Scripted languages, Markup languages) • Compiled programming languages • Query languages • Assembly language
- 4.2 Given a scenario, use programming organizational techniques and interpret logic.
  Organizational techniques (Pseudocode concepts, Flow chart concepts, Sequence) • Logic components (Branching, Looping)
- 4.3 Explain the purpose and use of programming concepts.
  Identifiers (Variables, Constants) • Containers (Arrays, Vectors) • Functions • Objects (Properties, Attributes, Methods)

Programming Logic

Apps, of whatever type, are created by programmers in a process of **software development**. Programmers (or coders) are individuals who work with one or more **programming languages** to write **code** that is used as the basis for the applications that you use on your computing device.

Program Sequence

A **program** is just a sequence of instructions for your computer to perform. For example, you might want to add two user-entered numbers together and display the sum on the screen. In plain English, the program might look something like this:

1) Clear the current display.
2) Ask the user for the first number and store that number for subsequent use.
3) Ask the user for the second number and store that number for subsequent use.
4) Retrieve the two stored numbers and add them together.
5) Display the result.

It's a simple set of instructions, but while English can tolerate ambiguity, programming generally cannot. In designing a program, we have to consider how input, processing, and output are all clearly defined. What if the user entered a word instead of a number? What if the user doesn't understand what's required? You could modify the program to address these issues:

1) Clear the current display.
2) Output to the screen the instructions for the operation.
3) Ask the user for the first number.
4) Verify that the entered value is a number:
   a) If it is, proceed.
   b) If it is not, remind the user what the valid range is and prompt again.
5) Store that number for subsequent use.
6) Ask the user for the second number.
7) Verify that the entered value is a number:
   a) If it is, proceed.
   b) If it is not, remind the user what the valid range is and prompt again.
8) Store that number for subsequent use.

9) Retrieve the two stored numbers and add them together.

10) Display the result.

Using a Flow Chart

As this restatement of the program is getting significantly more complex, it might help to visualize it. You could view the sequence as a graphical **flow chart** to help understand the processes.

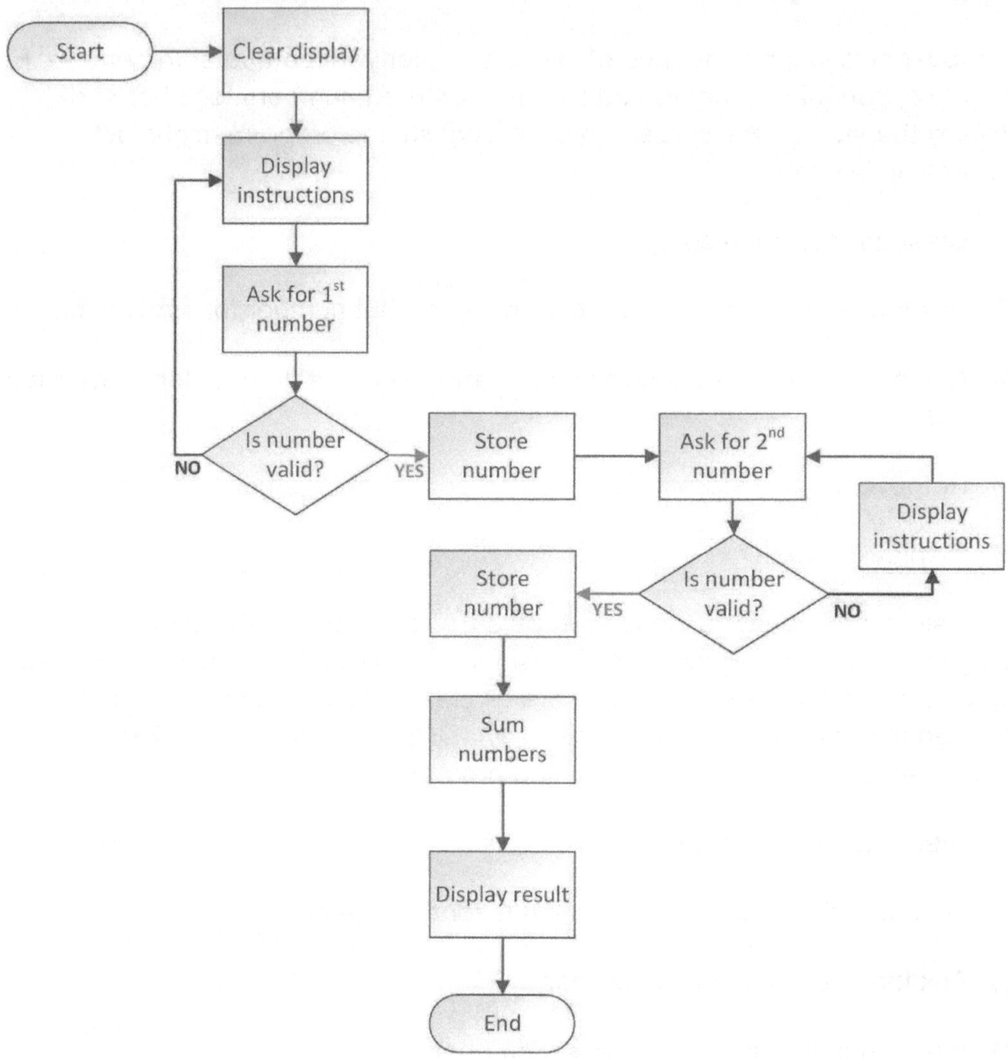

Flow chart of simple program.

With the steps shown visually in a diagram, it is easier to see that the program is not completely linear. There are branches and loops. Also notice that the program contains some duplicate steps; specifically, the verification steps and the display instructions steps. We can use the diagram to analyze the sequence of instructions and write better code to support that sequence.

"Better" code is a matter of some judgement, but it is desirable for a program to be as compact and efficient as possible. The fewer lines of code that can be used to perform the necessary instructions, the easier the code will be to maintain and update.

Writing Pseudocode

Having analyzed the structure of our program, we can switch from writing out the steps as a simple list and start to develop code blocks to support the program's function.

For example, where there are duplicate steps, you could write those as separate **subroutines** and then call them whenever needed.

```
'Main routine
Add It Up routine {
   clear display
   call Display Instructions routine
   prompt for first number
   call Verify subroutine
   store first number Variable1
   prompt for second number
   call Verify subroutine
   store second number Variable2
   sum (Variable1, Variable2)
   write sum to display
}
End routine
'Verify subroutine
Verify subroutine {
   verify user input is number
   if FALSE, call Display Instructions subroutine
   return
}
End routine
'Instructions subroutine
Display Instructions subroutine {
   clear display
   write "instruction text" to display
   prompt OK
   clear display
   return
}
End routine
```

Features of Programming Code

We haven't used the specific syntax of a particular programming language yet, but already, this is starting to look like a program (**pseudocode**). Note some of the features:

- The main routine calls some **subroutines**. Each routine is completed by an "End Routine" statement. This means (for example) when the program reaches the last step of the main routine, it closes rather than flowing through to try to execute the first subroutine.
- When a subroutine completes, it can **return** to the point in the main routine from where it was called, and the main routine continues execution. Note that when we use structures such as this, we have to be very careful not to create infinite loops in the code by mistake.
- There is a **conditional statement** (IF) that means part of the code only executes when certain conditions are true or false.
- There are **variables** to store data input by the user.
- There are **functions** (such as "sum" and "write") that we can assume are provided as features of the programming language. We don't need to code how to add two numbers together or write output to the display screen.
- There is a **user interface** that the program interacts with (prompting for input and displaying output).
- It contains **comments**, preceded by the `'` character. Comments are part of the programming code that are not executed by the computer but that help the developer read and maintain the code.

Programming Languages

Having created the logic behind your program, you must then code it using the appropriate **programming language**. It's important to consider what programming language to use. The choice that you make will be determined by many factors, including:

- What type of program you are writing.
- How experienced you are as a programmer.
- What type(s) of device(s) your users will be using.

A programming language provides the exact syntax for you to use for your code. For example, the character used for a comment or the way conditional statements are written out varies from language to language. Some languages provide more built-in functions than others.

There are many programming languages to choose from, but the most popular are:

- Java
- Python
- JavaScript
- C++
- C#
- PHP
- Perl
- Ruby

You can also divide programming languages into a number of broad categories, such as compiled, interpreted, and query languages.

Compiled Programming Languages

When you write a program using a **compiled programming language**, you must transform the code to an executable binary before it can run. Compiling converts the source code that you wrote to **machine code**. Machine code is the instructions converted to strings of ones and zeros for the CPU to process. A compiled program generally runs quickly (compared to interpreted code). However, a compiled program tends to be platform (CPU) specific; to run on other platforms, you must recompile the source code for the new platform. The following languages are compiled:

- C++
- C#
- COBOL
- PASCAL

Interpreted Programming Languages

When you write code with an interpreted language, you do not need to compile the program. It runs within the context of an **interpreter**, which converts the code into machine code at runtime. This means that the program probably runs more slowly but also means it is likely that you can run the program on any platform for which you have an interpreter. Examples of interpreted languages include scripting languages, such as JavaScript, Perl, and Python.

The interpreter can either be part of the operating system, or it can be provided as a virtual machine, such as the Java VM. With a Java VM, you develop the programming code in the Java environment and deploy it to your hosts. Each host OS (Windows versus Linux versus macOS for instance) has a different Java VM. When you package your Java program, your source code is compiled to a form called bytecode for the Java VM and the VM converts it to machine code to run on the hardware platform.

Some programming languages support both compiled and interpreted modes of execution.

Query Languages

Code written in a **query language**, such as Structured Query Language (SQL), is designed to retrieve specific records from a dataset. The code does not need to be compiled.

See Unit 2.4 for more information about query languages and databases.

Assembly Language

An **assembly language** represents machine code in human-readable text. An assembly language is typically specific to a particular hardware architecture. This is in contrast to compiled, interpreted, and query languages which you can use to write code that can be run on a number of platforms, assuming you have an appropriate compiler or interpreter. Even though it is in human-readable text, assembly code is very difficult to follow and is only really used by specialists trying to solve a very particular problem with an application. You would not choose an assembly language to start your new development project.

Markup Languages

A **markup language** is not a programming language but a means of making data in a document accessible to a program. A markup language, such as the HyperText Markup Language (HTML) or eXtensible Markup Language (XML), defines a series of nested tags that describe the structure and/or meaning of the tag contents.

For example, consider the following HTML markup:

```
<html>
<body>
<h1>Hello World</h1>
<p>Say hello back to <a href="mailto:support@comptia.org>
   CompTIA</a>!</p>
</body>
</html>
```

The tags tell a client application (such as a browser) how to structure the document:

- `html`—this top-level parent element identifies the type of document. All the other tags are nested within this one.

- `body`—indicates the main part of the content as a page to show to the client. HTML files can also have `head` sections, which would not be shown as part of the page display.
- `h1`—indicates that the content is a heading level.
- `p`—indicates the content is a paragraph-level block.
- `a`—indicates that the content links to another resource. In the example, this is an email address, but it could be another section of the page or another file or a page on another web server.

Note that each tag has a start and close element.

Programming Concepts

In order to write a program using a particular programming language, you must first understand the structure and syntax of the language. Most programming languages share similarities in their structure and syntax, but it is important to use the specific syntax correctly as any errors will cause the code not to compile or run. Without discussing the specifics of any particular language, the following topics list some of the basic building blocks and structures used.

Identifiers

An **identifier** is used in a program to access a program element, such as a stored value, class, method, or interface. For example, you might assign the identifier `FirstName` to a stored value that contains a user's first name. In essence, an identifier is a label for something within your program. If your identifier stores data, then it will be either a variable or a constant.

Variables

A **variable** contains a value that can change during the execution of the program. This value might be a text string, a number, or any other data type.

Variables are usually declared, defined as a particular data type, and given an initial value at the start of the routine in which they are used. It is often possible to use undeclared variables, but this can make code harder to read and more prone to errors.

Using our example of a first name, it's important to understand that although a person's name might not change, if you use a programmatic technique to refer to a user's name without knowing which user you're referring to, then, as far as the program is concerned, that is a variable. You can assign a value to a variable using fairly simple code.

For example, the following pseudocode declares our FirstName variable to store a string value with an initial value **Andy**, then sets it to a value from a data store:

```
declare FirstName as String = "Andy"
FirstName = find LastLoggedOnUser and get FirstNme
print FirstName
```

Running this code might produce the following output:

```
James
```

Constants

A **constant** is a specific identifier that contains a value that cannot be changed within the program. For example, you might want to store the numerical value for the screen dimensions or resolution.

Containers

Container can be used as a term for a special type of identifier that can reference multiple values (or **elements**). One example of a container construct is a simple **array**. For example, say that you want your program to store a list of user names who have logged on to the computer in the last 24 hours. You would declare the array with the data type of the values it will contain and the number of elements or "rows" that the array can contain:

```
declare Logons(9) as string
```

Elements in the array are counted from zero so the Logons(9) array contains up to 10 elements.

The following pseudocode would add a value to the first element in the array:

```
Logons(0) = find LastLoggedOnUser and get FirstName
```

In this example, the array has a single dimension. Arrays can also be multidimensional, which you can visualize as like a table with multiple columns. Note that all the elements must be the same data type. For example, the following code creates a two-dimensional array:

```
declare Logons(9,1) as string
```

The following pseudocode would populate the first "row" in the array, with the first name going into the first column and the logon time into the second:

```
Logons(0,0) = find LastLoggedOnUser and get FirstName
Logons(0,1) = find LastLoggedOnUser and get Time
```

One of the limitations of the array container type is that it cannot be resized. Most programming languages support container types called **vectors** that can grow or shrink in size as elements are added or removed.

Branches

Your program runs from the start to the end unless you instruct it to deviate from this path. One way of doing so is to create a **branch**; this is an instruction to your computer to execute a different sequence of instructions. You use branches to control the flow within your program. For example, you might create a branch based on a **condition**. We saw this in our earlier example when we verified a number had been entered correctly. If it had, then something happened, and if it had not, then something else happened. This is a conditional branch.

For example, in the following pseudocode, the value of a variable called `DisplayNumber` is compared to 25. If `DisplayNumber` is greater than 25, then a variable called `Count` is incremented by 1. If `DisplayNumber` is less than 25, no action occurs and the variable `Count` remains the same.

```
If DisplayNumber > 25 Then
   Count = Count+1
End If
```

Loops

Loops are similar to branches in as much as they deviate from the initial program path according to some sort of logic condition. However, with a loop, you instruct your computer to perform, or repeat, a task until a condition is met. For example, you might create a loop that continues until a certain amount of time has elapsed or until a counter reaches a certain level. Then, a predetermined action might occur, depending upon what you want. In the following example, the program loops around until the value of i is 5. Then the program proceeds to the next statement.

```
For i = 1 to 5
    print i
Next
```

As well as "For" structures, loops can also be implemented by "While" statements:

```
Do While i <= 100
   i = i + 1
   print i
Loop
```

As mentioned above, you need to make sure your code does not contain unintended or infinite loops. Without the statement to increment `i` in the Do loop example above, the loop would continue forever. An infinite loop will make the process hang.

Operators

Looping and branching structures depend on logical tests to determine whether to continue the loop or the branch to follow. A logical test is one that resolves to a TRUE or FALSE value. You need to be familiar with basic comparison operators:

- == is equal to (returns TRUE if both conditions are the same).
- != is not equal to.
- < less than.
- > greater than.
- <= and >= less than or equal to and greater than or equal to.

You might also want to test more than one condition at the same time. The logical operators are as follows:

- AND—if both conditions are TRUE, then the whole statement is TRUE.
- OR—if either condition is TRUE, then the whole statement is TRUE.
- XOR—if either condition is TRUE but *not both*, then the whole statement is TRUE.

You can also use the negation operator NOT to reverse the truth value of any statement.

Procedures and Functions

Both **procedures** and **functions** enable you to create segments of code that you will reuse. In our earlier example, we used a function to check that the user had entered a number. The key difference, in programming terms, between a procedure and a function is that the latter can **return** a value to whatever called it, whereas a procedure cannot. For example, the following is a procedure:

```
Verify subroutine {
    verify user input is number
    if FALSE, call Display Instructions subroutine
    return
}
```

Whereas, the following is a function:

```
Verify function {
    IsNumber = verify user input is number
    return IsNumber
}
```

In the function, the value of `IsNumber`, which will either be **TRUE** or **FALSE**, is returned to the main program for some further processing.

Comments

As noted above, it is important to use comments in code to assist with maintaining it. A comment line is ignored by the compiler or interpreter. A comment line is indicated by a special delimiter, such as double forward slash (`//`), hash (`#`), or apostrophe (`'`).

Object-Oriented Programming

Object-Oriented Programming (OOP) is a popular way of designing code. The idea is that creating recognizable *things* within the code and making them interact through defined methods makes the code easier to maintain and update. An object can have inner workings that other parts of the program cannot affect and outer or public values and things that the object can do that other parts of the program can read or ask the object to change or do.

Objects can have attributes (fields), properties, and methods:

- **Attributes** are values and data types that define the object. The attributes are stored within the object as fields or private variables. Other programs cannot access or change the fields directly. They must call a particular method (see below) to do that.

- **Methods** define what you can do to an object. For example, a Customer object might have a ChangeAddress method. When another part of the program calls the ChangeAddress method, it also passes a string (hopefully containing a well-formatted address) to the object because that is what the method expects. The object's code receives this string, checks that it can be used as a valid address, and updates its Address field. The object might then have another method (PrintAddress) allowing another part of the program to find out what the current value of the Address field is.

  The important part is that the external code cannot interact with the field directly.

- **Properties** represent an alternative way of accessing a field publicly. Using a method might be regarded as quite a "heavyweight" means of doing this, so properties allow external code to ask the object to show or change the value of one of its fields.

  While it's not mentioned in the syllabus, the concept of a class is also important to OOP. A class defines what a "thing" can be like, while an object is an instance of a thing created from a class.

Scripting Languages

We learned earlier that some of the interpreted programming languages are scripting languages. You can also make a distinction between the general purpose interpreted scripted languages, such as JavaScript or Perl, discussed above and *scripting* languages, such as Windows Command Prompt, Windows PowerShell, or Linux Bash. These languages support the automation and configuration of a particular operating system.

Just to confuse things, most languages can call (or "wrap") system commands as part of the code and can therefore also be used for scripting.

Whatever language is used to create it, a **script** is a smaller piece of code than a program. A script is generally targeted at completing a specific task, whether that task is based within a web-based application or is used by a network administrator to perform a repetitive administrative task. While a program usually provides some sort of unique functionality, anything a script does could usually be performed manually by a user.

Writing scripts is a good place to learn the basics about programming. They are usually simpler to learn, require no compiling, and are well documented on the Internet, should you require guidance or samples.

In Windows 10, you can create simple scripts using a number of different tools.

Batch Files

Batch files are a collection of command-line instructions that you store in a .CMD file. You can run the file by calling its name from the command line, or double-clicking the file in File Explorer. Generally, batch file scripts run from end to end and are limited in terms of branching and user input.

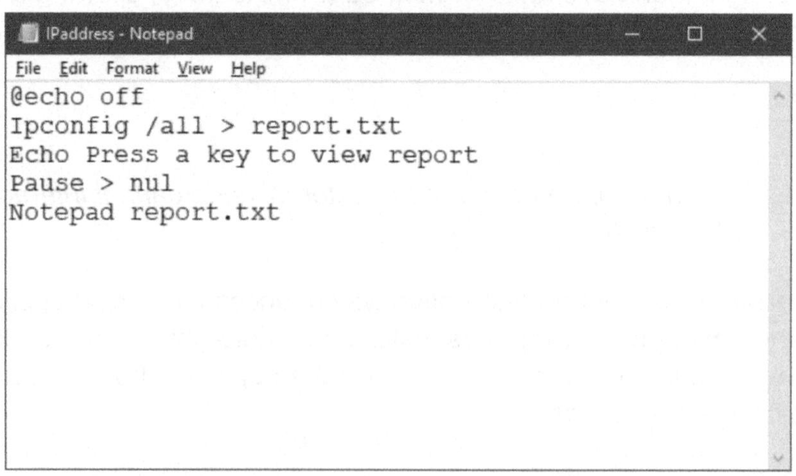


```
@echo off
Ipconfig /all > report.txt
Echo Press a key to view report
Pause > nul
Notepad report.txt
```

Windows batch file. Screenshot used with permission from Microsoft.

Windows PowerShell

Windows PowerShell enables you to perform management and administrative tasks in Windows 10 and Windows Server 2016 (and some earlier versions). It is fully integrated with the operating system and supports both remote execution and scripting. To help create and manage your Windows PowerShell scripts, Microsoft provides the Windows PowerShell Integrated Scripting Environment (ISE).

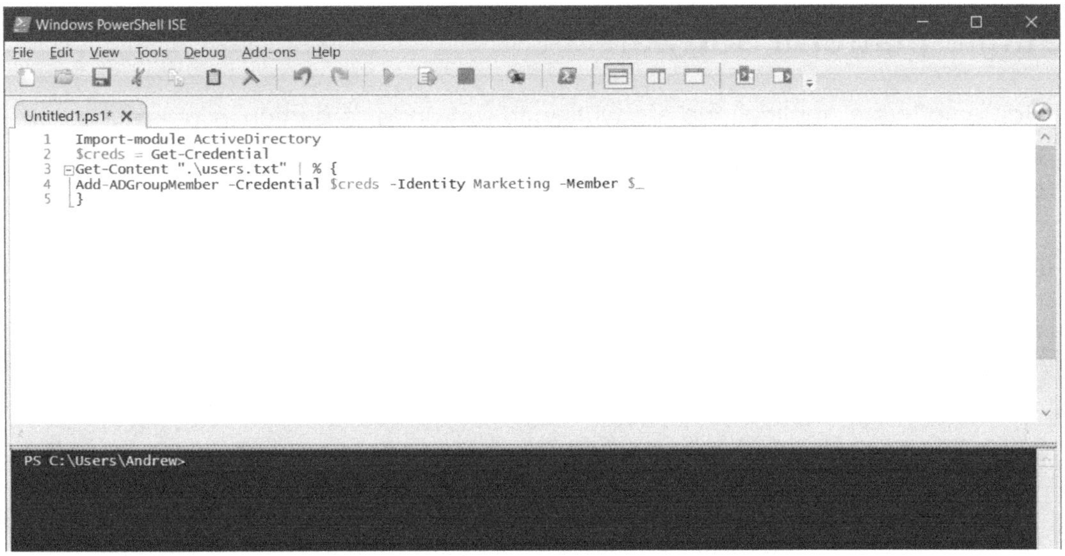

Windows PowerShell ISE. Screenshot used with permission from Microsoft.

VBScript

VBScript is a scripting language based on Microsoft's Visual Basic programming language. It provides similar functionality to JavaScript. VBScript is often used by network administrators to perform repetitive administrative tasks. With VBScript, you can run your scripts from either the command line or from the Windows graphical interface. Scripts that you write must be run within a host environment. Windows 10 provides Internet Explorer, IIS, and Windows Script Host (WSH) for this purpose.

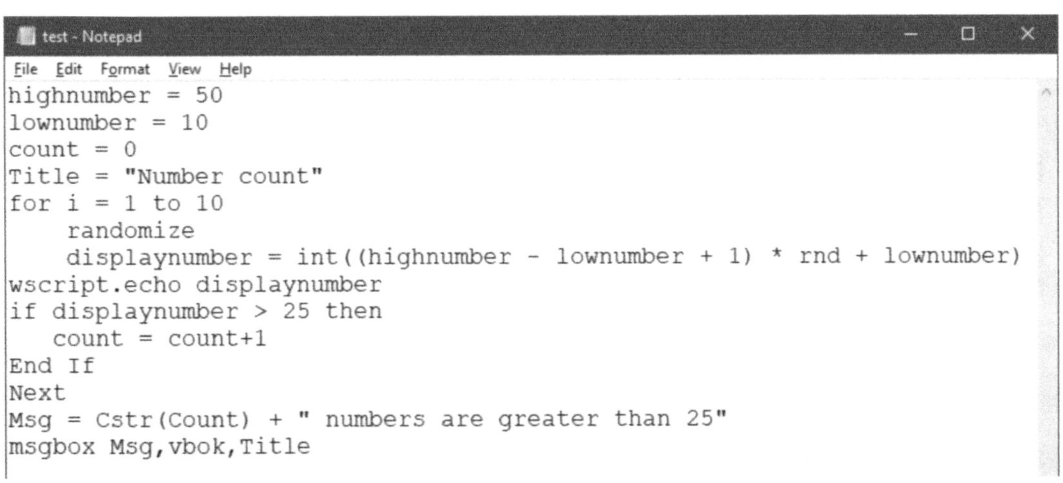

Visual Basic Script in Windows 10. Screenshot used with permission from Microsoft.

Application Platforms and Delivery

Once you have written and tested your code, you need to package it as an executable or script for deployment to the hosts that will run the software. There are many different ways of packaging and deploying software applications.

Single-platform Software

Some software applications are written to run under a particular operating system (and sometimes a particular version or set of versions of an OS). The software is written using a development environment suitable for that OS. The developer writes the application in program code using a particular programming language. When the application is compiled, it gets converted to machine code that can run (or execute) in the target OS environment.

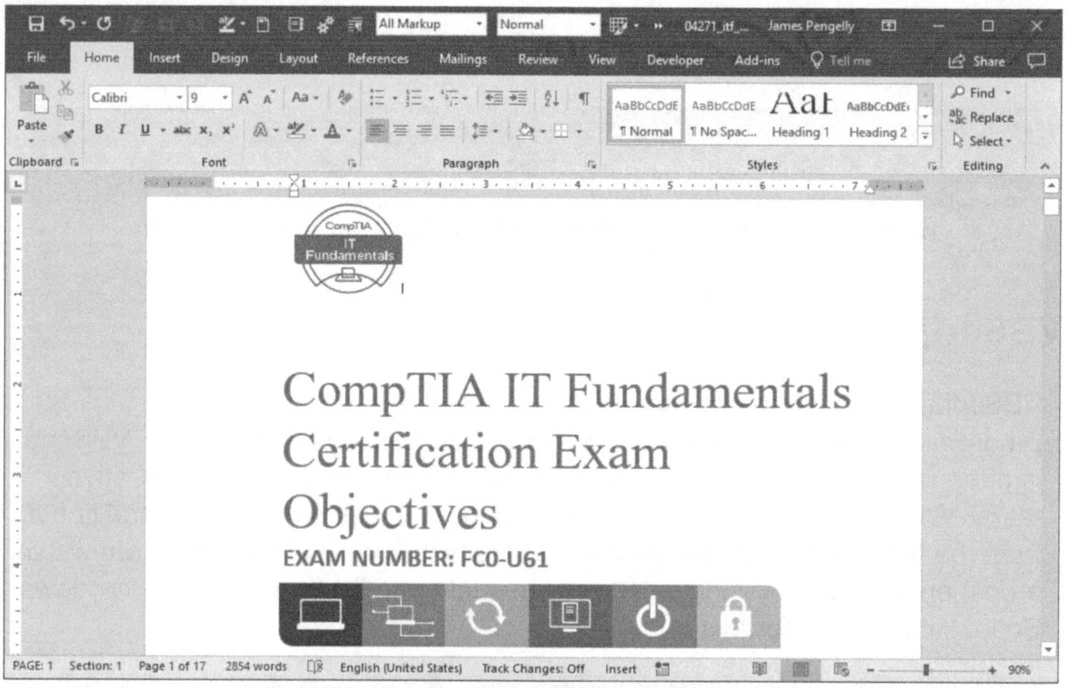

Editing a document in the Windows desktop edition of Microsoft Office. Screenshot used with permission from Microsoft.

This development model can be referred to as **single-platform software**. Because this model produces software that is optimized for a particular platform, it can perform better and be simpler to check for errors than cross-platform software. The drawback is that "porting" the software to a different platform (from Windows OS to Android for instance) can be very difficult.

Cross-platform Software

Software written for PCs and laptops ("desktop" applications) is being supplemented with software written for touch-based mobile devices and operating systems. These are often referred to as **apps**. There is usually plenty of interoperability between desktop and mobile platforms. For example, you could create a document in Microsoft Word on a PC and send it to someone to view on their smartphone.

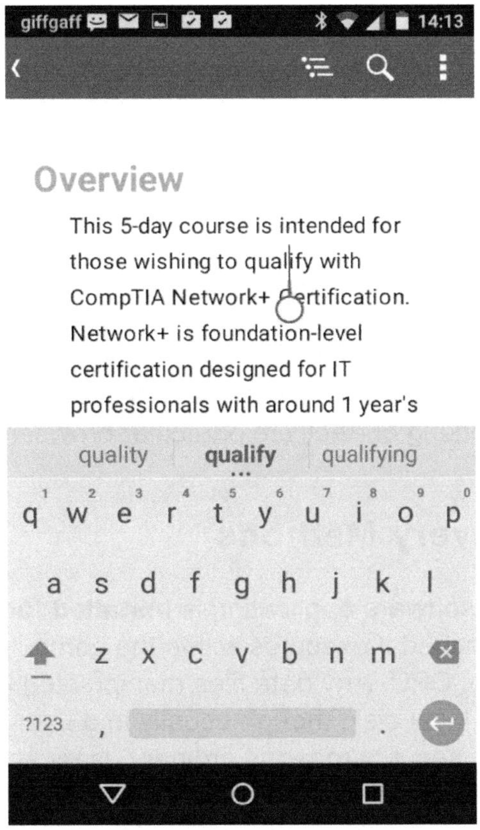

Editing a document in Office Mobile. Screenshot used with permission from Microsoft.

Another trend is for applications to be accessed over the web, often using a "cloud" deployment model. When software is run from a web server as a **web application**, it can usually support a wide range of different types of client operating systems and devices. Usually the only client required is a compatible web browser.

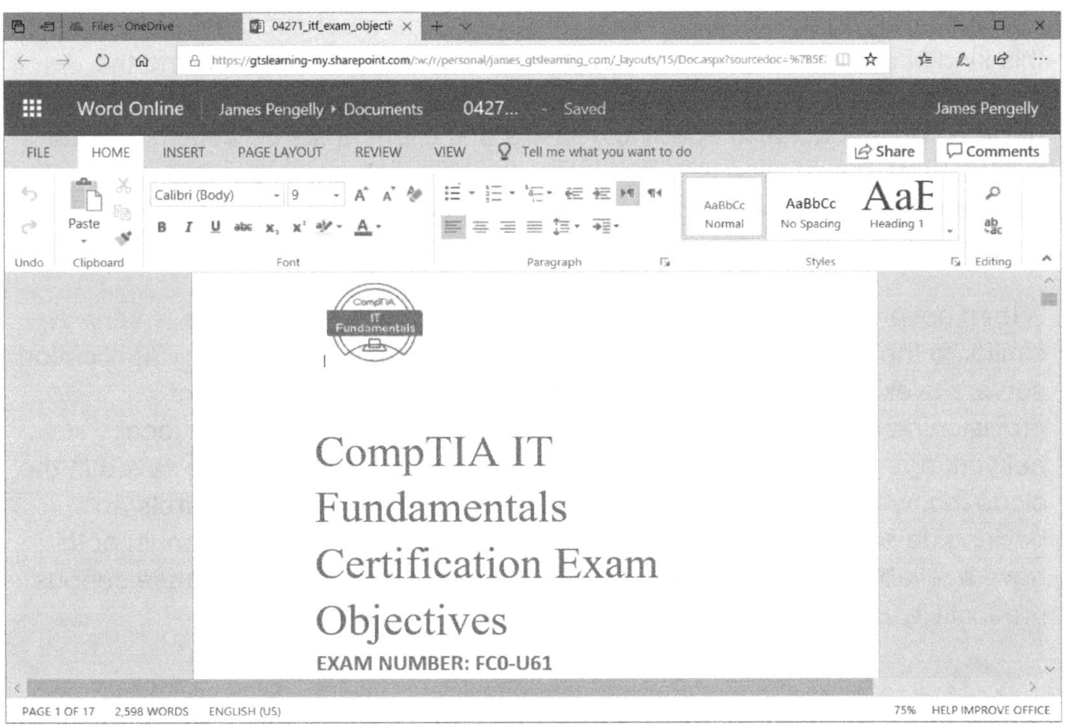

Editing a document in Word Online using a web browser. Screenshot used with permission from Microsoft.

This sort of cross-platform development is complicated by the different hardware interfaces for different computing devices. The interfaces supported by keyboard and mouse input devices for PCs and laptops do not always work well with the touchscreens used by smartphones. The wide range of display sizes, orientations, and resolutions are another factor making cross-platform design challenging. There can be performance problems when software is written for a "platform independent" environment, such as a Java virtual machine, rather than code run natively by the OS.

Compatibility issues can also affect web applications as different browser vendors can make slightly different interpretations of open standards that result in applications not working correctly in particular browsers or browser versions.

Application Delivery Methods

A traditional PC-type software application is **installed locally** to the computer's hard drive. When launched it executes within the computer's memory and is processed by the local CPU. Any data files manipulated by the application can also be stored on the local disk, though usually in a user folder rather than the application folder. For security reasons ordinary users should not be able to modify application folders.

A locally installed application such as this does not need network access to run, though obviously the network has to be present if the application makes use of network features.

For some enterprises, this locally installed model presents performance and security issues. Another option is for the application to be **installed to a network server** and executed on that server. Client workstations access the application using a remote terminal or viewer. The most successful example of this kind of application virtualization model is Citrix XenApp. Locating the application and its data files on a server is easier to secure and easier to backup. This model also does not require that client hosts be able to access the Internet. The drawback is that if there is no local network connection or the local network is heavily congested, users will not be able to use the application.

A third option for deploying apps is the **cloud hosted model**. This is very similar to the local network model except that clients connect to the application servers over the Internet. This provides a lot of flexibility in terms of provisioning the app to clients located in different regions. As with local network applications, user-generated data files would normally be saved in the cloud too, with the same benefits for creating security access controls and backing up easily. The drawback is that clients and cloud service must both have a reliable Internet connection. Outages on either side can cause serious productivity problems.

Actually, Internet access for cloud apps isn't always necessarily the case. There are different means of providing cloud services, some of which use local networks. But it is the most dominant model.

Review Questions / Module 2 / Unit 3 / Programming and App Development

Answer these questions to test what you have learned in this unit. You can review the model answers at the end of the book.

1) What shows the structure of code without using the specific syntax of any one language?
2) What is an interpreted language?
3) How is a markup language differ from a compiled language?
4) What are constants and variables examples of?
5) What type of programming concept allows for a variable size container?
6) You want to check whether a condition has been met, and if it has, perform one action. Otherwise, you want your program to perform a second action. What sort of programming operation would help achieve this?
7) In a program, what does a loop do?
8) What is the difference between a procedure and a function?
9) What three things define an object?
10) What three scripting options are commonly used in Windows 10 to perform administrative tasks?
11) True or false? You do not need to install a web application to your computer; it would be accessed via a browser.
12) What is the advantage of a local network hosted application, in terms of data storage?

Lab 8 / Using Scripting Tools

In this lab, you will practice creating scripts in three different Windows scripting environments.

Exercise 1 / Creating a Batch File

In this exercise, you will create simple batch file to automate the creation of a report of the local host's network configuration.

1) If necessary, start your computer and sign in.
2) Press `START`, type `notepad` and then press `ENTER`.
3) In the Untitled – Notepad window, type the following text:

   ```
   @echo off
   ipconfig /all > report.txt
   echo Press a key to view report
   pause > nul
   notepad report.txt
   ```

   Note the features of the script:

   - @echo off—suspends output being written to the command prompt.
   - ifconfig > report.txt—calls the system command to produce a network configuration summary (ifconfig) and redirects (or pipes) its output to a text file.
   - The remainder of the script waits for the user to press a key and then opens the report file in Notepad.
4) From the **File** menu, select **Save As**.
5) In the **Save as type** list, click **All Files**.
6) In the **File name** box, type `test.cmd`
7) In the navigation pane, click **Documents**.
8) Click **Save**.
9) Close Notepad.
10) Click **Start**, scroll down and expand **Windows System**, and then click **Command Prompt**.

11) In the command prompt window, type **`documents\test.cmd`** and then press **ENTER**.

Running the batch file. Screenshot used with permission from Microsoft.

12) When prompted to press a key, press **SPACEBAR**.

    A notepad window opens and displays the output from the ipconfig.exe command that you put in your batch file.

13) Close all open windows and apps.

Exercise 2 / Creating a Visual Basic Script

In this exercise, you will create and test a Visual Basic script.

1) Press **START**, type **`notepad`** and then press **ENTER**.

2) In the Untitled – Notepad window, type the following text:

```
for i = 1 to 5
    wscript.echo i
next
```

    This program creates a simple loop and uses the echo statement to show the current value of the variable i as the loop executes.

3) From the **File** menu, select **Save As**.

4) In the **Save as type** list, click **All Files**.

5) In the **File name** box, type **Test.vbs**.

6) In the navigation pane, click **Documents**.

7) Click **Save**.

8) Open Windows Explorer and navigate to your **Documents** folder.

9) Double-click the **Test.vbs**  file.

10) The script runs and a new window opens that displays the number 1. Click **OK**, and then number 2 displays in a new window. Continue until 5 has displayed.

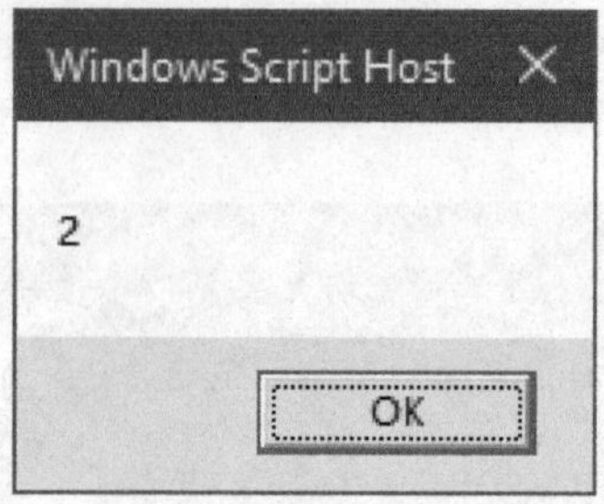

Running the VBScript file. Screenshot used with permission from Microsoft.

11) Click **Start**, scroll down and expand **Windows System**, and then click **Command Prompt**.

12) In the command prompt window, type **`cscript documents\test.vbs`** and then press **`ENTER`**.

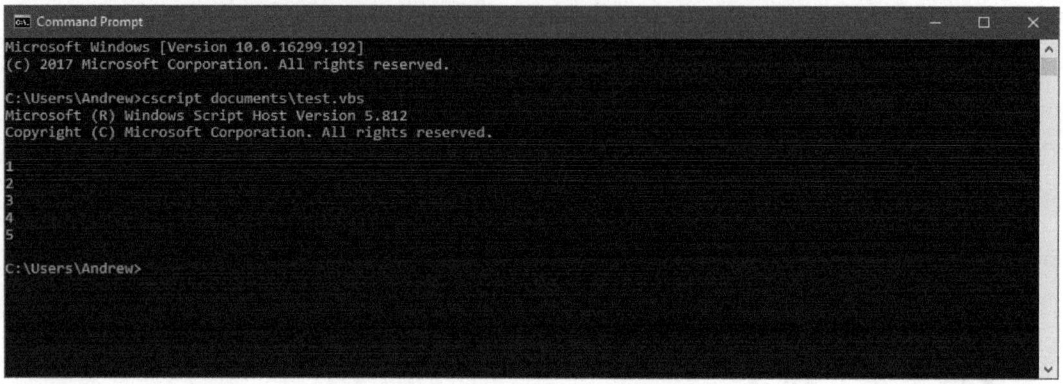

Running the VBScript from the command-line. Screenshot used with permission from Microsoft.

13) The script runs from the command line and displays each number in sequence.

14) Switch to the Notepad window and update the script to read as shown below:

```
iHigh = 50
iLow = 10
for i = 1 to 5
    randomize
    iDisplay = int((iHigh - iLow + 1) * rnd + iLow)
    wscript.echo iDisplay
next
```

15) Save the file.

This script uses some additional integer variables and built-in VBscript functions to return a random number between 10 and 50 during each iteration of the loop.

16) In the command prompt window, type **`cscript documents\test.vbs`** and then press **`ENTER`**.

Running the edited VBScript. Screenshot used with permission from Microsoft.

Five random numbers between 10 and 50 display.

17) What part of the code would you change to show 10 random numbers?

____

18) Edit this line and save the file:

```
for i = 1 to 10
```

19) Run the script again.

20) Switch to the Notepad window and update the script to read as shown below:

```
iHigh = 50
iLow = 10
iCount = 0
sTitle = "Number count"
for i = 1 to 10
    randomize
    iDisplay = int((iHigh - iLow + 1) * rnd + iLow)
    wscript.echo iDisplay
    if iDisplay > 25 then
        iCount = iCount + 1
    end if
next
sMsg = cstr(iCount) + " numbers are greater than 25"
msgbox sMsg,vbOK,sTitle
```

21) Save the file.

These modifications add another branch to increment a variable if another variable exceeds a certain value. Note how the branching statements are nested. We also use some string-type variables and a function to convert an integer (`iCount`) into a string for use as text output in a message box. Finally, note the use of `vbOK` in the last line. This is an example of a constant. It defines the type of message box to display (one with just an OK button).

22) In the command prompt window, run the script.

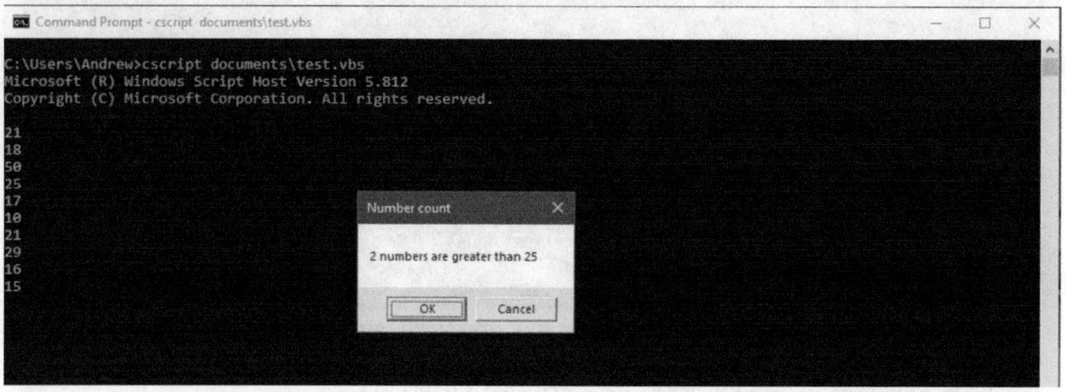

Running the modified VBScript from the command-line. Screenshot used with permission from Microsoft.

23) Close all open apps and windows.

Exercise 3 / Creating a Windows PowerShell Script

In this exercise, you will create and test a Windows PowerShell script.

1) Click **Start**, type **`Windows PowerShell`**, right-click **Windows PowerShell** and then click **Run as administrator**.

2) In the **User Account Control** window, click **Yes**.

3) In the **Windows PowerShell** window, type the following command (ignore the line break) and then press **`ENTER`**:

```
Get-WmiObject -Class Win32_OperatingSystem -
ComputerName localhost
```

4) Examine the returned results.

5) In the **Windows PowerShell** window, type the following command and then press **`ENTER`**:

```
Get-WmiObject -Class Win32_OperatingSystem -
ComputerName localhost | Select-Object -Property CSName
```

*To save a bit of time, you can press the **`UPARROW`** to select the original command and then edit it.*

Running a Windows PowerShell cmdlet. Screenshot used with permission from Microsoft.

6) Examine the returned results.

   Your computer name is displayed in a table. The command uses a pipe (|) to send the output from one command to another command.

7) In the Windows PowerShell window, type the following command and then press **ENTER**:

   ```
   Get-Service
   ```

8) Examine the returned results. A list of all services on your computer is displayed.

9) In the Windows PowerShell window, type the following command and then press **ENTER**:

   ```
   Get-Service | Select DisplayName
   ```

10) Examine the returned results. The same list of services is displayed but this time the output is filtered down to the service's "friendly" name.

11) In the Windows PowerShell window, type the following command and then press **ENTER**:

   ```
   Get-WmiObject win32_service | Select DisplayName, State
   | Sort State, DisplayName
   ```

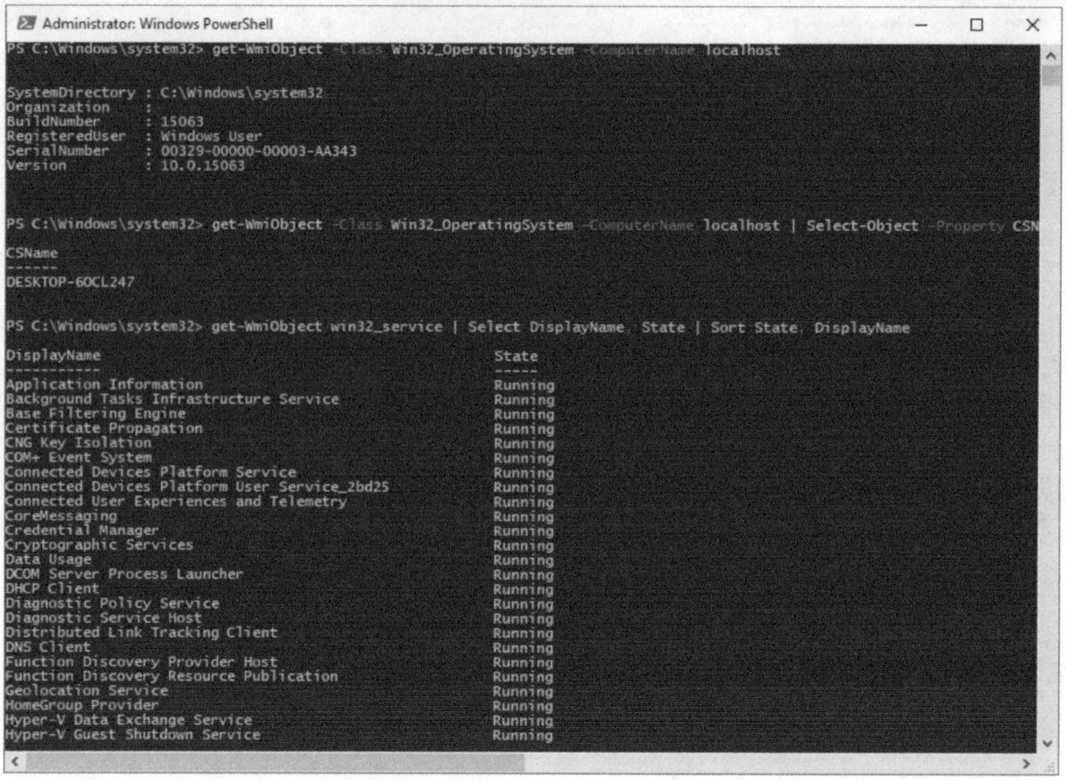

Running a piped Windows PowerShell cmdlet. Screenshot used with permission from Microsoft.

12) Examine the returned results. A list of all services on your computer is displayed, sorted by state and then display name.

    So far we have been running commandlets individually. You can also create PowerShell scripts in the editor environment and save them as files.

13) Click **Start**, type `Windows PowerShell`, right-click **Windows PowerShell ISE** and then click **Run as administrator**.

14) In the **User Account Control** window, click **Yes**.

15) In the Untitled1.ps1 area, type the following code as a single line:

```
Get-WmiObject -Class Win32_OperatingSystem –
ComputerName localhost | Select-Object -Property CSName
```

    Note that as you type, suggestion boxes appear helping you to autocomplete statements. Also notice that the editor applies color-coding to distinguish parts of your code. These features make a development environment much easier to work in than a plain text editor like Notepad.

16) On the toolbar, click **Save** .

17) In the **Save As** window, in the navigation pane, expand **This PC**.

18) Expand **Local Disk (C:)**, expand **Windows**, and then click **System32**.

19) In the **File name** box, type `Sample.ps1` and then click **Save**.

20) In the In the **Administrator: Windows PowerShell ISE** window, on the toolbar, click **Run** . You receive an error. This is because unsigned scripts are blocked by default. To enable scripts without a valid coding certificate to run, switch to the Windows PowerShell window.

21) In the Administrator: Windows PowerShell window, type the following command and then press **`ENTER`**:

    `Set-ExecutionPolicy RemoteSigned`

22) When prompted, type **`A`** and press **`ENTER`**.

23) Switch to **Windows PowerShell ISE** and click **Run**. Your simple one line script runs.

24) Switch to the Windows PowerShell window.

25) At the prompt, type **`Sample.ps1`** and then press **`Enter`**. Your simple one line script runs.

26) Close all open windows and apps.

Lab 9 / Using Programming Tools

In this lab, you will modify a sample Java program.

Exercise 1 / Installing Programming Tools

In this exercise, you will install the required components to allow you to create and test a sample program.

This lab involves downloading and installing a program from a third-party website. The authors and publisher believe the website and program to be reputable and pose no risk to your computer or personal information but cannot be held responsible for any loss or damage that may occur as a result of following the steps in this lab. If you have any concerns we recommend that you do NOT proceed.

1) Open a web browser and navigate to www.oracle.com/technetwork/java/javase/downloads/index.html

2) Click the NetBeans **DOWNLOAD** link to download NetBeans with JDK 8.

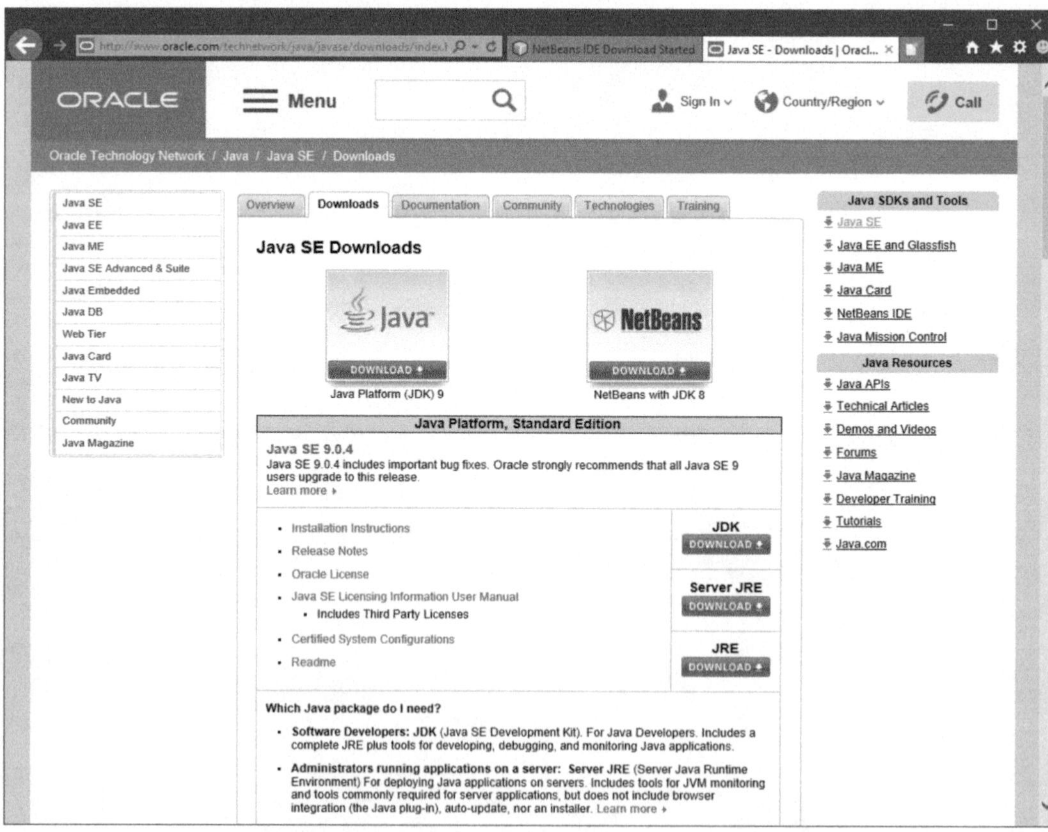

Downloading the NetBeans and JDK 8 from the Oracle website.

3) On the **Downloads** tab, click **Accept License Agreement**.

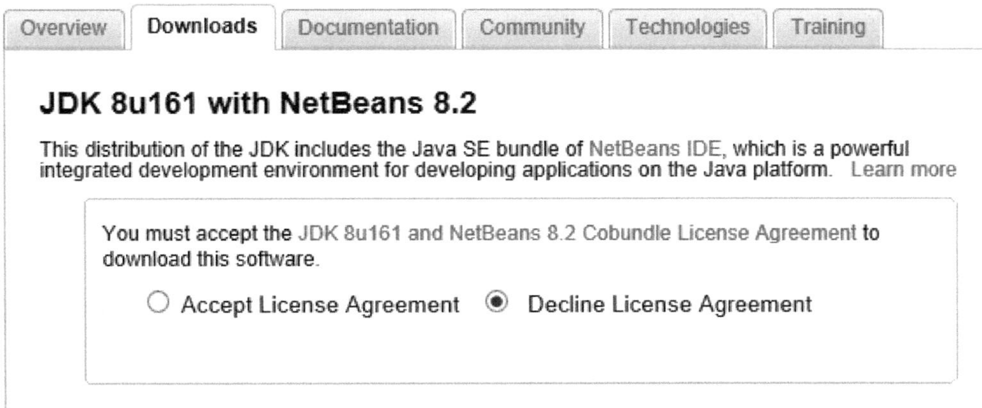

Accept the license agreement.

4) In the **Java SE and NetBeans Cobundle** table, click the link in the **Windows x86** row.

Java SE and NetBeans Cobundle (JDK 8u161 and NB 8.2)		
Product / File Description	File Size	Download
Linux x86	295.4 MB	jdk-8u161-nb-8_2-linux-i586.sh
Linux x64	290.36 MB	jdk-8u161-nb-8_2-linux-x64.sh
Mac OS X x64	362.7 MB	jdk-8u161-nb-8_2-macosx-x64.dmg
Windows x86	326.53 MB	jdk-8u161-nb-8_2-windows-i586.exe
Windows x64	337.9 MB	jdk-8u161-nb-8_2-windows-x64.exe

Select the Windows x86 download file.

We need to install the 32-bit version (x86), as we will use the Java Runtime Environment (JRE) with a 32-bit database application later in the course.

5) In the prompt at the bottom of the window, click **Save**. When download is complete, in the prompt, click **Run**.

6) In the **User Account Control** window, click **Yes**.

7) In the **Welcome to the JDK 8 Update 161 and NetBeans IDE 8.2 Installer** window, click **Next**.

8) On the **Install the JDK to:** page, click **Next**.

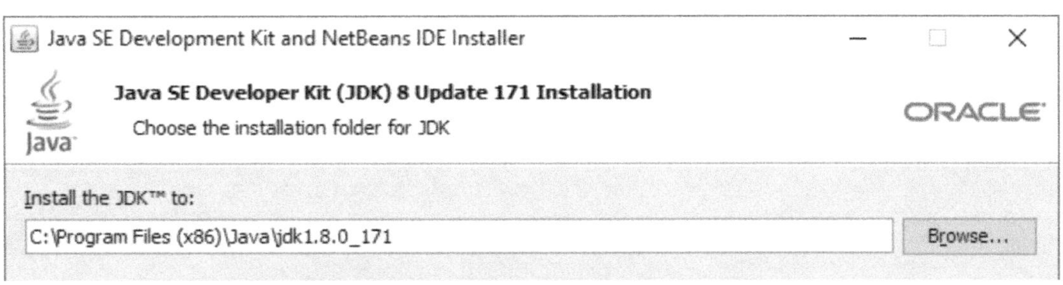

Selecting the installation path for the Java SDK.

9) On the **Install the NetBeans IDE to:** page, click **Next**.

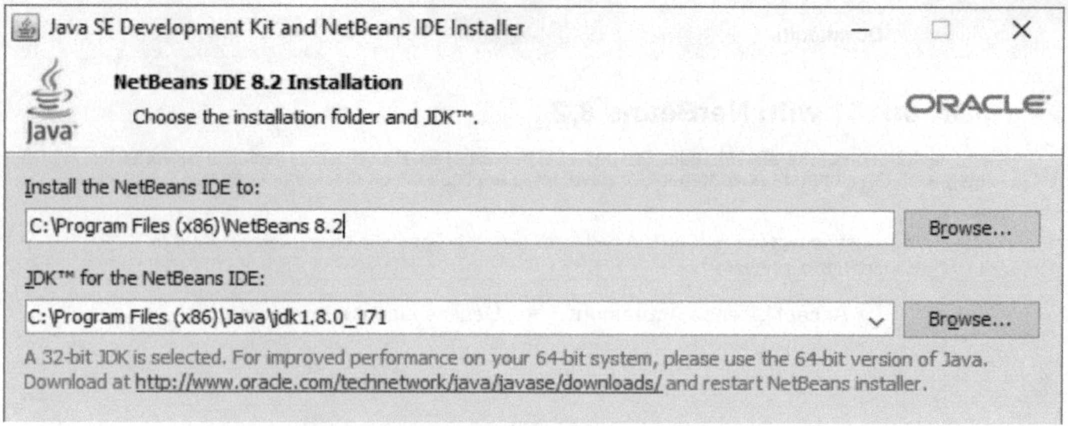

Selecting the installation path for NetBeans.

10) Clear the **Check for Updates** check box, and then click **Install**.

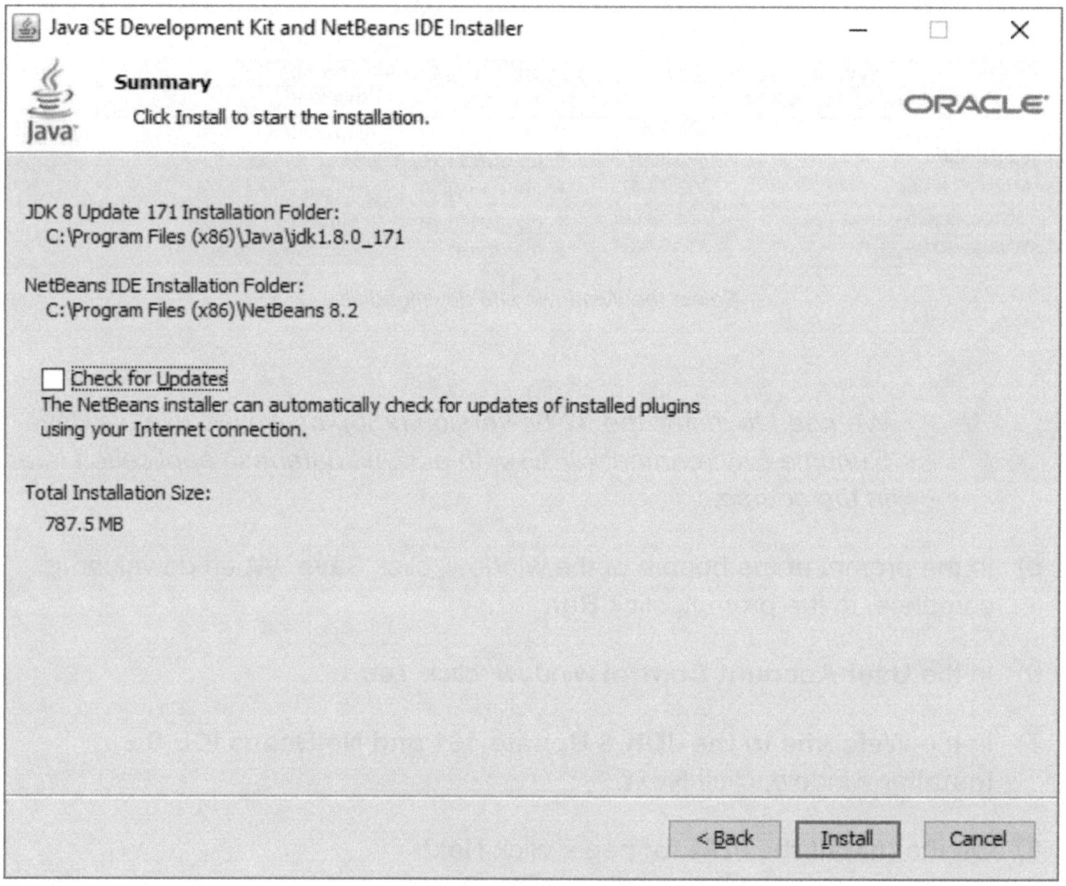

Do not install updates.

11) The required software installs. When prompted, clear the **Contribute to the NetBeans project** check box, and then click **Finish**.

Exercise 2 / Creating a Sample Program

In this exercise, you will examine the way a Java-based program works with form events and control structures and make some simple edits to the code.

1) On your computer's desktop, double-click **NetBeans IDE 8.2**.

2) In the **NetBeans IDE 8.2** window, click the **Try a Sample Project** link.

3) In the **Choose Project** window, expand **Samples**, click **Java**, and then in the **Projects** list, click **Client Editor** and then click **Next**.

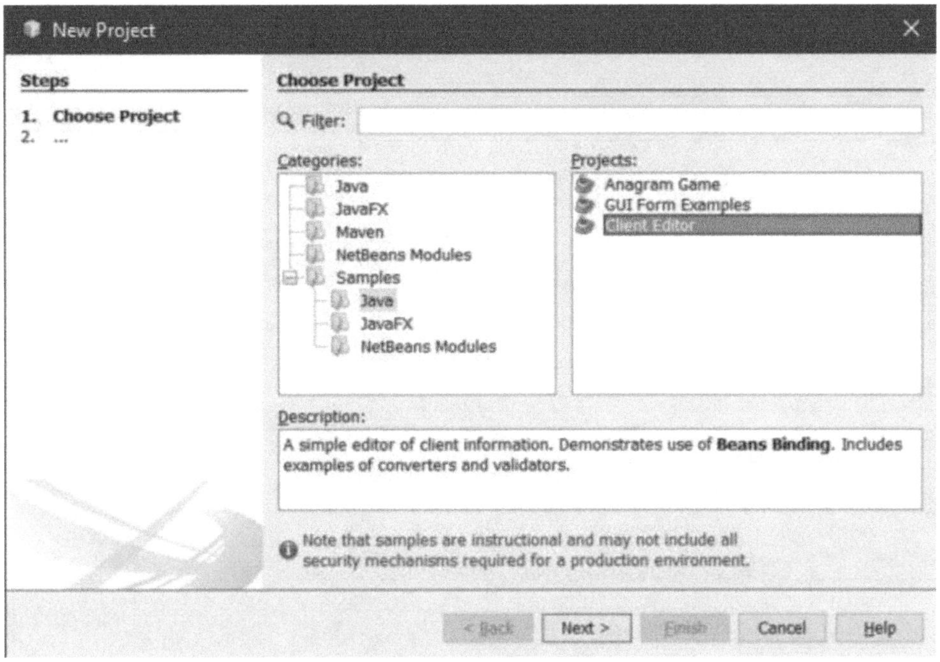

Select the Client Editor sample.

4) On the **Name and Location** page, click **Finish**.

5) On the **Projects** tab, click **ClientEditor**.

6) On the toolbar, click **Run** .

   The program runs. A new dialog box opens labeled Client Info: George Foo.

7) Hover your mouse over the **Marital status** list, currently set to Separated. Notice that no tip displays.

8) Click the **Marital status** list and notice there are four options.

9) Click in the **Age** box, and clear the current value (30). Notice the red text that displays indicating the valid range is 1–199.

10) Close the Client Editor dialog box and switch to the NetBeans interface.

11) In the navigation pane, if necessary, expand the **ClientEditor** node. Expand **Source Packages** and expand **clienteditor**.

12) Double-click ClientEditor.java. In the main tab, ensure the **Design** option is selected so that you can see the form.

13) Right-click the text box for the Age form field control and select **Bind > text**.

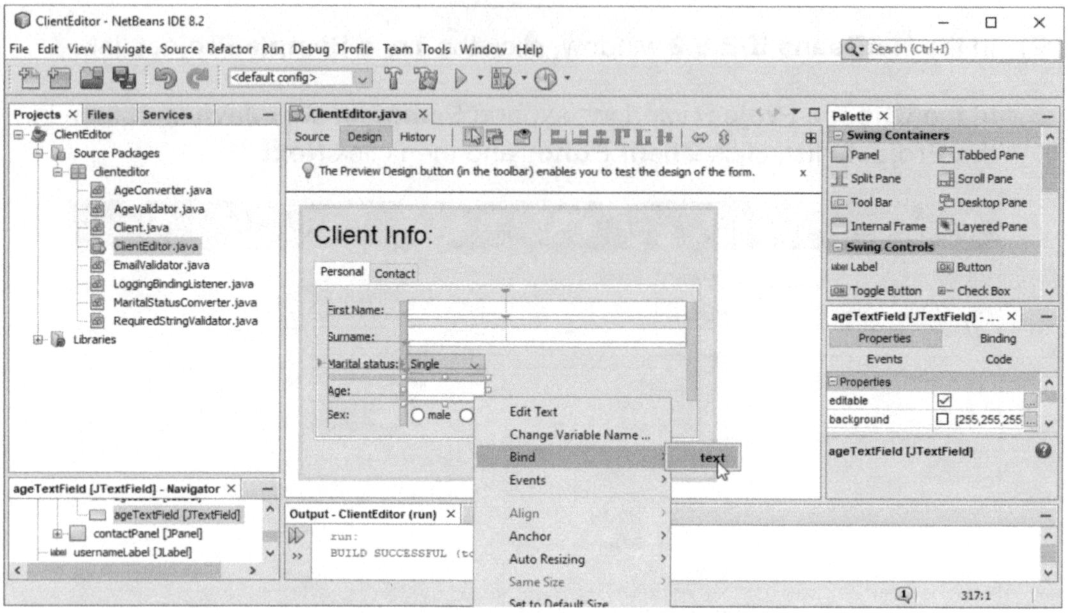

Checking the code for a form field.

14) Click the **Advanced** tab.

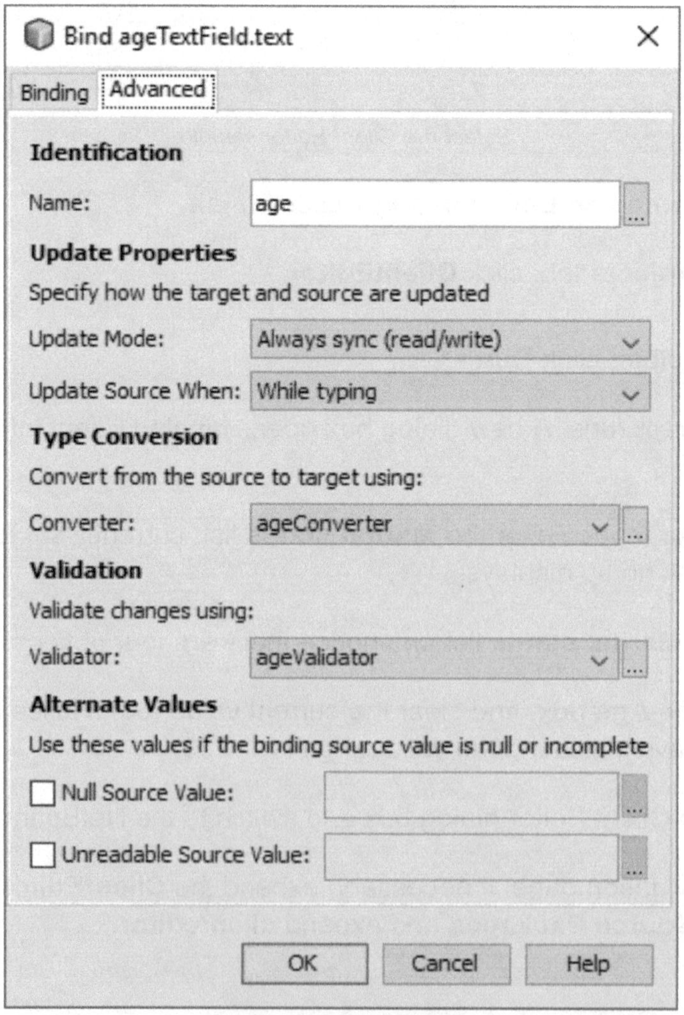

Binding for the age field.

Note that the control properties call a function called ageValidator when the value of the field changes.

15) Click **Cancel**.

16) In the left-hand pane, double-click **AgeValidator.java**.

Note that this code exists to check the values entered by the user into the "Age" box. Unlikely values are rejected.

17) In the details pane on the right, scroll down the listing shown.

18) Locate the text that reads:

```
public Validator.Result validate(Integer arg) {
   if ((arg < 1) || (arg > 199)) {
      return new Result(null, "Age range is 10-199");
```

The syntax of this code is a little difficult to follow, but in essence, it uses the OR logical operator (represented as `||`) to test for a value less than 1 or greater than 199. If either condition is TRUE, the function returns a message.

19) Edit the shaded text to read as follows:

```
public Validator.Result validate(Integer arg) {
   if ((arg < 1) || (arg > 125)) {
      return new Result(null, "Age range is 1-125");
```

20) In the navigation pane, double-click **MaritalStatusConverter.java**.

21) Scroll down the code on the right and locate the text that reads:

```
switch (arg) {
```

A switch or case select statement is another type of branching logic. With an If block, you can test for multiple conditions with fairly complicated logical operators and nested If statements. With a case select statement you can write out each condition to match more easily.

22) Add the shaded text (below) so that it reads as follows:

```
switch (arg) {
   case 0: value="Single"; break;
   case 1: value="Married"; break;
   case 2: value="Separated"; break;
   case 3: value="Divorced"; break;
   case 4: value="Won't say"; break;
```

23) Scroll down the details on the right and locate the text that reads:

```
public Integer convertReverse(String arg) {
```

This code performs conversion between the string values that the user can select and integer values for processing by some other code. This code uses nested If blocks—as you can see it is much more complex than the case block.

24) Add the shaded text (below) so that it reads as follows:

```
public Integer convertReverse(String arg) {
    int value = 0;
    if ("Single".equals(arg)) {
      value = 0;
    } else if ("Married".equals(arg)) {
      value = 1;
    } else if ("Separated".equals(arg)) {
      value = 2;
    } else if ("Divorced".equals(arg)) {
      value = 3;
    } else if ("Won't say".equals(arg)) {
       value = 4;
    }
    return value;
```

25) Select the **ClientEditor.java** tab.

26) Click the **Marital status** list on the dialog box.

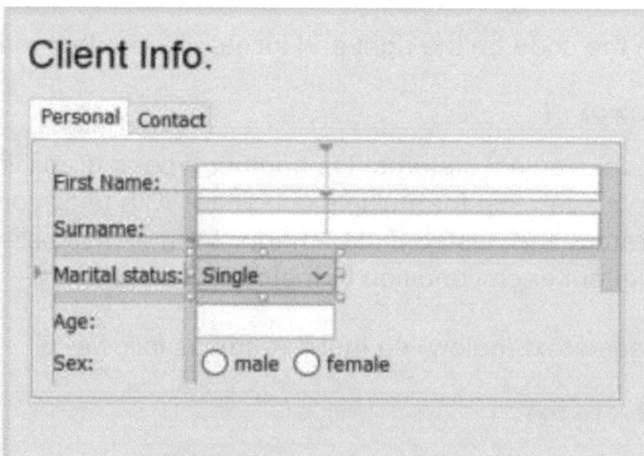

Modifying the Client Info dialog box.

27) On the right, click the **model** box.

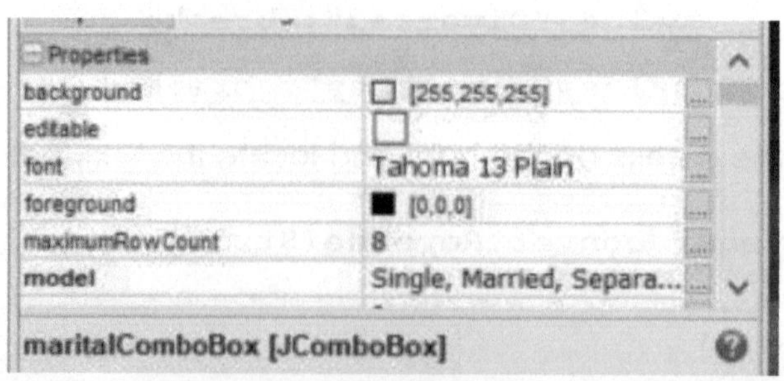

Updating properties.

28) Click the ellipse at the end of the model text box that contains Single, Married, Separated, Divorced.

29) In the new window, add the text **Won't say** on a new line.

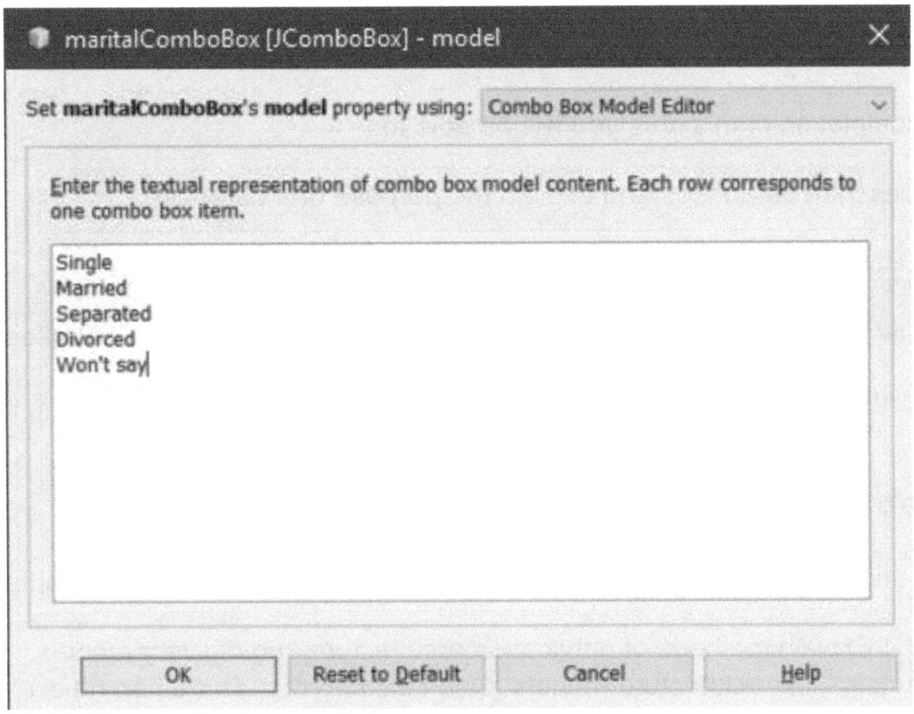

Update the selectable options.

30) Click **OK**.

31) In the far right pane, scroll down and locate the **toolTiptext** value. In the text box, type `Choose your marital status`. Press **ENTER**.

32) On the toolbar, click **Save All** .

33) From the **Run** menu, select **Clean and Build Project**.

34) On the **Projects** tab, click **ClientEditor**.

35) On the toolbar, click **Run** .

36) The program runs. A new dialog box opens labeled **Client Info: George Foo**.

37) Hover your mouse over the **Marital status** list, currently set to Separated. Notice that the new tool tip text displays.

38) Click the **Marital status** list and notice there are five options, including Won't say.

39) Click in the **Age** box, and enter `127`. Notice the red text that displays indicating the age range is 1–125.

40) Close the Client Editor dialog box.

41) Close NetBeans.

Module 2 / Unit 4
Using Databases

Objectives

On completion of this unit, you will be able to:

- □ Describe databases and explain the purpose of a database.
- □ List the relational methods used by structured databases.
- □ List the ways that users and applications can interface with databases.
- □ Distinguish application architecture models.

Syllabus Objectives and Content Examples

This unit covers the following exam domain objectives and content examples:

- □ 3.4 Explain methods of application architecture and delivery models.
  Application architecture models (One tier, Two tier, Three tier, n-tier)
- □ 5.1 Explain database concepts and the purpose of a database.
  Usage of database (Create, Import/input, Query, Reports) • Flat file vs. database (Multiple concurrent users, Scalability, Speed, Variety of data) • Records • Storage (Data persistence)
- □ 5.2 Compare and contrast various database structures.
  Structured vs. semi-structured vs. non-structured • Relational databases (Schema, Tables, Rows/records, Fields/columns, Primary key, Foreign key, Constraints) • Non-relational databases (Key/value databases, Document databases)
- □ 5.3 Summarize methods used to interface with databases.
  Relational methods (Data manipulation [Select, Insert, Delete, Update], Data definition [Create, Alter, Drop, Permissions]) • Database access methods (Direct/manual access, Programmatic access • User interface/utility access, Query/report builders) • Export/import (Database dump, Backup)

Database Concepts

Databases are used everywhere in today's connected world. Every time you make an online purchase with an e-commerce retailer, many databases are accessed by a variety of different applications in order to facilitate your purchase.

A **database** is an organized collection of information. The information is stored in a structured manner for easier access. Typically, a database consists of **tables** of information, organized into **columns** and **rows**. Each row represents a separate **record** in the database, while each column represents a single **field** within a record.

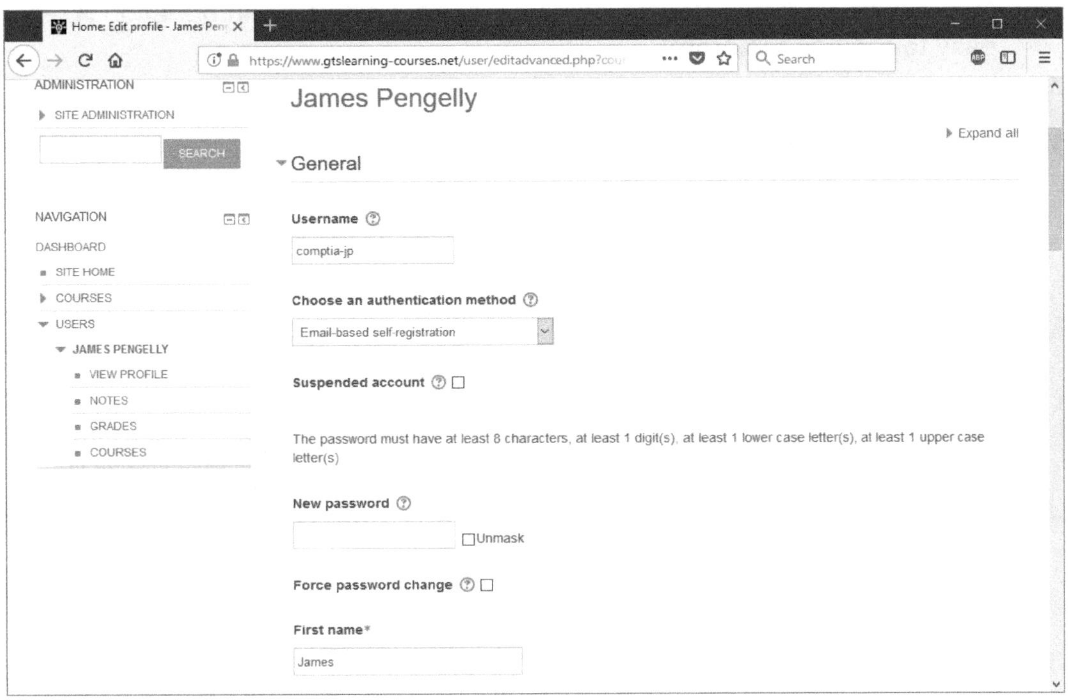

This user record is backed by a database. Each form field you can see shows and updates a column in a database table while this record is a row in the table.

Database Usage

A database is used both to store information securely and to report on the information it contains. Consequently, database usage involves the following processes and tools:

- Creation—this step involves defining what information the database will store, where it will be hosted, and how it will be accessed by clients.
- Import/input—once the database has been created, it must be populated with data records. Records can either be input and updated manually, usually using some type of form, or data might be imported from another source, or both.

- Storage (data persistence)—databases are often used with applications. While an application processes variables and other temporary data internally, this information is lost when the application is terminated. A database represents a way for an application to store data persistently and securely.
- Queries—it is possible in theory to read the information in each table manually, but in order to view information efficiently, a query is used to extract it. A query allows the user to specify criteria to match values in one or more fields and choose which fields to display in the results so that only information of interest is selected.
- Reports—a query might return a large number of rows and be just as difficult to read as a table. A report is a means of formatting and summarizing the records returned by a query so that the information is easy to read and interpret.

Flat File Systems

One common question asked when users are considering a database is, "Why can't I just use a spreadsheet such as Excel?" It's a fair question because Excel enables you to store your information in sheets, which are broadly analogous to tables, with rows and columns of data. This is an example of a **flat file** data storage and access system rather than a database.

Spreadsheets are not the only kind of flat file data store. Another example is a plain text file with delimiters for each column. A **Comma Separated Values (CSV)** file uses commas to identify the end of a column and a line feed for each row.

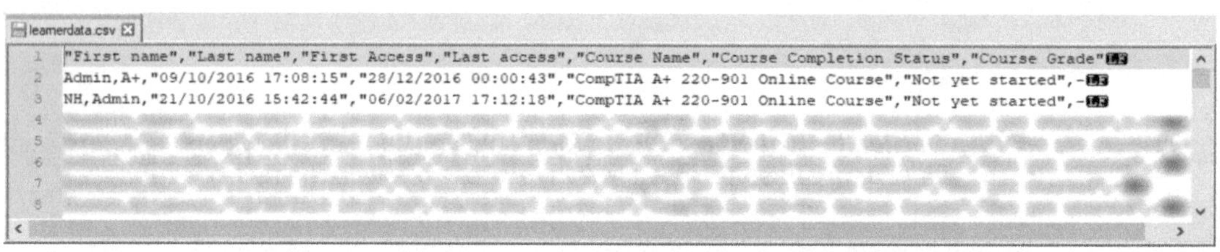

Comma Separated Values file—the column headers are shown at the top with commas separating each. Every line in the file corresponds to a row of data.

While flat file systems are easy to create they have many drawbacks compared to database systems.

Databases versus Flat File Systems

A flat file system might be useful for tasks such as simple order or sales databases used by a single person or small workgroup. A flat file is also a good way of exporting and importing information between systems. Dedicated database software has many advantages over flat files though.

- Databases can enforce data types for each column and validate information entered as fields and records. Spreadsheets can mimic some of this functionality but not as robustly. Databases consequently support a wider variety of data formats.

- Databases can manage multiple tables and link the fields in different tables to create complex schemas. In a flat file, all the information is stored within a single table.
- Databases can support tens, hundreds or thousands, or even millions of users concurrently. A single file-based data storage solution does not offer high enough speed for the volumes of transactions (adding and updating records) on enterprise-level systems.

In a file-based storage model, when one user opens the file it becomes locked to other users. They may be able to view the file but cannot change it (read-only). A database system supports concurrent users without locking the whole database. A particular record may be locked during a data entry transaction though.

- Databases are also more scalable. Scalability means being able to expand usage without increasing costs at the same rate. For example, in a non-scalable system, doubling the number of users would also double the costs of the system. Database architecture means that extra capacity can be added later with much less investment.
- Databases provide access controls to protect information from unauthorized disclosure and backup/replication tools to ensure that data can be recovered within seconds of it being committed.

Database Structures

There are different types of databases and data stores with different levels of structure.

Relational Databases

A **relational database** is the type we have been describing so far. A relational database is a highly **structured** type of database. Information is organized in **tables** (known as relations). A table is defined with a number of **fields**, represented by the table **columns**. Each field can be a particular data type. Each **row** entered into the table represents a data **record**.

Typically, **Relational Database Management Systems (RDBMS)** use **Structured Query Language (SQL)** to maintain and query data in the database. Examples of RDBMS include:

- Microsoft SQL Server.
- Oracle Database.
- MySQL.
- Microsoft Office Access.

Primary Key and Foreign Key

Attempting to store a complex set of data within a single table is impractical. For example, if you want to record who has borrowed books from a library, if you have a single LibraryLoans table, you have to duplicate information about the customer each time a loan record is created. It is likely that mistakes could be made inputting this information and the customer's details may change, resulting in inconsistencies in your data records. In a relational database, you can have multiple linked tables. If you design the database schema with one Customer table and one Loan table, you can link a single customer record to multiple loan records. If a customer record has to be updated, you can do that once in the Customer table rather than editing lots of records in a monolithic LibraryLoans table.

For this to work, in any given table, each record has to be unique in at least one way. This is usually accomplished by designating one column as a **primary key**. Each row in the table must have a unique value in the primary key field. This primary key is used to define the relationship between one table and another table in the database. When a primary key in one table is referenced in another table, then in the secondary table, that column is referred to as a **foreign key**.

The structure of the database in terms of the fields defined in each table and the relations between primary and foreign keys is referred to as the **schema**.

Relational Database Example

To give you an idea about a relational database, think again about a database supporting a lending library. Your database is designed to store and allow retrieval of data concerned with the management of book lending. This database might include a table that stored customer information, another that contained book title information, and finally a table that stored information about the actual lending.

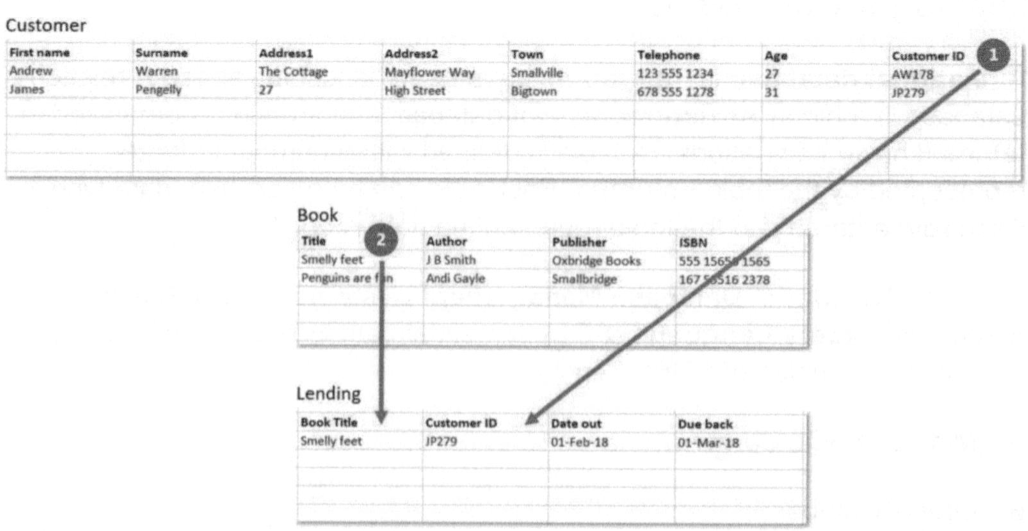

Relational database table model.

You can see that the customer information and book information that appears in the Lending table is drawn from the Customer and Book tables respectively. Specifically, the Customer ID is drawn from the Customer table and the Title is drawn from the Book table. The advantage of this approach is that if you must update customer information, you only need to do so in one place—the Customer table.

A query can be used to reconstruct the information. For example, if you want to check the customer associated with a particular lending record, your query would select the record from the Lending table then use the join between the Lending and Customer tables to show the values of the name and address fields from the related Customer table record.

Constraints

One of the functions of an RDBMS is to address the concept of **Garbage In, Garbage Out (GIGO)**. It is very important that the values entered into fields conform are consistent with what information the field is supposed to store.

When defining the properties of each field, as well as enforcing a data type, you can impose certain **constraints** on the values that can be input into each field. A primary key is an example of a constraint. The value entered or changed in a primary key field in any given record must not be the same as any other existing record. Other types of constraints might perform validation on the data that you can enter. For example, you could add constraints to prevent a field from being left blank, to define the format of a telephone number, or to check that the value entered to choose an order delivery date is not in the past. Another example of a constraint is to enter a default value in a field if the user makes no selection.

Constraints can be applied at different levels. As well as applying rules to fields, they can be used at the table and schema levels too.

Semi-structured and Unstructured Databases

When you store your information in a relational database, it is stored in a **structured** way. This structure enables you to more easily access the stored information and gives you flexibility over exactly what you access. For example, you can access all fields or only certain fields. Each field has a defined data type, meaning that software that understands the database language (SQL), can parse (interpret) the content of a field easily.

Unstructured data, on the other hand, provides no rigid formatting of the data. Images and text files, Word documents and PowerPoint presentations are examples of unstructured data. Unstructured data is typically much easier to create than structured data. Documents can be added to a store simply and the data store can support a much larger variety of data types than a relational database can.

Sitting somewhere between these two is **semi-structured** data. Strictly speaking, the data lacks the structure of formal database architecture. But in addition to the raw unstructured data, there is associated information called **metadata** that helps identify the data.

Document and Key/Value Pair Databases

A **document database** is an example of a semi-structured database. Rather than define tables and fields, the database grows by adding documents to it. The documents can use the same structure or be of different types. The database's query engine must be designed to parse each document type and extract information from it.

Documents would very commonly use markup language such as **XML (eXtensible Markup Language)** to provide structure.

Markup languages such as XML were discussed in *Unit 2.2.*

A **key/value pair database** is a means of storing the properties of objects without predetermining the fields used to define an object. A key/value pair table looks like the following:

Key	Value
user01_surname	Warren
user01_firstname	Andy
user01_age	27
user02_surname	Pengelly
user02_town	Bigtown
user_01_marketingconsent	TRUE
user_02_marketingconsent	FALSE

As you can see, not all properties have to be defined for each object. One widely used key/value format is JavaScript Object Notation (JSON). For example, "user01" could be expressed as the following JSON string:

```
{ "user01_surname" : "Warren", "user01_firstname" :
"Andy", "user01_age" : 27, "user01_marketingconsent" :
TRUE }
```

Document databases and key/value pair databases are **non-relational** because there are no formal structures to link the different data objects and files. This does not mean that relationships between the data items cannot be found though. Non-relational database systems use searches and queries to summarize and correlate data points.

Database engines dealing with a mixture of structured, unstructured, and semi-structured data are often referred to as NoSQL databases, which can stand either for "No SQL" or for "Not Only SQL."

Relational Methods

Database interfaces are the processes used to add/update information to and extract (or view) information from the database. In an RDBMS, the use of Structured Query Language (SQL) **relational methods** is critical to creating and updating the database.

These relational methods can be split into two types; those that define the database structure and those that manipulate information in the database.

Data Definition Methods

Data Definition Language (DDL) commands refer to SQL commands that add to or modify the structure of the database. Some examples of data definition commands are:

- `CREATE`—this command can be used to add a new database on the RDBMS server (`CREATE DATABASE`) or to add a new table within an existing database (`CREATE TABLE`). The primary key and foreign key can be specified as part of the table definition.
- `ALTER TABLE`—this allows you to add, remove (drop), and modify table columns (fields), change a primary key and/or foreign key, and configure other constraints. There is also an `ALTER DATABASE` command, used for modifying properties of the whole database, such as its character set.
- `DROP`—this is the command used to delete a table (`DROP TABLE`) or database (`DROP DATABASE`). Obviously, this also deletes any records and data stored in the object.
- `CREATE INDEX`—specifying that a column (or combination of columns) is indexed speeds up queries on that column. The tradeoff is that updates are slowed down slightly, or quite a lot if the column is not suitable for indexing. The `DROP INDEX` command can be used to remove an index.

There are also SQL commands allowing permissions (access controls) to be configured. These are discussed below.

Data Manipulation Methods

Data Manipulation Language (DML) commands allow you to insert or update records and extract information from records for viewing (a query):

- `INSERT INTO` *`TableName`*—adds a new row in a table in the database.
- `UPDATE` *`TableName`*—changes the value of one or more table columns. This can be used with a `WHERE` statement to filter the records that will be updated. If no `WHERE` statement is specified, the command applies to all the records in the table.
- `DELETE FROM` *`TableName`*—deletes records from the table. As with `UPDATE`, this will delete all records unless a `WHERE` statement is specified.

- `SELECT`—enables you to define a query to retrieve data from a database.

The following examples show some of the ways that a SELECT statement can be used to build a query:

```
SELECT * FROM Customers;
```

...enables you to select all data in the specified "Customers" table.

```
SELECT Name, Town FROM Customers;
```

...retrieves the values in the Name and Town fields for all records in the Customers table.

```
SELECT * FROM Customers
WHERE Town='Slough';
```

...retrieves all records from the Customers table where the value in the Town field is equal to "Slough."

```
SELECT * FROM Customers
WHERE Town='Slough'
 ORDER BY Name;
```

...as above but also sorts the results in alphabetical order by the contents of the Name field.

Permissions

SQL supports a secure access control system where specific user accounts can be granted rights over different objects in the database (tables, columns, and views for instance) and the database itself. When an account creates an object, it becomes the owner of that object, with complete control over it. The owner *cannot* be denied permission over the object. The owner can be changed however, using the **`ALTER AUTHORIZATION`** statement.

Other accounts can be granted specific rights over an object using the statement:

```
GRANT permission TO user
```

For example, the following statement grants use of the **`SELECT`** statement to the user "james."

```
GRANT SELECT ON Customers TO james
```

Rights can also be specifically denied a permission using:

```
DENY permission TO user
```

DENY overrides and GRANT permission, but cannot affect the owner, as mentioned above.

Permission statements can be considered as **Data Definition Language (DDL)** commands, like **`CREATE`** and **`DROP`**.

SQL also supports a **CONTROL** *permission where the user has all rights to the object by default but* can *subsequently be denied some rights.*

Database Access Methods

Database access methods are the processes by which a user might run SQL commands on the database server or update or extract information using a form or application that encapsulates the SQL commands as graphical controls or tools.

Direct/Manual Access

Administrators might use an administrative tool, such as phpMyAdmin, to connect and sign in to an RDBMS database. Once they have connected, they can run SQL commands to create new databases on the system and interact with stored data. This can be described as direct or manual access.

Query/Report Builder

There are many users who may need to interact closely with the database but do not want to learn SQL syntax. A query or report builder provides a GUI for users to select actions to perform on the database and converts those selections to the SQL statements that will be executed.

Programmatic Access

A software application can interact with the database either using SQL commands or using SQL commands stored as procedures in the database. Most programming languages include libraries to provide default code for connecting to a database and executing queries.

User Interface/Utility Access

An application might use a database in the background without the user really being aware of its presence. Alternatively, the application might provide a specific **Graphical User Interface (GUI)** or **form** to allow ordinary users to add and search records.

Backups and Data Export

As with any type of data, it is vital to make secure **backups** of databases. Most RDBMS provide stored procedures that invoke the **BACKUP** and **RESTORE** commands at a database or table level.

Backing up databases is complicated by the problem of gaining exclusive access to perform a consistent copy. SQL engines have tools to facilitate backup access to an online database. See *Unit 4.4* *for more information about backup issues.*

It may also be necessary to export data from the database for use in another database or in another type of program, such as a spreadsheet. A **dump** is a copy of the database or table schema along with the records expressed as SQL statements. These SQL statements can be executed on another database to import the information.

Most database engines support exporting data in tables to other file formats, such as Comma Separated Values (.CSV) or native MS Excel (.XLS).

Application Architecture Models

A database application can be designed for any sort of business function. Customer Relationship Management (CRM) and accounting are typical examples. If the application front-end and processing logic and the database engine are all hosted on the same computer, the application architecture can be described as **one-tier** or **standalone**.

A **two-tier** client-server application separates the database engine, or back-end or data layer, from the presentation layer and the application layer, or business logic. The application and presentation layers are part of the client application. The database engine will run on one server (or more likely a cluster of servers), while the presentation and application layers run on the client.

In a **three-tier** application, the presentation and application layers are also split. The presentation layer provides the client front-end and user interface and runs on the client machine. The application layer runs on a server or server cluster that the client connects to. When the client makes a request, it is checked by the application layer, and if it conforms to whatever access rules have been set up, the application layer executes the query on the data layer which resides on a third tier and returns the result to the client. The client should have no direct communications with the data tier.

In the terminology, a "layer" is a separate logical function, while a "tier" is an independent or compartmentalized processing function. While we describe tiers as "separate servers," they do not necessarily have to be physically separated machines. They could be implemented as virtual machines for instance.

An **n-tier** application architecture can be used to mean either a two-tier or three-tier application, but another use is an application with a more complex architecture still. For example, the application may use separate access control or monitoring services.

Review Questions / Module 2 / Unit 4 / Using Databases

Answer these questions to test what you have learned in this unit. You can review the model answers at the end of the book.

1) What are the structural elements of a database table?
2) What term is used to describe selecting and viewing information in a database?
3) How does an RDBMS such as Microsoft SQL Server differ from Microsoft Excel when used to store a dataset?
4) What language is usually used to request data from an RDBMS such as Oracle?
5) What is it that defines the relationship between tables in an RDBMS?
6) Give an example of unstructured data.
7) Give two examples of semi-structured data stores.
8) Is an INSERT statement an example of a definition or manipulation language statement?
9) You need a development environment with a library of database functions. What type of interface are you using?
10) How can a client-server application architecture be described if there is the potential for the structure of the application platform to be developed further?

Lab 10 / Creating and Using a Database

In this lab, you will use the database application bundled with Apache Open Office to create a database, use a form to input data, and build a query to select and view records.

Exercise 1 / Installing Apache Open Office

In this exercise, you will install Apache Open Office to make its database application available.

This lab involves downloading and installing a program from a third-party website. The authors and publisher believe the website and program to be reputable and pose no risk to your computer or personal information but cannot be held responsible for any loss or damage that may occur as a result of following the steps in this lab. If you have any concerns we recommend that you do NOT proceed.

1) If necessary, start your computer and sign in.

2) Open a browser and navigate to openoffice.org/download

3) Under the Download Apache OpenOffice heading, select **Windows (EXE)** and **English (US)**, then click **Download full installation**.

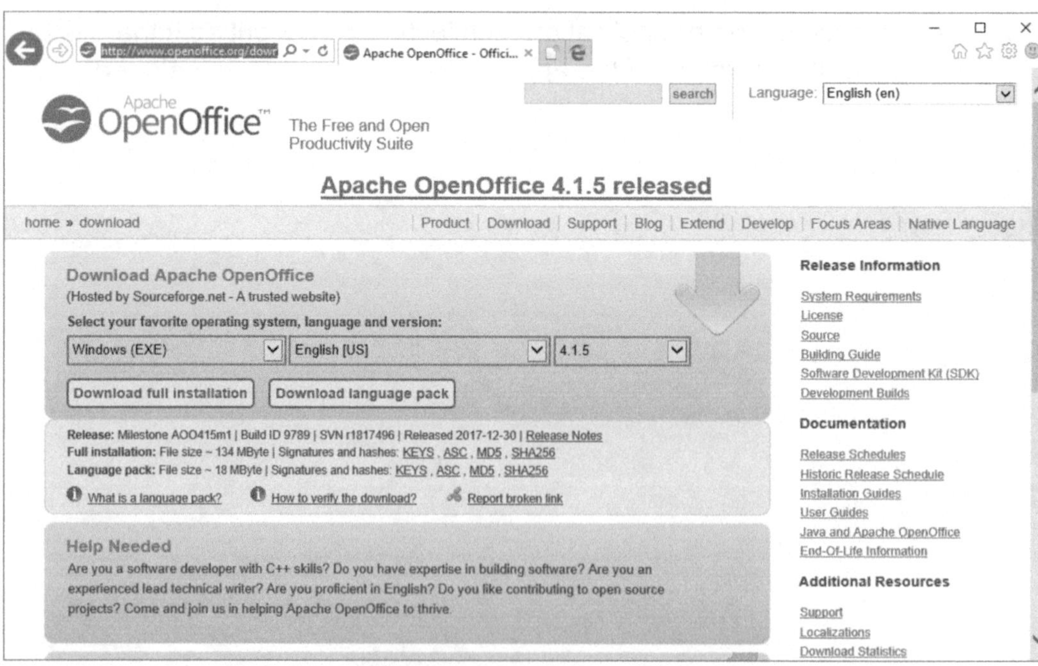

Downloading the Apache Open Office Windows executable.

4) In the prompt at the bottom of the window, click **Save**. When download is complete, in the prompt, click **Run**.

Windows does not trust the installer. In this case you have to trust the site that you downloaded the file from (sourceforge.net). You can find out more about how to verify the installer by browsing Open Office's FAQs (www.openoffice.org/security/faq.html#verify).

5) In the **User Account Control** window, read the warning but click **Yes**.

6) In the **OpenOffice 4.1.5 Setup** wizard, click **Next**.

7) On the **Choose Install Location** page, click **Install**.

8) On the **Welcome to the Installation Wizard for OpenOffice 4.1.5** page, click **Next**.

9) On the **Customer Information** page, click **Next**.

10) On the **Setup Type** page, click **Custom** and then click **Next**.

11) Review the components. Click **Next**.

12) On the **File Type** page, clear all check boxes and then click **Next**. This step is very important if you already have Microsoft Office installed.

13) On the **Ready to Install the Program** page, click **Install**.

14) When prompted, click **Finish**.

15) On the desktop, double-click the **OpenOffice 4.1.5** icon.

16) On the **Welcome** page, click **Next**.

17) Complete the User name information and then click **Finish**.

You require the Java Runtime Environment in order to use the database features of Open Office. This should have been installed as part of the programming labs earlier in this module.

18) From the **Tools** menu, select **Options**. In the **Options** dialog, select **Java**.

After a few seconds, the dialog should update to show a path to the Java runtime environment.

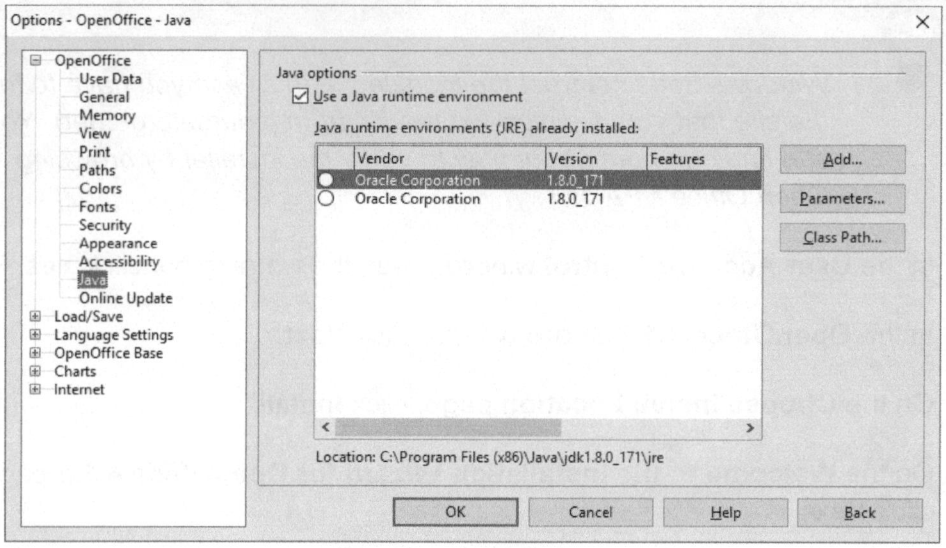

Verifying the Java path.

19) Click **OK**.

20) Close the Open Office window.

Exercise 2 / Creating a New Database

In this exercise, you will create a new database and create database tables.

1) On the desktop, double-click the **OpenOffice 4.1.5** icon.

2) In Open Office, click **Database**.

3) In the Database Wizard, on the **Select database** tab, click **Create a new database** and then click **Next**.

4) On the **Save and proceed** tab, click **Finish**.

5) In the **Save As** window, in the navigation pane, click **Documents**.

6) In the **File name** box, type `CompTIA` and then click **Save**.

7) In the open database window, click **Tables** and then click **Create Table in Design View**.

   As a first step, we will create a primary key for the table. As the primary key must always be unique, it is a good idea to use an automatically generated number for this field.

8) In the new table window, in the **Field Name** column, type `CustomerID`

9) In the **Field Type** column, select **Integer [INTEGER]**, and in the **Description** column, type `Primary key for the Customer table`

10) In the lower panel, from the **AutoValue** box, select **Yes**.

11) Click back in the field name area.

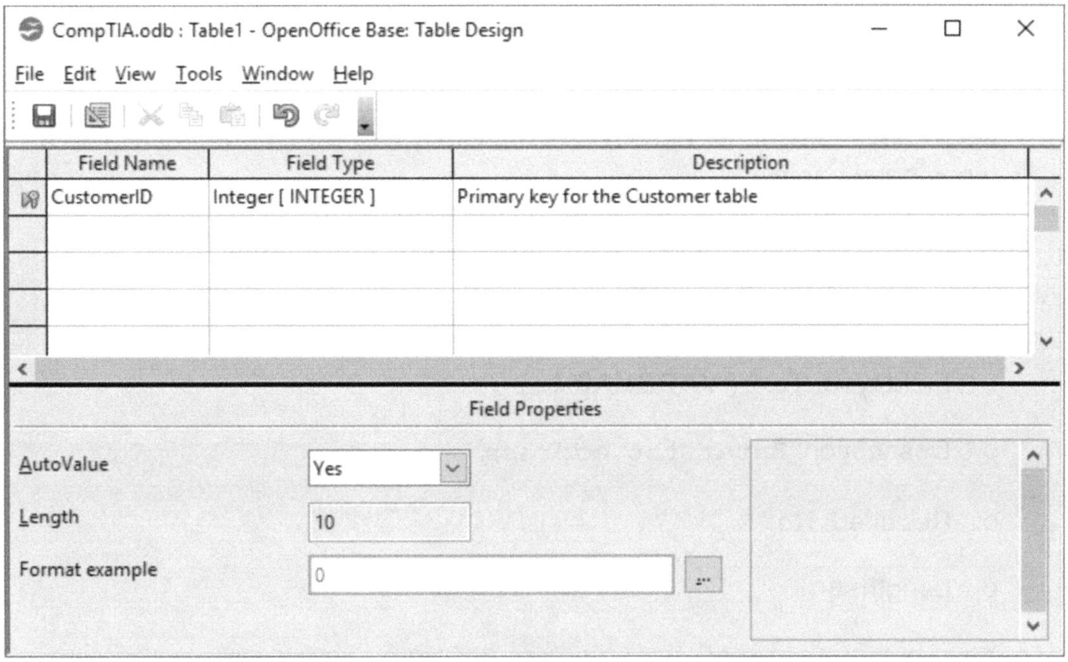

Creating a field to use as the primary key.

The database engine automatically picks this field to use as a primary key. A key icon appears in the row selector in the far left (the grey box) to show this.

12) Click in the **Field Name** column in the next row and type **`Name`**

13) In the **Field Type** column, leave **Text [VARCHAR]** selected, and in the **Description** column, type **`Enter the company name`**

    This creates a field with a string data type (variable number of characters).

14) In the lower panel, set the **Entry required** value to **Yes** and the **Length** to **`20`**

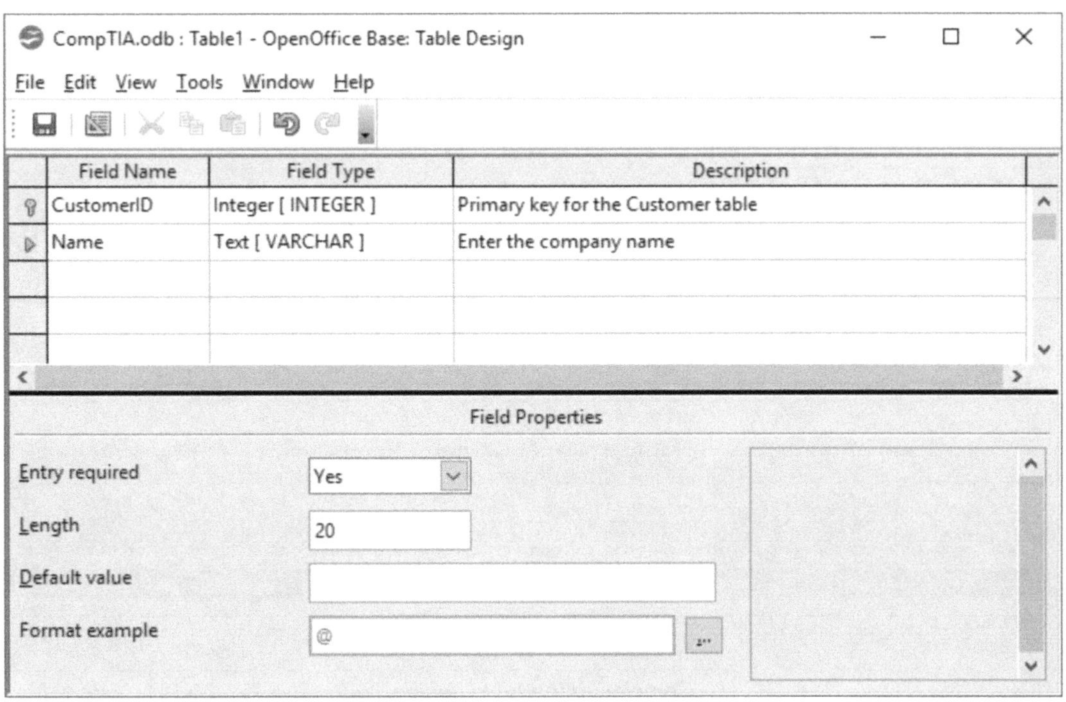

Defining a field with constraints.

This sets constraints for the field. Note that the length constraint sets a maximum length, so the user can enter fewer characters if needed. If we used a fixed length CHAR field data type, the same number of characters would have to be input each time—obviously that would not be suitable for a company name.

15) Add an address field to the table with the following properties:

- Field name: `Address`
- Field type: **Text [VARCHAR]**
- Description: `Enter the address`
- Required: **No**
- Length: `50`

16) Add a telephone field to the table with the following properties:

- Field name: `Telephone`
- Field type: **Number [NUMERIC]**
- Description: `Enter the phone number with no spaces`
- Required: **No**
- Length: `10`

Your table design should now look like this:

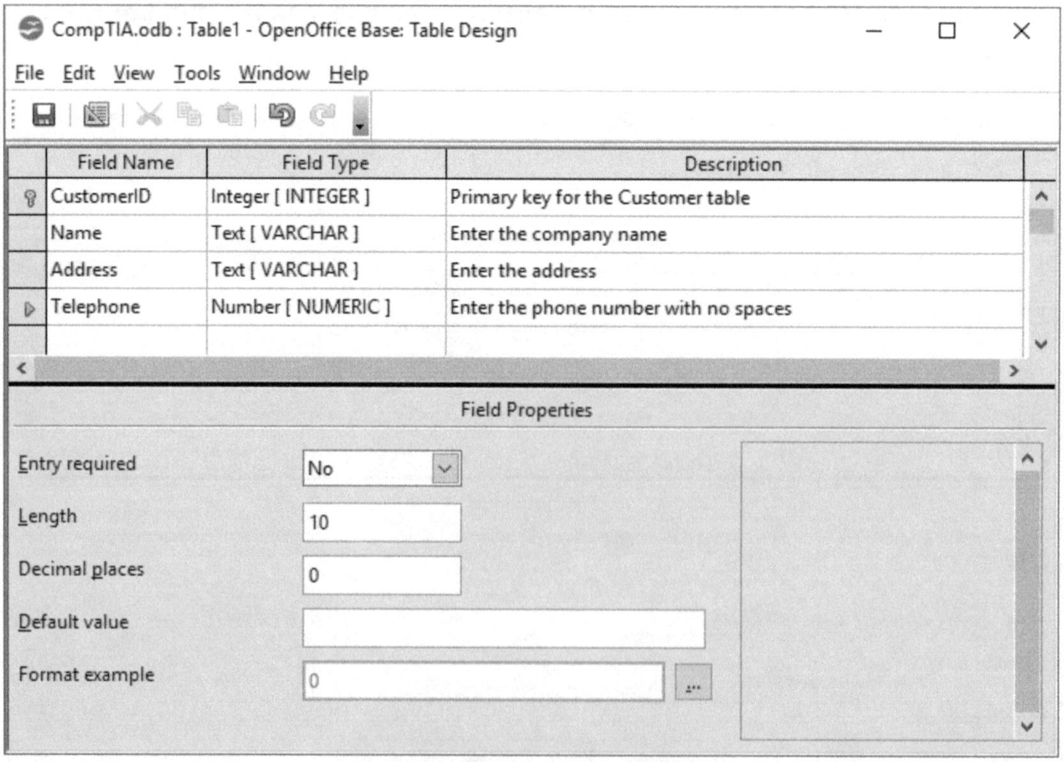

Completing the table design.

17) On the toolbar, click **Save**.

18) In the **Save As** box, type the name `Customer` and click **OK**.

19) Close the Customer table. In the database window, click **Create Table in Design View**.

20) In the new table window, in the **Field Name** column, type `ContactID`

21) In the **Field Type** column, select **Integer [INTEGER]**, and in the **Description** column, type `Primary key for the Contact table`

22) In the lower panel, from the **AutoValue** box, select **Yes**.

23) Click back in the field name area. The field is set as a primary key automatically.

As each contact will be connected with an associated company record, we now need to add the CustomerID field as a foreign key in the Contact table.

24) In the **Field Name** column, type `Customer`

25) In the **Field Type** column, select **Integer [INTEGER]**, and in the **Description** column, type `Select a customer record`

26) In the lower panel, from the **Entry required** box, select **Yes**.

27) Add a first name field to the table with the following properties:

- Field name: `FirstName`
- Field type: **Text [VARCHAR]**
- Required: **Yes**
- Length: `25`

28) Add a surname field to the table with the following properties:

- Field name: `Surname`
- Field type: **Text [VARCHAR]**
- Required: **Yes**
- Length: `25`

29) Click **Save**.

30) In the **Save As** window, in the **Table Name** box, type `Contact` and click **OK**.

31) Close the table window.

32) From the **Tools** menu, select **Relationships**.

33) In the **Add Tables** dialog, with **Customer** selected, click **Add** then select **Contact** and click **Add**. Click **Close**.

34) Drag the **CustomerID** field from the Customer table over the **Customer** field in the Contact table.

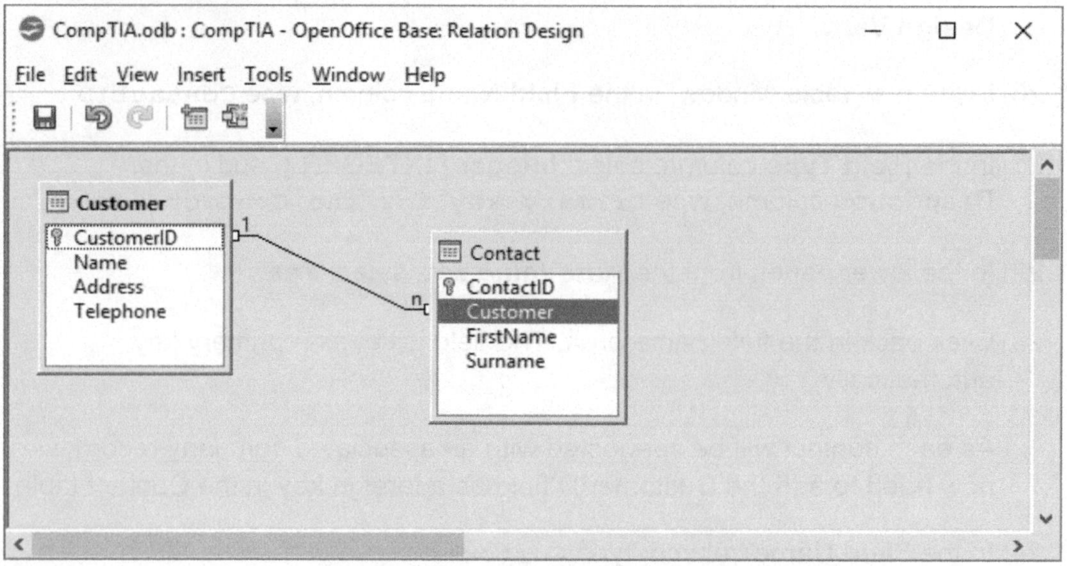

Creating a relationship between two tables.

Note the symbols on the join line. The customer table side is shown with a "1" while the contact side is labelled "n." This represents a one-to-many relationship. Each single record in the Customer table can have many related records in the Contact table. This is the most common type of relation.

35) Close the Table Relationships window. Click **Yes** to save when prompted.

36) On the menu bar, click **Save** to save the database tables.

Exercise 3 / Creating a Form and Entering Data

In this exercise, you will populate the database with sample records using a simple form.

1) With the **CompTIA** database open, click the **Forms** button.

2) in the **Tasks** list, click **Use Wizard to Create Form**.

3) In the **Form Wizard**, in the **Tables or queries** list, select **Table: Customer**.

4) In the **Available fields** list, select **Name**, **Address**, and **Telephone** then click **>** .

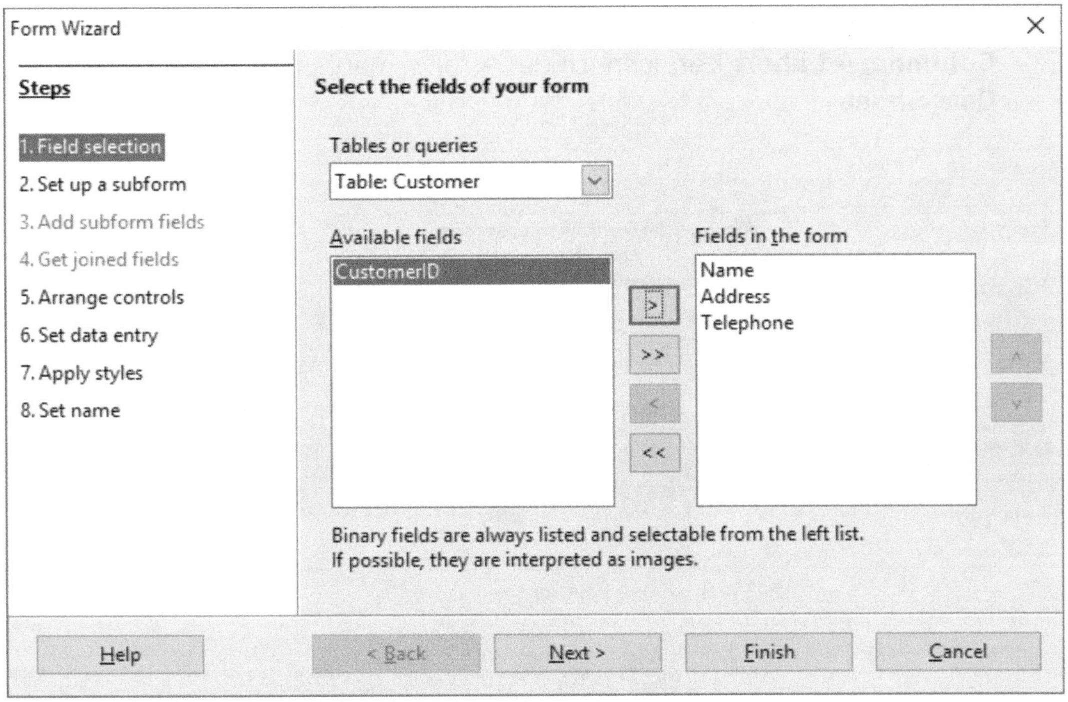

Creating a form with the wizard.

As the ID field is automatically generated for each new record, it does not need to be added to the form.

5) Click **Next**.

6) Check the **Add Subform** box and the **Subform based on existing relation** option button. Select **Contact**.

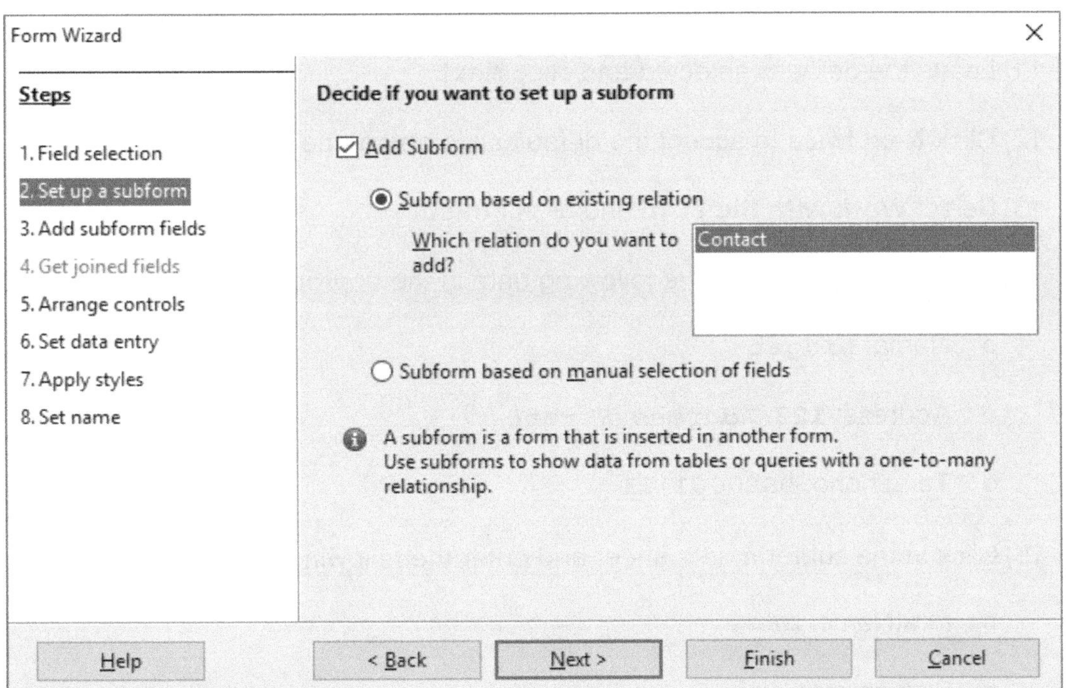

Adding a subform.

7) Click **Next**.

8) Add the **FirstName** and **Surname** fields then click **Next**.

9) On the **Arrange controls** tab, under **Arrangement of the main form**, click **Columnar – Labels Left** icon. Under Arrangement of the subform, click **As Data Sheet**.

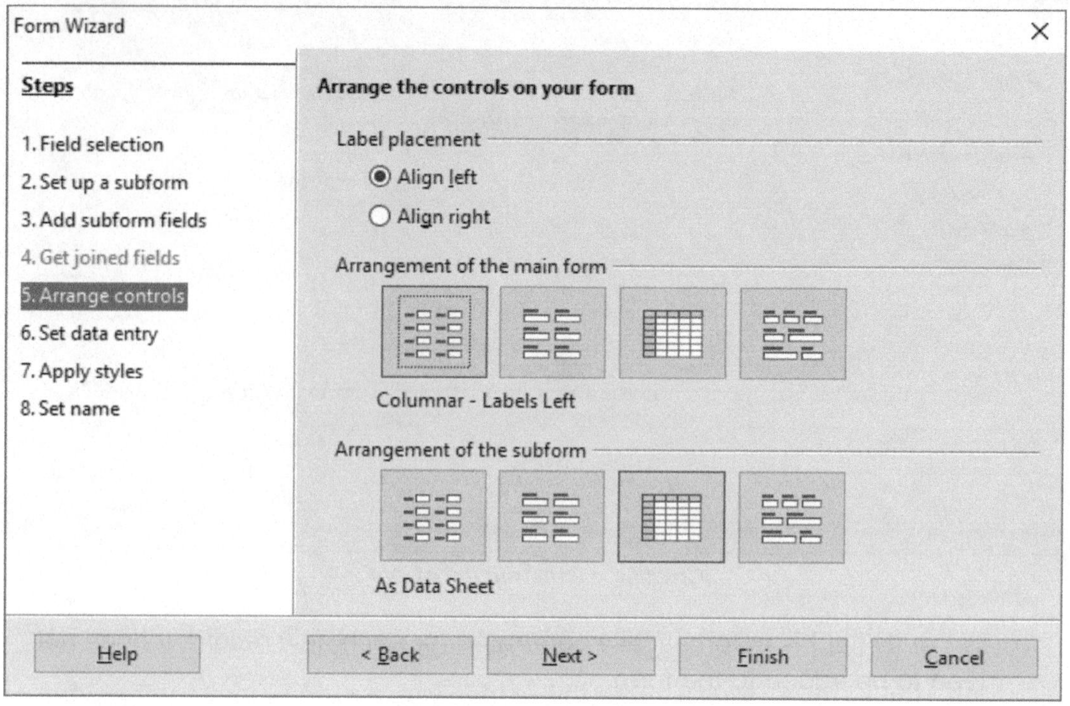

Defining the form layout.

10) Click **Next**.

    Forms can be configured to view only or with properties to prevent modification, addition, or deletion of data.

11) Leave the defaults selected and click **Next**.

12) Click **Next** twice to accept the default style and name.

13) Select **Work with the form** and click **Finish**.

14) In the open form, type the following data in the appropriate fields:

    - Name: `Widget`
    - Address: `123 Address Street`
    - Telephone: `9990001111`

15) Click in the subform data sheet and enter the following information:

    - FirstName: `Dave`
    - Surname: `Martin`

16) Type the following data in the next row:

    - FirstName: `Sue`
    - Surname: `Smith`

17) Click back in the main form (in the Name field for instance) then click the **New Record** button .

18) In the open form, type the following data in the appropriate fields:

- Name: `Grommet`
- Address: `321 Main Road`
- Telephone: `8880002222`

19) Click in the subform data sheet and enter one or two contacts.

20) Close the current form.

21) In the database window, select the **Tables** object. Open the **Customer** table. Make a note of the values in the CustomerID primary key field for the two records:

Widget: ______________________________

Grommet: ______________________________

22) Close the table.

23) Open the **Contact** table and check the Customer field—you should see the values you recorded above entered in the foreign key.

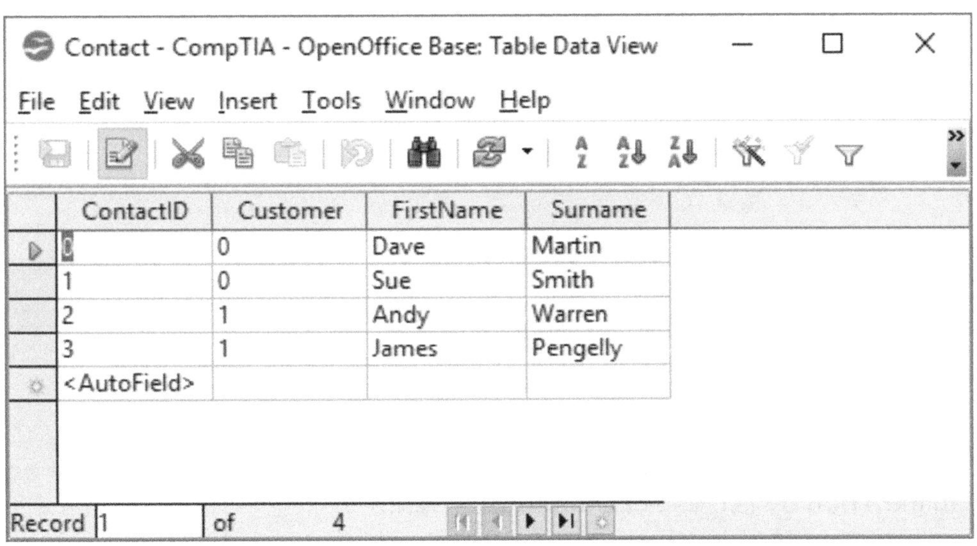

ContactID	Customer	FirstName	Surname
0	0	Dave	Martin
1	0	Sue	Smith
2	1	Andy	Warren
3	1	James	Pengelly
<AutoField>			

Values added to the Contact table foreign key Customer field.

These values are added automatically by the database engine because of the relationship you defined between the tables and between the form and subform.

24) Close the **Contact** table.

Exercise 4 / Working with Queries

In this exercise, you will use a query to extract data and display it using a report.

1) With the **CompTIA** database open, click the **Queries** button.

2) Click **Use Wizard to Create Query**.

3) In the **Query Wizard** window, from the **Tables** list, select **Table: Customer**.

4) Select all fields *except* CustomerID and then click **>**.

5) From the **Tables** list, click **Table: Contact**.

6) Select the **FirstName** and **Surname** fields then click **>**.

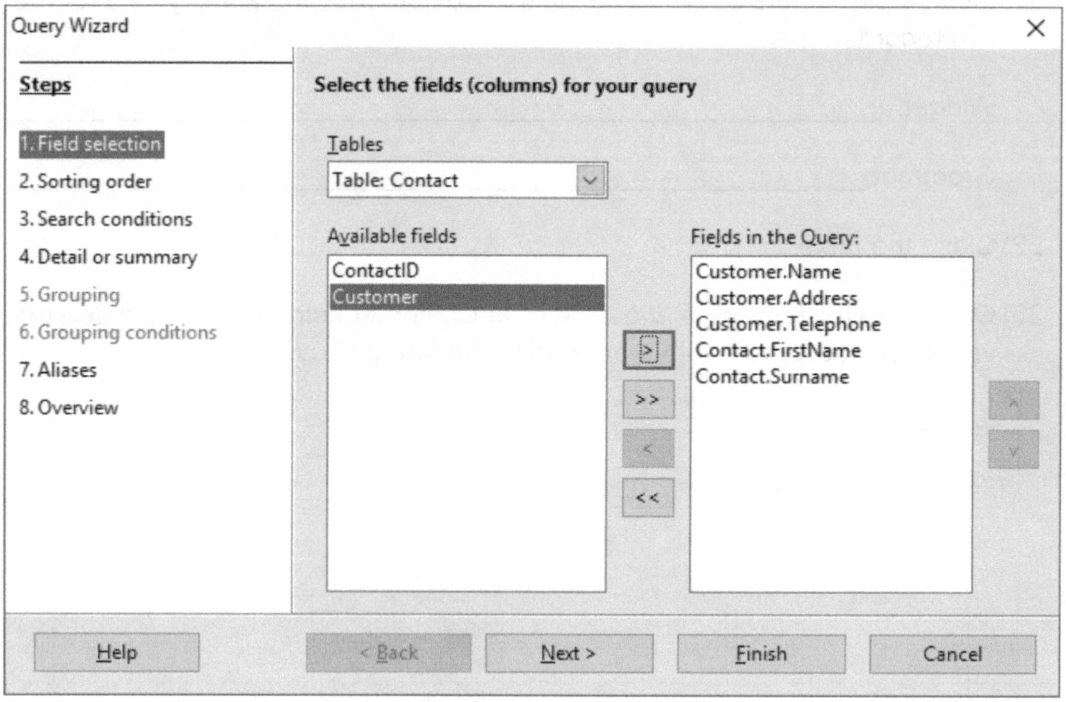

Defining fields to show in the query.

7) Click **Next**.

8) On the **Sorting order** tab, in the **Sort by** list, select **Customer.Name** and in the **Then by** list, select **Contact.Surname**.

9) Click **Next**.

10) With **Match all of the following** selected, from the **Fields** list box, select **Contact.FirstName**. From the **Condition** box, select **is not equal to**, and in the **Value** box, type `Dave`

11) Click **Finish**. What is wrong with the query results?

____

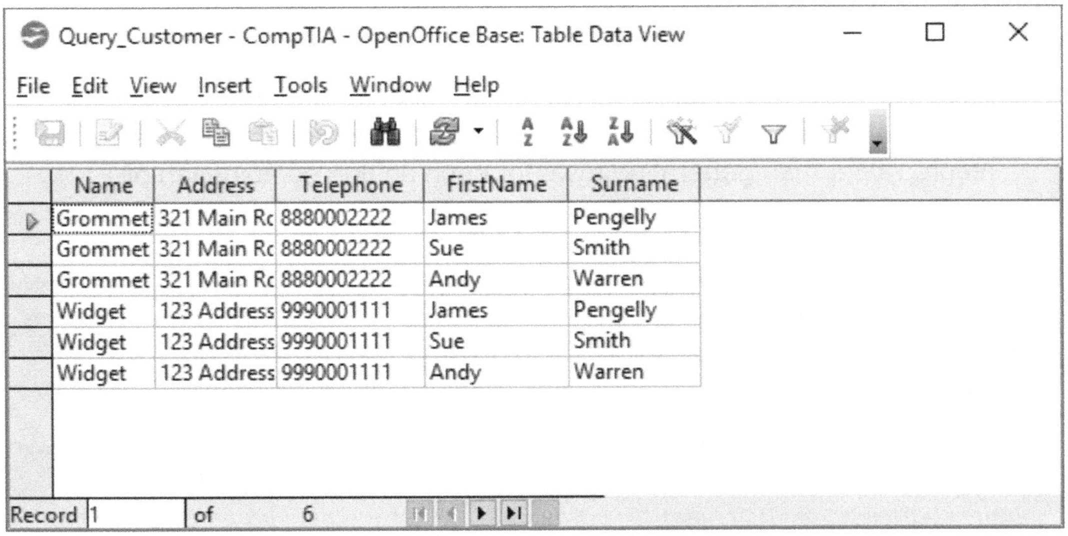

All of these people seem to have more than one job!

To fix the output, we need to re-state the join (relationship) between the tables in the query builder.

12) Close the query window. In the database window, right-click **Query_Customer** and select **Edit**.

13) Drag the **CustomerID** field from the Customer table over the **Customer** field in the Contact table.

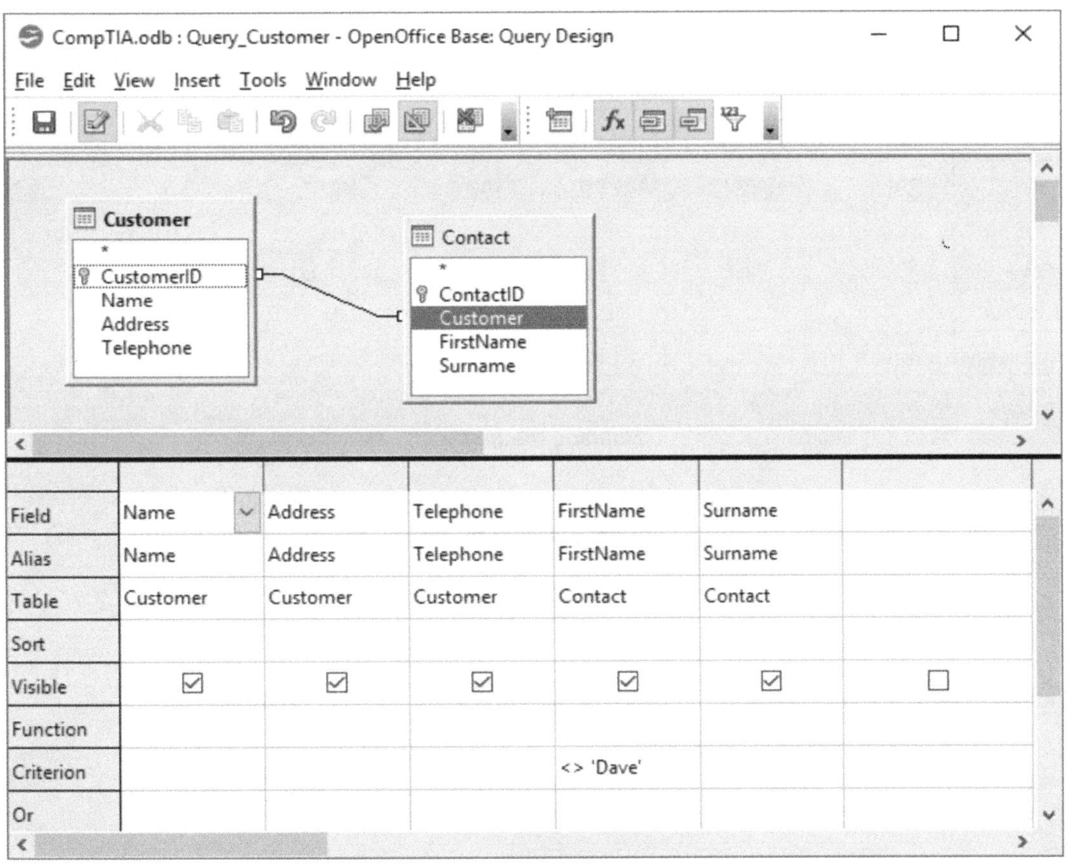

Setting the join in query design view.

14) Click the **Save** button then press **F5**.

    This runs the query within the builder interface. You should see that the join is now working properly and the query is returning one row per contact record rather than generating rows for each unique combination of customer and contact records.

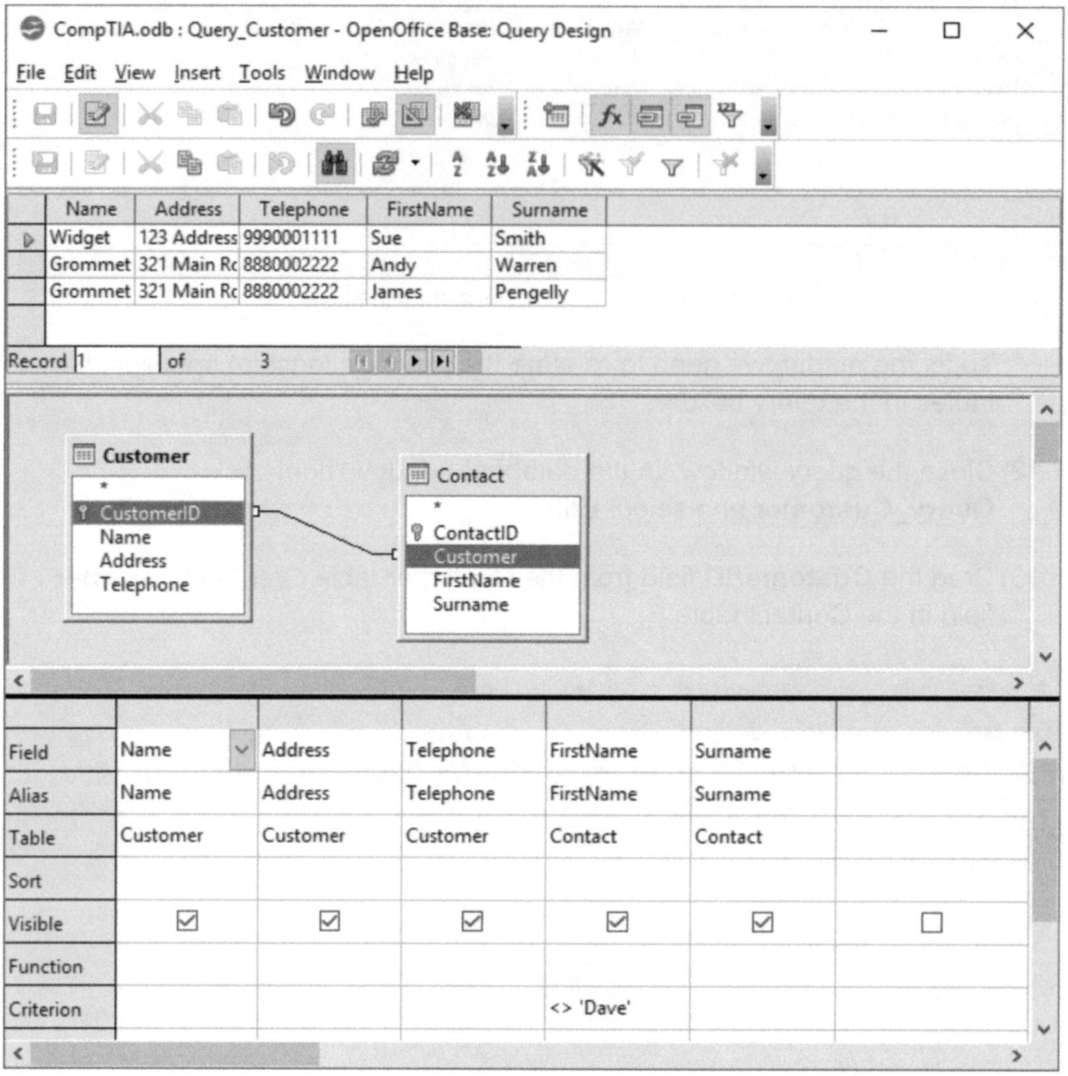

Running the query.

15) Close the query window. In the database window, right-click **Query_Customer** and select **Edit in SQL View**.

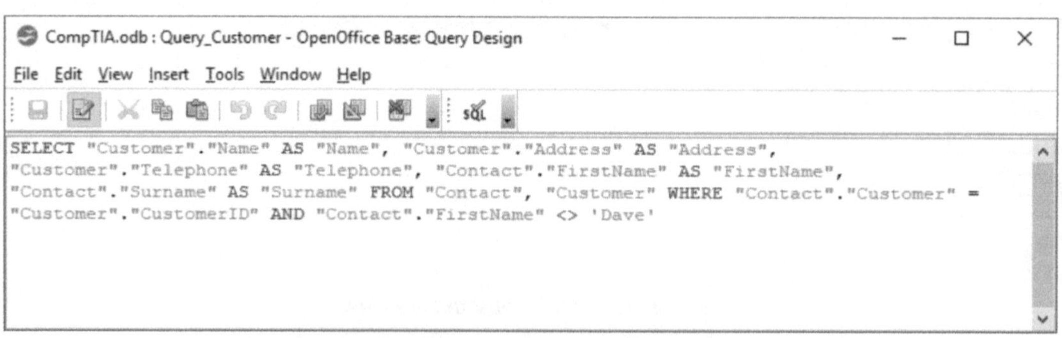

SQL statement underpinning the query.

Everything you have done in the database GUI is using underlying SQL. Note the features of this statement:

- The **SELECT** statement chooses records for viewing (data manipulation). It is followed by a list of column (field) names to use in the output. The **AS** keyword specifies an alias for each field.
- The **FROM** keyword lists the data sources (Customer and Contacts).
- The **WHERE** keyword states the join and the criteria excluding "Dave."

16) Close the SQL window.

17) Close Open Office, choosing to save changes when prompted.

This page left blank intentionally.

Module 2 / Summary
Using Apps and Databases

In this module you learned the basics of using a computer, Windows, and software applications.

Module 2 / Unit 1 / Using Data Types and Units

- Computers process binary data but this must often be converted to decimal or hexadecimal notation for use in programs and configuration dialogs.
- The fundamental bit value can be expressed in various multiples to describe storage and transfer rates (bits per second).
- Data must usually be declared as a particular type to be processed. Types include integers, floating point numbers, Boolean values, char values, and strings. Char and string types can use ASCII or Unicode representation.
- Data is a valuable asset and can be protected by legal mechanisms such as copyright, patent, and trademark.
- Consider the importance and use of data and analytics to defining business goals.

Module 2 / Unit 2 / Using Apps

- Plan software installation and upgrades carefully, making sure you read the documentation, verify system requirements, and check compatibility. Make sure you understand the implications of installing commercial, freeware, and shareware software.
- Be aware of the functions and features of productivity, collaboration, and business types of software.

Module 2 / Unit 3 / Programming and App Development

- Software development can progress through a sequence or flow chart of steps, to pseudocode, to the fully developed code written in the syntax of a particular programming language.
- Some programming languages require that you compile your programs before they can be run. However, others, including common scripting languages, run in an interpreter, which compiles at runtime. Note the use of other types of languages, such as query, markup, and assembly languages.
- Identifiers such as variables and constants, plus containers such as arrays and vectors allow programs to manipulate data. Branches and loops enable your program to deviate from its end-to-end run path.
- Procedures and functions enable you to create pieces of code that you will reuse within your program. Object oriented techniques help to design robust code.

- Applications can be packaged for standalone installation on a single computer but other architectures, such as network hosted and cloud hosted, are becoming more popular.

Module 2 / Unit 4 / Using Databases

- Make sure you understand the structure of relational databases and the processes of creation, import/input, storage, querying, and reporting involved in database usage.
- Flat file systems, such as Microsoft Excel, can be used to handle small volumes of data, and support one or two users. RDBMS-based databases typically support SQL and scale well to support high numbers of users and transactions. Also be aware of semi-structured datastores.
- You should know typical data definition and data modification commands and the basics of database permissions and access methods. Also consider how application architecture can use tiers to separate data from presentation and application layers.

Module 3 / Using Computer Hardware

The following CompTIA IT Fundamentals+ domain objectives and examples are covered in this module:

CompTIA ITF+ Certification Domains	Weighting
1.0 IT Concepts and Terminology	17%
2.0 Infrastructure	22%
3.0 Applications and Software	18%
4.0 Software Development	12%
5.0 Database Fundamentals	11%
6.0 Security	20%

Refer To	Domain Objectives/Examples
Unit 3.1 / System Components	**2.3 Explain the purpose of common internal computing components.** *Motherboard/system board • Firmware/BIOS • RAM • ARM CPU (Mobile phone, Tablet) • 32-bit CPU (Laptop, Workstation, Server) • 64-bit CPU (Laptop, Workstation, Server) • Storage (Hard drive, SSD) • GPU • Cooling • NIC (Wired vs. wireless, Onboard vs. add-on card)*
Unit 3.2 / Using Device Interfaces	**2.1 Classify common types of input/output device interfaces.** *Networking (Wired [Telephone connector (RJ-11), Ethernet connector (RJ-45)], Wireless [Bluetooth, NFC]) • Peripheral device (USB, FireWire, Thunderbolt, Bluetooth, RF) • Graphic device (VGA, HDMI, DVI, DisplayPort, Mini-DisplayPort)*
	2.2 Given a scenario, set up and install common peripheral devices to a laptop/PC. *Devices (Keyboard, Mouse)*
Unit 3.3 / Using Peripheral Devices	**2.2 Given a scenario, set up and install common peripheral devices to a laptop/PC.** *Devices (Printer, Scanner, Camera, Speakers, Display) • Installation types (Plug-and-play vs. driver installation, Other required steps, IP-based peripherals, Web-based configuration steps)*
	3.1 Manage applications and software. *Device management*
	3.2 Compare and contrast components of an operating system. *Drivers*
Unit 3.4 / Using Storage Devices	**2.2 Given a scenario, set up and install common peripheral devices to a laptop/PC.** *Devices (External hard drive)*
	2.5 Compare and contrast storage types. *Volatile vs. non-volatile • Local storage types (RAM, Hard drive [Solid state vs. spinning disk], Optical, Flash drive)*

Refer To	Domain Objectives/Examples
Unit 3.5 / Using File Systems	**3.2 Compare and contrast components of an operating system.** *File systems and features (File systems, NTFS, FAT32, HFS, Ext4) • Features (Compression, Encryption, Permissions, Journaling, Limitations, Naming rules) • File management (Folders/directories, File types and extensions, Permissions)*

Module 3 / Unit 1

System Components

Objectives

On completion of this unit, you will be able to:

- Explain the way in which system components determine performance and how to specify an appropriate computer system.
- Describe the types and functions of motherboards, processors, memory, and the expansion bus.
- Explain the importance of a cooling system and the components used.
- Identify the role of PC firmware and access the firmware setup program.

Syllabus Objectives and Content Examples

This unit covers the following exam domain objectives and content examples:

- 2.3 Explain the purpose of common internal computing components. Motherboard/system board • Firmware/BIOS • RAM • ARM CPU (Mobile phone, Tablet) • 32-bit CPU (Laptop, Workstation, Server) • 64-bit CPU (Laptop, Workstation, Server) • Storage (Hard drive, SSD) • GPU • Cooling • NIC (Wired vs. wireless, Onboard vs. add-on card)

Selecting a Computer

In this unit, you will look at the main components inside the PC and how they affect performance and upgrades. Computer performance is determined both by the type of components installed and how well matched the components are to one another. When considering performance, you need to understand how the main components in a PC work together.

Central Processing Unit (CPU)

The **Central Processing Unit (CPU)** is the device that "runs" software programs. Software is composed of many simple instructions. The CPU processes these instructions and directs other components to perform actions, such as displaying an image on the screen or printing a document.

Memory (System RAM)

When a program is started, its instructions are loaded into **system memory**. System memory uses a type of technology called **Random Access Memory (RAM)**. Having more RAM allows the PC to open more programs simultaneously and work on large files more efficiently. As well as system memory *size*, the *speed* of the memory subsystem is also important. The CPU fetches instructions from system memory as it needs them. This means that the bus between the CPU and memory, often referred to as the **Front Side Bus (FSB)**, must be as fast as possible. If the memory is slow and the CPU is fast, the CPU will not be supplied with enough instructions and become under-utilized.

Fixed Disk

Because RAM only works while the power is on, when the computer is turned off, programs and data are stored on a **Hard Disk Drive (HDD)** or **Solid State Drive (SSD)**. The type and specification of the mass storage drive such as an HDD or SSD is important for three reasons:

- If there is not enough space, fewer programs and data files can be stored on the computer.
- If the disk is not fast enough, performance will suffer when the computer tries to load programs and data files into memory (read operations) or write data from memory to files.
- The computer may use part of the hard disk to supplement system RAM (virtual memory). If the computer does not have much system RAM, it helps for the hard disk to be fast otherwise accessing virtual memory often will reduce performance even more than usual.

HDDs are based on a magnetic disk technology. SSDs use a type of transistor-based memory called flash memory and are much faster than HDDs.

See Unit 3.4 for more information about memory and storage devices.

Graphics Processing Unit (GPU)

Displaying a high-resolution image to the user requires a lot of processing power, especially if the image changes rapidly, as with video, or uses complicated 3D and texture effects, as with computer games. Consequently, display functions are often performed by a dedicated processor, referred to as the **Graphics Processing Unit (GPU)**. This might actually be part of the CPU package or a more powerful GPU might be provided on a plug-in expansion card.

See Unit 3.3 for notes on graphics and displays.

Network Interface

Computers, smartphones, and tablets are almost always used as part of a computer **network**. They can use the network to share information locally and to access data over the **Internet**. There are two main ways of making a network link:

- **Wired network**—on a home network, the computer will be connected to an Internet router via an **Ethernet** port. On a business network, the computer will be connected to the wider network via an Ethernet switch. The Ethernet port in the computer is provided by a **Network Interface Card (NIC)**. Almost all workstation computers come with a NIC on the motherboard (**onboard card**). Servers may have additional NICs supplied on expansion (or **add-on**) cards. The connection to the router is made using a cable with RJ-45 connectors on each end.
- **Wireless network**—most home networks support **Wi-Fi radio networking** so that computing devices do not have to be cabled to the Internet router to access the network. Most laptops, smartphones, and tablets have built in Wi-Fi adapters. Workstation computers more typically have a Wi-Fi add-on card. Most business networks support Wi-Fi via wireless access points.

An Internet router designed for home use actually combines the functions of an Internet modem or bridge, a router, an Ethernet switch, and a Wi-Fi access point. On a business network, these functions are more typically provided by separate appliances. Networking is discussed in more detail in Unit 4.1 and Unit 4.2.

Motherboard Components

If you open up a PC or a laptop, the main thing you will see is the **motherboard** (or **system board**). The motherboard is a **Printed Circuit Board (PCB)** with some built-in processors (the **chipset**), sockets and slots for upgradable components (CPU, RAM, adapter cards, disk drives), and wires (buses) to connect them together.

The motherboard determines the upgrade potential of the computer. If a component is not compatible with the motherboard, it cannot be installed. A component may not be compatible with the motherboard either because it does not *physically fit* in the type of sockets available or because it is too new for the motherboard's chipset to be able to *communicate* with it.

You could upgrade the motherboard itself, but this is rarely cost-effective.

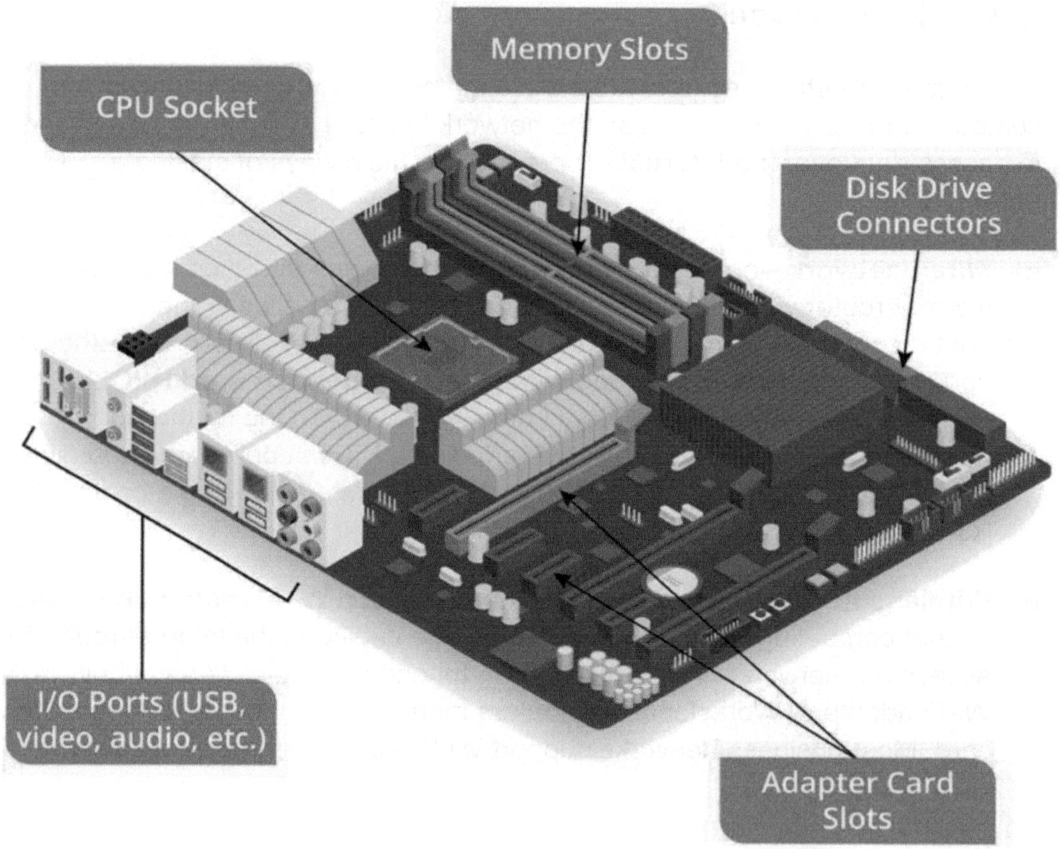

Main components on a PC motherboard. Image © 123rf.com.

The motherboard chipset provides "built-in" functions that might otherwise require an adapter card. Most motherboard chipsets support graphics, audio, and network adapter functions. An add-on card may still be used to upgrade those functions though.

Processors

A **microprocessor** (usually shortened to "processor") is a programmable **integrated circuit**—a silicon chip embedded on a ceramic plate. A silicon chip is a wafer of purified silicon doped with a metal oxide, typically copper or aluminum. The doping process creates millions of transistors and signal pathways within an area called the **die**, which provide the electrical on/off states that are the basis of binary computer systems.

PCs contain a number of processors, but the most important is the **Central Processing Unit (CPU)**. The CPU is commonly described as the "brains" of a computer; in fact, it is better thought of as a very efficient sorting office. The CPU cannot *think*, but it can process simple instructions very, very quickly and efficiently. A computer is only as "clever" as its software.

There have been numerous CPU architectures, developed by the vendors **Intel** and **AMD**, and, within each architecture, a number of different models and for each set of models a brand to position them within a particular market segment. For example, budget PCs, laptops, high-end workstations, and server computers would all be served by different CPU brands and models. The model names are used to market a CPU to consumers, but a model may go through several different versions. The "core" used for a version is given a codename, such as "Haswell," "Skylake," "Piledriver," or "Zen." You will see these names used on PC tech websites and in magazines.

The following list is designed to give you a brief overview of the main brands produced by Intel and AMD.

Intel CPU Brands

- Core—this is Intel's flagship desktop and mobile CPU series. The earliest models (Core Solo and Core Duo) were laptop-only chips. The Core 2 series introduced desktop versions plus 64-bit and multi-core support. The current product line is divided into Core i3, i5, and i7 brands, with i7 representing the best performing models. The Core i*X* brand has been based on successive generations of microarchitectures, named Nehalem, Sandy Bridge, Ivy Bridge, Haswell, Broadwell, and Skylake.

- Pentium—the Pentium used to be Intel's premium 32-bit CPU brand and you may still find Pentium 4-based computers in use. The Pentium brand has been reintroduced to represent "mid-range" CPU models based on the Core microarchitectures.

- Celeron—this has long been Intel's budget brand.

- Atom—this is a brand designating chips designed for low-power portable devices (smartphones and tablets).

- Xeon—this brand is aimed at the server/workstation market. Current Xeons are often differentiated from their Core i counterparts by supporting n-way multiprocessing and ECC memory and coming with larger caches.

AMD CPU Brands

Older AMD brands such as Athlon, Phenom, Sempron, and Turion have been phased out over the last few years. The following brands represent the company's Zen microarchitecture in different segments:

- Ryzen/Threadripper and Ryzen Mobile—this brand now represents AMD's pitch for the high-end enthusiast segment, replacing older AMD FX chips.
- Epyc—AMD's server-class CPU brand, replacing its long-standing Opteron series of chips.

ARM CPUs

CPUs and their chipsets for mobile phones/smartphones and tablets are often based on the **ARM (Advanced RISC Machine)** microarchitecture, such as the Apple A, Samsung Exynos, and nVIDIA Tegra, derivatives. RISC stands for Reduced Instruction Set Computing. RISC microarchitectures use simple instructions processed very quickly. This contrasts with Complex (CISC) microarchitectures, which use more powerful instructions but process each one more slowly. Intel's microarchitecture is CISC with RISC enhancements (micro-ops).

Features of Processors

The CPU is designed to run software programs. When a software program runs (whether it be an operating system, anti-virus utility, or word processing application), it is assembled into machine code instructions utilizing the fundamental **instruction set** of the CPU and loaded into system memory. The CPU then performs the following operations on these instructions:

- The **Control Unit** fetches the next instruction in sequence from system memory to the **pipeline**.
- The control unit decodes each instruction in turn and either executes it itself or passes it to the **Arithmetic Logic Unit (ALU)** or **Floating Point Unit (FPU)** for execution.
- The result of the executed instruction is written back to a **register** or to system memory. A register is a temporary storage area available to the different units within the CPU.

This overview is grossly simplified of course. Over the years, many different internal architectures have been developed to optimize the process of fetch, decode, execute, and writeback, while retaining compatibility with the basic **x86 instruction set**, which defines a CPU as IBM PC compatible.

Instruction Set (32- versus 64-bit)

The original version of x86 created in 1978 was designed for 16-bit CPUs. This means that each instruction is 16-bits "wide." The first 32-bit CPU was introduced in 1985 and the x86 instruction set was updated to a 32-bit version, called x86-32 or IA-32 (Intel Architecture).

AMD developed the AMD64/x86-64/x64 instruction set now used by most 64-bit CPUs in 2003. Intel refers to it as EM64T or Intel 64.

*Note that CPUs feature additional larger registers for floating point calculations and other specialized processing units. It is the **General Purpose (GP)** register size that makes a CPU 32- or 64-bit.*

The main advantage of 64-bit is the ability to use more system memory. 32-bit systems are limited to addressing up to 4 GB whereas systems with 64-bit CPUs can address 256 Terabytes (or more). A 64-bit CPU can run a 64-bit or 32-bit OS. A 32-bit CPU cannot run 64-bit software.

Most workstations and laptops now use 64-bit CPUs. Some budget models might come with a 32-bit chip, though this is increasingly unusual. Almost all server computers would use a 64-bit CPU with only very old servers relying on 32-bit. 64-bit also dominates the premium smartphone and tablet sector, though 32-bit is still prevalent on budget and midrange models.

Clock Speed and Bus Speed

A CPU's **clock speed** is the number of instructions it can process in one second. As a measure of frequency, this value is expressed in **Hertz (Hz)**. Early processors had clock speeds measured in Megahertz (MHz), or 1,000,000 times faster than 1 Hz. Modern CPUs run at 1 Gigahertz (GHz) or better. 1 GHz is 1000 times faster than 1 MHz.

When Intel or AMD release a new CPU, they produce a range of models clocked at different maximum speeds (2 GHz, 2.4 GHz, 2.8 GHz, and 3 GHz for instance). The speed at which the CPU runs is generally seen as a key indicator of performance. This is certainly true when comparing CPUs with the same architecture but is not necessarily the case otherwise. Dual-core CPUs (see below) run slower (up to about 3 GHz) than many earlier single core CPUs (up to about 4 GHz), but deliver better performance.

The core clock speed is the speed at which the CPU runs internal processes and accesses cache (see below). The **Front Side Bus** speed is the interface between the CPU and system memory. The speed of the bus is usually determined by the memory controller, which might be part of the motherboard chipset or part of the CPU.

While older bus speeds are typically measured in MHz, modern bus types and memory interfaces work at GHz speeds. Also, modern memory designs increase bandwidth by transferring data twice per clock cycle (Double Data Rate) and often by transferring data from two memory modules simultaneously (Dual-channel).

Multiprocessing and Dual-core

Trying to make the CPU work faster by increasing the clock speed has the drawbacks of using a lot of power and generating a lot of heat. A different approach to making a computer system faster is to use two or more physical CPUs, referred to as **Symmetric Multiprocessing (SMP)**. An SMP-aware OS can then make efficient use of the processing resources available to run application processes on whichever CPU is available.

SMP means physically installing two or more CPUs in a multi-socket motherboard. Obviously, this adds significantly to the cost and so is only implemented on servers and high-end workstations.

However, improvements in CPU manufacturing techniques have led to another solution: dual-core CPUs, or **Chip Level Multiprocessing (CMP)**. A dual-core CPU is essentially two processors combined on the same die. The market has quickly moved beyond dual-core CPUs to **multi-core** packages with four or eight processors.

System and Expansion Bus Technologies

A **bus** is circuitry that connects the various microprocessors and other components on the motherboard. If you look closely at a motherboard, you will see many tiny wires. These wires are the circuitry that makes up a bus imprinted on the **Printed Circuit Board (PCB)** that is the basis of a motherboard (there are actually multiple layers of circuitry in addition to what you can see on the surface). A bus carries four things:

- **Data**—the information being transferred between components.
- **Address** information—where the data is located in memory.
- **Timing** signal—as different components can work at different speeds, the system clock synchronizes the way they communicate over the bus.
- **Power**—electricity to run the component.

A PC system has two main types of bus: the system (or local) bus and the expansion bus.

- The **system** bus, also referred to as the **Front Side Bus (FSB)** or **local bus**, provides connections between the CPU and system memory.
- The **expansion** bus, also called the **Input/Output (I/O) bus**, provides connections between the CPU and add-on components, which can be integrated onto the motherboard, installed as expansion cards, or connected as peripheral devices.

The architecture of the expansion bus depends on what generation the motherboard and CPU platform are. Broadly speaking, since 1993, PC architecture has been based on one of **Peripheral Component Interconnect (PCI)**, **PCI with AGP (Accelerated Graphics Port)**, or **PCI Express (PCIe)**.

The main characteristics of these technologies are summarized below:

Bus	Bandwidth	Notes
PCI (32-bit)	133 MBps	Very old but still used on some desktops for compatibility; bandwidth is shared between all devices attached to the bus.
AGP	2133 MBps	Used for old graphics adapters only.
PCI Express (PCIe) 1.0	250 MBps per lane	Can use x1, x2, x8, or x16 lanes depending on the size of the slot; uses point-to-point links so each device gets the full bandwidth of the number of lanes it supports.
PCIe x16	4 GBps	Graphics adapters typically use x16 lanes.
PCIe 2.0	500 MBps per lane	Version 2 doubles the bandwidth per lane.
PCIe 2.0 x16	8 GBps	
PCIe 3.0	1 GBps per lane	Version 3 doubles the bandwidth per lane again.

A new computer would most likely have a PCIe x16 slot for a graphics adapter, one or two PCIe x1 slots, and one or two PCI slots for backward compatibility.

System Cooling

As a by-product of pushing electric current through the various electronic components in the computer, the system generates heat. The faster the components work, the more heat is produced. Excessive temperatures can cause the components to malfunction or even damage them. One of the most significant problems with CPUs (and RAM chips and graphics cards) is their thermal output. While Intel and AMD are both focusing on making new CPU designs more thermally-efficient, all CPUs require cooling. Also, a specific CPU model requires a specific cooling system, as some run hotter than others; the old Pentium 4 CPUs being a good example.

There are several ways of dissipating heat from the system case.

Heatsinks and Thermal Paste

A **heatsink** is a block of metal with fins. As the fins expose a larger surface area to the air around the component, a greater cooling effect by convection is achieved. The heatsink is "glued" to the surface of the chip using **thermal paste**, also referred to as thermal grease or compound, to ensure the best transfer of heat.

A heatsink is a **passive cooling** device. Passive cooling means that it does not require extra energy (electricity) to work. In order to work well, a heatsink requires good airflow around the PC. It is important to try to keep "cable clutter" to a minimum and to keep the PC interior free from dust.

As heatsinks are bulky objects with a lot of height, they cannot be used in laptops or other mobiles. Computers with thin cases use a **heat spreader** instead. This is a flat tube with liquid inside. As the component heats up the liquid, it moves to another part of the tube and is cooled down by a fan or other type of convection. The cooler liquid then passes back over the component, heats up again, and moves away, creating a constant cooling cycle.

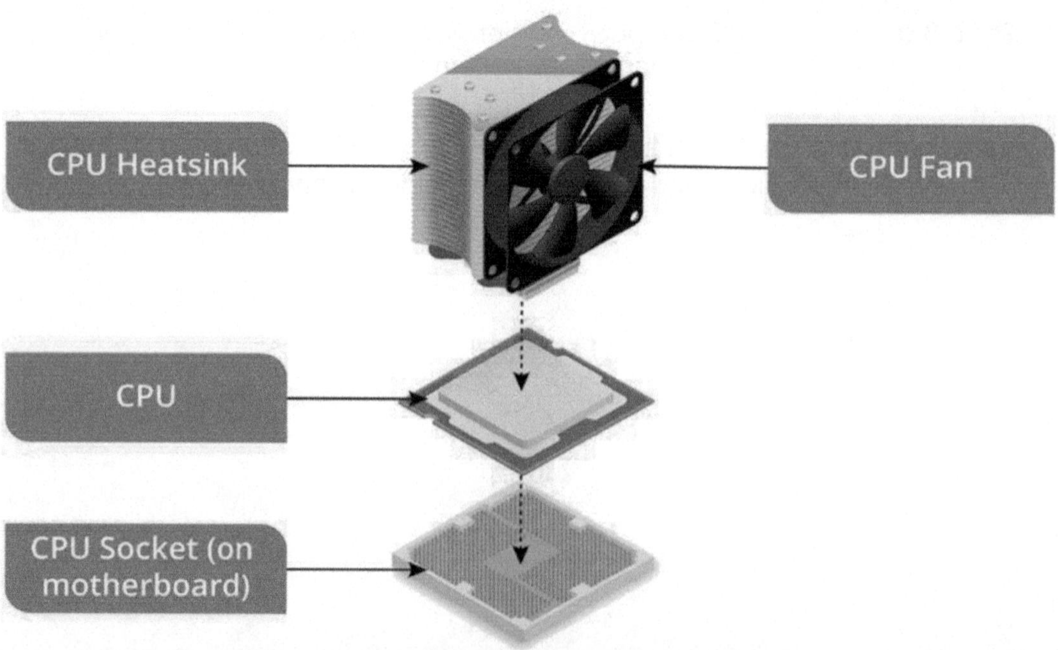

CPU heatsink and fan assembly. Image © 123rf.com.

Fans

Many PCs have components that generate more heat than can be removed by passive cooling. A **fan** improves air flow and so helps to dissipate heat. Fans are used for the power supply and chassis exhaust points. The fan system will be designed to draw cool air from vents in the front of the case over the motherboard and expel warmed air from the back of the case.

Fan for a PC case. Image © 123rf.com.

Typically, the speed of the fan is varied according to the temperature and sensors are used to detect whether a fan has failed.

Smaller fans may be used to improve the performance of the heatsink on the CPU, GPUs, and even hard disks.

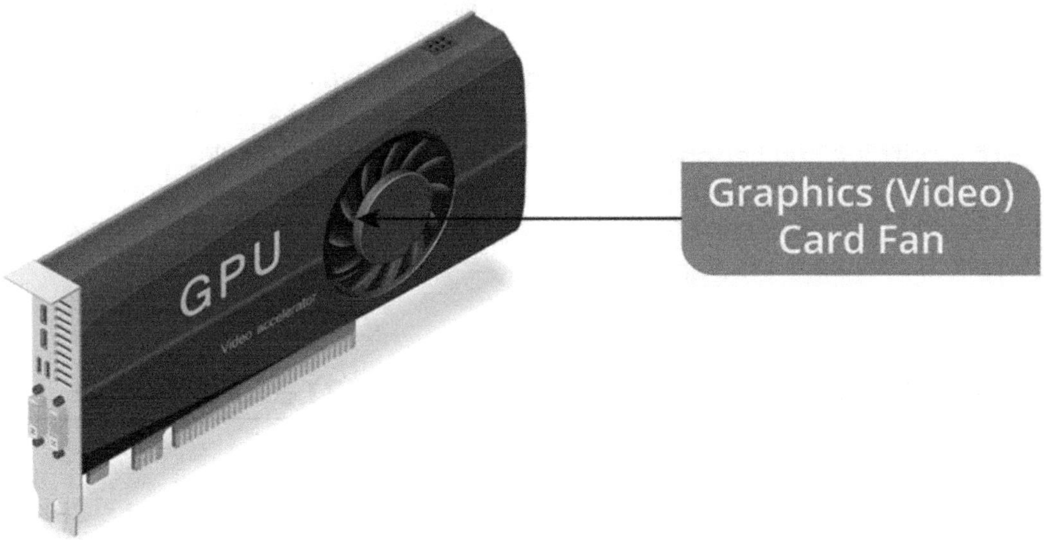

Fan assembly to cool the processor on a graphics (video) adapter card, Image © 123rf.com.

A fan is an **active cooling** device. It requires power to run. Power is supplied to a CPU or case fan by connecting its power connector to an appropriate header on the motherboard.

Liquid-based Cooling Systems

PCs used for high-end gaming, those with twin graphics cards for instance, and with overclocked components may generate more heat than basic thermal management can cope with. PCs used where the ambient temperature is very high may also require exceptional cooling measures.

Liquid-cooled PC design. Photo ©123rf.com.

Liquid-based cooling refers to a system of pumping water around the chassis. Water is a more effective coolant than air convection and a good pump can run more quietly than numerous fans. On the downside, liquid cooling makes maintenance and upgrades more difficult, requires comparatively more power to run, and is costly. Liquid cooling is an active cooling technology as the pump requires power to run.

BIOS and UEFI System Firmware

When a computer is powered on, it needs some standard means for the CPU to start processing instructions and initialize the other components. This is referred to as **bootstrapping** or more simply as **booting**. The bootstrapping process occurs before the operating system software is loaded and is enabled by a low-level operating system called **firmware**.

The **BIOS (Basic Input/Output System)** is one example of PC firmware. It provides industry standard program code to get the essential components of the PC running and ensures that the design of each manufacturer's motherboard is PC compatible.

Newer motherboards may use a different kind of firmware called **UEFI (Unified Extensible Firmware Interface)**. UEFI provides support for 64-bit CPU operation at boot, a full GUI and mouse operation at boot, and better boot security. A computer with UEFI may also support booting in a legacy BIOS mode.

System Firmware Setup Program

Low-level PC settings affecting the operation of the motherboard can be configured via the system firmware setup program. This may also be referred to as CMOS setup, BIOS setup, or UEFI setup.

The term "CMOS Setup" is still widely used because the settings used to be stored on a chip with CMOS RAM. CMOS RAM is obsolete but the term persists.

Press the key to enter setup before or during the memory count.

You can normally access the system setup program with a keystroke during the power-on (boot) process. The key combination used will vary from system to system; typical examples are `ESC`, `DEL`, `F1`, `F2`, or `F10`. The PC's documentation will explain how to access the setup program; often a message with the required key is displayed when you boot the PC.

One issue with modern computers is that the boot process can be very quick. If this is the case, you can `SHIFT`*+click the Restart button from the Windows logon screen to access UEFI boot options. Alternatively, the motherboard vendor may supply a tool for disabling fast boot or accessing the setup program.*

You navigate a legacy BIOS setup program using the keyboard arrow keys. Pressing **ESC** generally returns to the previous screen. When closing setup, there will be an option to exit and discard changes or exit and save changes. Sometimes this is done with a key (**ESC** versus **F10** for instance), but more often there is a prompt. There will also be an option to reload the default settings, in case you want to discard any customizations you have made.

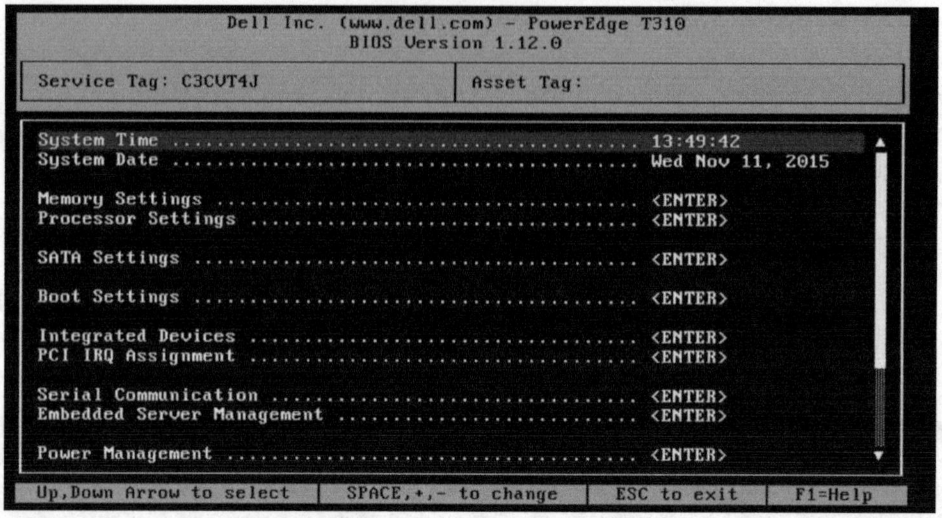

System firmware BIOS setup program.

UEFI Setup Programs

A UEFI setup program may feature a graphical interface with mouse support.

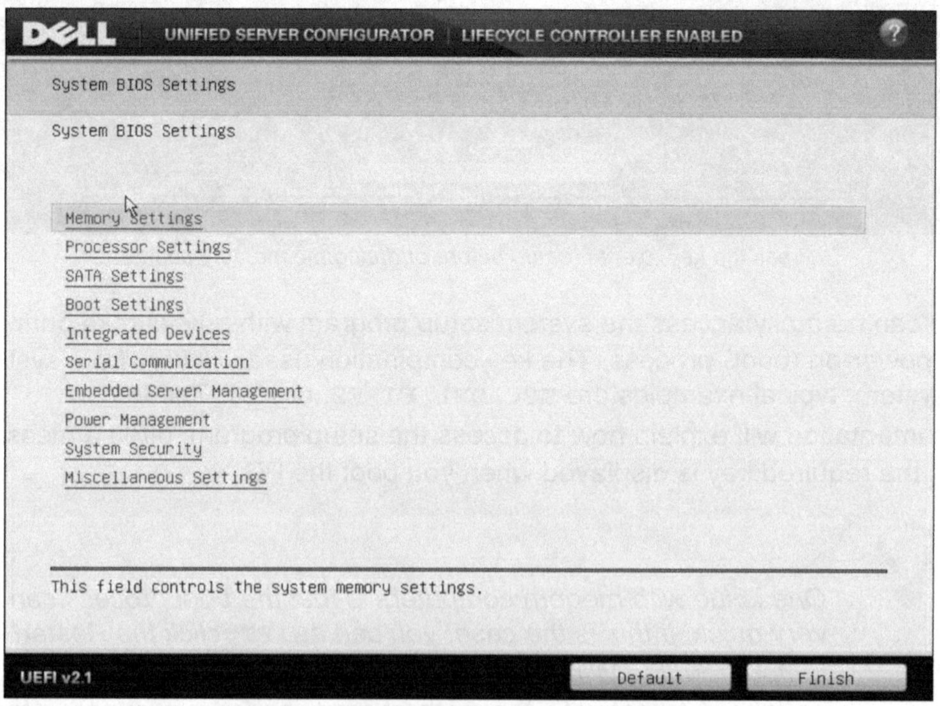

UEFI system setup software with a full GUI and mouse support.

Review Questions / Module 3 / Unit 1 / System Components

Answer these questions to test what you have learned in this unit. You can review the model answers at the end of the book.

1) What type of component provides persistent storage?
2) What computer component is most restrictive in terms of determining upgrade potential for a desktop computer?
3) True or false? A plug-in card is always required to support PC sound.
4) What is the main advantage of using a CPU in 64-bit mode?
5) What is a typical speed for a modern CPU to run at?
6) You want to purchase a computer with a fast graphics interface. What type of expansion slot should you look for?
7) What type of component provides a passive cooling solution?
8) How would you access the system setup program on a PC?

Lab 11 / Specifying PC Systems

You should make yourself familiar with the sort of cost associated with different types of desktop, laptop, netbook, and handheld computers. Vendors such as HP (hp.com) and Dell (dell.com) have online stores where you can build computers to order. Use one or two of the sites to try to obtain specifications for the following requirements (all budgets to *exclude* sales taxes and delivery).

- Tower case business system (no monitor required) for $300.
- Portable (laptop or netbook) for basic word processing, email, and web access for $500.
- Ultraportable business laptop with fast CPU and memory for $800.
- Desktop media center/gaming PC with high specification graphics and premium HD widescreen flat-panel display for $2000.

When you have obtained the specifications, use the component vendors' sites to compare some of the technologies (CPU and graphics card models for instance).

Module 3 / Unit 2
Using Device Interfaces

Objectives

On completion of this unit, you will be able to:

- Distinguish peripheral, graphics, and networking interfaces and their uses.
- Install and configure input devices.

Syllabus Objectives and Content Examples

This unit covers the following exam domain objectives and content examples:

- 2.1 Classify common types of input/output device interfaces.
  Networking (Wired [Telephone connector (RJ-11), Ethernet connector (RJ-45)], Wireless [Bluetooth, NFC]) • Peripheral device (USB, FireWire, Thunderbolt, Bluetooth, RF) • Graphic device (VGA, HDMI, DVI, DisplayPort, Mini-DisplayPort)
- 2.2 Given a scenario, set up and install common peripheral devices to a laptop/PC.
  Devices (Keyboard, Mouse)

Computer Port and Connector Types

Whether the computer is a desktop or laptop, the system case contains the computer **motherboard**. The motherboard connects all the other computer components together. One of its functions is to provide the **ports** used to attach peripheral devices and cabling to the computer. These **Input/Output (I/O)** ports are positioned so that they appear through holes cut in the case.

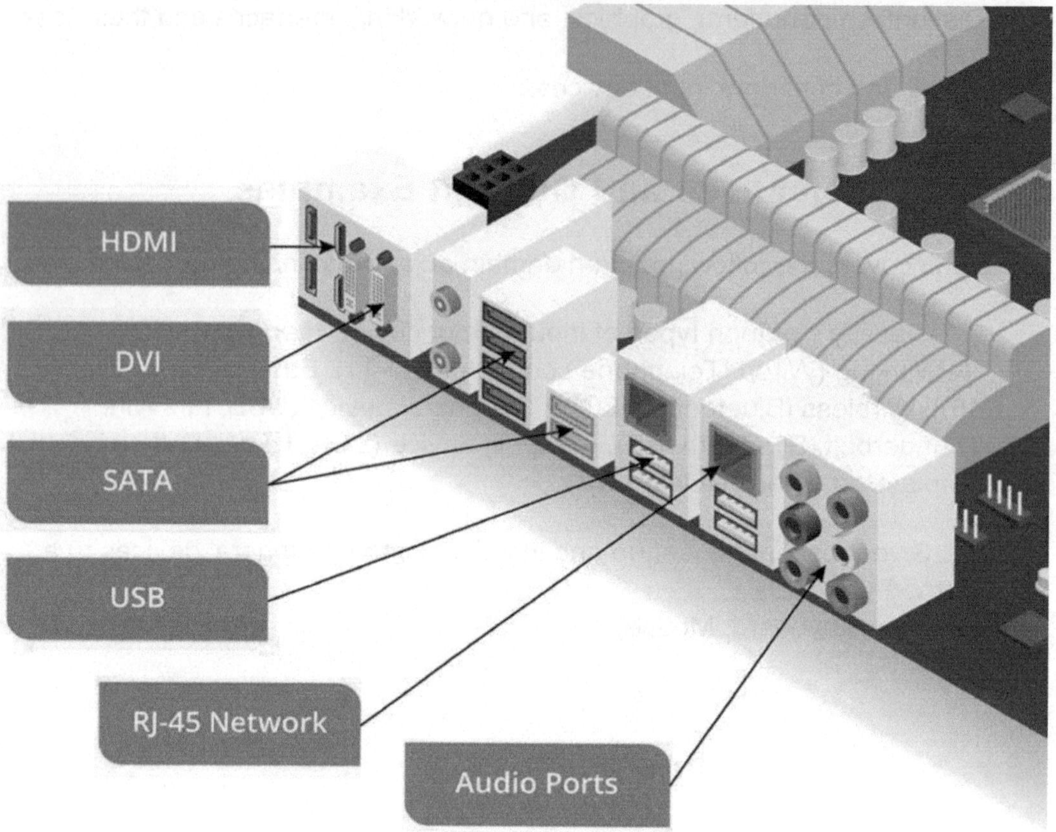

I/O ports on a motherboard. Image © 123rf.com.

Ports and connectors are described as male (pins) or female (holes). Connectors are usually male (with pins); ports are usually female (with holes).

On a desktop, there may be ports at the front and back of the computer. Laptop ports are positioned around the edge of the case.

USB and Firewire

The **Universal Serial Bus (USB)** has become the standard means of connecting peripheral devices to a computer. USB devices are **Plug-and-Play**. This means that when a device is connected via the port, Windows can identify the device and try to install a **driver** for it (make the device usable) automatically. Another feature of USB is that devices are **hot-swappable**. This means that Windows can detect and configure a device without requiring a restart.

As well as providing a data connection, USB can supply enough power (about 4.5W) over the cable to run small devices. Devices that require more power than this, such as optical drives or printers, must be connected to an external power supply.

USB Type A port and connector. Image © 123rf.com.

Devices supporting fast charging can supply 7.5W if the port is in charging mode (no data transfer is possible in charging mode). Devices conforming to the USB Power Delivery version 2.0 specification are able to deliver up to 100W of power.

USB Ports and Connectors

There are several types of USB connector:

- Type A—for connection to the host. The connector and port are shaped like flat rectangles.
- Type B—for connection to a device. The connector and port are square, with a beveled top. There are also small form factor versions of the type B connector and port:
    - Type B Mini—a smaller connector for connection to a device. This type of connector was seen on early digital cameras but is no longer widely used.
    - Type B Micro—an updated connector for smaller devices, such as smartphones and tablets. The micro connector is distinctively flatter than the older mini type connector.

- Type C—a new reversible connector type (can be inserted either way up).

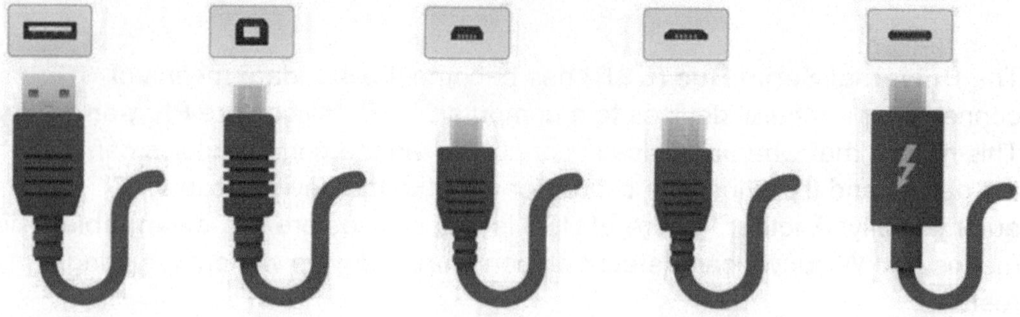

USB ports and connectors (from left to right): Type A, Type B, Mini Type B, Micro Type B, Type C. Image © 123rf.com.

Type A and B USB connectors are always inserted with the USB symbol ( ) facing up. Type C (USB-C) connectors are reversible (can be inserted either way up). There are various converter cables with different connector types on each end (for example, a USB Type A to USB-C cable).

USB Data Rates

The data rate for USB 1.1 is 12 Mbps (mega*bits* per second) while the **USB 2.0 (Hi-Speed)** standard has a nominal data rate of 480 Mbps. USB 2.0 uses the same connectors as USB 1.1 but a USB 1.1 device plugged into a USB 2.0 port will operate at the lower speed.

Note that this bandwidth is shared *between all devices attached to the same host.*

The USB 3.0 standard introduces a **SuperSpeed** mode. SuperSpeed improves the bus bandwidth tenfold (to 5 Gbps or 5000 Mbps) and makes the link full duplex, so a device can send and receive at up to 5 Gbps simultaneously. USB 3.x receptacles and connectors often have a blue connector tab or housing to distinguish them.

USB 3.1 defines a SuperSpeed+ mode with a data rate of 10 Gbps.

Firewire

The **Firewire** bus was based on the IEEE 1394 standard and the Small Computer System Interface (SCSI) communications protocol. Firewire was a competitor to USB but never received mainstream support amongst PC vendors. It was used on some Apple Mac computers. If you do encounter a Firewire device and the motherboard does not provide Firewire ports, an expansion card can be fitted.

This is the symbol used to denote a Firewire Port:

A single bus can connect up to 63 devices. Like USB, the bus is powered and supports hot swapping.

The Firewire 400 standard used 6-pin "alpha" connectors and cabling. The 6-pin connectors slightly resemble USB but have a beveled edge on one side. There is also a 4-pin unpowered connector.

The maximum transfer rate is 400 Mbps.

The IEEE 1394b (Firewire 800) standard supported transfer rates up to 800 Mbps. Firewire 800 used 9-pin ("beta") connectors and cabling.

Firewire ports and cables with "alpha" 6-pin connector on the left and 4-pin connector on the right. Image © 123rf.com.

Graphics Devices

While USB is used to connect a wide range of different peripheral devices, including keyboards, mice, scanners, cameras, and printers, it is not used to connect the **computer display** or **graphics device**. The graphics interface can be provided by a number of different technologies.

A computer's graphics system involves some sort of display unit, such as a flat-panel screen, connected to the computer via a **video card** (or **graphics adapter**). The video card generates the signals to send to the screen and provides support for one or more connection interfaces. Low-end graphics adapters are likely to be included as part of the motherboard or CPU. If a computer is to be used for 3D gaming or multimedia work, a better-quality **expansion adapter** is required. This is often one of the key features distinguishing budget desktops and laptops from premium versions.

Most graphics adapters are based on chipsets by ATI/AMD (Radeon chipset), nVIDIA (GeForce and nForce chipsets), SiS, VIA, and Intel.

Resolution and Color Depth

A computer image is made up of a number of **pixels**. The number of horizontal and vertical pixels gives the resolution of the image. Each pixel can be a different color. The total number of colors supported in the image is referred to as the **color depth** (or **bit depth**).

The other important component of video is the speed at which the display is refreshed, measured in Hertz (Hz). Increasing any one of these factors increases the amount of bandwidth required for the video signal and the amount of processing that the CPU or GPU (Graphics Processing Unit) must do and the amount of system or graphics memory required.

IBM created **VGA (Video Graphics Array)** as a standard for the resolution and color depth of computer displays. VGA specifies a resolution of 640x480 with 16 colors (4-bit color) at 60 Hz. The VGA standard is long obsolete but was further developed by the **Video Electronics Standards Association (VESA)** as **Super VGA (SVGA)**. SVGA was originally 800x600 @ 4-bit or 8-bit color. This was very quickly extended as the capabilities of graphics cards increased with the de facto **XGA** standard providing 1024x768 resolution, better color depths (16- and 32-bit), and higher refresh rates.

Resolutions for modern display systems use some variant of the XGA "standard" (in fact, these are labels rather than standards). Most computer displays now use a widescreen form factor (16:10) with a High Definition (HD) resolution such as 1280x720, 1360x768, 1600x900, or 1920x1080 (Full HD). Larger display devices are likely to use even higher resolution, such as 3840x2160 (4K or Ultra HD).

Consumer widescreen (for DVD movies) is 16:9 but many PC widescreen display formats are 16:10 to leave room for on-screen controls above or below the movie.

Graphic Device Interfaces

There are many different types of graphic device/display connectors and cabling. Many video adapters and display screens come with more than one type. When computers were primarily used with Cathode Ray Tube (CRT) monitors, the graphics adapter would generate an **analog** video signal to drive the monitor. Now that most screens use flat-panel technology, the video signal is usually **digital**.

High Definition Multimedia Interface (HDMI)

The **High Definition Multimedia Interface (HDMI)** is the most widely used graphic device interface. It is ubiquitous on consumer electronics, such as televisions and Blu-Ray players, as well as computer equipment. HDMI supports both video and audio digital streams, plus remote control (CEC) and digital content protection (HDCP).

HDMI cabling is specified to different HDMI versions, the latest being 2.1. Newer versions support higher bandwidths and consequently better resolutions (4K UHD for instance). HDMI uses a proprietary 19-pin (Type A) connector.

HDMI Type A port and connector. Image © 123rf.com.

HDMI v1.3 introduced the Mini HDMI connector (Type C) for use on portable devices, such as camcorders. This is more compact but has the same number of pins. HDMI v1.4 also introduces the even smaller Micro HDMI connector (Type D), still with 19 pins.

DisplayPort and Thunderbolt

HDMI was principally developed by consumer electronics companies (Hitachi, Panasonic, Sony, and so on) and requires a royalty to use. **DisplayPort** was developed by VESA, the organization largely representing PC graphics adapter and display technology companies. It is a royalty-free standard intended to "complement" HDMI.

DisplayPort uses a 20-pin connector. A **DP++** port allows a connection with DVI-D and HDMI devices (using a suitable adapter cable). There is also a mini DisplayPort format (MiniDP or mDP), developed by Apple and licensed to other vendors.

DP++ DisplayPort port and connector. Image © 123rf.com.

The **Thunderbolt (TB)** interface was developed by Intel and is primarily used on Apple workstations and laptops. Thunderbolt can be used as a display interface (like DisplayPort) and as a general peripheral interface (like USB or Firewire). In its first two versions, Thunderbolt uses the same physical interface as MiniDP and is compatible with DisplayPort, so that displays with a MiniDP port can be connected to a host via Thunderbolt. TB ports are distinguished from MiniDP by a lightning bolt icon.

Thunderbolt ports and connectors—on the left is the version 1 and 2 connector (same as MiniDP) while the image on the right shows the USB-C form factor adopted for Thunderbolt 3. Image © 123rf.com.

Version 2 of the standard supports links of up to 20 Gbps. Up to six devices can be connected to a single port by daisy-chaining the devices. You can also use a dock or hub device to channel a variety of ports (TB, USB, HDMI, and Ethernet for instance) via a single Thunderbolt port on the host PC or laptop.

Thunderbolt version 3 changes the physical interface to use the same port, connector, and cabling as USB-C. Converter cables are available to connect Thunderbolt 1 or 2 devices to Thunderbolt 3 ports. A USB device plugged into a Thunderbolt 3 port will function normally but Thunderbolt devices will not work if connected to a USB port. Thunderbolt 3 supports up to 40 Gbps over a short, high-quality cable (up to 0.5m/1.6ft).

Digital Visual Interface (DVI)

Digital Visual Interface (DVI) is a high-quality digital interface designed for flat-panel display equipment. There are several types of DVI. The pin configuration of the ports and connectors identifies what type of DVI is supported.

- Single- or dual-link—dual-link makes more bandwidth available. This may be required for resolutions better than HDTV (1920x1200).
- Analog and/or digital—DVI-I supports analog equipment (such as CRTs) and digital. DVI-A supports only analog equipment, and DVI-D supports only digital.

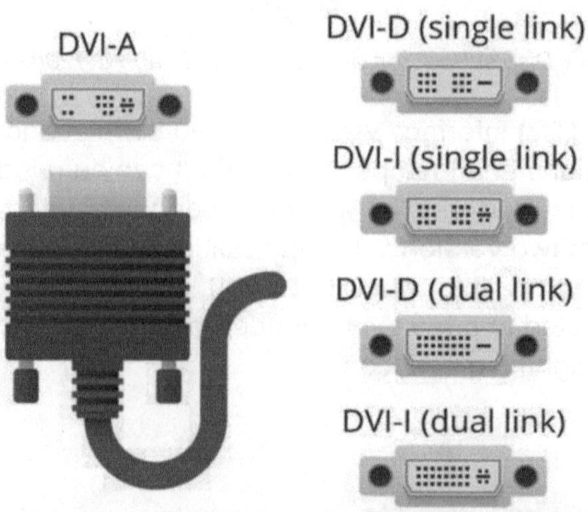

DVI port and connector types. Image © 123rf.com

DVI has been superseded by HDMI and DisplayPort/Thunderbolt but was very widely used on graphics adapters and computer displays. HDMI is backward-compatible with DVI-D using a suitable adapter cable. This means that (for example) a DVI-D graphics adapter could be connected to an HDMI port on the display device.

Video Graphics Array (VGA)

The distinctive blue, 15-pin **Video Graphics Array (VGA)** port (HD15F/DE-15) is a legacy analog video interface for PC devices. Many graphics adapters and display screens continue to support it.

VGA port and connector. Image © 123rf.com.

The connector is a D-shell type (HD15M) with screws to secure it to the port. The interface is analog, meaning that it carries a continuous, variable signal. The interface carries Red, Green, and Blue (RGB) component video signals. As this signal must be converted to work with digital displays, VGA is not very efficient and is not as reliable as other interfaces at supporting high resolutions.

Input Devices

Input devices, or **Human Interface Devices (HID)**, are peripherals that enable the user to enter data and select commands.

Keyboard

The **keyboard** is the longest serving type of input device. Historically, keyboards used the PS/2 interface, which had a round connector with pins. A keyboard PS/2 port is colored purple to differentiate it from the otherwise identical mouse connector. Modern keyboards use USB or Bluetooth ports however.

Extended PC keyboards feature a number of special command keys. These include **`ALT`** and **`CTRL`** plus keys such as **`PRINT SCREEN`**, **`NUM LOCK`**, **`SCROLL LOCK`**, **`START`**, **`SHORTCUT`**, and **`FUNCTION`**. Multimedia keyboards may also feature programmable keys and buttons that can be used for web browsing, playing CD/DVDs, and so on.

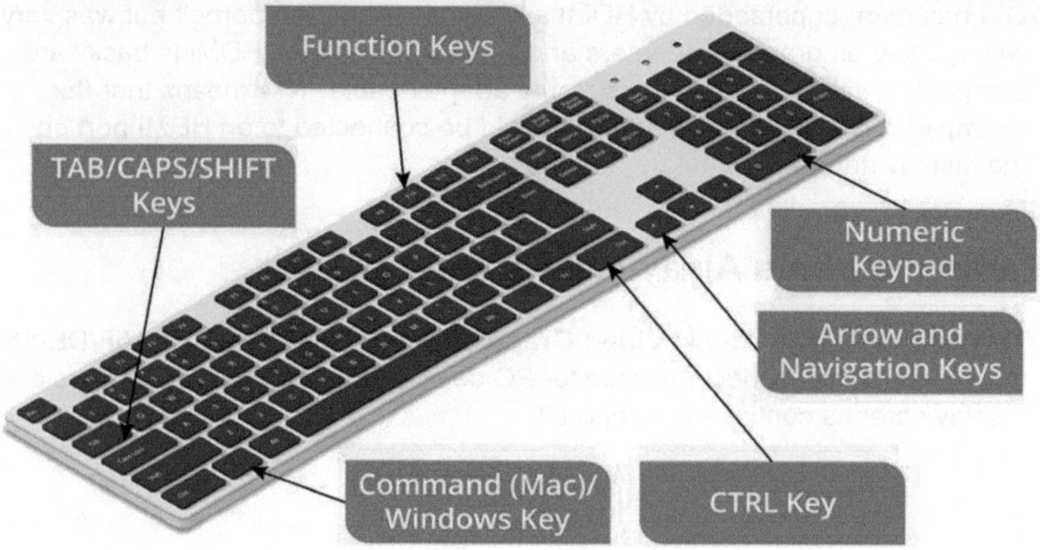

Special keys on a PC keyboard. Image © 123rf.com.

Mouse

The **mouse** is the main type of input device for graphical software. It is an example of a class of input devices described as **pointing devices**. A pointing device is used to move an on-screen cursor to select screen objects and text.

Mice can use PS/2 (the one for the mouse is color-coded green), USB, or Bluetooth connections. There are three distinct types of mice:

- Mechanical mouse—this contains rollers to detect the movement of a ball housed within the mouse case. As the user moves the mouse on a mat or other firm surface, the ball is moved and the rollers and circuitry translate that motion to move a cursor on the screen. Mechanical mice are no longer in production.
- Optical mouse—this uses LEDs to detect movement over a surface.
- Laser mouse—this uses an infrared laser, which gives greater precision than an optical mouse.

Another distinguishing feature of different mouse models is the number of buttons (between two and many), which can be customized to different functions, and the presence of a scroll wheel, used (obviously) for scrolling and as a clickable extra button. Mice are also distinguished by their size and shape. Smaller mice are useful with portable systems; some mice are marketed on the basis of their ergonomic shape.

Laptop Keyboards and Touchpads

Laptops have built-in keyboards. On smaller laptops, the keyboard may not feature full size keys, which can make typing difficult. Laptop keyboards do not often have numeric keypads either. Instead, the keypad functions are accessed using the `FN` (Function) key or by toggling `NUM LOCK`. The `FN` key also accesses laptop specific functions indicated by distinctive color-accented icons. These include switching the display output between the built-in screen and a connected monitor, adjusting the screen brightness, switching to battery power, disabling wireless functions, and so on.

A laptop also has a built-in **touchpad**, replicating the function of the mouse. To use a pad, you move your finger over the surface to move the cursor and tap the pad to click. Touchpads come with buttons and (usually) scroll areas to replicate the function of a mouse's scroll wheel.

None of the input devices on a laptop are really suitable for sustained use. An external keyboard and/or mouse can of course be connected using a USB or Bluetooth port.

Stylus Pen

A **stylus pen** can be used with a compatible touch display or graphics tablet. The stylus can be used like a mouse to select commands, but its main functions are for handwriting and drawing. Most touchscreens are now operated primarily with fingers rather than a stylus. Styluses for art applications can be fitted with nibs of different thicknesses and characters.

Digitizer and stylus. Image © 123rf.com.

Configuring Peripherals

Peripheral devices can be configured using a mixture of the properties dialogs provided for standard Windows device drivers and the vendor's own driver (if available).

Configuring a Mouse

Mice can be installed on PS/2, USB, or wireless ports depending on the model.

- PS/2—connect the mouse to the PS/2 port marked with a mouse icon (usually color-coded green) then switch on the PC.
- USB—connect the mouse to any USB port. USB is hot-swappable so you can attach the mouse when the computer is already switched on.
- Wireless—make sure the computer has a working wireless adapter and put a charged battery in the mouse. The mouse generally needs to be synchronized with the receiver using a push button (check the instructions for details) or paired with a Bluetooth receiver.

A standard mouse does not need a special driver installing and basic settings can be configured using the **Mouse** applet in **Control Panel/Settings**. However, to access and configure extra buttons on some mice you will need to install the manufacturer's driver.

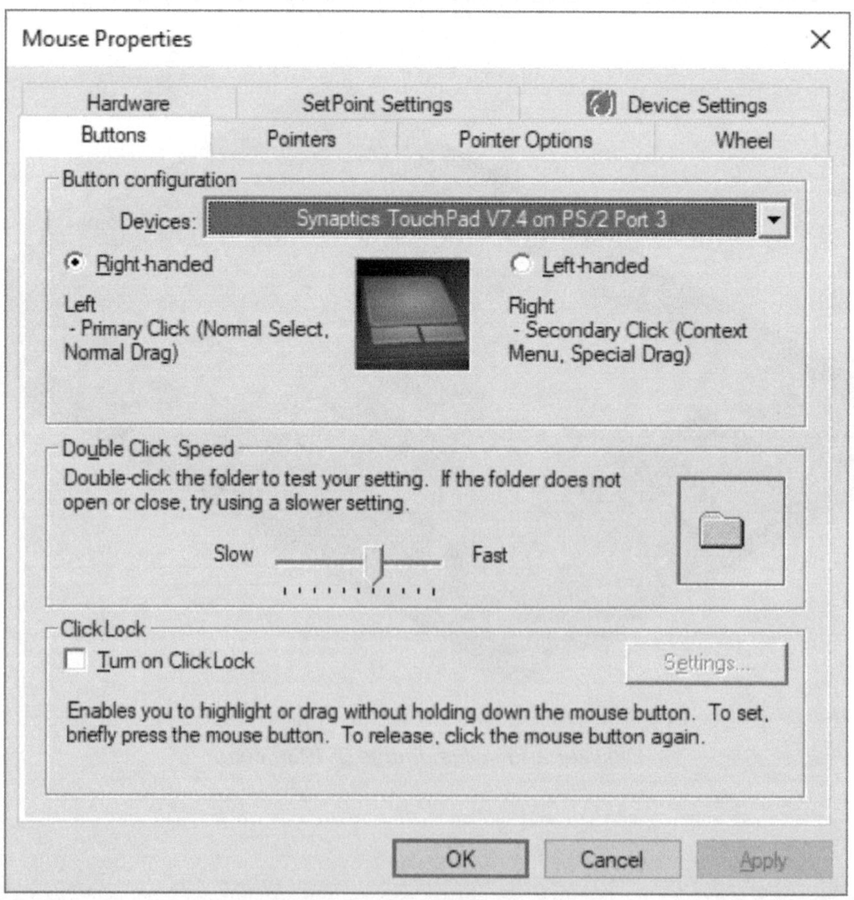

The Mouse applet in Control Panel allows you to configure both mice and touchpads. Installing the vendor's driver makes extra configuration settings available. Screenshot used with permission from Microsoft.

Configuring a Keyboard

A keyboard is connected in the same way as a mouse. You use the **Keyboard** applet in **Control Panel** to configure it.

The main options are to set the repeat rate and sensitivity for keys.

Multimedia keyboards will also have programmable keys and key combos.

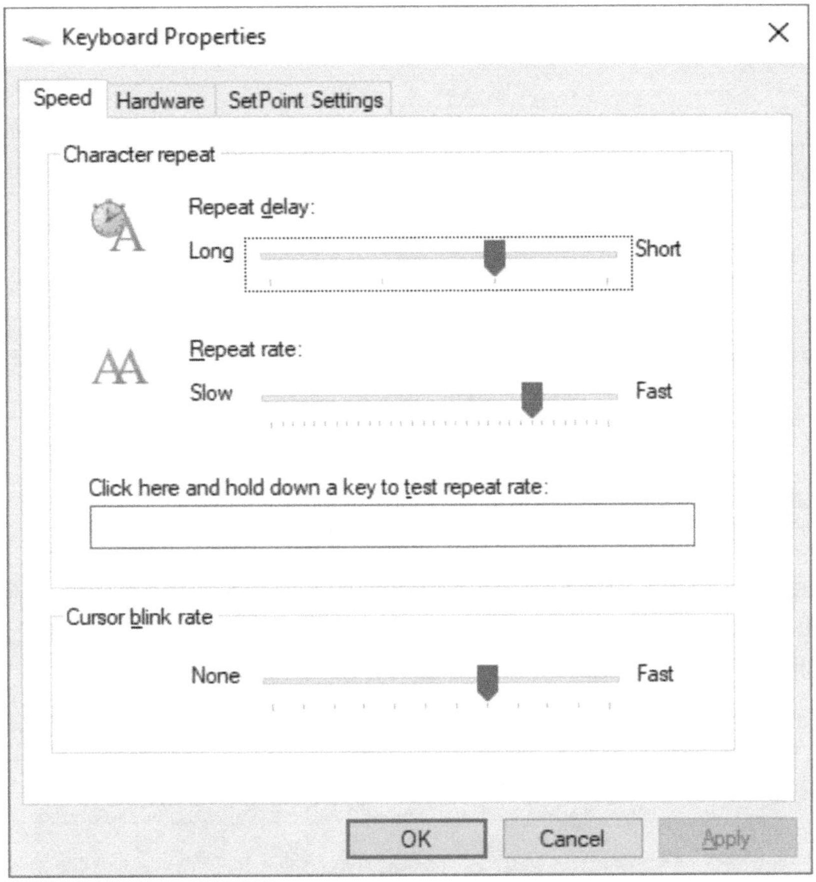

Keyboard applet in Control Panel. Screenshot used with permission from Microsoft.

Keyboard Regionalization

PC keyboards can vary from country to country. Where a country uses the Latin alphabet, the variations may be minor. For example, US and UK keyboards vary only in the location of some of the symbols. A keyboard that uses a non-Latin alphabet is considerably different of course. The type of keyboard layout is configured through the **Language** applet in Control Panel/Settings so that the computer knows which symbol to use when a particular key or key combination is pressed.

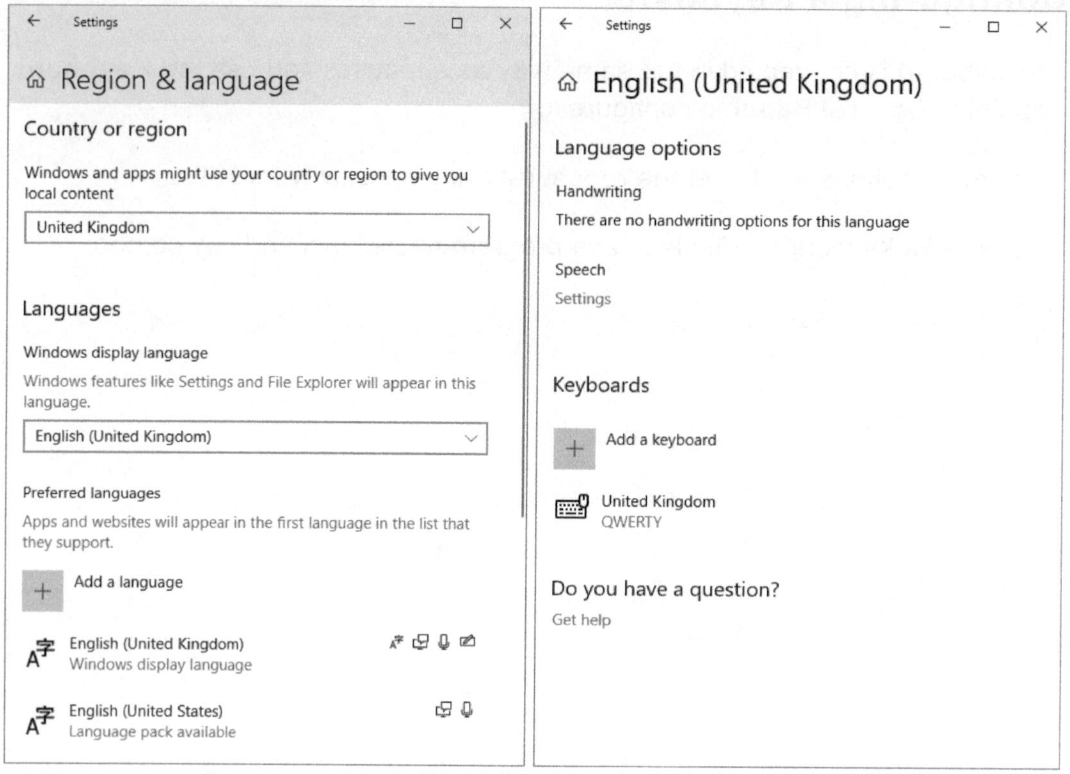

Adding language and input options using the Settings app in Windows 10. Screenshot used with permission from Microsoft.

If multiple layouts are enabled, a key combo (**START+SPACEBAR** in Windows 10) can be used to switch between them (and that this is quite easy to do by accident).

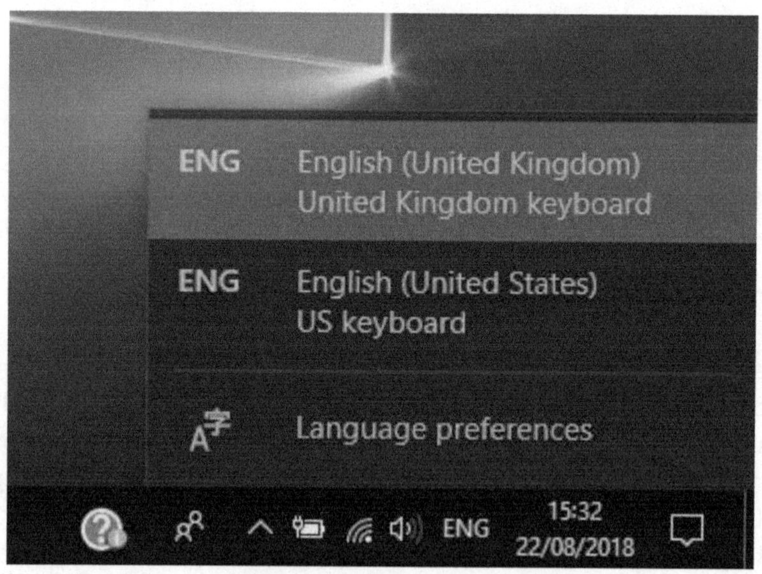

Switching keyboard layouts using the language icon in the notification area. Screenshot used with permission from Microsoft.

Configuring a Pen/Stylus

A **pen** (or **stylus**) can be used with a touchscreen to operate Windows and enter text. Handwriting recognition software can then convert this into characters that can be edited in word processing software.

Tablets can also be operated using touch and gesture recognition.

You configure the pen and gestures via the **Pen and Touch** applet in Control Panel.

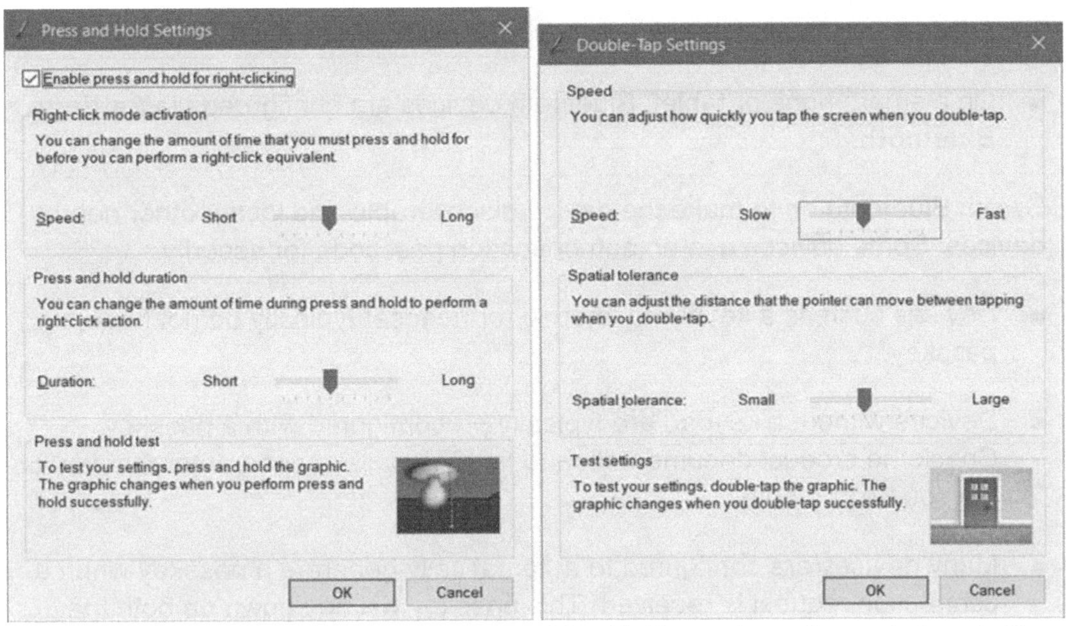

Pen and Touch settings for Press and Hold and Double-Tap gestures. Screenshot used with permission from Microsoft.

Bluetooth

Bluetooth is used for so-called Personal Area Networks (PAN) to share data with a PC, connect to a printer, use a wireless headset, connect to a wireless mouse/keyboard, and so on. Bluetooth is a radio-based technology but it is designed to work only over close range.

Bluetooth is quoted to work at distances of up to 10 meters (30 feet) for Class 2 devices or one meter (three feet) for Class 3 devices. There are also Class 1 devices that work at a range of 100m, but these are restricted to industrial applications. Devices supporting the **Bluetooth 2.0—Enhanced Data Rate (EDR)** standard have a maximum transfer rate of 3 Mbps; otherwise the maximum rate is 1 Mbps.

Bluetooth 3 supports a 24 Mbps HighSpeed (HS) mode, but this uses a specially negotiated Wi-Fi link rather the Bluetooth connection itself.

Configuring Bluetooth

To set up Bluetooth, you need to "pair" or "bond" the device with the computer. This is done by putting the devices into discoverable mode.

- On devices such as mice and keyboards this is normally done by pressing a recessed switch.
- In Windows, you manage Bluetooth devices using the **Settings** app. Click the **Devices** category and select the **Bluetooth & other devices** tab. There should also be an icon for Bluetooth in the notification area to provide easy access to the configuration settings.
- On a smartphone or tablet, Bluetooth devices are configured via **Settings > Bluetooth**.

Switch Bluetooth on to make the device discoverable and locate other nearby devices. Some devices use an authentication passcode for security.

- Devices such as a keyboard, mouse, or headset typically do not have a passkey.
- Devices without a keypad are typically preconfigured with a passkey. Check the product documentation to find the passkey and enter that key on the source computer.
- Many devices are configured to automatically generate a passkey when a connection request is received. This passkey will be shown on both the source and destination device. Input or confirm the key on both devices to accept the connection.

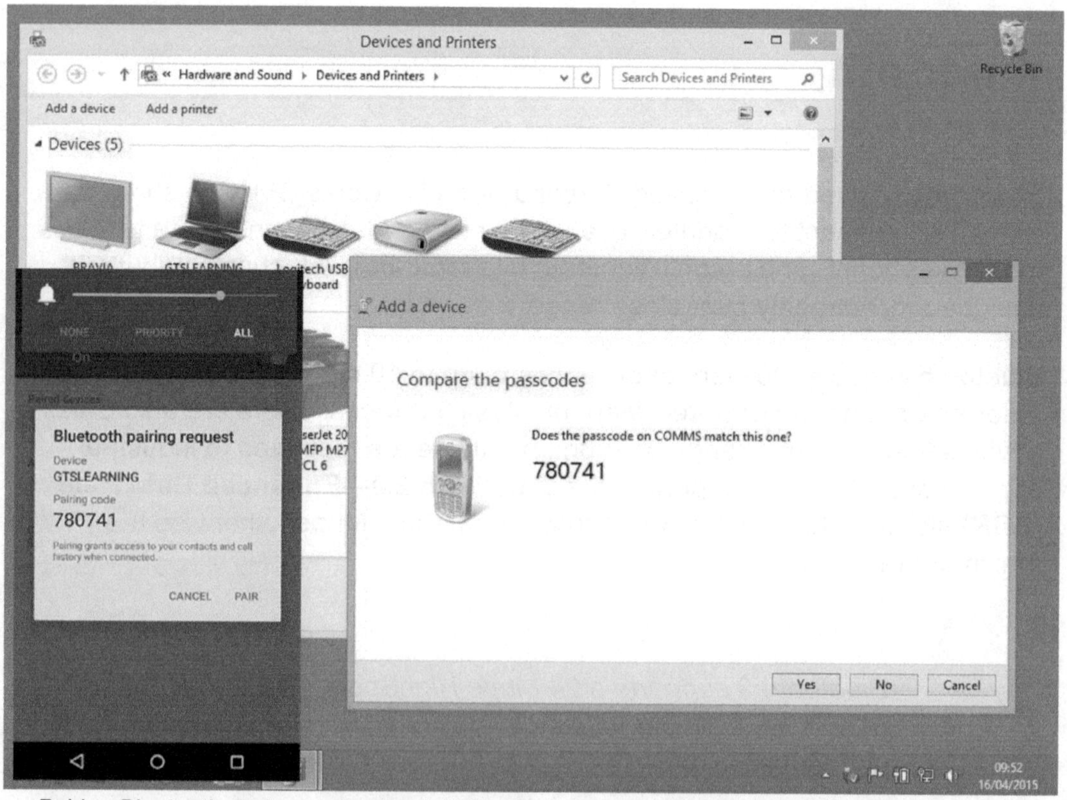

Pairing Bluetooth devices using the Add Device wizard and Bluetooth settings on an Android phone. Screenshot used with permission from Microsoft.

Disabling Bluetooth

Bluetooth can be disabled quickly via the notification shade in iOS or Android. On a PC, you can use the Bluetooth icon in the notification area to change settings and make the computer non-discoverable. The Bluetooth radio can also be switched on or off using the Wi-Fi adapter toggle.

RF and Near Field Communications (NFC)

Radio Frequency ID (RFID) is a means of tagging and tracking objects using specially-encoded **tags**. When an RFID **reader** scans a tag, the tag responds with the information programmed into it. A tag can either be an unpowered, passive device that only responds when scanned at close range (up to about 25m) or a powered, active device with a range of 100m. Passive RFID tags can be embedded in stickers and labels to track parcels and equipment and are used in passive proximity smart cards.

Near Field Communications (NFC) is a peer-to-peer version of RFID; that is, an NFC device can work as *both* tag *and* reader to exchange information with other NFC devices. NFC normally works at up to two inches (six cm) at data rates of 106, 212, and 424 Kbps. NFC sensors and functionality are starting to be incorporated into smartphones. NFC is mostly used for contactless payment readers, security ID tags and shop shelf edge labels for stock control. It can also be used to configure other types of connection (pairing Bluetooth devices for instance).

Networking Interfaces

Networking interfaces allow computers to be connected to exchange data. Most computers have a local network adapter or **Network Interface Card (NIC)** already installed as part of the motherboard chipset. A local network adapter (or Ethernet adapter) allows the computer to join a wired network with other nearby computers by connecting the devices to the same Ethernet switch, or switched fabric in an enterprise network. The computer is also likely to be able to access the Internet via the local network connection.

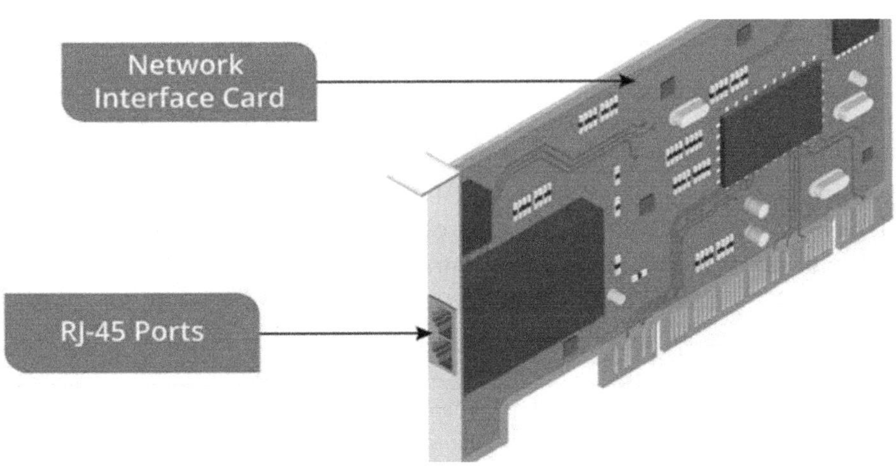

RJ-45 ports on a Network Interface Card (NIC). Image © 123rf.com.

Ethernet Connector (RJ-45)

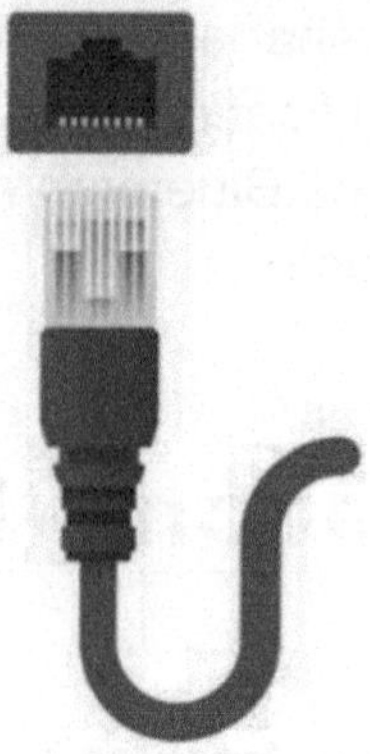

RJ-45 port and connector. Image © 123rf.com.

An Ethernet network adapter used with twisted pair cable will have an **RJ-45** port to connect the computer to the network, via another RJ-45 port in the network equipment. These ports will be marked "LAN" (Local Area Network). Twisted pair is a type of copper cabling where pairs of insulated conductors are twisted around one another, to minimize electrical interference.

Networking is discussed in more detail in Unit 4.1 and Unit 4.2.

Telephone Connector (RJ-11)

While local networking uses Ethernet technologies, some networking and communications functions depend on direct use of the telephone network. Not many computers and laptops ship with a **dial-up/analog modem** anymore, but they are still often a feature of "all-in-one" print/scan/fax devices. If required, a modem could be added to a PC using an expansion card or to a laptop using a USB fax modem adapter.

RJ-11 port and connector. Image © 123rf.com.

A fax modem uses twisted pair cabling with an **RJ-11** connector at the fax end and a connector suitable for use with the country's phone system at the other end. This could be another RJ-11 connector, but different connectors may be used in different regions; for example, a BT phone plug would be used in the UK.

The RJ-11 connector is smaller than the RJ-45 connector so you cannot plug one into the wrong port.

You are also likely to encounter RJ-11 ports on the DSL (Digital Subscriber Line) modem/router appliance used to connect a home network to the Internet. The Internet or Wide Area Network (WAN) port on the router will be the RJ-11 type. This is connected to the DSL port on the telephone master socket to create a fast, always-on "broadband" Internet link over the telephone line.

Review Questions / Module 3 / Unit 2 / Using Device Interfaces

Answer these questions to test what you have learned in this unit. You can review the model answers at the end of the book.

1) True or false? Mice and keyboards must be connected to a computer via PS/2 ports.

2) True or false? USB cables have the same connectors at either end.

3) A user has two USB drives connected to her PC. She complains that when she copies large files to both drives at the same time, it seems to take much longer. Why might this be?

4) You want to purchase a flat-panel monitor that can show widescreen movies. You are considering models with native resolutions of 1400x1050 and 1920x1200. Which should you choose?

5) True or false? HDMI is the only type of display interface that supports High Definition picture resolutions.

6) You are considering buying a new display device. The model you are considering accepts digital inputs only. Your computer's graphics adapter has a blue port with 15 holes. Would this flat-panel be a wise purchase?

7) You need to configure settings for an input device. What should be your first step?

8) A friend is asking for your help in using her computer. When he presses the key marked @, a different symbol appears. What could be the cause?

9) What type of mouse would you recommend for someone who uses their computer principally to play computer games and why?

Lab 12 / Configuring Input Devices

In this lab, you will look at the configuration options for input devices. As you may have noticed, in Windows 10 there are two interfaces for configuring the OS: the Settings app and Control Panel. The Settings app interface is for touchscreen-enabled configuration. Microsoft often moves a few controls to the Settings app with each feature update, but many configuration tasks on a desktop computer or laptop still have to be performed via a Control Panel applet. Similarly, newer hardware devices designed for Windows 10 might be managed using an app while older device drivers use Control Panel.

1) If necessary, start your computer and sign in.
2) Click **Start** then click the **Settings** icon .
3) Click **Devices** then from the left-hand panel, select **Mouse**.

   As you can see, the "app" settings for the mouse are fairly limited:

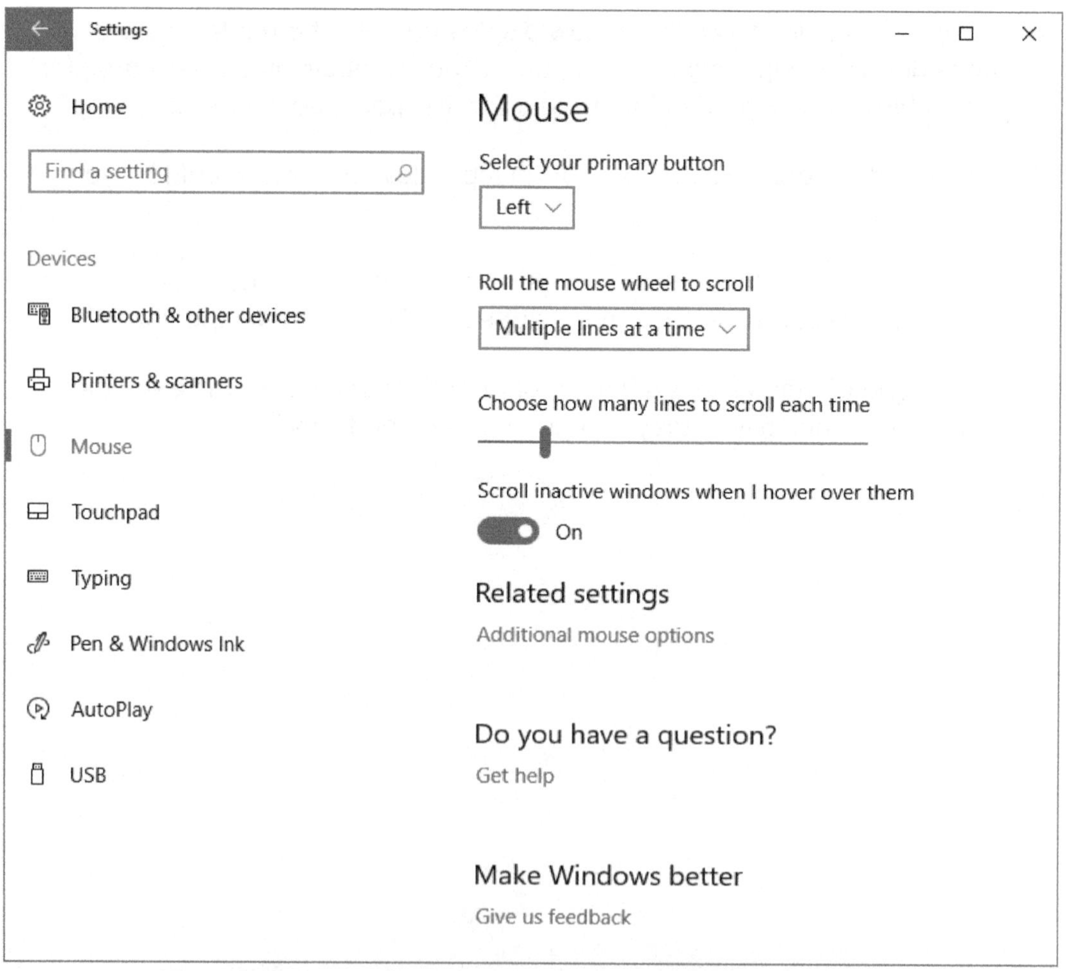

Mouse Settings app. Screenshot used with permission from Microsoft.

4) Click **Additional mouse options**.

The exact options presented here may be different on your computer as they depend on the hardware and driver software installed.

5) Click the **Buttons** tab.

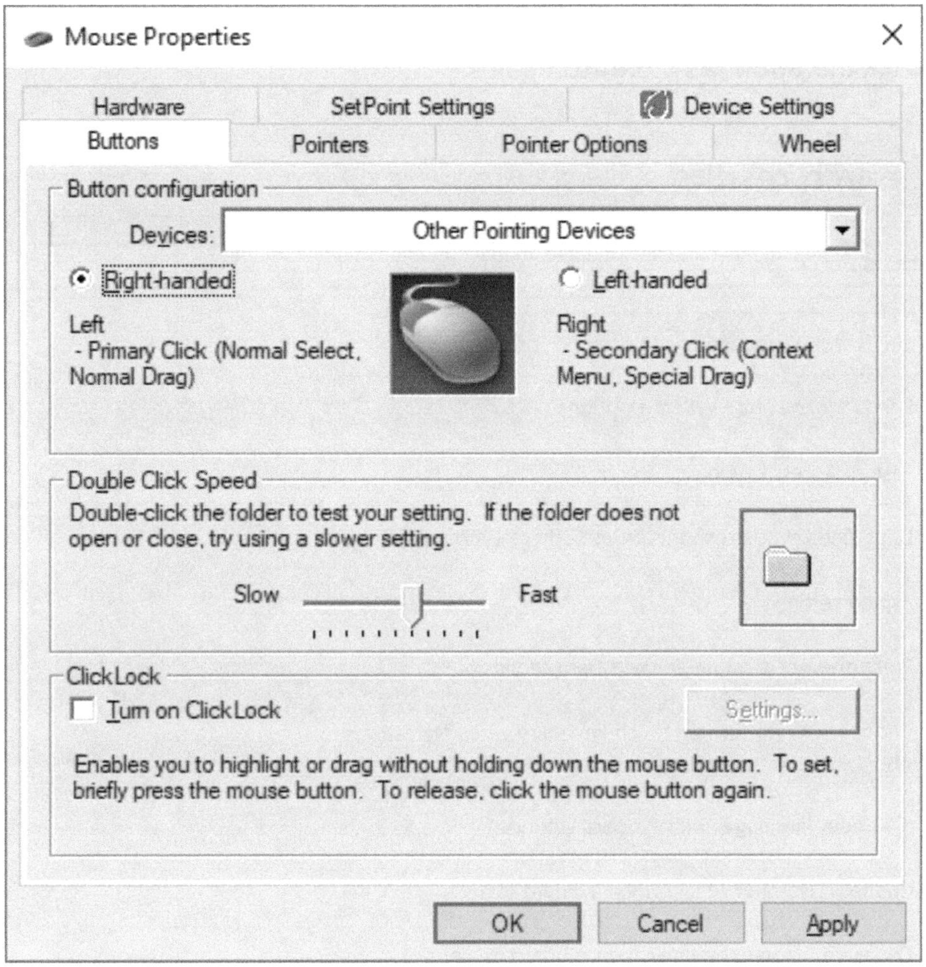

Typical mouse driver configuration page. On this computer you can switch between configuring the USB-attached mouse and the built-in laptop touchpad. Screenshot used with permission from Microsoft.

6) If you are left-handed, click the **Left-handed** button.

7) Adjust the **Double Click Speed** slider and test using the folder icon to get the response rate to a setting you are comfortable with. Click **Apply** if you make a change.

8) Click the **Pointers** tab and browse through the schemes available, picking a new one if you like. Again, click **Apply** if you have changed something.

9) Click the **Pointer Options** tab and set the cursor speed to whatever is comfortable for the way you use the mouse (faster speeds mean using smaller "sweeps" of the mouse). Enable any other options you want to use then click **Apply**.

10) If your mouse has a scroll wheel, use the **Wheel** tab to adjust the scroll speed.

11) Your mouse driver may make other settings available—take some time to explore these then close the dialog when you have finished.

12) In the Settings app, click **Typing** then from the left-hand panel.

    Note that these are primarily options for using an on-screen keyboard.

13) In the "Find a setting" box, type `keyboard`

14) Click the `Show all results` link.

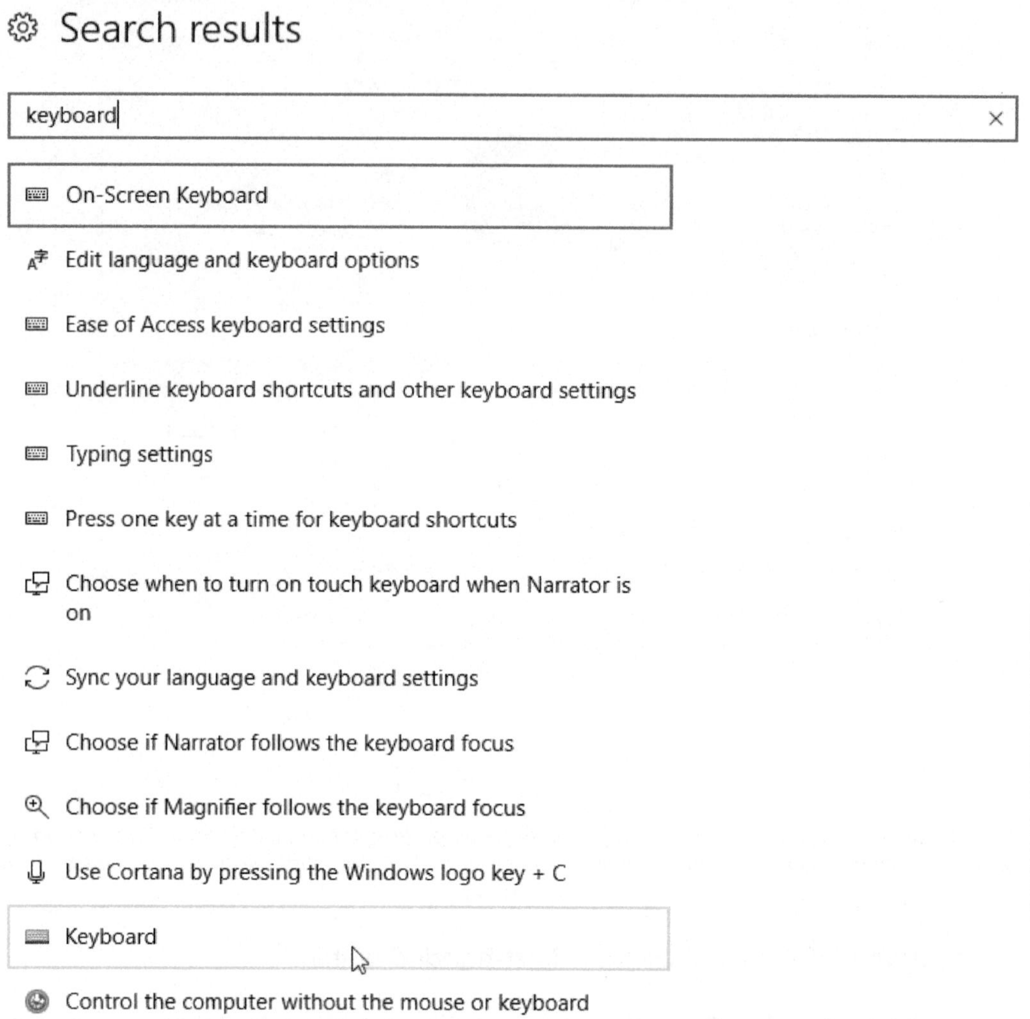

Searching the Settings app. Screenshot used with permission from Microsoft.

The search results contain links to pages within Settings *and* links to Control Panel applets and Windows troubleshooters.

15) From the search results, click the **Keyboard** icon (shown with the mouse cursor over it in the screenshot above).

16) Use the dialog to configure the repeat rate and delay to suit then click **OK**.

    As well as adjusting the way the keys respond, you may also need to reconfigure the keyboard input language.

17) In the Settings app, in the "Find a setting" box, type `region` and select the link to **Region & language**.

18) The "Country or region" setting should show the country you are in. Adjust it if you like.

    The "Languages" option provides support for using more than one display and input language.

19) Click the **Add a language** button.

20) Browse through the list to locate and select an alternative language, such as **English (United Kingdom)**.

21) When the language has been added, select it and click the **Options** button.

    Depending on the support available for the language, you can add packs to support using that language for the Windows interface or typing / handwriting in that language. You can also change the keyboard layout for the language, if necessary.

22) Optionally make any changes you want then click the **Back** button.

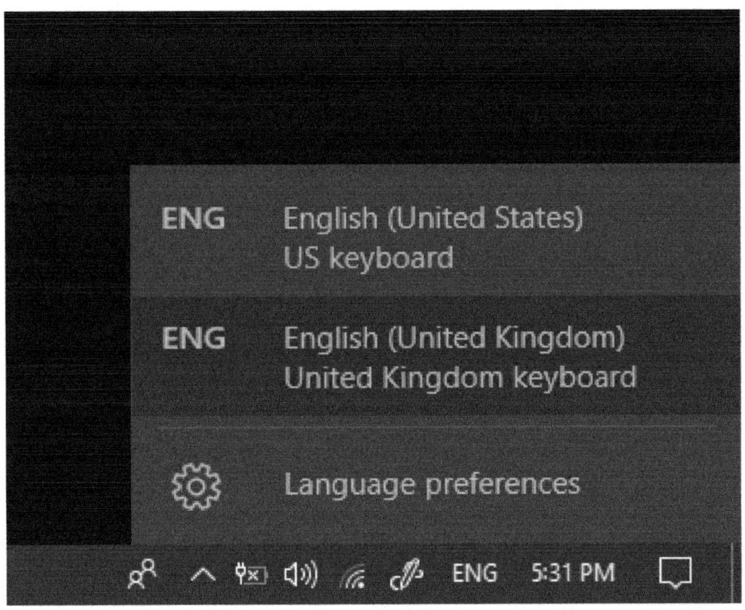

Language bar. Screenshot used with permission from Microsoft.

23) On the taskbar, locate the language bar in the notification area and click it.

    You can use this to switch between keyboard layouts. Note the key combo for switching (`START+SPACEBAR`).

24) Click **Start**, type `notepad`, and then press `ENTER`.

25) Type the following text, pressing `ENTER` after each line.

    @ Felicia Dorothea Hemans

    "The boy stood on the burning deck

    Whence all but he had fled;

    The flame that lit the battle's wreck

    Shone round him o'er the dead"

26) Press **START+SPACEBAR** and try to type the same text—what happens?

27) See if you can work out the correct keys to use to type the text using the "foreign" keyboard layout.

28) Press **CTRL+S** to save the document. If necessary, in the left pane, expand **This PC** and select the **Documents** folder.

29) In the "File name" box, type **Great Sea Battles** then click the **Save** button. Close Notepad.

30) Optionally, use the **Region & language** app to remove the foreign keyboard layout.

It's quite easy to switch input languages by mistake if you leave the key combo set to the default. Unless you need it, it's best to have only one keyboard layout installed.

31) Optionally, shut down your computer if you are not continuing to use it after this lab.

Module 3 / Unit 3
Using Peripheral Devices

Objectives

On completion of this unit, you will be able to:

- Use Plug-and-Play to install devices and understand the use of device drivers.
- Describe different display technologies and install and configure a PC display.
- Install and configure multimedia devices, such as sound cards, speakers, microphones, and webcams.
- Describe the features and capabilities of different types of printer and their associated interfaces.
- Install and configure a printers and scanners.

Syllabus Objectives and Content Examples

This unit covers the following exam domain objectives and content examples:

- 2.2 Given a scenario, set up and install common peripheral devices to a laptop/PC.
  Devices (Printer, Scanner, Camera, Speakers, Display) • Installation types (Plug-and-play vs. driver installation, Other required steps, IP-based peripherals, Web-based configuration steps)
- 3.1 Manage applications and software.
  Device management
- 3.2 Compare and contrast components of an operating system.
  Drivers

Installing and Uninstalling Peripherals

Peripheral devices are generally quite straightforward to install and remove.

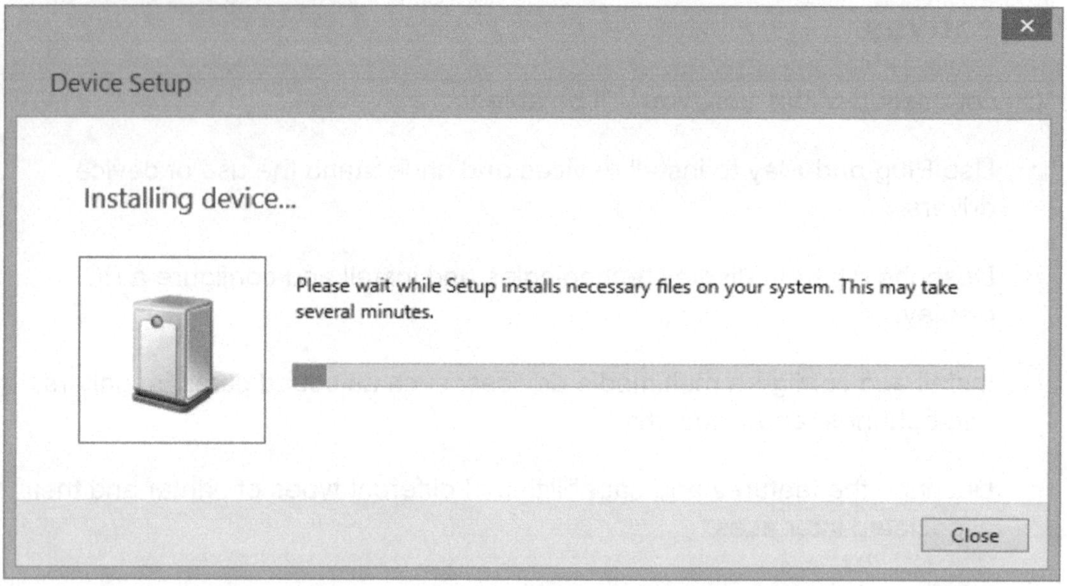

Installing device drive notification. When you connect a new device, Windows automatically locates and installs a driver. You may need to authorize the installation. Screenshot used with permission from Microsoft.

Plug-and-Play Installation

Windows devices are now all **Plug-and-Play**. This means that when you connect a new device, Windows identifies it and tries to install a **device driver**. The device driver makes the device work with the operating system and may come with software to allow the user to configure advanced settings or properties. The way this works varies between versions of Windows and from device to device. Often a device will be installed silently, at other times you may see a configuration message, and sometimes you will be prompted to locate driver files or configure settings.

Devices connected via USB are **hot-swappable**. This means that you can add or remove them when the system is running. If a device is not hot-swappable, you need to restart the system when adding it or shut down the system before removing it.

Manual Driver Installation

There may be occasions when Plug-and-Play does not work and you need to install driver software manually before the device can be recognized. Windows ships with a number of default drivers and can also try to locate a driver in the **Windows Update** website. If no driver is available from there, you need to obtain one from the device vendor. The device may come with setup software or you may be able to download a driver from the vendor's website.

Devices and Printers

Following installation there may be **other required steps** to complete configuration of the device. In Windows 7, Windows 8, and early versions of Windows 10, **Devices and Printers** is the location for the basic user-configurable settings for peripheral devices attached to the computer.

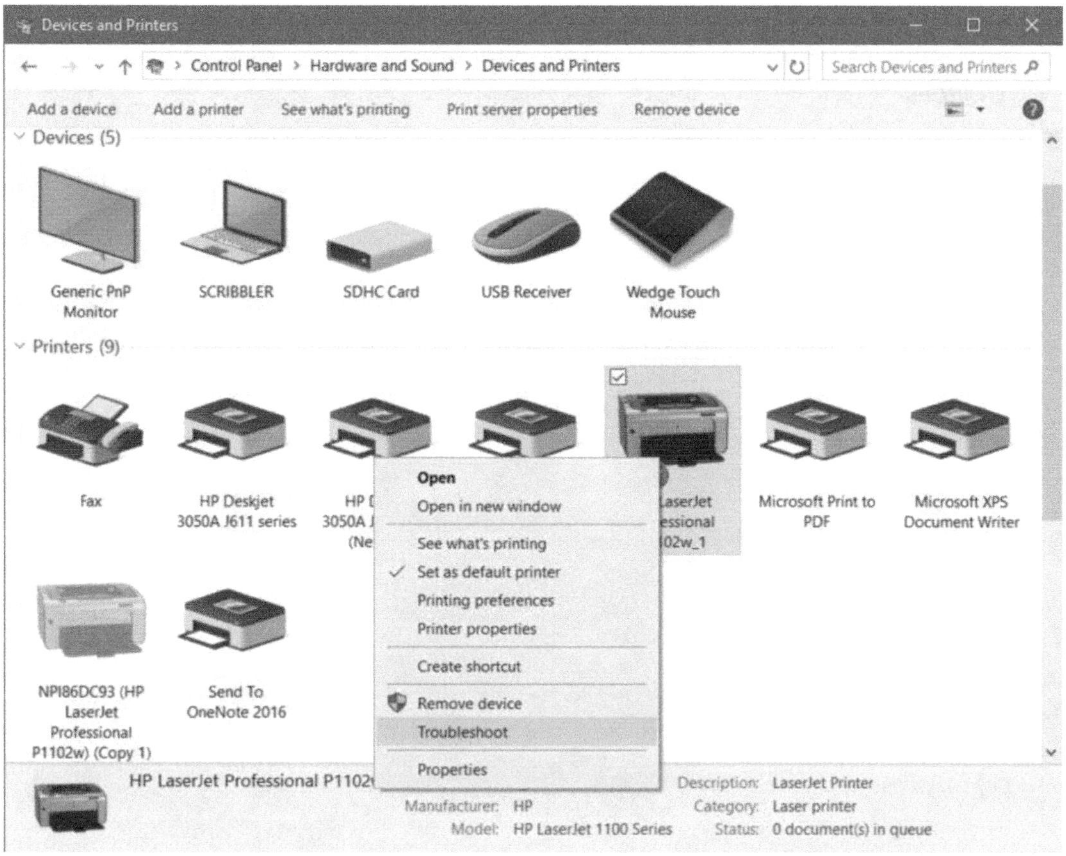

Devices and Printers. Screenshot used with permission from Microsoft.

Double-clicking an icon brings up the device's status page and available configuration options. The shortcut menu for each device also allows you to set configurable properties, start a troubleshooter (devices with a ⚠ icon are not working properly), or remove the device from the computer.

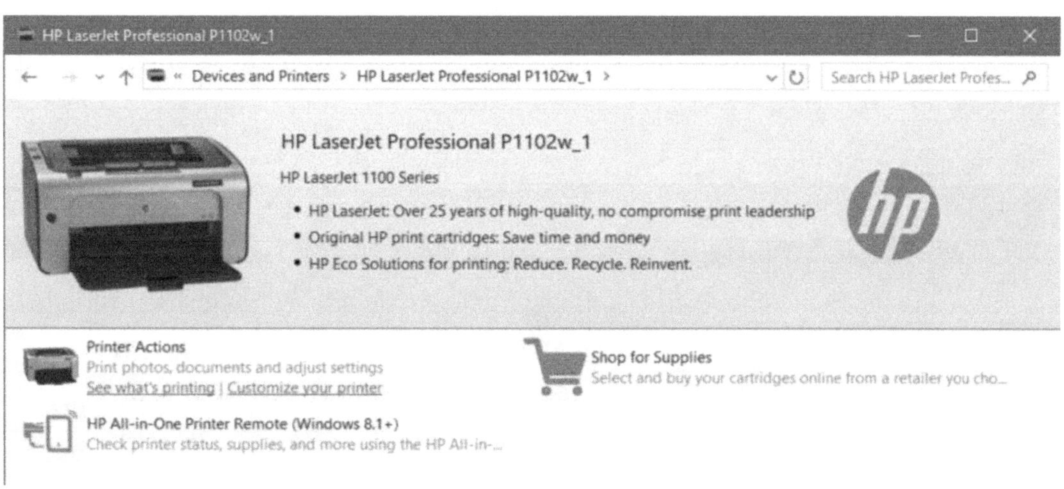

Device status page for an HP printer. Screenshot used with permission from Microsoft.

In Windows 10 version 1803, Devices and Printers is replaced by a simpler Devices page within the Settings app.

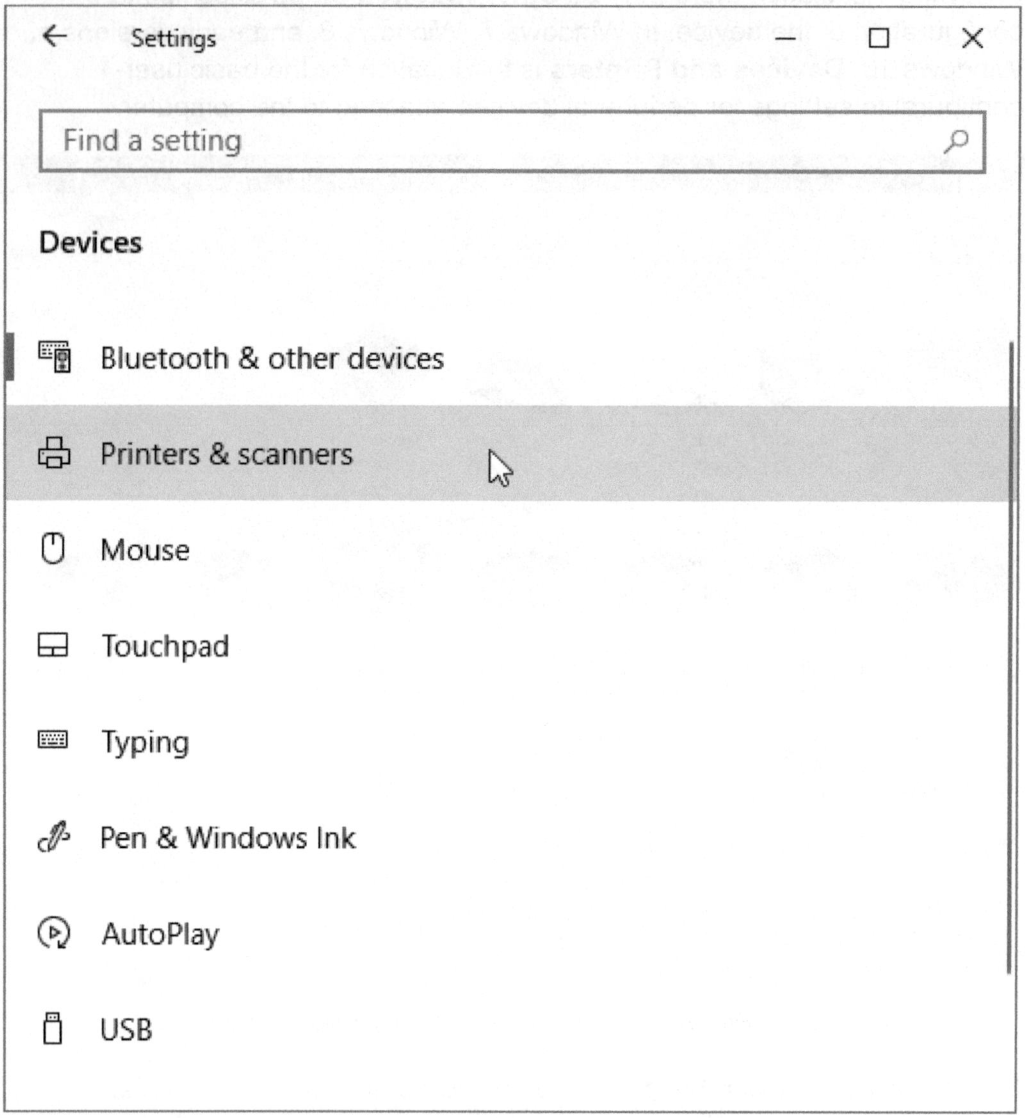

Devices page within the Settings app for Windows 10 (1803). Screenshot used with permission from Microsoft.

Removing and Uninstalling Devices

Windows detects when a device has been removed and will only load the driver for it when it is necessary. In some circumstances however you may want to completely uninstall a driver. Usually you can do this by uninstalling the software package used to install the driver in the first place. Alternatively, you can open **Device Manager** via the **START+X** menu, locate the device, then right-click and select **Uninstall**. A check box may allow you to remove the driver files from the system at the same time.

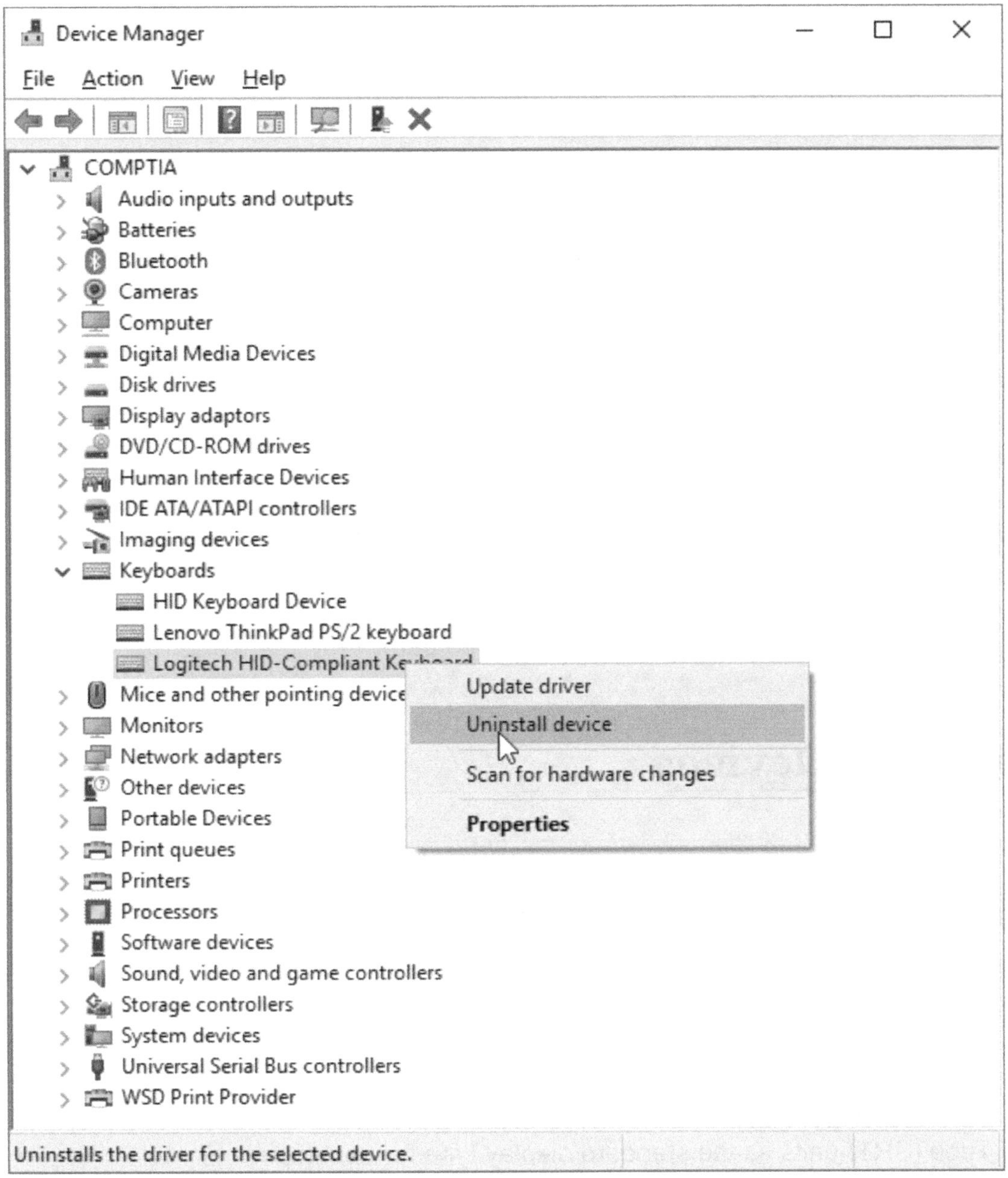

Uninstalling a keyboard using Device Manager. Screenshot used with permission from Microsoft.

IP-based Peripherals and Web Configuration

Some types of devices are not connected to the computer via a peripheral port but accessed over a network. Such a device will be configured with an **Internet Protocol (IP)** address. The device vendor will normally provide a tool to locate the device on the network and then open a web configuration page in a browser. You can use the configuration page to set device options.

Using a web configuration page to manage a Wi-Fi access point. The configuration page is accessed via the IP address 192.168.1.252.

Networking is discussed in more detail in Unit 4.1 and Unit 4.2.

Display Devices

Some notable manufacturers of display devices include Viewsonic, Iiyama, Sony, Panasonic, Toshiba, LG, Acer, Sanyo, and Mitsubishi.

Flat-screen Displays

Liquid Crystal Display (LCD) screens, or **flat-screen displays**, are used by portable computers and have also replaced the old and bulky Cathode Ray Tube (CRT) units as the standard display type for desktops.

Each picture element (pixel) in a color LCD comprises cells (or subpixels) with filters to generate the three primary colors (red, green, and blue) and transistors to vary the intensity of each cell, so creating the gamut (range of colors) that the display can generate.

The whole panel is illuminated by a fluorescent or LED (Light Emitting Diode) backlight.

Desktop computer with TFT display. Image © 123rf.com.

You will also see these displays referred to as TFT (Thin Film Transistor). TFT is a high-quality type of LCD.

Touchscreens

A **touchscreen** can be used for input where a mouse and/or keyboard are impractical. Typically, touchscreens are used on handheld portable devices, but they are also useful in industrial environments or for public terminals, such as kiosks, where mice or keyboards could be damaged, stolen, or vandalized.

Tablets and smartphones have integrated **capacitive** touchscreens. Capacitive touchscreens support **multitouch** events. This means that the screen (with compatible software) can interpret more complex hand and finger gestures as actions, such as rotating, scrolling, zooming, and moving objects. Laptop screens and full size flat-screen monitors may also be touch-enabled.

Digital Projectors

A video projector is a large format display, suitable for use in a presentation or at a meeting. The image is projected onto a screen or wall using a lens system. Some types of projector are portable; others are fixed in place. There are CRT and LCD versions but the top end of the market is dominated by **Digital Light Processing (DLP)**, developed by Texas Instruments. Projectors use the same HDMI, DVI, Thunderbolt, or VGA interfaces as other display equipment.

DLP projector. Image © 123rf.com.

Each pixel in a DLP device is represented by a mirror, which can be tilted toward or away from a light source and color filters to create the required shade.

Take care handling projectors. During use, the bulb becomes very hot and while it is hot, will be very fragile. Allow a projector to cool completely before attempting to move it.

Display Settings

You can customize almost any aspect of how Windows is displayed using options in the **Personalization** applet (right-click the desktop or open the applet in Control Panel/Settings). For example, you can change window colors and styles manually or using themes, adjust mouse pointers, change the sounds used for various events, and so on.

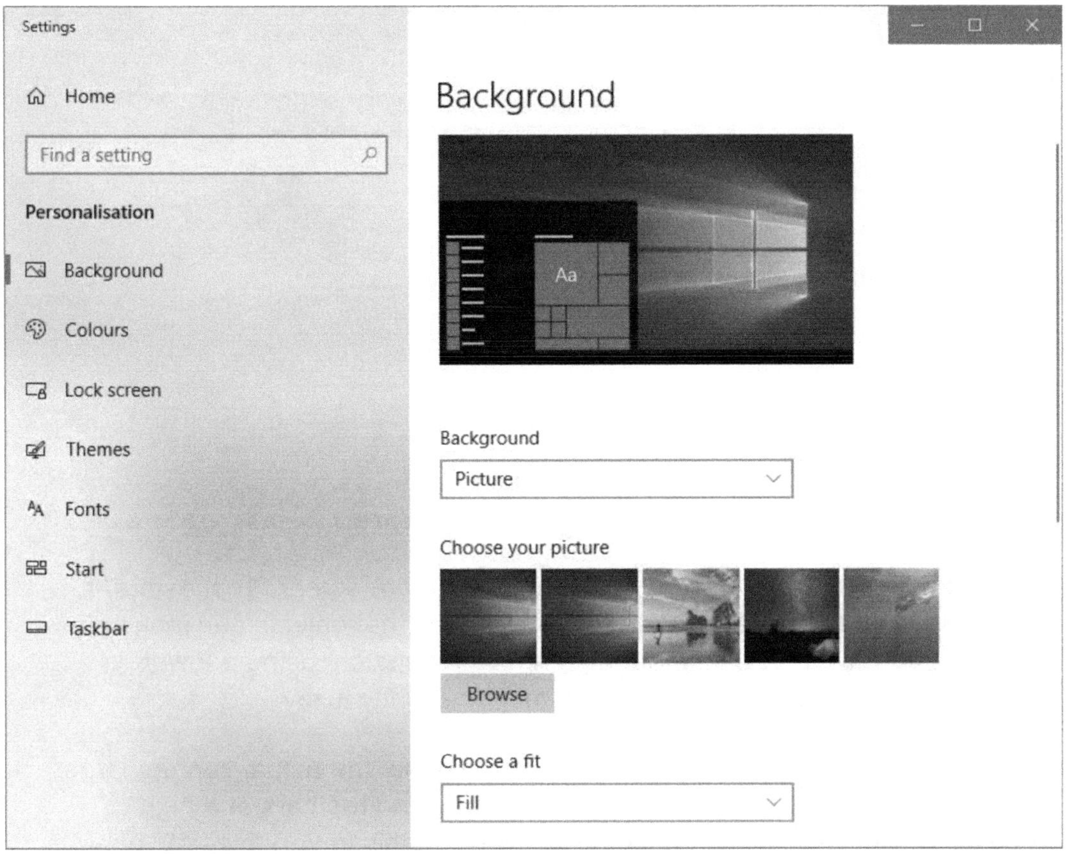

Personalization in Windows 10 settings app. Screenshot used with permission from Microsoft.

Screen Resolution

The screen resolution is the number of pixels used to create the screen image. It is measured as the number of pixels wide by the number of pixels high. Screen resolutions are either 4:3 (standard) aspect ratio or 16:10 (widescreen) aspect ratio.

To adjust screen resolution, open **Settings**, click **System** and then select the **Display** tab.

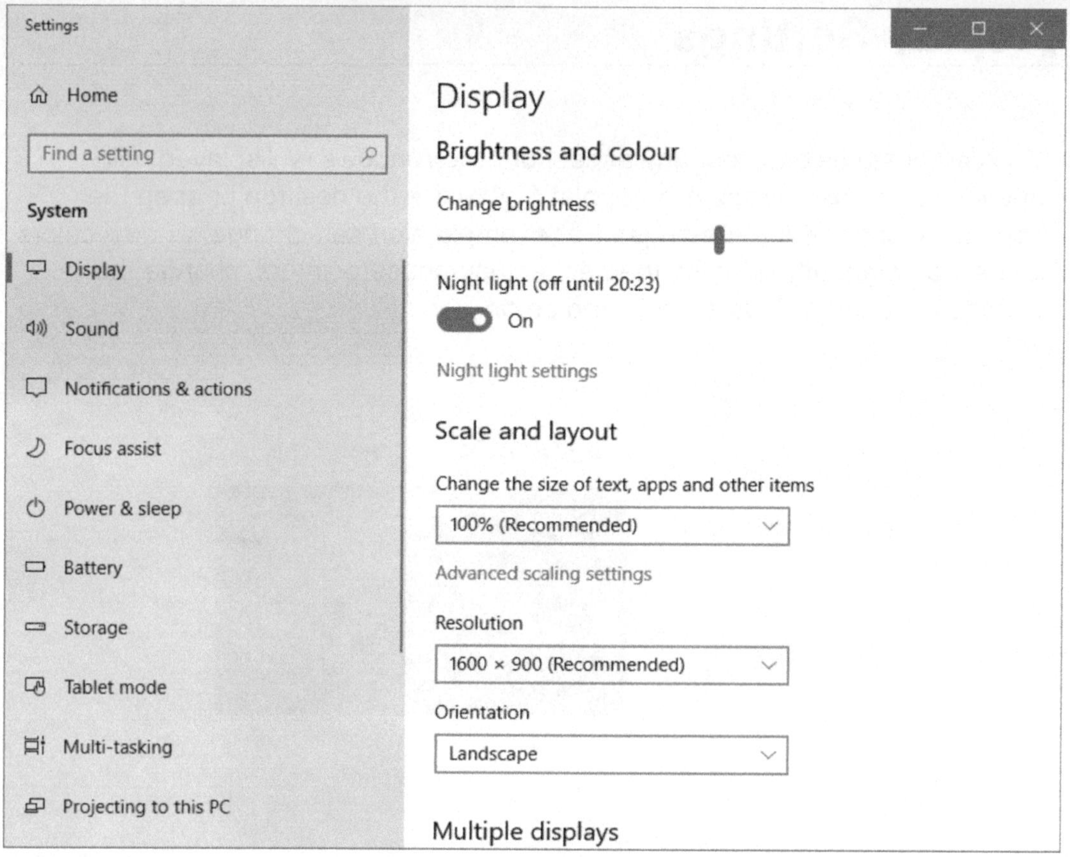

Display options in Windows 10 settings app. Screenshot used with permission from Microsoft.

Using a high screen resolution means there is more screen "real estate" to show windows and documents. The downside is that objects can look very small. If you have an LCD with a high native resolution, using a lower interpolated resolution makes screen images slightly fuzzy.

Most applications support a zoom function to make the actual content larger, but to increase the size of window text, menus, and toolbars at a high resolution, you can adjust the DPI setting. To do this in Windows 10, open **Settings**, select **System**, and on the **Display** tab, under the Scale and layout heading, click the drop-down list and select a scale in percent. You might need to sign out and sign back in for the change to take effect.

Installing and Configuring Dual Monitors

A PC (or laptop) can be set up to use two display devices. In terms of hardware, the PC requires either a graphics adapter with two display ports or two graphics adapters or a display interface that supports daisy-chaining (DisplayPort or Thunderbolt for instance). A laptop can also send the display to an external monitor or use both the built-in display and an external one.

Connect the extra display device and a dialog will be displayed automatically. You can also set the display mode later using the **Display** tab in the **System** node in the **Settings** app.

Dual monitors can be used in one of three modes:

- Display the same image on both devices—select the **Duplicate these displays** option (this mode is useful for delivering presentations).

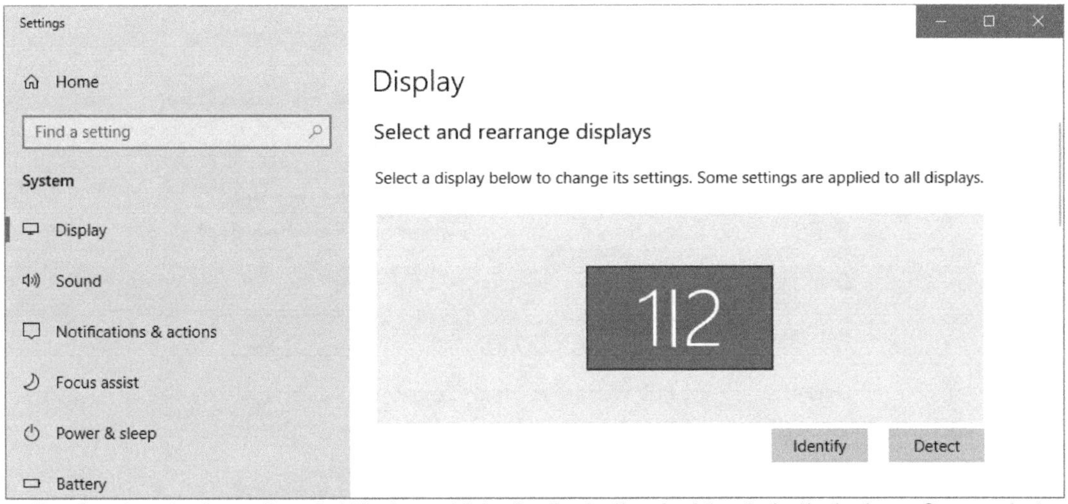

Configuring dual monitors in Windows 10 to duplicate the desktop to both devices. Screenshot used with permission from Microsoft.

- Display the desktop over both devices—select **Extend these displays** (this mode makes more screen "real estate" available and is useful for design, publishing, and programming work). Drag the displays in the box to position them correctly. You can put them to the left and right or above and below one another.

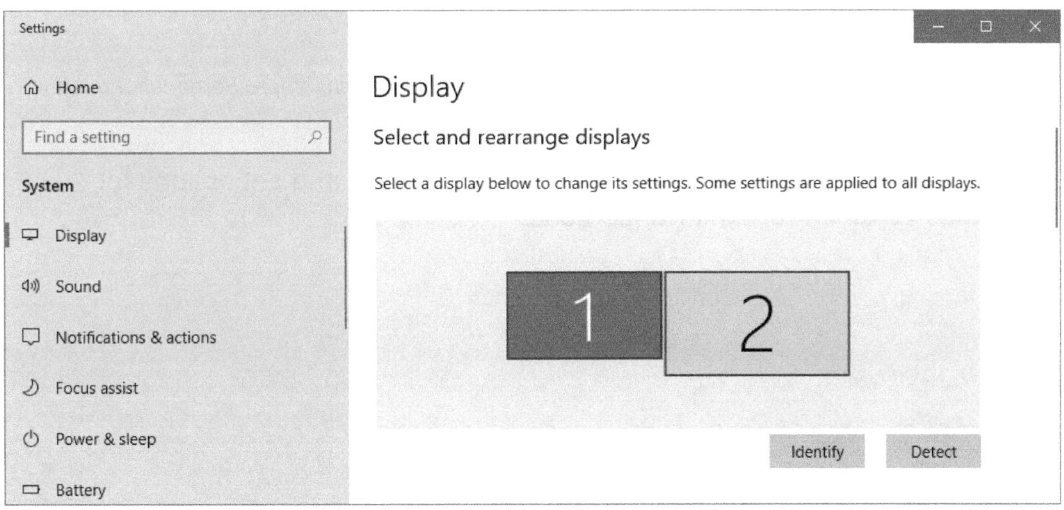

Configuring dual monitors in Windows 10 to extend the display - you can drag the icons around to reflect the physical position of your monitors. Screenshot used with permission from Microsoft.

- Display the desktop on one device only—select either **Show only on 1** or **Show only on 2**.

In Windows 10, you can select a multi-monitor mode quickly using **START+P**. *This causes a prompt to appear on the right side of the primary display listing the options: PC screen only, Duplicate, Extend, Second screen only.*

Configuring a Touchscreen

Touchscreen options are configured using the **Tablet PC Settings** and **Pen and Touch** applets.

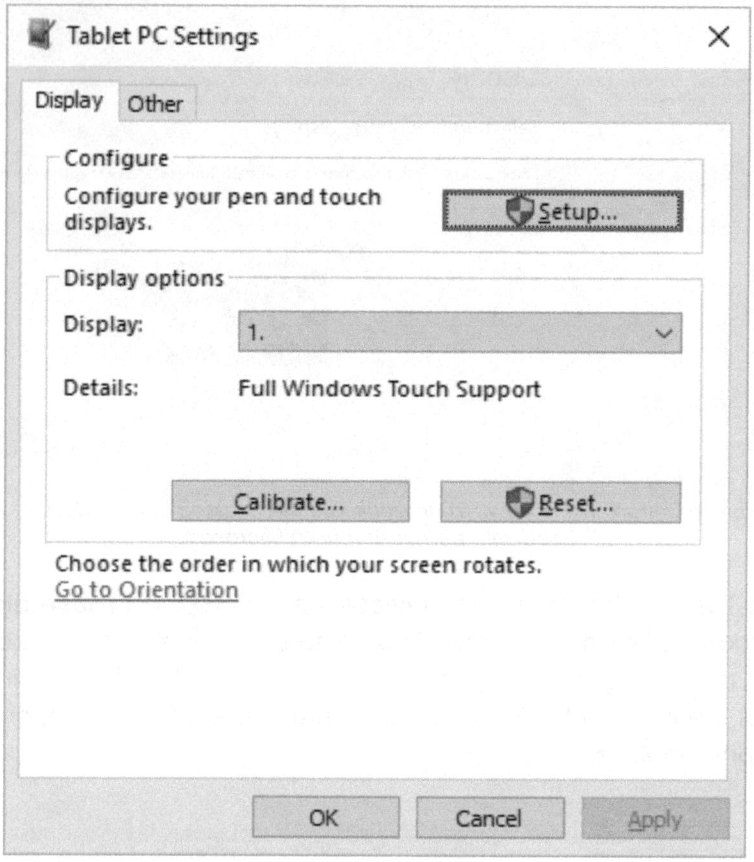

Use the Tablet PC Control Panel applet to set up or calibrate a touchscreen. Screenshot used with permission from Microsoft.

Tablet PC Settings allows you to calibrate the display and set options for orientation and left- or right-handed use.

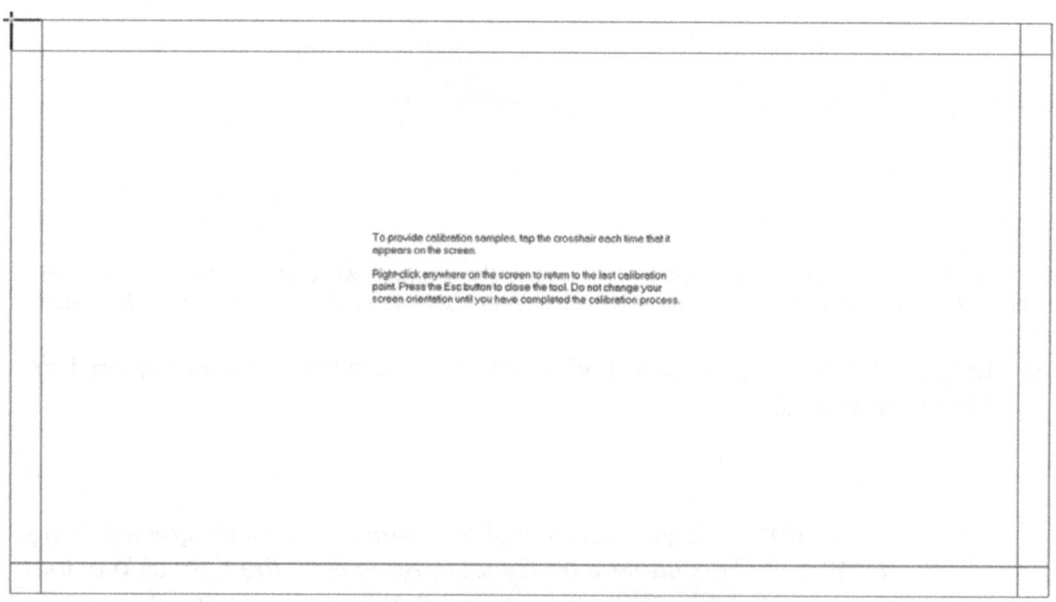

The calibration utility involves touching the crosshair at different points of the screen. Screenshot used with permission from Microsoft.

Pen and Touch allows you to configure gesture settings, such as using tap-and-hold to trigger a right-mouse click event.

Multimedia Ports and Devices

Multimedia refers to ports used to play and record audio and video from different inputs and outputs. One distinction that can be made between different types of multimedia ports is whether they are *analog* or *digital*. Analog signals need to be converted to digital to be processed by the computer, which can degrade the signal.

Audio Card

A computer's audio subsystem is made up of a **sound card** to process audio signals and provide interfaces for connecting equipment and one or more input (**microphone**) and output (**speaker**) devices. Most computers come with an audio or sound "card" as part of the chipset (embedded on the motherboard). An expansion card might be installed as an upgrade, to make better quality recordings or support surround sound for instance.

The basis of a sound card is the **Digital Signal Processor (DSP)** chip, which processes data from the computer to output a signal to drive the speakers and processes audio input from a microphone to convert it to computer data. Creative, Terratec, RealTek, and Turtle Beach are the most notable vendors of consumer sound cards, while E-MU, Yamaha, and Creative are noted for their professional-level cards.

Speaker and Microphone Jacks

A **microphone** allows for audio input and recording, while audio playback is achieved via **speakers** or **headphones**. A **headset** is a device with both microphone and headphones. Both analog and digital audio equipment is available.

Most analog audio connectors are 3.5 mm (⅛") jacks. A standard sound card will have a number of these for different equipment:

- **Audio in (light blue)**—audio in (or line in) is a low-level (1V) stereo signal as supplied by most tape decks, video players, tuners, CD players, and so on.
- **Microphone input (pink)**—this is generally a mono analog input.
- **Audio out (lime)**—audio out (or line out) is a low-level (1V) analog stereo signal suitable for feeding into an amplified speakers or headphones.

- **Audio out (black)**—signal for rear speakers in a surround sound system (see below).
- **Audio out (orange)**—signal for the subwoofer in a surround sound system.

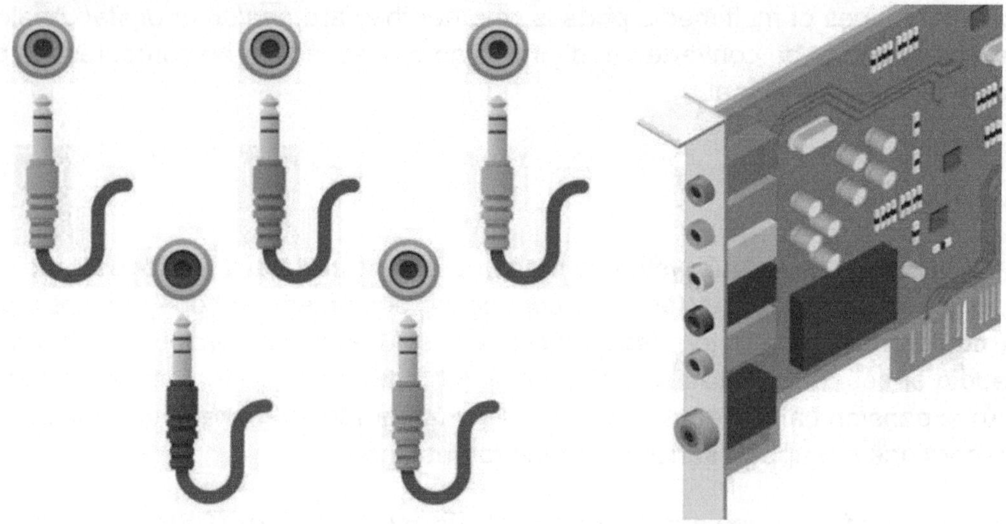

Audio jacks on a sound card. Image © 123rf.com.

Higher end sound cards will include an **S/PDIF (Sony/Phillips Digital Interface)** jack. S/PDIF can either use **coax** cabling with **RCA** connectors or **fiber optic** cabling and connectors. S/PDIF is most often used to carry digital signals for surround sound speaker systems.

RCA connectors are distinguished by a collar surrounding the connector, which makes the fit between plug and socket more secure.

Many models of microphone, headset, and speaker can also be attached via a USB port or wirelessly via Bluetooth.

Speaker Configurations

Sound cards supporting multiple output channels with an appropriate speaker system can provide various levels of playback, from stereo (left and right speakers) to some type of **surround sound**. Surround sound uses multiple speakers positioned around the listener to provide a cinematic audio experience. A 5.1 digital system (**Dolby Digital** or **Digital Theatre System [DTS]**) has three front (center, left, and right) speakers, and two rear (left and right) speakers, and a subwoofer for bass sounds. A 7.1 system (**Dolby Digital Plus** or **DTS-HD**) has two extra side speakers.

A speaker system will usually have controls for adjusting volume, bass, and treble plus optionally, an equalizer (EQ) or preset sound effects.

Audio Settings

To set up audio, connect the microphone, headset, or speakers to the appropriate ports on the card or motherboard.

Use the **Sound** applet in Control Panel/Settings to test the hardware and configure settings.

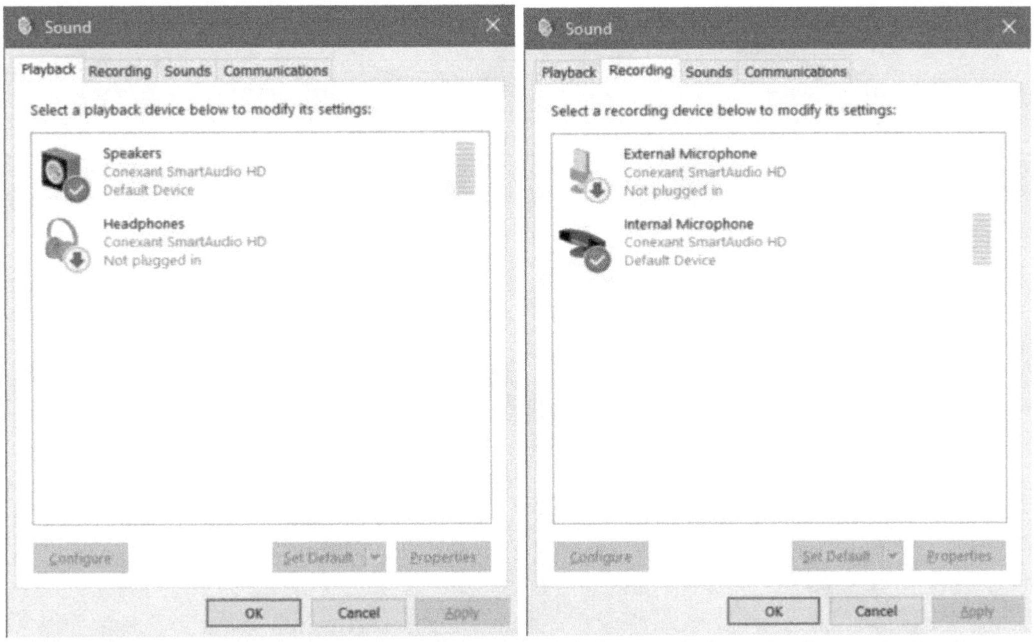

Configure audio properties using the Sound applet. Screenshot used with permission from Microsoft.

If you have multiple devices, you can choose the defaults here and test levels for audio input and output.

Changing the Volume

If you have a multimedia keyboard, there are usually keys for adjusting the volume. Also, laptops have push buttons and special **FN** keys to adjust the volume.

In Windows, use the icon in the Notification Area  to control the volume.

Windows volume control—drag the slider to adjust the volume and click the button to mute or unmute sound. Screenshot used with permission from Microsoft.

Webcams

Webcams record video images using a digital sensor and usually feature a microphone to record audio. They range in quality from models with low resolution and frame rates (25 fps [frames per second]) to models capable of High Definition resolution at 60 fps. Webcams are used for online video conferencing, as feeds for websites, and as surveillance devices. Webcams can be built into a laptop computer chassis or connected via USB.

Built-in and USB-attached webcam options. Image © 123rf.com.

Printer Types

Printing has always been associated with PC use. Reading from a screen is comparatively difficult compared to reading from paper. Printers also meet the need to keep hard copy records of important data.

A **printer technology** is the mechanism used to make images on the paper. The most widely-used technologies for general home and office use are **inkjet** and **laser**, though others are used for more specialized applications.

- A laser printer works by fixing a fine powder called **toner** to the page surface. The toner is applied using electrostatic charging then fixed using high heat and pressure in the **fuser unit**, creating a durable printout that does not smear or fade.

  A laser printer operates on the whole image as a single item. This means that laser printers need quite sophisticated processors and large amounts of memory.

- **Inkjets** (or **ink dispersion**) printers are often used for good quality color output. Inkjets are typically cheap to buy but expensive to run, with high cost consumables such as ink cartridges and high-grade paper. Compared to laser printers, they are slower and often noisier, making them less popular in office environments, except as a cheap option for low volume color printing.

  Color images are created by combining four inks: Cyan, Magenta, Yellow, and Black (K). The inks are stored in separate reservoirs, which may be supplied in single or multiple cartridges.

Inkjet (left) and laser (right) color printer types. Image © 123rf.com.

Some of the major vendors include HP, Epson, Canon, Xerox, Brother, OKI, Konica/Minolta, Lexmark, Ricoh, and Samsung.

Installing and Configuring a Printer

A local printer is usually connected to the computer via the USB interface. Some printers can be connected as network devices, either via wired Ethernet or Wi-Fi. Finally, a printer might be connected over a Bluetooth link.

As with any other device, the appropriate driver must be installed for a printer to function correctly. You can either use the setup software supplied with the printer or (in most cases) simply connect the printer and let Windows find a driver. When you connect a new Plug-and-Play printer, Windows installs drivers automatically, only prompting you if authorization is required or an appropriate driver cannot be found.

As with other types of hardware, the printer vendor may have a more up-to-date driver or setup software available on their website than the one supplied with Windows or available via Windows Update. Only use drivers from the genuine vendor or from Microsoft however.

Once the driver has been installed all applications will use it to send output to the printer.

Configuring Printers

Printers are configured using the **Devices and Printers** folder.

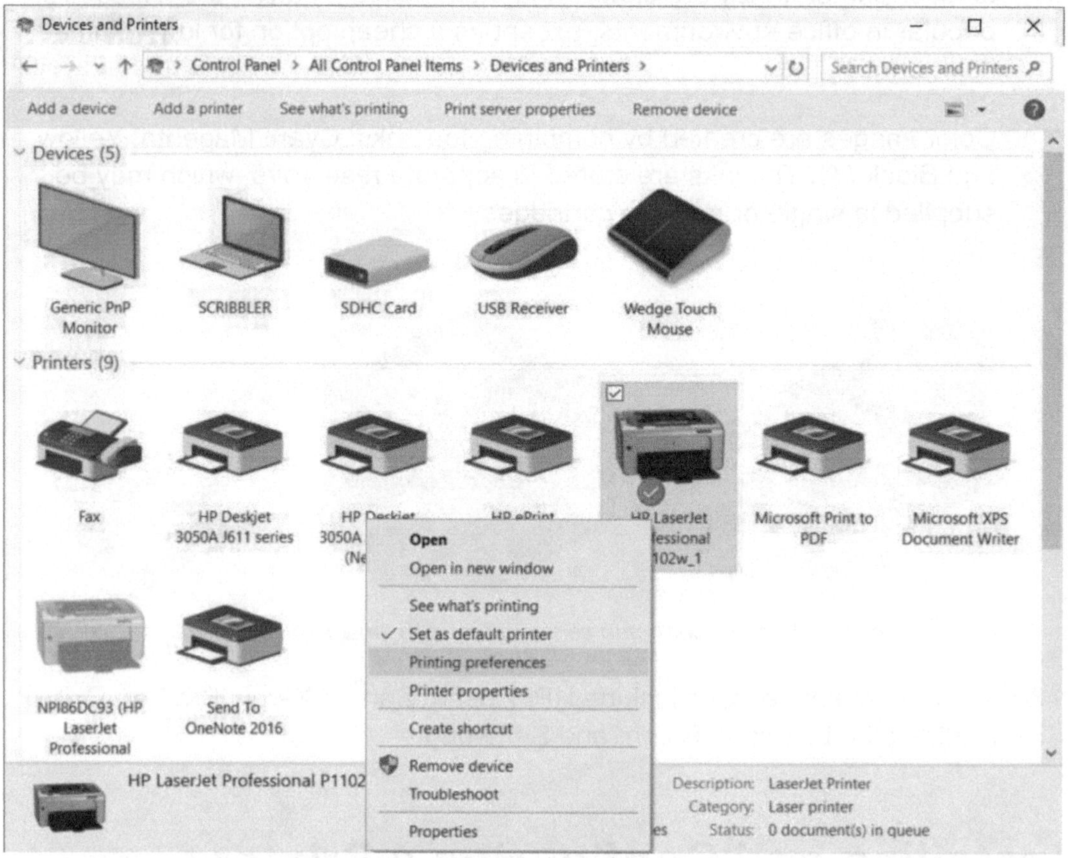

Choosing a default printer and configuring preferences through the Devices and Printers folder. Screenshot used with permission from Microsoft.

Opening a printer object displays its **status page** while the shortcut menu allows the selection of the default printer and configuration of sharing, properties, printing preferences, and management of the print queue (**See what's printing**).

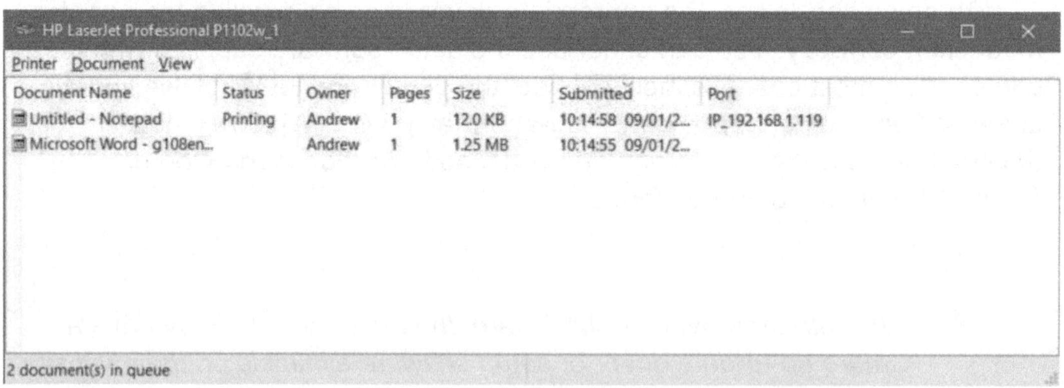

Print queue—use the shortcut menu to cancel or restart jobs or the Printer menu to pause the printer. Screenshot used with permission from Microsoft.

Printer Properties and Preferences

A local printer can be managed using **Printer Properties** and **Printing Preferences**. Properties allows you to update the driver, print to a different port, configure sharing and permissions, set basic device options (such as whether a duplex unit is installed), and configure default paper types for different feed trays. A duplex unit allows the printer to print to both sides of the paper. The unit turns the sheet over within the printer. Other options for printers include extra input and output trays and units that can collate output or bind or staple documents automatically.

This dialog also lets you print a test page (off the **General** tab). The **Print Test Page** command shows that a printer is installed and configured correctly.

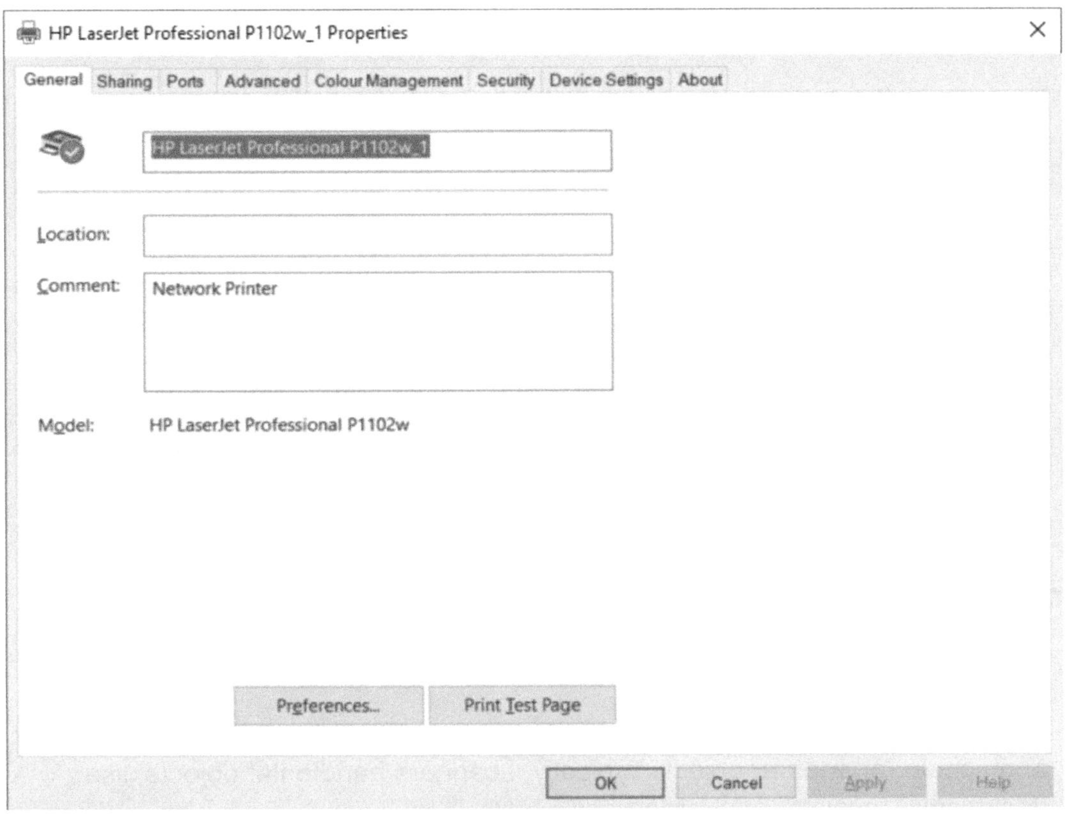

Printer properties—use the General tab to print a test page. Screenshot used with permission from Microsoft.

Preferences sets the **default** print options.

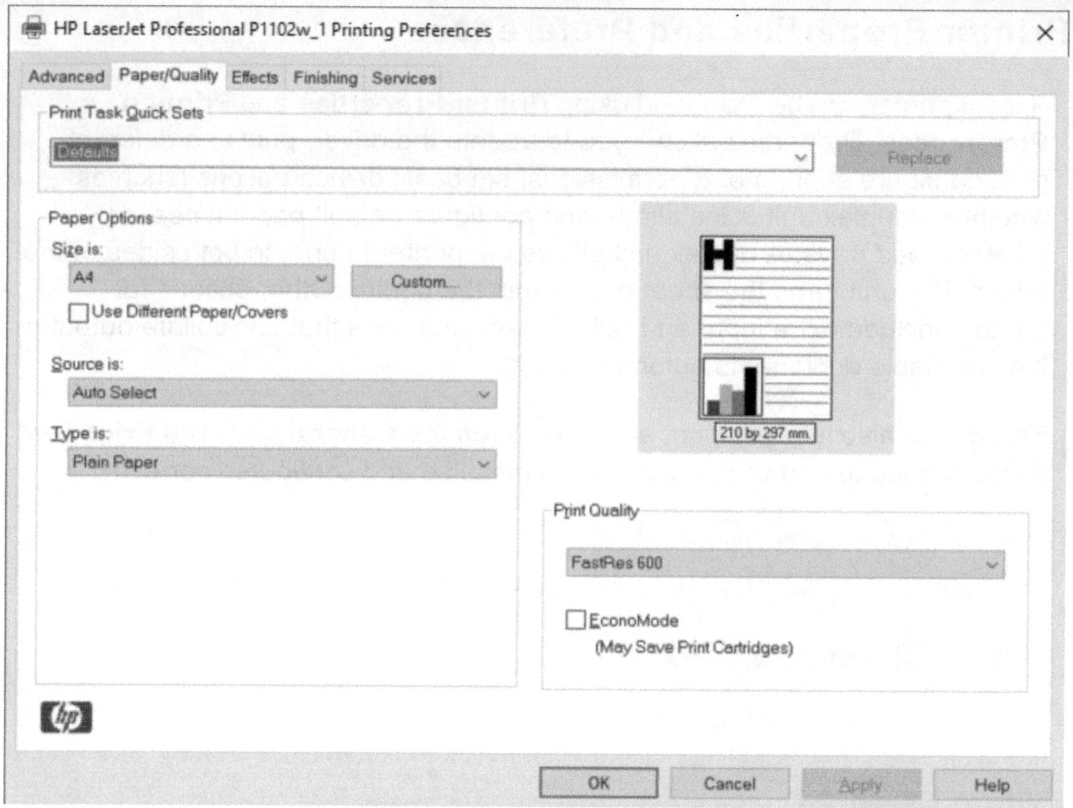

Printing preferences—this page lets you choose from a number of preset print settings templates. Screenshot used with permission from Microsoft.

These settings can also be changed on a **per-job** basis by clicking the **Properties** button in the application's **Print** dialog. Alternatively, the printer may come with management software that you can use to change settings.

Scanners and Cameras

A **scanner** is an imaging device, designed to create a digital file from a page of print, photo, or another object. Typically, scanners handle flat objects, like documents, receipts, or photographs.

Types of Scanners

A **flatbed scanner** works rather like a photocopier. The object to be scanned is placed on a glass faceplate and the cover closed to prevent ambient light affecting the image. A bright light, usually from a **Cold Cathode Fluorescent Lamp (CCFL)**, illuminates the object while the image is recorded using a **Charge Coupled Device (CCD)** array. A CCD is composed of picture elements (pixels) that generate an electrical charge in proportion to the intensity of light shined on them. This is used to create a digital image.

The quality of the scanner depends on its resolution (that is, the number of pixels in the CCD array). This is measured in pixels per inch (ppi). You may see dots per inch quoted instead, but this term is generally avoided to prevent confusion with a printer's output resolution.

Flatbed scanner. Image © 123rf.com.

Multi-function Devices (MFD) may use a **sheet-fed** scanner rather than a flatbed one. The main drawback of sheet-fed scanners is that they may only handle fairly thin paper objects.

Scanning a Document

When the scanner has been connected to the PC and configured by Plug-and-Play, it should become available to applications that can use the scan interface. Older scanners use TWAIN-based software; modern scanners are more likely to use WIA (Windows Image Acquisition). The software will present options for the image output format (PDF or JPEG for instance) and tools for selecting and correcting the image. Another option may be to use Optical Character Recognition (OCR) software to convert a text image into a computer-editable text document.

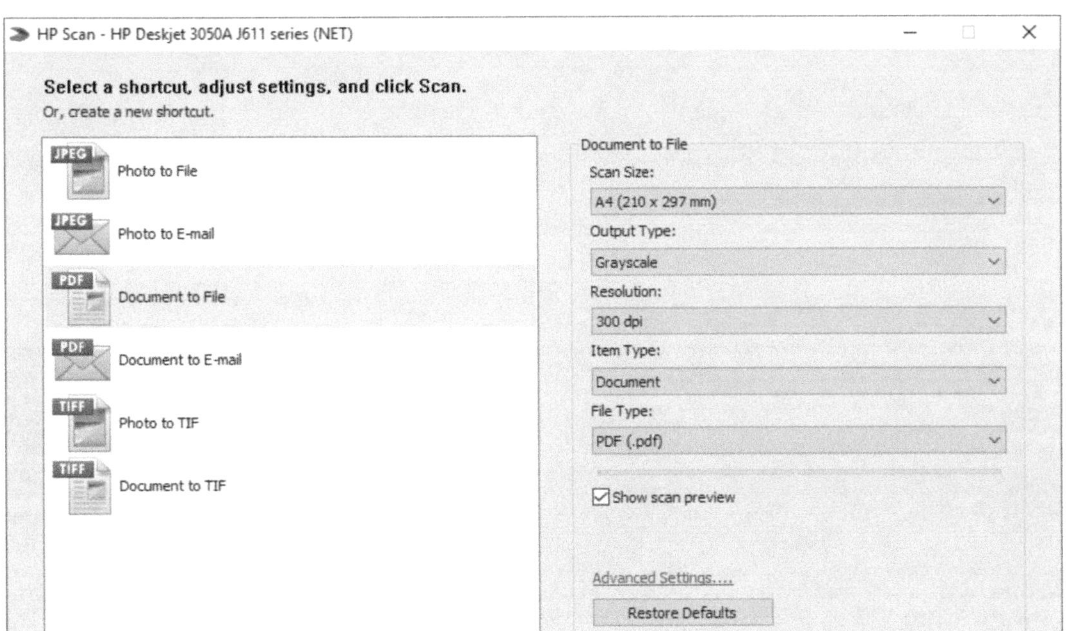

HP Scan image acquisition software.

TWAIN is an interface name and while it is always capitalized it is not an acronym, though the expansion Technology Without An Interesting Name has been suggested.

Digital Cameras

A digital camera stores images on a flash memory-based card, such as CompactFlash or Secure Digital. There are a number of ways to transfer the images stored on the card from the camera to the computer:

- Connect the camera to a USB port—this will mount the camera storage as a Windows drive and the pictures can be copied or moved using Explorer.
- Use a memory card slot—the memory card can be removed from the camera and inserted into a memory card reader on the PC, if available.
- Use Wi-Fi—a camera that supports wireless networking can make the images folder available as a shared folder on the network.

Review Questions / Module 3 / Unit 3 / Using Peripheral Devices

Answer these questions to test what you have learned in this unit. You can review the model answers at the end of the book.

1) Which Windows interface is used for advanced management and troubleshooting of devices?

2) What do you need to know to connect to a device that is configured over the network?

3) True or false? If you want to configure the DPI of a display device, you would do so via the Personalization app.

4) You are configuring dual monitors positioned side-by-side. You want to increase the amount of screen space available. Which multiple display option should you set?

5) You need to plug a microphone into a computer to make a recording. How would you identify which jack to use?

6) What, if any, type of printer uses a fuser?

7) What are the four inks used to produce color prints?

8) What type of wired interface is a printer MOST likely to use?

9) You want to configure a printer to use both sides of the paper (duplex) by default. You have alt-clicked the printer object—which command should you select to proceed?

10) What basic command demonstrates that a printer is connected properly to a computer and that its driver is installed correctly for Windows?

11) What function of a scanner would you use if you want to convert a letter that someone has mailed to you into a computer-editable document?

12) True or false? If your PC does not have a flash memory card reader, you should be able to connect the camera itself to the PC over USB to copy images off the card.

Lab 13 / Playing Audio

You will need a sound card and speakers or headphones for this lab.

1) Referring to the system documentation if necessary, connect the speakers or a pair of headphones to the appropriate output jack on your computer.

2) Press `START` and type `control panel` then click the **Control Panel** icon when it appears.

3) In the "Search" box, type `sound`

4) Click the **Sound** applet from the list of results.

5) On the **Playback** tab, select your speakers then click the **Configure** button.

6) Click **Test**—you should hear a sound from first one speaker then the other.

7) Cancel out of the dialogs.

8) Open the browser. Type the following URL into the address bar then press `ENTER`:

   `www.youtube.com/embed/rConxNFPn7g`

9) Press **Play** to start the video—as it plays, try adjusting the volume using the icon on the taskbar.

10) Optionally, shut down your computer if you are not continuing to use it after this lab.

Lab 14 / Using a Printer

You will need a printer to complete this lab.

1) If necessary, start your computer and sign in.

2) Read the documentation that accompanies the printer and complete any steps required to prepare the printer before plugging it in. The printer may come with setup software that you should install first. You should also check that the printer is loaded with paper properly.

3) Connect the printer using the appropriate port then switch it on. Allow Windows to install the driver.

4) When the printer has been installed, open **Settings > Devices > Printers and Scanners**. The printer should be the default, unless you have more than one.

5) Select the printer and then click **Manage**.

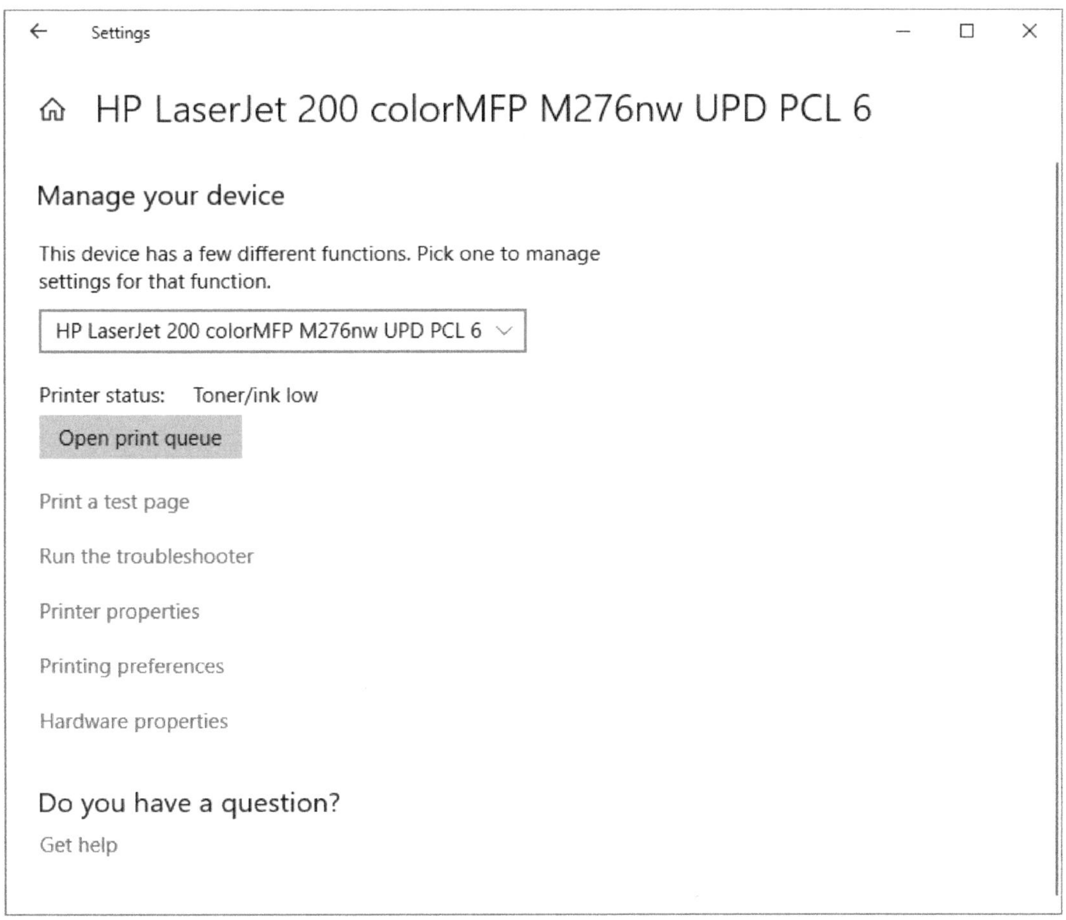

Printer management options. Screenshot used with permission from Microsoft.

6) Click the **Printing preferences** link. Browse the tabs in the dialog that opens to explore the features available on your printer. For example, find out if there are color or duplex options.

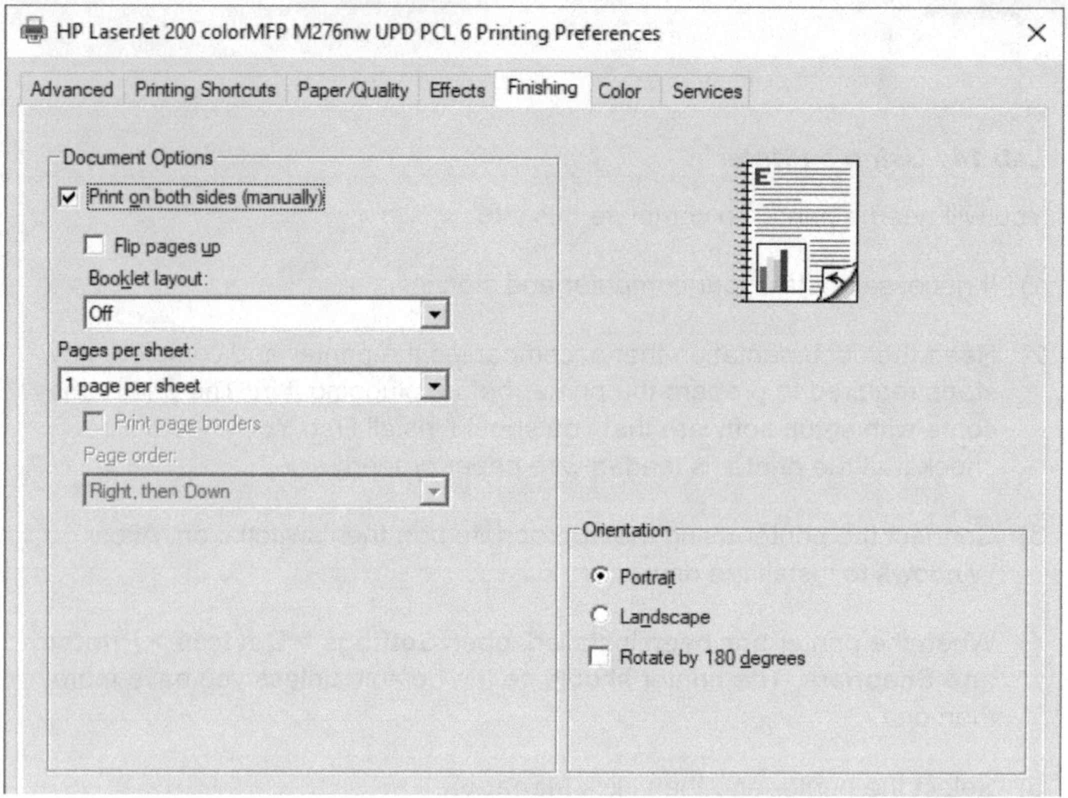

Printing preferences—this printer supports duplex (Finishing tab) but only manual duplex. Screenshot used with permission from Microsoft.

7) Click **Cancel** then in the **Settings** app, click **Open print queue**. From the **Printer** menu, select **Pause Printing**.

8) Right-click one of the picture files you created earlier and select **Print**.

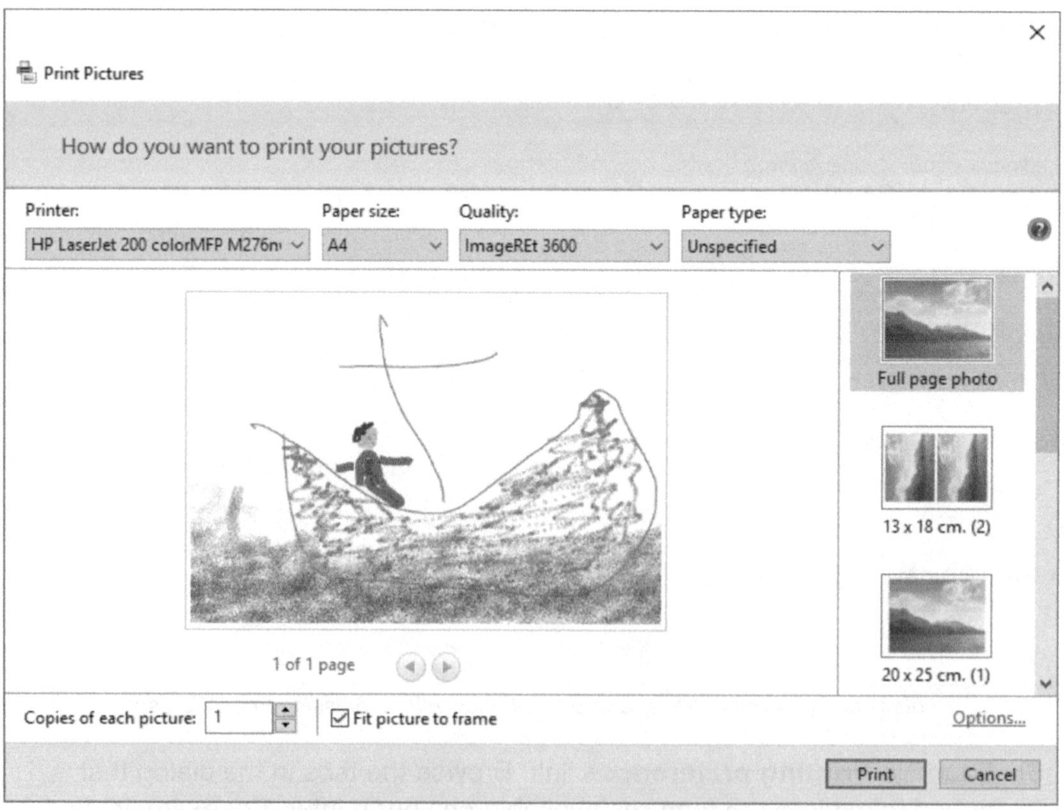

Selecting print options. Screenshot used with permission from Microsoft.

9) If necessary, select your printer from the **Printer** list box.

10) Choose the **Full Page Photo** option.

11) Click **Print**.

12) Switch to the print queue window and note that the job waits in the queue while the printer is paused. Right-click the job and note the options in the shortcut menu, but do not select any of them. Unpause the printer to allow the picture to print.

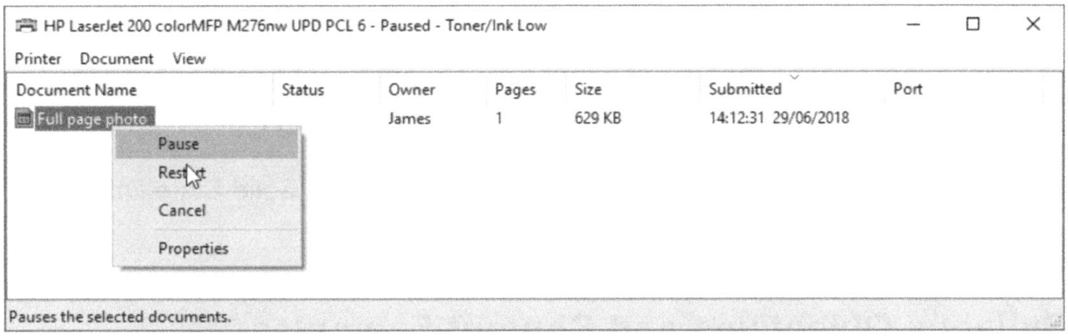

Managing the print queue. Screenshot used with permission from Microsoft.

13) Collect the print job then turn off the printer.

14) Close any open windows.

15) Optionally, shut down your computer if you are not continuing to use it after this lab.

Module 3 / Unit 4

Using Storage Devices

Objectives

On completion of this unit, you will be able to:

- Contrast volatile and non-volatile storage types.
- Describe the types of system memory modules used in PCs.
- Describe the types and features of Hard Disk Drives, Solid State Drives, optical drives, and flash memory.

Syllabus Objectives and Content Examples

This unit covers the following exam domain objectives and content examples:

- 2.2 Given a scenario, set up and install common peripheral devices to a laptop/PC.
  Devices (External hard drive)
- 2.5 Compare and contrast storage types.
  Volatile vs. non-volatile • Local storage types (RAM, Hard drive [Solid state vs. spinning disk], Optical, Flash drive)

System Memory

System memory is the main storage area for programs and data when the computer is running. System memory is necessary because it is much faster than accessing data in a mass storage system, such as a hard disk. System memory is a type of *volatile* memory called **Random Access Memory (RAM)**. Volatile means that data is only retained in the memory chips while there is a power source.

A large amount of system memory is essential for running a PC. The size of RAM determines a computer's ability to work with multiple applications at the same time and manipulate larger files. If there is not enough system RAM, the memory space can be extended by using disk space (virtual memory), but accessing the disk is very slow compared to accessing RAM.

Some notable RAM vendors include Kingston, Crucial (Micron), Corsair, PNY, and Integral.

DRAM

System RAM is a type of RAM called **Dynamic RAM (DRAM)**. DRAM stores each data bit as an electrical charge within a single **bit cell**. The electrical charge gradually dissipates, causing the memory cell to lose its information. In order to preserve the information, dynamic memory has to be refreshed periodically by accessing each cell at regular intervals.

SDRAM

Many different types of DRAM have been developed and become obsolete. Since the mid-1990s, variants of **Synchronous DRAM**, or SDRAM, have been used for system memory.

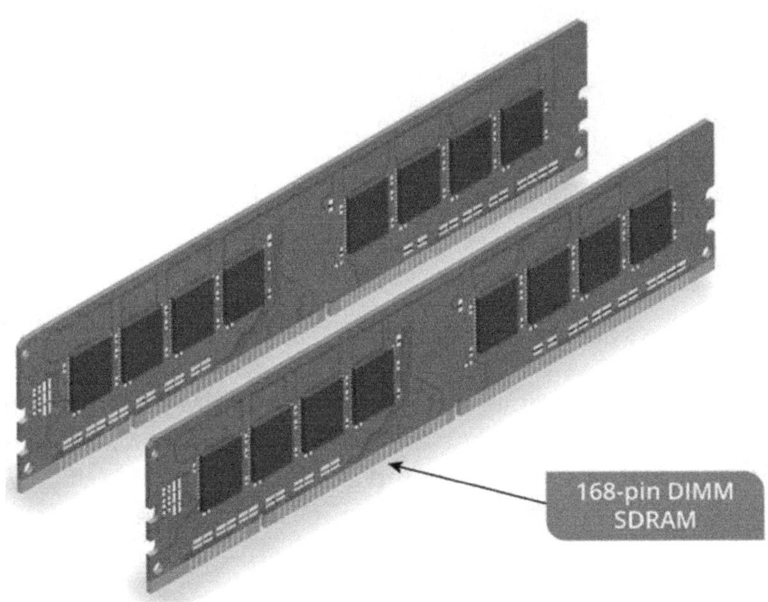

SDRAM packaged in 168-pin DIMMs. Image © 123rf.com.

SDRAM is synchronized to the system bus. It has a 64-bit data bus, meaning that in each clock cycle, 64 bits of information can be delivered to the CPU. Consequently, if the bus is running at 66 MHz, the bandwidth available to the memory controller is 66*64 or 4224 mega*bits* per second. Dividing by 8 gives the bandwidth in mega*bytes* per second (528 MBps).

SDRAM for desktop PCs is packaged in **DIMMs (Dual Inline Memory Module)**. Laptops use a smaller form factor called **Small Outline DIMM (SO-DIMM)**.

Double Data Rate SDRAM (DDR SDRAM)

Double Data Rate SDRAM (**DDR SDRAM**, or just **DDR**) is an updated type of SDRAM featuring "double pumped" data transfers. This means that 64 bits of information are transferred at the start of a clock cycle then another 64 bits at the end. For example, if the bus speed is 100 MHz, the maximum data rate would be ([64+64]*100)/8 = 1600 MBps (Mega*bytes* per second).

Since its first introduction, DDR has moved through **DDR2**, **DDR3**, and **DDR4** technology updates. These increase bandwidth by increasing the *bus* speed, as opposed to the speed at which the actual memory chips work. This produces scalable speed improvements without making the chips too unreliable or hot. The drawback is increased **latency**, as data takes longer to access on each chip. Latency is offset by improving the memory circuitry.

DDR3 SDRAM in 240-pin DIMMs. Image © 123.rf.com.

DDR2, DDR3, and DDR4 still use DIMM and SO-DIMM packaging, but the form factors of the edge connectors are different, so you must obtain modules that match the type of slots on the motherboard. For example, if you have a DDR4 motherboard, you *cannot* reuse older DDR3 modules with it.

Mass Storage Devices

Random Access Memory (RAM) is a **volatile** type of storage; it requires a constant power source to work. A **mass storage device** provides **non-volatile storage** where the data is preserved when the power is turned off. Every computing device has at least one internal mass storage device (or "fixed drive") to store the OS and application files plus user data.

Hard Disk Drives

Hard Disk Drives (HDD) are one of the most widely used type of mass storage device. Data on an HDD is encoded **magnetically** on specially coated glass or plastic **platters** accessed by **drive heads**. The platters are spun at very high speeds, giving rise to the term "spinning disk" drive. There are two formats for HDDs: 3.5" units are the type used in desktops; 2.5" form factors are used for laptops and as portable external drives.

3.5" form factor hard disk drive. Image © 123rf.com.

HDD Capacity and Performance

HDDs are available in a range of capacities. At the time of writing this ranges from 100 GB up to 10 TB (10,000 GB).

HDD performance is largely a measure of how quickly it can read and write data. One factor in determining read/write speeds is the speed at which the disks can spin, measured in **revolutions per minute (RPM)**. The higher the RPM, the faster the drive. High performance drives can reach 15,000 RPM; budget and midrange performance units are 5400 and 7200 RPM. RPM is one factor determining **access time** (measured in milliseconds), which is the delay that occurs as the read/write head locates a particular position on the drive. A high performance drive will have an access time below four ms; a typical drive might have an access time of around nine ms.

Some of the major hard drive vendors include Seagate, Western Digital, Maxtor, Hitachi, Fujitsu, Toshiba, and Samsung.

HDD Interfaces

Over the years, there have been several different standards for the controller and bus connecting an internal hard disk to a PC. These standards include EIDE/PATA, SATA, and SCSI. Modern PCs and laptops use the SATA (Serial ATA) interface. A SATA port can support a single drive. Most motherboards have at least four SATA ports.

External Hard Drives

HDDs are also available as external units. The drive is shipped in a special **enclosure**, which provides some combination of USB, Firewire, eSATA, and/or Thunderbolt ports. External units may be designed for desk use (3.5" drives) or to be portable (2.5" drives). 3.5" drives require a separate power supply too; consequently, most external drives now use the 2.5" form factor.

Standard	Bandwidth	Notes
USB 2	480 Mbps	Many devices were released to this older standard and remain in use.
USB 3 USB 3.1	5 Gbps 10 Gbps	Widely supported on devices released in the last few years.
Thunderbolt 2	20 Gbps	Uses MiniDP connector.
Thunderbolt 3	40 Gbps	Uses USB-C connector. Bandwidth only supported at up to 0.5m cabling.

An external drive can also be connected via a network. This is often referred to as Network Attached Storage (NAS). Often, NAS appliances can house multiple HDDs. NAS is covered in more detail in Unit 4.4.

Solid State Drives (SSD)

Solid State Drives (SSD) are designed to replicate or supplement the function of the hard drive. Solid state storage uses a type of non-volatile memory technology called **flash memory**. Flash memory is *non-volatile* because it does not need a power source to retain information even though it is a transistor-based technology. Compared to spinning disk storage, flash memory is very small and light and much faster. Mass manufacturing has seen prices fall to very affordable levels, though the cost per gigabyte of an SSD is still considerably higher than an HDD and it is unusual for SSDs to be supplied with more than 512 GB capacity.

While HDD specifically refers to a spinning disk drive, you may come across the term "hard drive" used to mean the main fixed disk in the computer, whether the drive format is HDD or SDD.

SSDs are available as either standalone units or hybrid drives. In a hybrid drive, the SSD portion functions as a large cache, containing data that is accessed frequently. The magnetic disc is only spun up when non-cached data is accessed. This reduces power consumption but can degrade performance.

2.5" form factor solid state drive. Image © 123rf.com.

SSDs can be packaged in the same 2.5" form factor with SATA connectors as HDDs. Better performance is obtained from SSDs installed as PCIe adapter cards or using the M.2 adapter interface, as the PCIe bus is much faster than SATA.

Optical Discs and Drives

Compact Discs (CDs), **Digital Video Discs** or **Digital Versatile Discs (DVDs)**, and **Blu-ray Discs (BDs)** are storage formats for consumer multimedia, such as music and video. They are referred to as "optical" drives because a laser is used to read data from the discs.

These formats have been adapted for data storage with PC systems. The CD/DVD/BD drives used with PCs and gaming consoles can also play consumer versions of the discs.

The data version of the CD (CD-ROM) became ubiquitous on PC systems as it has sufficient capacity (700 MB) to deliver most software applications. DVD is an improvement on CD technology and delivers substantially more capacity (up to about 17 GB). DVDs are used for some software installs and for games and multimedia. Blu-ray is the latest format for delivering High Definition movies and computer games.

Recordable and Rewritable Optical Discs

A **recordable** version of the CD (CD-R) was developed in 1999. Where an ordinary CD uses a premastered layer of foil with pits and lands to represent binary data, CD-Rs use a layer of photosensitive dye. A special laser is used to transform the dye, mimicking the structure of a normal CD, in a process called **burning**. Most ordinary CD players and drives can read CD-Rs, but they may not playback properly on older equipment.

CD-R is a type of **Write Once Read Many (WORM)** media. Data areas once written cannot be overwritten. If there is space, a new session can be started on the disc. However, this makes the disc unreadable in older CD-ROM drives. A **rewritable** (or **multisession**) disc format (**CD-RW**) has also been developed.

DVD Media

DVD is similar to CD but with better storage capacity. DVD discs can be dual-layer and/or double-sided. The different permutations result in the storage capacities listed below.

Standard	Capacity	Description
DVD-5	4.7 GB	Single layer/Single sided.
DVD-9	8.5 GB	Dual layer/Single sided.
DVD-10	9.4 GB	Single layer/Double sided.
DVD-18	17.1 GB	Dual layer/Double sided.
DVD-Video	Up to 17.1 GB	Commercially produced DVDs using MPEG encoding and chapters for navigation (can be single or dual layer and single or double sided).
DVD-Audio		Format for high quality audio (superior sampling rates and 5.1 surround sound for instance).

MPEG stands for Motion Picture Experts Group. Refer to *Unit 3.5* *for more information about file formats, encoding, and compression.*

Like CD, there are recordable and rewritable versions of DVD, some of which support dual layer recording. There are two slightly different standards for recordable and rewritable DVDs, referred to as DVD-R/DVD-RW versus DVD+R/DVD+RW. Most drives can read all formats but write in either + or - format. Many consumer DVD players can play DVD±R discs.

Consumer DVDs feature copy protection mechanisms (Digital Rights Management) and region coding. Region coding, if enforced, means that a disc can only be used in a player from the same region.

Blu-ray Discs

Blu-ray Discs (BD) are replacing DVD as the media for distributing consumer multimedia and video games.

Blu-ray is principally required to cope with the demands of High Definition video recording and playback. HD requires more bandwidth and storage space because it uses a much higher resolution picture (1920x1080 compared to 720x480 [NTSC]) and better audio quality (digital surround sound).

A standard BD has a capacity of 25 GB per layer. Dual-layer discs can store up to 50 GB and are readable in ordinary BD drives. Triple-layer 100 GB and quad-layer 128 GB discs are defined in the BD-XL specification. These require BD-XL compatible drives for writing *and* reading. There are currently no double-sided formats.

Like DVDs, consumer Blu-ray Discs are likely to be DRM-protected and may be region coded.

Optical Drive Units

A PC normally has an optical drive installed within the case, but it is now relatively uncommon for laptops to include optical drives. An optical drive can be connected via USB as an external unit.

Optical disc drive. Image © 123rf.com.

Optical drives are rated according to their data transfer speed. The original CD drives had a data transfer rate of 150 KBps. Subsequently, drives have been available that offer multiples of the original rate; this would be around 52x for new models, offering transfer rates in excess of 7 MBps.

Many optical drives also function as recordable/rewritable burners (or writers). Such drives feature three speeds, usually expressed as the Record/Rewrite/Read speed (for example, 24x/16x/52x).

DVDs feature a higher transfer rate, with multiples of 1.38 MBps (equivalent to 9X CD speed). The fastest models feature 16X read speeds. The base speed for Blu-ray is 36 MBps and the maximum theoretical rate is 12x (432 MBps). At the time of writing, most drives are 2x or 4x; 2x is the minimum required for movie playback.

Removable Flash Memory Devices

USB thumb drive (left) and SD memory card (right). Image © 123rf.com.

There are many ways of packaging flash memory other than fixed SSDs. One of the most popular is the USB drive (or thumb drive). This type of drive simply plugs into any spare USB port. Capacities are typically between 1 and 64 GB (128–512 GB thumb drives are available but are very expensive). Some USB drives may come with security features, such as encryption or fingerprint recognition.

Another popular type of packaging is the **memory card**, used extensively in consumer digital imaging products, such as digital still and video cameras. There are several proprietary types of memory card. Some popular examples include Secure Digital (SD) and Compact Flash (CF), plus formats such as Sony Memory Stick and xD Picture Card that are no longer produced. Memory cards are available in a number of sizes up to 256 GB capacity. There are 512 GB and even 2 TB cards but they are only available at a high price point.

SD cards also come in Mini (small) and Micro (smaller) form factors. The smaller form factors can be used with regular size readers using a caddy to hold the card.

Many PCs are fitted with **Multi-card Readers** with two or three slots that will accommodate most of the cards on the market. Some may have single slot readers that can only accept a single brand (typically SD).

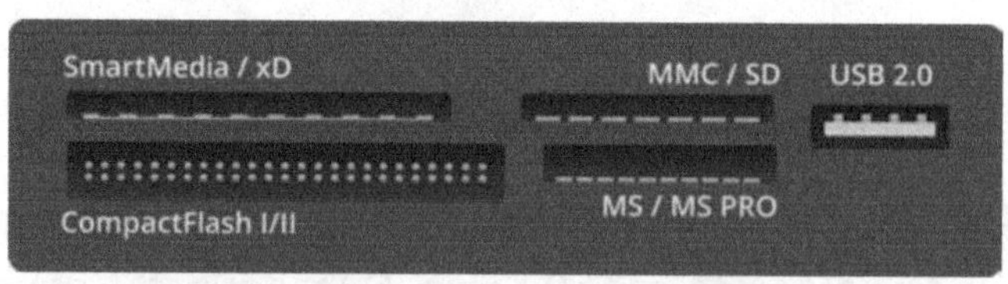

Multi-card reader. Image © 123rf.com.

Data transfer rates vary quite widely between different devices. The best-performing cards are about 312 MBps.

Another use for flash memory is as the main storage for electronic devices, such as tablets, smartphones, mobile media players (or mp3 players), handheld games consoles, and so on. Such devices typically have a few megabytes or gigabytes of internal flash memory that can be expanded using a memory card (though most will only support one particular brand of card).

Some of these devices may require special software to transfer music between the device and a PC (such as iTunes for Apple's range of iPod players). Very often though the device's flash memory will appear as a storage device when the media player is connected to the PC (via a USB port).

Review Questions / Module 3 / Unit 4 / Using Storage Devices

Answer these questions to test what you have learned in this unit. You can review the model answers at the end of the book.

1) You have a motherboard that is designed for DDR2 memory that works at a bus speed of 533 MHz. You have some DDR3 memory modules that also work at a bus speed of 533 MHz. Are the modules compatible with the motherboard?

2) Why can't you use memory modules designed for a desktop computer in a laptop?

3) A hard drive is rated at 10,000 RPM. What is the significance of this statistic?

4) What type of connector would you use for an external hard drive to connect to a Windows PC?

5) Your computer has 4 SATA ports. How many hard drives can be installed?

6) True or false? A single layer Blu-ray Disc has greater capacity than a dual-layer, double-sided DVD.

7) What sort of device would you need to transfer data from a "Memory Stick?"

8) What sort of device could you use to expand the storage capacity of a smartphone?

Lab 15 / Adding a Removable Drive

Removable storage devices are simple ways to extend storage capacity on a PC or transfer files. You can complete this lab if you have a USB stick, memory card, or removable hard drive. There are a number of different types of drive, but adding and removing them is usually straightforward. Check the instructions that came with the device if you are unsure.

1) If necessary, start your computer and log on.

2) If the device is connected by a cable, connect the smaller "B" connector on the USB cable to the device then the larger "A" connector to a USB port on the PC. Otherwise, plug a USB stick into a USB port or push a memory card into the multi-card reader.

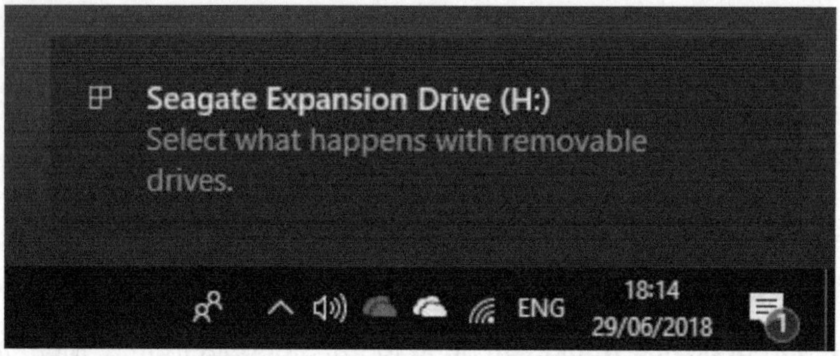

New drive detected notification. Screenshot used with permission from Microsoft.

3) After a few seconds, Windows will detect the device and begin configuring it. Click or tap the notification and an AutoPlay dialog is shown prompting you with different actions associated with the type of drive.

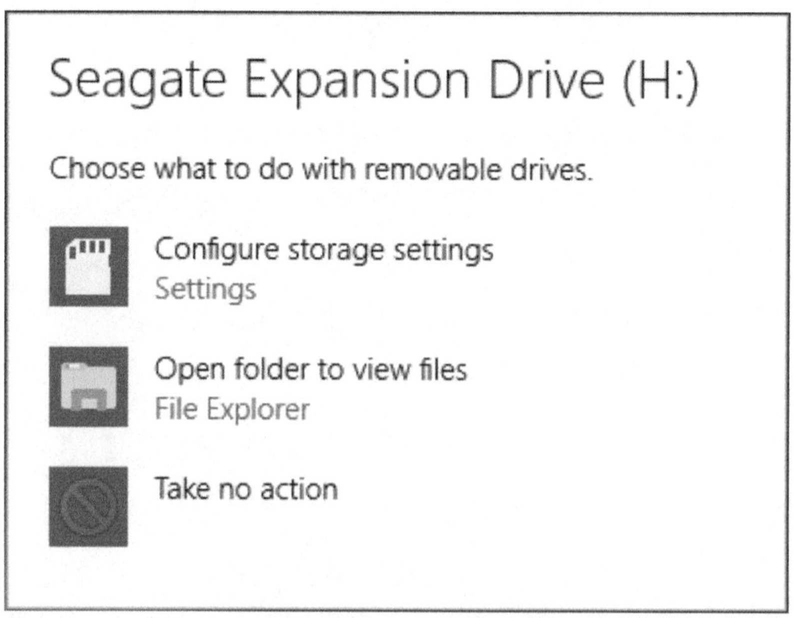

AutoPlay dialog for a USB-attached hard drive. Screenshot used with permission from Microsoft.

4) For now, just click the **Take no action** button to cancel the AutoPlay dialog.

5) Open **File Explorer** and make sure **This PC** is selected.

6) You should see that the drive is listed within under "Devices and drives" and has been assigned a drive letter in the left-hand pane.

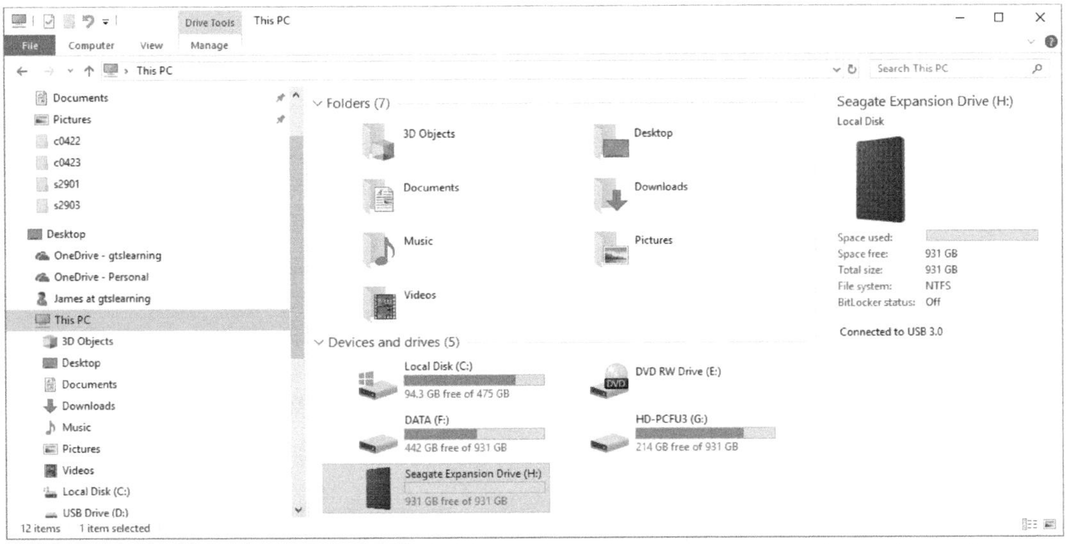

Locating the newly attached drive in File Explorer. Screenshot used with permission from Microsoft.

Note the capacity of the drive. In the screenshot above, you can see that what the vendor describes as a 1 TB drive has a formatted capacity of 931 GB. When the vendor uses the term "1 TB," they mean 1000^4 or one trillion bytes. Windows reports drive capacity using binary measurements (without using the proper notation), where 1 *tebibyte* would be 1024^4 bytes. Consequently, the capacity appears as a bit less than "1 TB."

7) Right-click the drive and note the options—for a read/write disk you should see the option to **Format**. Select **Properties**.

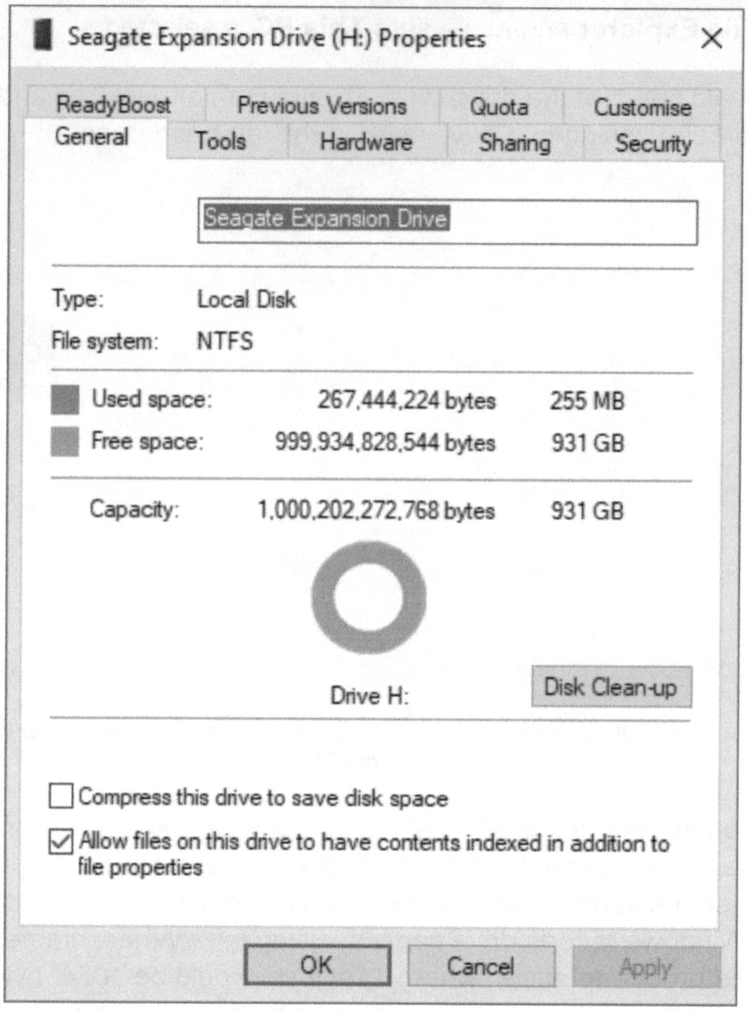

Disk properties dialog. Screenshot used with permission from Microsoft.

Note that you can confirm that the disk does have one trillion bytes of space (more or less).

8) Look through the dialog box to view the options available then click **Cancel**.

9) Double-click the drive to view its contents.

10) Close the **Computer** window.

11) Look in the Notification Area for the **Safely Remove Hardware** icon  (you may have to click the arrow to expand the area) then click it and select the **Eject** option.

12) Click **OK**.

13) Unplug the device.

14) Optionally, shut down your computer if you are not continuing to use it after this lab.

Module 3 / Unit 5
Using File Systems

Objectives

On completion of this unit, you will be able to:

- Describe the properties of file systems and select an appropriate file system for a given OS and usage.
- Use a file manager to create, open, move/copy, and delete files and folders/directories.
- Use search tools and view options to locate files quickly.

Syllabus Objectives and Content Examples

This unit covers the following exam domain objectives and content examples:

- 3.2 Compare and contrast components of an operating system.
  File systems and features (File systems, NTFS, FAT32, HFS, Ext4) • Features (Compression, Encryption, Permissions, Journaling, Limitations, Naming rules) • File management (Folders/directories, File types and extensions, Permissions)

Managing the File System

Non-volatile computer storage is based around mass storage drives. Every computer comes with a primary fixed disk (HDD or SSD). This stores the operating system and applications software that has been installed to the PC plus data files created by users.

The computer may also have a number of other storage devices, such as a secondary HDD or SSD, a CD/DVD/BD optical drive or writer, USB removable drives, or a flash memory card reader.

In order for the OS to able to read and write files to a drive, it must be **partitioned** and formatted with a **file system**.

Hard Disk Partitions

Partitioning a hard disk is the act of dividing it into logically separate storage areas. This may be done to improve the performance of the disk, to install multiple operating systems, or to provide a logical separation of different data areas. You must create at least one partition on the hard disk before performing a **format** to create a **file system**. Typically, this is done through Windows Setup when building a new PC or through Disk Management when adding an extra hard disk.

Historically, removable media such as USB thumb drives can only be formatted with a single partition using the Disk Management tool provided with Windows. However, the Windows 10 1703 update added support for creating multiple partitions on removable drives.

External hard drives usually come preconfigured with a partition and file system.

On the primary fixed disk, one of the partitions must be made **active**. This active partition is also referred to as the **system partition**. An active partition is used by the computer to boot. In Windows, the system partition is usually hidden from File Explorer and is not allocated a drive letter.

Windows Drives

In Windows, each formatted partition can be allocated a drive letter, from A through Z. The **boot partition** (containing the operating system files) is usually allocated the letter C. Each removable drive (CD/DVD/BD or flash memory card for instance) can also be allocated a drive letter.

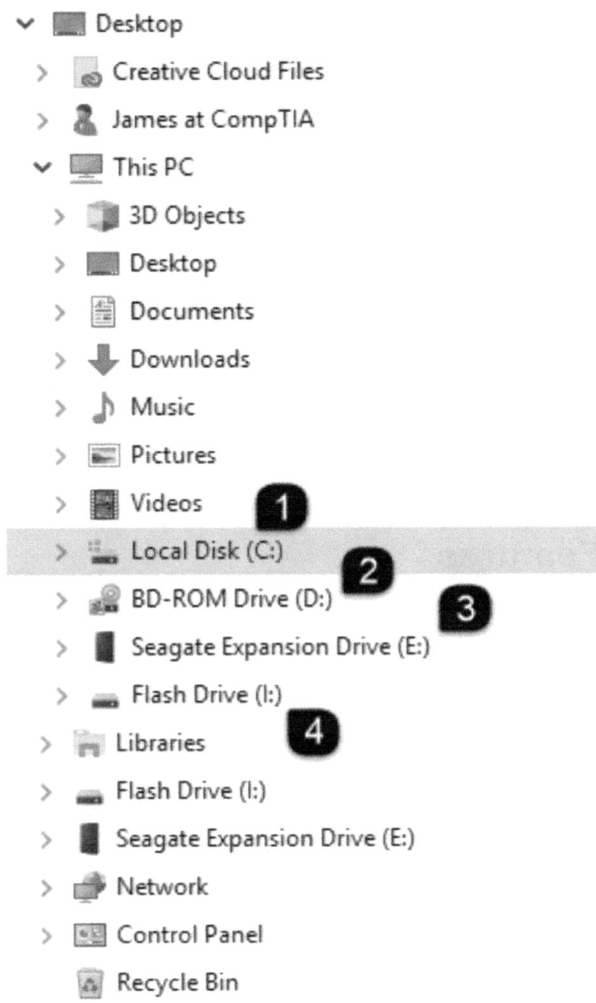

Windows drives—this computer has four: 1) The Local Disk (C:) drive is the boot partition on the hard disk; 2) D: is an optical drive; 3) E: represents an external USB-attached hard drive; 4) I: has been assigned to an SD memory card. Screenshot used with permission from Microsoft.

File Systems

Each partition can be formatted with a different **file system**. Under Windows, there is a choice between FAT and NTFS.

- **FAT (File Allocation Table)**—this was used for older versions of Windows and is preserved under Windows for compatibility. Typically, the 32-bit version (FAT32) is used. This permits a maximum file size of 4 GB and a maximum partition size of 32 GB.
- **NTFS (New Technology File System)**—as a 64-bit addressing scheme, NTFS allows much larger partitions (up to 2 TB) than FAT. NTFS also supports extended attributes, allowing for file-level security permissions, compression, and encryption. These features make NTFS much more stable and secure than FAT. Windows must be installed to an NTFS partition.

FAT32 is used for formatting most removable drives and disks as it provides the best compatibility between different types of computers and devices.

CDs and DVDs are often formatted using **Universal Disk Format (UDF),** though the older CD format **ISO 9660** (or **CDFS**) offers the best compatibility with legacy drives. Recordable media can be written to once only; rewritable media support deleting and adding files later, but to make the disc fully compatible with consumer DVD players, the session must be closed.

Most Linux distributions use some version of the **ext** file system to format partitions on mass storage devices. **ext3** is a 64-bit file system with support for journaling, which means that the file system tracks changes, giving better reliability and less chance of file corruption in the event of crashes or power outages. Support for journaling is the main difference between ext3 and its predecessor (ext2). **ext4** delivers significantly better performance than ext3 and would usually represent the best choice for new systems.

Apple Mac workstations and laptops use the extended **Hierarchical File System (HFS+),** though the latest macOS version is being updated to the Apple File System (APFS).

File System Features

You can evaluate file systems by considering which features they do or do not support:

- Compression—the file system can automatically reduce the amount of disk space taken up by a file. The file system applies a non-lossy algorithm to the file to find ways to store the data in it more efficiently without discarding any information. Note that file system compression only benefits files that are not already compressed. A file type such as JPEG that already applies compression will be significantly reduced in size.
- Encryption—the file system can automatically encrypt data in a file when it is saved. This means that the file can only be opened when there is access to the encryption key. If this is stored separately to the data and/or its use is protected by a password, the data on the drive is protected even if the disk is stolen and installed in another computer system.
- Permissions—the file system maintains an Access Control List (ACL) for each file or folder object. The ACL records which user accounts are allowed to read, write, or control the object.
- Journaling—the file system tracks changes or intended changes in a log. This means that if there is a sudden power cut and a particular write operation was interrupted, the journal may be used to recover the data or at least restore the file system to good working order (consistent state).
- Limitations—as noted in the table below, file systems have limits in terms of their maximum capacity and the size of individual files.

- Naming rules—very old file systems limited the size of a file name to eight characters plus a three-character extension. Modern file systems support longer file names (usually up to 255 characters) and complete directory paths, use of Unicode characters in the name, and support distinguishing the case of file name characters. File systems also have a number of reserved characters which cannot be used in a file name.

	FAT32	NTFS	HFS+	ext4
Compression	No	Yes	Yes	No
Encryption	No	Yes	No	Yes
Permissions	No	Yes	Yes	Yes
Journaling	No	Yes	Yes	Yes
Max File Size	4 GB	16 ExaBytes	8 EB	16 TB
Max Volume Size	8 TB	16 EB	8 EB	1 EB
Case-aware	No	Yes	Yes	Yes
Reserved characters	`" * / : < > ? \ | + , . ; = [ ]`	`" * / : < > ? \ |`	`: /`	`/`

Folders and Directories

The purpose of a drive is to store files. **Folders** are a means of organizing files on each drive to make them easier to find. Folders can also create distinct areas in terms of security access controls. Operating system files can be separated from user data files, and standard users can be prevented from modifying them. Also, each user can have a protected storage area that other standard users cannot access, unless the folder is shared.

Folders are created in a hierarchy of subfolders. The first level of the hierarchy is called the **root** folder. This is created when the drive is formatted. The root folder is identified by the drive label and a backslash. For example, the root folder of the C: drive is `C:\` The root folder can contain files and subfolders. The path to a subfolder is also separated by backslashes. For example, in `C:\WINDOWS\System32\`, `WINDOWS` is a subfolder of the root and `System32` is a subfolder of `WINDOWS`.

Windows System Folders

A default folder structure is created on the boot partition when Windows is installed. A default installation creates the following three system folders:

- **Windows**—the "system root," containing drivers, logs, add-in applications, system and Registry files (notably the System32 subfolder), and so on. System32 contains most of the applications and utilities used to manage and configure Windows.

- **Program Files**—subfolders for installed applications software.

A 64-bit version of Windows uses a "Program Files" folder for 64-bit applications software and a "Program Files (x86)" folder for 32-bit applications software.

- **Users**—storage for users' profile settings and data (Documents, Temporary Internet Files, Cookies, recent file shortcuts, desktop shortcuts, and so on).

The contents of Program Files and Windows should not be moved or changed except by using the proper Windows utilities and application installers. Moving or deleting files manually could cause serious problems. Ordinary users are denied access to system folders.

Linux Directories

"Folder" is a Windows-specific term. In Linux, these containers are called **directories**. Also, Linux uses the forward slash (`/`) to represent the root and as a directory delimiter. For example, in the directory path **`/home/andy`**, **`home`** is a subdirectory of the root directory and **`andy`** is a subdirectory of **`home`**.

Note that a forward slash will also work in Windows if you type it into the address bar or use one in a file path at the command prompt.

It is important to realize that *everything* available to the Linux OS is represented as a file in the file system, including devices. This is referred to as the **unified file system**. For example, a single hard drive attached to a SATA port would normally be represented in the file system by **`/dev/sda`**. A second storage device—perhaps one attached to a USB port—would be represented as **`/dev/sdb`**. There is no concept of "drive letters" in Linux. Everything is represented through the file system.

Think of the root file system representing everything on the computer as "THE" file system and a file system for a particular partition as just "A" file system.

A file system configured on a partition on a particular storage device is attached to a particular directory (**mount point**) within the unified file system using the **`mount`** command. For example:

```
mount /dev/sda1 /mnt/mydrive
```

...mounts partition 1 on the mass storage device **sda** to the directory **`/mnt/mydrive`**. Mountable file systems are listed in the **`/etc/fstab`** file.

File Explorer

In Windows, **File Explorer** (called **Windows Explorer** in previous versions and very widely just referred to as "Explorer") provides a visual means of navigating the file system. In the main pane, you can double-click a folder to open it. You can use the **Navigation** pane to expand and collapse objects or the **Breadcrumb** on the address bar and **Back** and **Forward** buttons on the toolbar.

Navigation Pane

When browsing the computer using File Explorer in Windows 10, two top-level categories are shown in the navigation pane. **Quick access** contains shortcuts to folders that are most useful. These can be modified by dragging and dropping. By default, it contains shortcuts to your personal Desktop, Downloads, Documents, and Pictures folders.

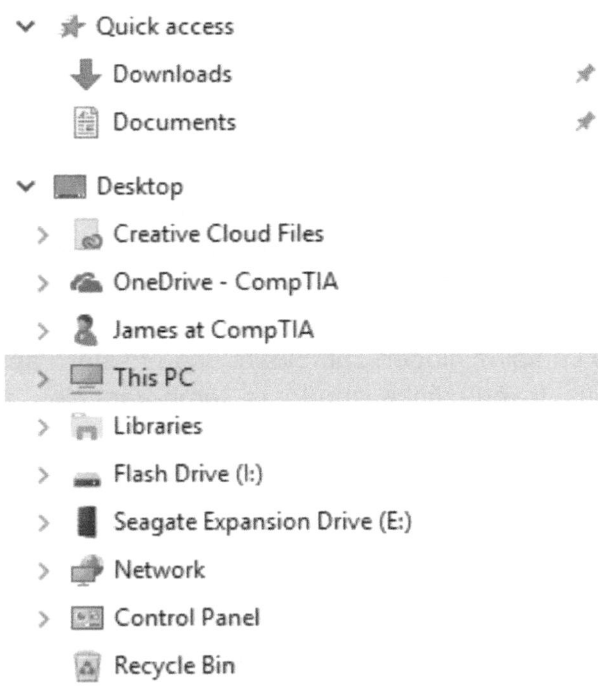

File Explorer navigation pane showing top-level categories. Screenshot used with permission from Microsoft.

The second top-level category is the **Desktop**. Under the "Desktop" object, you can find the following categories:

- **OneDrive**—if you sign into the computer with a Microsoft account, this shows the files and folders saved to your cloud storage service on the Internet. As you can see from the screenshot, other cloud service providers may add links here too.
- **User account**—the folders belonging to your account profile. For example, in the screenshot above the user account is listed as "James at CompTIA."

- **This PC**—access to user-generated files in the user's profile plus the hard drives and removable storage drives available to the PC.
- **Libraries**—these can be used to create views of folders and files stored in different locations and on different disks.
- **Network**—contains computers, shared folders, and shared printers available over the network.
- **Control Panel**—options for configuring legacy Windows features (most configuration is now performed via the Settings app rather than Control Panel).
- **Recycle Bin**—provides an option for recovering files and folders that have been recently deleted.

Earlier versions of Windows use different organizational principles for the top-level system objects. For example, Windows 7 has the user's name as the system object for accessing profile folders and the "Computer" object equivalent of "This PC" only shows drives.

User Profiles and Libraries

Each user has his or her own profile folder, stored under the **Users** system folder. Files in each user's profile are private (though a user with administrative privileges can still access them). Each profile folder contains subfolders for different types of file (documents, music, pictures, video, and so on). The profile folder also contains hidden subfolders used to store application settings and customizations, favorite links, shortcuts, temporary files, and so on.

Windows also configures a **Public** profile to allow users of the PC to share files between them (a **local share**).

*Folders can also be made available over a network (a **network share**). See Unit 4.4 for more information about folder sharing.*

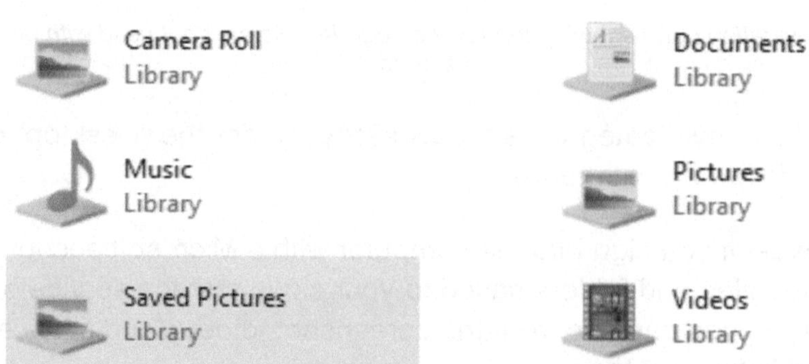

Browsing libraries. Screenshot used with permission from Microsoft.

In Windows 10, **libraries** are used to provide easy access to different kinds of documents that may be stored in different places. For example, you may store pictures in your pictures folder, on a flash drive, and on a network. You can view all these pictures in one location by adding the locations to a library. Libraries work as a kind of "virtual" folder.

By default, each profile contains libraries for Documents, Music, Pictures, and Videos. You can create new libraries using the toolbar or by right-clicking in the **Libraries** folder. Right-clicking a library icon allows you to set the locations (folders) it includes and optimize the library display settings for a particular type of file.

You can also set the default save location (the physical folder used when you save a file to a library)

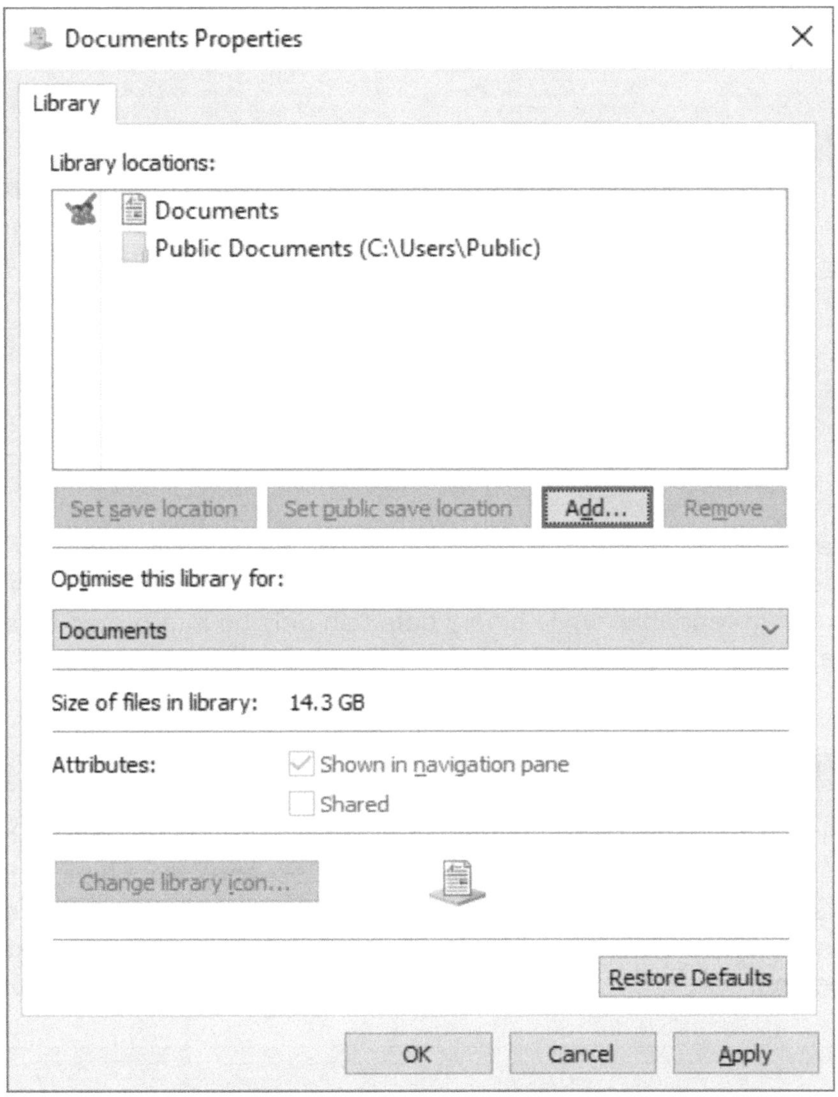

Customizing a library. Screenshot used with permission from Microsoft.

The shortcut menus for folders have the **Include in Library** *option, providing another way of adding them to a library.*

Creating a Folder

You can use the shortcut or File menus to create a new folder within another object. Windows has various folder naming rules that must be followed when modifying the folder structure:

- No two subfolders within the same folder may have the same name. Subfolders of *different* folders may have the same name though.
- Folder names may not contain the following reserved characters:
  `\ / : * ? " < > |`
- The full path to an object (including any file name and extension) may not usually exceed 260 characters.

A warning message is displayed if these rules are not followed and the user is prompted to enter a new folder name.

Folder and file names are case aware, *which means that the system preserves case in the name as entered but does not regard the case as significant for operations such as detecting duplicate names or indexing.*

Files

Files are the containers for the data that is used and modified through the operating system and applications. Files store either **text** or **binary** data; text data is human-readable, while binary data can only be interpreted by a software application compatible with that file type.

File Types and Extensions

Files follow a similar naming convention to folders, except that the last part of the file name represents an **extension**, which describes what type of file it is and is used by Windows to associate the file with an application. The extension is divided from the rest of the file name by a period. By convention, extensions are three characters. By default, the extension is not shown to the user.

Linux (and Android) use file permissions rather than extensions to determine whether a file is executable. Many Linux GUI file managers do use extensions to make opening a file within a suitable application easier though.

You can use a period as part of the main part of the file name too. It is the last *period that delimits the file extension.*

Creating and Opening Files

System and application files are created when you install programs. User files are created when you use the **Save** or **Save As** function of a program.

As you can see, the File Explorer tools are available in an application's Save dialog to navigate between folders. Most applications let you save the file in one of several file formats, accessed through the **Save as type** box.

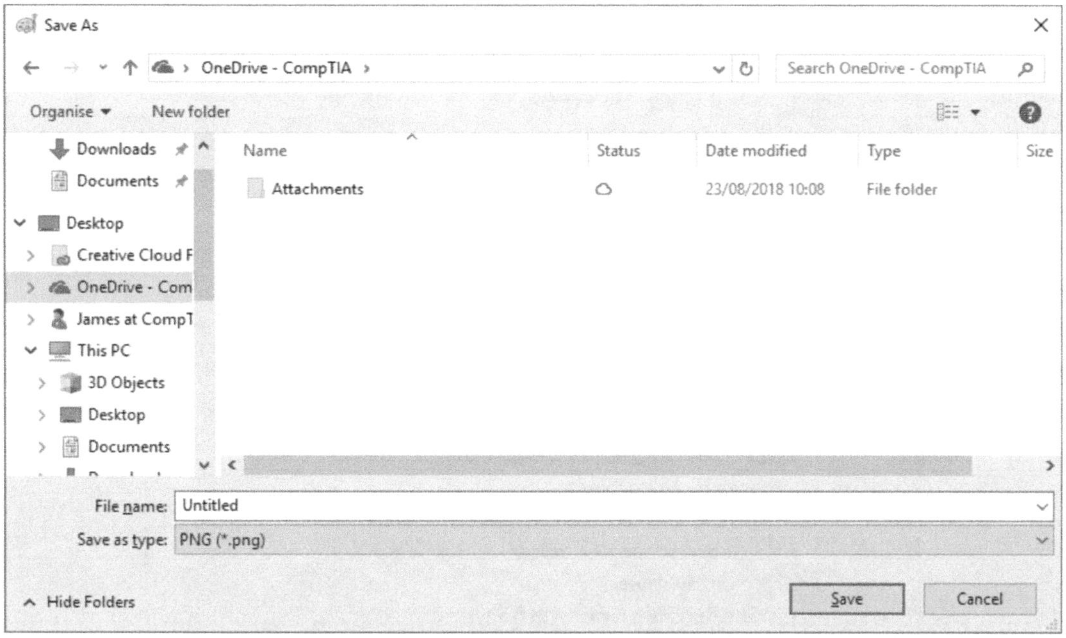

Save As dialog. Screenshot used with permission from Microsoft.

You can also create certain types of file in Explorer by right-clicking in a folder and selecting **New**, followed by the type of file you want to create.

Files are usually opened by double-clicking them. You may want to open a file in a software product other than the default however. When you right-click a file, the shortcut menu displays a list of suitable choices, or you can choose **Open With** and browse for different application. You can also use the **Default Programs** applet to configure file associations. When creating and editing text files, you must be careful to use a plain text file format, such as that used by Notepad (a Windows accessory). If you convert a plain text system file to a binary format, it will become unusable.

Some files can have different associations for the **Open** *and* **Edit** *commands. For example, a picture file might open in the Photos app when you double-click it, but if you right-click and select* **Edit,** *it will open in Paint.*

You must also use the **Save** command to retain any changes you make while editing a document. If you want to keep both the original document and the edited version, use the **Save As** command to create a new file with a different name and/or stored in a different folder.

File Explorer Options

The **File Explorer Options** applet in Control Panel controls how Explorer works. The **General** tab contains options for opening files by single-clicking and for opening folders in the same or new windows.

Folder Options dialog—View settings tab. Screenshot used with permission from Microsoft.

The **View** tab contains a long list of options affecting how folders and files are displayed in Explorer (such as whether to show **hidden** files or **file extensions**). View settings (such as whether to show thumbnail icons or details) are retained on a per-folder basis but can be reset using the buttons on the **View** tab.

Renaming Files and Folders

To rename a file or folder, select it, press `F2`, then type the new name. You can also right-click the file and select **Rename**.

Do not change a file's extension if it is shown. If you delete or change the extension, the file will not be associated with the correct program for opening it.

Copying and Moving Files

Explorer supports multiple methods of moving or copying files. These include:

- Use the **Edit > Cut/Copy/Paste** commands from the main menu or shortcut menu or their keyboard shortcuts (`CTRL+X`, `CTRL+C`, `CTRL+V`).
- Drag and drop the object, holding down `CTRL` to copy or `SHIFT` to move (or `CTRL+SHIFT` to create a shortcut).

The default action (no key press) for drag and drop is to move *the selection if the destination is a* local *drive or* copy *it if the destination is a* network *or* removable *drive.*

It is simplest to have the destination folder visible before you start to drag and drop, but you can cause a window to scroll up or down during the drag process or make a minimized window active by dragging the selection over the window's taskbar icon.

- Right-click drag the object and select an option from the shortcut menu displayed when you release the mouse button.
- Use the **Edit > Move to Folder/Copy to Folder** commands.
- Use the **Send To** command from the main menu or shortcut menu to copy a file to a disk or send it by email.

If a folder contains a file with the same name as the file being pasted, a confirmation dialog is shown:

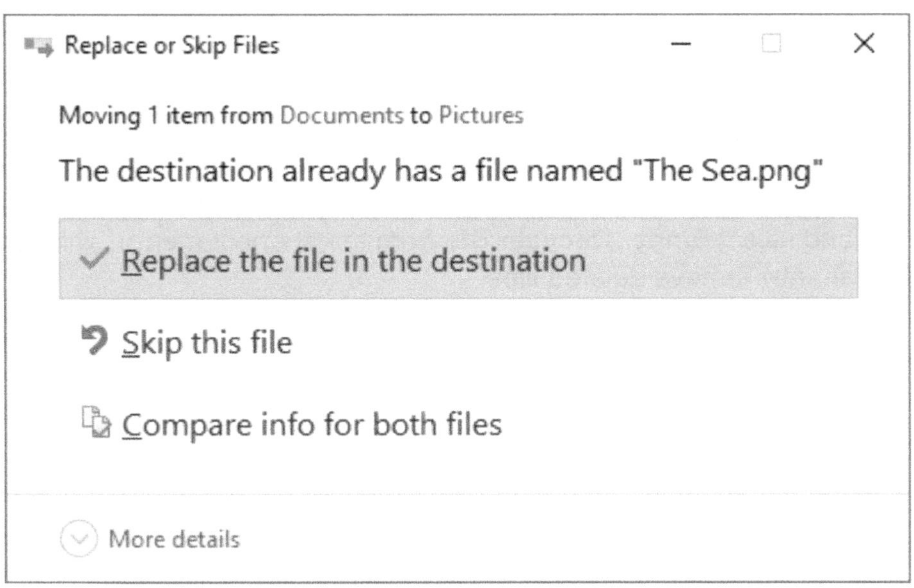

Replace or Skip Files confirmation dialog. Screenshot used with permission from Microsoft.

You can choose to overwrite the destination file, cancel the paste operation, or keep both files by renaming the one you are moving or copying (in Windows 8, choose the **Compare info for both files** option to do this). If doing this with several files, there is also a check box to choose the same option for all conflicts.

Deleting Files and the Recycle Bin

To delete a file using Explorer, select it then press `DEL` (or use the shortcut menu). Confirm the action using the prompts.

If you accidentally delete a file or folder from a *local hard disk*, you can retrieve it from the **Recycle Bin**. A retrieved file will be restored to the location from which it was deleted. The size of the Recycle Bin is limited by default to 10% of the drive's capacity. If large numbers of files are deleted, those files that have been in the Recycle Bin the longest will be permanently deleted to make room for the newly deleted files.

To recover a file, open the **Recycle Bin** 

, right-click the icon(s) to recover, and select **Restore**.

Recycle Bin. Screenshot used with permission from Microsoft.

If disk space is low, the Recycle Bin can be emptied (right-click the **Recycle Bin** icon and select **Empty Recycle Bin** from the shortcut menu). This process will permanently remove deleted files.

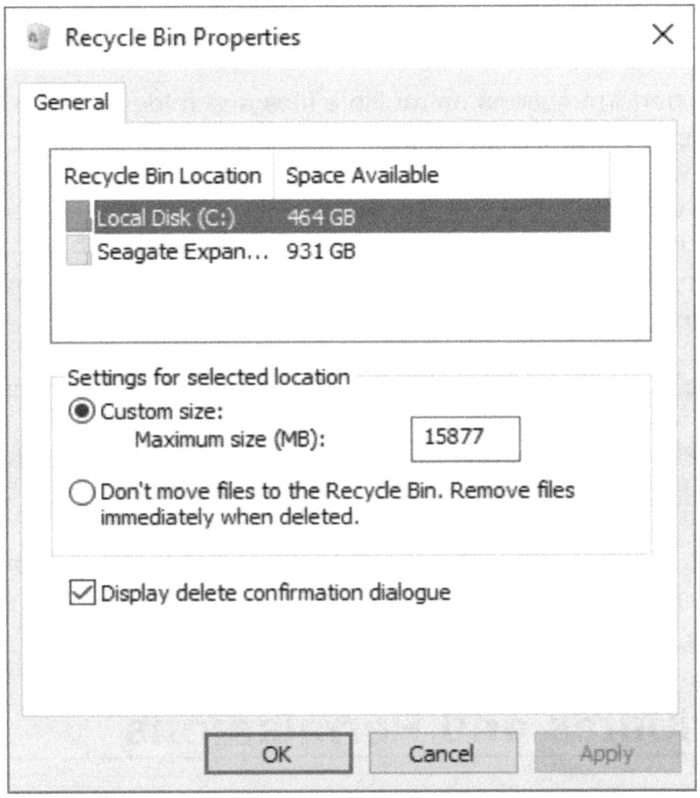

Recycle Bin properties—note that on this PC there are two hard drives, each with its own recycle bin. Screenshot used with permission from Microsoft.

From a security point of view, note that the data is not actually erased until that area of disk is overwritten by different data. Third-party utilities can recover files that have been "deleted" in this way. Other file "shredding" utilities are available to properly erase confidential data.

You can set the amount of space to use on a per-drive basis or set one Recycle Bin for all local drives. You can also choose to suppress the use of delete confirmation dialogs.

To set these options, right-click the **Recycle Bin** and select **Properties**.

There is also an option not to use the Recycle Bin. If you want to delete a particular file without using the bin, hold down the `Shift` *key as you delete it.*

The Recycle Bin works only for local hard drives, including USB-connected hard drives but not with flash memory thumb drives, removable media, or network folders. Files deleted from these locations are deleted permanently, though on a network, the administrator may be able to recover a file from the server itself.

Selecting Multiple Files and Folders

You can also perform actions on multiple files and folders. To do so, you need to be able to select the icons you want. There are various ways of doing this:

- Click and drag the mouse cursor around a block of files or select the first icon then hold **SHIFT** and click the last icon to select a block. You may want to sort the icons into a particular order first (see the "Searching for Folders and Files" topic below).
- Select the first icon then hold **CTRL** and select any other icons you want.
- Use **SHIFT** with the **ARROW** keys to select a block of files using the keyboard.
- Use **CTRL** with the **ARROW** keys to keep your existing selection, using the **SPACEBAR** to add icons to it.

File Attributes and Permissions

A file's name is just one of its **attributes**. Other attributes include the date the file was created, accessed, or modified, its size, its description, and the following markers, which can be enabled or disabled:

Attribute	Usage
Read-only (R)	Prevent changes being saved back to the file. The user will be prompted to create another file containing the modified data.
Hidden (H)	Specifies whether the file is visible in the default view (it is possible to adjust Windows to display hidden files and folders though).
System (S)	Specifies that the file should not be accessible to ordinary users.
Archive (A)	Shows whether a file has changed since the last backup.

Files stored on an NTFS partition have **extended attributes**, including permissions, compression, and encryption.

File Properties Dialog

You can set some attributes manually using the file or folder's properties dialog. To open the properties dialog for a file or folder, right-click and select **Properties**. The properties for a folder will show the size of all the files in that folder (plus any subfolders). The properties for a file (or selection of multiple files) will show the file size.

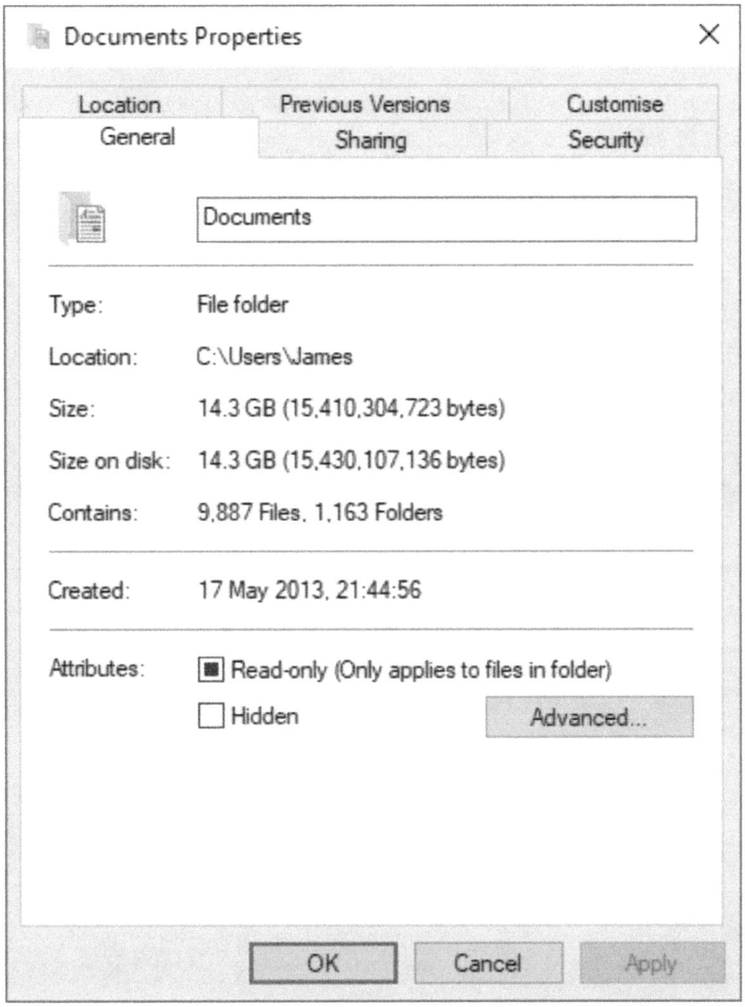

Properties dialog for a folder. Screenshot used with permission from Microsoft.

Note there is an actual file size and a size on disk shown. The size on disk is usually larger due to the way storage locations (or clusters) are created on the disk.

You can also view file and folder information in the Details Pane in File Explorer or in Details view (see below).

Folder and File Permissions

To view, create, modify, or delete a file in a folder, you need the correct **permissions** on that folder. Permissions can also be applied to individual files. Administrators can obtain full permissions over any file, but standard users can generally only view and modify files stored either in their profile or in the public profile. If a user attempts to view or save a file with insufficient permissions to do so, Windows displays an **Access Denied** error message.

Custom permissions can be configured for a file or folder using the **Security** tab in its properties dialog.

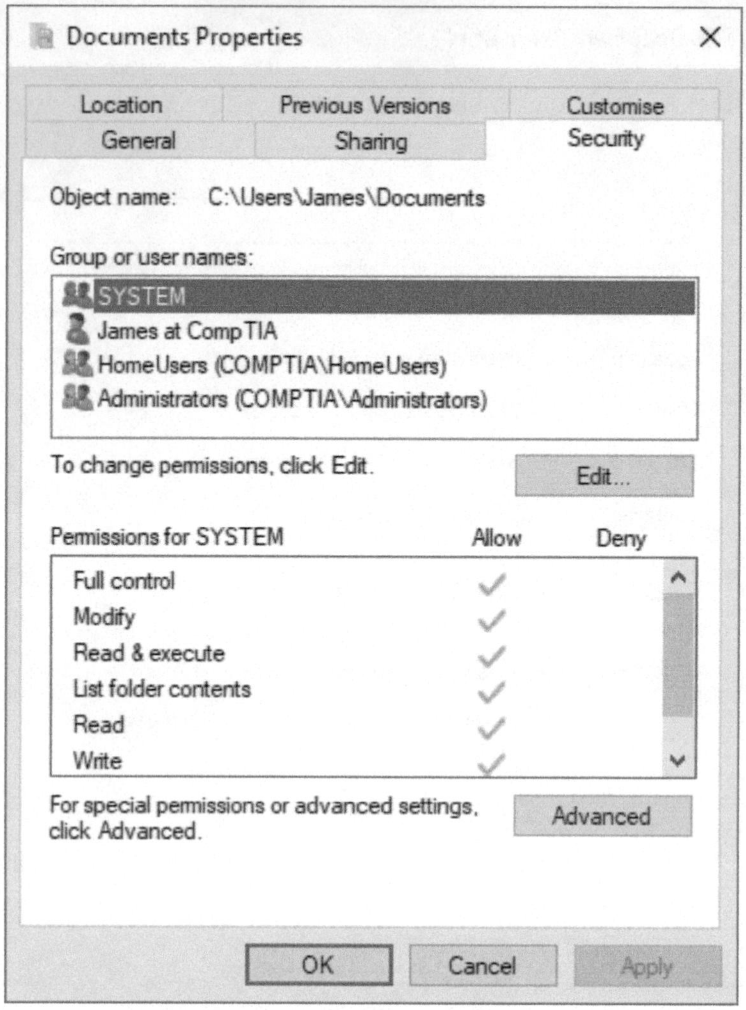

Viewing permissions for a folder object. Screenshot used with permission from Microsoft.

Remember that permissions can only be configured if the file system is NTFS. FAT does not support permissions.

To configure permissions, you first select the account to which the permissions apply. You can then set the appropriate permission level. In simple terms, the permissions available are as follows:

- Full control—allows the user to do anything with the object, including change its permissions and its owner.
- Modify—allows the user to do most things with an object but not to change its permissions or owner.
- Read/list/execute—allow the user to view the contents of a file or folder or start a program.
- Write—allows the user to read a file and change it, or create a file within a folder, but not to delete it.

Searching for Folders and Files

Windows **Search** enables you to locate files and information located in on your computer, within apps, such as email, or on the web. Search makes automatic use of file and folder properties (or metadata) and file contents. In Windows 10, the simplest way to search is to press the **START** key and type a search phrase. Files, programs, apps, messages, and web pages that match your search are displayed instantly:

Windows 10 search box. Screenshot used with permission from Microsoft.

In Windows 10, the search box is located next to the Start button. You can type your search text straight into the box, or you can use vocal commands to initiate a search by using Windows Cortana, Windows 10's digital assistant.

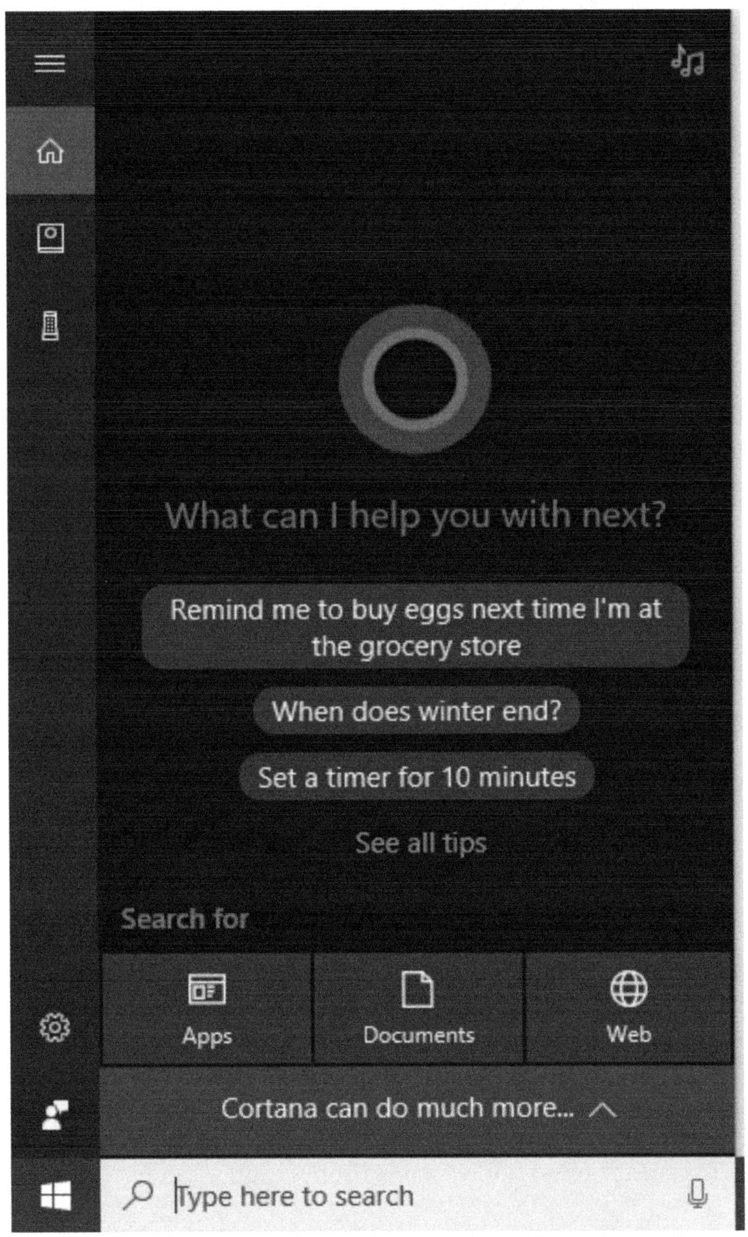

Cortana. Screenshot used with permission from Microsoft.

Type the required search string, and if necessary, click the Apps, Documents, or Web tab to filter results accordingly.

File Explorer Search

To search for files, you can also use File Explorer. The Explorer search box is located in the top-right corner of the window. Pressing **F3** in Explorer activates the search box.

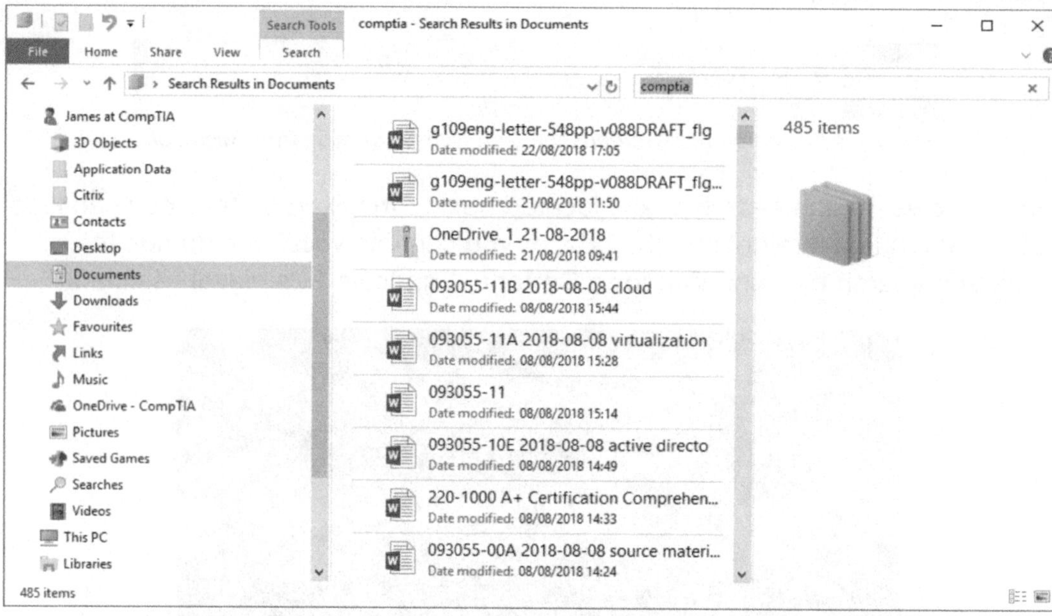

Performing a file search. Screenshot used with permission from Microsoft.

You can open, rename, delete, move, and copy files from the search results as normal. If a basic search does not locate the file you want, you can add a filter to reduce the number of results:

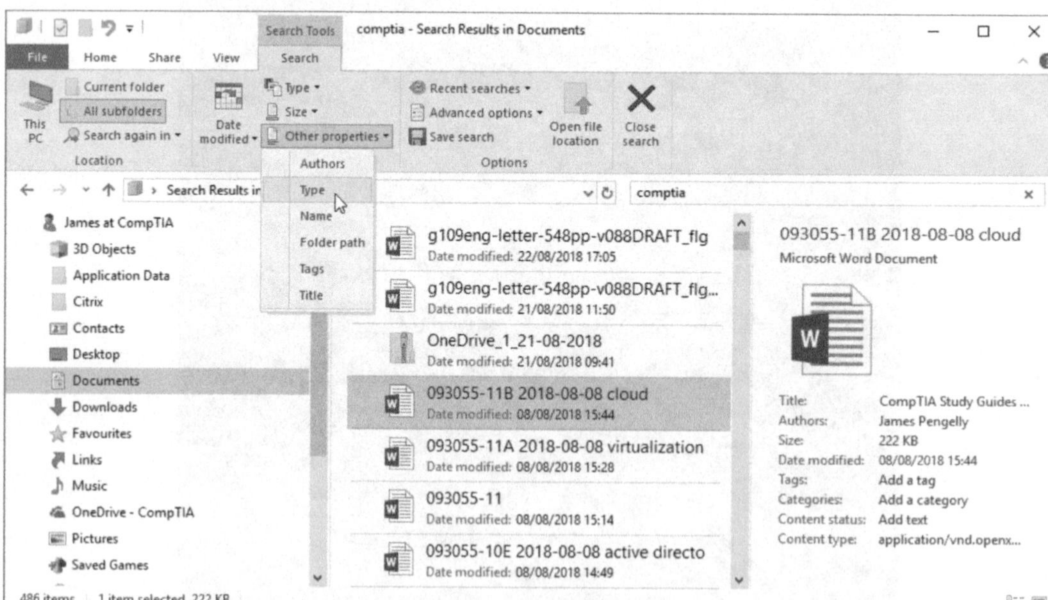

Search filter options. Screenshot used with permission from Microsoft.

View, Group, and Filter Options

In any folder, you can also use the view options to make finding a file or files easier. The view options set how large icons are, and you can use **Details** view to show information about each file in columns. The column headers allow you to sort files in ascending or descending order (or in other views you can right-click and select **Sort By**).

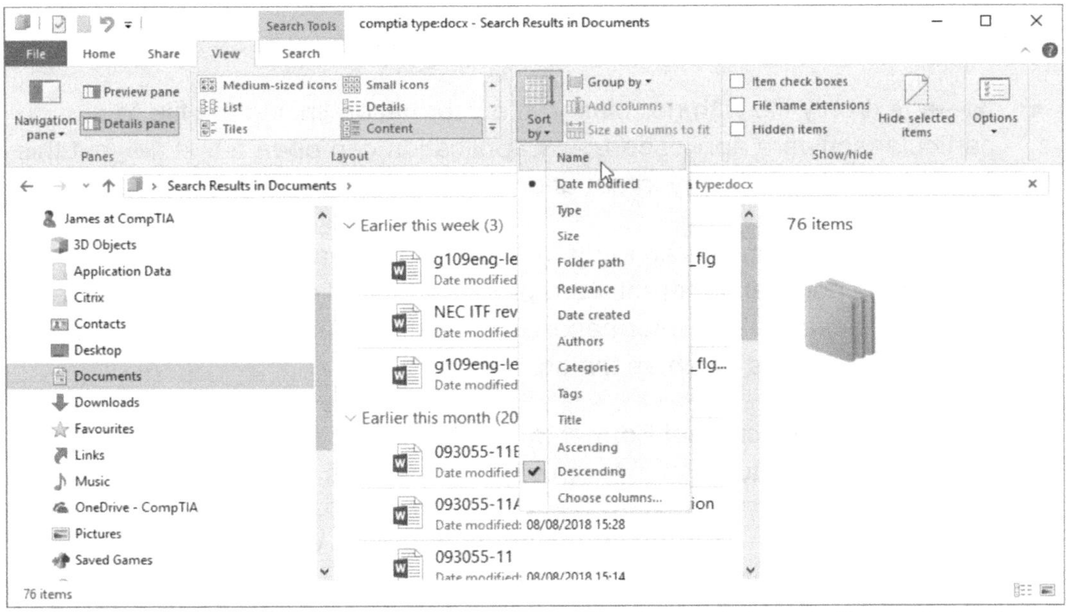

Applying view options to group and sort search results. Screenshot used with permission from Microsoft.

The column headers or right-click menu also allow you to group and filter by the information in that field:

- Group—show icons in groups with dividers between them (for example, all files with names beginning "A," then all files beginning with "B," and so on).
- Filter—show only the files that match the selected criteria.

The contents of libraries display an **Arrange By** *option, allowing you to stack files in virtual folders according to the chosen field (Author or Type for instance).*

The Windows Search service indexes files and folders in the background. Indexing (and re-indexing) files can slow the computer down, so you may need to configure **Indexing Options** *from* **Control Panel**.

File Types and Extensions

It is worth knowing some of the extensions used to identify common file types.

Word Processing Software

The following file formats are often used by word processing software:

- txt—a text-only file with no "binary" file information linking the file to a particular software application. Any application can open a text file, but this file type cannot store any information about formatting or layout.
- rtf—Rich Text Format is an early "generic" file format for sharing documents between different word processing applications. It is capable of storing basic formatting information, such as font and paragraph formatting, and layout features, such as tables.
- odf—the Open Document Format is an XML-based specification with better support for the features of modern word processors than RTF.
- doc/docx—this format is the one used by Microsoft Word. The docx XML-based format was introduced in Word 2007.

Spreadsheet Software

Microsoft's Excel spreadsheet software saves files with an xls or xlsx (Excel 2007 and up) file extension.

Presentation Software

Microsoft's PowerPoint presentation software saves files with a ppt or pptx (PowerPoint 2007 and up) file extension.

PDF Viewers and Creators

Adobe's **Portable Document Format (PDF)** is a file format for distributing documents. It is now an open standard, so different productivity applications can use it. For example, you could save a Microsoft Word document to PDF format and then open it in the Adobe Reader PDF viewer application. Most web browsers have plug-in PDF viewers. PDF was envisaged as a "final" format for the distribution of a published document. A PDF should look the same on-screen as it does when printed. It is possible to edit PDFs (using special applications) or to export a document from PDF to another format. In most cases though, it is important to keep a copy of the document in its "native" format. For example, having published a PDF from a Word document file, you would also save the latest changes to the Word file and keep it as the source file for any future changes.

Image File Types

DTP and graphic design applications (and most productivity software) can make use of images in digital file formats. A number of different image file formats have been developed for use in different scenarios:

- jpg/jpeg (Joint Pictures Expert Group)—this lossy compression format is the most widely used for photographic pictures. The lossy compression method relies on dithering the image to some extent (changing the color value of some pixels). The user can select a level of compression when saving the file, trading picture quality for reduced file size.

  A lossy compression method irreversibly discards some of the original data. This will, for example, reduce the quality of an image. Lossless compression is fully reversible because no information is discarded (it is just stored more efficiently).

- gif (Graphics Interchange Format)—this is an old lossless compression format. It only supports up to 8 bits per pixel, seriously limiting the available color palette. An 8-bit image can have up to 256 color values. Modern image formats support up to 24 bits per pixel, allowing a palette of millions of color values.
- tiff (Tagged Image File Format)—this is a popular format for exchanging images between editing applications. It can use lossless or JPEG compression.
- png (Portable Network Graphics)—this is a full-color (24-bit) lossless format designed to replace GIF. It also supports transparency.
- bmp—this is a Windows-only lossless format. It is not widely used due to its lack of compatibility with other operating systems.

Video File Types

- mpg—this is an early MPEG (Motion Pictures Expert Group) standard for video files with lossy compression.
- mp4—the MPEG-4 standard audio/video file format. The format acts as a container for audio and video media streams (plus additional media, such as subtitles). A number of different encoding methods (or codecs) are available. One of the most widely used is H.264.
- flv—another container file format designed to deliver Flash Video. This is video created in the Adobe Flash developer tool. It can be viewed through the free Flash Player browser plug-in. Flash was once ubiquitous on the web but its use is declining since Apple refused to support it on the iPhone and iPad. The HTML5 web page coding language provides a standards-based alternative to Flash.
- wmv (Windows Media Video)—a video container file format developed by Microsoft. It is well supported by media players and can also be used as the format for DVD and Blu-ray Discs.

- avi—a legacy Windows-only video format. It is a limited format with not much ongoing support.

Audio File Types

- mp3—developed from MPEG, this remains one of the most popular formats for distributing music and is almost universally supported by media players. The only drawback is that it is a lossy compression format, which means that some of the audio information is discarded.
- aac (Advanced Audio Coding)—developed from MPEG as a successor to mp3. This format is also widely supported.
- m4a—this is an audio-only file format deriving from the MPEG-4 standards track. It usually uses AAC compression, though other methods are available (including lossless ones).
- flac (Free Lossless Audio Codec)—as the name suggests, this format achieves file size compression without discarding audio data. The only drawback is that it is not quite as widely supported by media players.
- wav—this is an early Windows audio file format. It is not widely supported by media players but may be used by audio editing applications.

Executable Files

An **executable file** is one that contains program code. Unlike a data file, program code can make changes to the computer system. Most operating systems enforce permissions to restrict the right to run executable code to administrator-level users.

- exe—this is the basic type of program file in Windows.
- msi—this is a Windows Installer file used to install and uninstall software applications under Windows.
- app—this is the equivalent of an exe file for macOS.
- bat/cmd/vbs/js/ps1—contains a sequence of commands either from the operating system's command interpreter or from a scripting language supported by the OS. A script is slightly different from program code in that it is not compiled into executable code. Instead, the script runs within an interpreter.

Compression Formats

Often, to send or store a file it needs to be compressed in some way, to reduce the amount of space it takes up on the storage media or the bandwidth required to send it over a network. There are a number of compression utilities and formats.

- zip—this format was developed for the PKZIP utility but is now supported "natively" by Windows, Mac OS X, and Linux. "Natively" means that the OS can create and extract files from the archive without having to install a third-party application.
- tar—this was originally a UNIX format for writing to magnetic tape (tape archive) but is still used with gzip compression (tgz or .tar.gz) as a compressed file format for UNIX, Linux, and macOS. A third-party utility is required to create and decompress tar files in Windows.
- rar—this proprietary format is used by the WinRAR compression program.
- 7z—this type of archive is created and opened using the open-source 7-Zip compression utility.

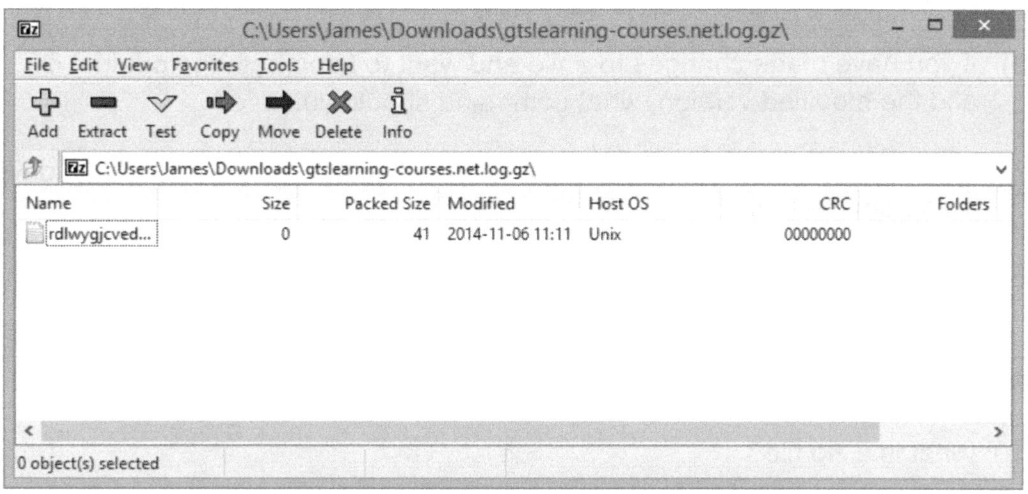

Extracting .gz files in Windows using the 7-zip utility.

- gz—this type of archive is created and opened by the gzip utility, freely available for UNIX and Linux computers. A number of Windows third-party utilities can work with gzip-compressed files.
- iso—this is a file in one of the formats used by optical media. The main formats are ISO 9660 (used by CDs) and UDF (used by DVDs and Blu-Ray Discs). Many operating systems can mount an image file so that the contents can be read through the file browser.
- vhd/vmdk—these are disk image file formats used with Microsoft Hyper-V and VMware virtual machines respectively. A disk image is a file containing the contents of a hard disk, including separate partitions and file systems. Like an ISO, such a file can often be mounted within an OS so that the contents can be inspected via the file browser.
- dmg—this is a disk image file format used by Apple macOS.

Review Questions / Module 3 / Unit 5 / Using File Systems

Answer these questions to test what you have learned in this unit. You can review the model answers at the end of the book.

1) In Windows, you can access data via letter-labeled "drives." Do these correspond exactly to physical disks?
2) What type of file system must the partition that Windows files are installed on use?
3) What default installation folders contain system and application files that should not normally be deleted or modified manually?
4) What is the file path to the Documents folder for a user named "David," assuming Windows is installed to a hard disk with a single partition using the default settings?
5) How is a Windows library different from a folder?
6) If you have made changes to a file and want to keep both the original file and the modified version, what command should you use?
7) Why should you be more careful about deleting files from a USB flash drive than from the main hard drive?
8) What view options could you use to show files of a particular type sorted by date?
9) What kind of data would you expect to find in a file with a TIFF extension?
10) What is a zip file?

Lab 16 / Using File Explorer

In this lab, you will investigate the Windows file system and practice some typical file management tasks.

Exercise 1 / The Windows File System

In this exercise, you will investigate the user profile folders, navigate the Windows directory structure, and look at how libraries can be used to consolidate multiple file locations into one view.

1) If necessary, start your computer and sign in.

2) Press `START+E` to open File Explorer.

   File Explorer opens the "Quick Access" object by default. This contains shortcuts to frequently-used folders (you can change these by dragging new shortcuts into the menu) and also a list of recently opened files.

3) Double-click the **Desktop** folder. This folder contains shortcuts, files, or folders that you have added to the desktop folder in your profile, plus any shortcuts added by setup programs (it may be empty).

4) Click the **Up One Folder** button ↑ or click the **This PC** segment in the address bar breadcrumb.

   "This PC" contains the drives connected to the computer and the main profile folders. There are default folders designed for storing different types of data (Documents, Pictures, Music, Video, and so on).

5) Click the **Up One Folder** button ↑ again or click the arrow on the breadcrumb root icon and select **Desktop** (note the different icon)

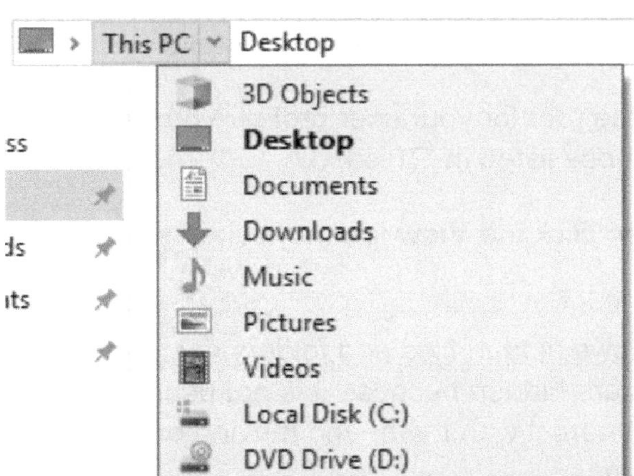

Using the breadcrumb. Screenshot used with permission from Microsoft.

   This selects the system-level desktop object. This contains all the system objects you can see in the left-hand navigation pane plus the shortcuts from your "personal" desktop folder.

6) Right-click in some empty space here and select **New > Text Document**. Type the name `Navigating the Desktop` then press `ENTER`.

7) Press `START+D` to show the desktop. You should be able to see the text document you just created. Press `START+D` again to restore the File Explorer window.

8) Right-click the desktop and then click **Personalize**.

9) In the left-hand pane, select **Themes**, and then scroll down to click **Desktop icon settings**.

10) In the "Desktop Icon Settings" dialog, select the **Computer** and **User's Files** check boxes, and then click **OK**.

11) Close the Settings app.

12) On the desktop, double-click the icon for your user account .

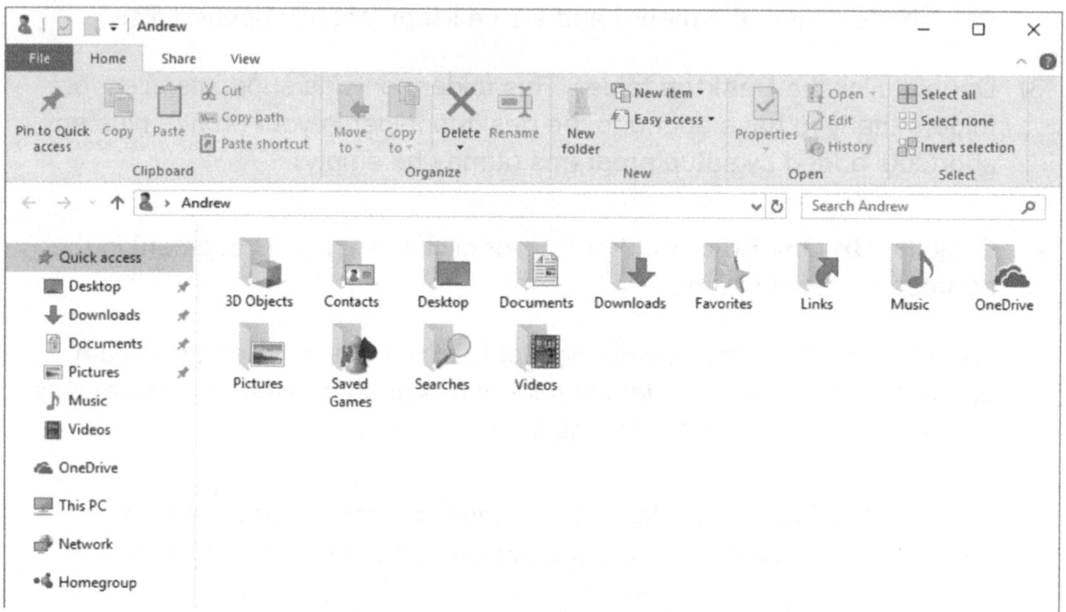

User home folder. Screenshot used with permission from Microsoft.

This folder is the root for your user profile. You will see extra folders compared to those listed in "This PC."

13) In File Explorer, click the **View** tab menu then select the **Hidden items** check box.

This option shows hidden files and folders, such as the AppData folder. These objects are hidden because it is not usually necessary for standard-level users to interact with them, and moving or deleting them might cause system problems.

14) Open the **Pictures** folder. You should see the Paint picture you created earlier. Make a note of the navigation objects shown in the breadcrumb.

____

15) Click in an empty part of the breadcrumb and note the directory path. It will be something like "C:\Users*YourName*\Pictures."

In the navigation pane, expand **This PC**, and then click **Local Disk (C:)**.

The drive should be shown with a Windows logo over it . This indicates that it is the **boot volume** or the drive that Windows is installed to.

You can now see the folders stored on the root of the main hard drive, including the **Windows** system folder, **Program Files** folders for software applications, and the **Users** folder. You will also be able to see some hidden folders.

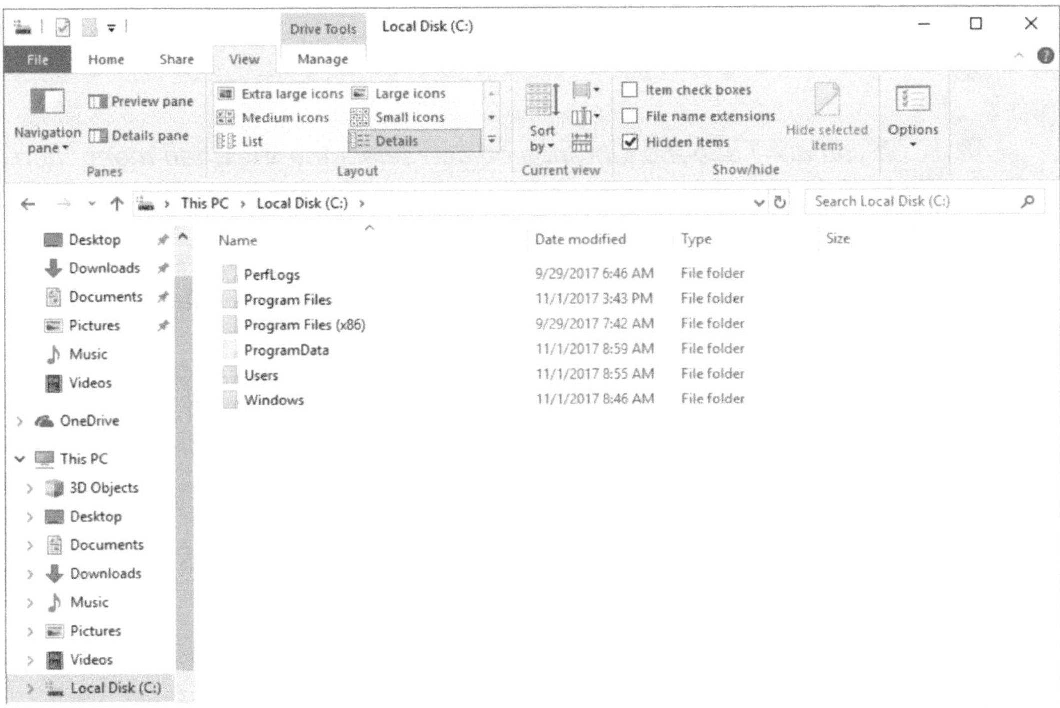

Browsing the root of the boot volume. Screenshot used with permission from Microsoft.

16) Open the **Users** folder. You should see a folder named after your user account and a "Public" folder. Open the folder for your user account.

You'll also see a hidden "Default" folder. This controls the profile settings for new user accounts.

17) Open the **Pictures** folder. You should see the Paint picture you created earlier. Make a note of the navigation objects shown in the breadcrumb:

You are in the same folder as before, but the breadcrumb shows the different route you have taken to get there.

18) Click in an empty part of the breadcrumb then overtype the existing file path with `C:\Users\Public` and press **ENTER**.

Files stored in a user's home folder are private to that user, though the computer administrator can always view them. The "Public" folder is a means for different users of the same PC to share files.

19) Press **START** then type **paint** and press **ENTER**. Draw a picture of a seaside scene then press **CTRL+S** to save the file.

When you save a file for the first time, the Save As dialog provides you with a mini File Explorer to use to choose a location in which to save your file.

20) In the "Save As" dialog, click in an empty part of the breadcrumb then overtype the existing file path with **C:\Users\Public\Pictures** and press **ENTER**.

21) In the "File name" box, overtype the existing file name with **The Beach**. Click the **Save** button.

22) Press **ALT+F4** to close Paint.

23) In the navigation pane, select the **Libraries** object.

If you don't see the Libraries object, select the **View** *tab menu then click the* **Navigation pane** *list button and select* **Show libraries**.

24) Open the **Pictures** library. You may now see both Paint pictures you have created or just one, depending on how your computer was set up.

To show both pictures, the library must be set up to include the Public Pictures folder. If your computer was upgraded from Windows 7, this will be the case by default but not if Windows 10 was "clean installed."

25) In the navigation pane, right-click the **Pictures** library object and select **Properties**.

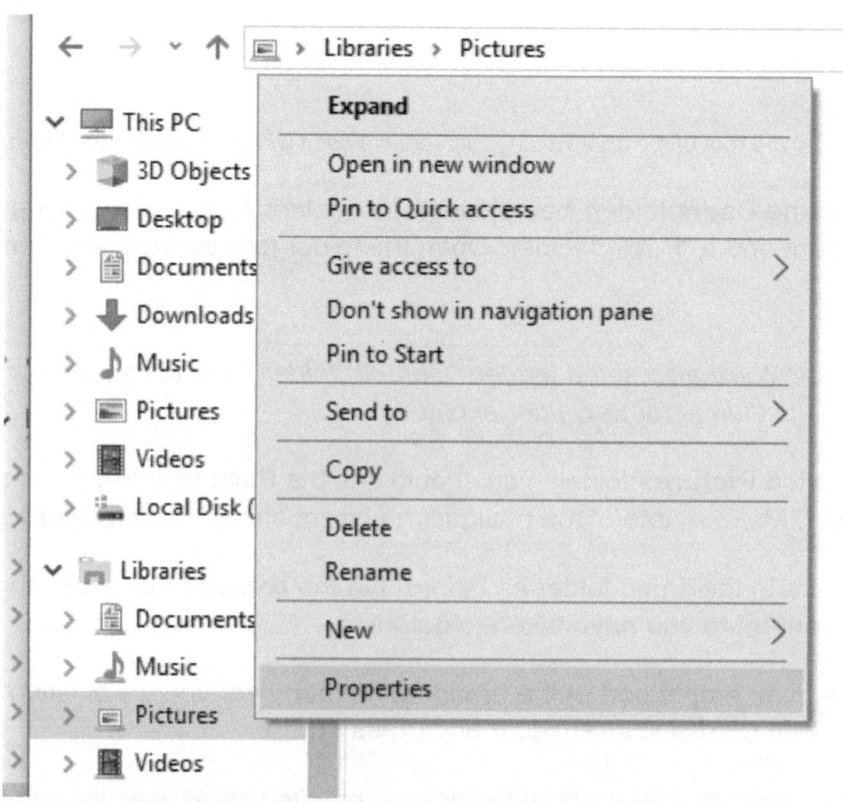

Opening library properties. Screenshot used with permission from Microsoft.

26) In the dialog, click the **Add** button. Open `C:\Users\Public` then select the **Public Pictures** folder and click the **Include folder** button. Click **OK**.

You should now see both pictures. Note the "Arrange By" view showing the real folder in which each image is located.

27) In File Explorer, click the **View** tab menu then clear the **Hidden items** check box.

Exercise 2 / Creating, Renaming, and Copying Folders and Files

Each user can create new folders and files within their own folders and in the public folders. Creating folders and files outside these areas may require administrator privileges.

1) Open your **Pictures** library, right-click and select **New > Bitmap image**. Enter the name `Sunny Day`.

2) Right-click the new file and select **Edit**.

3) Create a picture of a sunny day in the countryside—the paintbrush tool is a good choice. Save and close when you are done.

4) Click **Start**, type **WordPad**, and press `ENTER`. Use the **Picture** button on the ribbon to add the picture you created. Write a caption or heading for it, making sure you use the word `holiday`, then save and close the document in the **Documents** folder as `Day Out`.

5) Right-click some empty space within your **Documents** folder then select **New > Folder**. Type the name `Holidays` and press `ENTER`.

6) Select the **Day Out** file then click-and-drag it over the "Holidays" folder—do not release the mouse button yet...

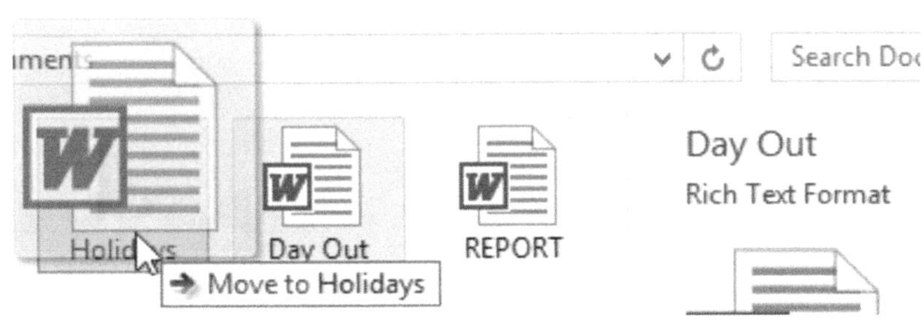

Click-and-drag to move an object on the same disk—hold down Ctrl to copy the object. Screenshot used with permission from Microsoft.

7) Note that the default action shown in the tooltip is to move the file. Hold down the `CTRL` key and note that the tooltip now reads "Copy to holidays." Release the mouse button then the `CTRL` key.

8) Open the **Pictures** *library* from the navigation pane but ensure that the "Holidays" folder is still expanded.

9) You should have two picture files (Sunny Day and The Sea). To select multiple objects individually, `CTRL`+click them.

10) With both files selected, hold down `CTRL` then click-and-drag the selection to the **Holidays** folder.

11) Open the **Holidays** folder. Open the **Day Out** file and make some amendments to it, making sure you use the word `beach`. Save and close the file when done.

12) Select all the files (you can press `CTRL+A` to do this quickly). Drag and drop the selection over the **Documents** folder in the navigation pane.

13) Note that because the destination folder contains a file with the same name, you are prompted whether to replace it or not. Select the **Compare info for both files** option.

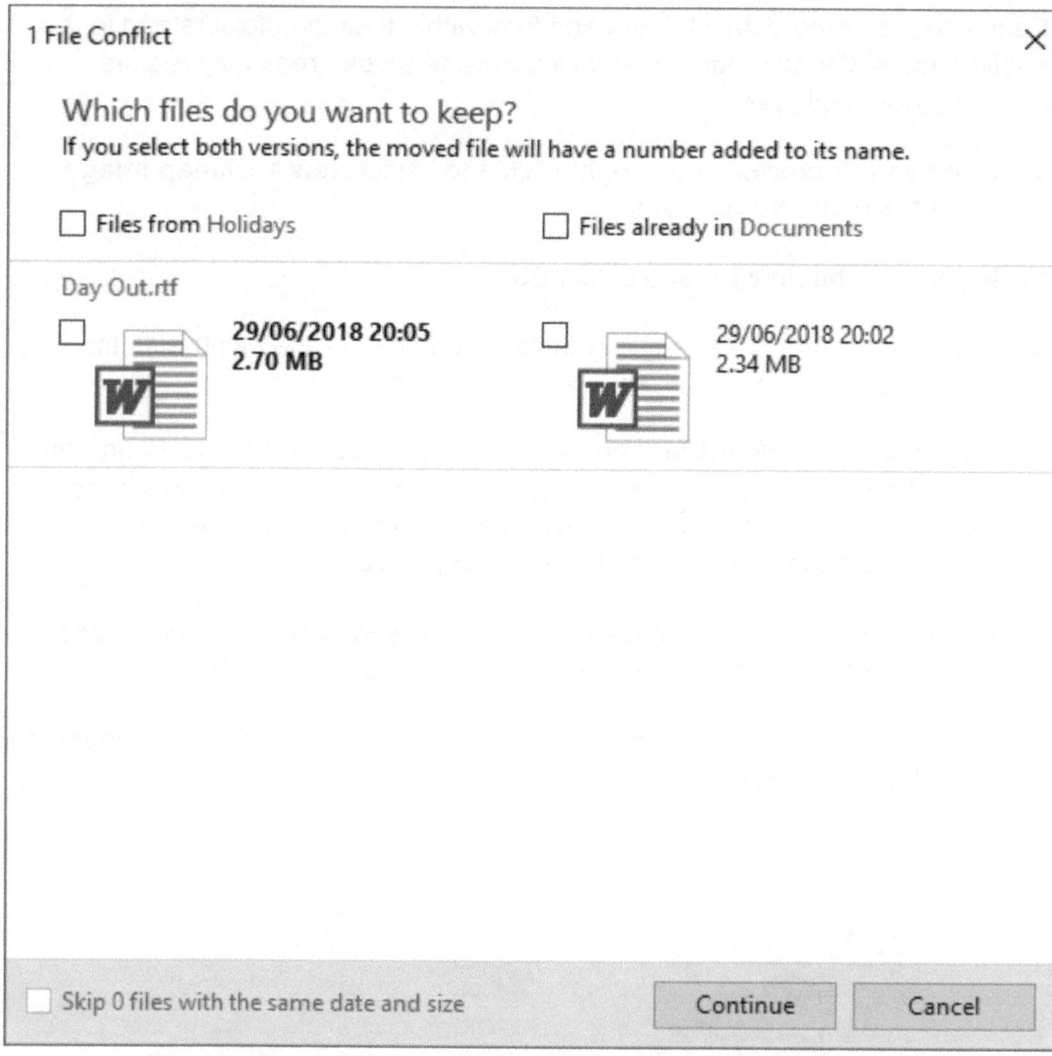

Resolving file conflicts. Screenshot used with permission from Microsoft.

14) In the **File Conflict** dialog, note the different file details (such as date modified and size). Check both boxes to keep both versions of the file where there is a name conflict. Click **Continue**.

15) Open the **Documents** folder and select the **Day Out (2)** file. Press `F2` then type the new name `Another Sunny Day`.

16) Move all the files back into the **Holidays** folder.

Exercise 3 / View Options and Search

When you have a lot of files and folders to manage, you can use view options and the search function to assist with locating individual and groups of files quickly.

1) Open the **Holidays** folder. Select the **View** menu tab and cycle through the different options in the "Layout" panel, leaving the folder set to using **Details**.

2) Click the column headers to sort by different file properties in ascending and descending order.

3) Right-click the column headers and look at the fields that you can add to the view. You can also add or remove fields by right-clicking a header and selecting **More**.

4) In the **Choose Details** dialog, check the box for **Attributes** and click **OK**.

5) From the **View > Options** list button select **Change folder and search options**.

6) Click the **View** tab. Click the **Apply to Folders** button then click **Yes** to confirm.

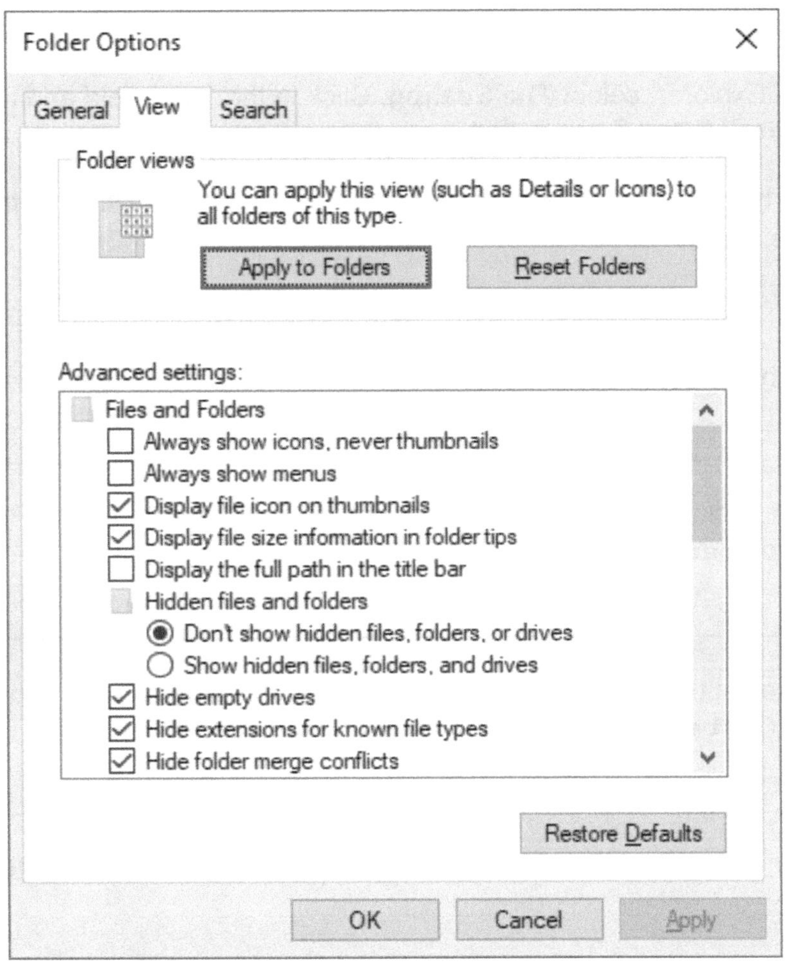

Folder Options dialog—View tab. Screenshot used with permission from Microsoft.

7) On the same tab, note some of the options, such as whether to preserve folder customizations, launch new windows when opening folders, show pop-up descriptions, and so on. Click **OK**.

8) Open your **Pictures** folder. Note that this is a different type of folder to Documents (optimized for viewing images) so the default view settings you just configured have not been applied.

9) Open the **Holidays** folder again. On the "View" tab, experiment with different options from the **Group by** list box. Try sorting with different group options applied.

10) Select the **The Sea** image file. From the **View** tab, select **Details pane**.

    Note that this file format has no editable details fields.

11) Right-click **The Sea** and select **Edit**. In Paint, from the **File** menu, select **Save As**.

12) From the **Save as type** box, select **JPEG**. Use the Explorer tools to select the Holidays folder. Click the **Save** button.

13) Click **OK** to the warning about transparency.

14) Close Paint.

    Note that you have two files with the same name ("The Sea") but different extensions.

15) In File Explorer, select **The Sea.jpg**. Click in the **Tags** field and type `beach`. Click the **Save** button.

16) Press the `START` key then type `beach` then press `ENTER`. Note the search results.

    ____

17) Click the Documents icon to filter the results. Are any files found now?

    ____

18) Switch back to File Explorer and select the **Documents** folder. Press `F3` and type `beach` in the search box. Note the results:

    ____

19) Now select the top-level **Desktop** icon under "Favorites" and repeat the search for `beach` and note the results:

    ____

20) Finally, select **This PC** and repeat the search for `beach` and note the results:

    ____

    As you can see, file search operations outside the user document folders can be a bit inconsistent. Also, searching in non-indexed locations such as subfolders of "This PC" can take a long time.

Exercise 4 / Compressing Files

If your drive is getting low on space, you can compress files and folders. You can either make the file system apply compression automatically or you can add folders and files to zip archives (though you won't save any space this way unless you delete the original files).

1) In File Explorer, open the **Documents** folder.
2) Right-click the **Holidays** subfolder and select **Send to > Compressed (zipped) folder**.
3) Change the name of the zip file to `HolidaysArchive`.
4) Right-click the **Holidays** folder and select **Properties**.
5) Make a note of the **Size on disk**:

   ____

6) Click the **Advanced** button.
7) Check **Compress contents to save disk space** and click **OK**.
8) Click **OK** then **OK** again.
9) Check the folder properties again—how much space does it take up now?

   ____

10) How does the size of the zip file compare to the uncompressed and compressed folder size?

    ____

11) Open the zip file and then open one of the files. Change some text then try to save—what happens?
12) Cancel the save and close the document.
13) Close any open windows.

Exercise 5 / Deleting and Recycling Files

Files deleted from the local disk are not removed completely but put in the Recycle Bin.

1) Right-click the **Recycle Bin** icon on the Desktop and select **Properties**.

   Note the options here to suppress use of the bin, change its size, and suppress use of delete confirmations. Click **Cancel**.

2) Open the **Documents** folder and delete all the contents.

3) Open Recycle Bin. Restore the **Holidays** folder. Check the restored folder in Explorer to see what it contains.

4) Close all open windows.

5) Optionally, shut down your computer if you are not continuing to use it after this lab.

Module 3 / Summary

Using Computer Hardware

In this module you learned about the different types of peripheral and system components that make up a computer. You also learned the basics of file management.

Module 3 / Unit 1 / System Components

- CPU performance is measured by a combination of its clock speed and internal architecture. Multiple CPUs (SMP) or multi-core CPUs (CMP) represent another way to boost performance. Most new CPUs can work in 32- or 64-bit mode; 64-bit mode allows for much larger amounts of system memory but there are currently not many 64-bit software applications.

- The amount of system memory affects the ability of the computer to open multiple applications and work efficiently with larger files. The main types of memory are SDRAM and DDR/DDR2/DDR3/DDR4, packaged in DIMM modules for desktops or SO-DIMM modules for laptops.

- The motherboard determines the compatibility of all the other components (including CPU, memory, storage devices, and support for expansion cards). The motherboard chipset provides memory and I/O controllers plus any integrated peripherals (such as sound and video) and ports (such as USB, parallel, serial, and network). The chipset and connectors provide support for different I/O bus standards (PCI, PCIe, and AGP).

- The motherboard can be configured using the low-level firmware (BIOS or UEFI) setup program.

Module 3 / Unit 2 / Using Device Interfaces

- You learned about the various interfaces used to connect peripheral devices to computers. Most PCs and laptops use USB (and to a lesser extent Firewire). Computers can also use wireless Bluetooth links for peripheral devices. Make sure you learn the characteristics and capabilities of these interfaces.

- Make sure you can distinguish the types and features of input devices and their configuration settings, usually accessed via Control Panel or the Settings app.

- The display signal is generated by the graphics adapter, which will determine the supported resolution, color depth, and special effects capabilities of the system. There are a number of display connectors, including VGA (analog) and DVI/HDMI/DisplayPort (digital).

- Local network (Ethernet) connections are made using a cable connected to the RJ-45 port. Modem cables for the fax function of a compatible printer are connected via an RJ-11 port. The RJ-11 port is also used with DSL Internet services.

Module 3 / Unit 3 / Using Peripheral Devices

- Devices interface with the system using a device driver. Devices and Printers and Device Manager provide tools for verifying and configuring devices. You can use them to update drivers, check device properties, and enable/disable devices.
- Most computers use flat-screen displays but be aware that these now often come with touchscreen capability. Computers can also use alternative displays, such as projectors.
- Multimedia devices allow for audio recording and playback and video recording. Audio ports come in different sizes and types to allow the connection of equipment such as microphones and speakers.
- Printers for home and office use are usually either based on a laser print process or an inkjet print process.
- Printers use standard peripheral connections (typically USB or wireless/Bluetooth) and can also be connected via a wired or wireless network.
- Printer installation is quite straightforward, but make sure you know how to access the different configuration options and printing preferences. Similarly, learn the output options for scanners.

Module 3 / Unit 4 / Using Storage Devices

- Computers use system memory (RAM) for fast but volatile storage. Mass storage devices such as HDDs and SSDs provide persistent storage when the computer is turned off.
- A number of types of removable drive and media provide extra storage capacity, backup, and data transfer. Some examples include CD/DVD/Blu-ray Disc (read-only, recordable, and rewritable) and flash memory (memory cards, and USB drives). Make sure you know the characteristics and capacities of these storage devices.

Module 3 / Unit 5 / Using File Systems

- Hard disks can be divided into a number of partitions and each partition must be formatted to make a drive accessible under Windows. Each partition can be assigned a drive letter.
- Windows creates three main folders during installation: Windows, Program Files, and Users. Each profile stored in Users is divided into a number of subfolders for different types of file.
- Files and folders can be managed using File Explorer. Files are associated with applications using a period plus three-character extension on the end of the file name.
- Files also have attributes, such as Read-Only or Archive, and permissions that restrict access to authorized users.
- Make sure you can use file search and viewing tools effectively.

Module 4 / Using Networks

The following CompTIA IT Fundamentals+ domain objectives and examples are covered in this module:

CompTIA ITF+ Certification Domains	Weighting
1.0 IT Concepts and Terminology	17%
2.0 Infrastructure	22%
3.0 Applications and Software	18%
4.0 Software Development	12%
5.0 Database Fundamentals	11%
6.0 Security	20%

Refer To	Domain Objectives/Examples
Unit 4.1 / Networking Components	**2.7 Explain basic networking concepts.** *Basics of network communication (Basics of packet transmission, DNS, URL-to-IP translation, LAN vs. WAN) • Device addresses (IP address, MAC address) • Basic protocols (HTTP/S, POP3, IMAP, SMTP)*
Unit 4.2 / Connecting to a Network	**2.4 Compare and contrast common Internet service types.** *Fiber optic • Cable • DSL • Wireless (Radio frequency, Satellite, Cellular)*
	2.7 Explain basic networking concepts. *Devices (Modem, Router, Switch, Access point)*
	2.8 Given a scenario, install, configure and secure a basic wireless network. *802.11a/b/g/n/ac (Older vs. newer standards, Speed limitations, Interference and attenuation factors) • Best practices (Change SSID, Change default password, Encrypted vs. unencrypted [Open, Captive portal, WEP, WPA, WPA2])*
Unit 4.3 / Secure Web Browsing	**2.7 Explain basic networking concepts.** *Devices (Firewall)*
	3.5 Given a scenario, configure and use web browsers. *Caching/clearing cache • Deactivate client-side scripting • Browser add-ons/extensions (Add, Remove, Enable/disable) • Private browsing • Proxy settings • Certificates (Valid, Invalid) • Popup blockers • Script blockers • Compatible browser for application(s)*
	6.2 Explain methods to secure devices and best practices. *Securing devices (Host firewall, Safe browsing practices)*

Refer To	Domain Objectives/Examples
Unit 4.4 / Using Shared Storage	**2.5 Compare and contrast storage types.** *Local network storage types (NAS, File server) • Cloud storage service*
	6.7 Explain business continuity concepts. *Backup considerations—data [File backups, Critical data, Database, OS backups], Backup considerations—location [Stored locally, Cloud storage, On-site vs. off-site]*
Unit 4.5 / Using Mobile Devices	**This unit does not cover specific exam domain objectives or content examples.**

Module 4 / Unit 1

Networking Concepts

Objectives

On completion of this unit, you will be able to:

- Describe the components and functions of computer networks.
- List the protocols and technologies used for addressing on computer networks.
- Connect a computer to a wired or wireless network.
- Describe the uses of common application protocols.

Syllabus Objectives and Content Examples

This unit covers the following exam domain objectives and content examples:

- 2.7 Explain basic networking concepts.
  Basics of network communication (Basics of packet transmission, DNS, URL-to-IP translation, LAN vs. WAN) • Device addresses (IP address, MAC address) • Basic protocols (HTTP/S, POP3, IMAP, SMTP)

Network Components

A **network** is two or more computer systems linked together by some form of transmission medium that enables them to share information. The network technology is what connects the computers, but the purpose of the network is to provide services or resources to its users. These services may include access to shared files and folders, printing, and database applications.

Networks are built from media, appliances, and protocols but they exist to provide services and resources to users. (Image by Svetlana Kurochkina © 123rf.com.)

Network Clients and Servers

Network **clients** are computers and software that allow users to request resources shared by and hosted on **servers**.

LANs and WANs

Networks of different sizes are classified in different ways. A network in a single location is often described as a **Local Area Network (LAN)**. This definition encompasses many different types and sizes of networks though. It can include both residential networks with a couple of computers and enterprise networks with hundreds of servers and thousands of workstations. Typically, most of the equipment and cabling used on a LAN is owned and operated by the company or organization using the LAN.

Networks in different geographic locations but with shared links are called **Wide Area Networks (WAN)**. A WAN is more likely to make use of a **service provider** network. Companies that operate national telephone networks are called **telecommunications companies** or **telcos**. Companies that specialize in providing Internet access are called **Internet Service Providers (ISP)**. Telcos operate as ISPs themselves but also make parts of their networks available to smaller ISPs.

Network Media

A network is made by creating communications pathways between the devices on the network. Network endpoints can be referred to as **nodes** or **hosts**. Communications pathways are implemented using an **adapter** installed in the host to transmit and receive signals and network **media** between the interfaces to carry the signals. There are two main types of local network connections:

- **Wired** data connections use cabling and either electrical signals over copper wire or light signals over fiber optic to connect nodes. Most local networks use a wired network standard called Ethernet to implement these links.

- **Wireless (Wi-Fi)** data connections use radio signals to transmit signals over the air. With Wi-Fi, a node usually connects to an access point at a range of up to about 30m.

Wide area networks can also use copper or fiber optic cabling and various types of wireless networking, including point-to-point radio, cellular radio, and satellite communications.

Addressing and Protocols

Network signals must be packaged in such a way that each host is able to understand them. Also, each host must have a means of recognizing the location of other hosts on the network. These functions are provided by a network **protocol**. A network protocol identifies each host on the network using a unique address. It also defines a **packet** structure. A packet is a wrapper for each data unit transmitted over the network. A packet generally consists of a **header** (indicating the protocol type, source address, destination address, error correction information, and so on) and a **payload** (the data).

Networks use multiple protocols. The packet from one protocol can be wrapped within the packet from another (encapsulation).

The overwhelming majority of networks use TCP/IP to perform these functions.

TCP/IP

In an age when even your refrigerator is connected to the Internet, it's important that you understand the basics of networking, specifically, how the **Transmission Control Protocol/Internet Protocol (TCP/IP)** *suite* of protocols works to provide the apps and services we increasingly rely on.

Packet Transmission

The original research underpinning TCP/IP was performed in the late 1960s and early 1970s by the **Advanced Research Projects Agency (ARPA)**, which is the research arm of the **US Department of Defense (DoD)**. The DoD wanted to build a network to connect a number of military sites. The prototype was a research network called ARPANET, first operational in 1972. This connected four university sites using a system described as a **packet switching network**.

Prior to this development, any two computers wanting to communicate had to open a direct channel, known as a **circuit**. If this circuit was broken, the computers would stop communicating immediately. Packet switching introduces the ability for one computer to **forward** information to another. To ensure information reaches the correct destination, each packet is addressed with a source and destination address and then transferred using any available pathway to the destination computer. A host capable of performing this forwarding function is called a **router**.

A packet switching protocol is described as "robust" because it can automatically recover from communication link failures. It re-routes data packets if transmission lines are damaged or if a router fails to respond. It can utilize any available network path rather than a single, dedicated one.

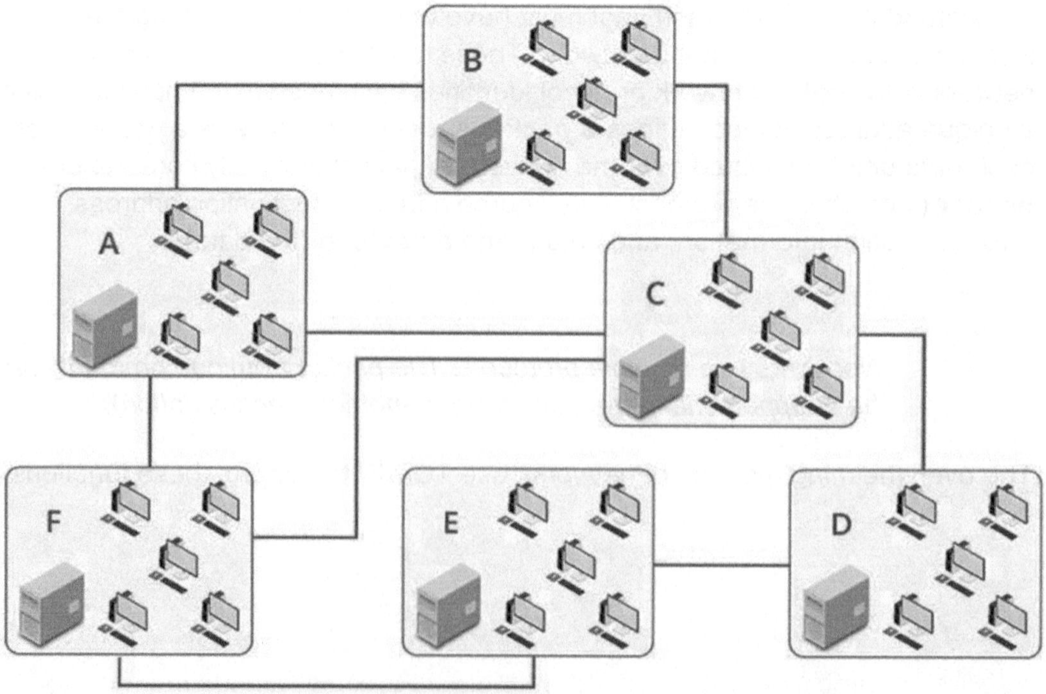

Packet switching internetwork. Image © 123rf.com.

The figure above shows an example of an internetworking system. A packet being sent from Network A to Network D may be sent via Network C (the quickest route). If this route becomes unavailable, the packet is routed using an alternate route (for example, A-F-E-D).

As well as the forwarding function and use of multiple paths, data is divided into *small* chunks or packets. Using numerous, small packets means that if some are lost or damaged during transmission, it is easier to resend just the small, lost packets than having to re-transmit the entire message.

TCP/IP Protocol Suite Layers

The major benefit in utilizing TCP/IP is the wide support for the protocol. It is the primary protocol of the Internet and the World Wide Web. It is also the primary protocol for many private internets, which are networks that connect Local Area Networks (LANs) together.

As mentioned above, TCP/IP is a suite or set of network transport protocols. When considering network technologies and protocols, it is helpful to conceive of them as working in **layers**. The TCP/IP model consists of four layers, each with defined functions. At each layer are protocols within the TCP/IP suite, or its supporting technologies, that make *use* of the protocols in the layer below and provide *services* to the protocols in the layer above:

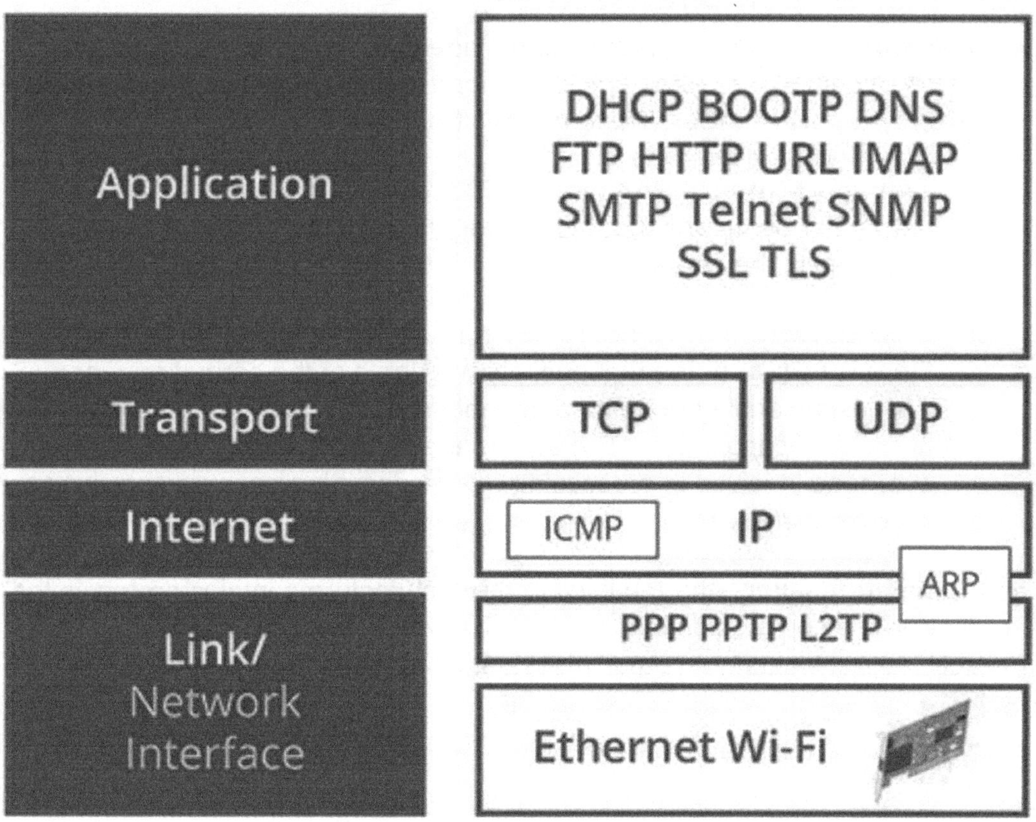

Layers in the TCP/IP protocol suite.

The four layers are as follows:

- **Link or Network Interface layer**—responsible for putting frames onto the physical network. This layer does not contain TCP/IP protocols as such. At this layer, different networking products and media can be used, such as Ethernet or Wi-Fi. Communications on this layer take place only on a local network segment and not between different networks. Data at the link layer is packaged in a unit called a **frame**.
- **Internet layer**—encapsulates packets into Internet **datagrams** and deals with routing between different networks. Three key protocols are used at this layer:
  - **Internet Protocol (IP)**—the main protocol in the TCP/IP suite is responsible for logical addressing and routing of packets between hosts and networks.
  - **Address Resolution Protocol (ARP)**—used for hardware address resolution. Each host has a link or network interface layer address, usually called the Media Access Control (MAC) address, to identify it on the local physical network. To deliver packets, this local MAC address must be resolved to a logical IP address using ARP.
  - **Internet Control Message Protocol (ICMP)**—sends messages and reports on errors regarding packet delivery.
- **Transport layer**—these protocols provide communication sessions between computers. Each application protocol is identified at the transport layer by a **port number**. There are two transport protocols:
  - **Transport Control Protocol (TCP)** provides connection-oriented delivery. This means that the delivery is reliable and that packets are delivered in the correct sequence.
  - **User Datagram Protocol (UDP)** provides connectionless delivery – there is no guarantee that packets will arrive in the correct sequence. Any issues arising from the unreliable nature of UDP must be dealt with at the application layer. The advantage of UDP is that there is less overhead involved in processing and transmitting each packet and so it is faster than TCP.
- **Application layer**—the top level of the architecture contains protocols that provide the communications formats for exchanging data between hosts, such as transmitting an email message or requesting a web page.

Internet Protocol

The **Internet Protocol (IP)** is the primary protocol responsible for the forwarding function we defined above. It provides packet delivery for all higher-level protocols within the suite. It provides best effort delivery between hosts on a local network or within an internetwork of an unreliable and connectionless nature.

Delivery is not guaranteed and a packet might be lost, delivered out of sequence, duplicated, or delayed.

IP Packet Structure

At the IP layer, any information received from the transport layer is wrapped in a **datagram**. The transport layer datagram is the payload and IP adds a number of fields in a header to describe the payload and how to deliver it:

Field	Explanation
Source IP address	Identifies the sender of the datagram by IP address.
Destination IP address	Identifies the destination of the datagram by IP address.
Protocol	Indicates whether the data should be passed to UDP or TCP at the destination host.
Checksum	Verifies the packet's integrity upon arrival at the destination.
Time to Live	The number of seconds a datagram is allowed to stay on the network before being discarded, otherwise packets could endlessly loop around an internet. A router will decrease the TTL by at least one second when it handles the packet, and is required to decrement the TTL by at least the time spent in the router.

Once the fields have been added, the IP datagrams are packaged into a suitable frame format and delivered over the local network segment.

IP Addresses

As you can see from the fields in the datagram, an **IP address** is used to logically identify each device (host) on a given network. An IP address is a 32-bit binary value. To make this value easier to enter in configuration dialogs, it is expressed as four decimal numbers separated by periods: 172.30.15.12 for instance. Each number represents a byte value, that is, an eight-character binary value, also called an octet, or a decimal value between 0 and 255. This is referred to as **dotted decimal notation**.

Recall that you can convert between binary and decimal by setting out the place value of each binary digit. For example, you can convert `172` as follows:

```
  128     64     32     16      8      4      2      1
    1      0      1      0      1      1      0      0
128*1   64*0   32*1   16*0    8*1    4*1    2*0    1*0
  128  +   0  +  32  +   0  +   8  +   4  +   0  +   0
= 172
```

Refer back to Unit 2.1 for the topic on binary and decimal notation.

This information relates to IP version 4. IP version 6 (IPv6) defines longer addresses (128 bit compared to 32 bit). These are expressed in hex notation (2001:db8::abc:0:def0:1234 for example).

Network Prefixes and Subnet Masks

An IP address encodes *two* pieces of information:

- The network number (network ID)—this number is common to all hosts on the same IP network.
- The host number (host ID)—this unique number identifies a host on a particular network or logical subnetwork.

In order to distinguish the network ID and host ID portions within an address, each host must also be configured with a **network prefix length** or **subnet mask**. This is combined with the IP address to determine the identity of the network to which the host belongs.

The network prefix is also a 32-bit number. It contains a contiguous series of binary ones where the matching bit of the IP address is a part of the network ID. The rest of the mask is zeroes and represents the host ID bits in the IP address. For example, the prefix `/8` would contain eight binary ones followed by 24 binary zeros. The prefix could also be expressed as a subnet mask by converting it to dotted decimal (`255.0.0.0`).

IPv6 only uses network prefixes to identify the network portion of the address.

Packet Delivery and Forwarding

The Internet Protocol (IP) covers addressing and forwarding at a "logical" level between networks with distinct IDs (network layer). Actual delivery of information takes place at the lower physical/data link layer. The IP datagram is put into a **frame**. Frames can only be delivered over a local network segment.

MAC Addresses

Frames use a *different* addressing method than IP. At the data link layer, each host is identified by the address of its network interface. This is called a **hardware address** or a **Media Access Control (MAC)** address. The MAC address is assigned to the network adapter at the factory. It is a 48-bit value expressed in hex notation. It is often displayed as six groups of two hexadecimal digits with colon or hyphen separators or no separators at all (for example, `00:60:8c:12:3a:bc` or `00608c123abc`) or as three groups of four hex digits with period separators (`0060.8c12.3abc`).

Address Resolution Protocol (ARP)

If two systems are to communicate using IP, the host sending the packet must map the IP address of the destination host to the hardware address of the destination host. The **Address Resolution Protocol (ARP)** is the protocol that enables this process of local address discovery to take place. Hosts broadcast ARP messages onto the local network to find out which host MAC address "owns" a particular IP address. If the destination host responds, the frame can be delivered. Hosts also *cache* IP:MAC address mappings for several minutes to reduce the number of ARP messages that have to be sent.

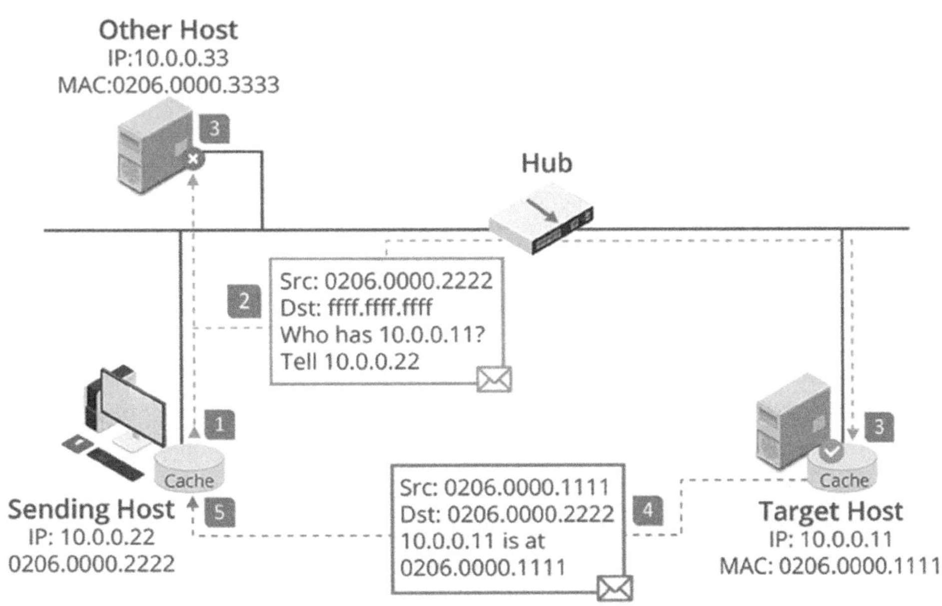

Using ARP for local address resolution.

Routing

If the destination IP address is a local one (with the same network ID as the source), the host uses ARP messaging to discover the local destination host. If the network IDs are different, the sending host uses ARP messaging to discover a **router** on the local segment (its **default gateway**) and uses that to forward the packet. The router forwards the packet to its destination (if known), possibly via intermediate routers.

DNS and URLs

As we have seen, network addressing uses 48-bit MAC values at the data link layer and 32-bit IP addresses at the network layer. Computers can process these numbers easily, but they are very difficult for people to remember or type correctly.

People find it much easier to address things using simple **names**. Consequently, there are protocols to assign names to hosts and networks and to convert these names into IP addresses. The name resolution protocol used with the TCP/IP suite is called the **Domain Name System (DNS)**.

Domain Name System (DNS)

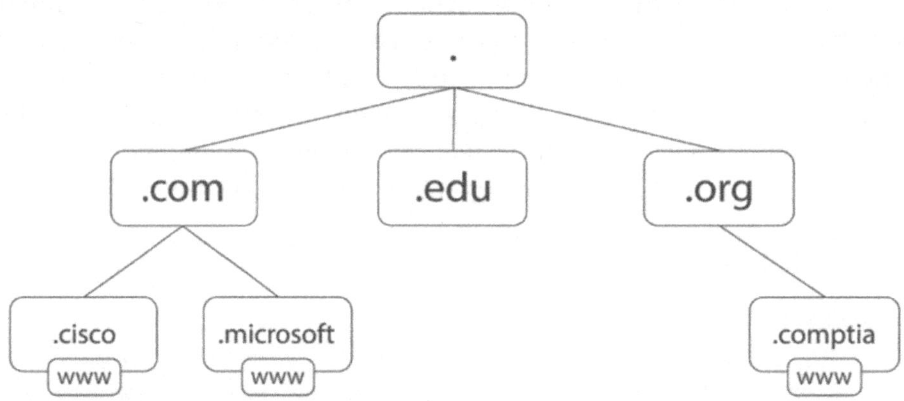

DNS name resolution hierarchy.

The **Domain Name System (DNS)** is a hierarchical, client/server-based distributed database name management system. The purpose of the DNS database is to resolve resource names to IP addresses. In the DNS, the clients are called resolvers and the servers are called name servers. The DNS database is distributed because no one DNS server holds all possible DNS records. This would be far too much information for a single server to store. Instead, the hierarchical nature of the DNS namespace enables DNS servers to query one another for the appropriate record.

The namespace is structured like an inverted tree, starting at the root, and working down. Below the root are a set of Top Level Domains (TLD) that define broad classes of entities (`.com` versus `.gov`, for instance) or national authorities (`.uk` versus `.ca`, for instance). Within the TLDs, entities such as companies, academic institutions, non-profits, governments, or even individuals can all register individual domains. An organization may also create sub-domains to represent different parts of a business. Domains and sub-domains contain resource records. These records contain the host name to IP address mapping information used to resolve queries.

Any computer holding records for a part of the namespace is said to be a name server. Name servers that contain the requested resource records for a particular namespace are said to be authoritative. If they are not authoritative for a namespace, they will have pointers to other name servers which might be authoritative.

Resolvers are software programs running on client computers. For example, name resolution is a critical part of web browsing, so web browser software will implement a resolver.

Hostnames and Fully Qualified Domain Names

A **hostname** is just the name given to an IP host. A hostname can be configured as any string with up to 256 alphanumeric characters (plus the hyphen), though most hostnames are much shorter. The hostname can be combined with information about the domain in which the host is located to produce a **Fully Qualified Domain Name (FQDN)**. For example, if `www` is a host name, then the FQDN of the host `www` within the `comptia.org` domain is `www.comptia.org`.

DNS Query Example

In the graphic below, a client needs to establish a session with the `www.comptia.org` web server.

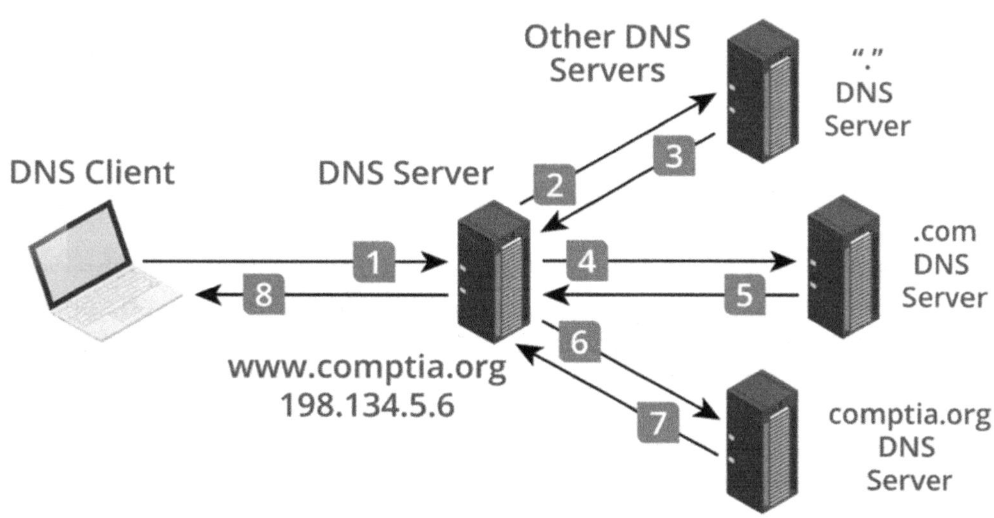

Resolving a hostname using DNS.

1) The resolver (client) sends a recursive DNS query to its local DNS server asking for the IP address of `www.comptia.org`. The local name server checks its DNS data corresponding to the requested domain name.

   A recursive query makes the local name server responsible for resolving the name and means it cannot just refer the resolver to another name server.

2) It then sends a query for `www.comptia.org` to a root name server.
3) The root name server has authority for the root domain and will reply with the IP address of a name server for the `.org` top level domain.
4) The local name server sends an iterative query for `www.comptia.org` to the .org name server.

   An iterative query means that the local name server does not expect the .com name server to return a record and that it will accept a referral to another name server. Name servers that are authoritative for domains will only typically respond to iterative queries.

5) The .com name server doesn't have a resource record `www.comptia.org` but it can provide the IP address of the name server responsible for the `comptia.org` domain.
6) The local name server now queries the comptia.org name server for the IP address of `www.comptia.org`.
7) The comptia.org name server replies with the IP address corresponding to the FQDN `www.comptia.org`.
8) The local name server sends the IP address of `www.comptia.org` back to the original resolver.

Note how each query brings the local name server closer to the IP address of www.comptia.org.

Uniform Resource Locators (URL)

When a web browser is used to request a record from a web server, the request must have some means of specifying the location of the web server and the resource on the web server that the client wants to retrieve. This information is provided as a **Uniform Resource Locator (URL)**.

The URL (or web address) contains the information necessary to identify and (in most cases) access an item.

1 2 3
http://store.comptia.org/itf/index.htm

URL with 1) Protocol; 2) Host location; 3) File path.

A URL consists of the following parts:

1) **Protocol**—this describes the access method or service type being used. URLs can be used for protocols other than HTTP/HTTPS. The protocol is followed by the characters ://
2) **Host location**—this could be an IP address, but as IP addresses are very hard for people to remember, it is usually represented by a Fully Qualified Domain Name (FQDN). DNS allows the web browser to locate the IP address of a web server based on its FQDN.
3) **File path**—specifies the directory and file name location of the resource, if required. Each directory is delimited by a forward slash. The file path may or may not be case-sensitive, depending on how the server is configured. If no file path is used, the server will return the default (home) page for the website.

Internet Application Services

The protocols we have discussed so far all involve supporting communications with addressing formats and forwarding mechanisms. At the application layer, there are protocols that support services, such as publishing, e-commerce, or messaging. The TCP/IP suite encompasses a large number and wide range of application layer protocols. Some of the principal protocols amongst these are discussed below.

HTTP and HTML

HyperText Transfer Protocol (HTTP) is the basis of the World Wide Web. HTTP enables clients (typically web browsers) to request resources from an HTTP server. A client connects to the HTTP server using its TCP port (the default is port 80) and submits a request for a resource using a **Uniform Resource Locator (URL)**. The server acknowledges the request and returns the data.

To run a website, an organization will typically lease a server or space on a server from an ISP. Larger organizations with their own Internet Point-of-Presence may host websites themselves. Web servers are not only used on the Internet however. Private networks using web technologies are described as **intranets** (if they permit only local access) or **extranets** (if they permit remote access).

HTTP is usually used to serve **HTML** web pages, which are plain text files with coded tags (**HyperText Markup Language**) describing how the page should be formatted. A web browser can interpret the tags and display the text and other resources associated with the page, such as picture or sound files. Another powerful feature is its ability to provide **hyperlinks** to other related documents. HTTP also features forms mechanisms (GET and POST) whereby a user can submit data from the client to the server.

The functionality of HTTP servers is often extended by support for scripting and programmable features (web applications).

SSL/TLS

One of the critical problems for the provision of early e-commerce sites was the lack of security in HTTP. Under HTTP, all data is sent unencrypted and there is no authentication of client or server. **Secure Sockets Layer (SSL)** was developed by Netscape and released as version 3.0 in 1996 to address these problems. SSL proved very popular with the industry and is still in widespread use. **Transport Layer Security (TLS)** was developed from SSL and ratified as a standard by IETF. TLS is now the version in active development, with 1.2 as the latest version.

SSL/TLS is closely associated with use of the HTTP application, referred to as **HTTPS** or **HTTP Over SSL** or **HTTP Secure** but can also be used to secure other TCP/IP application protocols.

HTTPS operates over port 443 by default. HTTPS operation is indicated by using https:// for the URL and by a padlock icon shown in the browser.

Essentially, a server is assigned a **digital certificate** by some trusted **Certificate Authority**. The certificate proves the identity of the server, assuming that the client trusts the Certificate Authority. The server uses the digital certificate and the SSL/TLS protocol to encrypt communications between it and the client. This means that the communications cannot be read or changed by a third party.

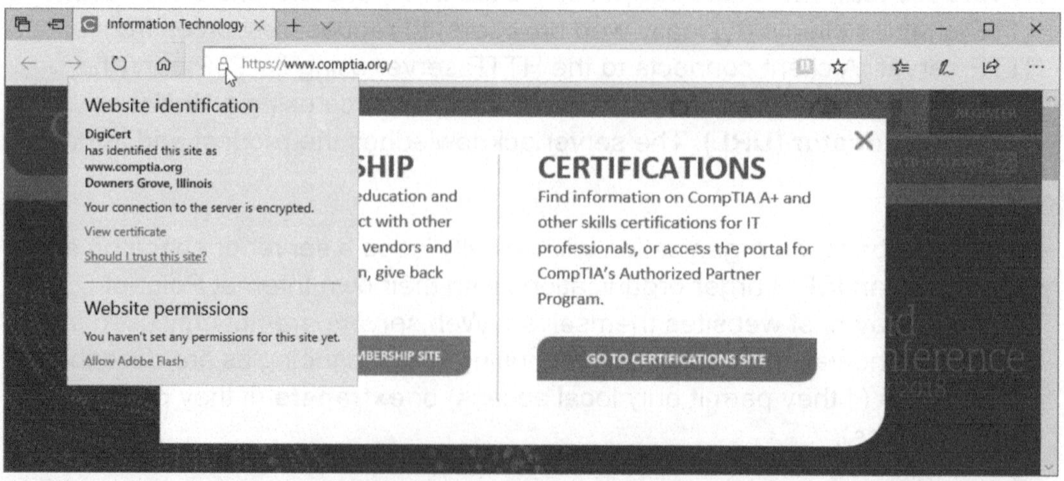

Use the padlock icon displayed next to a secure web address to verify the identity of the certificate holder.

Electronic Mail (Email)

Email is a messaging system that can be used to transmit text messages and binary file attachments encoded using **Multipurpose Internet Mail Extensions (MIME)**. Email can involve the use of multiple protocols. The following process illustrates how an email message is sent from a typical corporate mail gateway, using the Microsoft Exchange mail server, to a recipient with dial-up Internet access:

1) The email client software on the sender's computer (`sender@widget.com`) sends the message to the Exchange email server using Microsoft's **MAPI (Message Application Programming Interface)** protocol. The mail server puts the message in a queue, waiting for the next **Simple Mail Transfer Protocol (SMTP)** session to be started.

2) When the Exchange SMTP server starts to process the queue, it first contacts a DNS server to resolve the recipient's address (for example, `recipient@othercompany.com`) to an IP address for the `othercompany.com` email server, listed as an **MX (Mail Exchanger)** record in DNS.

3) It then uses SMTP to deliver the message to this email server. The delivery usually requires several "hops," from the mail gateway to the sender's Internet Service Provider (ISP), then to the recipient's ISP. The hops taken by a message as it is delivered over the Internet are recorded in the message header.

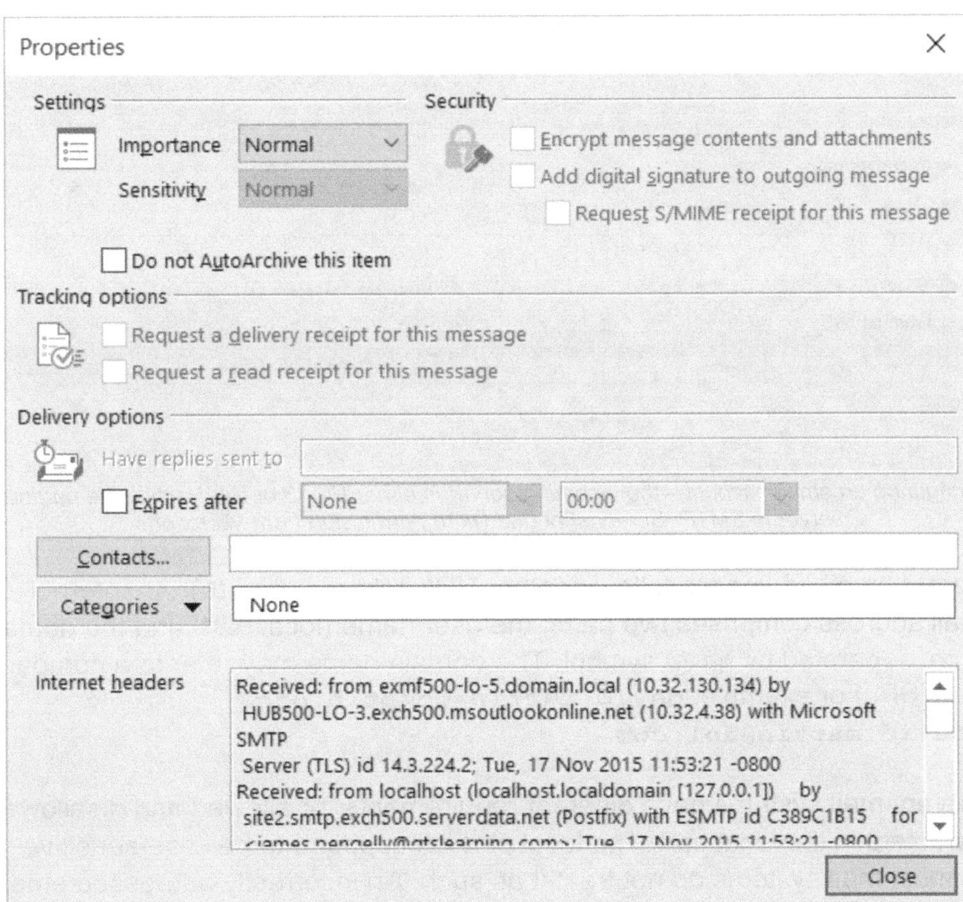

Viewing SMTP Internet headers for a mail message. Screenshot used with permission from Microsoft.

4) The message is put in the message store on the recipient's mail server. To retrieve it, the recipient uses his or her mail client software to connect with the mailbox on the server, using the **Post Office Protocol v3 (POP3)** or **Internet Message Access Protocol (IMAP)**.

   When using POP3, the messages are usually deleted from the server when they are downloaded, though some clients have the option to leave them on the server. IMAP supports permanent connections to a server and connecting multiple clients to the same mailbox simultaneously. It also allows a client to manage the mailbox on the server, to organize messages in folders and control when they are deleted for instance, and to create multiple mailboxes.

Email communications between a client and server would normally be protected with SSL/TLS security.

Configuring Email

To configure an email account, you need the user name, password, and default email address, plus incoming and outgoing server addresses and protocol types from the ISP.

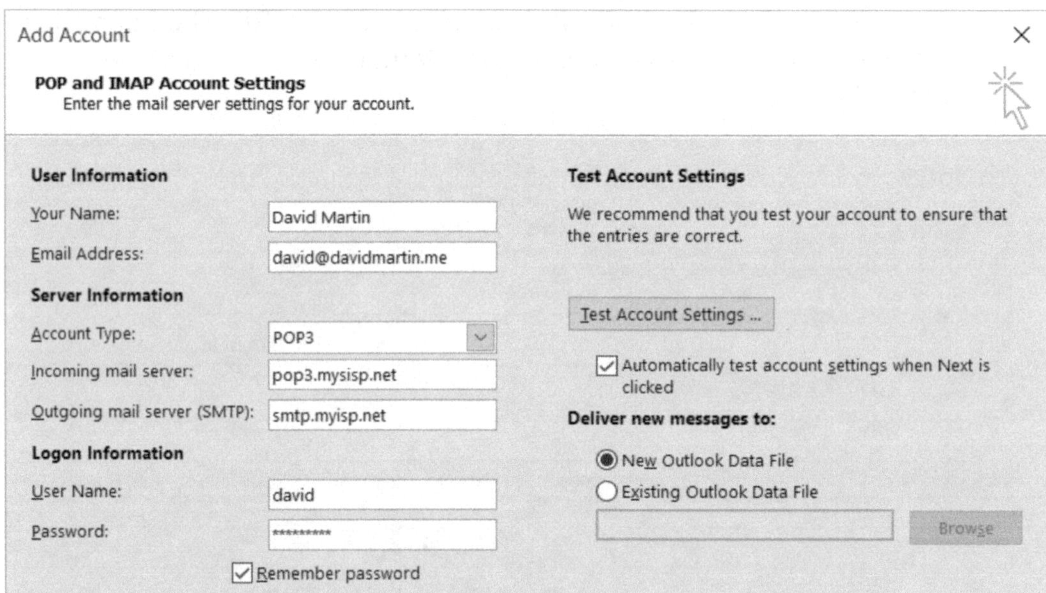

Configuring an email account—the incoming server is either POP3 or IMAP while the outgoing server is SMTP. Screenshot used with permission from Microsoft.

Internet email addresses follow another URL scheme (**mailto**). An Internet email address comprises two parts; the user name (local part) and the domain name, separated by an @ symbol. The domain name may refer to a company or an ISP. For example, `david.martin@comptia.org` or `david.martin@aol.com`.

Different mail systems have different requirements for allowed and disallowed characters in the local part. The local part is supposed to be case-sensitive, but most mail systems do not treat it as such. An incorrectly addressed email will be returned with a message notifying that it was undeliverable. Mail may also be rejected if it is identified as spam or if there is some other problem with the user mailbox, such as the mailbox being full.

Review Questions / Module 4 / Unit 1 / Networking Concepts

Answer these questions to test what you have learned in this unit. You can review the model answers at the end of the book.

1) What is a WAN?
2) What is a packet made up of?
3) What are the key features of a packet switching network?
4) What protocol is usually used to provide logical addressing on networks?
5) What type of address identifies a network interface in the context of the local network segment only?
6) What type of device is used to transfer packets between different networks?
7) Which protocol allows people to use names/labels to address network resources rather than numeric addresses?
8) Which of the following parts of a web address is usually depends on a name resolution service: protocol type, host location, file path?
9) What does HTTP stand for?
10) Which email protocol(s) are used to download messages from a mail server?

Module 4 / Unit 2

Connecting to a Network

Objectives

On completion of this unit, you will be able to:

- Identify the roles of different network devices in providing local and Internet network connectivity.
- Distinguish the advantages and disadvantages of Internet connection types.
- Connect a computer to a wired or wireless network.
- Configure a wireless access point to use secure network settings.

Syllabus Objectives and Content Examples

This unit covers the following exam domain objectives and content examples:

- 2.4 Compare and contrast common Internet service types.
  Fiber optic • Cable • DSL • Wireless (Radio frequency, Satellite, Cellular)
- 2.7 Explain basic networking concepts.
  Devices (Modem, Router, Switch, Access point)
- 2.8 Given a scenario, install, configure and secure a basic wireless network.
  802.11a/b/g/n/ac (Older vs. newer standards, Speed limitations, Interference and attenuation factors) • Best practices (Change SSID, Change default password, Encrypted vs. unencrypted [Open, Captive portal, WEP, WPA, WPA2])

Internet Service Types

The sort of equipment and networks used at home and in small businesses are often described as **SOHO (Small Office Home Office)**. A SOHO network is typically based around a single **multifunction device**. This type of network device can perform the following sort of functions:

- **Switch**—connects four or eight computers together in an Ethernet LAN using RJ-45 network ports and twisted-pair cabling.
- **Access Point (AP)**—creates a Wi-Fi wireless network (WLAN) between computers and mobile devices equipped with suitable adapters and also switches communications between the wired and wireless networks.
- **Internet router/modem**—connects the wired and wireless network clients to the Internet via a WAN link.

Typical SOHO Internet router/modems—the antennas visible on the one on the left show that it can also function as a wireless access point. (Image © 123rf.com.)

These devices are often simply referred to as "routers." It is possible for the modem and the router to be separate appliances. The function of the modem is to transmit frames across the WAN link, while the function of the router is to forward packets between the local network and the Internet.

There are various ways in which the WAN link can be provisioned.

Digital Subscriber Line (DSL)

Digital Subscriber Line (DSL) is one of the most popular SOHO Internet service types. DSL works over an ordinary telephone line, providing the line is of sufficient quality. The DSL modem/router is connected to the telephone line using a cable with RJ-11 connectors between the WAN port on the router and the telephone point. Data is transferred over the line using the high frequency ranges that voice calls don't need to use. The telephone point is fitted with a microfilter to prevent the data signals interfering with voice calls and vice versa.

Most residential DSL services are asymmetric (ADSL), meaning that the uplink (up to about 1.4 Mbps) is slower than the downlink (up to about 24 Mbps). The speeds achievable are heavily depending on the quality of the telephone wiring and the distance to the local telephone exchange. The maximum supported distance is about three miles.

Fiber Optic

Faster Internet services can be provisioned using **fiber optic** networks. Fiber optic cables perform much better over long distances and are not affected by noise in the way that electrical signals over copper cable are. Unfortunately, providing a fiber cable all the way to customer premises, referred to as **Fiber to the Home (FTTH)**, requires substantial investment by the telecom providers and is not widely available.

Fiber to the Curb (FTTC) is a compromise solution widely deployed in urban and some rural areas. FTTC means that the telecom provider has installed a fiber network terminating at a cabinet somewhere in a nearby street. Each residence is connected to the fiber network over the ordinary copper telephone cabling using **Very High Bit Rate DSL (VDSL)**. VDSL supports a downlink of up to 52 Mbps and an uplink of 16 Mbps at a distance of up to about 300m. VDSL2 also specifies a very short range (100m/300 feet) rate of 100 Mbps (bi-directional). The VDSL Internet modem/router is connected in much the same way as an ADSL modem/router.

Cable

Where FTTC is offered by providers with origins in the telephone network, a **cable** Internet connection is usually provided as part of a **Cable Access TV (CATV)** service. These networks are often described as **Hybrid Fiber Coax (HFC)** as they combine a fiber optic core network with coax links to customer premises equipment. Coax is another type of copper cable but manufactured in a different way to twisted pair.

The cable modem or modem/router is interfaced to the computer through an Ethernet adapter and to the cable network by a short segment of coax, terminated using an **F-connector**.

Cable based on the **Data Over Cable Service Interface Specification (DOCSIS)** version 3.0 supports downlink speeds of up to about 1.2 Gbps. Most service providers packages do not offer those kinds of speeds however, with about 100 Mbps being typical of a premium package at the time of writing.

Each Internet access type requires a specific modem or router/modem. You cannot use an ADSL router/modem to connect to an FTTC or HFC service for instance.

Verifying a Wired Connection

When you connect a Windows computer to a wired network, the network icon in the notification area of the taskbar should show a valid connection. A red cross on the icon indicates that either the cable is not connected properly, is faulty, or the network switch/router is faulty. A yellow alert on the icon indicates that the link has not been configured properly with IP address information and cannot connect to the Internet.

Network status icons showing (left-to-right) a working connection, a disconnected cable, and a connection with unknown or incomplete address information. Screenshot used with permission from Microsoft.

The Internet Protocol (IP) address information is usually configured by the router, using a service called the **Dynamic Host Configuration Protocol (DHCP)**. You would need to investigate either the settings on the adapter or the switch/router.

You can test an Internet connection quite simply by trying to browse a website.

Wireless Internet Services

While a cabled Internet service will usually offer the best bandwidth, they are not always available. Wireless services can be used in areas where it is too difficult or expensive to lay cable.

Microwave Satellite

Satellite systems provide far bigger areas of coverage than can be achieved using other technologies. The microwave dishes are aligned to orbital satellites that can either relay signals between sites directly or via another satellite. The widespread use of satellite television receivers allows for domestic Internet connectivity services over satellite connections. Satellite services for business are also expanding, especially in rural areas where DSL or cable services are less likely to be available.

Satellite connections experience severe **latency** problems as the signal has to travel thousands of miles more than terrestrial connections, introducing a delay of 4–5 times what might be expected over a land link. For example, if accessing a site in the US from Europe takes 200ms over a land (well, undersea) link, accessing the same site over a satellite link could involve a 900ms delay. This is an issue for real-time applications, such as video conferencing, voice calling, and multi-player gaming.

To create a satellite Internet connection, the ISP installs a satellite dish (antenna) at the customer's premises and aligns it with the orbital satellite. The satellites all orbit the equator, so in the northern hemisphere the dish will be pointing south. The antenna is connected via coaxial cabling to a DVB-S (Digital Video Broadcast Satellite) modem. This can be installed in the PC as an expansion card or as an external box connected via a USB or Ethernet port.

Cellular Radio

Cellular data connections use radio transmissions but at greater range than Wi-Fi. Cellular data is more closely associated with Internet access for cell phones and smartphones than with computers.

That said, a cell phone can share its Internet connection with a computer (tethering), if the computer has no other means of Internet access.

A cellular phone makes a connection using the nearest available transmitter (cell or base station). Each base station has an effective range of up to five miles (eight km). The transmitter connects the phone to the mobile and PSTN networks. Cellular radio works in the 850 and 1900 MHz frequency bands (mostly in the Americas) and the 900 and 1800 MHz bands (rest of the world).

Cellular digital communications standards developed in two competing formats, established in different markets:

- **GSM (Global System for Mobile Communication)**-based phones. GSM allows subscribers to use a **SIM (Subscriber Identity Module)** card to use an unlocked handset with their chosen network provider. GSM is adopted internationally and by AT&T and T-Mobile in the US.
- **TIA/EIA IS-95 (cdmaOne)**-based handsets. With CDMA, the handset is managed by the provider not the SIM. CDMA adoption is largely restricted to the telecom providers Sprint and Verizon.

There are many different cellular Internet service types, marketed in terms of "generations" (3G, 4G, and 5G). Support for a particular type is dependent on the local cell tower. Some of the technologies used include:

- **GPRS/EDGE (General Packet Radio Services/Enhanced Data Rates for GSM Evolution)** is a precursor to 3G (2.5G) with GPRS offering up to about 48 Kbps and EDGE about 3–4 times that.
- **Evolved High Speed Packet Access (HSPA+)** is a 3G standard developed via several iterations from the **Universal Mobile Telecommunications System (UMTS)** used on GSM networks. HSPA+ nominally supports download speeds up to 168 Mbps and upload speeds up to 34 Mbps. HSPA+-based services are often marketed as 4G if the nominal data rate is better than about 20 Mbps.
- **CDMA2000/Evolution Data Optimized (EV-DO)** are the main 3G standards deployed by CDMA network providers. EV-DO can support a 3.1 Mbps downlink and 1.8 Mbps uplink.

- **Long Term Evolution (LTE)** is a converged 4G standard supported by both the GSM and CDMA network providers. LTE has a maximum downlink of 150 Mbps in theory, but no provider networks can deliver that sort of speed at the time of writing, with around 20 Mbps far more typical of the speed that might actually be obtained.
- **LTE Advanced (LTE-A)** is intended to provide a 300 Mbps downlink, but again this aspiration is not matched by real world performance. Current typical performance for LTE-A is around 40 Mbps.

Radio Frequency

As noted above, **Radio Frequency (RF)** is a means of provisioning a wireless local network using Wi-Fi standard equipment. While this isn't a means of Internet service provision in itself, it is a means for a client to connect to a wireless router offering Internet access.

As well as the wireless router in your home network, you could use an **open** or **public access point** to get on the Internet. You have to be careful to secure the connections you open when doing this and to avoid using public access points that have been set up for malicious purposes.

When using an open access point, only use web servers supporting the HTTPS secure protocol if transferring information. Similarly, ensure that your connection to your email provider uses a secure type of SMTP and POP3/IMAP.

Setting Up a Wireless Network

A typical SOHO network appliance provides four wired Ethernet ports to connect hosts to the local network via a built-in switch and, via a built-in router and WAN modem, to the Internet. Most consumers need to connect more than four devices to the network, and it is not very convenient to have to use those devices only in locations where they can be cabled to the router. Consequently, most SOHO networks rely heavily on wireless (Wi-Fi) networking.

Wireless Standards and Compatibility

"Wireless networking" is generally understood to mean the IEEE's 802.11 standards for **Wireless LANs (WLAN)**, also called **Wi-Fi**. There are several versions of the standard, starting with the legacy 802.11a and 802.11b, which supported data rates of 54 Mbps and 11 Mbps respectively. Subsequently, 802.11g acted as an upgrade path for 802.11g, working at 54 Mbps but also allowing support for older 802.11b clients. 802.11a was not as widely adopted but does use a less crowded frequency band (5 GHz) and is considered less susceptible to interference than the 2.4 GHz band used by 802.11b/g.

The 802.11n standard can use either frequency band and deliver much improved data rates (nominally up to 600 Mbps). The latest 802.11ac standard is now widely supported. 802.11ac access points can deliver up to 1.7 Gbps throughput at the time of writing. 802.11ac works only in the 5 GHz range with the 2.4 GHz band reserved for legacy standards support (802.11b/g/n).

Standard	Maximum Transfer Rate	Band
802.11a (1999)	54 Mbps	5 GHz
802.11b (1999)	11 Mbps	2.4 GHz
802.11g (2003)	54 Mbps	2.4 GHz
802.11n (2009)	72.2 Mbps/stream (Single Channel) 150 Mbps/stream (Bonded Channels)	2.4/5 GHz
802.11ac (2013)	1.7 Gbps (at time of writing)	5 GHz

Most SOHO routers support 802.11g/n or 802.11g/n/ac. This means that you can have a mix of client devices. For example, you might have a new router that supports 802.11ac but computers and tablets with wireless adapters that only support 802.11n. You can use the access point in compatibility mode to allow these devices to connect.

Compatibility modes can slow the whole network down, especially if 802.11b clients have to be supported. If possible, use newer standards only.

Configuring an Access Point

To configure an access point, you connect a PC or laptop to one of the LAN ports on the SOHO router. The SOHO router should assign the computer's adapter an **Internet Protocol (IP)** address using a service called the **Dynamic Host Configuration Protocol (DHCP)**. If this has worked properly, you should see the network status icon in the notification area.

Look at the SOHO router's setup guide to find out the router's IP address. Open a web browser and type the router's IP address into the address bar. This should open a management page for you to log on. Enter the user name and password listed in the router's setup guide. Most routers will invite you to complete the configuration using a wizard, which guides you through the process.

Use the **System** page to choose a new **admin** password. The admin password is used to configure the router. It is vital that this password be kept secret and secure. You must choose a strong password that cannot be cracked by password-guessing software. Use a long, memorable phrase of at least 12 characters.

You must always change the default password (typically "default," "password," or "admin") to prevent unauthorized access.

Use the **Wireless** settings page to configure the router as an access point. Having checked the box to enable wireless communications, you can adjust the following settings from the default.

It is best practice not to enable services you do not need, especially on a multifunction device such as this. Most devices are now shipped in "security-enabled" configurations, meaning that you explicitly have to choose to enable services that you want to run.

- SSID (Service Set ID)—a name for the WLAN. This is usually set by default to the router vendor's name. It is a good idea to change the SSID from the default to something unique to your network. Remember that the SSID is easily visible to other wireless devices, so do not use one that identifies you personally or your address. The SSID can be up to 32 characters.

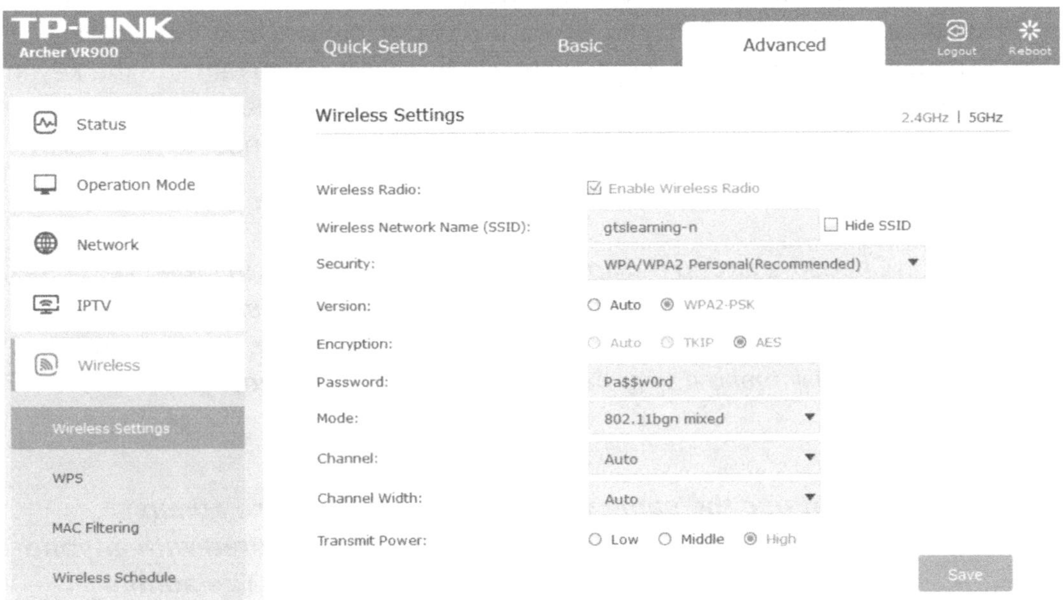

Configuring a SOHO access point.

- Wireless mode—enable compatibility for different 802.11 devices.

Configuring Wireless Security

To prevent snooping, you should enable **encryption** on the wireless network. Encryption scrambles the messages being sent over the WLAN so that anyone intercepting them is not able to capture any valuable information. An encryption system consists of a **cipher**, which is the process used to scramble the message, and a **key**. The key is a unique value that allows the recipient to decrypt a message that has been encrypted using the same cipher and key. Obviously, the key must be known only to valid recipients or the encryption system will offer no protection.

Following our SOHO router configuration example, under **Encryption**, you would select the highest security mode supported by devices on the network.

- **WEP (Wired Equivalent Privacy)**—this is an older standard. WEP is flawed and you would only select this if compatibility with legacy devices and software is imperative.

- **Wi-Fi Protected Access (WPA)**—this fixes most of the security problems with WEP. WPA uses the same weak RC4 (Rivest Cipher) cipher as WEP but adds a mechanism called the **Temporal Key Integrity Protocol (TKIP)** to make it stronger.
- **WPA2**—this implements the 802.11i WLAN security standard. The main difference to WPA is the use of the **AES (Advanced Encryption Standard)** cipher for encryption. AES is much stronger than RC4/TKIP. The only reason not to use WPA2 is if it is not supported by devices on the network. In many cases, devices that can support WPA can be made compatible with WPA2 with a firmware or driver upgrade.

See Unit 5.3 for more information about ciphers and encryption.

On a SOHO network, you would also generate a **Pre-Shared Key (PSK)** using a **wireless password**. When you type a password into the box, the router converts it into an encryption key to use with the cipher. You can see the key in the screenshot above expressed as hex numerals. The same wireless password must be entered on client devices for them to connect to the WLAN.

Choose a strong passphrase and keep it secret. In order to generate a strong key, use a long phrase (at least 12 characters). The passphrase can be up to 63 characters long, but making it too long will make it very hard for users to enter correctly.

Do not use the same wireless password as the admin password. The wireless password can be shared with anyone you want to allow to connect to the network. The admin password must be kept secret.

Open Authentication and Captive Portals

Selecting open authentication means that the client is not required to authenticate. This mode would be used on a public AP (or hotspot). This also means that data sent over the wireless network is **unencrypted**.

Open authentication may be combined with a secondary authentication mechanism managed via a browser. When the client associates with the open hotspot and launches the browser, the client is redirected to a **captive portal**. This will allow the client to authenticate to the hotspot provider's network (over HTTPS so the login is secure). The portal may also be designed to enforce terms and conditions and/or take payment to access the Wi-Fi service.

Configuring a Wireless Client

To connect a Windows computer to a wireless network, click the network status icon in the notification area . Select the network name and then click **Connect**. If you leave **Connect automatically** selected, Windows will save the password and always try to connect to this SSID when it is in range. In the next panel, enter the wireless password (PSK):

Connecting to a network and entering the network security key (password). Screenshot used with permission from Microsoft.

When you connect to a new network, you are prompted to set its **location**. If the link is configured as **Public** (selecting **No** in Windows 10), your computer is hidden from other computers on the same network and file sharing is disabled. If it is configured as **Private** (home or work) by selecting **Yes**, the computer is discoverable and file sharing is enabled.

The computer should now be part of the SOHO network and able to connect to the Internet. To verify, test that you can open a website in the browser.

Speed Limitations (Attenuation and Interference)

A device supporting the Wi-Fi standard should have a maximum indoor range of up to about 30m (100 feet), though the weaker the signal, the lower the data transfer rate. The distance between the wireless client (station) and access point determines the **attenuation** (or loss of strength) of the signal. Each station determines an appropriate data rate based on the quality of the signal using a mechanism called **Dynamic Rate Switching/Selection (DRS)**. If the signal is strong, the station will select the highest available data rate, determined by the 802.11 standard. If the signal is weak, the station will reduce the data rate to try to preserve a more stable connection.

Radio signals pass through solid objects, such as ordinary brick or drywall walls but can be weakened or blocked by particularly dense or thick material and metal. Other radio-based devices and nearby Wi-Fi networks can also cause **interference**. Other sources of interference include devices as various as fluorescent lighting, microwave ovens, cordless phones, and (in an industrial environment) power motors and heavy machinery. Bluetooth uses the 2.4 GHz frequency range but a different modulation technique, so interference is possible but not common.

Connecting to an Enterprise Network

An enterprise network uses the same sort of switch, access point, and router technologies as a SOHO network. In a SOHO network, these technologies are likely to be combined within a single multifunction appliance. On an enterprise network, multiple switch, access point, and router appliances will be used.

Cabled Enterprise Network Access

An office building is likely to be flood wired with cabling so that there are network ports at every desk. A computer can be connected to the network via an RJ-45 patch cable (or possibly a fiber optic patch cable) plugged into one of these network ports.

Modular wall plate with an RJ-45 patch cord connected. Image by Nikolai Lebedev © 123rf.com.

The cabling from each port is routed back to a telecommunications room where it is connected to an Ethernet switch. While the switch in a SOHO Internet router usually provides four ports, a single enterprise switch will support 20 ports or more. Modular enterprise switches can support hundreds of ports. Furthermore, the switches can be interconnected to create a switched fabric supporting thousands of ports within the same LAN.

Cisco Catalyst 3650 Series workgroup switch. Image © and Courtesy of Cisco Systems, Inc. Unauthorized use not permitted.

Wireless Enterprise Network Access

Wireless enterprise network access also works in the same basic way to SOHO but at a bigger scale. Enterprise access points can support more devices than consumer-level ones.

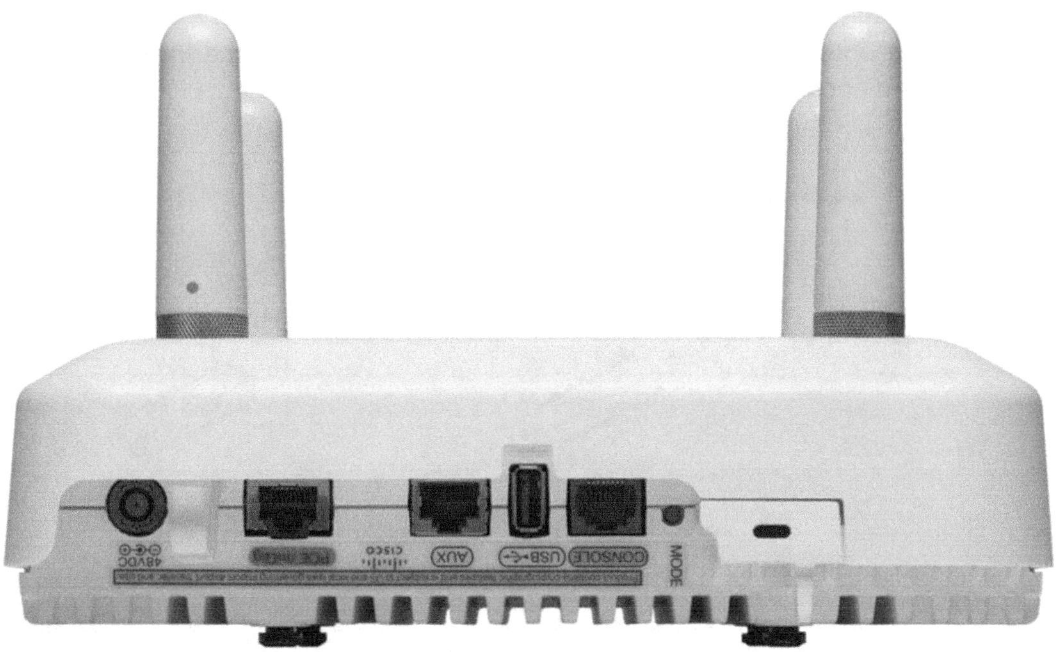

Cisco Aironet access point. Image © and Courtesy of Cisco Systems, Inc. Unauthorized use not permitted.

Enterprise Network Routers

While the switches and access points can provide thousands of ports and network connections, it is inefficient to have that many connections to the same "logical" network. The ports are divided into groups using a technology called Virtual LAN (VLAN) and each VLAN is associated with a different subnet. Communications between different VLANs have to go through a router.

Cisco 1000 Series Advanced Services Router. Image © and Courtesy of Cisco Systems, Inc. Unauthorized use not permitted

The graphic below illustrates how the network components described above might be positioned. The whole network is connected to the wider Internet via a **router**. The router is also used to divide the network into two **subnets** (A and B). Within each subnet, a **switch** is used to allow **nodes** to communicate with one another and, through the router, to the other subnet and the Internet. The link between each node and the switch is a **segment**.

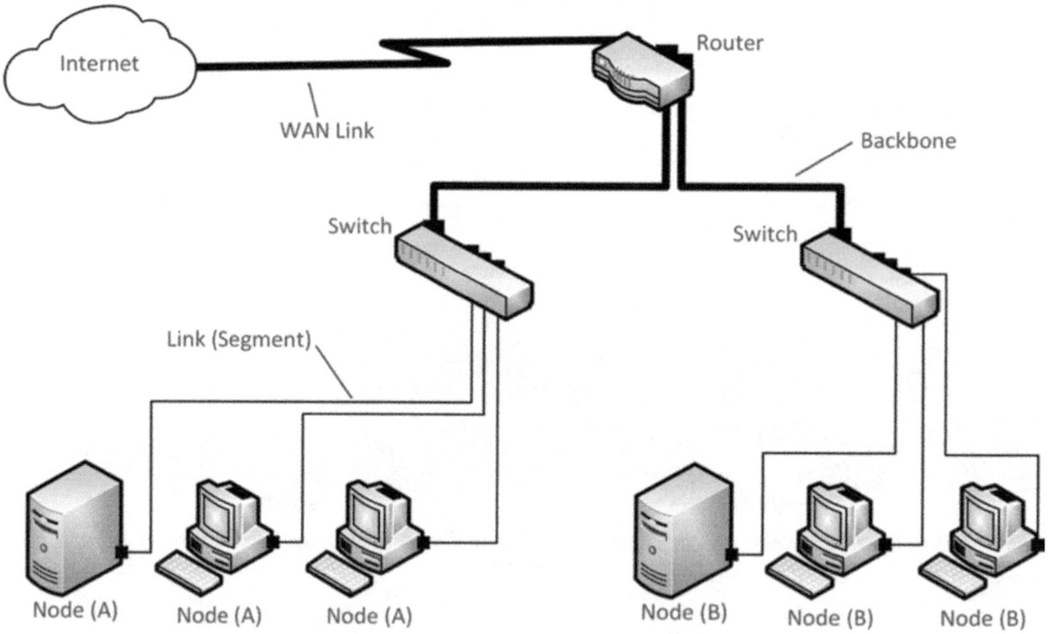

Positioning network components.

High bandwidth **backbone segments** are used between the router and the Internet and between the router and the two switches.

Note that this diagram is very much simplified. An enterprise network might use hundreds of switches and tens of router appliances. The routers used within the network and for Internet access are also likely to be separate appliances.

Review Questions / Module 4 / Unit 2 / Connecting to a Network

Answer these questions to test what you have learned in this unit. You can review the model answers at the end of the book.

1) What device is used to connect computers together in an Ethernet network?

2) What is the difference between a modem and a router?

3) Can you list at least four Internet access methods?

4) What is the latest Wi-Fi standard and which frequency band(s) does it use?

5) What information do you need to configure a wireless connection manually?

6) What is the risk of using a free Wi-Fi network to make an order from an online shop?

7) What does attenuation mean?

Lab 17 / Network Settings

In this lab, you will verify the network connection between your computer and your Internet router. This lab assumes that you have a SOHO router configured to connect to the Internet and assign local network settings to connected computers.

1) If necessary, start your computer and sign in.

2) If you have a wired connection to the router, make the following checks:

    - The router is powered on and connected to the telephone point. Also verify that its "Internet," "WAN," or "DSL" LED is green.

    - The computer is connected to the router via a cable connecting the RJ-45 ports on the two devices.

    - The network status icon in the notification area shows a connected symbol and pointing at the icon reveals an "Internet access" tooltip.

    If there is a warning icon the connection has not been correctly configured by the router or the router is not connected to the Internet. If there is a red cross icon then the cable is faulty or not connected properly.

    - If you open the web browser then you can view a website such as `www.comptia.org`.

3) If you have a wireless connection to the router, make the following checks:

    - The network status icon in the notification area shows a connected symbol and pointing at the icon reveals an "Internet access" tooltip.

    - If the icon shows that connections are available , click it, select your wireless network name (SSID) and click **Connect**, then input the passkey.

    - If you open the web browser then you can view a website such as `www.comptia.org`.

4) Right-click the network status icon and select **Open Network & Internet Settings**.

    From here, you can configure Wi-Fi or Ethernet (as appropriate) settings, and also create and configure Dial-up and VPN connections. You can also configure your computer as a mobile hotspot.

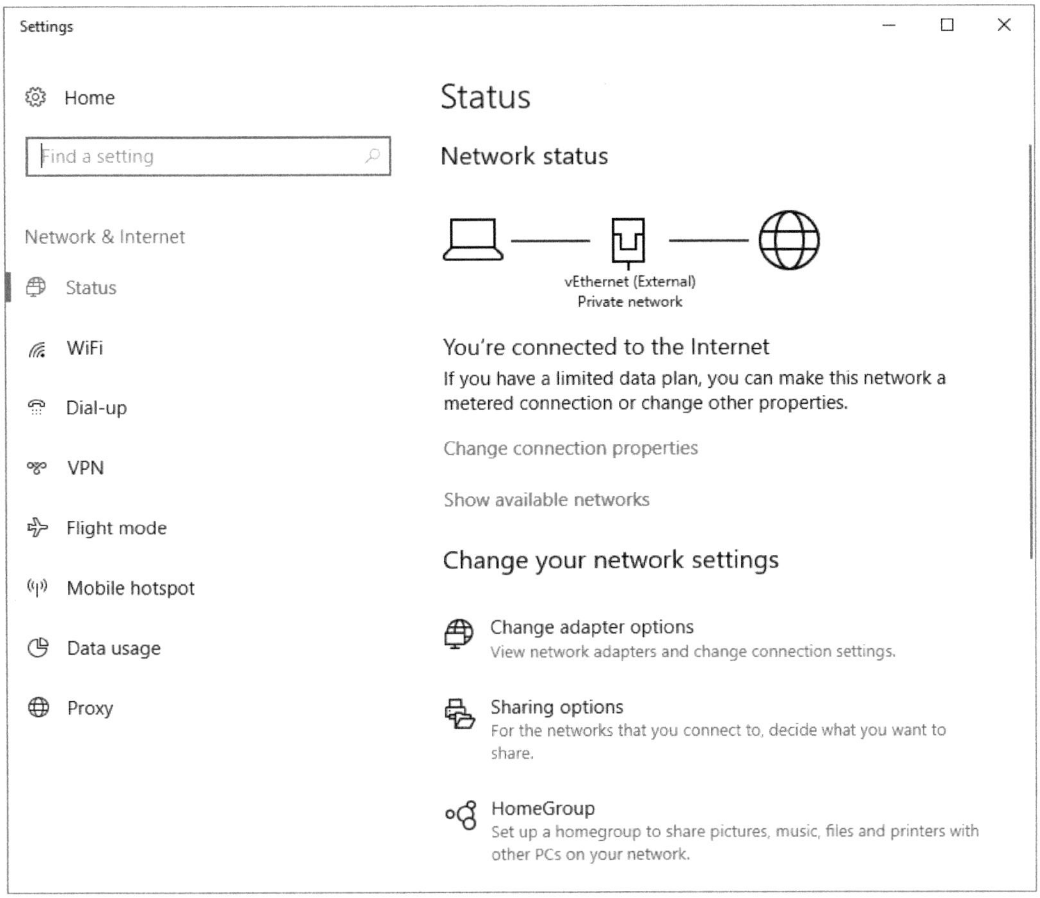

Network & Internet Settings. Screenshot used with permission from Microsoft.

5) Click the **WiFi** or **Ethernet** tab (depending on whether your computer has a wireless or wired connection).

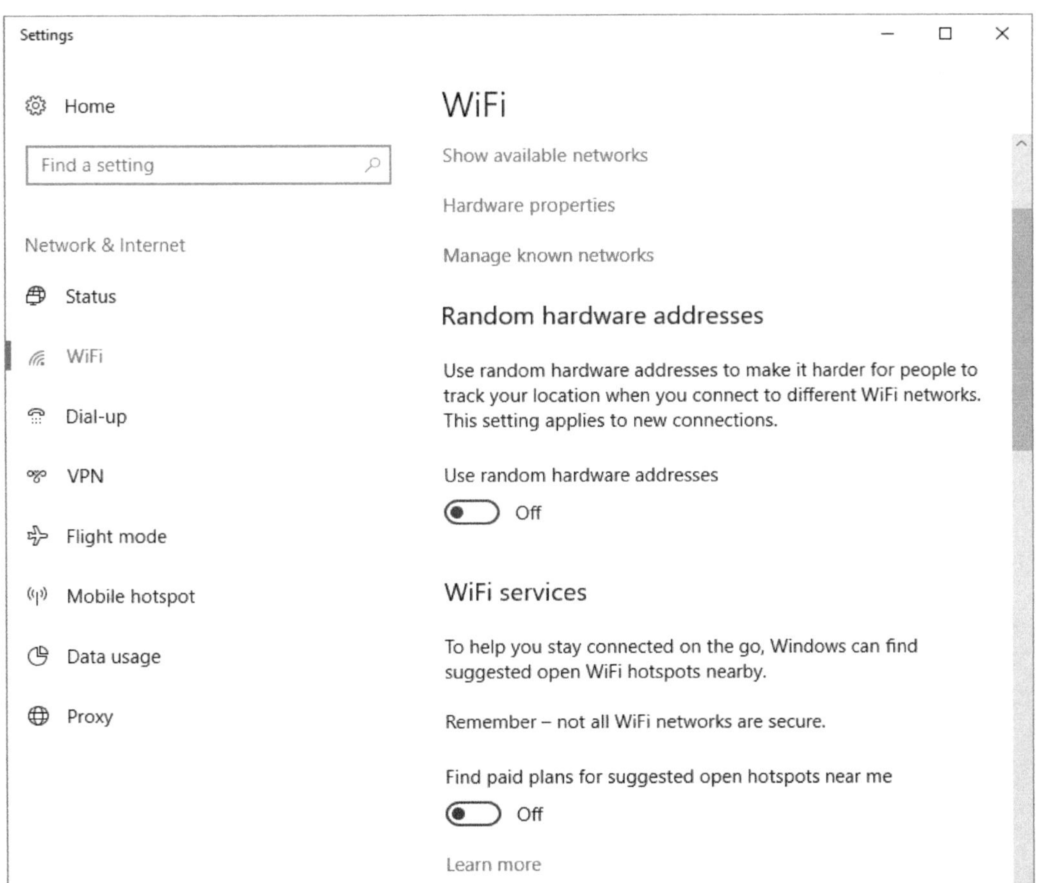

WiFi tab. Screenshot used with permission from Microsoft.

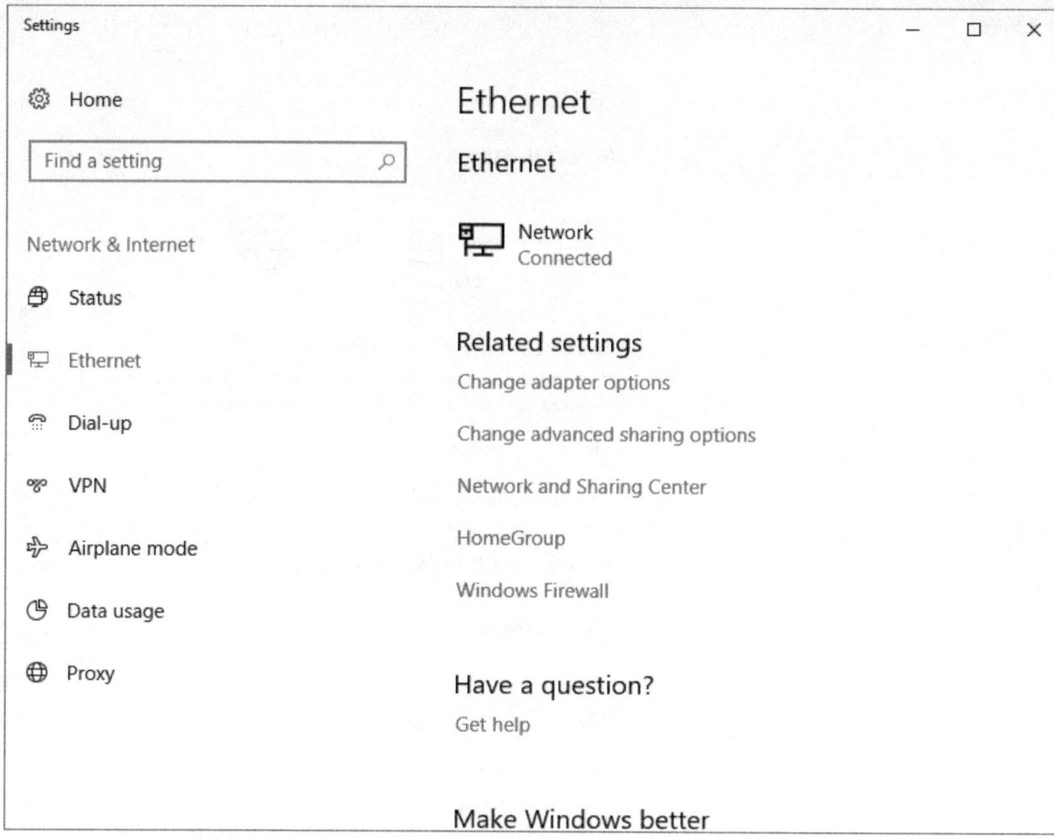

Ethernet tab. Screenshot used with permission from Microsoft.

6) Click **Network and Sharing Center**.

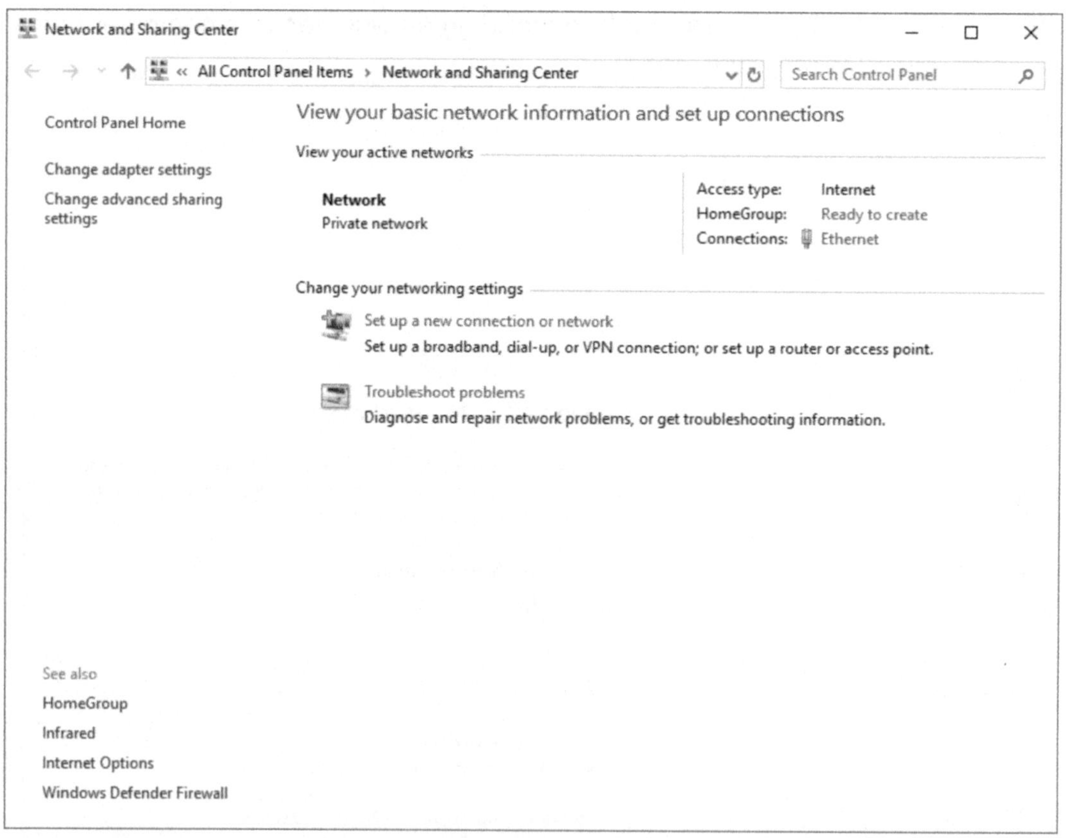

Network and Sharing Center. Screenshot used with permission from Microsoft.

7) Under "view your active networks," click the **Ethernet** link or the ***SSID*** (depending on whether your link is wired or wireless). This displays a **Status** dialog showing the protocol used by the connection and the link speed

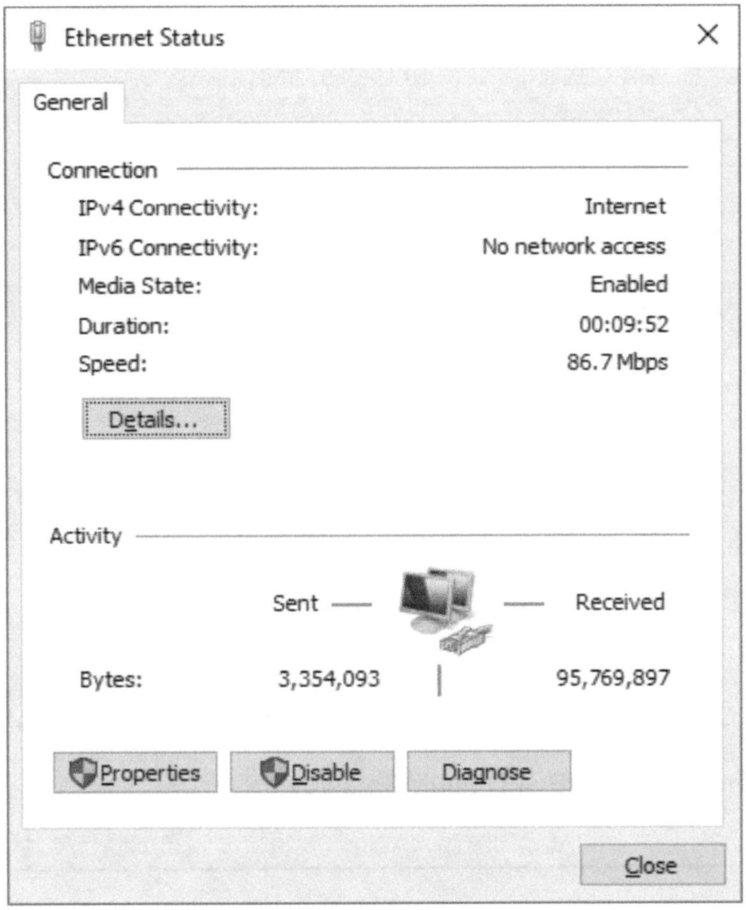

Ethernet Status dialog. Screenshot used with permission from Microsoft.

8) Click the **Details** button. This shows the configuration of the link, including the Internet Protocol (IP) address (**`192.168.1.127`** in the example below) and the IP address of the default gateway—your Internet router (**`192.168.1.254`**).

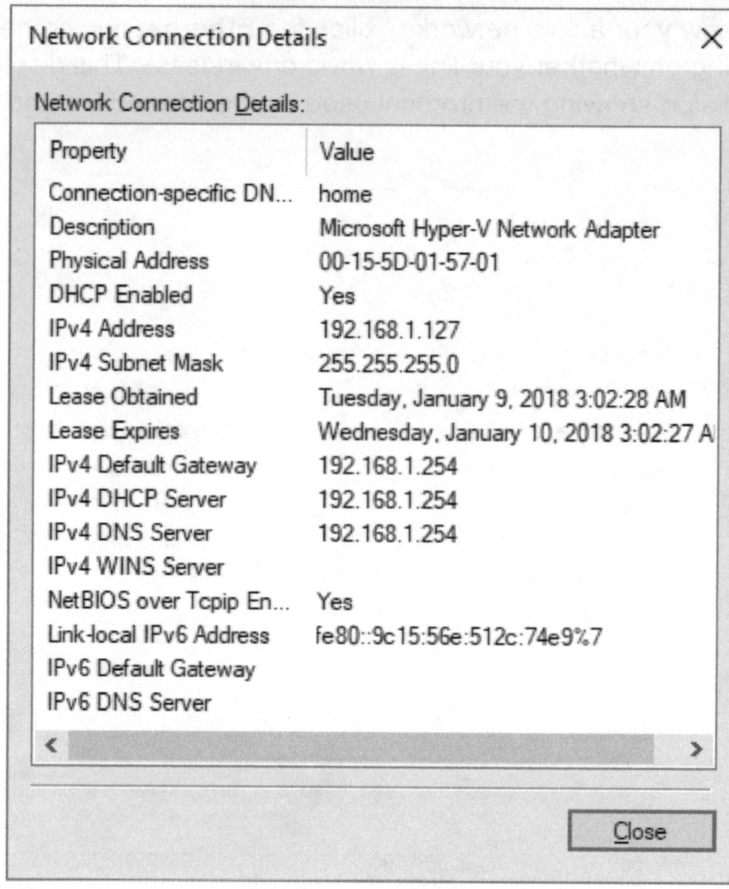

Network Connection Details dialog. Screenshot used with permission from Microsoft.

9) Make a note of the "IPv4 Default Gateway":

____

10) Click **Close** then **Close** again to close both dialogs.

11) Open the web browser then type the IP address of your default gateway into the address bar.

    This should load the configuration page for your Internet router. You could log on here using the administrative credentials supplied with your router to change settings or investigate problems.

12) Optionally, shut down your computer if you are not continuing to use it after this lab.

Module 4 / Unit 3
Secure Web Browsing

Objectives

On completion of this unit, you will be able to:

- Explain risks of using open Internet access methods.
- Describe safe browsing practices and configure browser security/privacy features.
- Identify the use and basic configuration parameters of a firewall.

Syllabus Objectives and Content Examples

This unit covers the following exam domain objectives and content examples:

- 2.7 Explain basic networking concepts.
  Devices (Firewall)
- 3.5 Given a scenario, configure and use web browsers.
  Caching/clearing cache • Deactivate client-side scripting • Browser add-ons/extensions (Add, Remove, Enable/disable) • Private browsing • Proxy settings • Certificates (Valid, Invalid) • Popup blockers • Script blockers • Compatible browser for application(s)
- 6.2 Explain methods to secure devices and best practices.
  Securing devices (Host firewall, Safe browsing practices)

Safe Browsing Practices

When you use a computer and web browser to access pages and other resources over the Internet, you must consider the ways you can keep any information you transmit secure and prevent any malicious software (**malware**) from infecting your computer. There are a number of **safe browsing practices** that you should be aware of.

Using Free/Open Networks

Sometimes people connect to the Internet via an **open or free network**. This may be a commercial Wi-Fi network, operated by a cafe or made available in an airport or railway terminal, or wired Internet access available from a "web cafe." You might also find that your neighbor is operating an open Wi-Fi network or discover several open networks when you use your laptop in a park or other public space. It is important to realize that any data you transfer over a free network could be intercepted by anyone else connected to the network and by the person that owns the network. To mitigate this, use a security-enabled protocol (SSL/TLS) that encrypts the link between your client and the web or mail server.

It is also worth noting that any data you transfer over an Internet connection is processed and may be stored on the ISP's computers. When you use an ISP, you are trusting them not to snoop on your unencrypted Internet traffic.

When using a public workstation, you should always be alert to the possibility that it could be infected with malware. Clear the browser cache before shutting down or logging off, and make sure you do not allow passwords to be cached.

If you operate a wireless network, it is important to secure it so that others do not make malicious use of it, for which you could be held responsible. Most ISPs make it a condition of service that you use your wireless router in a secure configuration.

An ISP's terms and conditions aside, it is also illegal to use open networks (those not protected by a password) without explicit permission from the owner, though the chances of a prosecution being launched are very low. If you try to guess or crack the password of someone's network, perhaps one that has been configured with the default password for instance, you are committing an illegal act.

Malware Threats

The web browser is one of the most well-exploited *vectors* for infecting a system with malware or stealing information. **Malware** is malicious software threats and tools designed to vandalize or compromise computer systems. Malware can be categorized in a number of ways:

- Viruses and worms—malware principally designed to spread to other PCs.
- Trojan Horse—an apparently legitimate application that conceals malicious functions, such as spyware or a bot allowing remote control of the PC.

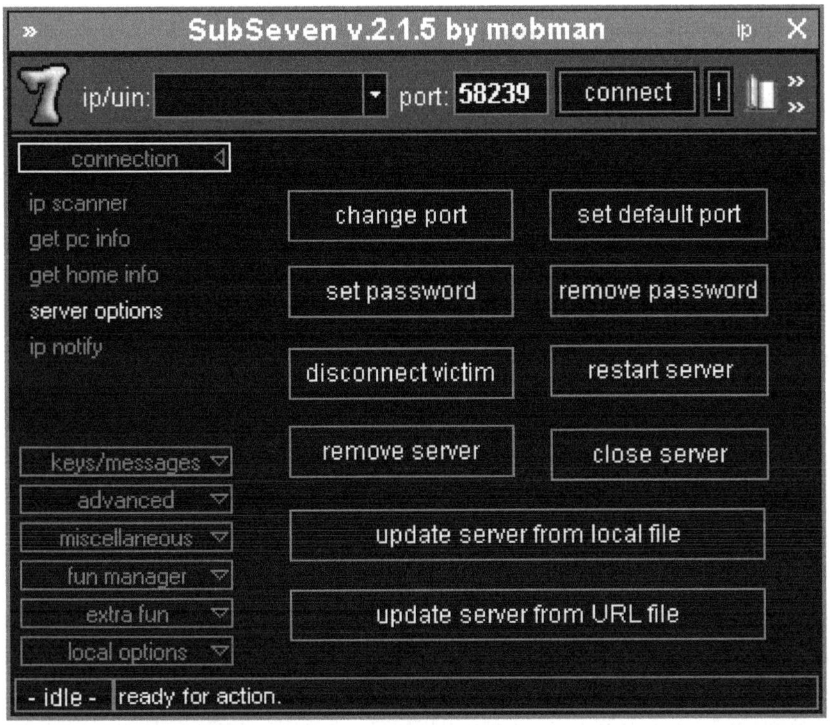

SubSeven RAT management console—the attacker could use this interface to snoop or exploit the infected host. Image courtesy (CCAS4.0 International) J.SA13D034 from Wikimedia Commons.

- Adware—software or configuration files installed with your agreement that helps a company track what pages you visit and display personalized adverts to you.
- Spyware—malware installed covertly, possibly as a Trojan or as a result of a virus or worm infection, that tries to track everything you use the computer for. Spyware might record keystrokes, take screenshots of the desktop, or even hack the computer's camera and microphone.

The lines between useful utilities, adware, and spyware are not completely clear-cut, but if something is there that the user (or IT department) did not explicitly sanction, then it's best to get rid of it.

Consequently, it is important to use the latest browser software versions. Legacy browsers are more likely to be susceptible to malware. Also, ensure that the browser software and any plug-in software used by the browser (see below) is updated with the latest security patches.

Refer to Unit 5.2 for notes on software updates and malware.

As well as faults in the browser client software, web applications can be vulnerable to faults in web server and database software and poor programming practice.

Spyware and Adware Symptoms

Malware, such as adware and spyware, is designed with commercial or criminal intent rather than to vandalize the computer system. It can therefore be difficult to identify whether a computer is infected, because the malware may be designed to remain hidden.

Obvious symptoms of infection by spyware or adware are pop-ups or additional toolbars, the home page or search provider changing suddenly, searches returning results that are different from other computers, slow performance, and excessive crashing (faults). Viruses and Trojans may spawn pop-ups without the user opening the browser.

Another symptom is redirection. This is where the user tries to open one page but gets sent to another. This may imitate the target page. Redirection attacks often target Internet search engines. In adware, redirection is just a blunt means of driving traffic through a site, but spyware may exploit it to capture authentication details.

You should also be wary of suspicious banner ads. A banner ad is an area of a website set aside for third-party advertising. The advert is inserted into a frame and can be hosted on a different server to that of the main site. Adverts for free anti-virus, or virus infection warnings, or system performance warnings are all likely to be bogus. In the worst cases, the ads could contain malicious code that will attempt to exploit any vulnerabilities in your OS or browser/plug-in software to infect your computer (a drive-by download).

Configuring Browser Security

Malware may be able to infect your computer because OS or browser software is not up to date and is therefore vulnerable to some sort of **exploit**. You can only mitigate this type of threat by installing the latest software patches. There are other browser settings you can configure to ensure you are using the best safe browsing practices though.

Choosing a Compatible Browser

Historically, browsers varied quite widely from the standards agreed for the way HTML and associated formats, such as Cascading Style Sheets (CSS). Microsoft's Internet Explorer (IE) browser was particularly notorious for this. Many websites and web applications used custom or proprietary features of IE that meant other browsers might fail to run the web application properly.

While the mainstream browsers are now much more standards-based, compatibility problems can still arise. It is often the case that you will need to have more than one browser installed on your computer. This is not ideal in security terms, as it is better to install as few applications as possible, but circumstances may demand it.

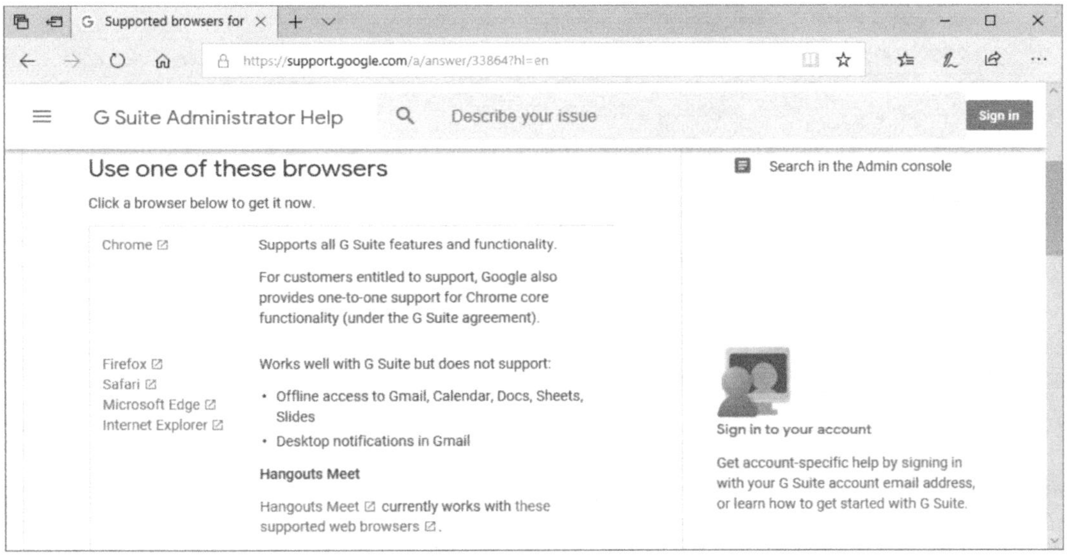

Browser compatibility advice for Google's G Suite cloud applications.

Compatibility aside, your choice of browser is largely down to personal preference. Do make sure you choose a browser whose developer is active in monitoring security issues and providing software updates to fix them.

Active Content Types

HTTP is a limited protocol in terms of serving any content other than text and pictures. Many websites use active content to play video or add animated and interactive features. There are several ways of creating this type of content:

- **Scripting**—scripts can run either on the server or on the client (browser) to perform quite sophisticated actions. Scripting is usually based on JavaScript. JavaScript can also be used to create browser add-ons.
- **Add-ons**—animated or interactive content often uses a browser add-on. These are mini applications that work within the browser. There are many different add-ons, each working with a different type of content. Add-ons can also be used to extend or change the functionality of the browser by adding a custom toolbar for instance.
- **Flash/Silverlight**—these are two rival development environments, created by Adobe and Microsoft respectively, used to provide interactive web applications and video. The browser must have the Flash or Silverlight plug-in installed to view this type of content.
- **Java**—unlike JavaScript, this is a fully-featured programming language used to develop sophisticated web applications. Java applications require the Java Virtual Machine to be installed on Windows and for the Java plug-in to be enabled in the browser.

All of these technologies pose some degree of risk as they can be used for malicious purposes. When a web page needs to use active content and it is either not permitted to by current security settings or because the required plug-in is not installed, the browser displays a warning. Click the bar to install the component or change security settings.

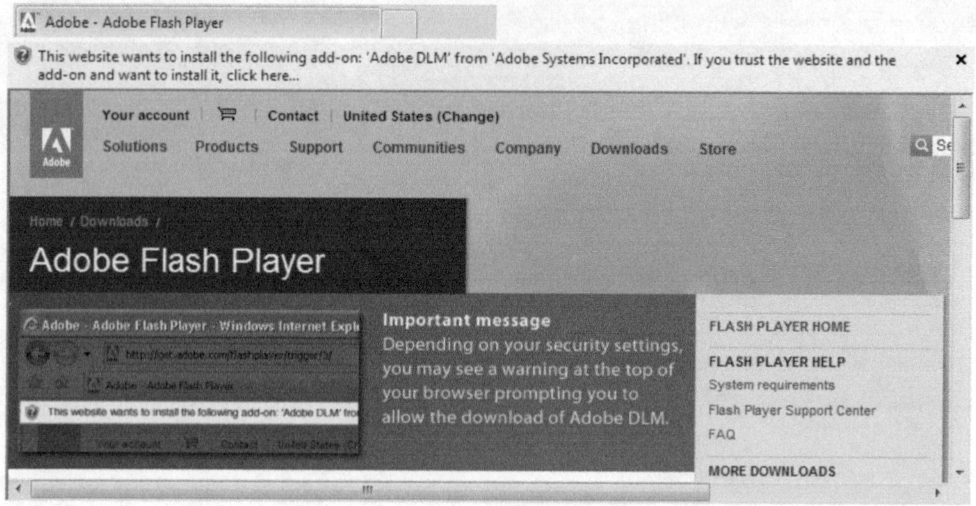

Installing an add-on—the yellow information bar will tell you if the publisher is trusted (has a valid digital certificate) and prompts you whether to install the add-on. Screenshot used with permission from Microsoft.

Generally speaking, you should only install add-ons where the browser can identify that the publisher is a trusted source.

Flash, Silverlight, and client-side Java have fallen out of favor with web developers. Most modern sites use scripting for interactive content.

Disabling Client-side Scripting

Most sites will use **server-side scripting**, meaning that code runs on the server to display the page you are looking at. There is no way to disable this. Many sites also depend on **client-side scripting**. This means that code is placed in the page itself and runs within the browser to change the way it looks or provide some other functionality.

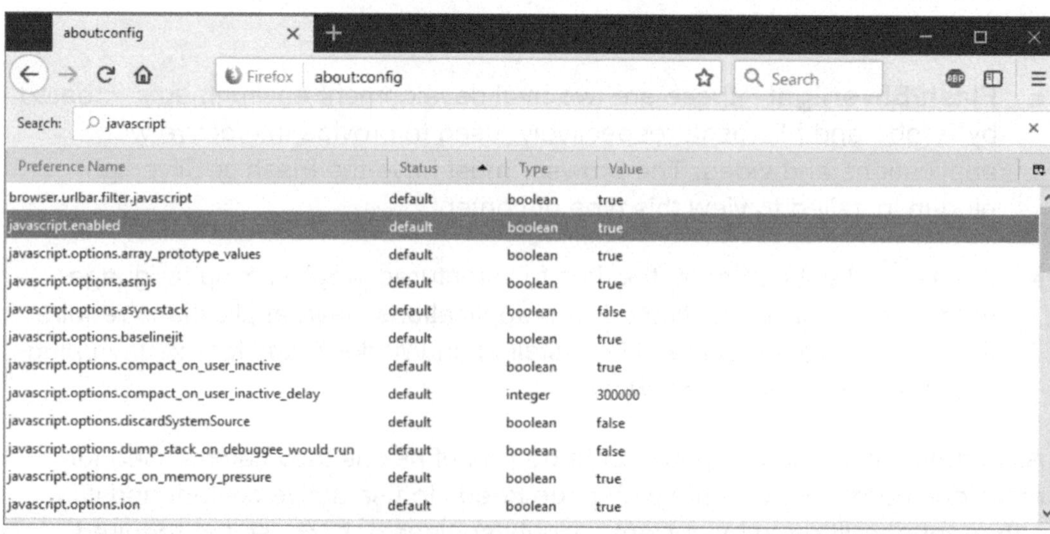

Disabling scripting in the Firefox browser requires the advanced options configuration interface and cannot be configured on a site-by-site basis.

Deactivating client-side scripting tends to break most of the websites published on the Internet because they depend very heavily on the functionality that scripting allows. In theory, enabling scripting should not be significantly risky. Modern browsers "sandbox" the scripts running on a page or browser tab so that they cannot change anything on other tabs or on the computer (at least, not without explicit authorization from the user). Scripting can be disabled in some browsers by configuring settings, but others, Microsoft's new Edge browser for instance, do not allow scripts to be disabled.

It is also possible to install a **script blocker** add-on. This provides more control over which websites are allowed to run scripts.

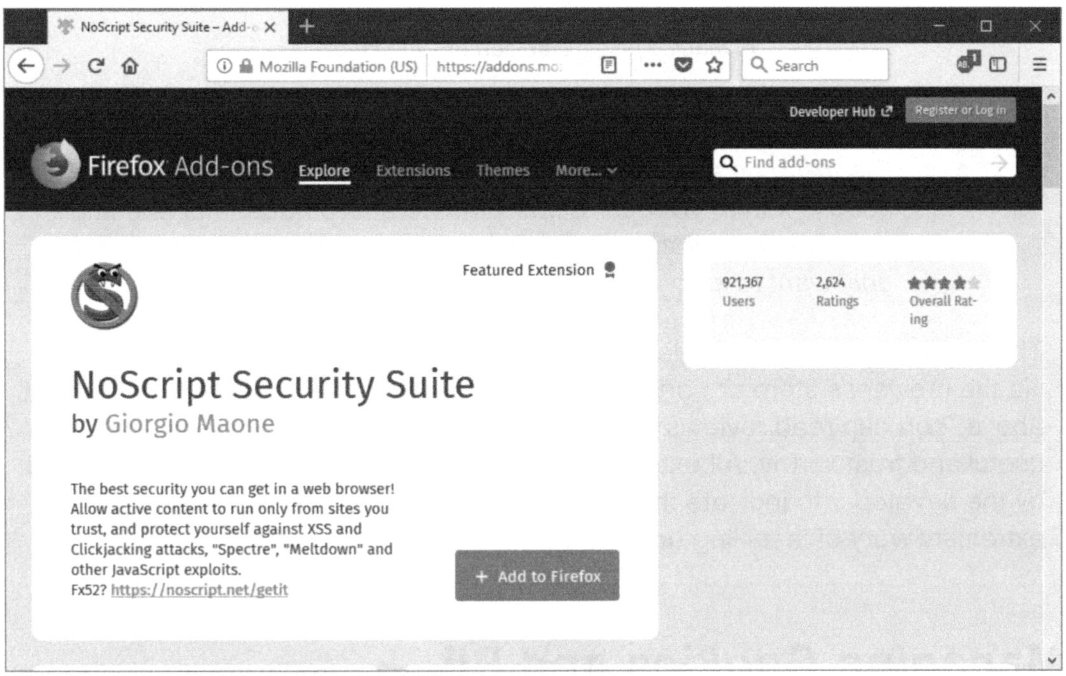

You could use a script blocker extension such as NoScript (noscript.net) to manage active content instead. Make sure the extension is maintained by a reputable developer!

Managing Add-ons

While scripting is usually left enabled, all browsers provide tools for managing **add-ons**. Add-ons come in several different types:

- **Extensions**—these can add functionality to the browser. They might install a toolbar or change menu options. They can run scripts to interact with the pages you are looking at.
- **Plug-ins**—these are designed to play some sort of content embedded in a web page, such as Flash, Silverlight, or other video/multimedia format. The plug-in can only interact with the multimedia object placed on the page so is more limited than an extension.
- **Themes**—these change the appearance of the browser using custom images and color schemes.

You can view installed add-ons and choose to remove or enable/disable them using the browser settings button or menu.

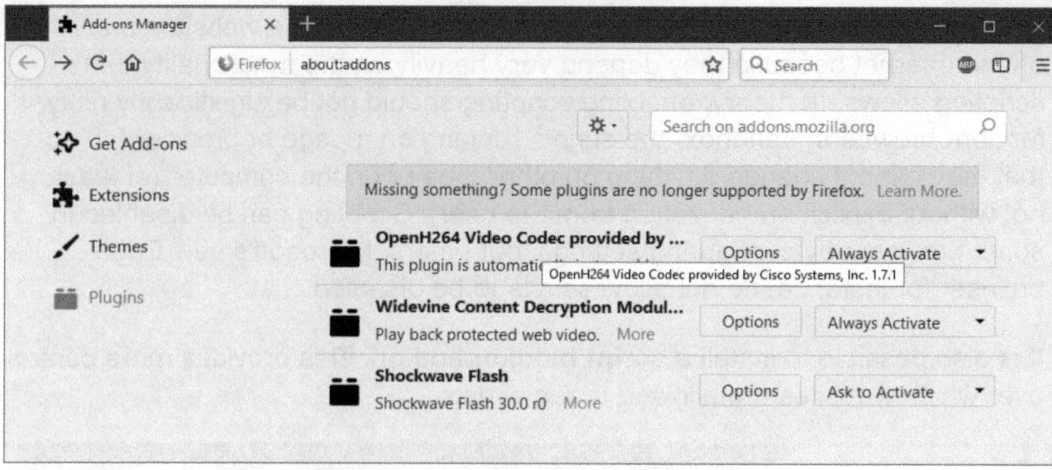

Managing plugin type add-ons in Firefox.

Disabling an add-on rather than removing it means the application code is left on your computer, but the add-on does not execute when the browser starts. You would use the disable option if you only want to stop using the add-on temporarily.

The interface will also provide an option for browsing and installing add-ons, via the browser's store or portal, using the **Get Add-ons** link in the screenshot above. You can read reviews of the add-on and determine whether it will be useful and trustworthy. All extensions and plug-ins should be **digitally signed** by the developer to indicate that the code is as-published. You should be extremely wary of installing unsigned add-ons.

Managing Cookies and PII

As well as protecting against risks from malware and malicious add-ons, you also need to consider how the way your browser stores data and interacts with websites protects, or doesn't protect, your personal information.

Cookies

A **cookie** is a plain text file created by a website when you visit it. The purpose of cookies is to store session information so that the website can be personalized for you. For example, cookies may record information you type into forms, preferences you choose for the way the site works, and so on. They may also be used to display targeted advertising to you or collect information (metadata) about the browser you are using, your IP address, the links you click, how often you visit a site, and so on. An IP address can often be tied quite closely to a geographic location.

This sort of information is referred to as **Personally Identifiable Information (PII)**. Anyone able to collect this information might be able to track the sites you visit and work out where you live. You can configure browser settings to try to limit the way sites can gather PII from your browser.

There are two classes of cookies:

- First-party cookies—set by the domain you visit. For example, if you browse comptia.org and the server creates a cookie owned by comptia.org then this is a first-party cookie.
- Third-party cookies—set by another domain. For example, if you browse comptia.org and a widget on the site tries to create a cookie for ad-track.com, this is a third-party cookie.

Cookies have the following privacy and security issues:

- The site may record more information about you than you are aware, and information in the cookies may be shared with other sites. Sites should generally publish a privacy policy describing what information is collected and how it is used.
- Cookies cannot spread malware, but if your computer is infected with a virus or a Trojan, it may be able to steal the information contained within cookies.
- Spyware and adware may make use of cookies to track what sites you visit and display targeted adverts.
- Cookies should normally expire (self-delete) after a given date, but some try to set a date in the very distant future.
- Confidential information, such as a password, should only be stored in a secure cookie (readable only under the SSL/TLS session it was created in).

Do not type passwords into unsecure sites (any site not using the HTTPS protocol). If you must use a password with an unsecure site, do not reuse that password in any other context. While sharing passwords between sites is not recommended generally, sharing a password between encrypted and unencrypted sites is doubly risky.

Pop-up Windows

A **pop-up** is a "sub-window" that appears over the main window. Pop-ups can be implemented using scripts or add-ons. A pop-up can be opened automatically by a script running on the page or in response to clicking a link. A different kind of overlay pop-up can be implemented using Cascading Style Sheets (CSS), which is HTML's extended formatting language. These don't open a new window but place some content in a layer above the main content so that you cannot view it without waiting for a timer to end or clicking a close icon.

Most of the time pop-ups are designed to be helpful to the user. For example, a form might use a pop-up window to explain what you are supposed to enter in a particular field without having to navigate away from the form and lose the information you have already entered.

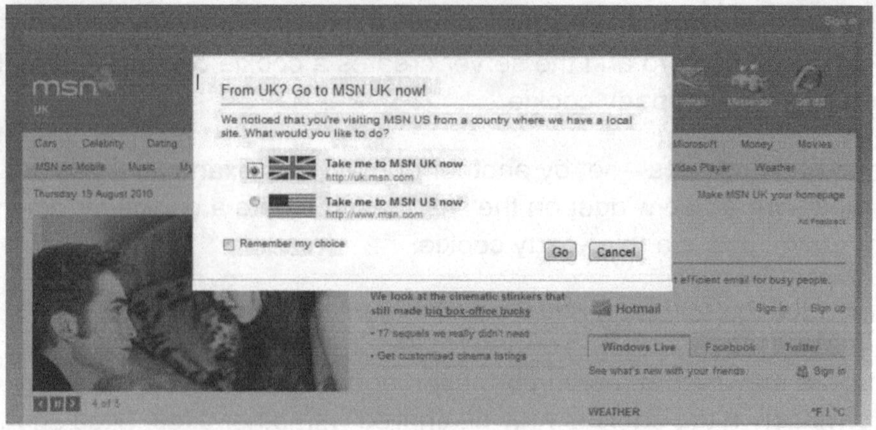

Example of a pop-up window—this one is trying to direct the user to the appropriate site home page.

Pop-ups are also used for advertising however. For example, a site may have some content you want to read and pop an advertising window over the top of it, so that you cannot read the content without first looking at the advert and closing it, or as the advertiser hopes, perhaps reading it, buying the product, then returning to the article. They are also used by subscription-based sites to prompt you to sign in with your account before you can view the content.

Aggressive use of pop-up windows is associated with spyware and adware. These spawn pop-ups when you open the browser, on every site you visit, and when you try to close the browser. They may even re-spawn when you try to close them. Malicious software can also use misleading pop-ups; for example, the Close button may try to execute a script that installs a virus or Trojan or the window may be designed to look like a Windows alert dialog ("Viruses have been detected on your computer—click OK to remove them").

The User Account Control (UAC) feature in Windows should protect you against malicious scripts such as this. The script should not be able to change the computer configuration without your explicit authorization through UAC.

Controlling Cookies and Pop-ups

You can control the use of cookies by the websites you visit using browser settings. There will be options to set what type of cookies to accept and how long to keep them. You can also configure exceptions so that certain domains are always or never allowed to create cookies. Finally, you can view which sites have created cookies and clear any data that you do not want to keep.

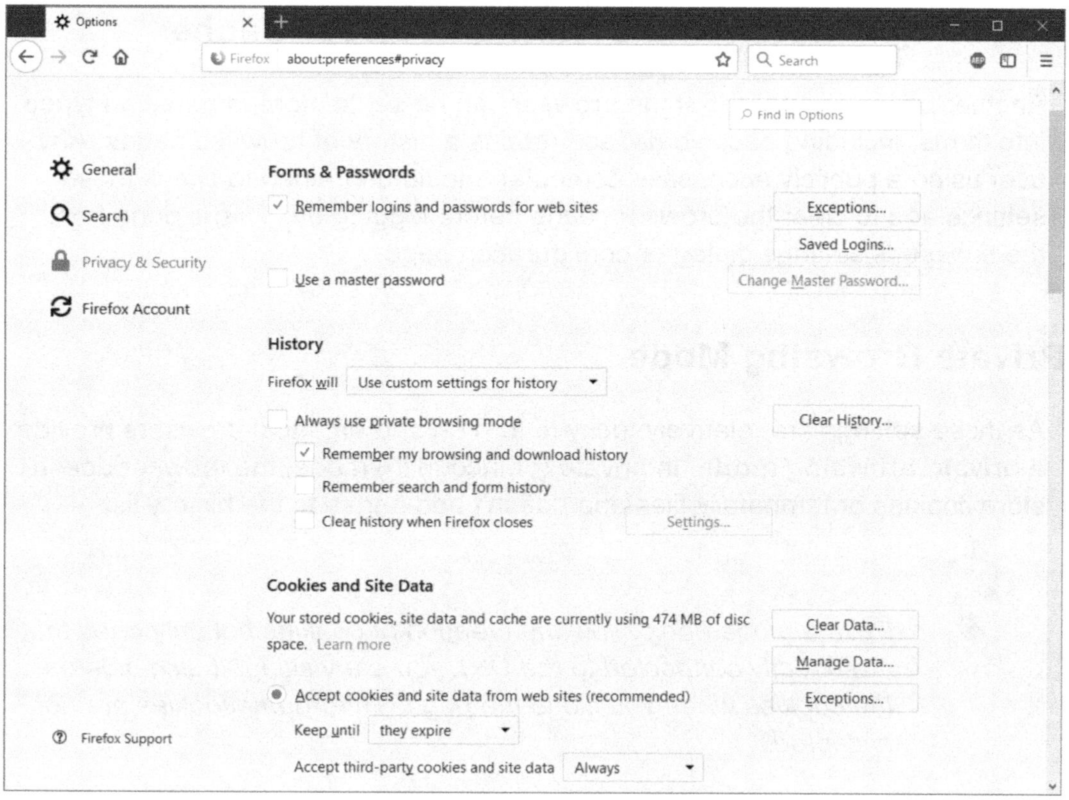

Configuring privacy settings in Firefox.

As with scripting, disabling first-party cookies is likely to leave a website, and certainly a web application, unusable. Sites that depend on advertising can detect when you are blocking third-party cookies, pop-ups, and other advertising features and refuse to show the page content.

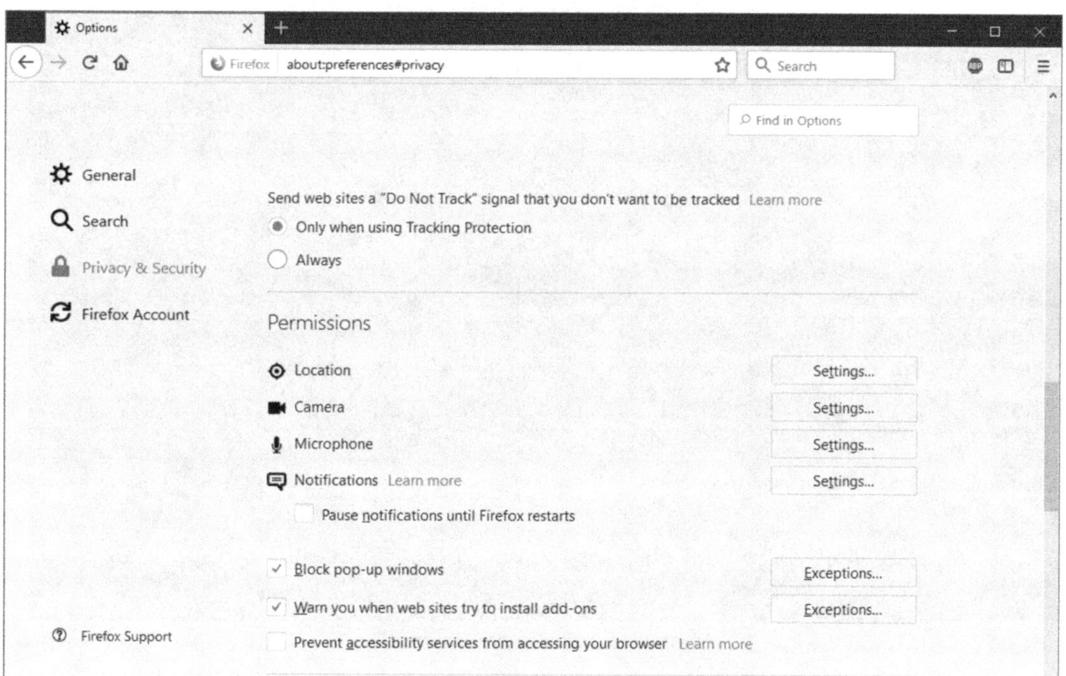

Configuring browser permissions in Firefox.

You can also choose to prevent sites from creating pop-up windows and configure exceptions for this rule. Note that this will not block all types of overlay pop-ups or advertising. If you want to have closer control over advertising on a site you need to install a suitable browser extension.

Disabling AutoFill and Clearing Browser Cache

Another privacy issue is that the browser can be set to store information typed into forms, including passwords, and retains a history of browsed pages. Any user using a publicly accessible computer should be trained to check these settings and to clear the browser cache before logging off. This is done from the browser's settings dialog or configuration page.

Private Browsing Mode

As these settings are relatively tricky to turn on and off, most browsers provide a **private browsing mode**. In private (or incognito) mode, the browser doesn't store cookies or temporary files and doesn't add pages to the history list.

Private mode does allow the creation of cookies but only ones that are directly connected to the URL you are visiting. It also deletes the cookies when you close the page. Third-party cookies are not accepted.

You can usually open a private browser tab by pressing **CTRL+SHIFT+P**. Private mode is indicated by a different icon and darker theme colors.

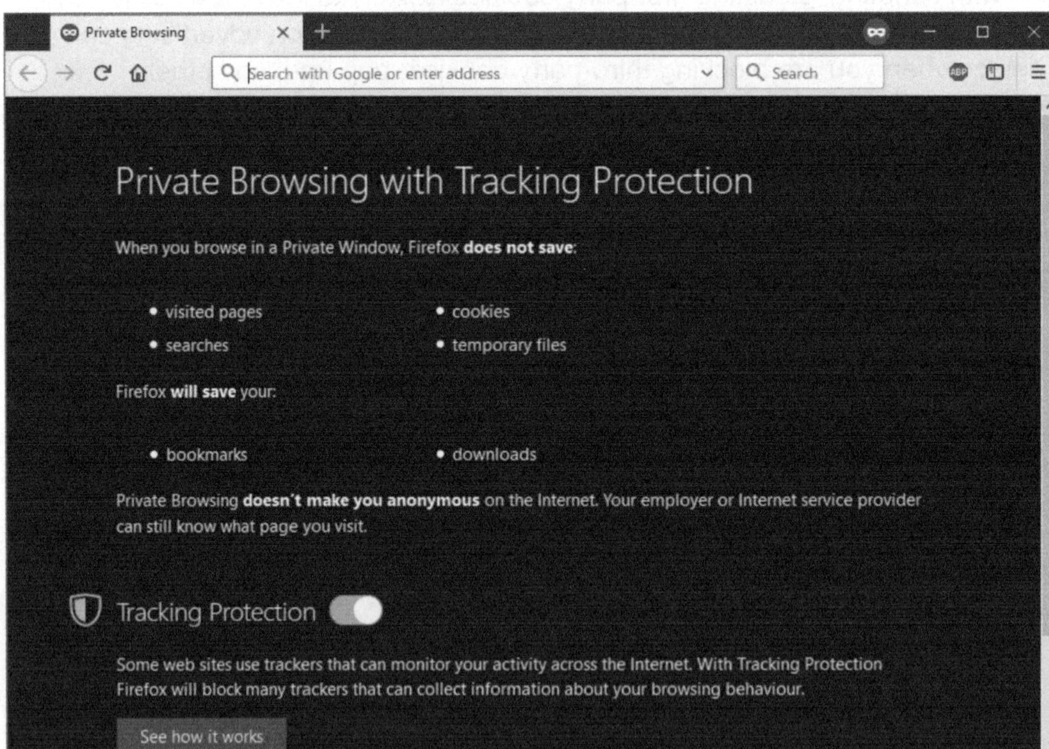

Running Firefox in private mode.

Private mode does not stop the browser from sending some information to the website. You cannot avoid the website discovering your IP address for instance. For fully "anonymous" browsing, you have to use some sort of Virtual Private Network (VPN) or proxy.

Digital Certificates and Anti-phishing

When a web browser communicates with a secure (HTTPS) server, it accepts the server's digital certificate to use its public key to encrypt communications. Because of the special way that the keys are linked, the public key *cannot* be used to decrypt the message once encrypted. Only the linked private key can be used to do that. The private key must be kept secret. This is referred to as asymmetric encryption.

Having a certificate is not in itself any proof of identity. The browser and server rely upon a third-party—the **Certificate Authority (CA)**—to vouch for the server's identity. This framework is called **Public Key Infrastructure (PKI)**.

A browser is pre-installed with a number of **root certificates** that are automatically trusted. These represent the commercial CAs that grant certificates to most of the companies that do business on the web.

Windows has a certificate store that Microsoft Internet Explorer and Edge browsers use, but third-party browsers such as Firefox and Chrome maintain their own stores.

Valid and Invalid Certificates

When you browse a site using a certificate, the browser displays the information about the certificate in the address bar:

- If the certificate is valid and trusted, a padlock icon is shown. Click the icon to view information about the certificate and the Certificate Authority guaranteeing it.

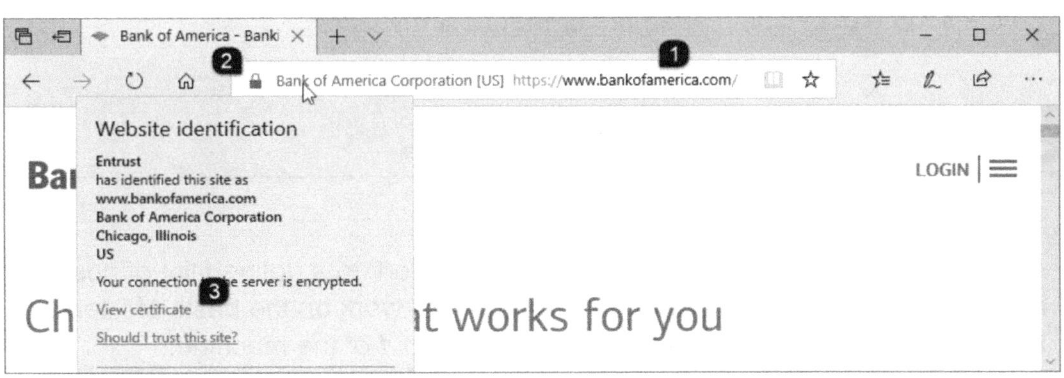

Browsing a secure site: 1) Check the domain name as highlighted in the address bar; 2) Only enter confidential data into a site using a trusted certificate; 3) Click the padlock to view information about the certificate holder and the CA that issued it and optionally to view the certificate itself.

- If the certificate is highly trusted, the address bar is colored green. High assurance certificates make the website owner go through a (even) more rigorous identity validation procedure.

- If the certificate is untrusted or otherwise invalid, the address bar is colored maroon and the site is blocked by a warning message. If you want to trust the site anyway, click through the warning.

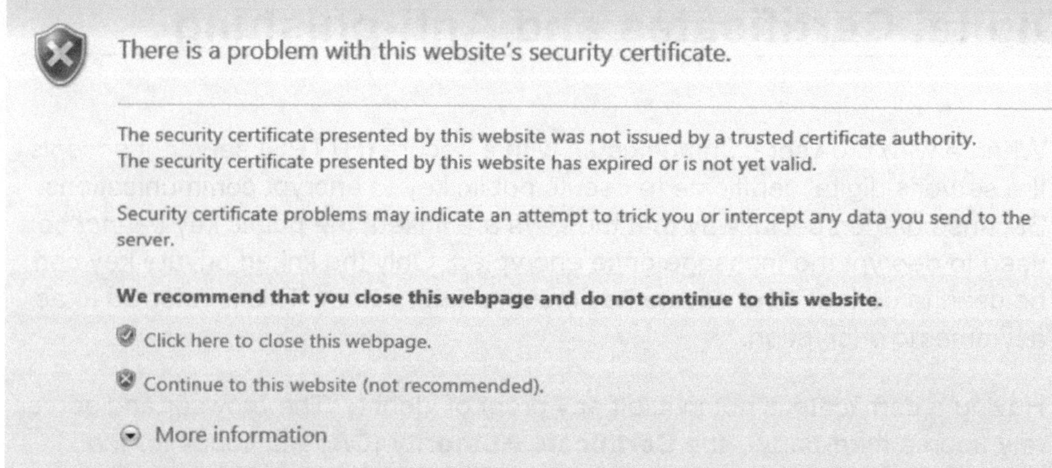

Untrusted certificate warning. Screenshot used with permission from Microsoft.

Digital certificates are also used to verify the identity of software publishers. If a certificate has not been issued by a one of the trusted root CAs, Windows will warn you that the publisher cannot be verified when you try to install an add-on or other type of application.

Suspicious Links and URLs

Another important step in validating the identity of a site is to confirm its domain name. Techniques to direct users to fake or manipulated websites are called phishing and pharming. These depend on making a fake site look like the real one. One trick is to use well-known subdomains as part of the address. For example, "comptia.phishing.org" has nothing to do with "comptia.org" but may fool the unwary into thinking it does. The browser highlights the registered domain part of the address so that you can verify it.

Most browsers run anti-phishing protection to block access to URLs known to be the source of phishing attempts or that host malware.

Enabling a Firewall

A **firewall** restricts access to a computer or network to a defined list of hosts and applications. Basic **packet filtering** firewalls work on the basis of filtering network data packets as they try to pass *into* or *out of* the machine.

Types of Firewall

On a TCP/IP network, each host is identified by an IP address, while each application protocol (HTTP, FTP, SMTP, and so on) is identified by a **port number**. Packet filters on a firewall can be applied to IP addresses and port numbers.

A more advanced firewall (**stateful inspection**) can analyze the *contents* of network data packets, so long as they are not encrypted, and block them if any suspicious signatures are detected and identify suspicious *patterns* of activity.

A **hardware** firewall is a dedicated appliance with the firewall installed as **firmware**. A **software** firewall is installed as an application on a workstation or server. Most Internet routers also feature a built-in firewall, configured via the web management interface.

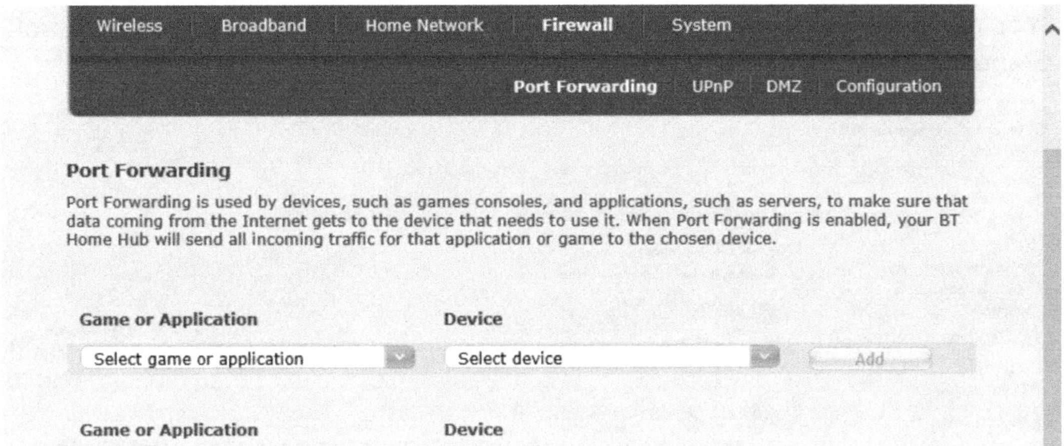

Configuring a firmware-type firewall on DSL router.

A simple **host** firewall (or **personal** firewall) may be installed on a client PC to protect it. Windows features such a firewall. There are also numerous third-party host firewalls.

Configuring the Windows Defender Firewall

Windows Defender Firewall is enabled on all network connections by default unless it has been replaced by a third-party firewall. It is not a good idea to run two host firewalls at the same time because they can conflict with each other, would be unnecessarily complex to configure, and more difficult to troubleshoot.

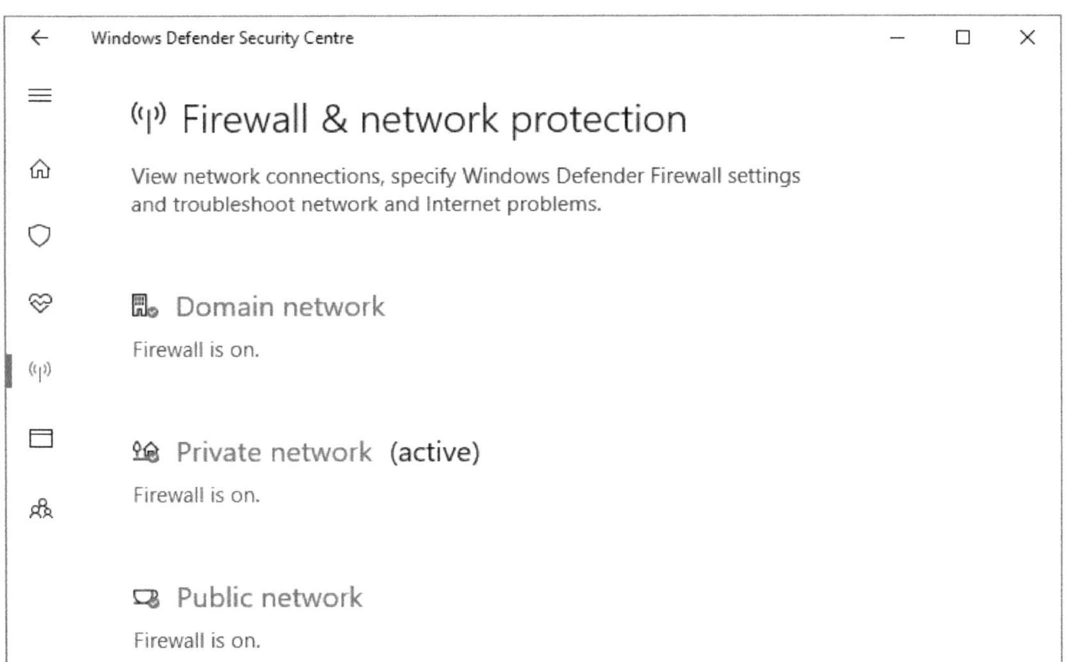

Checking the status of Windows Defender Firewall. Screenshot used with permission from Microsoft.

To configure the firewall, open **Windows Defender Security Center** and then click the **Firewall & network protection** node. Use the links to configure the settings. For example, to allow an app through the firewall, click **Allow an app through the firewall**.

You can also access Windows Defender Firewall settings by using the Control Panel Windows Defender Firewall applet.

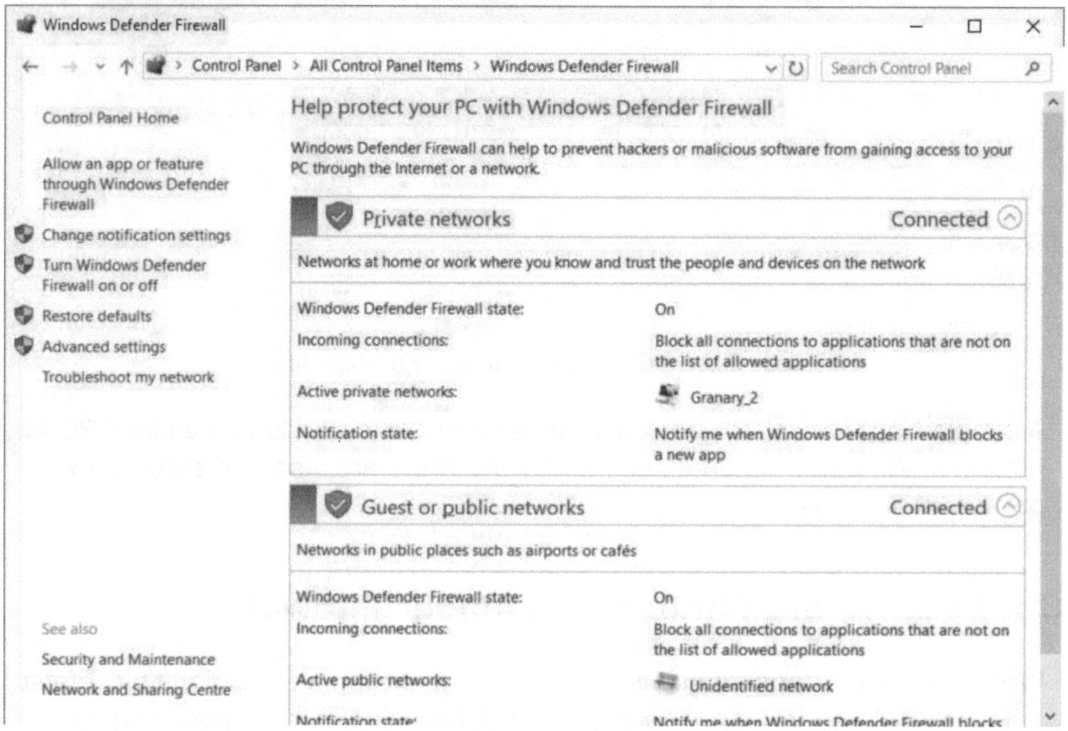

Checking the status of Windows Defender Firewall. Screenshot used with permission from Microsoft.

To turn off the firewall, which is only advisable if you are using an alternative host firewall software product, in Settings, click the active network and then click the **On** button to turn off the firewall. In Control Panel, click the **Turn Windows Defender Firewall on or off** link. You can then configure the required settings, as shown below.

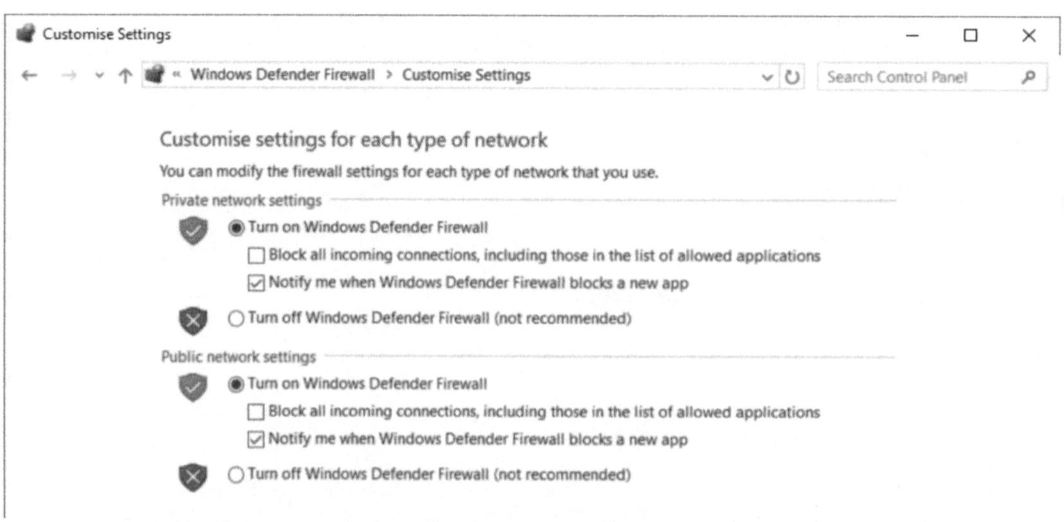

Configuring the firewall state for links to private and public networks. Screenshot used with permission from Microsoft.

The **Allow an app or feature** link lets you configure applications that are allowed to accept incoming Internet connections.

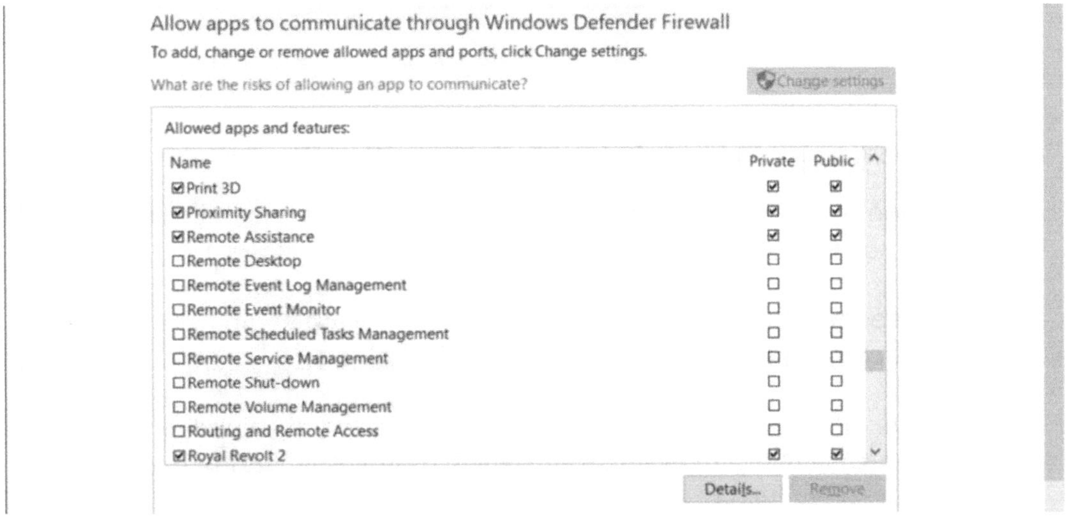

Allowed Programs configuration dialog of the Windows Firewall. Screenshot used with permission from Microsoft.

When a new (unlisted) program attempts to accept an Internet connection, a warning is displayed prompting the user to allow or block the program, unless the firewall is configured not to display notifications.

Configuring Proxy Settings

On an enterprise network, a network firewall is likely to be deployed to monitor and control all traffic passing between the local network and the Internet. On networks like this, clients might not be allowed to connect to the Internet directly but forced to use a **proxy server** instead. The proxy server can be configured as a firewall and apply other types of content filtering rules.

Some proxy servers work transparently so that clients use them without any extra configuration of the client application. Other proxies require that client software, such as the browser, be configured with the IP address and port of the proxy server. This information would be provided by the network administrator.

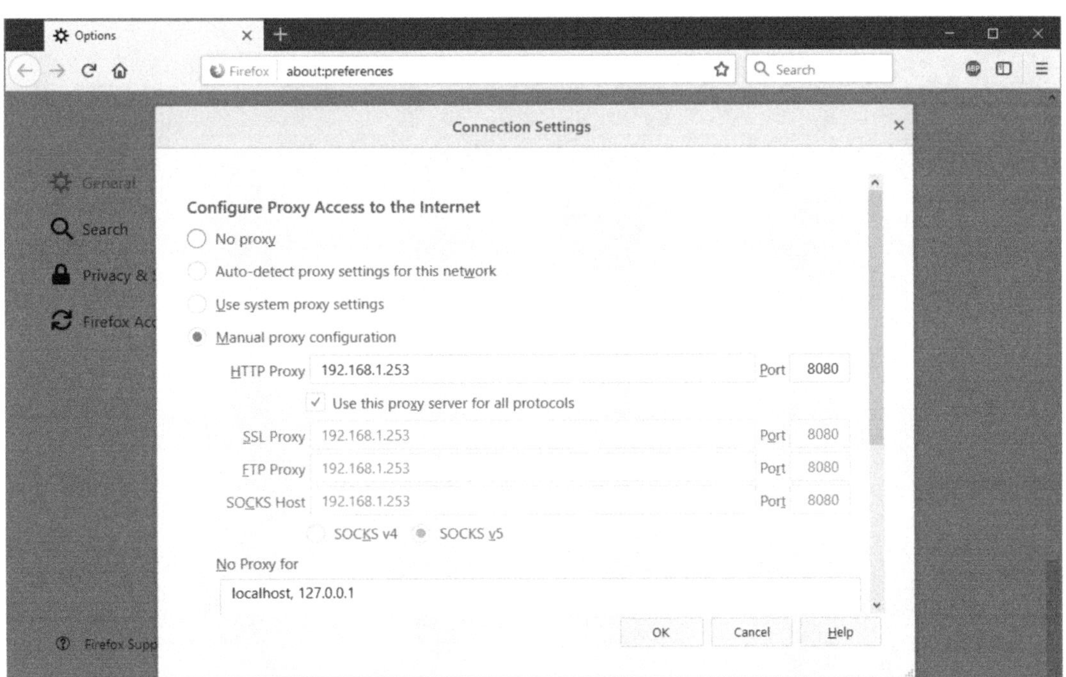

Configuring Firefox to use a proxy by entering its IP address and port number. Any requests will be passed to the proxy for processing rather than trying to contact a web server directly.

Review Questions / Module 4 / Unit 3 / Secure Web Browsing

Answer these questions to test what you have learned in this unit. You can review the model answers at the end of the book.

1) If you use an open network, what email configuration setting should you ensure is enabled?
2) You have installed a screensaver application. Later, after updating your anti-virus software, a malicious program is found. This appears to have infected your system at the same time as the screensaver was installed. What class of malware is this?
3) You want to use a website that hosts training modules in a custom media format. What type of add-on would you need to install to play this media?
4) What type of file might a website use to track whether you have visited it before?
5) True or false? Browser pop-up windows are definite symptoms of virus infection.
6) You are using a computer in an Internet cafe. What should you do at the end of the session?
7) What identifies a website as using the secure HTTPS protocol with a valid certificate?
8) You want to restrict access to a computer on your network to a single Internet host running a particular application. What two things do you need to configure in your firewall's access control list?

Lab 18 / Web Security

To use the web and the Internet safely, you need to ensure that the operating system and Internet applications and plug-ins are patched to the latest version, configure browser security settings to prompt you before running untrusted code, and understand how to spot spoof or malicious sites.

Exercise 1 / Browser Security Settings

In this exercise you will investigate browser security settings.

1) If necessary, start your computer and sign in.

2) Open the **Internet Options** applet in **Control Panel**.

3) Click the **Security** tab. Check that the settings for the Internet zone are **Medium-High**.

4) Click the **Privacy** tab then click the **Advanced** button. Note that the default policy is to accept all kinds of cookies.

5) Click **Cancel**. Note the check box for the "Pop-up Blocker." Click the **Settings** button next to it.

   This dialog allows you to specify sites that are allowed to show pop-ups, regardless of the default policy.

6) Click **Close**.

7) Click the **Content** tab then the **Settings** button next to **AutoComplete**. The checked boxes represent data that Internet Explorer is caching. If you are using a public computer, you should make sure all these boxes are unchecked.

   When using an unfamiliar computer, it is also worth checking which add-ons are installed (Programs tab).

8) Close the **Internet Options** dialog and start Internet Explorer.

9) Open the home page for the online store **`amazon.com`**.

10) This takes you to a secure page—look for the protocol (HTTPS not HTTP) and the padlock icon. Click the icon to view the CA (the company that issued the certificate) and confirmation that the certificate matches the web address shown in the bar.

Internet Explorer highlights the "important" part of the domain name. Phishing sites use various tricks to disguise the domain name. For example, they may use a spelling variant such as "amazoon.com" or a misleading subdomain such as "amazon.ama.com." Also, be wary of pop-ups on a secure site—never enter confidential information into a pop-up—and pages that do not display an address bar or status bar.

11) Open the page for `bankofamerica.com`.

    Notice that this secure site is highlighted in green; this means that the certificate has undergone "extended validation" by the CA. Compare the certificate details with those of Amazon.

12) Press **CTRL+SHIFT+H** and note the record of the sites you have visited. Select the **Safety** button then click **Delete Browsing History**.

13) Note the different options—delete whatever cached data you want or click Cancel if you want to keep it for now.

14) Press **CTRL+SHIFT+P**. This opens Internet Explorer in a special InPrivate mode. In this mode, the cache is deleted automatically at the end of the session, and add-ons are blocked from recording your web activity.

15) Open a couple of sites in InPrivate mode then close both browsers.

16) Open Internet Explorer and check the browser history—the sites you just visited will not be listed.

    The Edge browser uses different security settings to Internet Explorer. Changes you make in "Internet Options" only affect Internet Explorer, not the Edge browser.

17) Start the Edge browser then click the **More Actions** ellipse ... icon and select **Settings**.

18) Under "Clear browsing data," click the **Choose what to clear** button.

19) Note the different types of browsing data that can be deleted then click the Back chevron.

20) Click **View advanced settings** and scroll through the list of options.

    Edge does not support ActiveX at all, so there is no option to configure it. You can choose to enable Flash or not. JavaScript is always supported and can only be disabled using an advanced Windows configuration tool (Group Policy). There are also options for managing cookies and whether passwords are cached.

21) Close the browser.

Exercise 2 / Installing a Plug-in

Plug-ins (referred to as "extensions" by Edge) are used to extend the functionality of the browser to block ads, make notes, save form content and passwords, and so on. You have to be careful only to install plug-ins from reputable sources. Generally speaking, if Windows cannot verify the publisher of a plug-in (or other "active" content) you should not trust it.

One of the most widely used plug-ins is Flash Player, published by Adobe.

1) If necessary, start your computer and sign in.
2) Open `cnet.com` in the Edge browser. Click the **Reviews > Laptops** link.
3) Look around the page to identify the banner ads.
4) Click the **More Actions** ellipse ... icon and select **Extensions** then click the **Get extensions from the Store link**.
5) Take a minute to browse the different plug-ins available. Click the link for **Ghostery**. On the product page, click the **Get** button.
6) When setup is complete, click the **Launch** button. In Edge, click the **Turn it on** button.
7) Switch to the `cnet.com` tab and refresh the page.

   The website displays a notification requesting that you allow ads to enable the website owner to continue to receive revenue for running the site.
8) Click **Continue without whitelisting**. Note that the banner ads are now no longer present.
9) Optionally, use **Apps and Features** to uninstall Ghostery.
10) Optionally, shut down your computer if you are not continuing to use it after this lab.

Module 4 / Unit 4
Using Shared Storage

Objectives

On completion of this unit, you will be able to:

- List ways to share files and storage on a local network.
- Describe means of sharing files and services on the Internet.
- Explain the importance of backups and configure simple backup options.

Syllabus Objectives and Content Examples

This unit covers the following exam domain objectives and content examples:

- 2.5 Compare and contrast storage types.
  Local network storage types (NAS, File server) • Cloud storage service
- 6.7 Explain business continuity concepts.
  Backup considerations—data [File backups, Critical data, Database, OS backups], Backup considerations—location [Stored locally, Cloud storage, On-site vs. off-site]

Local Network Sharing and Storage

One of the main uses of a network is to share files. There are a number of different methods for making shared storage available on a local network.

File Server (Direct Attached Storage)

All computers have at least one internal hard disk, or SSD, for storing the operating system and software applications plus user data. Additional storage can be added to the computer as internal or external hard drives or flash drives.

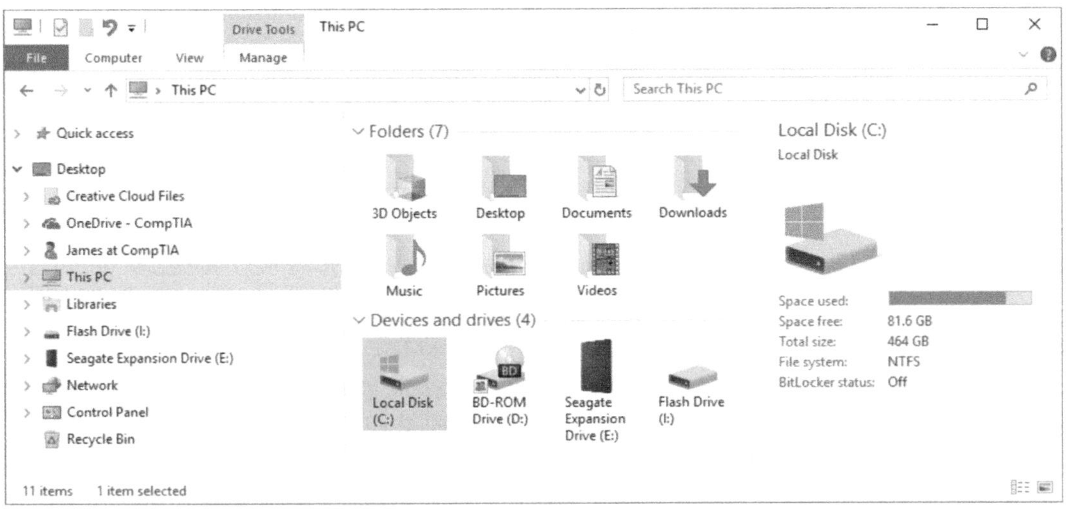

Direct attached storage—this computer has a local hard drive and optical drive and a USB-attached hard drive and removable SD memory card. Any of these drives can be shared on the network. Screenshot used with permission from Microsoft.

When the computer is on a network, any internal or external local drives can be shared with other computers. When a computer shares an attached hard drive, or folder on an attached drive, it can be referred to as **Direct Attached Storage**. The computer is acting as a file server.

On a SOHO network, any workstation can act both as a server and as a client. This is referred to as peer-to-peer. On an enterprise network, dedicated server computers are reserved for server functions such as file sharing. This provides centralized control over the servers.

Network Attached Storage (NAS)

A **Network Attached Storage (NAS)** appliance is one or more hard drives housed in an enclosure with basic server firmware, usually running some form of Linux. The NAS appliance provides access to its storage devices using various file sharing protocols. The appliance is accessed over the network using a wired Ethernet port. In a SOHO network you would plug it into a LAN port on the SOHO router. A NAS appliance may also support wireless (Wi-Fi) networking.

Network Attached Storage (NAS) server appliance—the display shows the device's IP address while the housings beneath allow the installation of up to six hard disks. There are also two USB ports on the left. Image © 123rf.com.

The NAS appliance can be configured by connecting to its web management page. Like a SOHO router, open a web browser then input the IP address assigned to the NAS device.

Network Printer Sharing

There are two main options for sharing a printer on the network, similar to the direct attached and network attached options for storage:

- Share the printer via Windows—an administrator can share any locally installed printer via its **Sharing** tab in the **Properties** dialog. Locally installed means that Windows communicates with the print device directly over the relevant port. It does not matter whether the port is wired (USB or Ethernet) or wireless (Bluetooth or Wi-Fi). The main disadvantage of this approach is that both the printer and the Windows PC must be switched on for other devices to be able to access the printer.
- Use a hardware print server—some printers come with an embedded print server, allowing client computers to connect to them over the network without having to go via a server computer. If the print server supports wired connections, it needs to be attached to a switch or home router via an RJ-45 cable. If the printer has a wireless adapter, it can be joined to a wireless network using the printer's control panel. You can also purchase print servers or use a solution such as a Network Attached Storage (NAS) device that supports print sharing.

Windows File Sharing

For Windows to connect to a network and share resources with other computers, the computers must have appropriate **client software** installed. This is no problem for a network where all the computers run Windows, as the Windows client software is installed by default. It allows the computer to connect to workgroups or, in the case of the Professional or Enterprise editions, to Active Directory domain networks.

Joining a Workgroup or Domain

Information about the network the computer is joined to is shown in **System** properties, which you can open from **Control Panel** or by right-clicking the **This PC** object (**Computer** object in older versions of Windows) and selecting **Properties**. Each computer is given a name to identify it on the network.

Using the System applet to view the network name configuration—this PC is called "COMPTIA" and is joined to the default workgroup. Screenshot used with permission from Microsoft.

An administrator can change the network computer name and domain or workgroup membership by clicking **Change settings**.

In Windows 10, you can also use the **Access work or school** page from the Settings app.

A computer can belong to either *a workgroup* or *a domain but not both. In addition, the computer can only belong to one domain.*

File and Printer Sharing

As long as the network location/Windows firewall settings have been configured to allow it, any file or folder on a Windows computer can be shared with other computers. To share an object, right-click it and select **Give access to**. You can then select the user accounts allowed to access the share and whether they can modify files in it or not. You can choose to share an object with the **Everyone** special account to grant access to all users.

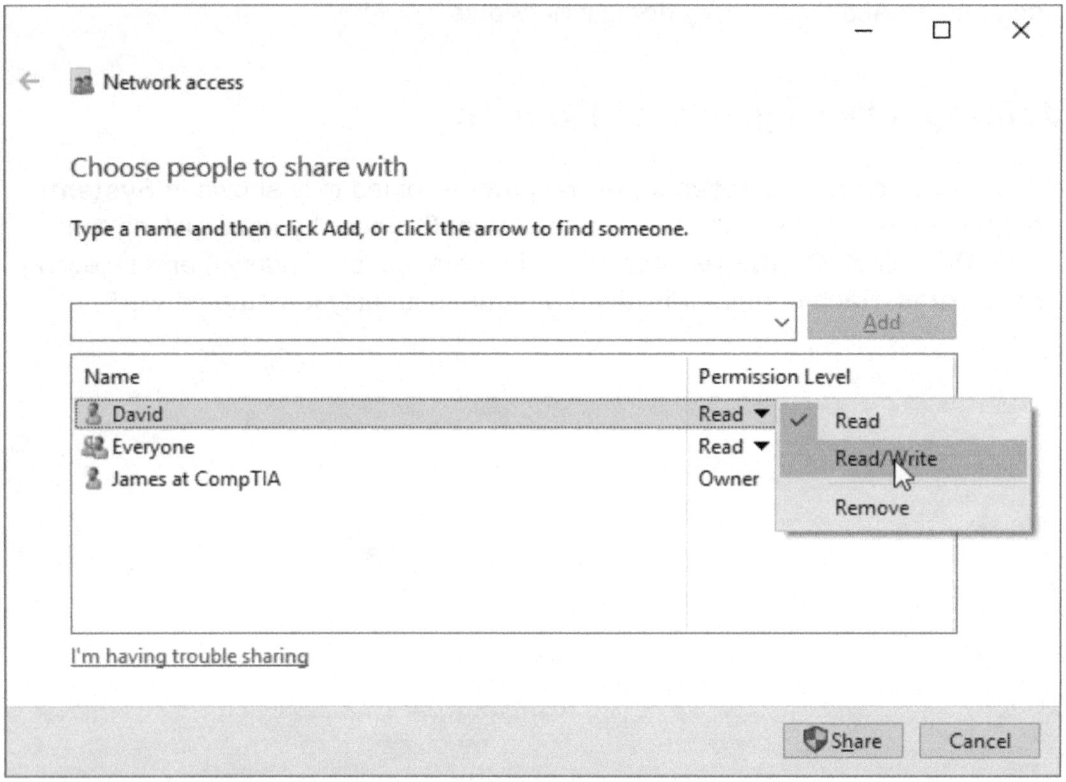

Basic folder sharing in Windows 10—select an account then set the permission level for that account. Note that an account can be a specific user (like David) or a group of users (like Everyone). Screenshot used with permission from Microsoft.

When configuring file sharing like this, it is important for users to have matching user accounts, with the same user name and password, on both the host and client computer. This can become very complex to manage.

To allow unauthenticated access, you can enable the **Guest** account via the User Accounts applet. Alternatively, you can disable password-protected file sharing by opening the **Network and Sharing Center** from **Control Panel** and clicking **Advanced sharing settings**. Neither of these options are very secure however.

Microsoft also provided a Homegroup feature to try to simplify file sharing with Windows 10 but that has been discontinued in the 1803 version update. PCs with a Bluetooth adapter can use the new Nearby Devices sharing feature to quickly send a file over the network.

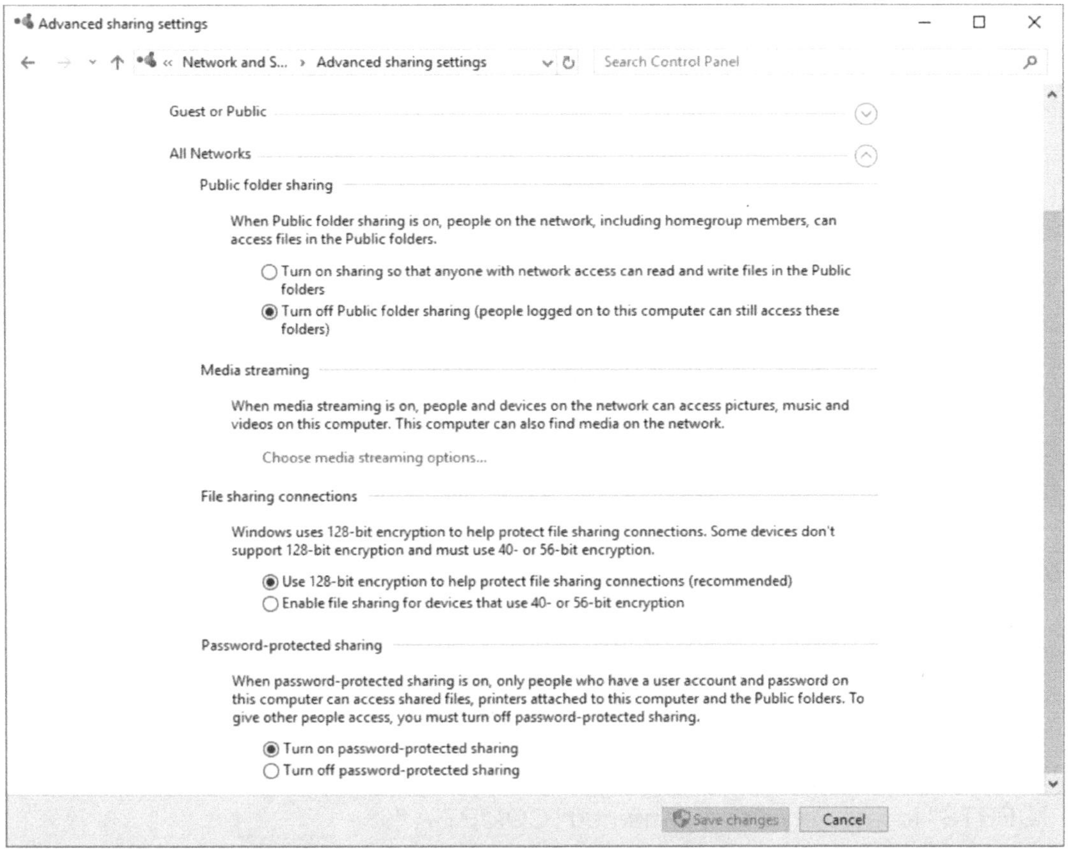

Windows 10 Advanced sharing settings dialog—you can use this to disable password-protected sharing or use the public folders to share files with anyone with network access. Screenshot used with permission from Microsoft.

Browsing Network Shares and Drives

When a folder has been shared, the host computer will be visible on the network.

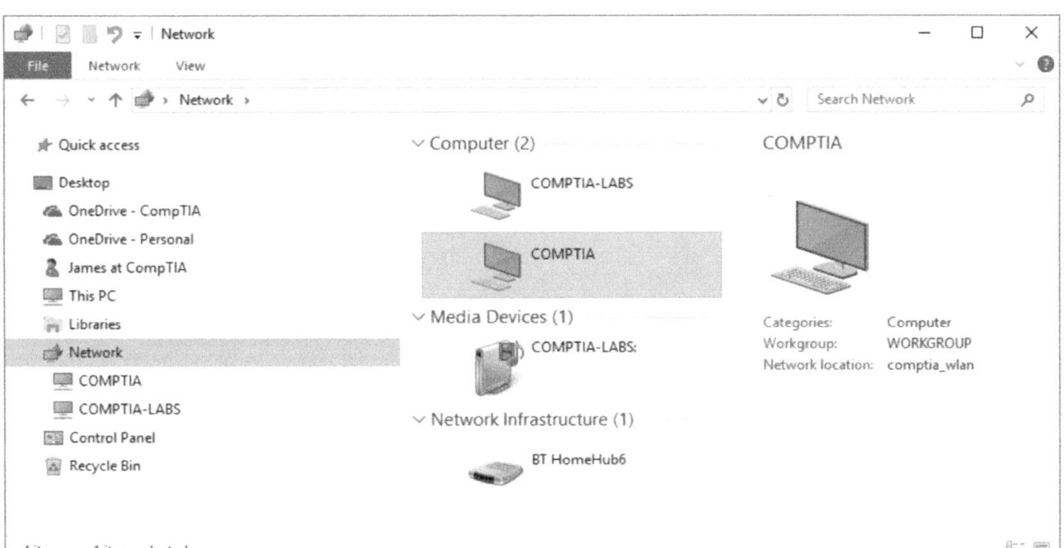

Browse network resources via the Network object. Screenshot used with permission from Microsoft.

Opening a computer object shows the shares available. Browse into a share to view the files and subfolders it contains.

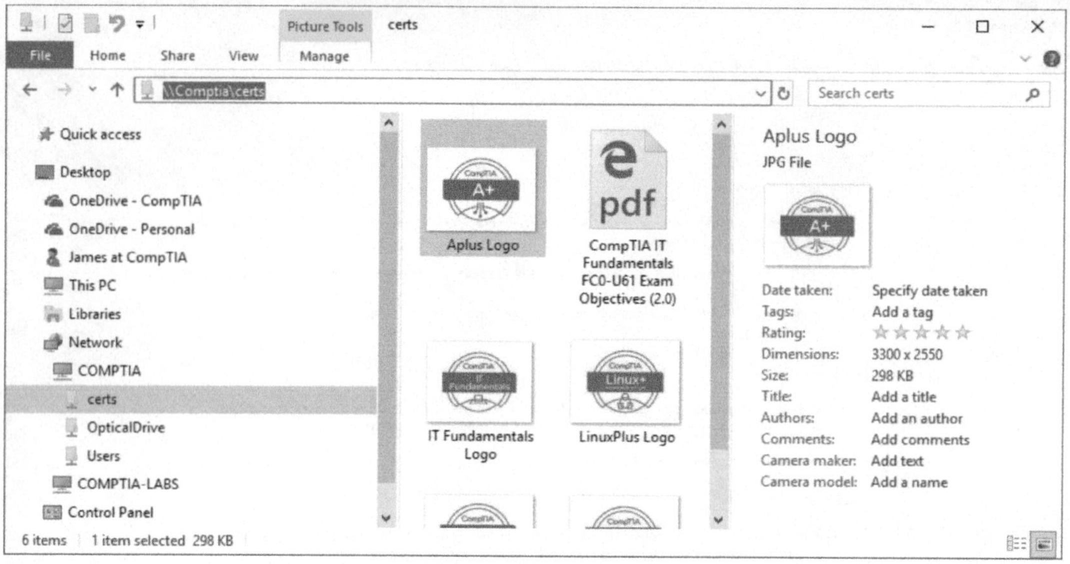

Browsing a network share—note the UNC path selected in the address bar. Screenshot used with permission from Microsoft.

You can also access a shared folder by entering its UNC (Universal Naming Convention) in the address bar. A UNC is composed of a double slash (\\) followed by the server name and then a single slash and the shared folder name. For example, `\\COMPTIA\CERTS` is the UNC of a folder named "CERTS" located on a server named "COMPTIA."

If you access a share often, you can map it as a network drive. To do so, right-click the share and select **Map network drive**:

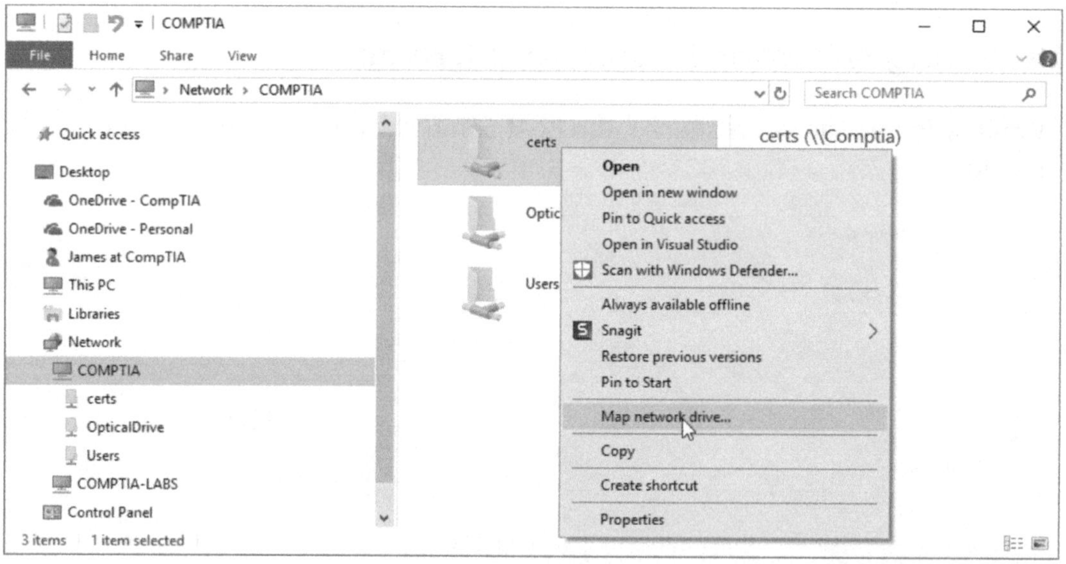

Mapping a network drive. Screenshot used with permission from Microsoft.

Select a drive letter then click **Finish**. The network drive will now appear under the **Computer/This PC** object in Explorer:

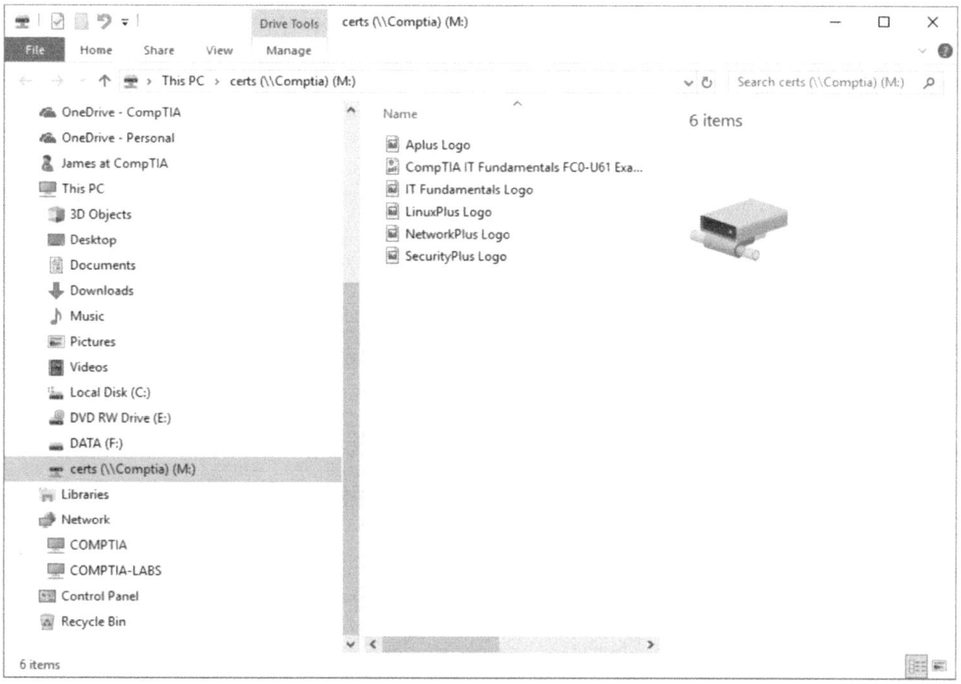

The "CERTS" share has been mapped as drive M on the local PC. Screenshot used with permission from Microsoft.

Hosted Sharing and Storage

The sharing and storage options discussed above make resources available to computers on the same local network. If you want to make resources available over a wider network, such as the Internet, you likely need to make use of a hosted storage solution.

HTTP/HTTPS and File Downloads

A powerful feature of HTTP is the capability to provide **hyperlinks** to other related documents. As well as web pages, hyperlinks can point to any type of file. This means that a web server can be used to host any type of **file download**.

File Transfer Protocol (FTP)

The **FTP (File Transfer Protocol)** is used to upload and download files between clients and servers. For example, it is widely used to update the files constituting a website from the designer's PC to the web server. An FTP server can also be configured with a number of public directories (accessed anonymously) and private directories, requiring a user account. FTP is more efficient compared to email file attachments or HTTP file transfer.

Like plain HTTP, FTP has no security mechanisms. All authentication and data transfers are communicated as plain text. An FTP session can be protected using encryption protocols.

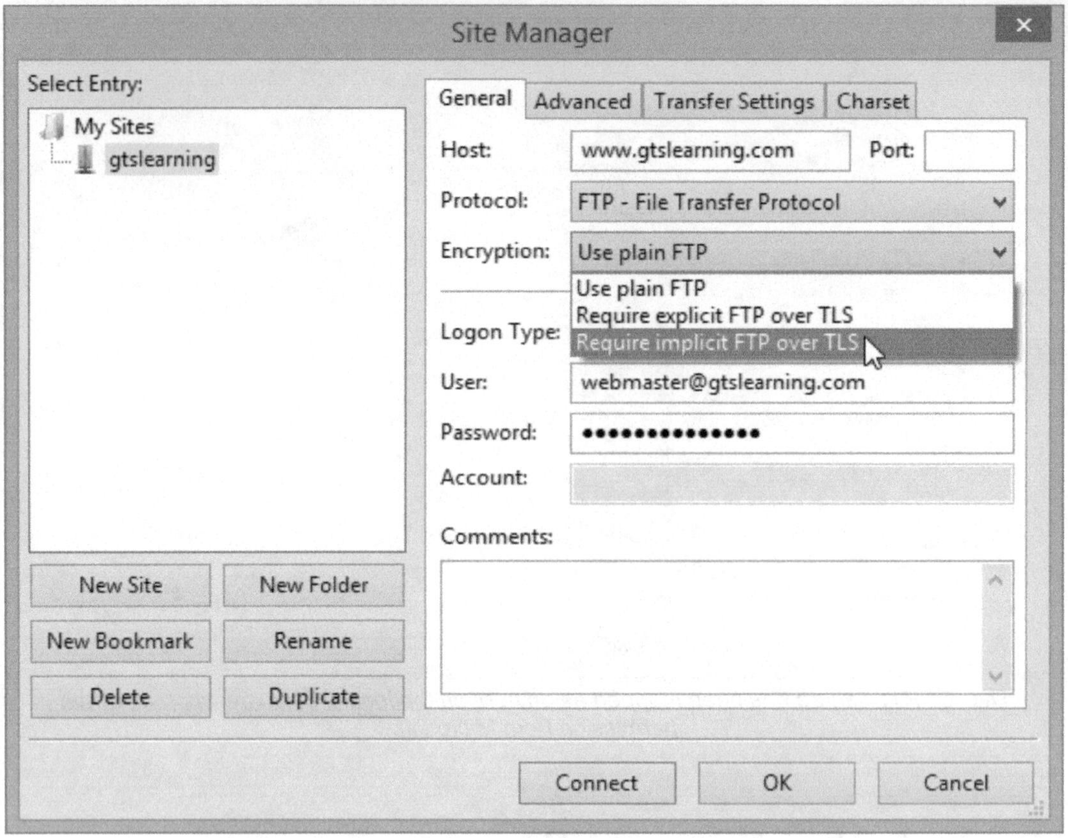

Configuring the FileZilla FTP client to use a secure server.

Cloud Computing

Hosted storage means leasing a web server from a service provider. Hosted services can also be provided as a "cloud." **Cloud computing** has lots of different definitions but generally refers to any sort of computing resource provided to the customer on a pay-per-use basis. The customer is not responsible for configuring and provisioning the computing resource within the cloud.

Among other benefits, the cloud provides **rapid elasticity**. This means that the cloud can scale quickly to meet peak demand. For example, a company may operate a single web server instance for most of the year but provision additional instances for the busy Christmas period and then release them again in the New Year. This example also illustrates the principles of **on-demand** and **pay-per-use**; key features of a cloud service (as opposed to a hosted service). On-demand implies that the customer can initiate service requests and that the cloud provider can respond to them immediately. This feature of cloud service is useful for project-based needs, giving the project members access to the cloud services for the duration of the project, and then releasing the cloud services back to the provider when the project is finished. This way, the organization is only paying for the services for the duration of the project.

The provider's ability to control a customer's use of resources through **metering** is referred to as **measured service**. The customer is paying for the CPU, memory, disk, and network bandwidth resources they are actually consuming rather than paying a monthly fee for a particular service level.

In order to respond quickly to changing customer demands, cloud providers must be able to provision resources quickly. This is achieved through **resource pooling** and **virtualization**. Resource pooling means that the hardware making up the cloud provider's data center is not dedicated or reserved to a particular customer account. The layers of virtualization used in the cloud architecture allow the provider to provision more CPU, memory, disk, or network resource using management software, rather than (for instance) having to go to the data center floor, unplug a server, add a memory module, and reboot.

Cloud-based Storage

Cloud-based storage solutions are very popular, both for home and business use. Vendors such as Apple, Google, and Microsoft (plus many ISPs) offer users a certain amount of free cloud-based storage. There are also business-oriented solutions, such as DropBox and Amazon. These services are typically operated with a browser or smartphone/tablet app. In Windows 10, a cloud storage client (OneDrive) is built into the OS and can be accessed via File Explorer.

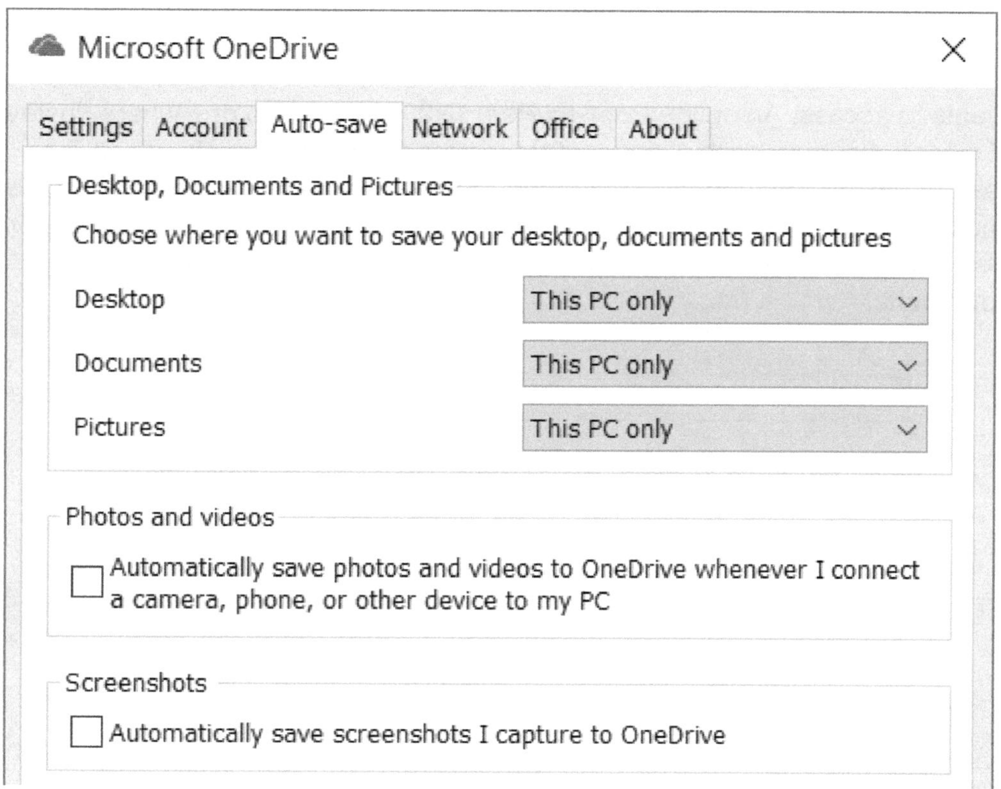

Microsoft's OneDrive cloud-based storage product. Screenshot used with permission from Microsoft.

Cloud-based Collaborative Applications

As well as dedicated storage solutions, many different types of software applications can be delivered using the cloud computing model. Office suites, such as Microsoft Office 365, Google G Suite, and Smartsheet, allow access to word processing, spreadsheets, and presentations with just a web browser installed on the client. These suites have tools to allow multiple users to access and collaborate on documents.

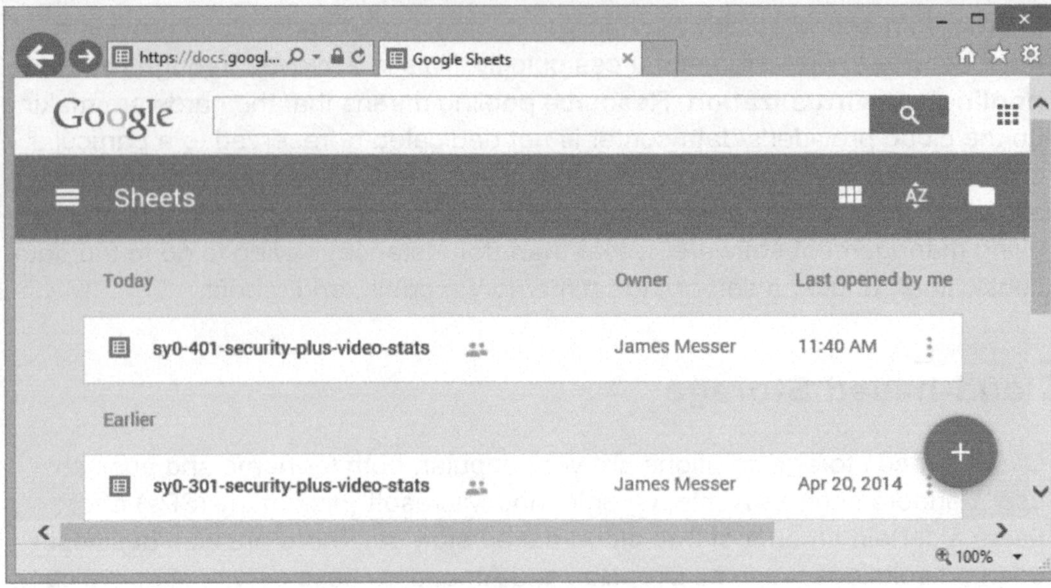

Google G Suite online word processing, spreadsheet, and presentation software that multiple users can collaborate on over the web.

Peer-to-Peer File Sharing

The hosted storage solutions described above rely on a central server for clients to access. An online **Peer-to-Peer (P2P)** network is one where, instead of a central server, each client contributes resources to the network. In the case of P2P file sharing, clients contribute a certain amount of storage space and bandwidth. Each client can then search for, download, or upload files. The files are split between the available clients and rebuilt by the P2P client for download.

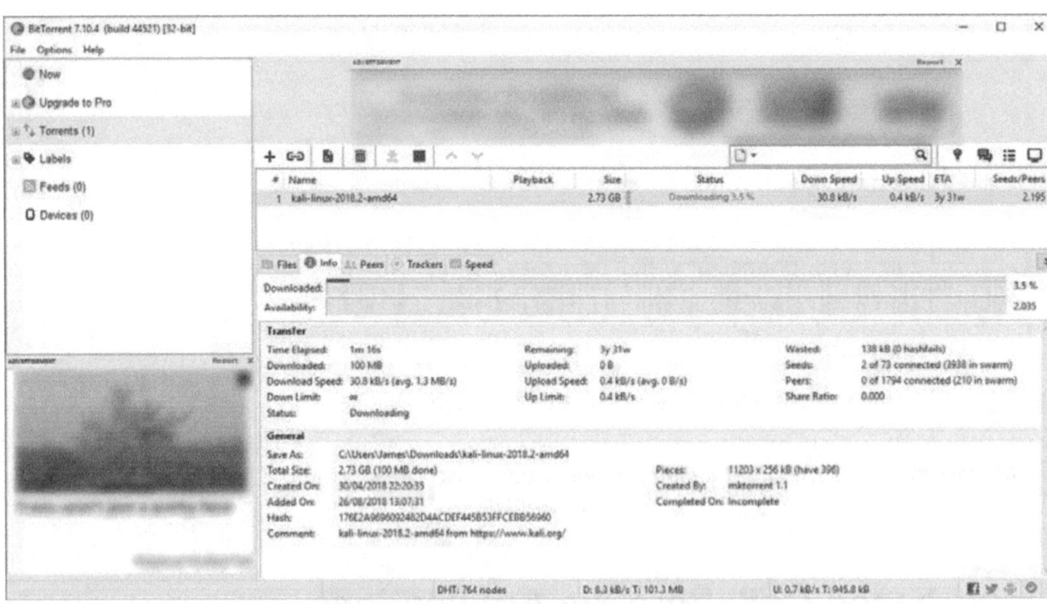

Using BitTorrent to download a copy of KALI Linux.

P2P networks, such as BitTorrent, may use servers to coordinate clients. Other P2P networks do not rely on any sort of servers, and some try to operate with complete anonymity, referred to as the darknet or deep web.

P2P networks have often been used to distribute music and video without respecting copyright. There is also the risk of files being infected with malware. Most companies prevent the use of P2P file sharing software on corporate networks.

Backups

Whenever you consider a storage solution, you must also consider backup. It is essential to make a **backup** of **data files**. Making a backup of the **system configuration** is also important, as reinstalling Windows, software applications, and reconfiguring custom settings can be very time consuming.

Backup Considerations

You should understand the main principles of backups:

- Keep at least one backup in a different location to the computer. This protects data against theft, fire, and flood. A backup stored in the same location as the original data is called **on-site**, while one kept in a different location is called **off-site**.
- Keep the device or media used to store backup data in a secure location.
- Keep more than one copy of data—if you delete or accidentally change a file then make a backup, you will not be able to restore the file. You need multiple backups going back to different points in time to recover from this type of data error.
- Make a backup regularly—the frequency depends how often your data files change, but most people should consider making a backup every week. Data in an office is typically backed up every day. Make a system backup whenever you install new software or perform an upgrade.

Backup Storage Types

Any of the storage media discussed in this unit could be suitable for making a backup:

- Locally attached storage—use hard disks or flash drives attached to the local PC or server.
- Network Attached Storage—use a NAS appliance to allow multiple machines to back up to the same location.
- Offsite/cloud-based—back up over the Internet to cloud-based storage. Keeping offsite copies of data is very important in mitigating against the risk of fire or theft. This method might require substantial bandwidth. You also need to be able to trust the cloud provider with your data.

It is a good idea to use a combination of methods, to cover both on-site and off-site backups for instance. You could back up often to locally attached storage or NAS and then copy the backups to a cloud storage solution for off-site security.

Enterprise networks with very large amounts of data to backup may use more specialized media, such as tape drives.

File Backups and Critical Data

A **file backup** is an ordinary backup job. You configure the backup software to select certain folders or individual files to include in the backup job and a schedule for performing the backup.

When configuring backups, you need to understand that not all **critical data** may be stored in files within a user folder or shared folder. Critical data could be stored in a settings file outside of the normal data areas or be located within a database or message store. You also have to consider that critical data might include confidential, proprietary, and/or personal information. When you make a copy of such information by making a backup, you need to ensure that the copy is subject to the same security policies and access controls as the original.

Unit 5.3 has more information about access controls.

Database Backups

If the data that you're considering backing up is part of a RDBMS (Relational Database Management System), such as SQL data, or a messaging system, such as Exchange, then the data is probably being used all the time. Each change in the database is referred to as a **transaction**. Transactions that add, amend, or retrieve a record might comprise several read/write operations. These operations are bundled as transaction to ensure that the data records remain consistent and are not corrupted by partially completed write operations. Ordinary file copy backup methods are not "transaction-aware" and so cannot be reliably used to back up a database. Consequently, database backup requires the use of software dedicated to that purpose.

One of the ways of backing up a database is called **replication**. A replica is a copy (or mirror) of the database hosted on a separate server. When a transaction is posted, it must typically be committed to both the master database and its replica before the transaction can be considered complete. This provides redundancy in the case that the master database server is damaged.

Replication doesn't protect you from errors such as accidentally deleting a record, however. If the error is accepted as a valid transaction, it will be propagated amongst all the replicas at the next scheduled replication interval. You still have to back up the replicated data therefore, so that you can restore data to a point-in-time. An RDBMS keeps a **transaction log**. It is critical to include the transaction log along with the database tables in backup operations to support rollback of mistaken transactions and recovery from critical disasters.

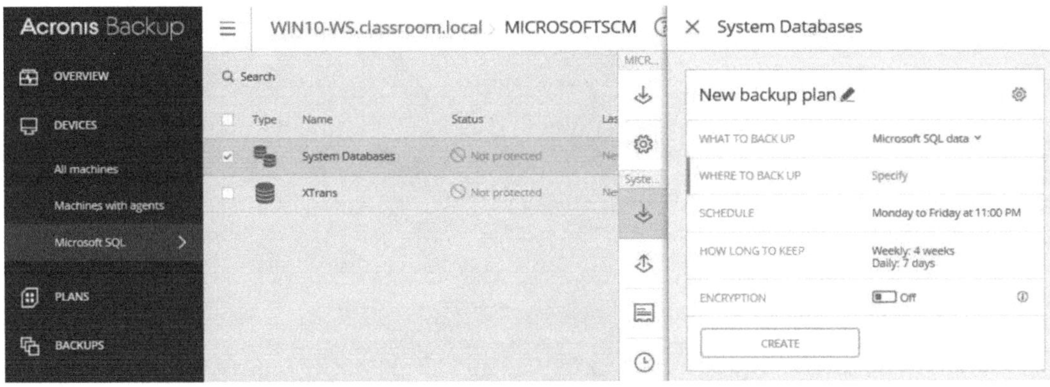

Backing up an SQL Server using Acronis Backup (acronis.com).

You may also want to make **read-only** copies of the database. This is supported through **snapshots**. A snapshot-based backup might be useful for keeping historical records of changes to the database or for recovering from really serious administrative errors that cannot be corrected through transaction rollbacks.

OS Backups

An **OS** or **system backup** makes a copy of the OS and installed applications so that a workstation or server can be recovered without having to manually reinstall software and reconfigure settings. Older methods of system backup could involve lengthy recovery procedures. Typically, the operating system would have to be reinstalled, then the backup applied to the new OS to recover the old configuration.

A **bare metal** backup is one that can be applied directly to a partitioned drive without the separate step of reinstalling the OS. Bare metal backups typically work by making an **image**. The backup software provides a recovery boot disk which enables the system to connect to the recovery media (an external hard drive or network drive for instance). The only drawback to this method is that system images require multi-gigabyte storage media.

A system image can also be quite time-consuming to create, so this method works best if the system configuration is kept fairly static and user data is stored separately from the OS volume.

Windows Backup

In Windows, there are a number of options for backing up your files, and for providing for file recovery. These are:

- **Backup and Restore** (Windows 7)—enables you to perform selective, scheduled, and ad-hoc backups.

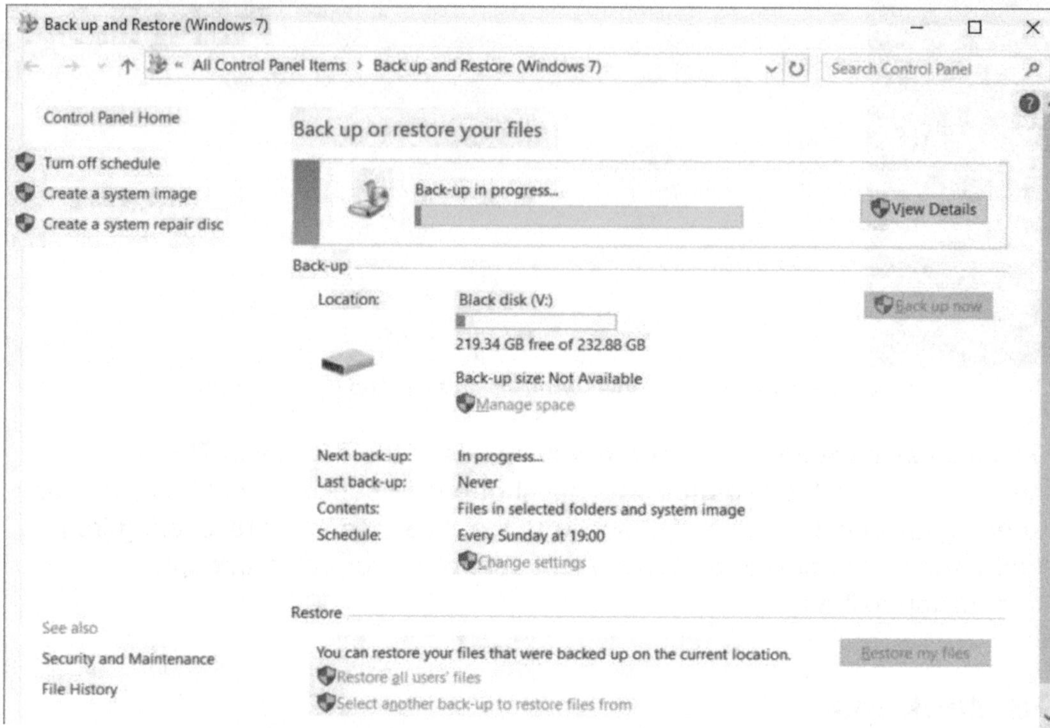

Backup and Restore (Windows 7). Screenshot used with permission from Microsoft.

- **File History** (Windows 8 and Windows 10)—enables automated backups. As files are modified, the versions are tracked and backed up automatically.

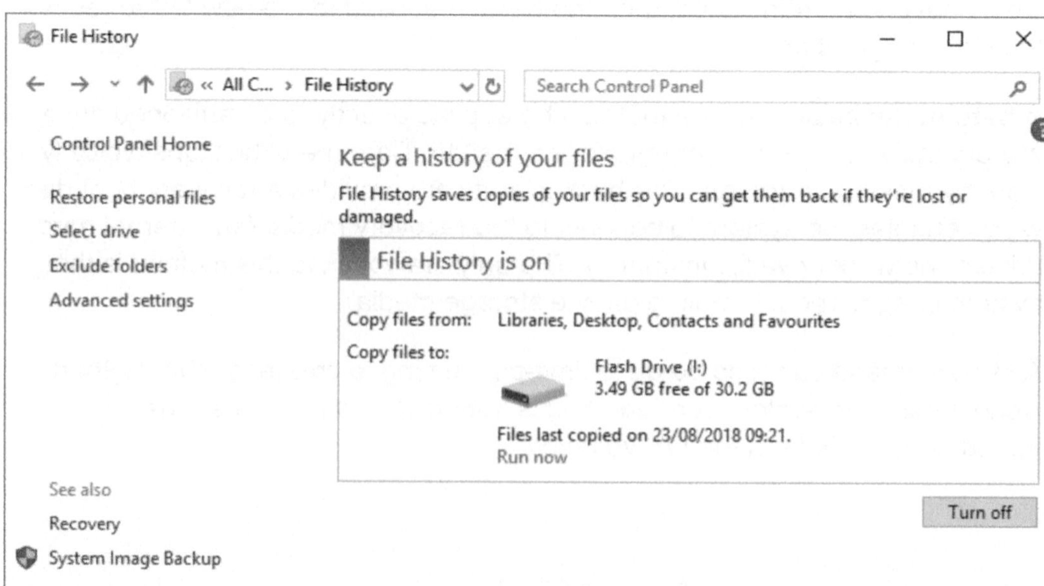

File History app in Windows 10. Screenshot used with permission from Microsoft.

These are accessible from the **Backup** tab in the **Update & Security** category in the **Settings** app.

Scheduling and Frequency

Having selected the type of backup and what files to include, you then need to define a schedule on which to run the backup and work out how frequently to make backups.

With tape-based backup on an enterprise network, backing up data can take a long time and tapes have to be carefully managed to balance their limited capacity with the amount of data to preserve. For a typical personal computer, there is not so much data to backup, and hard-disk based storage is fast and very high capacity. As you can see, the default for File History is to make copies of files every hour.

On a SOHO network, backup jobs are often scheduled to run overnight, minimizing any performance problems the backup might cause, especially if using cloud-based storage. Most businesses would make a backup at least once every day.

You also need to consider whether you need to keep backups to a certain point in time. If you delete or change a file by accident, then make a backup, there will be no way to restore the file from the last backup. To do so, you would have to have made an earlier backup and gone back to that. To keep multiple backups, you will need multiple drives (ideally) or enough space on a single drive to store multiple backups.

As well as making scheduled backups, make a backup whenever you install or upgrade software or hardware, just in case the installation causes serious problems with your PC. It is also worth making a backup before you uninstall software.

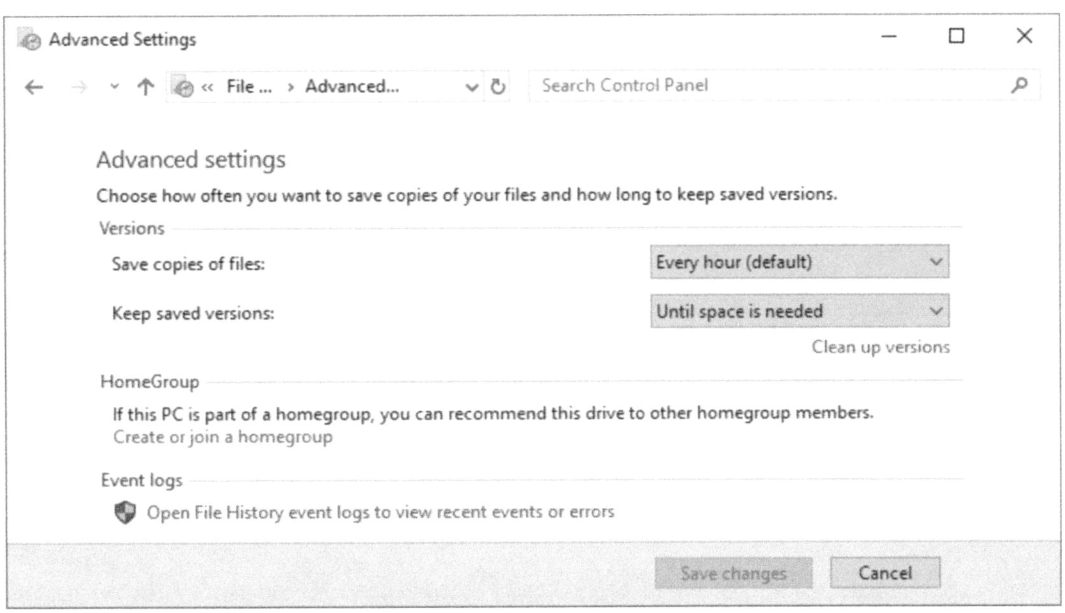

Choosing a backup schedule. Screenshot used with permission from Microsoft.

Restoring Data and Verifying Backups

It is *critical* to test that backup operations work properly. There can be no worse feeling in IT than turning to the backups you have been happily making for the last six months only to discover that a critical data file has never been included in the job! The following represent some of the main backup verification and testing issues:

- **Error detection**—problems with the backup media or configuration can cause backup jobs to fail. Depending on the error, the whole job may be cancelled, or some data may not get backed up. Backup software usually has the facility to verify a backup. This makes the backup operation longer though. The software should also be able to report errors to a log file.
- **Configuration**—when setting up a new job (and periodically thereafter), it is wise to check to ensure that all the expected data has been backed up.
- **Test restore**—another option is to test that a restore operation can be performed successfully. This is important when using new backup software, to test old backup media, to check a new job, and to carry out random spot checks. When you do a test restore, you *redirect* the data to a different folder, to avoid overwriting live data.

As well as completing test restores, you should review the status report to confirm that the backup ran successfully.

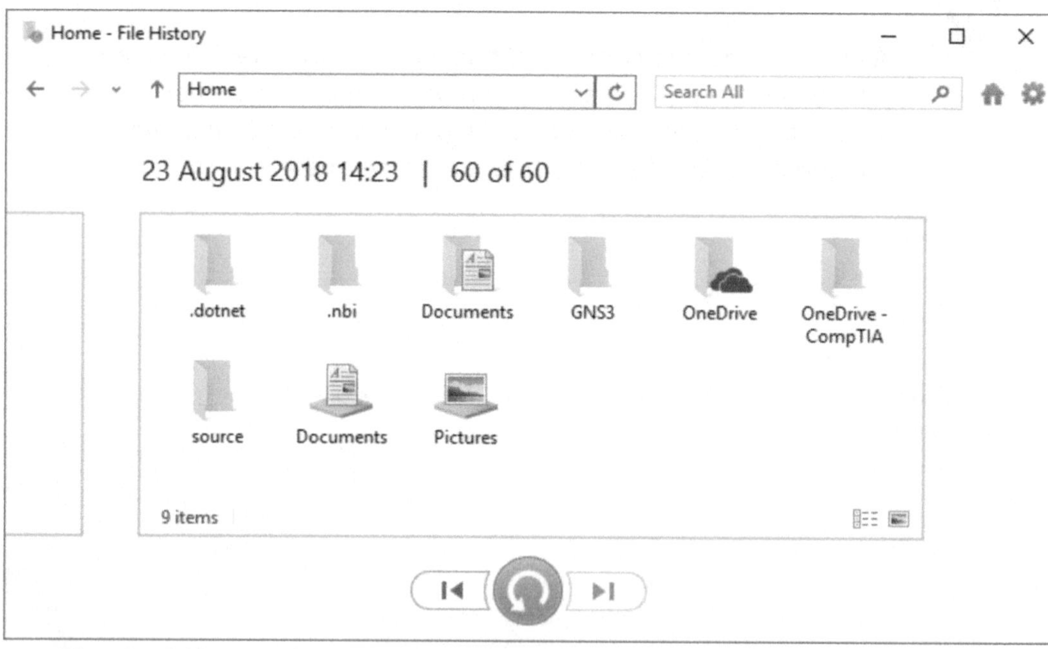

Choosing folders and files to restore from a particular point in time. Screenshot used with permission from Microsoft.

Review Questions / Module 4 / Unit 4 / Using Shared Storage

Answer these questions to test what you have learned in this unit. You can review the model answers at the end of the book.

1) True or false? A hard disk connected to a computer via a USB port could be described as "Direct Attached Storage."
2) What type of connection would a NAS device use?
3) Which admin tool or screen would you use to configure a Windows computer to join a domain?
4) True or false? Any version or edition of Windows can be used to share files with other users.
5) How could you access a network folder called DATA on a network server called TOWER1 using the Explorer address bar?
6) What is a mapped drive?
7) What protocol would be used to provide encrypted file downloads from a web server?
8) You have made a backup of system data using a removable hard disk. What should you do next?

Lab 19 / File Sharing

In this lab, you will investigate workgroup settings and configure a shared folder. If you have a second computer, you can use that to browse the network; if not, you can still investigate the settings and network shares on the local machine.

1) If necessary, start your computer and sign in.

2) Click **Start**, click **Settings**, click **System** and then select the **About** node.

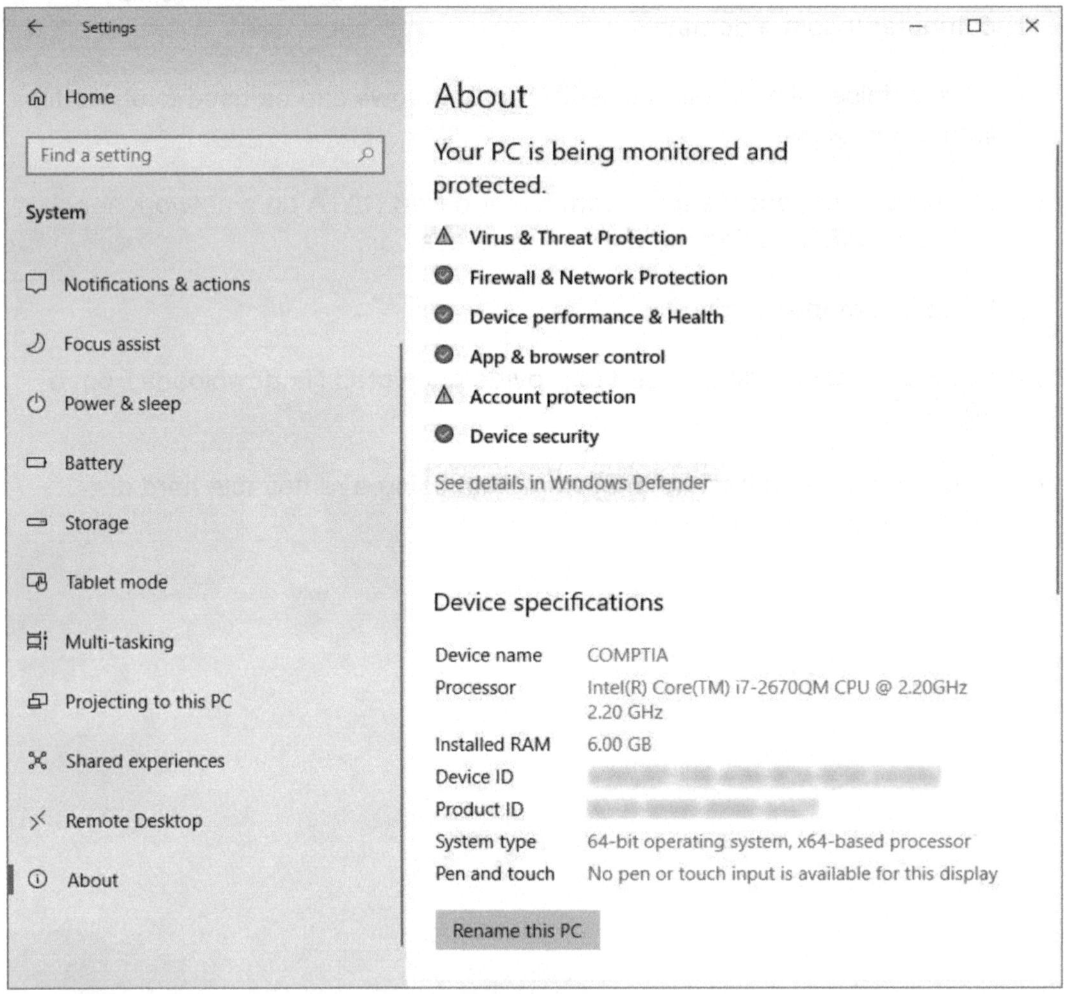

Using the Settings app to view system information. Screenshot used with permission from Microsoft.

3) Under "Device specifications," make a note of the device name:

____

4) Open **Control Panel**, and click **System and Security**, then click **System**. The same computer name is listed.

5) The computer should be part of a workgroup name "Workgroup." If it is not, complete the following additional steps:

    - Click **Change settings**.
    - Click the **Change** button.
    - Type `WORKGROUP` in the **Workgroup** box.
    - Click **OK** then **OK** again.
    - Click **Close**.
    - Click **Restart Now**.
    - When the computer has restarted, sign in again.

6) Right-click the network status icon on the taskbar, and then click **Open Network & Internet settings**.

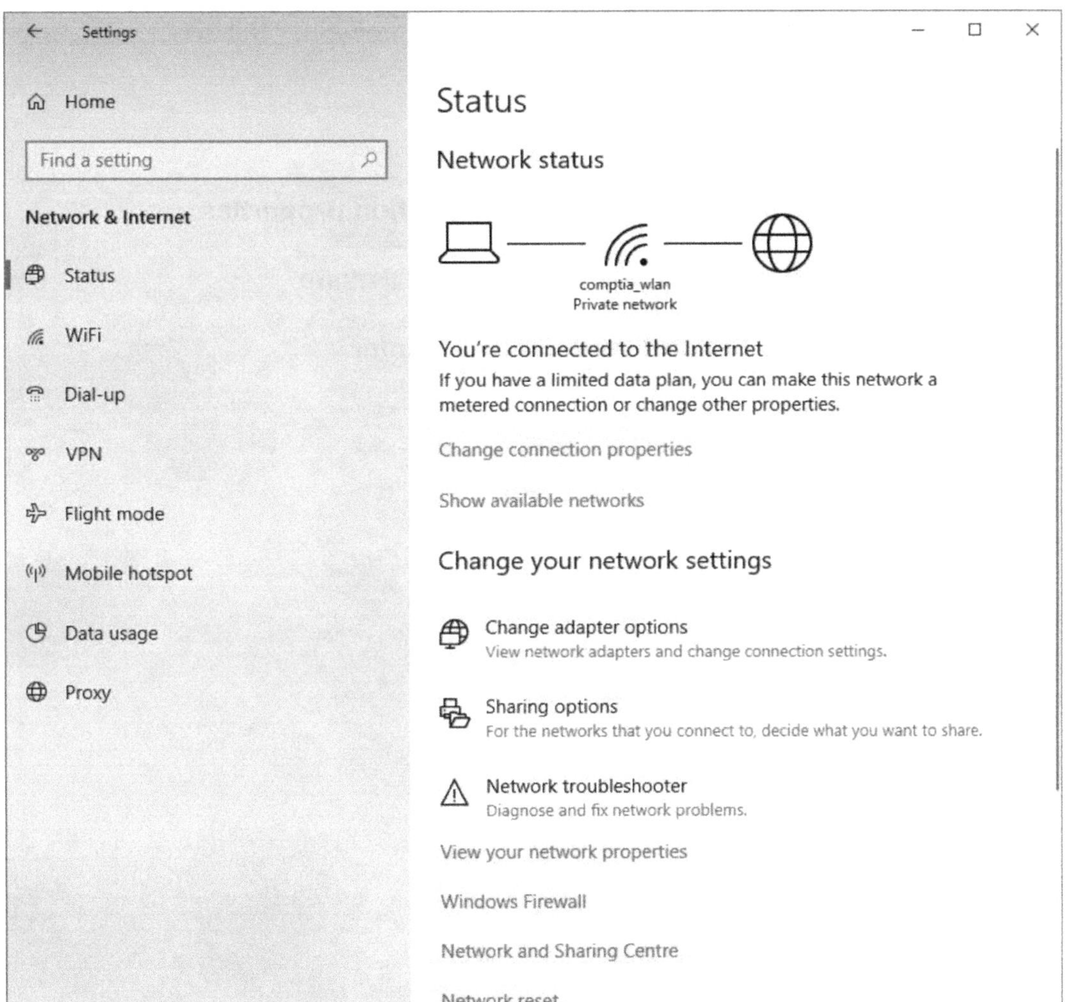

Settings app—network status information and options. Screenshot used with permission from Microsoft.

7) With the **Status** node selected, scroll down and click **Network and Sharing Center**.

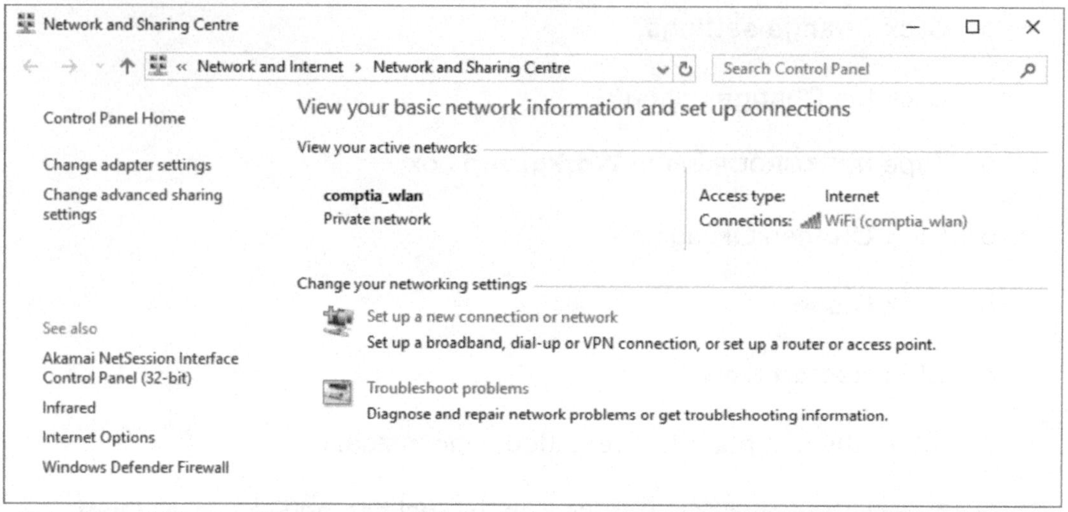

Network and Sharing Center—under "View your active networks," check that the network type is set to "Private network." Screenshot used with permission from Microsoft.

8) Check that the network type is set to "Private network." If it is not, complete the following steps:

    - Switch to **Settings**.
    - On the **Status** tab, click **Change connection properties**.
    - Under the **Network profile** heading, click **Private**.
    - Switch back to **Network and Sharing Center**.

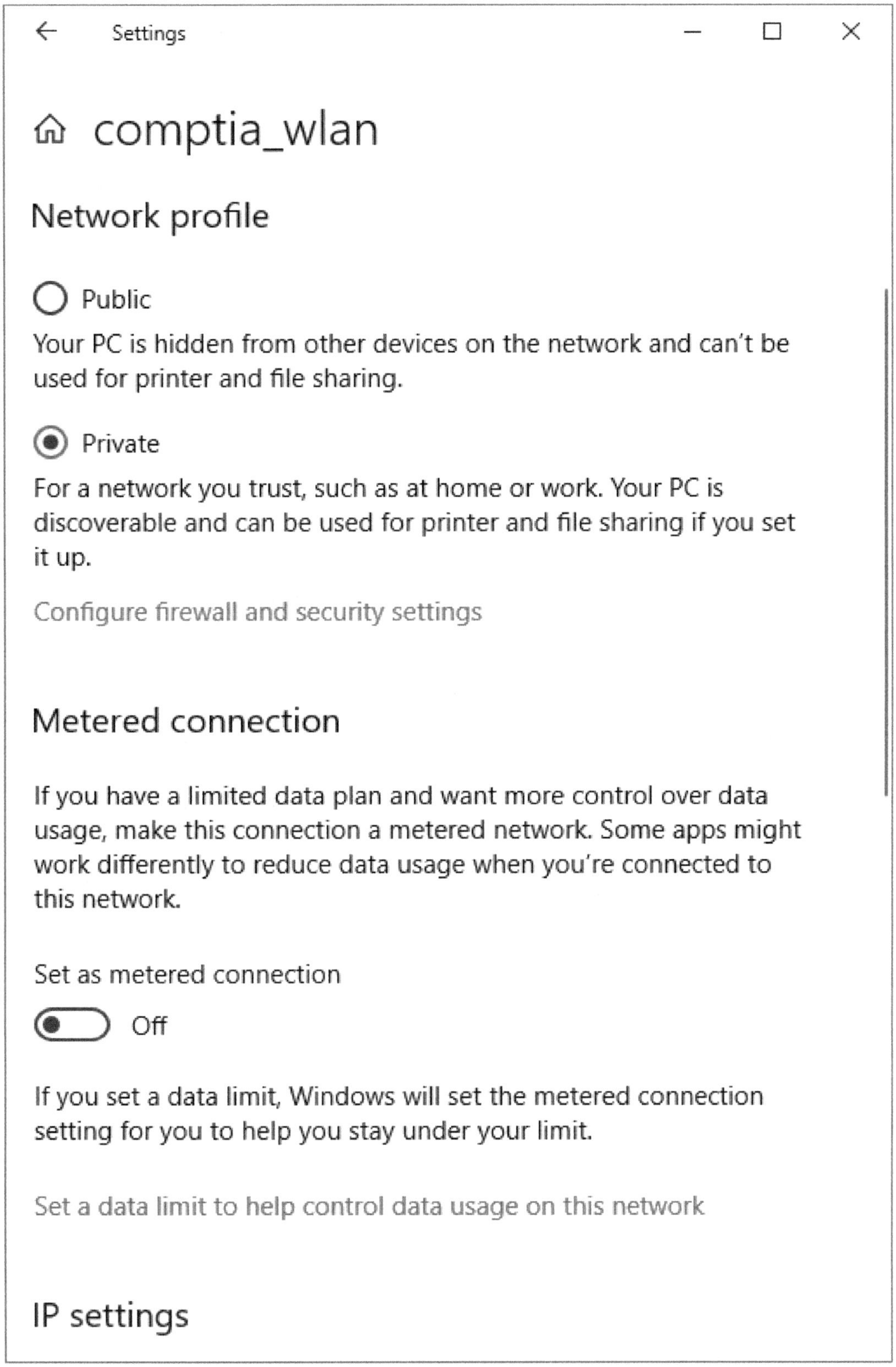

Viewing network connection properties via the Settings app. Screenshot used with permission from Microsoft.

Note that this page gives you another way to view the adapter's address configuration. Also, you can use the Copy button here to obtain the information for pasting into a document or an email. This is useful if you need a user to give you the computer's current network configuration.

9) Select the **Change advanced sharing settings** link.

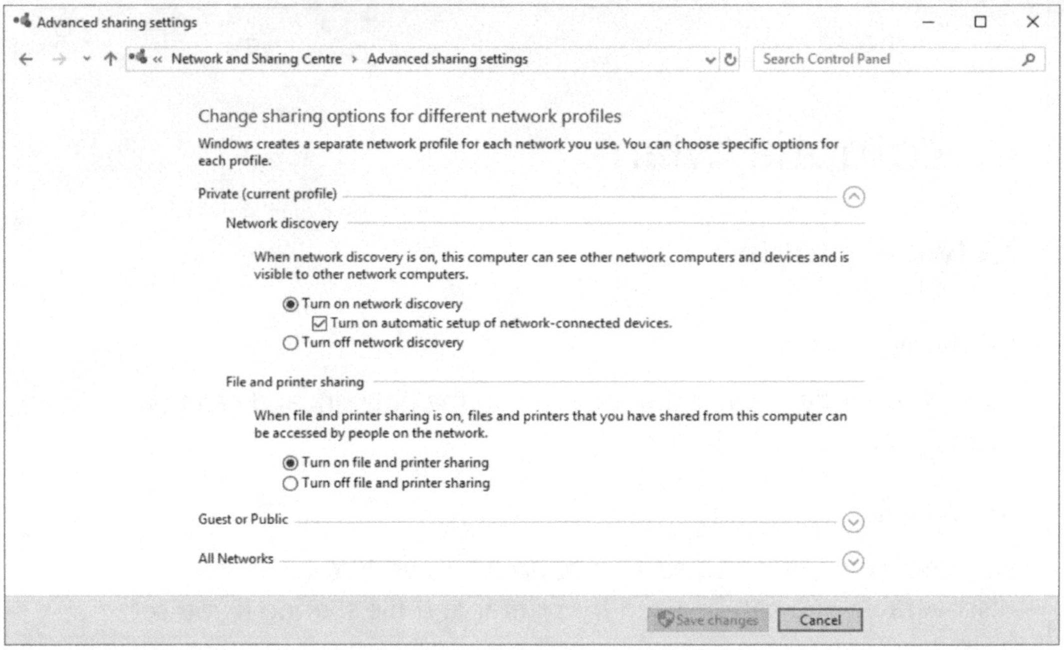

Advanced sharing settings—check that network discovery and file and printer sharing are enabled. Screenshot used with permission from Microsoft.

10) If necessary, select **Turn on network discovery** and **Turn on file and printer sharing**.

11) Click in the window address bar, type `documents`, then press `Enter`.

12) In the **Documents** folder, right-click the **Holidays** folder and select **Give access to > Specific people**.

13) In the "Network access" dialog, select **Everyone** from the list box then click **Add**.

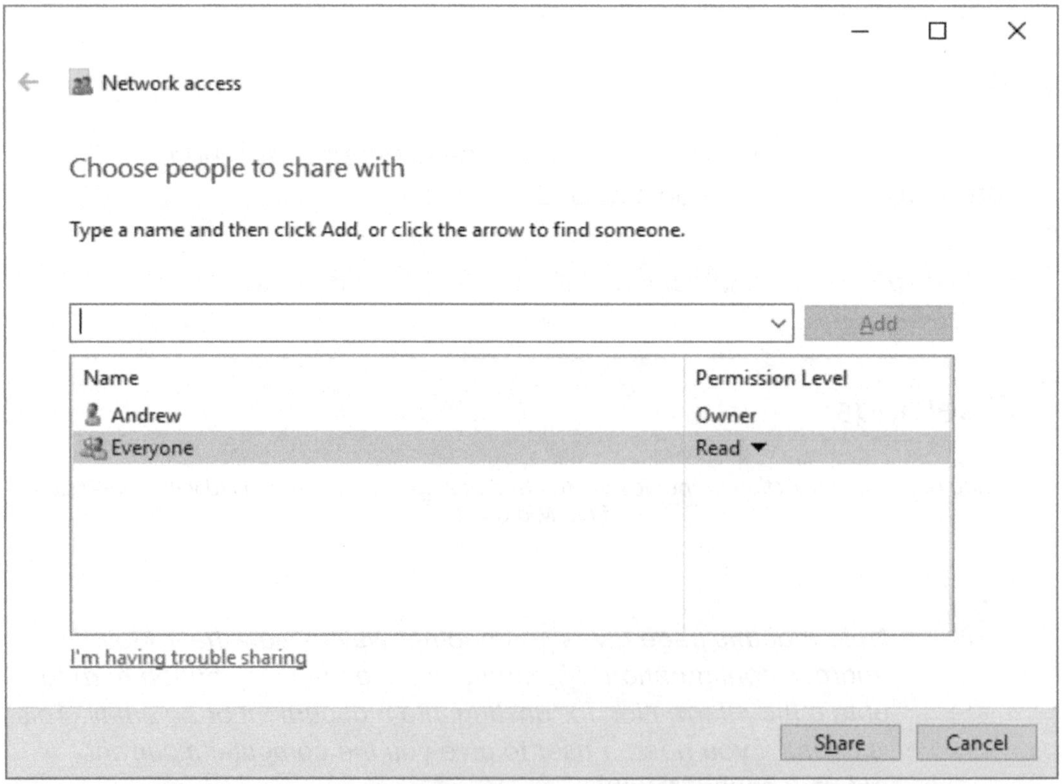

Network access dialog. Screenshot used with permission from Microsoft.

14) Leave the permission level set to "Read" and click the **Share** button. Note the UNC share path. Click **Done** to finish.

    If you have a second computer, complete the following steps. If not, just use your first PC, but be aware that you will receive different results when viewing the shared folder and testing the permissions you have.

    Also, this lab assumes you are accessing the second PC with a user account with a different name and password.

    - Open File Explorer and expand the **Network** object from the navigation pane. You should see both computer names listed.
    - Double-click the icon for your first computer. You should see a "Holidays" shared folder.
    - Click in the address bar and type `\\`***`ServerName`***`\Holidays`, where *ServerName* is the name of your first computer, and press **`ENTER`**.
    - Test that you have only view permissions on this folder by trying to delete one of the existing files and create a new file.

15) Back on your first PC, in File Explorer, right-click the **C:\Holidays** folder and select **Share with > Stop sharing**.

16) Optionally, shut down your computer if you are not continuing to use it after this lab.

Module 4 / Unit 5

Using Mobile Devices

Objectives

On completion of this unit, you will be able to:

- Identify the key features of different types of mobile devices and mobile operating systems.
- Configure network, email, and data transfer settings on mobile devices.

Syllabus Objectives and Content Examples

This unit does not cover specific exam domain objectives or content examples.

Using a Mobile Device

A touchscreen allows the user to control the OS directly through the screen (or with a stylus) rather than using navigation buttons or a scroll wheel.

Gesture-based Interaction

Modern mobile devices use capacitive touchscreens. These capacitive displays support **multitouch**, meaning that gestures can be interpreted as events and responded to by software in a particular way.

- Tap—usually the equivalent of a main button mouse click.
- Tap-and-hold—usually the equivalent of a right-button mouse click.
- Swiping—typically used to switch between documents or apps. Some devices and software can distinguish between one-, two-, and three-finger swiping.
- Pinch and stretch—typically used to zoom out (bring your fingers together) and zoom in (spread your fingers).
- Sliding—move objects around the screen.

Kinetics and Screen Orientation

Kinetics can refer either to operating a device by moving it around or using a camera in the device to recognize your hand movements.

Mobile devices use **accelerometers** and **gyroscopes** to detect when the device is moved and change the screen orientation between portrait and landscape modes. Often this can happen inappropriately so the screen orientation can also be locked to a particular setting.

Kinetics can also be used as a more advanced control mechanism. For example, a driving game could allow the tablet itself to function as a steering wheel or shaking the device could be interpreted as an "undo" event in a software application.

Speech Recognition and Hands Free

Speech recognition is another important interface for controlling a mobile device. All three of the major vendors have speech recognition built into the OS (Apple's Siri, Google Now, and Microsoft's Cortana) and are working hard to create interfaces that can correctly interpret users' natural language requests. Speech recognition is one part of allowing **hands free** use of a mobile device. Using a Bluetooth or wired headset also means that the device can be kept in a pocket (while walking for instance) or used in a motor vehicle safely.

Passcode Locks

If an attacker is able to gain access to a smartphone or tablet, they can obtain a huge amount of information and the tools with which to launch further attacks. Quite apart from confidential data files that might be stored on the device, it is highly likely that the user has cached passwords for services such as email or remote access networks and websites. In addition to this, access to contacts and message history (SMS, email, and IM) greatly assists social engineering attacks.

Consequently, access to a mobile device should always be protected by a **screen lock**. The screen lock can be configured to activate whenever the power button is pressed and/or to lock when the sleep timer activates (or some time afterward). Once the phone locks, it has to be unlocked by entering the appropriate credentials. A simple passcode requires the user to enter a PIN; a more complex password-based lock can use letters and symbols too. Android can use a graphical "join-the-dots" lock. Some devices can use biometric authentication via a fingerprint reader.

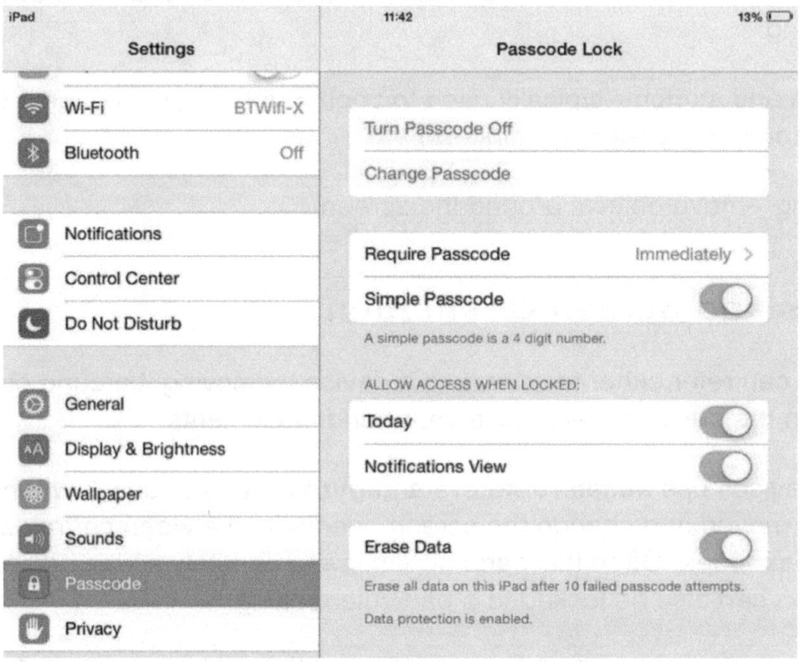

Configuring a passcode lock on iOS.

The screen lock can also be configured with a **lockout** policy. This means that if an incorrect passcode is entered, the device locks for a set period. This could be configured to escalate, so the first incorrect attempt locks the device for 30 seconds while the third locks it for 10 minutes for instance. This deters attempts to guess the passcode.

Another possibility is for the phone to support a **remote wipe** or "kill switch." This means that if the handset is stolen, it can be set to the factory defaults or cleared of any personal data. Some utilities may also be able to wipe any plug-in memory cards too. The remote wipe could be triggered by a number of incorrect passcode attempts or by enterprise management software. Other features include backing up data from the phone to a server first and displaying a "Lost/stolen phone—return to XX" message on the handset.

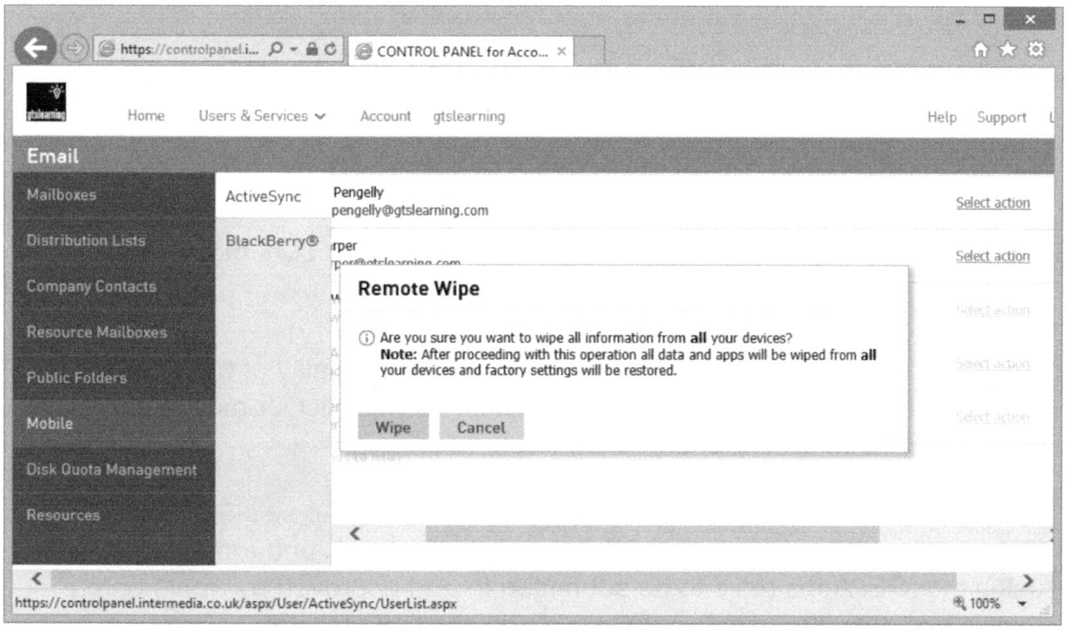

Most corporate messaging systems come with a Remote Wipe feature, allowing mail, calendar, and contacts information to be deleted from mobile devices.

A thief can (in theory) prevent a remote wipe by ensuring the phone cannot connect to the network then hacking the phone and disabling the security.

Full Device Encryption

All but the early versions of mobile device OS for smartphones and tablets, such as Android and iOS, provide **full device encryption**.

In iOS 5 (and up), there are various levels of encryption.

- All user data on the device is always encrypted, but the key is stored on the device. This is primarily used as a means of wiping the device. The OS just needs to delete the key to make the data inaccessible rather than wiping each storage location.
- Email data and any apps using the "Data Protection" option are also encrypted using a key derived from the user's passcode (if this is configured). This provides security for data in the event that the device is stolen. Not all user data is encrypted; contacts, SMS messages, and pictures are not, for example.

In iOS, Data Protection encryption is enabled automatically when you configure a password lock on the device. In Android, you need to enable encryption via Settings > Security. Android uses full-disk encryption with a passcode-derived key. When encryption is enabled, it can take some time to encrypt the device.

The encryption key is derived from the PIN or password. In order to generate a strong key, you should use a strong password. Of course, this makes accessing the device each time the screen locks more difficult.

With the release of Android Nougat, full device encryption is being deprecated in favor of file-level encryption.

Mobile Applications and App Stores

Apps are installable programs that extend the functionality of the mobile device. An app must be written and compiled for a particular mobile operating system (Apple iOS, Android, or Windows).

Third-party developers can create apps for iOS using Apple's Software Development Kit (SDK). The SDK can only be installed and run on a computer using macOS. Apps have to be submitted to and approved by Apple before they are released to users. Apps are made available for free or can be bought from the **App Store**.

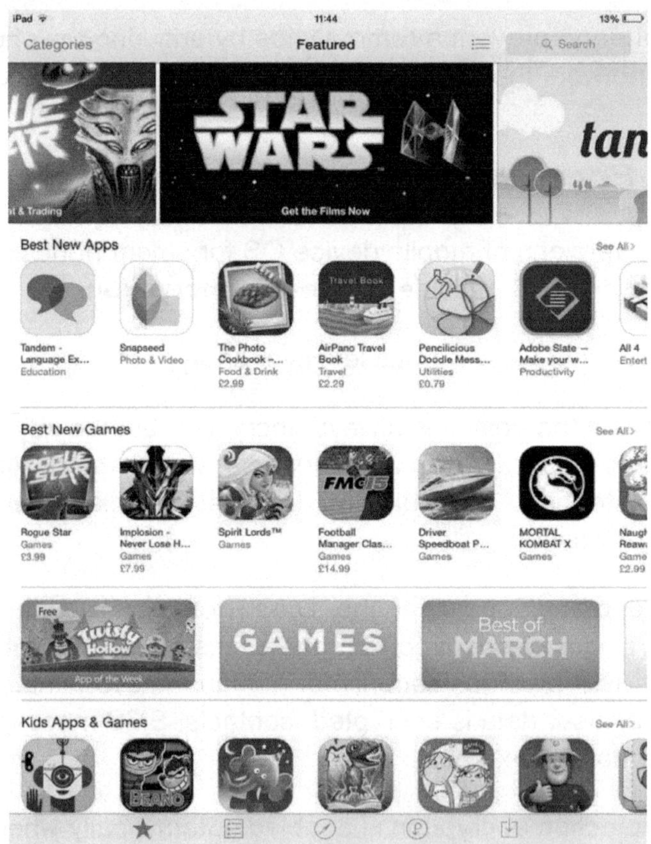

Apple's App Store.

Android's app model is more relaxed, with apps available from both Google Play and third-party sites, such as Amazon's app store. The SDK for Android apps is available to install on Linux, Windows, and macOS development machines.

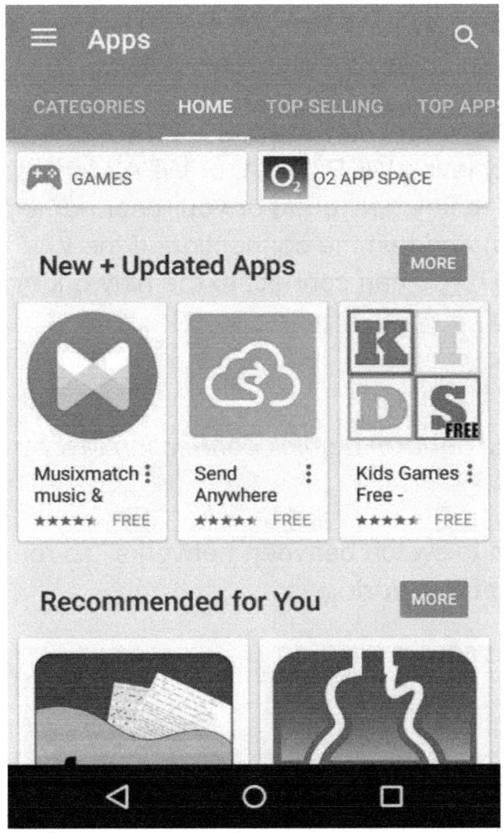

Google Play app store.

Apps are supposed to run in a sandbox and have only the privileges granted by the user.

Network Connectivity

There are generally two choices for connecting a smartphone or tablet to the Internet:

- Use mobile data access (the cellular provider's network).
- Use a nearby Wi-Fi network.

In iOS, cellular network options are configured via **Settings > General > Network**. In Android, the options are configured via **Settings > Data usage**.

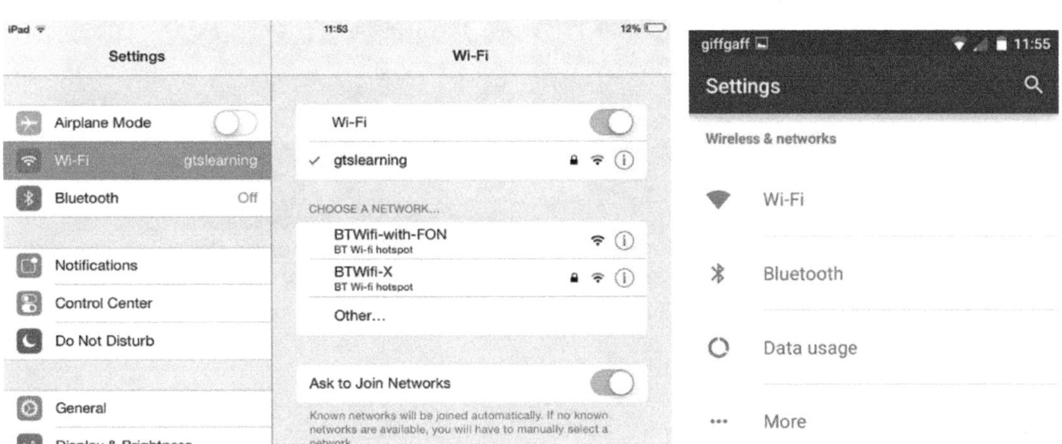

Configuring mobile data options in iOS (left) and Android (right).

Devices default to using Wi-Fi if it is available. The indicator on the status bar at the top of the screen shows the data link in use.

Wi-Fi networks can be setup via **Settings > Wi-Fi**. Choose the SSID and configure the security level (WEP, WPA, or WPA2 for instance). Enter either the key (for pre-shared key networks) or your user name and password (Enterprise networks) and test the connection. If the Wi-Fi network is not broadcasting its SSID, you can connect to the network by entering the network name manually.

You could perform a quick connection test by trying to browse a website.

Use the Wi-Fi screen to switch between networks. To remove a network, select it, then choose **Forget Network**.

Airplane Mode

Most airlines prevent flyers from using radio-based devices while onboard a plane. A device can be put into "airplane mode" to comply with these restrictions, though some carriers insist that devices must be switched off completely at times such as takeoff and landing. Airplane mode disables all wireless features (cellular data, Wi-Fi, GPS, and Bluetooth). On some devices, some services can selectively be re-enabled while still in airplane mode.

Both iOS and Android provide a notification or toggle shade with some quick configuration options, including toggles for wireless options.

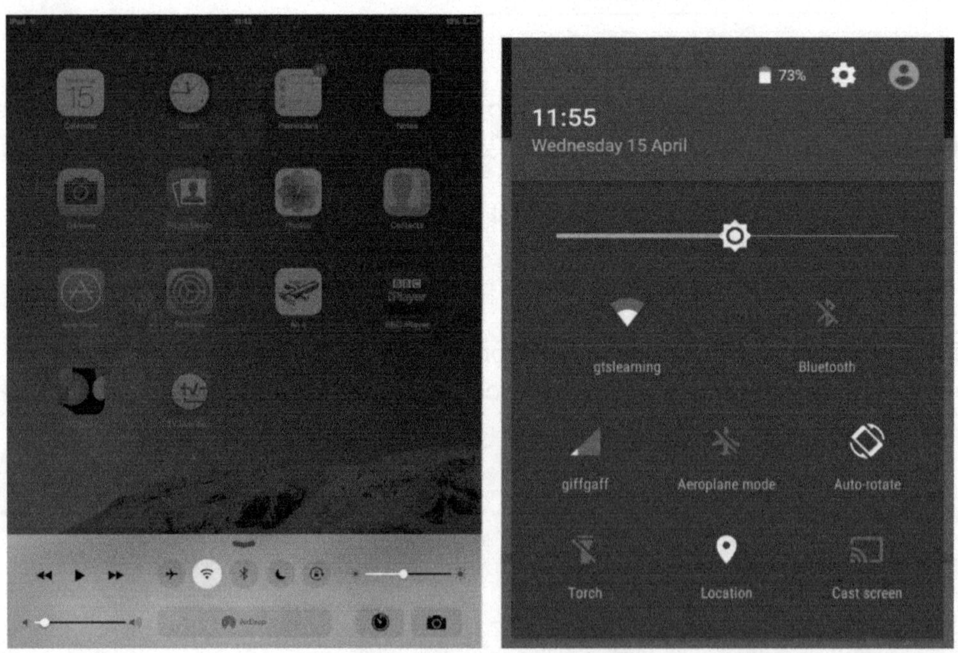

Wireless options can be quickly switched on or off in iOS and Android using the toggle shades. Swipe up from the bottom of the screen in iOS or down from the top of the screen in Android.

Email Configuration

One of the most important features of smartphones is the ability to receive and compose email. The settings are configured on the phone in much the same way you would set up a mail account on a PC. For example, in iOS, open **Settings > Mail, Contacts, Calendars** then click **Add Account**. In Android, the configuration is performed via **Settings > Accounts**.

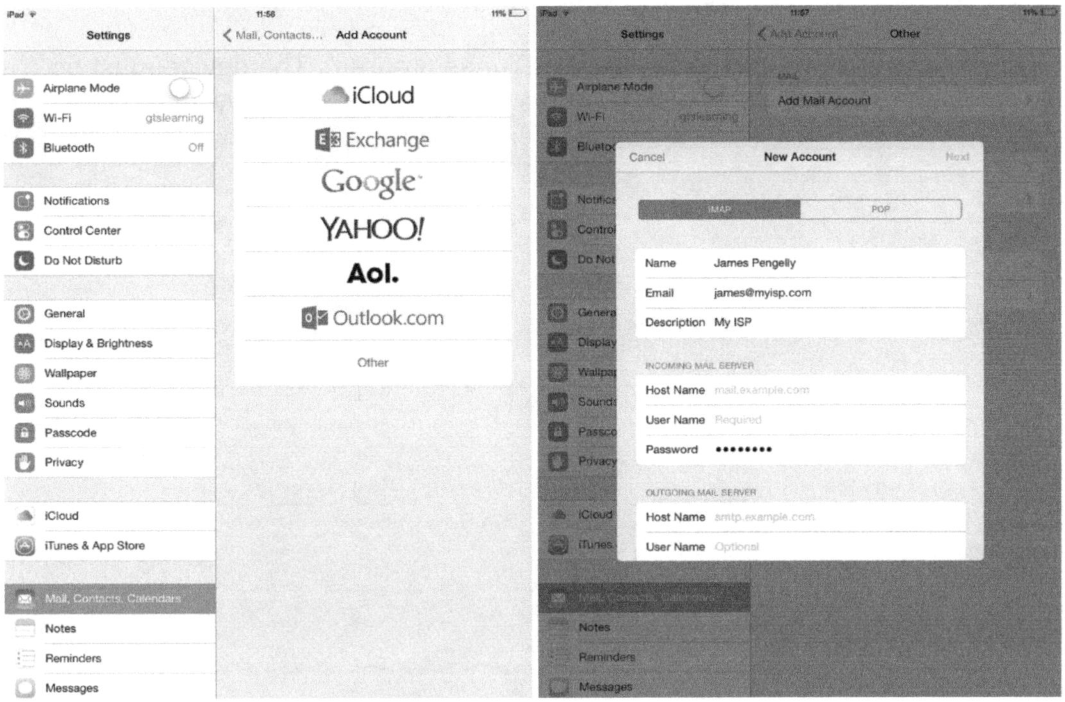

Configuring a mail account in iOS.

Choose the mail provider (Exchange, Gmail, and so on) then enter your user credentials and test the connection. If the mail provider is not listed, you can enter the server address manually by selecting **Other,** then inputting the appropriate server addresses.

- The incoming mail server will either be an Internet Message Access Protocol (IMAP) or a Post Office Protocol (POP) server. Both of these protocols are designed to allow a mail client to download messages from a mail server. IMAP has better functionality than POP, allowing the user to manage messages and folders on the server.

- The outgoing mail server will be a Simple Mail Transfer Protocol (SMTP) server. The client sends a new message to an SMTP server, which then handles the process of transferring the message to the recipient's SMTP server.

The other important option is to enable SSL/TLS. This option should always be chosen if the server supports a secure link.

SSL/TLS protects confidential information such as the account password and is necessary if you connect to mail over a public link, such as an open Wi-Fi "hotspot."

Synchronization and Data Transfer

Mobile device synchronization refers to copying data back and forth between a PC and phone or tablet. This method can be used to share email, calendar, and contacts with a locally installed mail application, though setting up an "over the air" server or cloud service sync, as described above for email, is generally preferable. It can also be used to share media files between devices—camera pictures, downloaded music tracks or videos, and so on.

iOS can synchronize with a PC via the iTunes program. The device must be connected to the PC via a USB to Apple Lightning cable or a Wi-Fi link.

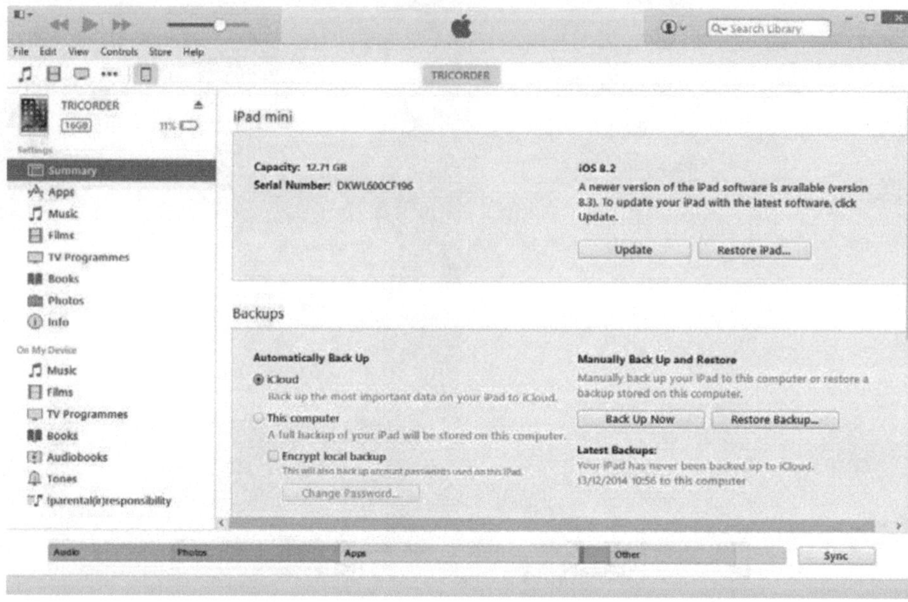

Using iTunes to sync data between an iPhone and a PC.

Android-based phones are primarily set up to sync with Google's Gmail email and calendar/contact manager services. You can usually view the phone from Windows (Android phones use standard USB ports) and allow drag and drop or copy and paste for file transfer with a Windows PC using the Picture Transfer Protocol (PTP) or Media Transfer Protocol (MTP).

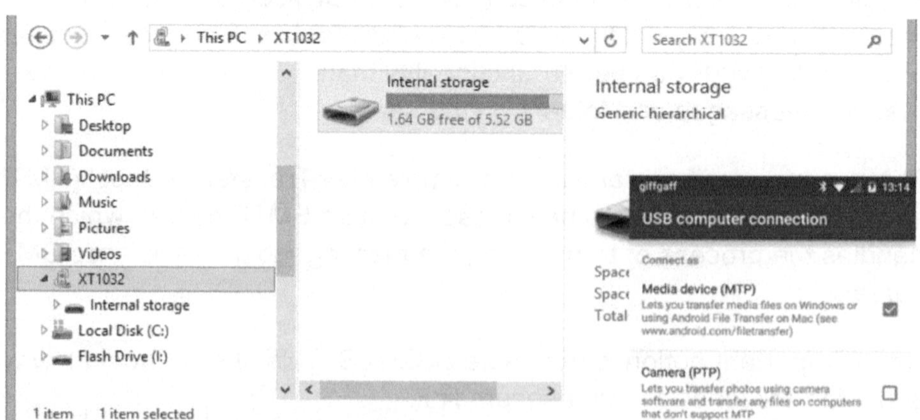

Connecting to an Android smartphone's storage folders via Windows. The inset shows the connection options available from the Android device (choosing between MTP and PTP).

Remote Backup

While devices can often store gigabytes of data, improved Internet bandwidth means that it can be feasible to back this data up to a cloud storage provider. As well as keeping a security copy, this can allow files to be shared and synchronized between multiple devices. Notable service providers include Apple's iCloud, Dropbox, Microsoft's OneDrive, and Google's Cloud Platform.

Configuring iCloud backup and synchronization options.

Review Questions / Module 4 / Unit 5 / Using Mobile Devices

Answer these questions to test what you have learned in this unit. You can review the model answers at the end of the book.

1) What type of gesture is typically used for zooming on a touchscreen?
2) What is the purpose of an accelerometer, as fitted in a mobile device?
3) What feature allows data to be removed from a device if is lost or stolen?
4) True or false? A smartphone cannot join a Wi-Fi network if the SSID is not being broadcast.
5) What is "airplane mode?"

Module 4 / Summary
Using Networks

In this module you investigated the components and protocols used to create networks and how to configure basic SOHO networks and file sharing.

Module 4 / Unit 1 / Networking Concepts

- Ethernet LANs are based on switches and cabled media to connect computers together; wireless networks use IEEE 802.11 standards. At this data link layer, hosts are identified by a MAC address.
- Packet transmission uses routers to forward small packets over any available network path, making the network more resilient to link failures. At this network layer, hosts are identified by an IP address. The IP address contains a network ID, masked by a network prefix, and a host ID.
- DNS provides a means for people to use plain names or labels to access resources. DNS maps these labels to IP addresses.
- Make sure you can match application protocols in the TCP/IP suite to functions such as web browsing and email.

Module 4 / Unit 2 / Connecting to a Network

- Home/small office networks are usually configured with a multifunction network device, combining the function of switch, access point, WAN modem, and router.
- Typical Internet access methods include DSL, cable/HFC, FTTC, satellite, and cellular.
- Make sure you know the configuration parameters for setting up a wireless network, such as standards support, SSID, and encryption type.

Module 4 / Unit 3 / Secure Web Browsing

- Using effective browser security settings is imperative in protecting the computer against malicious sites. Make sure you understand how to control cookie and cache settings to ensure privacy.
- Digital certificates are a means of validating the identity of a web server or software publisher.
- Firewalls are another essential component of a secure system as they restrict network communications to authorized hosts, applications, and protocols.

Module 4 / Unit 4 / Using Shared Storage

- Local file and print sharing can use direct attached storage (file server) or a Network Attached Storage appliance.
- Windows network client settings are configured via the System Properties or Settings. Shared resources can be browsed using the Network object in File Explorer or the share's UNC. A shared folder can also be mapped as a drive.
- Hosted sharing can be implemented using HTTP/HTTPS, FTP, cloud, streaming, and P2P services.
- Make sure you understand the issues and procedures surrounding backing up and restoring data files, especially different kinds of backup (data, database, OS) and the need for off-site storage.

Module 4 / Unit 5 / Using Mobile Devices

- Make sure you know how to operate a mobile device using gestures and kinetics and about the basic options for securing the device.
- Understand the capabilities of different network connection methods and how to enable and disable them.
- Make sure you know how to set up email and data synchronization services.

Module 5 / Security Concepts

The following CompTIA IT Fundamentals+ domain objectives and examples are covered in this module:

CompTIA ITF+ Certification Domains	Weighting
1.0 IT Concepts and Terminology	17%
2.0 Infrastructure	22%
3.0 Applications and Software	18%
4.0 Software Development	12%
5.0 Database Fundamentals	11%
6.0 Security	20%

Refer To	Domain Objectives/Examples
Unit 5.1 / Security Concerns	**6.1 Summarize confidentiality, integrity, and availability concerns.** *Confidentiality concerns (Snooping, Eavesdropping, Wiretapping, Social engineering, Dumpster diving) • Integrity concerns (Man-in-the-Middle, Replay attack, Impersonation, Unauthorized information alteration) • Availability concerns (Denial of service, Power outage, Hardware failure, Destruction, Service outage)*
	6.7 Explain business continuity concepts. *Fault tolerance (Replication, Redundancy [Data, Network, Power], Contingency plan) • Disaster recovery (Data restoration, Prioritization, Restoring access)*
Unit 5.2 / Using Best Practices	**6.2 Explain methods to secure devices and best practices.** *Securing devices (mobile/workstation) (Anti-virus/Anti-malware, Changing default passwords, Enabling passwords, Patching/updates) • Device use best practices (Software sources, Validating legitimate sources, Researching legitimate sources, OEM websites vs. third-party websites, Removal of unwanted software, Removal of unnecessary software, Removal of malicious software)*

Refer To	Domain Objectives/Examples
Unit 5.3 / Using Access Controls	**6.4 Compare and contrast authentication, authorization, accounting, and non-repudiation concepts.** *Authentication (Single factor, Multifactor, Examples of factors [Password, PIN, One-time password, Software token, Hardware token, Biometrics, Specific location, Security questions], Single sign-on) • Authorization (Permissions, Least privilege model, Role-based access [User account types], Rule-based access, Mandatory access controls, Discretionary access controls) • Accounting (Logs, Tracking, Web browser history) • Non-repudiation (Video, Biometrics, Signature, Receipt)*
	6.5 Explain password best practices. *Password length • Password complexity • Password history • Password expiration • Password reuse across sites • Password managers • Password reset process*
	6.6 Explain common uses of encryption. *Plain text vs. cipher text • Data at rest (File level, Disk level, Mobile device) • Data in transit (Email, HTTPS) • VPN • Mobile application*
Unit 5.4 / Behavioral Security Concepts	**6.3 Summarize behavioral security concepts.** *Expectations of privacy when using: (The Internet [Social networking sites, Email, File sharing, Instant messaging], Mobile applications, Desktop software, Business software, Corporate network) • Written policies and procedures • Handling of confidential information (Passwords, Personal information, Customer information, Company confidential information)*

Module 5 / Unit 1
Security Concerns

Objectives

On completion of this unit, you will be able to:

- Distinguish threats to the confidentiality, integrity, and availability of information processing systems.
- Identify social engineering techniques.
- Describe the importance of business continuity and how to make systems fault tolerant.
- Explain the importance of disaster recovery plans.

Syllabus Objectives and Content Examples

This unit covers the following exam domain objectives and content examples:

- 6.1 Summarize confidentiality, integrity, and availability concerns.
  Confidentiality concerns (Snooping, Eavesdropping, Wiretapping, Social engineering, Dumpster diving) • Integrity concerns (Man-in-the-Middle, Replay attack, Impersonation, Unauthorized information alteration) • Availability concerns (Denial of service, Power outage, Hardware failure, Destruction, Service outage)
- 6.7 Explain business continuity concepts.
  Fault tolerance (Replication, Redundancy [Data, Network, Power], Contingency plan) • Disaster recovery (Data restoration, Prioritization, Restoring access)

Computer Security Basics

Security is the practice of controlling access to something (a **resource**). Computer security has become a vital competency as the risks from threats such as malware, hacking, and identity fraud become better recognized and increasingly serious. Security must be balanced against **accessibility** however. If a system is completely secure, then no one has access to it, and it is unusable.

Confidentiality, Integrity, and Availability (CIA)

Secure information has three properties, often referred to by the "CIA Triad."

- **Confidentiality**—this means that the information should only be known to authorized users.
- **Integrity**—this means that the information is stored and transferred as intended and that any modification is authorized.
- **Availability**—this means that the information is accessible to those authorized to view or modify it.

Security Threats

Most organizations would like to think their networks were secure. They have set up user accounts, they have a stringent accounts policy, and they even audit security related events. But is that all there is to it? To understand security, you must understand the types of **threats** that your network faces.

There can be attempts to circumvent your security that come from within and without your network. These attacks could be malicious or simply implemented by the curious. They could be very technically sophisticated, or laughably simple, exploiting an oversight on your part for instance.

Let's look at some of the more common forms of attack, and examples of such attacks.

Confidentiality Concerns

Confidentiality means that information is only revealed to authorized people. This can be compromised in a number of ways:

- **Snooping**—this is any attempt to get access to information on a host or storage device (data at rest) that you are not authorized to view. An attacker might steal a password or find an unlocked workstation with a logged-on user account, or they might install some sort of spyware on the host.

- **Eavesdropping/wiretapping**—this is snooping on data or telephone conversations as they pass over the network. Snooping on traffic passing over a network is also often called **sniffing**. It can be relatively easy for an attacker to "tap" a wired network or intercept unencrypted wireless transmissions. Networks can use segmentation and encryption to protect data in-transit.

- **Social engineering/dumpster diving**—this means getting users to reveal information or finding printed information. We'll discuss this topic in more detail later in this unit.

As well as "active" attacks and threats, you should also consider "passive" threats, such as configuration errors or user error. Copying data to an unsecure storage location or attaching the wrong file to an email are just as likely to threaten data confidentiality as hackers.

Integrity Concerns

Integrity means that the data being stored and transferred has not been altered without authorization. Some threats to integrity include the following attacks:

- **Man-in-the-Middle (MitM)**—where a host sits between two communicating nodes, and transparently monitors, captures, and relays all communications between them. A MitM may be able to change the messages exchanged between a sender and receiver without them realizing. To protect against this, senders and receivers must authenticate themselves and use encryption to validate messages.

One of the most serious frauds to hit consumers is for criminals to hijack money transfers between a client and solicitor. If the criminal learns about an upcoming major transaction, such as a house purchase, they can try to send or modify the details of the client account used to fund the purchase so that the unwitting client pays money into a fraudulent account. You should always try to confirm account details with your representative in person when making this kind of transaction.

- **Replay**—where a host captures another host's response to some server and replays that response in an effort to gain unauthorized access. Replay attacks often involve exploiting an access token generated by an application. The application needs to use encryption and time-stamping to ensure that the tokens cannot be misused.

- **Impersonation**—a common attack is where a person will attempt to figure out a password or other credentials to gain access to a host. The attacker can then hijack the authorizations allocated to the account and generally masquerade as that user. There are numerous ways to perform impersonation attacks, but an obvious one is to capture password packets in transit and work out which bit the password is. Many vendors have addressed this issue, to some extent, by encrypting the password packets. But the encryption systems used are not strong enough, and various utilities are available that allow users to break even encrypted password packets through brute force, given enough time.

Availability Concerns

Availability means keeping a service running so that authorized users can access and process data whenever necessary. Availability is often threatened by accidents and oversights as well as active attacks.

- **Denial of Service (DoS)**—this is any situation where an attacker targets the availability of a service. A DoS attack might tamper with a system or try to overload it in some way. On the web, a Distributed Denial of Service (DDoS) uses hosts compromised with bot malware to launch a coordinated attack against a web service. The size of the botnet determines how easily the attacker can overwhelm the service.

- **Power outage**—if you lose power, then clearly your computers cannot run. Using standby power can help mitigate this issue. It's also common for data corruption to occur when a computer is turned off rather than being shut down. Using an Uninterruptible Power Supply (UPS) can provide a means to safely close down a server if building power is interrupted.

- **Hardware failure**—if a component in a server fails, then the server often fails. A hard disk contains moving parts and will eventually fail. If a disk fails, you will likely lose access to the data on the failed disk and quite possibly lose the data. You can compensate against hardware failure by provisioning redundant components and servers. The service is then configured to failover to a working component or server without interruption.

- **Destruction**—the loss of a service or data through destruction can occur for a number of reasons. At one extreme, you might lose a data center through a fire or even an act of terrorism. At the other end of the spectrum, you might lose access to a server when a person accidentally spills coffee on a server or a malicious person deliberately smashes a computer. Either way, putting your servers in a physically secure room and controlling access to that room can help protect against these issues.

- **Service outage**—any of the situations above can lead to service unavailability. Many organizations use online, cloud-based apps and services these days. You need to consider how third-party service failures may affect your data processing systems. When you decide which cloud provider to use, consider the options they provide for service availability and fault tolerance.

Authorization, Authentication, and Auditing

To guard against these threats to confidentiality and integrity, data and data processing systems are protected by **access controls**. An access control system normally consists of one or more of the following types of controls:

- **Authentication** means one or more methods of proving that a user is who they say they are and associates that person with a unique computer or network user account.
- **Authorization** means creating one or more barriers around the resource such that only authenticated users can gain access. Each resource has a permissions list specifying what users can do. Resources often have different access levels, for example, being able to read a file or being able to read and edit it.
- **Accounting** means recording when and by whom a resource was accessed.

One of the key points to note from the above is "one or more." A security system that depends on one mechanism only is often not very effective. Providing multiple controls of different types offers much better security.

Social Engineering

Attackers can use a diverse range of techniques to compromise a security system. A pre-requisite of many types of attack is to obtain information about the security system. **Social engineering** refers to means of getting users to reveal confidential information or obtaining unauthorized physical access to a resource.

Often, malicious people can start to gain access to your network resources through the use of seemingly innocuous data. For example, accessing an address list, or contact directory can provide a starting point for attempting to sign in to your network.

It is also important to note that gaining access to a network is often based on a series of small steps rather than a single large step. That is, knowing the SSID of a wireless access point enables a person to attempt to connect to a network. If the connection is ultimately successful, accessing a discarded email message might help a malicious person to determine the user ID of a standard user. At this stage, the malicious person is well on their way to gaining access to your network.

Impersonation

Impersonation (pretending to be someone else) is one of the basic social engineering techniques.

The classic impersonation attack is for an attacker to phone into a department, claim they have to adjust something on the user's system remotely, and get the user to reveal their password.

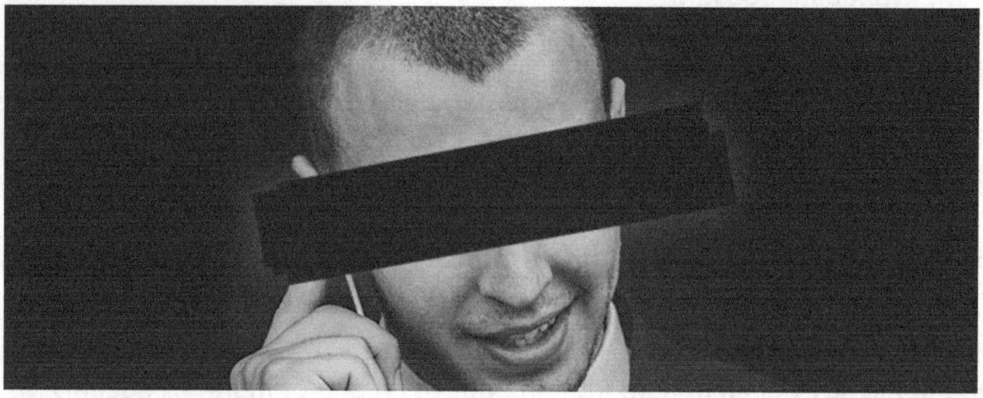

Do you really know who's on the other end of the line? (Photo by Uros Jovicic on Unsplash)

Attackers will generally try one of the following methods:

- Intimidate the target by pretending to be someone senior in rank.
- Intimidate the target by using spurious technical arguments and jargon.
- Coax the target by engaging them in friendly conversation.

Trust and Dumpster Diving

Being convincing or establishing **trust** usually depends on the attacker obtaining privileged information about the organization. For example, an impersonation attack is much more effective if the attacker knows the user's name. As most companies are set up toward customer service rather than security, this information is typically easy to come by. Information that might seem innocuous, such as department employee lists, job titles, phone numbers, diary, invoices, or purchase orders, can help an attacker penetrate an organization through impersonation.

Another way to obtain information that will help to make a social engineering attack credible is by obtaining documents that the company has thrown away. **Dumpster diving** refers to combing through an organization's (or individual's) refuse to try to find useful documents (or even files stored on discarded removable media).

Remember that attacks may be staged over a long period of time. Initial attacks may only aim at compromising low-level information and user accounts, but this low-level information can be used to attack more sensitive and confidential data and better protected management and administrative accounts.

Identity Fraud

Identity fraud can either mean compromising someone's **computer account** or **masquerading** as that person.

To perform the first type of attack, the attacker must discover and subvert the person's authentication credentials. **Strong authentication** makes this type of attack much more difficult to perform. Most specific identity frauds are aimed at getting someone to reveal their logon, or other secure information, through a phishing or other social engineering attack.

Masquerading effectively means subverting the account creation process. It can be mitigated by performing rigorous **identity checks** when setting up a new account.

Identity theft is also facilitated by the careless transmission, storage, and disposal of **Personally Identifiable Information (PII)**.

PII includes things such as full name, birth date, address, Social Security number, and so on. PII may also be defined as responses to **challenge questions**, such as "What is your favorite color/pet/movie?" Some bits of information, such as a Social Security number, are unique to an individual and once lost cannot easily be changed. Others uniquely identify an individual in combination, such as full name with birth date and street address.

PII is often used for password reset mechanisms and to confirm identity over the telephone.

Shoulder Surfing

Shoulder surfing refers to stealing a password or PIN, or other secure information, by watching the user type it. Despite the name, the attacker may not have to be in close proximity to the target. They could use high-power binoculars or CCTV to directly observe the target remotely.

Defeating Social Engineering Attacks

Social engineering is best defeated by training users to recognize and respond to these kinds of situations. Users should understand what constitutes secure information and know in what circumstances, if any, it should be revealed to other people.

Users should also have a good understanding of the technical support process, so that it cannot be compromised.

Train users in secure behavior. (Image by dotshock © 123rf.com.)

Users should learn always to lock their workstations and mobile devices when leaving them unattended. This helps prevent so-called "lunchtime attacks," where an attacker gets access to an account via an open desktop. This could allow someone to masquerade as the user—sending email or starting IM conversations under their user name. Windows can be locked by pressing **`START+L`** or by selecting the option from Start. You can also set the display properties to use a password-protected screen saver to time out the desktop after so many minutes of inactivity. Users should also take care when entering a password or PIN in the presence of others.

In terms of physical security, employees need to be trained to be confident enough to challenge unrecognized people or those without an appropriate security badge. Care should be taken when moving between areas not to leave security doors open or unlocked.

Business Continuity

Most organizations are reliant to a greater or lesser extent on the availability of their apps and data to continue trading. Many are also reliant on the continued availability of services, such as cloud storage or apps, that are used within their organization. Without continuous access to these data and apps, whether held on-premises on in the cloud, organizations cannot function properly. There can be a significant cost implication for an organization during an outage. Consequently, it is important that you understand possible risks and common mitigations.

Fault Tolerance and Contingency Planning

To help protect against losing access to a computer system when a component fails, you must implement **fault tolerance**. Fault tolerant systems are those that contain additional components to help avoid **single points of failure**. Business continuity plans will start with analysis of business processes and assets to identify critical workflows and resources plus vulnerabilities in those systems. These vulnerabilities can be mitigated by creating **contingency plans** and resources that allow the system to be resilient to failures and unexpected outages. Most contingency plans depend on providing **redundancy** at both the component and system level. If a component or system is not available, redundancy means that the service can **failover** to the backup either seamlessly or with minimum interruption.

Contingency planning does not just involve hardware systems. You might put in place plans for staff to adopt different working procedures, by temporarily using pen-and-paper records rather than a computer system for instance.

Data Redundancy

Combining hard disks into an array of disks can help to avoid service unavailability due to one or more disks failing. The **Redundant Array of Independent Disks (RAID)** standard has evolved to offer a variety of fault tolerant solutions. Different RAID solutions are defined in numbered levels. Two of the most common levels use redundancy solutions called mirroring and striping:

- RAID 1—known also as disk mirroring. RAID 1 uses two disks. Each write operation is performed on both disks so that one is a mirror of the other. Read operations can use either disk. If one of the disks fails, the array will continue to work.
- RAID 5—known as striping with parity. At least three disks are combined into a single logical drive. Data is written in stripes across all disks in the set. A calculation is performed to determine what is known as **parity** information. The parity data is written to a different disk with each write operation. In the event of a single disk failure, the parity information in each stripe of data is used to determine the missing data. If a second disk fails however, then the whole array will fail.

RAID is not a substitute for backups. A disaster, such as a fire, that destroys the whole array will result in total data loss without a backup. Refer back to Unit 4.4 for more information about backup procedures.

Network Redundancy

Without a network connection, a server is not of much use. As network cards are cheap, it is commonplace for a server to have multiple cards (adapter fault tolerance). Multiple adapters can be configured to work together (adapter teaming). This provides fault tolerance—if one adapter fails, the network connection will not be lost—and can also provide **load balancing** (connections can be spread between the cards).

Network cabling should be designed to allow for **multiple paths** between the various servers, so that during a failure of one part of the network, the rest remains operational (**redundant connections**). Routers are great fault tolerant devices, because they can communicate system failures and IP packets can be routed via an alternate device.

Power Redundancy

Network appliances and servers require a stable power supply to operate. Electrical events such as voltage spikes or surges can crash computers and network appliances, while loss of power from brownouts or blackouts will cause equipment to fail. **Power redundancy** means deploying systems to ensure that equipment is protected against these events and that network operations can either continue uninterrupted or be recovered quickly.

- Dual power supplies—enterprise servers and networking equipment are often provisioned with two power supply units so that if one fails, it does not cause power loss.
- Redundant circuits—critical infrastructure might provision multiple power circuits so that if one fails, there will not be total power loss across all systems.
- Uninterruptible Power Supply (UPS)—a UPS is a large battery that can continue to provide power to connected devices for a few or possibly tens of minutes in the event of building power loss.
- Backup power generator—as UPS batteries cannot provide power indefinitely, they will not be able to maintain service during an extended period of building power loss. A local power generator provides redundancy for this sort of eventuality.

Site Redundancy and Replication

To guard against these risks, you must consider implementing service and data **replication** between multiple data centers. Replication is the process of synchronizing data between servers and potentially between sites. This replication might be real-time or bundled into batches for periodic synchronization.

Disaster Recovery

Business continuity and contingency plans put systems and working methods in place to be resilient to failure. **Disaster recovery** has a different emphasis; it creates workflows and resources to use when a specific disaster scenario affects the organization. A disaster could be anything from a loss of power or failure of a minor component to man-made or natural disasters, such as fires, earthquakes, or acts of terrorism. For each high-risk scenario, the organization should develop a plan identifying tasks, resources, and responsibilities for responding to the disaster.

Prioritization

In a large-scale disaster, numerous systems that the company depends upon could fail. After a disaster, resources are likely to be scarce and time pressures severe. Consequently, disaster recovery plans should identify priorities for restoring particular systems first. This process has to be conditioned by dependencies between different systems. The servers running the website front-end might not be able to operate effectively if the servers running the database are not available.

Data Restoration

If a system goes down, there may be data loss. Data can either be restored from backup or by switching over to another system to which data has been replicated. It is vital that the integrity of the data be checked before user access is re-enabled. If the data is corrupt or the database system is not working properly, trying to add more data to it could result in even more severe problems.

Restoring Access

Once the integrity of the failover or restored system has been verified, you can re-enable user access and start processing transactions again. You might try to restrict user numbers initially, so that the system can be monitored and verified as working normally.

Review Questions / Module 5 / Unit 1 / Security Concerns

Answer these questions to test what you have learned in this unit. You can review the model answers at the end of the book.

1) Which property of secure information is compromised by snooping?
2) An attacker has used a rogue access point to intercept traffic passing between wireless clients and the wired network segment. What type of attack is this?
3) What type of access mechanism is MOST vulnerable to a replay attack?
4) Which specific attack uses a botnet to threaten availability?
5) What does AAA stand for?
6) Why should a security policy instruct users not to reveal their password to technical support staff?
7) How might someone masquerade as someone else when using email or Instant Messaging?
8) In considering availability concerns, what use might a lockable faceplate on a server-class computer be?
9) What are the three main areas where redundancy should be provisioned?
10) Why is prioritization a critical task for disaster recovery?

Module 5 / Unit 2
Using Best Practices

Objectives

On completion of this unit, you will be able to:

- Describe basic principles for hardening computer systems against attack.
- Distinguish types of malware and use anti-malware software.
- Identify spam and phishing threats.
- Install software patches and updates from secure sources.

Syllabus Objectives and Content Examples

This unit covers the following exam domain objectives and content examples:

- 6.2 Explain methods to secure devices and best practices.
  Securing devices (mobile/workstation) (Anti-virus/Anti-malware, Changing default passwords, Enabling passwords, Patching/updates) • Device use best practices (Software sources, Validating legitimate sources, Researching legitimate sources, OEM websites vs. third-party websites, Removal of unwanted software, Removal of unnecessary software, Removal of malicious software)

Securing Devices

Device **hardening** refers to a set of policies that make mobile and workstation computers and network appliances more secure. Some options for hardening mobile devices, configuring a screen lock out and encrypting data for instance, were discussed earlier. Some other typical hardening policies are as follows:

- **Anti-virus/anti-malware**—malware is software that aims to damage a computer or steal information from it. Anti-malware software can detect the presence of malware and prevent it from running. This is discussed in more detail later in this unit.

- **Patching/updates**—OS files, driver software, and firmware may be exploitable by malware in the same way as applications software. It is important to keep computers and other devices configured with up-to-date patches and firmware.

- **Enabling passwords**—most operating systems *allow* the use of an account *without* a password, PIN, or screen lock, but this does not mean it is a good idea to do so. It makes the device highly exploitable in the event of theft. It could also allow other users to impersonate the user. All computing devices should be protected by requiring the user to input credentials to gain access.

- **Default/weak passwords**—network devices such as wireless access points, switches, and routers ship with a default management password, such as "password," "admin," or the device vendor's name. These should be changed on installation. Also, the password used should be a strong one—most devices do not enforce complexity rules so the onus is on the user to choose something secure.

  It is now standard practice for devices to be shipped with individually configured default credentials, usually placed on a label on the device or in the instruction manual, or for devices to require a change of password as part of their initial setup.

- **Disabling unused features**—any features, services, or network protocols that are not used should be disabled. This reduces the attack surface of a network device or OS. **Attack surface** means the range of things that an attacker could possibly exploit in order to compromise the device. It is particularly important to disable unused administration interfaces (and to secure those that are used).

- **Removing unwanted/unnecessary software**—new computers ship with a large amount of pre-installed software, often referred to as **bloatware**. These applications should be removed if they are not going to be used. Similarly, if an application has been installed in the past but is no longer necessary, it should be removed too.

Most device exploits depend on the attacker having physical access to the unit, though some vulnerabilities can be exploited over a network link.

Malware

Malware is a catch-all term to describe malicious software threats and tools designed to vandalize or compromise computer systems.

Computer Viruses

Computer **viruses** are programs designed to *replicate* and spread amongst computers. Viruses are classified by the different ways they can infect the computer. For example:

- **Program viruses**—these are sequences of code that insert themselves into another executable program or script**.** When the application is executed, the virus code becomes active.
- **Macro viruses**—these viruses affect Microsoft Office documents exploiting the macro programming language Visual Basic for Applications (VBA) used to automate tasks.
- **Worms**—memory-resident viruses that replicate over network resources, such as email, by exploiting faults in software programs.

A virus's **payload** can be programmed to perform many different actions, especially in the case of program and macro viruses. A virus payload may be programmed to display silly messages, corrupt or delete documents, damage system files, or to install some sort of spyware to snoop on the user.

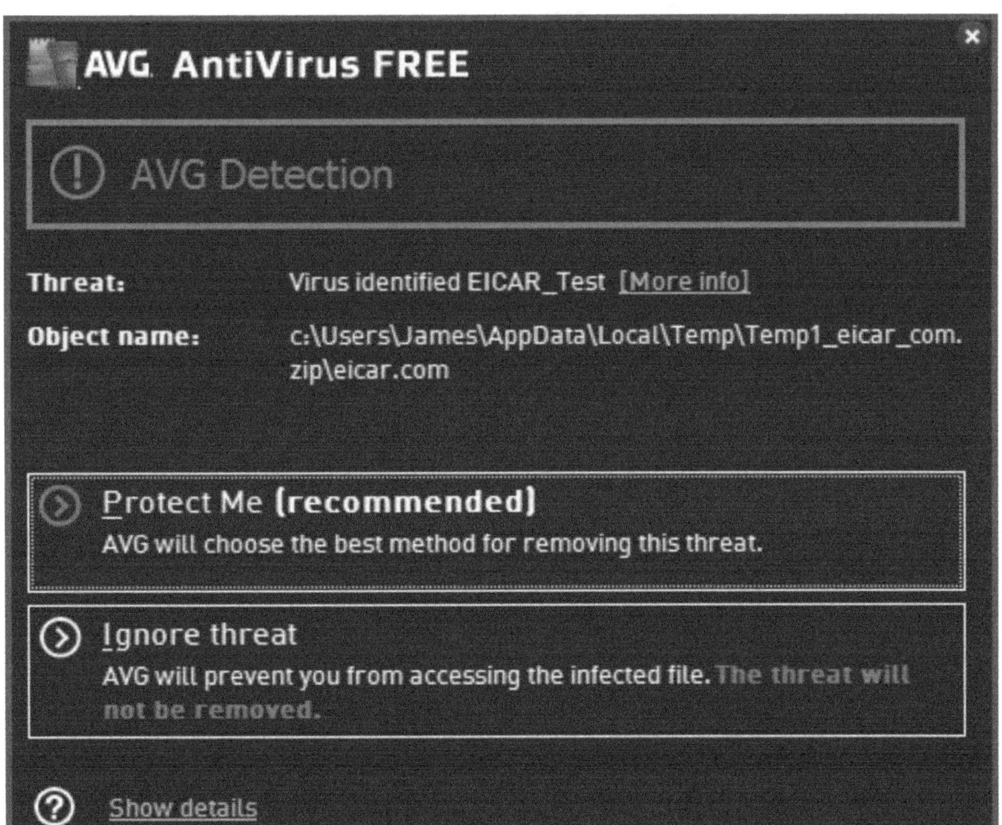

The EICAR test string is used to test anti-virus software. If the string appears in a file the software should detect it as a threat.

Most viruses must be activated by the user and thus need some means to *trick* the user into opening the infected file. **Email attachment viruses**, usually program or macro viruses in an attached file, often use the infected host's electronic address book to **spoof** the sender's address when replicating. For example, Jim's computer is infected with a virus and has Alan's email address in his address book. When Sue gets an infected email apparently sent by Alan, it is the virus on Jim's computer that has sent the message.

Malware can also be distributed on removable media, such as CD/DVD or USB flash drives. Such media may give a virus an opportunity to infect the PC if the user chooses to allow the infected application to run via its AutoPlay default action.

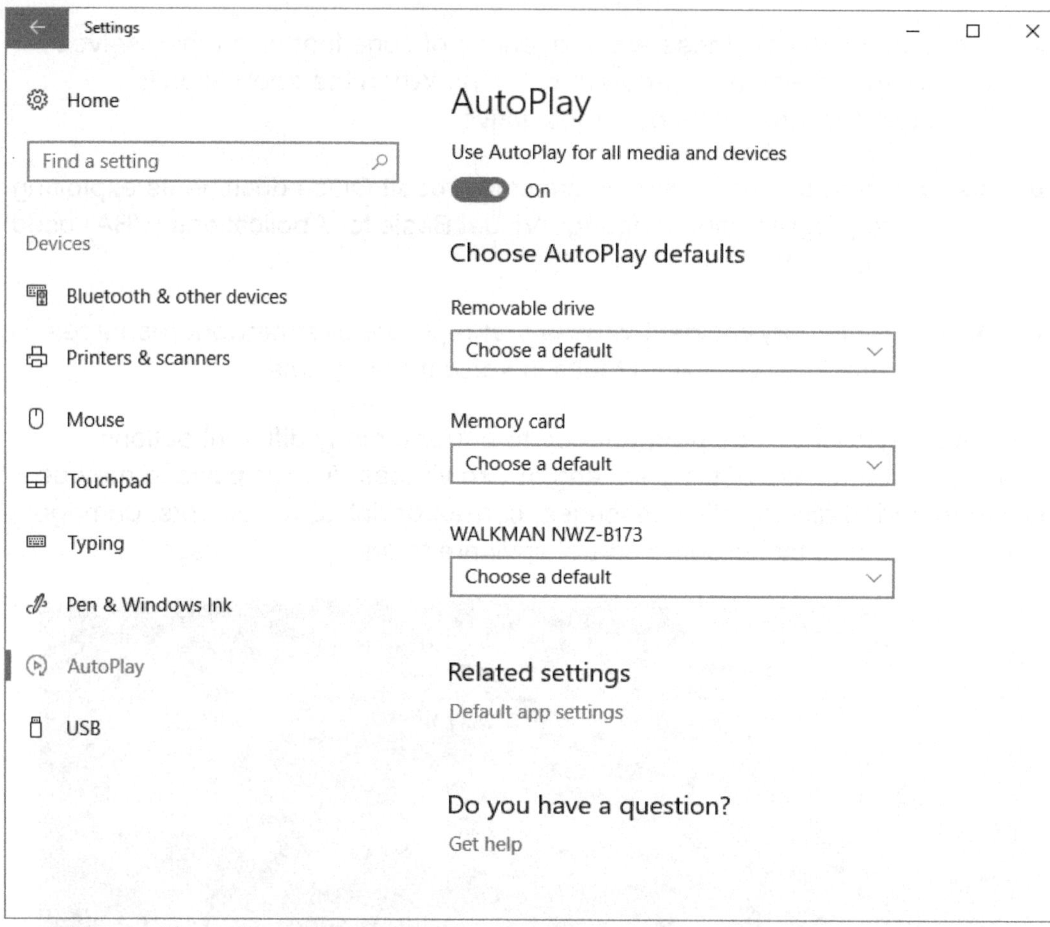

Removable media can be configured to AutoRun or prompt when it is connected to the computer—do not run untrusted programs. Screenshot used with permission from Microsoft.

Windows' User Account Control (UAC) and AutoPlay configuration settings help mitigate the chances of malware infection as the user has to explicitly confirm any attempt to install or modify software.

Viruses can also use **application exploits** to replicate without user intervention, in some circumstances. The most common scenario is for the malware to be uploaded to a compromised website and to try to trigger exploits in the clients visiting the site via vulnerabilities in the OS, the web browser, or web browser plug-in. This is referred to as a **drive-by download**.

Trojans

Other types of malware are not classed as viruses as they do not necessarily try to make copies of themselves. They represent an even greater security threat than viruses however. A **Trojan Horse**, often simply called a **Trojan**, is a program that pretends to be something else. For example, you might download what you think is a new game, but when you run it, it deletes files on your hard drive; or when you install what you think is a screensaver, the program includes a hidden process that sends your saved passwords to another person. There is also the case of **rogueware** or **scareware** fake anti-virus, where a web pop-up claims to have detected viruses on the computer and prompts the user to initiate a full scan which installs the attacker's Trojan.

Many Trojans function as **backdoor** applications. Once the Trojan backdoor is installed, it allows the attacker to access the PC, upload files, and install software on it. This could allow the attacker to use the computer in a **botnet**, to launch Distributed Denial of Service (DDoS) attacks or mass-mail spam. Trojans are also used by attackers to conceal their actions as attacks appear to come from the corrupted computer system.

Spyware

Spyware is a program that monitors user activity and sends the information to someone else. It may be installed with or without the user's knowledge. Aggressive spyware or Trojans known as "key loggers" actively attempt to steal confidential information; capturing a credit card number by recording key strokes entered into a web form for example. Another spyware technique is to spawn browser pop-up windows to try to direct the user to other websites, often of dubious provenance.

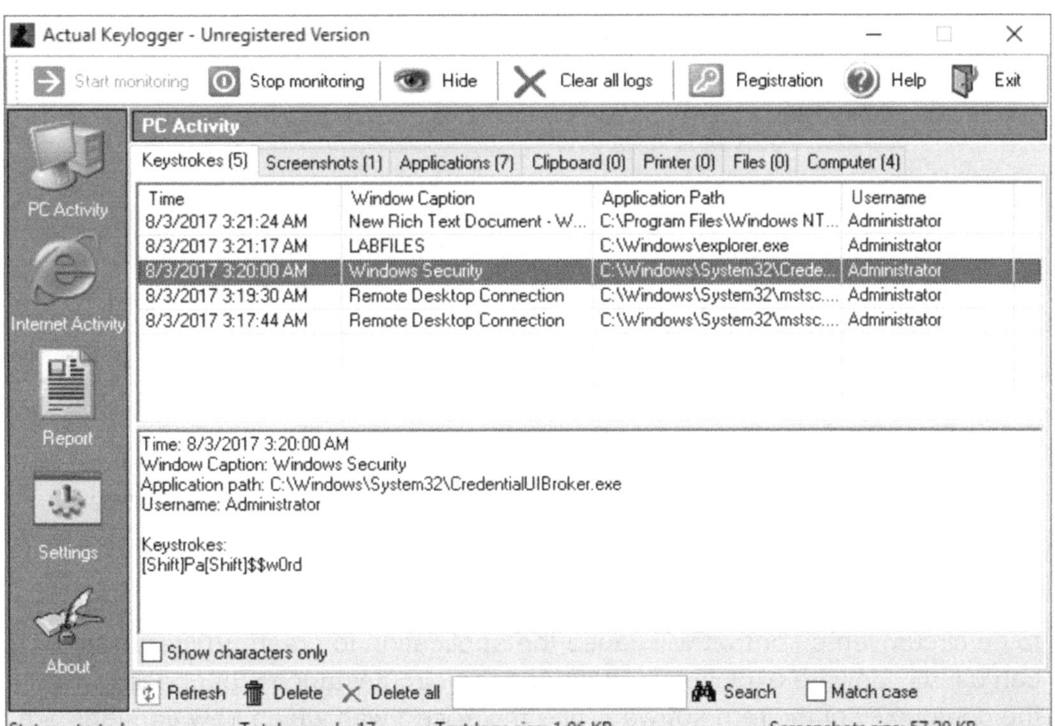

Actual Keylogger—Windows software that can run in the background to monitor different kinds of computer activity (opening and closing programs, browsing websites, recording keystrokes, and capturing screenshots [actualkeylogger.com]).

Ransomware

Ransomware is a type of malware that tries to extort money from the victim. One class of ransomware will display threatening messages, such as suggesting that Windows must be reactivated or suggesting that the computer has been locked by the police because it was used to view child pornography or for terrorism. This may block access to the computer by installing a different shell program, but this sort of attack is usually relatively simple to fix. Another class of ransomware attempts to encrypt data files on any fixed, removable, and network drives. If the attack is successful, the user will be unable to access the files without obtaining the private encryption key, which is held by the attacker. If successful, this sort of attack is extremely difficult to mitigate unless the user has up-to-date backups of the encrypted files.

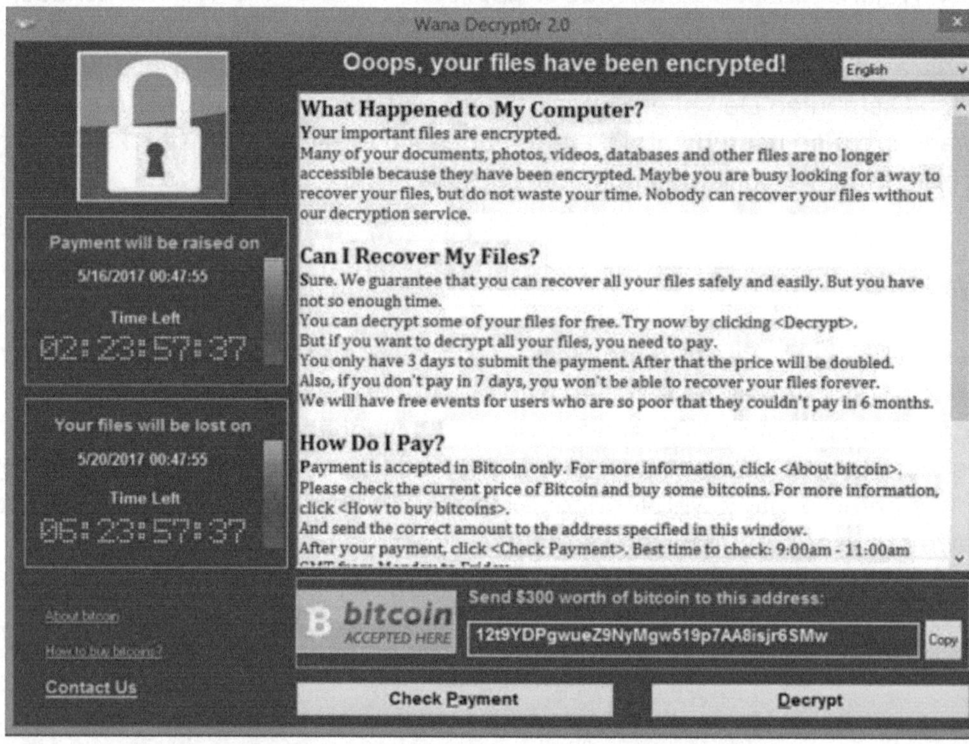

WannaCry ransomware. Wikimedia Public Domain image.

Ransomware uses payment methods such as wire transfer, bitcoin, or premium rate phone lines to allow the attacker to extort money without revealing his or her identity or being traced by local law enforcement.

Operating System Vulnerabilities

Many attacks and types of malware exploit vulnerabilities in OS or application software. Typically, applications such as web servers, web browsers and browser plug-ins, email clients, and databases are targeted.

A vulnerability is a design flaw that can cause the application security system to be circumvented or that will cause the application to crash. Vulnerabilities can usually only be exploited in quite specific circumstances, but because of the complexity of modern software and the speed with which new versions are released to market, almost no software is free from vulnerabilities.

Software vendors release **security updates** (or **patches**) when such vulnerabilities and exploits are identified.

Preventing Malware Infections

There are numerous sources of malware infection. The route by which malware infects a computer is called the **vector**. Some of the main ones are:

- Visiting "unsavory" websites with an unpatched browser, low security settings, and no anti-virus software.
- Opening links in unsolicited email.
- Infection from another compromised machine on the same network.
- Executing a file of unknown provenance—email attachments are still the most popular vector, but others include file sharing sites, websites generally, attachments sent via chat/Instant Messaging, autorun USB sticks and CDs, and so on.
- Becoming victim to a "zero day" exploit. A zero day is some infection mechanism that is was unknown to software and anti-virus vendors. This means that there may be a substantial delay before the vendors can develop a software patch or anti-virus detection signatures that can mitigate the exploit mechanism.

A number of steps can be taken to reduce the risk and impact of malware infection.

- Carry out regular backups that allow data to be recovered, in case of loss due to a virus infection.
- Apply operating system and application security patches.
- Install and use security (anti-virus) software. This must be kept up to date with updated **signatures** (or **definitions**), since viruses and other malware are continually being developed and the latest signatures offer the most protection.
- Select security software that scans automatically (on-access). This provides much more reliable protection against web and email attachment threats.
- Do not log on with administrative privileges except where necessary. Limit administrative privileges to a few, selected accounts. Choose strong passwords for these accounts, and keep them secure.
- Exercise care before installing new software, downloading files from the web, opening file attachments, or clicking links in email messages.

Anti-virus Software

Anti-virus is software that can detect malware and prevent it from executing. The primary means of detection is to use a database of known virus patterns, called **definitions**, **signatures**, or **patterns**. Another technique is to use **heuristic** identification. "Heuristic" means that the software uses knowledge of the sort of things that viruses do to try to spot (and block) virus-like behavior.

Security software tends to come as either personal security suites, designed to protect a single host, or network security suites, designed to be centrally managed from a server console. Most anti-virus software is designed for Windows PCs and networks, as these are the systems targeted by most virus writers, but software is available for Linux and Apple macOS as well.

Some of the major vendors are Symantec (including the Norton brand), McAfee, Avast/AVG, Trend Micro, Sophos, Kaspersky, ESET, and BitDefender.

AVG Anti-Virus FREE edition.

On-access Scanning

Almost all security software is now configured to scan **on-access**. This reduces performance somewhat but is essential to maintaining effective protection against malware. When a user or system process accesses a file, the anti-virus software scans the file and blocks access if it detects anything suspicious.

Most types of software can also scan system memory to detect worms and scan email file attachments, removable drives, and network drives. Many scanners can also detect websites with malicious scripts or coding.

When configuring anti-virus software, it is vital to configure the proper exceptions. Real-time scanning of some system files and folders can cause serious performance problems.

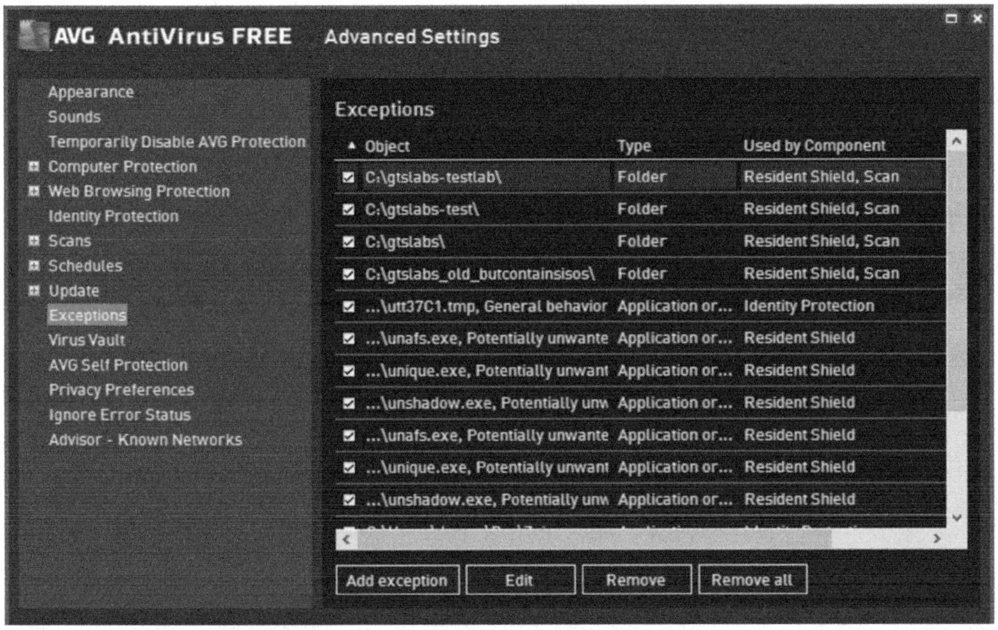

Configure file types and exceptions for on-access scanning so as not to impact PC performance adversely.

Scheduled Scans

As well as on-access scanning, you can initiate a whole computer scan. This might be configured to inspect more file types than on-access scanning. As this can impact performance, such scans are best run when the computer is not being used intensively.

Scanning the computer for threats.

Scans can also be scheduled to run automatically.

Quarantining and Remediating Infected Systems

Malware such as worms propagate over networks. This means that one of the first actions should be to disconnect the network link.

If a file is infected with a virus, most of the time the anti-virus software will detect the virus and take the appropriate action. You can configure the default action that software should attempt when it discovers malware as part of a scan. You can use anti-virus software to try to **remove** the infection (**cleaning**), **quarantine** the file (the anti-virus software blocks any attempt to open it), or **erase** the file.

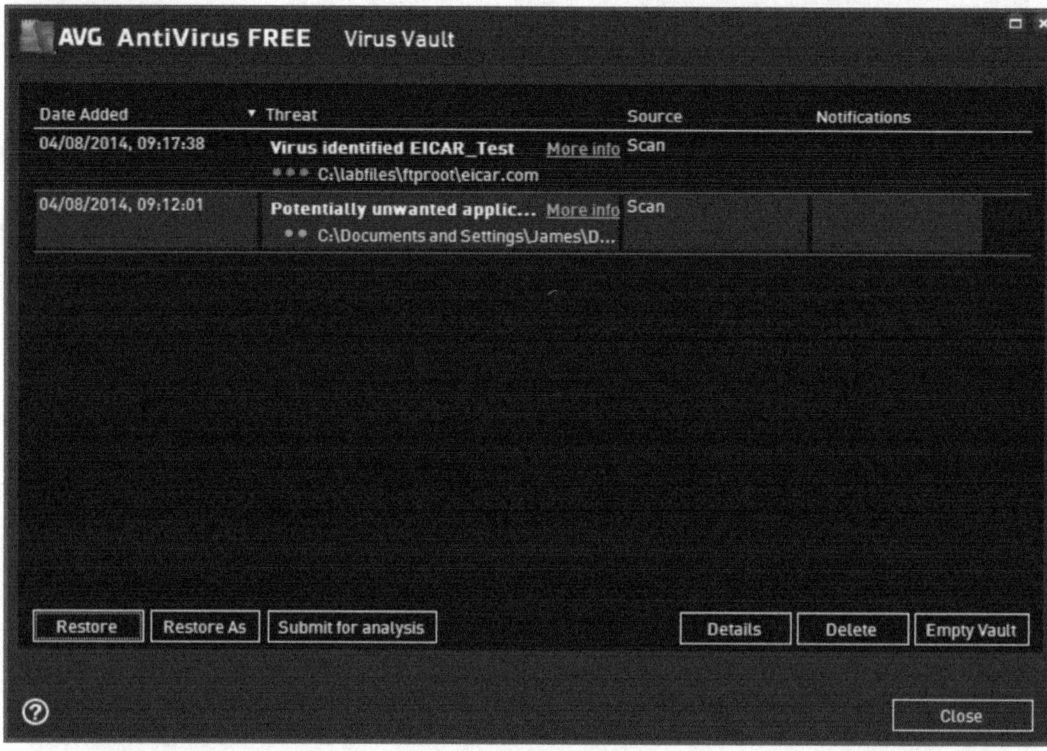

Viewing infected files.

If you cannot clean a file or if the anti-virus software does not detect it and allows the virus to infect the computer, you should get help by **escalating** the problem to a support professional, who will research the virus and identify ways of removing it manually and (possibly) recovering data files.

Windows Defender

Windows 10 is tightly integrated with Windows Defender. This anti-virus and anti-malware software combines with Windows Firewall to help protect your computer from the threats outlined earlier. Microsoft has integrated the two elements in a single, unified app called Windows Defender Security Center.

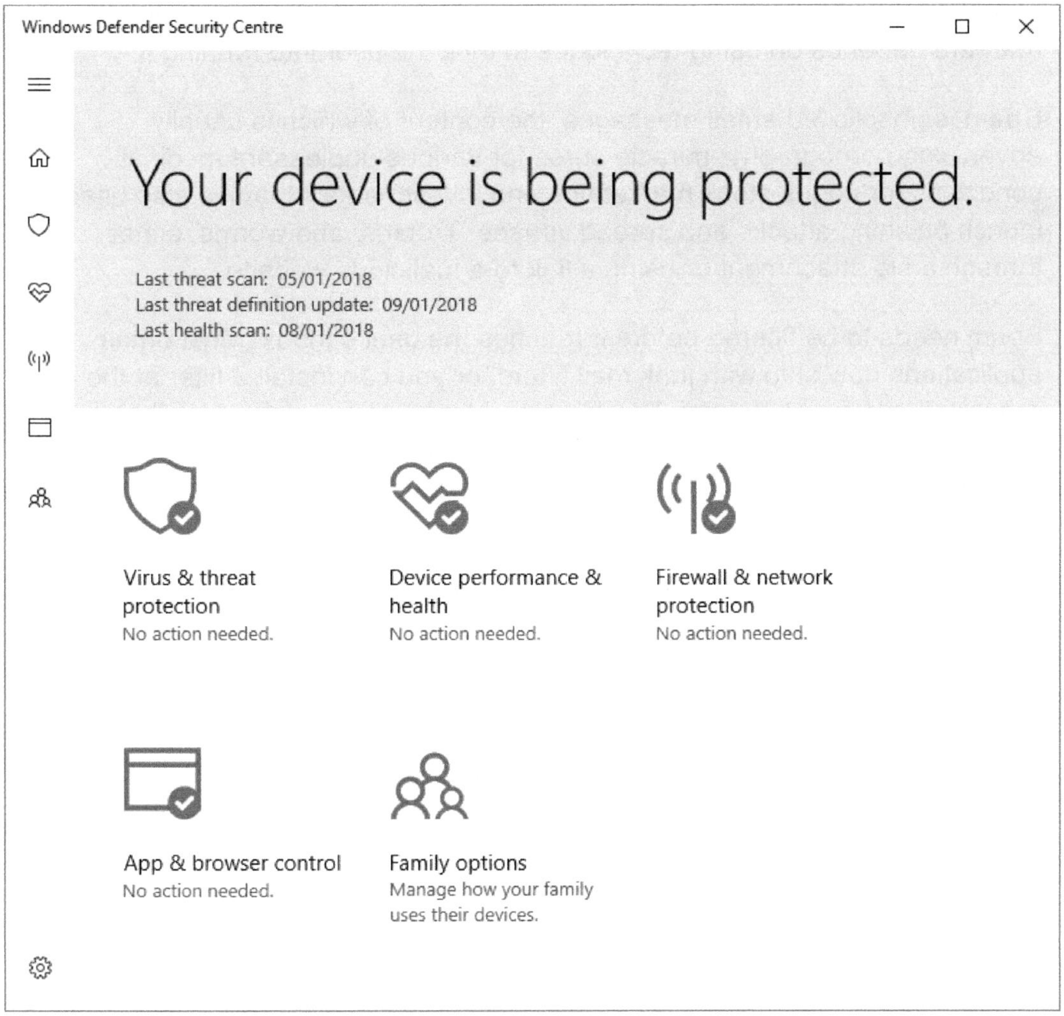

Windows Defender Security Center. Screenshot used with permission from Microsoft.

You can use the tiles in Windows Defender Security Center to access configuration options for the various security features.

Spam

Sometimes a malware writer can exploit a serious vulnerability in an OS or application to execute their malware without the user doing anything. While these exploits are extremely serious, they also tend to be fairly rare, and patches against them are made available quickly. Consequently, a lot of malware depends on using techniques to trick the user into running it.

Spam is unsolicited email messages, the content of which is usually advertising pornography, miracle cures for various unpleasant medical conditions, or bogus stock market tips and investments. Spam is also used to launch phishing attacks and spread viruses, Trojans, and worms, either through a file attachment or using a link to a malicious website.

Spam needs to be filtered before it reaches the user's inbox. Most email applications now ship with junk mail filters, or you can install a filter at the organization's mail gateway. The main problem with spam filters is that they can block genuine messages too, leading to missed communications. Spammers also develop ways to circumvent filters, such as using images or file attachments.

Consequently, you should learn how to recognize suspicious emails and identify potentially hazardous content.

- Attachments—any type of executable code is potentially hazardous. Legitimate applications should be digitally signed with a trustworthy certificate. Other types of files, including office documents and even images, can be used to try to infect a computer with malware. Often these attacks use some kind of vulnerability discovered in the software application or operating system.

  While performing regular system updates and using anti-malware software will protect against many malicious file attachment threats, you should only open attachments that you were expecting to receive. Unsolicited file attachments should be confirmed with the sender first.

- Hyperlinks—malicious code can also be put on a website to try to infect any visiting computers (a drive-by download). Again, these attacks often depend on exploiting a vulnerability in the browser software or OS. Hyperlinks may also be disguised and try to divert you from a real website to a fake one with the intention of stealing your credentials.

  You should inspect the web address used in a link carefully. It is always safer to retype the address in the browser address bar, rather than clicking the link.

Phishing

Phishing is a technique for tricking a user into revealing confidential information by requesting it in an official-looking email, perhaps pretending to come from a bank or online store. The email will contain a link to a counterfeit site or to a valid site that the attacker has been able to compromise. The user is prompted to input confidential data, such as online bank account numbers and passwords, which are then stolen.

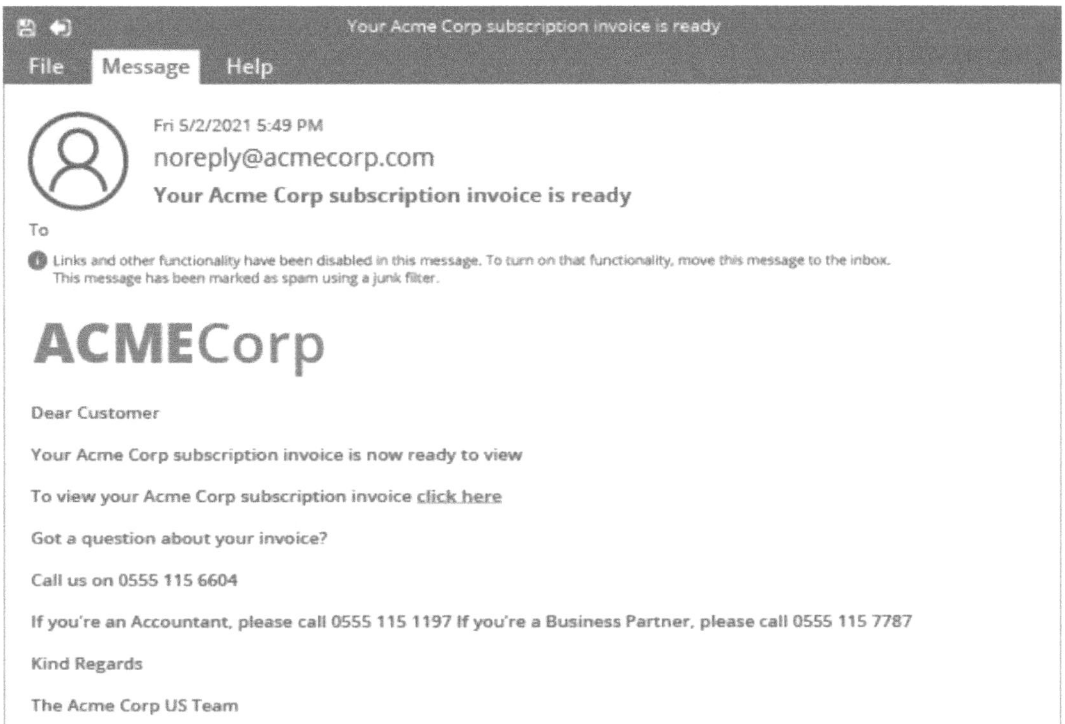

If a phishing message is displayed with its intended formatting, it can look like a genuine request from a company that the user may well know and do business with.

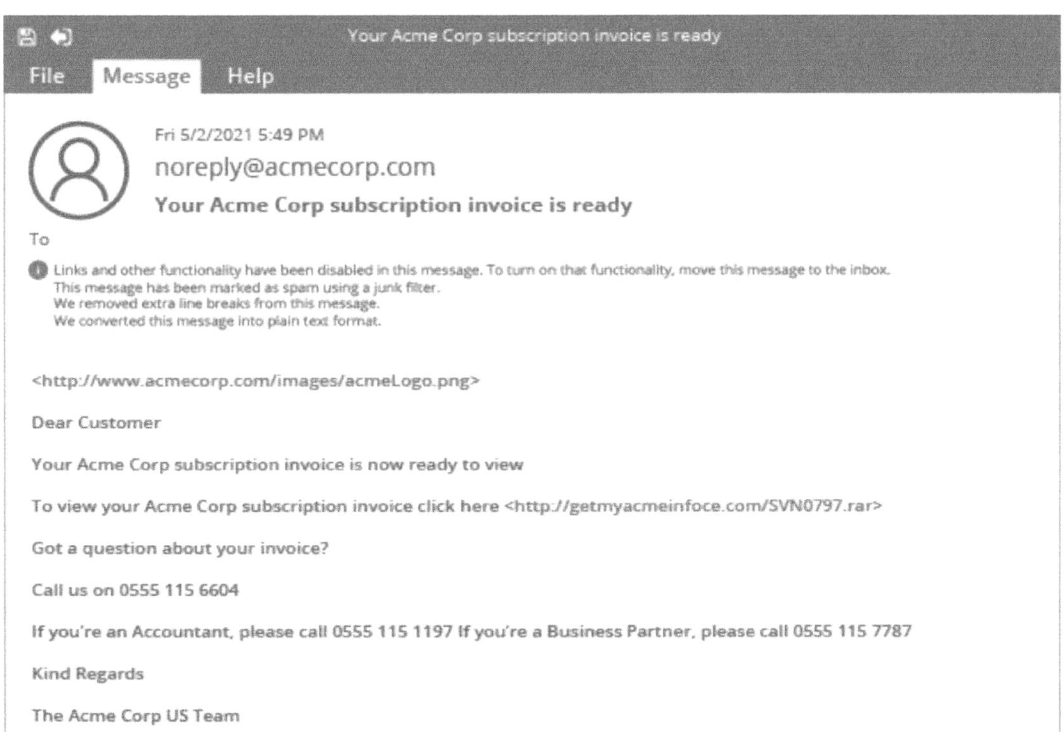

With formatting stripped out, the hyperlink is shown not to point to the expected domain.

Another technique is to spawn a pop-up window when a user visits a genuine banking site to try to trick them into entering their credentials through the pop-up. This sort of attack often employs a technique called "cross-site scripting," where the attacker uses a flaw in one website to attack or snoop upon another.

A related attack, called **pharming**, attempts to redirect web traffic to a counterfeit page, usually by corrupting the way the computer resolves the website name used in the web address to the IP address of a particular server.

Anti-spam

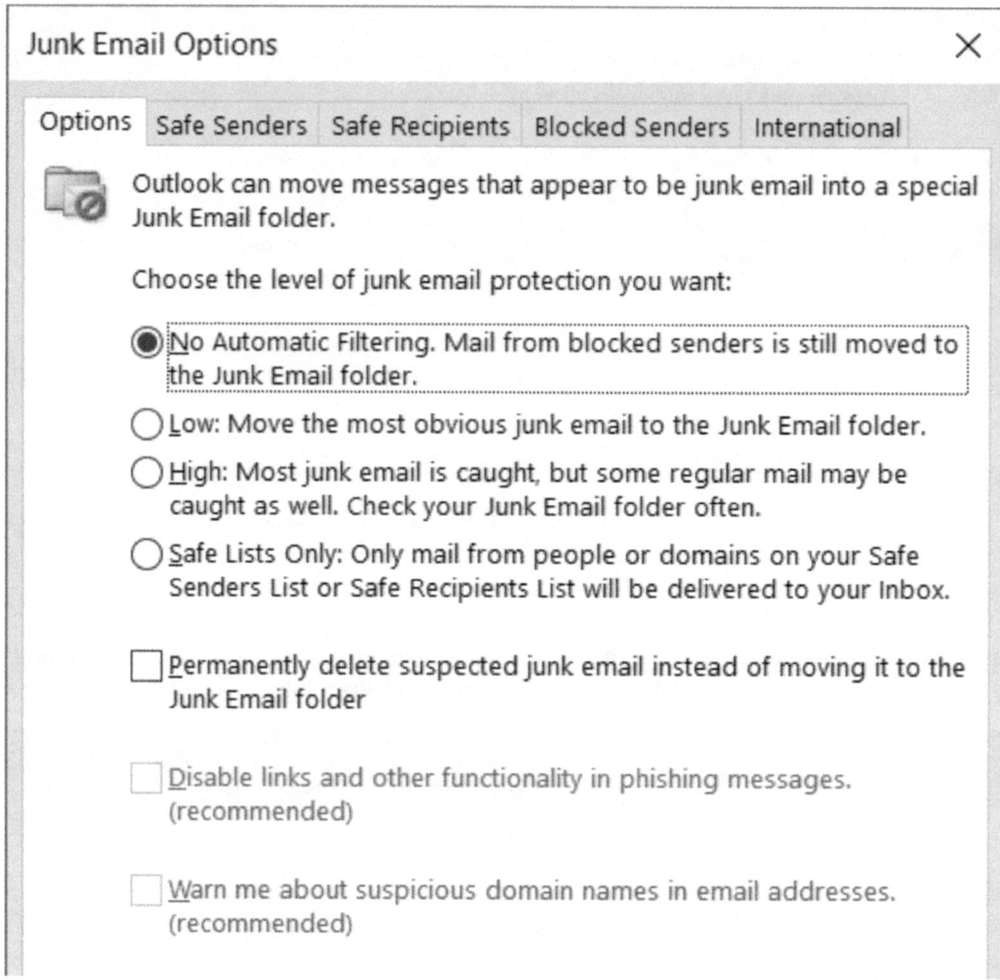

Configuring anti-spam options in Microsoft Outlook. Screenshot used with permission from Microsoft.

Most email software comes with a built-in filter for junk email. You can typically set how aggressive the filter is in terms of blocking messages, configure sender "whitelists" and "blacklists," and determine whether spam is quarantined (moved automatically to a junk mail folder) or deleted.

Using high protection settings will probably increase the number of false positives (genuine messages marked as junk); decreasing the protection level will increase the number of false negatives (junk messages not marked as spam).

Another important option is disabling links, scripting, and attachments in email marked as suspicious. This helps to defeat phishing attacks and attempts to infect the computer with viruses.

The same sort of functionality is now starting to be incorporated in Instant Messaging and Voice over IP (VoIP) applications. Junk IM messages are sometimes referred to as SPIM.

Authentication presents another challenge for secure communications. It is possible to spoof an email address so that it appears to come from someone else. IM and VoIP applications generally have better protection against this, but it can still be difficult to verify the actual identity of a contact.

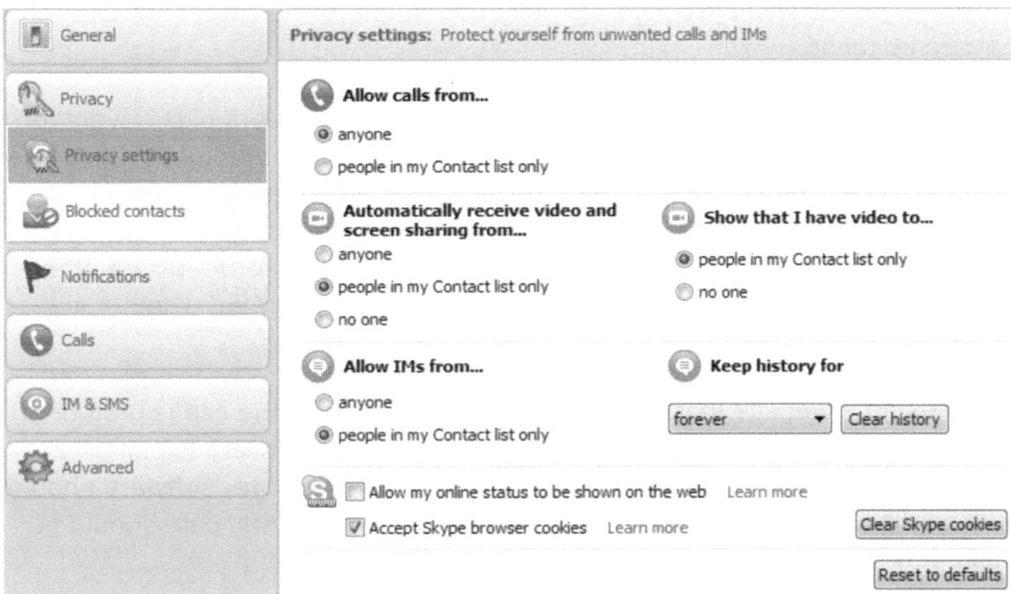

Configuring privacy options and blocked contacts in Skype VoIP software. Screenshot used with permission from Microsoft.

Email and IM/VoIP can be used with digital certificates to prove identity and encrypt communications, but both people have to be using the same system of digital certificates. Consequently, they are not in widespread use.

Also, if a virus or Trojan has infected a user's computer, it can easily send messages while masquerading as that user.

Even if you think you know the sender—do not open links or attachments in messages if you were not expecting to receive them.

Software Sources and Patch Management

When installing new software applications or drivers, it is important to obtain the setup files from a **legitimate source**. Reputable sources include:

- Vendor app stores (for example, Windows Store, Google Play Store, Apple App Store).
- Merchant app stores, such as Amazon Appstore.
- Authorized resellers, Original Equipment Manufacturer (OEM) vendors, and managed service providers. If in any doubt, check the reseller or OEM's accreditation.

There are third-party sites claiming to host up-to-date drivers plus drivers for systems that have been "abandoned" by the original manufacturer. If you need to use a driver from a site such as this, try to research it as much as you can. Search for references to the site on the web to find out if anyone has posted warnings about it. If you trust the site overall, check for a forum where other users might have tried a specific driver package and indicated whether it is legitimate or not.

When using a website to install software, always ensure the site is protected and identified by a valid digital certificate and that the software is being downloaded over a secure HTTPS connection. Ideally, driver software should also be digitally signed by the vendor, and the vendor's certificate should be trusted by your computer.

Patch Management

Patch management is an important maintenance task to ensure that PCs operate reliably and securely. A patch or update is a file containing replacement system or application files. The replacement files fix some sort of coding problem in the original file. The fix could be made to improve reliability, security, or performance.

A **Service Pack (SP)** is a collection of previous updates but may also contain new features and functionality. While SPs are not paid for, they do require you to follow the upgrade process to ensure that software and, to a lesser extent, hardware will be compatible. You should also make a backup before applying a service pack. Service packs can be installed via Windows Update, downloaded from Microsoft's website, or shipped on disc. The later manufacturing releases of the setup media tend to include the latest service pack.

Microsoft products are subject to their support lifecycle policy. Windows versions are given five years of mainstream support and five years of extended support, during which only security updates are shipped. Support is contingent on the latest Service Pack being applied. Non-updated versions of Windows are supported for 24 months following the release of the SP.

Windows Update

Windows Update is the website (update.microsoft.com) that Windows uses to manage updates. Windows Update hosts security patches to fix vulnerabilities in Windows and its associated software plus optional software and hardware updates to add or change features or drivers.

Only use updates from Microsoft's website. Similarly, only use updates for third-party software applications and device drivers from the vendor's website. Software and drivers hosted on other sites could be infected with malware.

You can view and configure the Windows Update settings by using the Settings app. Select the **Update & Security** category, and then click the **Windows Update** tab.

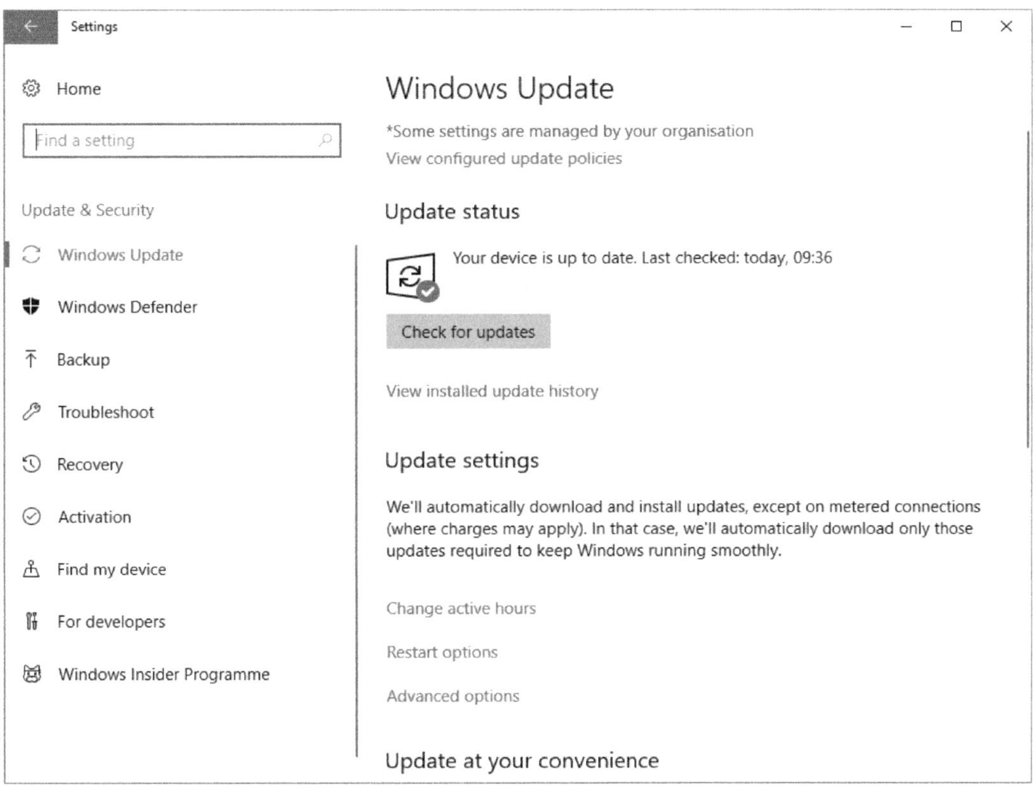

Windows Update. Screenshot used with permission from Microsoft.

In the screenshot, you can see that some settings are managed by the organization. This is typical in large organizational networks where it is important to exert more control over the update process.

You can configure Windows Update to always install updates or to check for approval first and set a schedule for downloading and installing them. You can also view the update history, which is useful if you need to confirm whether a specific update has been installed.

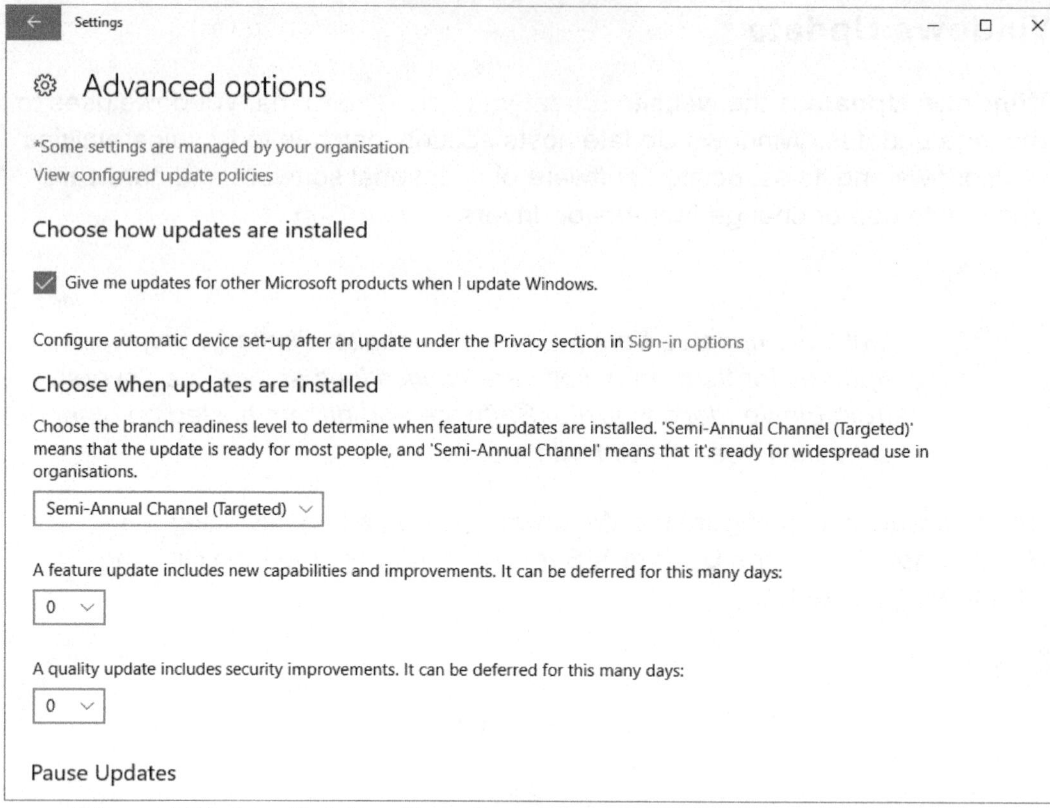

Advanced Windows Update settings. Screenshot used with permission from Microsoft.

Windows Update Scheduling and Frequency

Security and critical updates, known as **quality updates**, should normally be installed automatically without deferring them. If updates are not installed promptly, there is a greater risk of the computer being infected by malware. For example, Windows Defender updates are released daily.

Feature updates introduce new functionality, and therefore pose a small risk to compatibility with other apps or drivers. For enterprise networks, it is best practice to test feature updates before deploying them, but for small networks and home users this is impractical.

Microsoft recognizes this issue and have responded by making updates available in a number of different servicing channels. These are:

- **Windows Insider Program**—enables users to get early access to feature updates. Not recommended for most production machines.
- **Semi-annual channel (targeted)**—updates are ready for most people. The only configurable option (aside from Insider Program) for Windows 10 Home editions. Users receive feature updates as soon as they're released.
- **Semi-annual channel**—updates are ready for widespread use and have been in use for a period of time by those on the semi-annual channel (targeted). There is less risk posed by updating this way. This option is available for Windows 10 Pro and Enterprise editions.

- **Long term servicing channel**—only available for Windows 10 Enterprise editions on the LTSB channel. This defers feature updates for a significant period of time and is ideal for specialist devices, such as ATMs, running embedded versions of Windows.

For further information, read the following website page: docs.microsoft.com/en-us/windows/deployment/update/waas-overview#servicing-channels.

Application Updates

Software applications, especially those with browser plug-ins, may also need updating with the latest patches. Applications can contain security vulnerabilities in the same way as the OS. In fact, applications are targeted more aggressively than Windows itself as attackers recognize that they are less likely to be patched than the OS. Microsoft applications, such as Microsoft Office, can be updated as part of Windows Update. Applications from other vendors either use their own tools to detect and install new versions or rely on the user to check manually.

Updating Anti-virus Software

It is particularly important that anti-virus software (or any other type of malware-blocking software) be updated regularly. Two types of updates are generally necessary:

- Virus definitions/patterns/signatures—this is information about new viruses. These updates may be made available daily or even hourly.
- Scan engine/components—this fixes problems or makes improvements to the scan software itself.

There is usually an option within the software program to download and install these updates automatically.

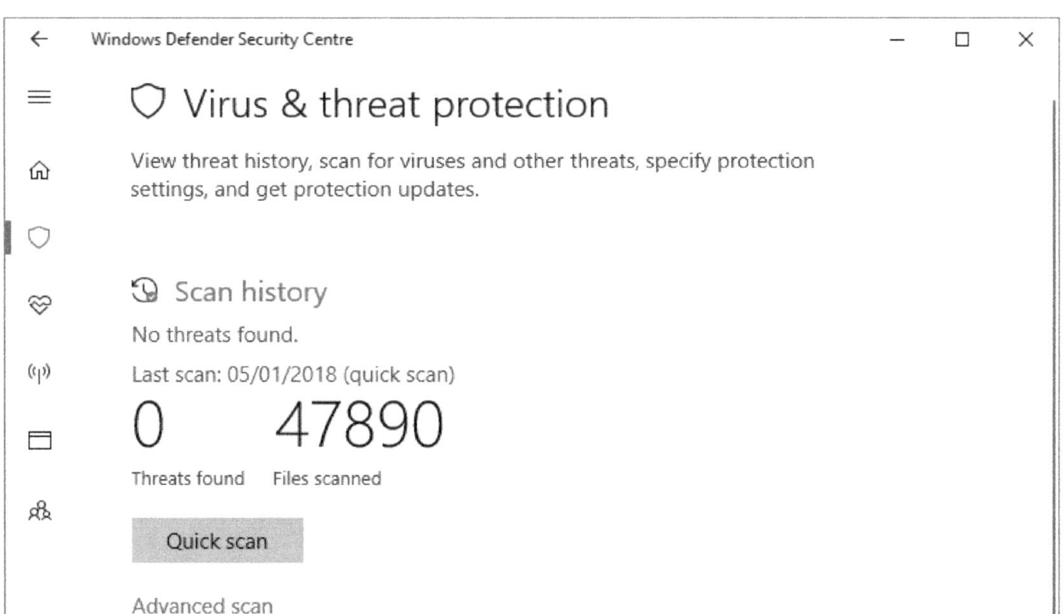

Configuring Windows Defender. Screenshot used with permission from Microsoft.

Driver Updates

Windows ships with a number of core and third-party hardware drivers. Updates for these devices can be obtained via Windows Update, though they will be listed as optional updates and might not install automatically. Most of the time, third-party drivers should be obtained from the vendor's website. To update, you download the driver files and install them using the supplied setup program or extract them manually and save them to the hard disk. You can then use the device's property dialog in Device Manager to update the driver. You can either scan for the update automatically or point the tool to the updated version you saved to the hard disk.

Review Questions / Module 5 / Unit 2 / Using Best Practices

Answer these questions to test what you have learned in this unit. You can review the model answers at the end of the book.

1) Part of host hardening is to reduce the attack surface. What configuration changes does reducing the attack surface involve?

2) What is the main difference between virus and worm malware?

3) How might malware hosted on a website be able to infect your computer simply by your browsing the site?

4) How might spyware be able to steal a password?

5) What type of malware is being described? The malware encrypts the user's documents folder and any attached removable disks then extorts the user for money to release the encryption key.

6) True or false? Most anti-virus software can remediate a system by blocking access to an infected file but not actually deleting it.

7) What is the main means by which anti-virus software identifies infected files?

8) What are the two main ways that spam might expose recipients to hazardous content?

9) Your friend sent you an email link, which you have opened, and now the browser is asking whether you should install a plug-in to view all the content on the page. Should you proceed?

10) True or false? An OEM site is a reputable source of management software and drivers for a particular system.

Lab 20 / Using Windows Defender and Windows Update

In this lab, you will investigate the Windows Defender anti-malware product bundled with Windows and look at the settings available in the Windows Update client.

You will download an anti-virus test signature called EICAR to trigger a virus alert. Note that EICAR is NOT a virus.

1) If necessary, start your computer and sign in.
2) Click **Start** and then type `Windows Defender` then from the list of results, click **Windows Defender Security Center**.
3) Click **Virus & threat protection**.
4) Click the **Scan now** button to run a quick scan.
5) While the scan is running, open the browser and open the following address:

   `https://secure.eicar.org/eicar_com.zip`
6) In the notification banner at the bottom of the window, click **Save**.
7) Windows Defender will detect the presence of a suspect file. Click the pop-up banner or else click Notifications and then click the message from Windows Defender.

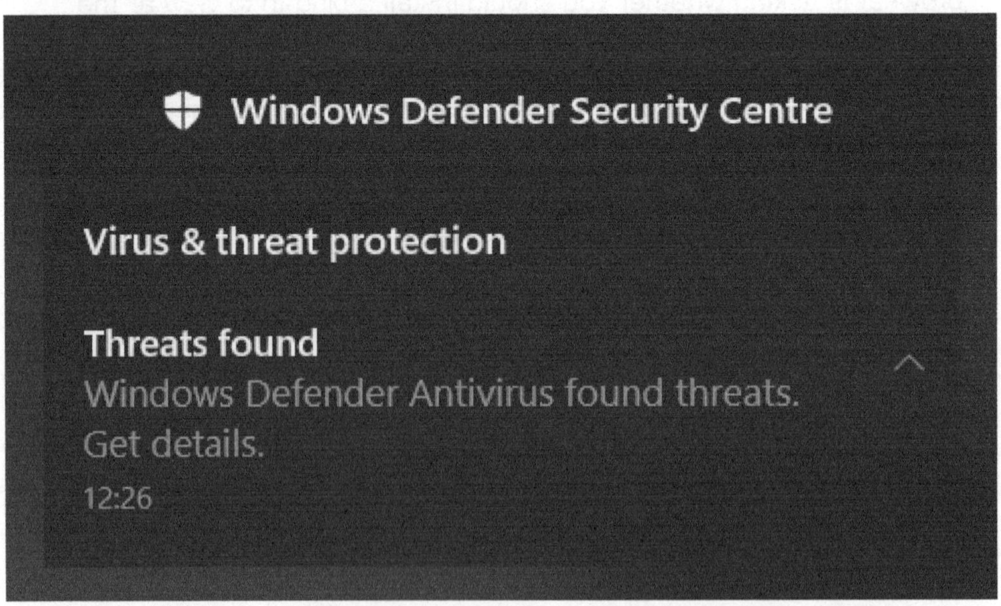

Windows Defender warning. Screenshot used with permission from Microsoft.

8) In the Windows Defender window, you should see the suspicious file.

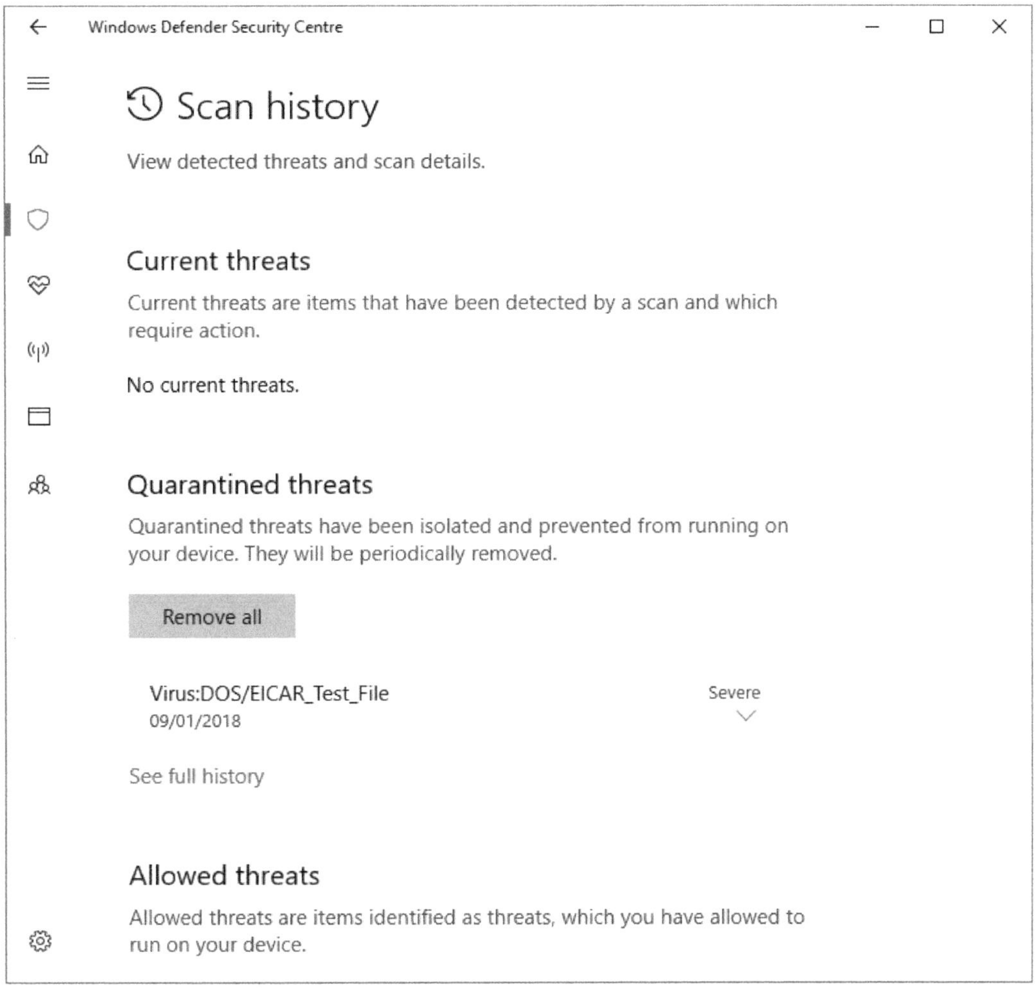

Suspicious file. Screenshot used with permission from Microsoft.

EICAR is not actually a virus. It is a test string that any properly configure anti-virus software should identify as a virus. You can find out more at eicar.org.

9) Click **Remove all** then click **Yes**.

10) Close the browser.

11) In Windows Defender Security Center, click the shield button and then click **Virus & threat protection updates**.

12) Click **Check for updates**. It is likely to be up to date.

13) Close the Windows Defender Security Center window.

14) Open **Settings** and then click **Update & Security**.

15) On the **Windows Update** tab, click **Check for updates**.

16) Click the **View update history link**. Look through the list for any failed updates and check that they have been successfully installed subsequently.

Often when Windows attempts to install multiple updates at the same time, one or two will fail due to file dependencies or locking. Windows will then attempt to reinstall the update later.

17) Click the **Back** button. From the main "Windows Update" page, if there are any optional updates, click the link to view them. Check to see if there are any driver updates included in the list.

18) Optionally, shut down your computer if you are not continuing to use it after this lab.

Module 5 / Unit 3
Using Access Controls

Objectives

On completion of this unit, you will be able to:

- Distinguish between identification, authentication, authorization, and accounting in access control systems.
- Identify different authentication factors and understand their use in providing strong authentication.
- List best practices when choosing passwords.
- Explain how encryption technologies are used for authentication and access control.

Syllabus Objectives and Content Examples

This unit covers the following exam domain objectives and content examples:

- 6.4 Compare and contrast authentication, authorization, accounting, and non-repudiation concepts.
  Authentication (Single factor, Multifactor, Examples of factors [Password, PIN, One-time password, Software token, Hardware token, Biometrics, Specific location, Security questions], Single sign-on) • Authorization (Permissions, Least privilege model, Role-based access [User account types], Rule-based access, Mandatory access controls, Discretionary access controls) • Accounting (Logs, Tracking, Web browser history) • Non-repudiation (Video, Biometrics, Signature, Receipt)
- 6.5 Explain password best practices.
  Password length • Password complexity • Password history • Password expiration • Password reuse across sites • Password managers • Password reset process
- 6.6 Explain common uses of encryption.
  Plain text vs. cipher text • Data at rest (File level, Disk level, Mobile device) • Data in transit (Email, HTTPS) • VPN • Mobile application

Access Controls

An **access control system** is the set of technical controls that govern how subjects may interact with objects. **Subjects** in this sense are users or software processes or anything else that can request and be granted access to a resource. **Objects** are the resources; these could be networks, servers, databases, files, and so on. In computer security, the basis of access control is usually an **Access Control List (ACL)**. This is a list of subjects and the rights or **permissions** they have been granted on the object.

An access control system is usually described in terms of four main processes:

- **Identification**—creating an account or ID that identifies the user or process on the computer system.
- **Authentication**—proving that a subject is who or what it claims to be when it attempts to access the resource.
- **Authorization**—determining what rights or permissions subjects should have on each resource and enforcing those rights.
- **Accounting**—tracking authorized and unauthorized usage of a resource or use of rights by a subject.

Least Privilege and Implicit Deny

The more privileges and permissions that you allocate to more users, the more you increase the risk that a privilege will be misused. Authorization policies help to reduce risk by limiting the allocation of privileges as far as possible. This principle is referred to as **least privilege**. This means that a user should be granted rights necessary to perform their job and no more.

As part of least privilege, access controls are usually founded on the principle of **implicit deny**. This means that unless there is a rule specifying that access should be granted (explicit authorization), any request for access is denied.

This principle can be seen clearly in firewall policies. A firewall filters access requests using a set of rules. The rules are processed in order from top to bottom. If a request does not fit any of the rules, it is handled by the last (default) rule, which is to refuse the request.

Authorization Access Models

An important consideration in designing a security system is to determine *how* users receive rights; or, to put it another way, how Access Control Lists (ACL) are written. Access control or authorization models are generally classed as one of the following:

- **Discretionary Access Control (DAC)** stresses the importance of the **owner**. The owner is originally the creator of the resource, though ownership can be assigned to another user. The owner is granted **full control** over the resource, meaning that he or she can modify its ACL to grant rights to others.

- **Role-based Access Control (RBAC)** adds an extra degree of administrative control to the DAC model. Under RBAC, a set of organizational roles are defined and users allocated to those roles. You can see a simple version of RBAC working in the division of Windows user account types into Administrators and Standard Users.

- **Mandatory Access Control (MAC)** is based on the idea of security clearance levels. Rather than defining access control lists on resources, each object and each subject is granted a clearance level, referred to as a **label**. If the model used is a hierarchical one (that is, high clearance users are trusted to access low clearance objects), subjects are only permitted to access objects at their own clearance level or below. Alternatively, each resource and user can be labeled as belonging to a domain (compartmentalized). A user may only access a resource if they belong to the same domain. This is an instance of a "Need to Know" or least privilege policy put into practice.

- **Rule-based** access control is a term that can refer to any sort of access control model where access control policies are determined by system-enforced rules rather than system users. As such, RBAC and MAC are both examples of rule-based (or non-discretionary) access control. Another instance of rule-based access control is continuous authentication. For example, with the Windows User Account Control (UAC) feature, just because the user has signed in does not mean that Windows fully trusts the account to exercise its privileges. When the account tries to do something protected by UAC, such as installing an app, the user must confirm the action with a prompt. This protects against account hijacking by a malicious script or similar.

Accounting and Non-repudiation

The accounting part of the access control system provides an audit log of how users have authenticated to the network and used their access privileges. Accounting is usually provided for by **logging** events. Computer systems support logging of pretty much any kind of event. Examples of events are a user signing in or attempting to modify a file or install an app. Another example is the history of URLs visited kept by a web browser. This allows the accounting system to **track** what users are doing within the system.

Accounting is an important part of ensuring **non-repudiation**. Non-repudiation is the principle that the user cannot *deny* having performed some action. Apart from logging, several mechanisms can be used to provide non-repudiation:

- Video—surveillance cameras can record who goes in or out of a particular area.

- Biometrics—strong authentication can prove that a person was genuinely operating their user account and that an intruder had not hijacked the account.
- Signature—similarly, a physical or digital signature can prove that the user was an author of a document (they cannot deny writing it).
- Receipt—issuing a token or receipt with respect to some product or service is proof that a user requested that product and that it was delivered in a timely manner.

User Account Types

Part of the identification process is to allocate each user with their own account on the computer system and network.

User Accounts

A **user account** ensures that the identity of someone using a computer is validated by the operating system at log on. This validation is typically achieved by entering a user account name and a secret password but could use a different type of credentials. Requiring the user to log on before accessing the computer or network is called **mandatory logon**.

When Windows is installed, a number of **default** user accounts are created. The main ones are:

- **Administrator** user account—as a member of the Administrators group this account has complete control over the local computer. This account should be protected by a strong password. The account is disabled by default.
- **Guest** user account—this account is also disabled by default. It can be enabled on "professional" versions of Windows but should not generally be used. If the guest account is enabled, anyone can use the computer without needing to enter a password.
- A user account created during setup—this can either be a local account or a Microsoft account, used to access Microsoft online services, such as Office 365. By default, it is a member of the local Administrators group and should be protected by a strong password.

The administrative user created during setup may also create extra user accounts for the people who are going to use the computer. Generally speaking, these should be configured as standard user accounts.

The administrative user should create a standard user account for themselves. Even with User Account Control, it is best practice not to use an account with administrative privileges for day-to-day tasks, such as web browsing or using Office applications.

Group Accounts

User accounts can be assigned directly to security policies, but if there are a large number of users, this can be difficult to manage. Administration is simplified by the use of **group accounts**. A user can belong to one or more group accounts and inherit security permissions through privileges allocated to the groups.

As noted above in the discussion of user accounts, Windows creates several default group accounts. The only two we need to consider here are administrators and standard users:

- **Administrators**—user accounts belonging to this group have complete control over the computer. This group should be used sparingly.
- **Standard users**—this group allows use of Microsoft Store apps and basic configuration of display and input settings, but tasks such as installing software, configuring hardware, or changing system properties are restricted.

Windows makes use of a simplified access control system when it is part of a workgroup. The only group accounts are Computer Administrators and Standard Users. The use of additional group accounts is associated more with domain networks. You cannot create group accounts in the "home" editions of Windows.

Authentication Factors

Authentication is the process of ensuring that each account is only operated by its proper user. There are many different authentication technologies. They can be categorized as something you **know** (such as a password), something you **have** (such as a smart card), or something you **are** (such as a fingerprint). These different ways of authenticating a subject are referred to as **factors**. Each factor has advantages and drawbacks.

Something You Know Authentication

The typical "something you know" technology is the logon or sign-in. A sign-in comprises a **username** and a **password**. The username is typically not a secret, though it should not be published openly, but the password must be known only to the account holder. A **passphrase** is a longer password comprising a number of words. This has the advantages of being more secure and easier to remember. A **Personal Identification Number (PIN)** is another example of something you know as is the response to a **pattern lock**.

Another important concept in authentication based on facts that a person knows is **Personally Identifiable Information (PII)**. PII is often used as **security questions** for password reset mechanisms and to confirm identity over the telephone. For example, PII may be defined as responses to challenge questions, such as "What is your favorite color/pet/movie?"

Something You Have Authentication

Password-type credentials are generally seen as not providing adequate security for high-risk applications, such as corporate network logons or online banking. One solution is to provide each user with a unique **hardware token** to prove their identity.

There are various ways to authenticate a user based on "something they have." The most widely used is the **smart card** or **USB fob**, which contains a chip with authentication data, such as a **digital certificate**. The card must be presented to a card reader before the user can be authenticated. This is typically combined with a user name/password logon or Personal Identification Number (PIN) code. This protects the token against unauthorized use in the event that it is lost or stolen.

Another hardware authentication device is the SecurID token, developed by RSA. This generates a number code synchronized to a code on a server for the user to enter to log on, again combined with a secret PIN, in case the device is stolen. The code changes every 60 seconds or so. This is an example of a **one-time password**.

Key fob token generator. Image © 123rf.com.

A **software token** is generated by an application and stored on the user's computer or smartphone, as a web cookie for instance. It is important that such tokens use encryption so that they cannot be misused.

The main concerns with token-based technologies are loss and theft and the chance that the device can be counterfeited or that a software token can be replayed. There are also extra setup and maintenance costs.

Something You Are Authentication

"Something you are" authentication means employing some sort of **biometric** recognition system. Many types of biometric information can be recorded, including fingerprint patterns, iris or retina recognition, or facial recognition. The chosen biometric information is scanned and recorded and stored as a **template** in a database. When the user wants to access a resource, they are re-scanned and the scan compared to the template. If they match, access is granted.

Using a biometric entry system with fingerprint reader.
Image by Narinthon Phaiboonsombat © 123rf.com.

The main problems with biometric technology are that users find it intrusive and threatening to privacy, the setup and maintenance costs, and the chance that the technology can be counterfeited. Biometrics can also be prone to **false negatives**, where a valid user is refused access, and **false positives**, where an intruder is misidentified as a valid user or one user is mistaken for another.

Windows 10 provides support for biometric authentication through the use of an architecture known as Windows Hello. If your computer is Windows Hello capable, you will see the option in ***Settings > Accounts > Sign-in options*** *under the* ***Windows Hello*** *heading.*

Somewhere You Are Authentication

Location-based authentication measures some statistic about "where" you are (your presence in a **specific location**). This could be a geographic location, measured using **GPS (Global Positioning System)** and/or **IPS (Indoor Positioning System)**, or it could be by IP address. The IP address could also be used to refer to a logical network segment or it could be linked to a geographic location using **geoip**.

Location-based authentication is not used as a primary authentication factor, but it may be used as a continuous authentication mechanism or as an access control feature. For example, if a user enters the correct credentials at a remote network access gateway but their IP address shows them to be in a different country than expected, access controls might be applied to restrict the privileges granted or refuse access completely.

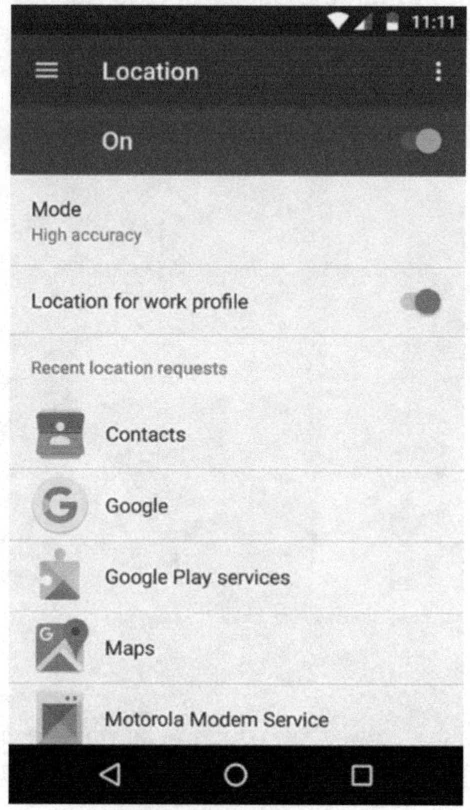

Location services, such as those provided by Android on this smartphone, can support access control systems.

Multifactor and Two-factor Authentication

An authentication product is considered "strong" if it combines the use of more than one authentication data type. This is called **multifactor authentication**. **Single-factor authentication** systems can quite easily be compromised: a password could be written down or shared, a smart card could be lost or stolen, and a biometric system could be subject to high error rates.

Two-factor authentication combines something like a smart card or biometric mechanism with "something you know," such as a password or PIN. Three-factor authentication combines all three technologies. An example of this would be a smart card with integrated thumb or fingerprint reader. This means that to authenticate, the user must possess the card, the user's fingerprint must match the template stored on the card, and the user must input a PIN.

Multifactor authentication requires a combination of different *technologies. For example, requiring a PIN along with Date of Birth may be stronger than entering a PIN alone, but it is not multifactor.*

Single Sign-On

Single Sign-On (SSO) means that a user only has to authenticate to a system once to gain access to all its resources—that is, all the resources to which the user has been granted rights. An example is the Kerberos authentication and authorization model used on Windows enterprise networks. This means, for instance, that a user who has authenticated with Windows is also authenticated with the Windows domain's database and email services.

The advantage of single sign-on is that each user does not have to manage multiple user accounts and passwords. The disadvantage is that compromising the account also compromises multiple services.

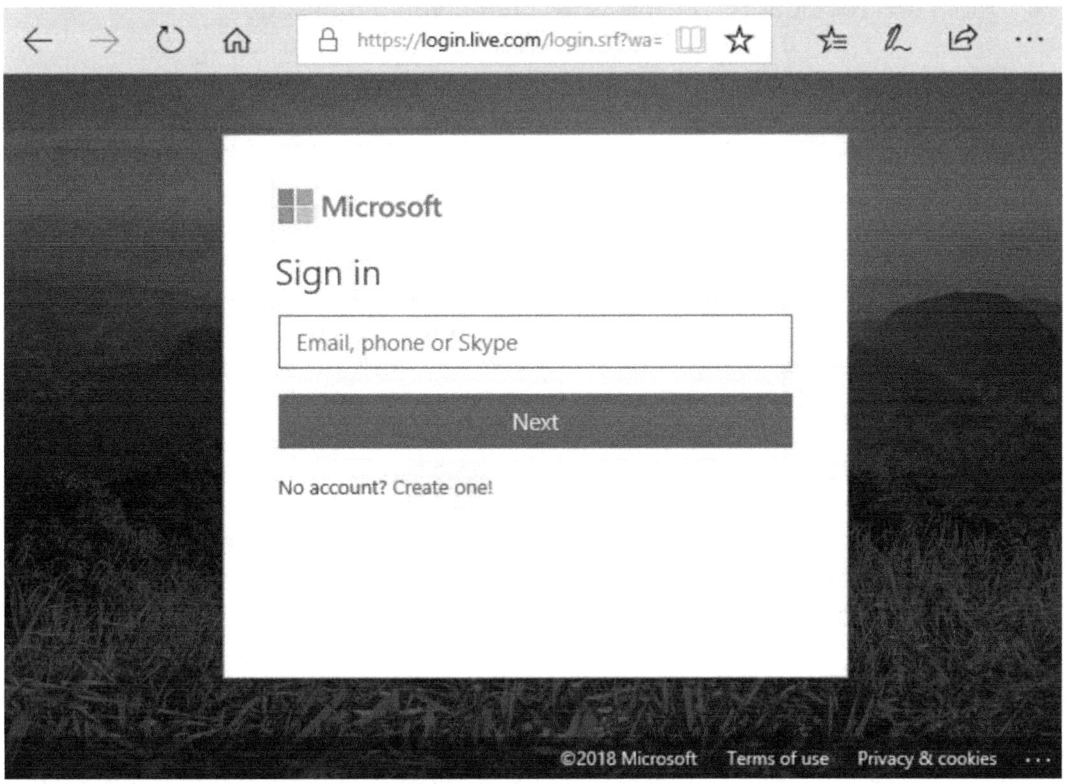

Microsoft accounts allow SSO to multiple Microsoft and third-party services. Screenshot used with permission from Microsoft.

It is critical that users do not re-use work passwords or authentication information on third-party sites. Of course, this is almost impossible to enforce, so security managers have to rely on effective user training.

Uses of Encryption

Encryption is an ancient technique for hiding information. Someone obtaining an encrypted document, or **cipher text**, cannot understand that information unless they possess a **key**. The use of encryption allows sensitive data to travel across a public network, such as the Internet, and remain private. Even if an eavesdropper could intercept and examine the data packets, the content would be unreadable.

The following terminology is used to discuss cryptography:

- Plain text (or clear text)—this is an unencrypted message.
- Cipher text—an encrypted message.
- Cipher—this is the process (or algorithm) used to encrypt and decrypt a message.

It is also important to understand that there are different types of encryption and cryptographic processes. These include cryptographic hashing, symmetric encryption, and asymmetric encryption. Often two or more of these three different types are used together in the same product or technology.

Symmetric Encryption

In symmetric encryption, a single **secret key** is used to both encrypt and decrypt data. The secret key is so-called because it must be kept secret. If the key is lost or stolen, the security is breached.

Symmetric encryption is also referred to as single-key or private-key. Note that "private key" is also used to refer to part of the PKI process (see below), so take care not to confuse the two uses.

The main problem with symmetric encryption is secure distribution and storage of the key. This problem becomes exponentially greater the more widespread the key's distribution needs to be. The main advantage is speed, as symmetric key encryption is less processor and system memory intensive than asymmetric encryption.

Symmetric encryption is used to encode data for storage or transmission over a network. Some examples of symmetric encryption technologies or ciphers are 3DES, AES, RC (Rivest Cipher), IDEA, Blowfish/Twofish, and CAST.

One of the principal measures of the security of an encryption cipher is the size of the key. Early ciphers used between 32- and 64-bit keys. Currently, 1024-bit keys would be selected for general use, with larger keys required for highly sensitive data. The larger the key however, the more processing is required to perform encryption and decryption.

Asymmetric Encryption

In asymmetric encryption, or Public Key Cryptography, a secret **private key** is used to *decrypt* data. A mathematically related **public key** is used to *encrypt* data. This public key can be widely and safely distributed to anyone with whom the host wants to communicate, because the private key *cannot* be derived from the public key. Also, the public key *cannot* be used to decrypt a message that it has just encrypted.

A key pair can be used the other way around. If the private key is used to encrypt something, only the public key can then decrypt it. The point is that one type of key cannot reverse the operation it has just performed.

Asymmetric encryption is mostly used for authentication technologies, such as digital certificates and digital signatures, and key exchange. **Key exchange** is where two hosts need to know the same *symmetric* encryption key without any other host finding out what it is. Symmetric encryption is much faster than asymmetric, so it is often used to protect the actual data exchange in a session. Asymmetric encryption is more complex, taking longer for a computer to process, and so typically only used on small amounts of data, such as the authentication process to set up the session.

Most asymmetric encryption technologies use the RSA cipher.

Public Key Infrastructure (PKI)

Asymmetric encryption is an important part of **Public Key Infrastructure (PKI)**. PKI is a solution to the problem of authenticating subjects on public networks. Under PKI, users or server computers are validated by a **Certificate Authority (CA)**, which issues the subject a digital certificate. The digital certificate contains a public key associated with the subject embedded in it. The certificate has also been signed by the CA, guaranteeing its validity. Therefore, if a client trusts the signing CA, they can also trust the user or server presenting the certificate.

The client can then send the server (comptia.org for example) data (their credit card details for example) encrypted using the public key, safe in the knowledge that only that particular server will be able to decrypt it (using its private key). A similar technique can be used to encrypt the contents of emails. The sender uses the recipient's public key to encrypt the data with the assurance that only the linked private key can be used to decrypt the data again. PKI can also be used by mobile applications to encrypt any data sent between the client and the server.

Digital certificates are also used for secure authentication to computer networks. The certificate is stored with the private key on a smart card hardware token. To authenticate, the card provides the certificate to the authentication server, which checks that it is valid and trusted. It then uses the public key in the certificate to issue an encrypted challenge to the user. The smart card should be able to decrypt this challenge using the private key and send an appropriate response.

Digital Signatures

Public/private key pairs can use the reverse encryption/decryption relationship to **sign** messages. In this scenario, the user uses his or her private key to *encrypt* a message signature then distributes the linked public key wrapped in a digital certificate to the message recipient. The fact that the public key embedded in the certificate can *decrypt* the signature proves that the sender signed it, because the encryption must have been performed with the linked private key.

Cryptographic Hashes

A **hash** is a short representation of data; you take a variable amount of information and the hash function converts it to a fixed length string. A **cryptographic hash** is designed to make it impossible to recover the original data from the hash and ensure that no two pieces of information produce the same hash.

Cryptographic hashing can be used to prove that a message has not been tampered with. For example, when creating a digital signature, the sender computes a cryptographic hash of the message and then encrypts the hash with his or her private key. When the recipient receives the message and decrypts the hash, the recipient computes its own hash of the message and compares the two values to confirm they match.

Cryptographic hashes are also used for secure storage of data where the original meaning does not have to be recovered—passwords for instance.

Two of the most commonly used cryptographic hash algorithms are SHA-1 and SHA-2 (Secure Hash Algorithm) and MD5 (Message Digest).

Data States

When deploying a cryptographic system to protect data assets, thought needs to be given to all the ways that information could potentially be intercepted. This means thinking beyond the simple concept of a data file stored on a disk. Data can be described as being at rest or in transit:

- **Data at rest**—this state means that the data is in some sort of persistent storage media. In this state, it is usually possible to encrypt the data using techniques such as whole disk encryption, mobile device encryption, database encryption, and file- or folder-level encryption.
- **Data in transit** (or **data in motion**)—this is the state when data is transmitted over a network, such as communicating with a web page via HTTPS or sending an email. In this state, data can be protected by a **transport encryption** protocol, such as Secure Sockets Layer (SSL)/Transport Layer Security (TLS).

Virtual Private Networks (VPN)

A **Virtual Private Network (VPN)** connects the components and resources of two private networks over another public network or connects a remote host with an Internet connection to a private local network. A VPN is a "tunnel" through the Internet or any other network. It uses special connection protocols and encryption technology to ensure that the tunnel is secure and the user is properly authenticated.

Password Cracking and Management

"Something You Know" authentication is vulnerable to attempts to learn the password or passwords used to gain access to a host or network. Passwords can be discovered via social engineering or because a user has written one down. It is also possible to capture password packets in transit. If the protocol uses **cleartext credentials,** then the attacker's job is done. Most credentials are only sent using some sort of cryptographic protection however.

Password Crackers

Even if the credentials are only transmitted with cryptographic protection, the attacker might be able to use password cracking software to decipher it. This type of software uses different methods to obtain the password from a **cryptographic hash**:

- **Dictionary**—the software matches the hash to those produced by ordinary words found in a dictionary. This could also include information such as user and company names, pet names, or any other words or simple phrases that people might naively use as passwords.

- **Brute force**—the software tries to match the hash against one of every possible combination it could be. If the password is short (under seven characters) and non-complex (using only letters for instance), a password might be cracked in minutes. Longer and more complex passwords increase the amount of time the attack takes to run—to years if the password is long and complex enough.

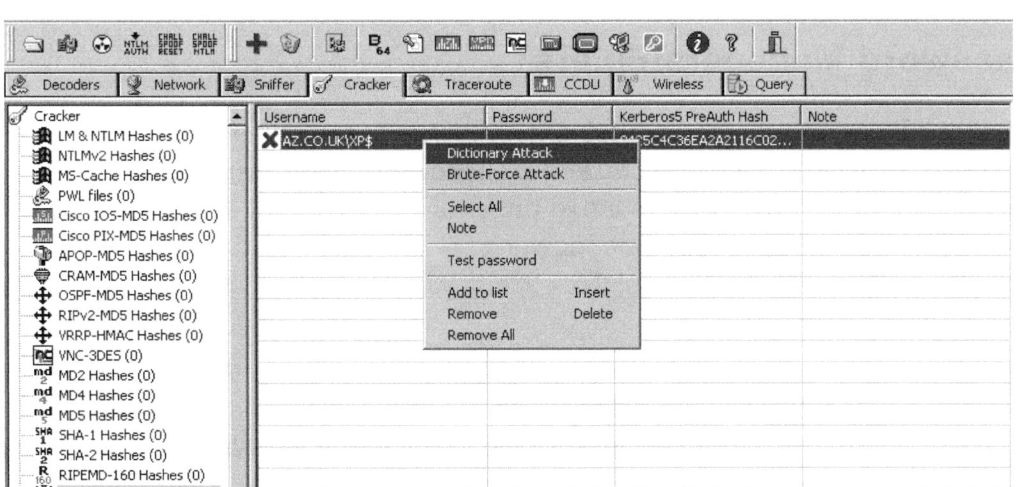

Cain and Abel password cracker.

Password Best Practices

For a system to be secure against password crackers, strong passwords are required. The following rules make passwords difficult to guess or crack:

- **Length**—a longer password is more secure. Around 9–12 characters is suitable for an ordinary user account. Administrative accounts should have longer passwords (14 or more characters).
- **Complexity** can improve the security of a password:
    - No single words—better to use word and number/punctuation combinations.
    - No obvious phrases in a simple form—birthday, user name, job title, and so on.
    - Mix upper and lowercase (assuming the software uses case-sensitive passwords).
- **Memorability**—artificial complexity makes a password hard to remember, meaning users write them down or have to reset them often. Using a long phrase, perhaps with one or two symbols and numerals mixed into it, can offer a good balance between complexity and memorability.
- **Maintain confidentiality**—do not write down a password or share it with other users.
- **History/expiration**—change the password periodically. Many systems can automatically enforce password expiration, meaning users have to choose a new password. Such a system may also keep a history of previously used passwords and prevent the user from choosing the same one again.
- **Reuse across sites**—a typical user might be faced with having to remember tens of logons for different services at work and on the Internet and resort to reusing the same password for each. This is unsecure, as your security becomes dependent on the security of these other (unknown) organizations. Users must be trained to practice good password management, or at the very least not to re-use work passwords for web accounts.

Password Managers/Fillers

A password policy should balance ensuring that users select strong passwords, which cannot be cracked by password-guessing software, and ensuring that they select memorable passwords and do not resort to reusing them across sites or writing them down.

If users are permitted to write passwords down, they must at the very least be stored securely. If a note containing a password is lost, the IT department should be informed and the password reset as soon as possible.

There are also various hardware and software password "fillers" that can store passwords for multiple accounts.

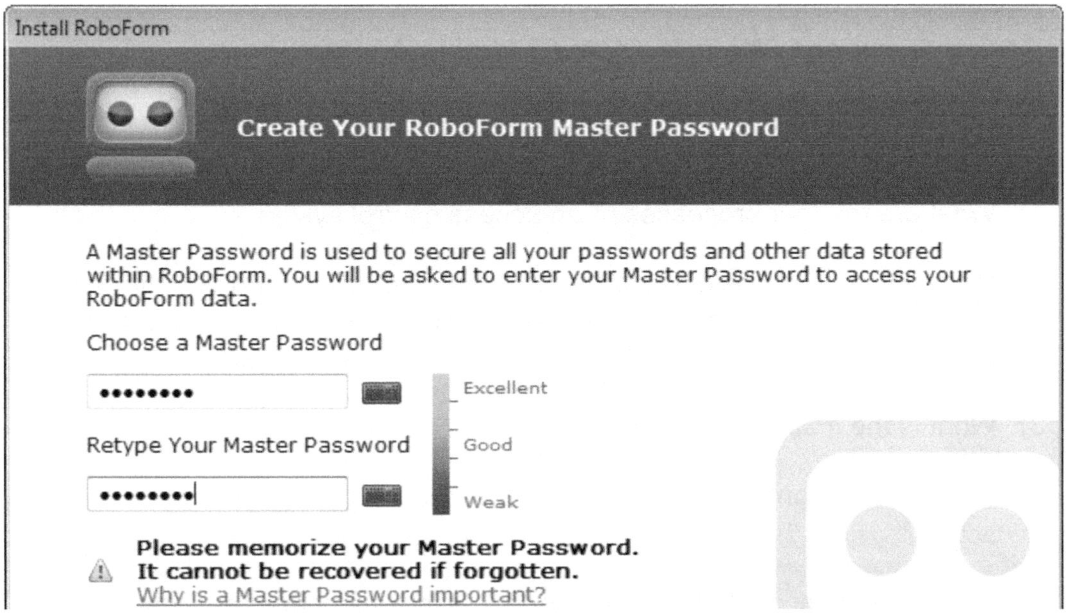

A password filler such as RoboForm is configured with one master password.

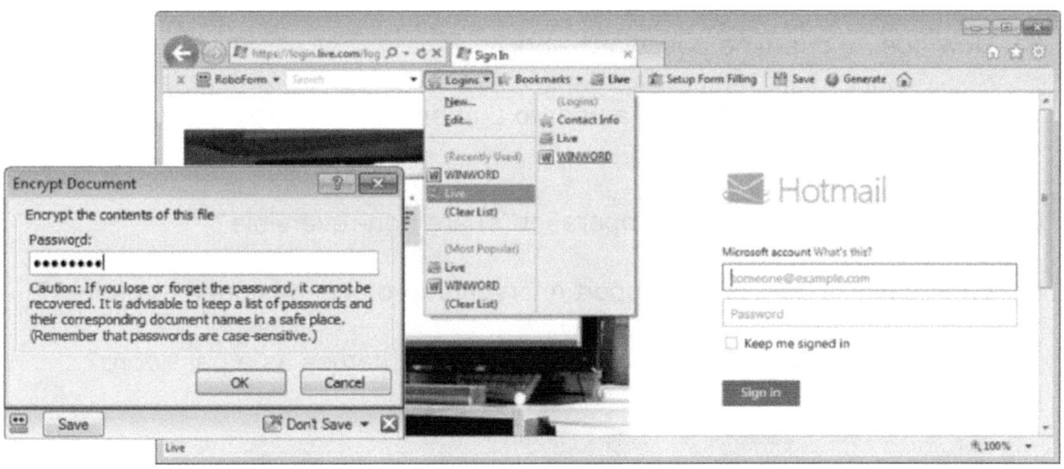

The password filler can be used to record passwords for different applications and websites.

Password Reset

A **password reset** mechanism allows a user who has forgotten a password to self-select a new one. This mechanism must obviously be well protected to prevent a malicious user from obtaining a new password for the account. As noted above, reset mechanisms may depend on security question challenges such as, "Who was your best friend at school?" Another popular mechanism is to register an alternative contact method, such as a cell phone number or secondary email address. The reset mechanism sends a link or code to this contact to authorize use.

The reset mechanism should also log the action and inform the user via their registered email address or cell number that a reset has taken place.

Review Questions / Module 5 / Unit 3 / Using Access Controls

Answer these questions to test what you have learned in this unit. You can review the model answers at the end of the book.

1) What are the four processes of an access control system?
2) Users should only be granted the minimum sufficient permissions. What system policy ensures that users do not receive rights unless granted explicitly?
3) What is the main type of non-discretionary access control?
4) What type of control prevents a user from denying they performed an action?
5) What sort of account allows someone to access a computer without providing a user name or password?
6) How does a one-time password work?
7) What type of system allows a user to authenticate once to access multiple services?
8) What type of cryptographic operation(s) are non-reversible?
9) What class of data is a transport encryption protocol designed to protect?
10) Why is it important not to use simple words or names as a password?

Module 5 / Unit 4
Behavioral Security Concepts

Objectives

On completion of this unit, you will be able to:

- Explain the importance of written policies and procedures in ensuring behavioral security.
- Describe basic principles for handling confidential information.
- List some privacy and usage issues for corporate systems and Internet/social media sites.

Syllabus Objectives and Content Examples

This unit covers the following exam domain objectives and content examples:

- 6.3 Summarize behavioral security concepts.
  Expectations of privacy when using: (The Internet [Social networking sites, Email, File sharing, Instant messaging], Mobile applications, Desktop software, Business software, Corporate network) • Written policies and procedures • Handling of confidential information (Passwords, Personal information, Customer information, Company confidential information)

Policies and Procedures

As a vital component of a company's IT infrastructure, employees must understand how to use computers and networked services securely and safely and be aware of their responsibilities. To support this, the organization needs to create **written policies and procedures** to help staff understand and fulfill their responsibilities and follow best practices.

The value of a comprehensive policy is that it removes any uncertainty that employees may have about what to do in a given situation. For example, if you work for a large company and meet someone you do not recognize in your work area, should you smile and say hello or smile, say hello, ask them where they want to be, and then escort them to that place? If there is a company policy saying that visitors to the workplace must be escorted at all times, it will be much easier for employees to take it upon themselves to "act the policeman" in this sort of circumstance.

Standards, Procedures, and Guidance

Policy is an overall statement of intent. In order to establish the correct working practices, three different mechanisms can be put in place:

- Standard—a standard is a measure by which to evaluate compliance with the policy.
- Procedure—a procedure, often referred to as a SOP (Standard Operating Procedure), is an inflexible, step-by-step listing of the actions that must be completed for any given task. Most critical tasks should be governed by SOPs.
- Guidance—guidelines exist for areas of policy where there are no procedures, either because the situation has not been fully assessed or because the decision-making process is too complex and subject to variables to be able to capture it in a procedure. Guidance may also describe circumstances where it is appropriate to deviate from a specified procedure.

Personnel Management Policies

Human Resources (HR) is the department tasked with recruiting and managing the organization's most valuable and critical resource: people. Personnel management policies can be conceived as applying in three phases:

- Recruitment (hiring)—locating and selecting people to work in particular job roles. Security issues here include screening candidates and performing background checks.

- Operation (working)—it is often the HR department that manages the communication of policy and training to employees, though there may be a separate training and personal development department within larger organizations. As such, it is critical that HR managers devise training programs that communicate the importance of security to employees.
- Termination or separation (firing or retiring)—whether an employee leaves voluntarily or involuntarily, termination is a difficult process with numerous security implications.

Operational policies include privilege management, data/information handling, incident response, and the use of company devices and services, such as Internet access. One function of HR is to draft and communicate these written policies to employees, including any updates to the policies. Another function is to enforce disciplinary measures, perhaps in conjunction with departmental managers.

Handling Confidential Information

Any document or information processed by a company must be classified depending on how sensitive it is. Employees should be trained to understand what information is confidential and how to handle it correctly.

Passwords

Users must keep their work passwords known only to themselves. This means not writing down the password, not telling it to anyone else, and not using it to authenticate to any other services or websites.

See Unit 5.3 for more information about password management

Personally Identifiable Information (PII)

The rise in consciousness of **identity theft** as a serious crime and growing threat means that there is an increasing impetus on government, educational, and commercial organizations to take steps to obtain, store, and process Personally Identifiable Information (PII) more sensitively and securely.

Staff should be trained to identify PII and to handle personal or sensitive data appropriately. This means not making unauthorized copies or allowing the data to be seen or captured by any unauthorized people. Examples of treating sensitive data carelessly include leaving order forms with customers' credit card details in view on a desk or putting a credit card number in an unencrypted notes field in a customer database.

Company Confidential Information

Any of the business information used to run a company could be misused in the wrong hands. This sort of information includes product designs or plans, marketing plans, contracts, procedures and workflows, diagrams and schematics, and financial information. This information must not be disclosed to unauthorized people and should always be stored on media that are subject to network access controls and/or encrypted. Paper or electronic copies of this sort of information that are no longer needed should be destroyed rather than discarded.

Customer Confidential Information

The same rules apply to information provided by customers (and suppliers or partners for that matter). When a business requests information from a customer, they should obtain explicit consent to process and store that information. This consent process should inform the customer how the information will be used and for how long it will be retained.

Acceptable Use Policies

An **Acceptable Use Policy**, or **Fair Use Policy**, sets out what someone is allowed to use a particular service or resource for. Such a policy might be used in different contexts. For example, an acceptable use policy could be enforced by a business to govern how employees use equipment and services, such as telephone or Internet access, provided to them at work. Another example might be an ISP enforcing a fair use policy governing usage of its Internet access services. Enforcing an acceptable use policy is important to protect the organization from the security and legal implications of employees (or customers) misusing its equipment. Typically, the policy will forbid the use of equipment to defraud, defame, or to obtain illegal material. It is also likely to prohibit the installation of unauthorized hardware or software and to explicitly forbid actual or attempted intrusion (snooping). An organization's acceptable use policy may forbid use of Internet tools outside of work-related duties or restrict such use to break times.

Rules of Behavior

The equipment used to access the Internet in the workplace is owned by the employer. Many employees expect relatively unrestricted access to Internet facilities for personal use. In fact, employees' use of social networking and file sharing poses substantial risks to the organization, including threat of virus infection or systems intrusion, lost work time, copyright infringement, and defamation. If an employee breaks copyright laws or libels someone using an organization's equipment, the organization itself could be held liable.

To avoid confusion, an employee's handbook should set out the terms under which use of web browser/email/social networking/P2P software is permitted for personal use and what penalties infringements could incur. Employers are within their rights to prohibit all private use of Internet services.

Users should be aware that any data communications, such as email, made through an organization's computer system are liable to be stored within the system, on servers, backup devices, and so on. Consequently, employees should not use computers at work to send personal information, for their own security and privacy if nothing else.

Use of Personally Owned Devices in the Workplace

Portable devices, such as smartphones, USB sticks, media players, and so on, pose a considerable threat to data security as they facilitate file copying. Camera and voice recording functions are other obvious security issues.

Network access control/endpoint security and data loss prevention solutions can be of some use in preventing the attachment of such devices to corporate networks. Some companies may try to prevent staff from bringing such devices on site. This is quite difficult to enforce though.

Privacy Policy

The right to privacy is one expected by citizens of most countries. However, the right to privacy has to be balanced against the need for the companies we work for and shop with to receive and process, and in some cases keep, information about us.

For example, an e-commerce company needs to know your address in order to deliver goods to you. When you tell them your address, you might expect them to use it only for delivering goods that you have ordered and not to use it to contact you about other products or to pass it to another company without your permission.

In order to protect their business, employers claim a responsibility to monitor the way employees put **business software** and the **corporate network** to use. Employees claim rights deriving from human rights legislation that they should not be treated cruelly or unusually. The balance between these rights and responsibilities is not always clearly defined in law, though as workplace privacy becomes more of an issue, laws and company guidelines are being instituted to account for it. A **contract of employment** may set out what an employee must agree to as a condition of employment.

Workplace surveillance can be divided into several categories:

- **Security assurance**—monitoring data communications and employees' behavior to ensure they do not divulge confidential information or compromise the security of the organization. Employers may also use security systems such as CCTV to prevent theft.
- **Monitoring data**—analyzing data communications to measure an employee's productivity. For example, a contact management system may record the frequency and duration of telephone contacts.
- **Physical monitoring**—recording employees' movement, location, and behavior within the workplace, often using CCTV and drugs/alcohol testing.

A good employer will make the procedures for workplace surveillance clear and unambiguous. To this end, a contract of employment or staff handbook should make clear the rules for employee conduct, as regards security, refreshment breaks, and use of equipment. It should likewise define prohibited actions and appropriate disciplinary procedures and punishments. Each employee should be given the opportunity to read these guidelines, and the employer should check that the employee understands them.

Additionally, some thought needs to be given to guests and callers, where the issue of consent is even more ambiguous.

Expectations of Privacy

As well as use of the Internet and business/corporate applications in a work setting, you should also understand privacy issues around use of social networking, communications services (email and Instant Messaging), and file sharing services.

One privacy issue with such sites is understanding what is published publicly and what is uploaded for private use only. Any personal information or content you post to such sites can usually either be marked as public and accessible to anyone or private and accessible only to your contacts or friends, or possibly to a subset of the closest contacts. Sites should provide tools to allow you to review what information and content you have made public. If you make something public accidentally, it can be very difficult to stop people from continuing to publish it elsewhere. Such information can also be archived and continue to appear in web searches. Consequently, you need to take care when updating your profile and posting messages or new content.

The other major privacy issue is understanding to what uses the service provider may put the data you supply to it. Most providers of "free" services will take the opportunity to scan any content they process on your behalf (social media posts, emails, file uploads, and so on) and extract metadata from it. Metadata is "information about information." Examples of metadata might include the date and time a message was sent, the language it used, and the regions associated with the sender's and recipient's domains. It might also include keywords or frequency of keywords. The service provider will aggregate and summarize this data for advertising and marketing/demographic analysis and may sell it to other companies, typically in an anonymized form.

The processes used to mask or anonymize personal identities from a dataset are not always completely reliable. There is often the risk that individuals could continue to be identified from information within the dataset.

This type of privacy consideration should also affect your choice of Internet Service Provider (ISP) and web search engines. Your browsing and search history reveal an enormous amount of very personal information. While the actual content of what you view or send to a site might be protected by encryption, the URL or web address of the site is not.

The acquisition, processing, storage, and transmission of personal data is sometimes governed by laws. If subject to such laws, you will be able to obtain redress against a company that does not obtain consent for the ways in which it uses and stores your data. Whether or not there is legislation to comply with, companies should have a privacy policy setting out what uses they can put your data to. It is in your interest to only use service providers that properly respect your right to privacy.

Privacy issues do not just affect websites, social media sites, ISPs, and search providers. It is also possible that this type of data will be collected from mobile apps and desktop software. It is typical for software such as Windows or Office to prompt you to allow usage and troubleshooting data to be sent back to the vendor (Microsoft) for analysis for example. Any software allowed to transmit data back to its vendor should be governed by a privacy policy.

Review Questions / Module 5 / Unit 4 / Behavioral Security Concepts

Answer these questions to test what you have learned in this unit. You can review the model answers at the end of the book.

1) What is a SOP?
2) Apart from passwords and PII, what other type(s) of confidential information should be governed by classification and handling procedures?
3) Why might a company ban use of the corporate network and desktop software for personal communications?
4) What two main privacy issues arise from using a social networking site?

Module 5 / Summary
Managing Security

In this module you learned about threats to computer security and some of the countermeasures and procedures that can be used to use computers safely.

Module 5 / Unit 1 / Security Concerns

- Secure information has the properties of confidentiality, integrity, and availability. Make sure you know which attacks threaten these properties.
- Social engineering is an important security concept to understand. Know how to identify different attack strategies and that security technologies need to be backed up by education and training for users to make them effective.
- Companies make their systems resilient to security threats and other risks by designing them to be fault tolerant, with redundancy for data, networks, and power. Disaster recovery planning sets out procedures and resources to use to respond to severe incidents.

Module 5 / Unit 2 / Using Best Practices

- Device hardening policies can mitigate against the risks of physical theft of computers and exploits designed to compromise software and security systems.
- Learn the different types malware and what risks they pose for computer and Internet users plus the countermeasures that can be put in place by installing anti-virus software.
- Learn the risks posed by spam, including suspicious attachments and hyperlinks, plus ways to filter junk email.
- It is vital to check for updates to system files, drivers, malware detection, and applications using secure sources. Windows Update provides an automated system for doing this for Windows systems and Microsoft software.

Module 5 / Unit 3 / Using Access Controls

- You can classify access control security systems as providing identification, authorization, authentication, and accounting (auditing). Authorization means granting permissions to users. There are different models for doing this on either a discretionary or mandatory/rules-based way.
- Accounting systems use logs and other technologies to track what users do and enforce non-repudiation.
- Understand the use of group accounts to assign system permissions and privileges and the difference between fundamental group types, such as administrators versus standard users.

- Authentication is often based on a user name/password log on but can also use tokens and biometric data. Recognize the risks posed by weak passwords.
- Cryptography underpins many security mechanisms. Understand the differences between symmetric and asymmetric encryption and cryptographic hashes. Appreciate the way they can be used in products such as digital certificates and transport encryption.

Module 5 / Unit 4 / Behavioral Security Concepts

- Technical security controls are usually insufficient. Behavioral security is important too and must be shaped by written policies and procedures.
- Make sure you understand the reasons for information handling and classification and the types of confidential information a business may process.
- Employees use of corporate systems and customers use of Internet services raise many privacy issues. Being informed about privacy is a key component of digital citizenship.

Taking the Exam

When you think you have learned and practiced the material sufficiently, you can book a time to take the test.

Preparing for the Exam

We've tried to balance this course to reflect the percentages in the exam so that you have learned the appropriate level of detail about each topic to comfortably answer the exam questions. Read the following notes to find out what you need to do to register for the exam and get some tips on what to expect during the exam and how to prepare for it.

Questions in the exam are weighted by domain area as follows:

CompTIA ITF+ Certification Domains	Weighting
1.0 IT Concepts and Terminology	17%
2.0 Infrastructure	22%
3.0 Applications and Software	18%
4.0 Software Development	12%
5.0 Database Fundamentals	11%
6.0 Security	20%

The objectives and content examples are covered in units in the course as listed in the table below. You can also use the index at the back of the book to look up specific content examples:

Domain Objectives/Examples	Refer To
1.1 Compare and contrast notational systems. *Binary • Hexadecimal • Decimal • Data representation (ASCII, Unicode)*	Unit 2.1 / Using Data Types and Units
1.2 Compare and contrast fundamental data types and their characteristics. *Char • Strings • Numbers (Integers, Floats) • Boolean*	Unit 2.1 / Using Data Types and Units
1.3 Illustrate the basics of computing and processing. *Input • Processing • Output • Storage*	Unit 1.1 / Common Computing Devices
1.4 Explain the value of data and information. *Data and information as assets • Importance of investing in security • Relationship of data to creating information • Intellectual property (Trademarks, Copyright, Patents) • Digital products • Data-driven business decisions (Data capture and collection, Data correlation, Meaningful reporting)*	Unit 2.1 / Using Data Types and Units

Domain Objectives/Examples	Refer To
1.5 Compare and contrast common units of measure. *Storage unit (Bit, Byte, KB, MB, GB, TB, PB) • Throughput unit (bps, Kbps, Mbps, Gbps, Tbps) • Processing speed (MHz, GHz)*	Unit 2.1 / Using Data Types and Units
1.6 Explain the troubleshooting methodology. *Identify the problem (Gather information, Duplicate the problem, if possible, Question users, Identify symptoms, Determine if anything has changed, Approach multiple problems individually) • Research knowledge base/Internet, if applicable • Establish a theory of probable cause (Question the obvious, Consider multiple approaches, Divide and conquer) • Test the theory to determine the cause (Once the theory is confirmed [confirmed root cause], determine the next steps to resolve the problem, If the theory is not confirmed, establish a new theory or escalate) • Establish a plan of action to resolve the problem and identify potential effects • Implement the solution or escalate as necessary • Verify full system functionality and, if applicable, implement preventive measures • Document findings/lessons learned, actions and outcomes*	Unit 1.5 / Troubleshooting and Support
2.1 Classify common types of input/output device interfaces. *Networking (Wired [Telephone connector (RJ-11), Ethernet connector (RJ-45)], Wireless [Bluetooth, NFC]) • Peripheral device (USB, FireWire, Thunderbolt, Bluetooth, RF) • Graphic device (VGA, HDMI, DVI, DisplayPort, Mini-DisplayPort)*	Unit 3.2 / Using Device Interfaces
2.2 Given a scenario, set up and install common peripheral devices to a laptop/PC. *Devices (Keyboard, Mouse)*	Unit 3.2 / Using Device Interfaces
Devices (Printer, Scanner, Camera, Speakers, Display) • Installation types (Plug-and-play vs. driver installation, Other required steps, IP-based peripherals, Web-based configuration steps)	Unit 3.3 / Using Peripheral Devices
Devices (External hard drive)	Unit 3.4 / Using Storage Devices
2.3 Explain the purpose of common internal computing components. *Motherboard/system board • Firmware/BIOS • RAM • ARM CPU (Mobile phone, Tablet) • 32-bit CPU (Laptop, Workstation, Server) • 64-bit CPU (Laptop, Workstation, Server) • Storage (Hard drive, SSD) • GPU • Cooling • NIC (Wired vs. wireless, Onboard vs. add-on card)*	Unit 3.1 / System Components
2.4 Compare and contrast common Internet service types. *Fiber optic • Cable • DSL • Wireless (Radio frequency, Satellite, Cellular)*	Unit 4.2 / Connecting to a Network
2.5 Compare and contrast storage types. *Volatile vs. non-volatile • Local storage types (RAM, Hard drive [Solid state vs. spinning disk], Optical, Flash drive)*	Unit 3.4 / Using Storage Devices

Domain Objectives/Examples	Refer To
Local network storage types (NAS, File server) • Cloud storage service	Unit 4.4 / Using Shared Storage
2.6 Compare and contrast common computing devices and their purposes. *Mobile phones • Tablets • Laptops • Workstations • Servers • Gaming consoles • IoT (Home appliances, Home automation devices, Thermostats, Security systems, Modern cars, IP cameras, Streaming media devices, Medical devices)*	Unit 1.1 / Common Computing Devices
2.7 Explain basic networking concepts. *Basics of network communication (Basics of packet transmission, DNS, URL-to-IP translation, LAN vs. WAN) • Device addresses (IP address, MAC address) • Basic protocols (HTTP/S, POP3, IMAP, SMTP)*	Unit 4.1 / Networking Components
Devices (Modem, Router, Switch, Access point)	Unit 4.2 / Connecting to a Network
Devices (Firewall)	Unit 4.3 / Secure Web Browsing
2.8 Given a scenario, install, configure and secure a basic wireless network. *802.11a/b/g/n/ac (Older vs. newer standards, Speed limitations, Interference and attenuation factors) • Best practices (Change SSID, Change default password, Encrypted vs. unencrypted [Open, Captive portal, WEP, WPA, WPA2])*	Unit 4.2 / Connecting to a Network
3.1 Explain the purpose of operating systems. *Interface between applications and hardware • Types of OS (Mobile device OS, Workstation OS, Server OS, Embedded OS, Firmware, Hypervisor [Type 1])*	Unit 1.3 / Using an OS
Disk management • Process management/scheduling (Kill process/end task) • Memory management • Access control/protection	Unit 1.4 / Managing an OS
Application management	Unit 2.2 / Using Apps
Device management	Unit 3.3 / Using Peripheral Devices
3.2 Compare and contrast components of an operating system. *Services • Processes • Utilities (Task scheduling) • Interfaces (Console/command line, GUI)*	Unit 1.4 / Managing an OS
Drivers	Unit 3.3 / Using Peripheral Devices
File systems and features (File systems, NTFS, FAT32, HFS, Ext4) • Features (Compression, Encryption, Permissions, Journaling, Limitations, Naming rules) • File management (Folders/directories, File types and extensions, Permissions)	Unit 3.5 / Using File Systems

Domain Objectives/Examples	Refer To
3.3 Explain the purpose and proper use of software. *Productivity software (Word processing software, Spreadsheet software, Presentation software, Web browser, Visual diagramming software) • Collaboration software (Email client, Conferencing software, Instant messaging software, Online workspace, Document sharing) • Business software (Database software, Project management software, Business-specific applications, Accounting software)*	Unit 2.2 / Using Apps
3.4 Explain methods of application architecture and delivery models. *Application delivery methods—locally installed (Network not required, Application exists locally, Files saved locally) • Application delivery methods—Local network hosted (Network required, Internet access not required) • Application delivery methods—Cloud hosted (Internet access required, Service required, Files saved in the cloud)*	Unit 2.3 / Programming and App Development
Application architecture models (One tier, Two tier, Three tier, n-tier)	Unit 2.4 / Using Databases
3.5 Given a scenario, configure and use web browsers. *Caching/clearing cache • Deactivate client-side scripting • Browser add-ons/extensions (Add, Remove, Enable/disable) • Private browsing • Proxy settings • Certificates (Valid, Invalid) • Popup blockers • Script blockers • Compatible browser for application(s)*	Unit 4.3 / Secure Web Browsing
3.6 Compare and contrast general application concepts and uses. *Licensing (Single use, Group use/site license, Concurrent license, Open source vs. proprietary, Subscription vs. one-time purchase, Product keys and serial numbers) • Software installation best practices (Reading instructions, Reading agreements, Advanced options)*	Unit 2.2 / Using Apps
Single-platform software • Cross-platform software (Compatibility concerns)	Unit 2.3 / Programming and App Development
4.1 Compare and contrast programming language categories. *Interpreted (Scripting languages, Scripted languages, Markup languages) • Compiled programming languages • Query languages • Assembly language*	Unit 2.3 / Programming and App Development
4.2 Given a scenario, use programming organizational techniques and interpret logic. *Organizational techniques (Pseudocode concepts, Flow chart concepts, Sequence) • Logic components (Branching, Looping)*	Unit 2.3 / Programming and App Development

Domain Objectives/Examples	Refer To
4.3 Explain the purpose and use of programming concepts. *Identifiers (Variables, Constants) • Containers (Arrays, Vectors) • Functions • Objects (Properties, Attributes, Methods)*	Unit 2.3 / Programming and App Development
5.1 Explain database concepts and the purpose of a database. *Usage of database (Create, Import/input, Query, Reports) • Flat file vs. database (Multiple concurrent users, Scalability, Speed, Variety of data) • Records • Storage (Data persistence)*	Unit 2.4 / Using Databases
5.2 Compare and contrast various database structures. *Structured vs. semi-structured vs. non-structured • Relational databases (Schema, Tables, Rows/records, Fields/columns, Primary key, Foreign key, Constraints) • Non-relational databases (Key/value databases, Document databases)*	Unit 2.4 / Using Databases
5.3 Summarize methods used to interface with databases. *Relational methods (Data manipulation [Select, Insert, Delete, Update], Data definition [Create, Alter, Drop, Permissions]) • Database access methods (Direct/manual access, Programmatic access • User interface/utility access, Query/report builders) • Export/import (Database dump, Backup)*	Unit 2.4 / Using Databases
6.1 Summarize confidentiality, integrity, and availability concerns. *Confidentiality concerns (Snooping, Eavesdropping, Wiretapping, Social engineering, Dumpster diving) • Integrity concerns (Man-in-the-Middle, Replay attack, Impersonation, Unauthorized information alteration) • Availability concerns (Denial of service, Power outage, Hardware failure, Destruction, Service outage)*	Unit 5.1 / Security Concerns
6.2 Explain methods to secure devices and best practices. *Securing devices (Host firewall, Safe browsing practices)*	Unit 4.3 / Secure Web Browsing
Securing devices (mobile/workstation) (Anti-virus/Anti-malware, Changing default passwords, Enabling passwords, Patching/updates) • Device use best practices (Software sources, Validating legitimate sources, Researching legitimate sources, OEM websites vs. third-party websites, Removal of unwanted software, Removal of unnecessary software, Removal of malicious software)	Unit 5.2 / Using Best Practices

Domain Objectives/Examples	Refer To
6.3 Summarize behavioral security concepts. *Expectations of privacy when using: (The Internet [Social networking sites, Email, File sharing, Instant messaging], Mobile applications, Desktop software, Business software, Corporate network) • Written policies and procedures • Handling of confidential information (Passwords, Personal information, Customer information, Company confidential information)*	Unit 5.4 / Behavioral Security Concepts
6.4 Compare and contrast authentication, authorization, accounting, and non-repudiation concepts. *Authentication (Single factor, Multifactor, Examples of factors [Password, PIN, One-time password, Software token, Hardware token, Biometrics, Specific location, Security questions], Single sign-on) • Authorization (Permissions, Least privilege model, Role-based access [User account types], Rule-based access, Mandatory access controls, Discretionary access controls) • Accounting (Logs, Tracking, Web browser history) • Non-repudiation (Video, Biometrics, Signature, Receipt)*	Unit 5.3 / Using Access Controls
6.5 Explain password best practices. *Password length • Password complexity • Password history • Password expiration • Password reuse across sites • Password managers • Password reset process*	Unit 5.3 / Using Access Controls
6.6 Explain common uses of encryption. *Plain text vs. cipher text • Data at rest (File level, Disk level, Mobile device) • Data in transit (Email, HTTPS) • VPN • Mobile application*	Unit 5.3 / Using Access Controls
6.7 Explain business continuity concepts. *Backup considerations—data [File backups, Critical data, Database, OS backups], Backup considerations—location [Stored locally, Cloud storage, On-site vs. off-site]*	Unit 4.4 / Using Shared Storage
6.7 Explain business continuity concepts. *Fault tolerance (Replication, Redundancy [Data, Network, Power], Contingency plan) • Disaster recovery (Data restoration, Prioritization, Restoring access)*	Unit 5.1 / Security Concerns

Registering for the Exam

CompTIA Certification exams are delivered exclusively by Pearson VUE.

- Log on to VUE (pearsonvue.com/comptia) and register your details to create an account.
- To book a test, log in using your account credentials then click the link to schedule an appointment.
- The testing program is CompTIA and the exam code is FC0-U61.
- Use the search tool to locate the test center nearest you then book an appointment.
- If you have purchased a voucher or been supplied with one already, enter the voucher number to pay for the exam. Otherwise, you can pay with a credit card.
- When you have confirmed payment, an email will be sent to the account used to register, confirming the appointment and directions to the venue. Print a copy and bring it with you when you go to take your test.

Arriving for the Exam

- Arrive at the test center at least 15 minutes before the test is scheduled.
- You must have two forms of ID; one with picture, one preferably with your private address, and both with signature. View certification.comptia.org/testing/test-policies/candidate-id-policy for more information on CompTIA's candidate ID policy and examples of acceptable forms of ID.
- Books, calculators, laptops, cellphones, smartphones, tablets, or other reference materials are not allowed in the exam room.
- You will be given note taking materials, but you must not attempt to write down questions or remove anything from the exam room.
- It is CompTIA's policy to make reasonable accommodations for individuals with disabilities.
- The test center administrator will demonstrate how to use the computer-based test system and wish you good luck. Check that your name is displayed, read the introductory note, and then click the button to start the exam.

Taking the Exam

CompTIA has prepared a Candidate Experience video (www.youtube.com/embed/kyTdN2GZiZ8). Watch this to help to familiarize yourself with the exam format and types of questions.

- There are up to 75 multiple-choice questions, which must be answered in 60 minutes. The passing score is 650 on a scale of 100–900.
- Read each question and its option answers carefully. Don't rush through the exam as you'll probably have more time at the end than you expect.
- At the other end of the scale, don't get stuck on a question and start to panic. You can mark questions for review and come back to them.
- As the exam tests your ability to recall facts and to apply them sensibly in a troubleshooting scenario, there will be questions where you cannot recall the correct answer from memory. Adopt the following strategy for dealing with these questions:
  - Narrow your choices down by eliminating obviously wrong answers.
  - Don't guess too soon! You must select not only a *correct* answer, but the *best* answer. It is therefore important that you read all of the options and not stop when you find an option that is correct. It may be impractical compared to another answer.
  - Utilize information and insights that you've acquired in working through the entire test to go back and answer earlier items that you weren't sure of.
  - Think your answer is wrong—should you change it? Studies indicate that when students change their answers they usually change them to the wrong answer. If you were fairly certain you were correct the first time, leave the answer as it is.
- Don't leave any questions unanswered! If you really don't know the answer, just guess.
- The exam may contain "unscored" questions, which may even be outside the exam objectives. These questions do not count toward your score. Do not allow them to distract or worry you.
- The exam questions come from a regularly updated pool to deter cheating. Do not be surprised if the questions you get are quite different than someone else's experience.

Good Luck!

Do not discuss the contents of the exam or attempt to reveal specific exam questions to anyone else. By taking the exam, you are bound by CompTIA's confidentiality agreement.

After the Exam

- A score report will be generated and a copy printed for you by the test administrator.
- The score report will show whether you have passed or failed and your score in each section. Make sure you retain the report!
- Five days after passing the exam, go to comptia.org/careerid and create an account (or log on to an existing account) using the information in your score report. You can use this site to order your certificate and ID card.
- If six weeks have passed after taking your exam and you haven't received a copy of your certificate, contact our customer service team at 866.835.8020 / 630.678.8300 from 7 a.m. to 7 p.m. CT, Monday through Friday. You may also visit our help.comptia.org to see FAQs and submit a help request.
- You can use your Career ID to track your certification progress on CompTIA's website order duplicate certificates, and download certification logos in various image file formats.

Retaking the Test

If you do fail the certification test on the first attempt, then you can retake it at your convenience. However, should you fail the test at the second, third, or subsequent attempts, you will not be able to retake the exam for at least 30 days after your last attempt. Study your score report to see which areas of the exam you were weak on.

This page left blank intentionally.

Career Advice

The CompTIA IT Fundamentals+ certificate is a great thing to show employers that you know the basics of PC support, but it is not a golden ticket into employment. To get a job, you need to know where to look, how to write a good resume and application letter, how to prepare for an interview, and generally how to impress potential employers.

This module contains tips to help you do this. There are also sample job-hunting resources, such as a resume and covering letter, on the support website.

Making a Career Plan

To make a career plan, first you need to think about where you are and where you want to be. Then you identify the steps you need to take to get from one situation to the other.

No Job Experience

It is likely that you will not have any formal job experience. However, completing the ITF+ certification is an excellent way to demonstrate that you have the necessary skills and that you have the enthusiasm to pursue a career in this area. If you have completed the practical activities, you will also have some evidence of practical experience.

Already Working in the IT Industry

If you work in the IT industry in a customer services or administrative role, you may want to move into (or up to) a support role. Passing the ITF+ certification is an excellent way to demonstrate that you have the necessary skills and enthusiasm to pursue a career in this area. You should also be able to demonstrate customer service skills from your current job.

If you are already working in PC support and want to move further up the ladder, your job experience and CompTIA qualifications will serve you well in proving that you have acquired basic skills and aptitudes. In a help desk environment, there might be scope for you to be promoted to Senior Technician level. Alternatively, you may look at Network Support or an applications or programming role.

For any of these options, you are going to need to acquire the relevant technical skills and possibly certifications. More information on these can be found under the "Continuing Education" topic below.

Working in another Industry

IT is a popular career choice for many "job changers." As described above, you can use CompTIA credentials as evidence of your aptitude and enthusiasm for IT support and use your career to date as evidence of your skills in communication and professionalism.

IT Support Job Roles

IT support is provided in a number of ways. In planning your career, you should first recognize the range of organizations that recruit IT support staff and the sort of job roles available within each.

IT Technicians

"IT Technician" describes the traditional PC service role, where a technical support department provides assistance to a number of users. Typically, this involves both remote and client-facing support. Apart from technical support within medium-size and large companies, this role is also important to the third-party IT support service industry. These businesses range widely in size and turnover, from sole traders to stock market listed companies. IT support technicians working in smaller companies are likely to need a broader range of skills, including server and network management.

PC technicians need to demonstrate a full range of technical skills. Apart from troubleshooting and maintenance, typical activities are completing hardware and OS upgrades, performing simple network configuration, and training and supporting users. The **CompTIA A+** certification validates the skills and knowledge of professional support technicians with 12 months' job experience (or equivalent training).

Apart from PC technicians, the CompTIA A+ skill set is also useful to those in a PC or software sales role. Sound technical knowledge enables sales staff to discuss benefits of products authoritatively and understand client needs.

PC support and application support are typically the entry-level positions within an IT support department or help desk. Roles may be divided between two levels, with senior technicians taking more responsibility in resolving problems, making decisions and recommendations, and providing team leadership.

More senior roles take responsibility for network support and then network and application service design and management.

Remote Support

Remote support is now a specialist function within many IT support departments and contact centers. Technicians are usually graded, with Level 1 techs providing telephone and remote support and more experienced Level 2 techs handling any desk-side or client-facing jobs. This type of role is increasingly important as more and more software and hardware vendors realize that providing cost-effective technical support is a key product differentiator. Managed services IT providers also use remote support to proactively manage a customer's IT infrastructure, rather than responding to support incidents.

Traditionally, remote support was very much telephone-based. However, the technologies available for remote configuration have improved to the extent that many incidents are now dealt with using email or chat messaging plus Remote Assistance-style tools. These tools are highly cost-effective, greatly reducing the number of incidents that require a site visit.

In terms of technical skills, remote support is more focused on software troubleshooting and configuration.

Contact Centers

A **contact center** (or **help desk**) is a division responsible for receiving, initiating, and managing customer contacts. A contact center may be a unit within a business or may be a business in itself. The concept of a contact center is to provide a proper framework for the supply of services to customers.

Contact center job roles are usually divided between:

- Customer service operators—take initial contacts, deal with basic queries, or direct calls to the appropriate service area.
- Analyst/Service Technician—provide advice and troubleshooting. This role may be graded between first and second line support.

Service technician.

- Team leader—responsibility for leading and motivating a team or department. Managers must demonstrate a variety of skills, including being able to recruit, develop, and motivate staff, design efficient procedures and operations, monitor and evaluate service quality and performance, and deal with change and crisis.
- Contact Center Manager/Operations Manager—the senior role within the contact center, with responsibility for setting policy, managing the budget, managing day-to-day operations, providing staff and equipment resources, and ensuring compliance (adherence to legal requirements).

Managed Services

Managed Services companies provide a completely outsourced IT solution to businesses. The advantage for the business is that it does not need to retain in-house expertise or employees.

Managed services typically use remote support to handle monitoring and basic troubleshooting and configuration of computer systems. Site visits may be required for new installations or complex troubleshooting, but the focus is on proactively managing the IT infrastructure rather than responding to incidents.

Depot Technicians

The depot (or bench) technician role is one that involves the least direct client contact. Depot technicians will perform PC troubleshooting, maintenance, and optimization that cannot be performed in the field. Consequently, the emphasis is on hardware systems building, troubleshooting, and maintenance skills.

This role may exist as a specialist part of the support services in larger companies, but most jobs are with PC and hardware vendors.

Self-employed Technicians

Starting your own business is another IT support career option. There is a huge market for assisting home users and small businesses with new PC sales and troubleshooting. As with any small business though, you need to be able to handle marketing, accounting, and legal issues to make the business successful—in addition to developing your technical and customer service skills.

Searching for Vacancies

To summarize from the section above, you will be searching for vacancies such as "PC Support Technician," "PC Engineer," "Support Engineer," "Support Specialist," or "Systems Administrator" for hands-on roles or "Help Desk Technician" or "Call Center Technician" for remote support.

The most likely recruiters are medium to large companies with internal support departments of any size or third-party IT support specialists.

A simple approach to job seeking is to sign on with recruitment agencies. Many companies use agencies to handle recruitment, so you may find that job advertisements are placed by an agency anyway. Make sure you choose agencies that specialize in IT support.

The next simplest option is to browse advertised vacancies and post your resume to a recruitment website. Some popular sites include itjobs.com, careerbuilder.com, computerjobs.com, and hotjobs.com. You should also look at the job ads in local newspapers.

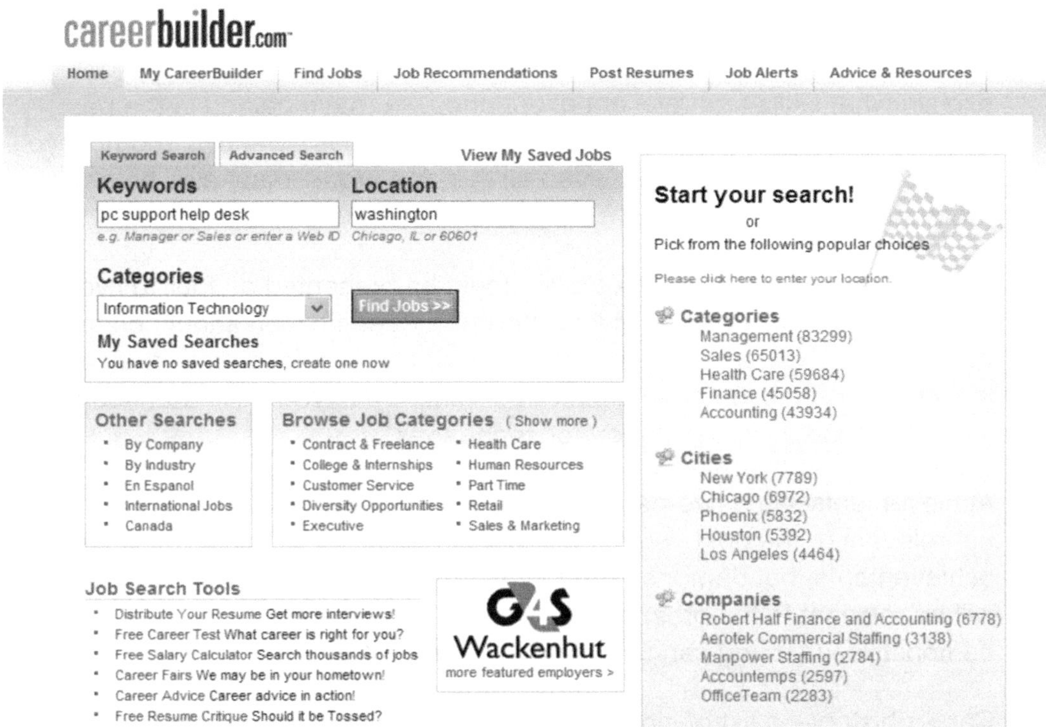

careerbuilder.com.

If these approaches do not turn up anything, you can try the following:

- Ask family, friends, and teachers for contacts or introductions.
- Approach local companies speculatively (see "Cold calling employers" below).

Approaching Employers

When you respond to a vacancy you have seen advertised, you will normally submit your resume (with a covering letter) or possibly complete an application form and might then attend an interview.

Resume

Your resume is the key tool to get you into work. A resume is a description of your skills and career history. You must make sure that your resume is factually correct, contains no spelling or grammatical errors, advertises the skills and experience employers will be interested in, and has a simple and attractive layout. Your resume should be no longer than two pages. If you do not have much previous experience, use a one-page resume rather than trying to stretch it to two pages.

You can either organize a resume to focus on career history or on skills. As you are probably entering the job market for the first time, the latter approach is probably best. The typical layout is as follows:

- Personal details—make sure your name and contact details (address, telephone, and email) are clearly printed. Do *not* include your date of birth, marital status, gender, or a photograph.

- Profile—this explains why you are looking for a job in IT support. Try to tell your story to make yourself interesting to employers. The profile should explain what skills and relevant experience you have gained in the past, why you are a great candidate for an IT support position now, and how you plan to develop your career. Given all this, the profile must also be short (no more than 4–5 lines).
- Key skills/qualifications—key skills should be presented as four to five bullet points, each of a single line. Your ITF+ certification should be top of the list. Other key skills should relate to what an employer says they are looking for in their job advertisement or other skills you have that could be valuable, such as speaking foreign languages.
- Achievements—in a two-page resume or if your career history is short and not relevant to the post you are seeking, present a list of four to five key achievements that demonstrate that you have some of the experience that will be relevant to the prospective employer. Achievements should also demonstrate that you can use your skills effectively.
- Career history—a list of significant employment and/or voluntary work in reverse chronological order. List the job title, company, date, and key achievements. Do not try to make inflated claims for minor jobs, but do try to show that you have gained at least some experience in all the areas that will interest prospective employers (specific IT experience, team working, and customer support).

In a career-focused resume, career history will come before key skills. If there are long gaps (over one month) in your employment history, try to find ways to explain them in your resume. For example, show that you were doing voluntary work or traveling. Be prepared to be asked about gaps at an interview.

- Education—list academic education, with the name of each school or college, dates attended, and key qualifications. Also list any relevant professional training.
- Hobbies—only list hobbies if you have spare space and they are genuinely interesting, reflect some concrete achievement, or demonstrate your character.
- References—you do not need to include previous employer or character references unless specifically requested by the prospective employer. Do state that references can be provided on request.

You will need two to three references and cannot use members of your family. If you do not have a previous employer, ask teachers or friends of good professional standing. Give your referees a copy of your resume.

When you have finished your resume, hold it at arm's length for 10 seconds—what part of it stands out? Does the resume make it clear that you want a career in IT support and have skills (ITF+ certification) and some experience? Get other people to give you their opinion about your resume and ideally to help you check it for any mistakes.

When you print your resume, use good quality paper (*not* colored) and a decent printer. It may be worth getting copies printed professionally. If you submit your resume online or by email, Microsoft Word, RTF, or PDF format is probably best. If submitting an electronic file, stick to common fonts to avoid formatting problems.

If you post your resume to recruitment websites, remember to re-upload it each week so that employers know you are still in the job market.

Application Forms

The challenge of an application form is to leverage the material in your resume to the format required by the form.

When completing a form by hand (required by some employers), print and fill out a draft copy first and work on it until you are happy with the text. Spell check what you have written carefully.

Cover Letter

A resume or application form should normally be accompanied by a cover letter, especially if applying for a job speculatively. The cover letter should be hand-written if this is specifically requested by the employer (unlikely for jobs in IT support).

The purpose of a cover letter is to show that you want the job, that you are interested in the company, and to draw out the key skills and achievements from your resume that demonstrate that you are a capable candidate for the job. The covering letter should fit on one page and consist of three to four paragraphs of four to five lines each.

Cold Calling Employers

If you do not see many vacancies advertised, you may wish to approach companies speculatively by cold calling them. This is very hard work and you must prepare to face many rejections, but it does demonstrate your commitment and confidence.

1) Make a list of likely companies in your area. Remember the companies with the most potential are likely to be medium to large companies with internal support departments of any size or third-party IT support specialists. You should be able to locate third-party IT support companies via the Yellow Pages and the larger companies close to where you want to work should be quite easy to identify.

Be methodical when cold calling companies. Make sure you make a list of who you have called already!

2) Research the company using their website and social networking sites. Find out what they sell and to whom. If possible, find out who is responsible for recruitment (obviously also check if they are advertising any jobs!).

3) Phone the company and ask the receptionist who (if anyone) manages IT or computers or computer support in the company. Make sure you get their name (correctly spelled) and job title. Remember to thank the receptionist.

You want to try to approach the person responsible for IT support rather than an HR manager.

4) Adapt your resume and cover letter to write a speculative application to work with the company in a support role. Make it clear that you have researched and understand their business.

5) Follow-up the letter (around three to five days after sending it) by calling the IT or support manager. Ask if they have had a chance to look at your resume and whether any opportunities are available, now or in the future. If there are no opportunities, ask whether they know of any other firms that might have openings and whether you can use their name to approach them (a referral).

Social Networking

Use a social networking profile to present a positive image of yourself, using information from your resume and covering letter. Make sure that anything that might cause you embarrassment in a work context is restricted to private contacts (or removed completely).

Preparing for an Interview

To prepare for an interview, you should anticipate questions you may be asked. Interview questions will focus on the skills and requirements that are listed in the job advertisement. The interviewer(s) will want either evidence of previous experience or to be convinced that you are competent enough to learn quickly and to assess your character and personality.

Interviewers are also likely to ask questions based on your resume. For example, "I see you have passed the ITF+ certification, but you haven't worked in IT support before. Do you have any practical experience of maintaining PCs?" They may also ask questions designed to confirm that you really have the skills and experience that you are claiming.

Some of the standard questions to prepare answers for include:

- Why do you want this job? Why do you want to work for this company?
- What are your strengths and weaknesses?
- How would you cope with…?

Prepare and memorize four to five little scenarios that demonstrate practical experience of IT troubleshooting, configuring or specifying a computer system, dealing with customers, working on a team, showing resourcefulness when faced with a problem, and dealing with a difficult or challenging situation. These should be things you have actually done—do not make anything up. You should be able to deploy these scenarios to answer most of the questions you will be asked. Try not to repeat yourself. Show that you understand the realities of working in support and that you have taken the time to research the prospective employer's business. Your weakness is likely to be obvious (lack of professional experience), but show that you understand that and are resourceful enough to have acquired skills in other ways and that you can learn quickly.

A lot of people with no professional experience will say they have experience from helping with friends' and family's PCs. If you have to rely on this type of experience, be specific about what sort of problems you have fixed and make it clear that you also understand that professional IT support is a more pressured environment.

Also prepare any questions you might have about the post, both in terms of responsibilities and pay and benefits. These may be covered in the course of the interview, but you will also be asked if you have any questions. Only ask a *good* question; do not ask one for the sake of it.

On the day of the interview, dress smartly and check your appearance in a mirror. Make sure you arrive on time. Bring a couple of copies of your resume with you.

When you walk in, keep your head up and make eye contact with the people in the room. Shake hands and introduce yourself. When you answer questions, try to keep making eye contact. Sit up straight and try not to fidget, but do use hand gestures to reinforce what you are saying.

At the end of the interview, get up and shake hands with each interviewer, thanking them for their time.

Continuing Education

PC support is an entry-level position within the field of IT job opportunities. You should start to think early about how to progress your career.

PC Support

The **CompTIA A+ certification** validates the skills and knowledge of professional support technicians with 12 months' job experience (or equivalent training). Completing the ITF+ certification is an excellent foundation for pursuing the more advanced training or on-the-job experience necessary to prepare to take the A+ certification exams. You have to pass two exams to become A+ certified.

Application Support

Application support means assisting users with software applications and troubleshooting errors. The **Help Desk Analyst (HDA)** qualification validates general support skills. **Microsoft Office Specialist (MOS)** and **Microsoft Certified Solutions Associate (MCSA)** certifications are available for those supporting Windows and Office environments. More specialized support is provided for database applications customized to a particular function (Line of Business applications). At this level, there are numerous vendor certifications for different application products.

Network Support

A typical route from PC support is into network support. **CompTIA's Network+** and **Server+** certifications provide entry-level qualifications. Most network support technicians and engineers will progress to **Microsoft Certified Solutions Expert (MCSE)** and/or **Cisco Certified Network Associate (CCNA)** certifications.

Security is an increasingly important specialization, both within network support and for specific job roles within IT. **CompTIA's Security+** certification provides an entry-level qualification.

Answers to Review Questions

Module 1 / Unit 1 / Common Computing Devices

1) True or false? All types of computers use CPU and system memory.

    a) **True.**

2) What type of computer is most likely to need peripheral devices?

    a) **Desktop computer—you could also call this a Personal Computer (PC) or a workstation. An All-in-one PC also uses peripheral devices, with the obvious exception of a monitor.**

3) What type of computer is best suited for using in a job where you have to make notes and be able to move around easily?

    a) **A tablet or smartphone or possibly a hybrid laptop/tablet. Note-taking is supported by a touchscreen-based device.**

4) Why don't laptops make good servers?

    a) **There is no room for expansion and you are paying for components and design (maximum portability) you do not need.**

5) Why isn't a smartphone a good tool for writing a report?

    a) **Touchscreen or mini keyboards are not optimized for writing lots of text, though it is possible to attach them as peripheral devices.**

6) What type(s) of IoT appliance are less likely to be controlled via a home automation hub?

    a) **Modern cars and medical devices are unlikely to interface via a hub. Home automation hubs link to kitchen and domestic appliances, streaming media players, and potentially security systems.**

Module 1 / Unit 2 / Using a Workstation

1) What should you do before attempting to set up a new computer system?

   a) **Verify that the environment is suitable and that the installation will be safe.**

2) When setting up a desktop computer, what factor should you consider when deciding on the location of the system case?

   a) **You do not want to leave trailing wires over walkways so you need to consider the position of power outlet(s) and where peripheral devices will be placed. You also want to ensure adequate air flow around the system unit.**

3) What factors should you consider when positioning input and output devices?

   a) **Ensure that they can be used without exerting strain, especially on the arms/wrists and back/neck. Ensure that cabling is not a trip hazard. Avoid locations that cause excessive screen glare.**

4) You have to sign in to Windows—does it matter if the CAPS LOCK light on the keyboard is activated?

   a) **Yes—passwords are case-sensitive.**

5) You have to open a word processing application but you cannot see an icon on the desktop. What should you do?

   a) **Look for the shortcut in Start Menu or Start Screen—not all programs add shortcuts on the Desktop.**

6) Your colleague has to run many applications at the same time and finds it difficult to know which icon to choose when switching between them. What alternative method could you suggest?

   a) **Press Alt+Tab—this shows previews of the window. Windows can also show previews of the window contents when pointing at the taskbar icon.**

7) Your colleague is using a laptop and you notice that he laboriously clicks the mouse repeatedly to scroll through the document you are co-editing. What technique could he use to be more productive?

   a) **Use the mouse scroll wheel (or if it doesn't have one drag the scroll button in the scroll bar).**

Module 1 / Unit 3 / Using an OS

1) What function of an operating system is performed by the "shell?"

    a) **Interface between the user and the computer.**

2) What type of file in an OS is the main means of providing coordination of hardware components?

    a) **A driver (or device driver).**

3) What is an example of an open source operating system?

    a) **Linux, Chromium, or Android.**

4) What type of computing device(s) is macOS designed for installation on?

    a) **Desktop computers/workstations and laptops.**

5) True or false? Windows 10 is the first 64-bit edition of Windows.

    a) **False—Windows 10 is better described as a version than edition and there have been 64-bit editions of Windows versions since Windows XP.**

6) You have to open a file located on a network server. What should be your first step?

    a) **Open the Network object from Explorer and locate the server (computer) hosting the file.**

7) What is the technical term for a web address?

    a) **Uniform Resource Locator (URL). In fact, Uniform Resource Identifier (URI) is now preferred in web standards documentation but URL is more widely known and used.**

8) What key combination can you use to force the browser to ignore any locally cached files when refreshing a page?

    a) **Ctrl+F5.**

Module 1 / Unit 4 / Managing an OS

1) What is the registry and how does it distinguish Windows and Linux?

   a) **The registry is a database of configuration settings supporting the Windows OS. Linux uses individual text files to store settings.**

2) What term is used to describe terminating a process that is not responding to user input?

   a) **This is often called "killing" the process.**

3) Why might you use the Services snap-in to manage background processes rather than Task Manager?

   a) **Task Manager allows you to start and stop services but the Services snap-in also allows you to configure service properties.**

4) The Task Scheduler allows you to run a process automatically in Windows. What is a widely-used Linux equivalent?

   a) **cron is widely used to run tasks automatically in Linux.**

5) What part of the system memory setup is most user-configurable?

   a) **Use of virtual memory or a pagefile, where disk space is used to supplement system RAM.**

6) What two things are configured on a disk to make storage space on the disk available to the Windows OS?

   a) **The disk must contain at least one partition, typically allocated a drive letter, and the partition must be formatted with a suitable file system.**

7) What is a CLI?

   a) **A Command Line Interface allows the user to interact with the OS using typed commands or scripts rather than a GUI.**

8) What protection feature in Windows is designed to prevent a script or software from making unauthorized changes to the OS configuration?

   a) **User Access Control (UAC). UAC means that the user must input their credentials or click through an authorization prompt before the configuration change can be made.**

9) True or false? A standard user cannot change their own password.

   a) **False—ordinary users can change their own password but cannot change anyone else's.**

Module 1 / Unit 5 / Troubleshooting and Support

1) You are advising a colleague about best practices when troubleshooting. You have identified the following techniques to use to identify a problem: gather information, duplicate the problem, question users, identify symptoms, and approach multiple problems individually. If you are following CompTIA's troubleshooting model, what other piece of advice should you give?

   a) **Determine if anything has changed—this is one of the most useful troubleshooting techniques.**

2) You have asked a senior manager to authorize your plan of action for resolving a fault in a software application. What name is given to the process you are following?

   a) **This is escalating the problem. You might escalate a problem to more experienced staff or seek help with a solution plan that is beyond your authority to put into action.**

3) You are setting up a new computer, but it doesn't seem to be working. Should you check anything or contact the manufacturer?

   a) **It would be best to double-check you have connected the cables correctly (especially power).**

4) Your computer locks up periodically and feels hot to the touch. Could these things be related?

   a) **Yes, many lockup problems are caused by overheating. The first step would be to clean the fan exhaust vents of dust.**

5) What crucial piece of information would you need when trying to locate support information about a computer system on the manufacturer's website?

   a) **The model number or a service code.**

6) If you do not have a support contract, what is likely to be the best option for obtaining advice about a problem with an application?

   a) **A product support or community forum.**

7) You are looking for content on a topic but your search is returning millions of matches that are not particularly helpful. What two methods could you use to get better search results?

   a) **Use more search keywords (ideally with 'uncommon' words) or search for an exact phrase by enclosing it in quotes.**

8) You want to find something on a particular website, but the site does not have a search tool. Could you use a general search engine, and if so, how?

   a) **Yes—you use an advanced search form or use the site: operator (for example 'certification site:comptia.org').**

Module 2 / Unit 1 / Using Data Types and Units

1) Which notation system supports presenting the largest numbers using the fewest digits: Binary, Decimal, or Hexadecimal?

   a) **Hexadecimal. Each hex digit can store 16 bits of information. A single decimal digit stores 4 bits while binary obviously stores 1 bit.**

2) What is the decimal number 75 in binary and hexadecimal?

   a) **0100 1011 in binary and 4B in hex. Hex notation is often indicated using 0x to precede the hex digits, so you may see this written like 0x4b. To work out the answer without a calculator, write out the place values for each notation system. For binary you'd have columns for 64, 32, 16, 8, 4, 2, and 1 and put a 1 in each column you need to add up to 75 and a 0 in the others. For hex you only need 16 and 1 (75 divided by 16 is 4 remainder 11, which is represented as "B" in hex).**

3) Which data type provides for whole numbers only?

   a) **Integer.**

4) What is the difference between the char and string data types?

   a) **Char stores a single textual character in a fixed length field (typically 1 byte). A string is a variable length field for storing a sequence of characters.**

5) Which data representation format can encode the widest range of characters?

   a) **Unicode can represent millions of characters (glyphs). ASCII's 7-bit data structure can only support 128 characters, some of which are non-printable control characters.**

6) What type of legal protection could be obtained for a novel software algorithm?

   a) **Patent provides the best protection as it can enforce ownership even if someone tries to write the algorithm in a slightly different way. Software code is often protected both by patent and by copyright however.**

7) What data protection technology could you implement in order to restrict the type of activity that users could employ on digital products that they have purchased or rented?

   a) **Digital Rights Management (DRM).**

8) What part of the process of data analytics is most closely supported by meaningful reporting?

   a) **Insights are the "end product" of the analytic process. Humans need a suitable reporting format to make best use of insights.**

1) What compatibility information should you confirm before installing a software application?

    a) **That it works with the version of Windows that you have and that your computer meets the system (hardware) requirements.**

2) Following installation of a program written for an older version of Windows, you receive an alert that it might not have installed correctly. What feature could you use to make the program run correctly?

    a) **Use the program's Compatibility tab to use settings for the older Windows version.**

3) Why would Windows prompt you to enter a password if you try to install a software application?

    a) **Installing an application requires administrator privileges and is an action protected by User Account Control. If you were logged on as an administrator already, you might have to enter the password on a domain; if you were logged on as an ordinary user, you would have to enter the administrator's user name and password.**

4) Windows comes with web server software but it is not enabled by default. How would you install this software?

    a) **Use the Turn Windows features on or off dialog from Programs and Features.**

5) Following installation of an application, another program on your computer has stopped working. What could you do to try to fix it?

    a) **Try using the Repair option in Programs and Features (if available) or re-installing the program.**

6) Why might one of your first tasks on receiving a new computer be to remove software applications?

    a) **The computer may be bundled with pre-installed software that you do not want.**

7) In order to obtain support, the software vendor wants to know the application's product ID. How would you locate this information?

    a) **Usually via the Help > About menu.**

8) What is the difference between freeware and open source software?

    a) **Open source means that the programming code used to design the software is also made available (and you must make it available in turn if you sell or distribute any part of it). Freeware means the software product costs nothing to use but this does not mean that the code is made available too or that you could modify the software and distribute it yourself.**

9) What type of software would you use to configure a server by connecting to it over the network?

   a) **Remote Desktop.**

10) What type of software manages tasks, dependencies, and timelines?

   a) **Project management software.**

Module 2 / Unit 3 / Programming and App Development

1) What shows the structure of code without using the specific syntax of any one language?

   a) **Pseudocode.**

2) What is an interpreted language?

   a) **Interpreted languages do not need to be compiled. They run within the context of an interpreter which converts the code to machine code during runtime.**

3) How is a markup language differ from a compiled language?

   a) **Markup doesn't provide instructions for the CPU to run as such. Markup is a way of using nested tags within a document to describe its structure and contents.**

4) What are constants and variables examples of?

   a) **Programming identifiers.**

5) What type of programming concept allows for a variable size container?

   a) **A vector is a variable size container while an array is a fixed size one.**

6) You want to check whether a condition has been met, and if it has, perform one action. Otherwise, you want your program to perform a second action. What sort of programming operation would help achieve this?

   a) **A conditional branch, such as an If...Then statement.**

7) In a program, what does a loop do?

   a) **A loop performs one or more instructions until (or while) a condition is met.**

8) What is the difference between a procedure and a function?

   a) **A procedure does something while a function does something and then returns a value to the main program.**

9) What three things define an object?

   a) **Properties, attributes, and methods.**

10) What three scripting options are commonly used in Windows 10 to perform administrative tasks?

    a) **Batch files, Windows PowerShell scripts, and VBScripts.**

11) True or false? You do not need to install a web application to your computer; it would be accessed via a browser.

    a) **True.**

12) What is the advantage of a local network hosted application, in terms of data storage?

    a) **If data is stored on the server not on the local workstation, it is easier to apply access controls and to back it up.**

Module 2 / Unit 4 / Using Databases

1) What are the structural elements of a database table?

    a) **Each table stores information about records (rows in the table) in fields (columns in the tables).**

2) What term is used to describe selecting and viewing information in a database?

    a) **Query.**

3) How does an RDBMS such as Microsoft SQL Server differ from Microsoft Excel when used to store a dataset?

    a) **Excel is an example of a flat file system. These do not scale well, and usually support a single user only. RDBMS platforms enable many hundreds or thousands of users to connect concurrently, and can support very large datasets. Also, an RDBMS can enforce data types for each column and validate information entered as fields and records.**

4) What language is usually used to request data from an RDBMS such as Oracle?

    a) **Structured Query Language (SQL) is used to query RDBMS-based database platforms.**

5) What is it that defines the relationship between tables in an RDBMS?

    a) **Each table contains a primary key whose value is unique for each record in the table. A foreign table can use the value of a primary key as a relation, storing the value in a foreign key field.**

6) Give an example of unstructured data.

    a) **Images and text files and other document formats are unstructured data.**

7) Give two examples of semi-structured data stores.

   a) **Key/value pair databases and markup language document stores.**

8) Is an INSERT statement an example of a definition or manipulation language statement?

   a) **Manipulation language—it depends on the structure of a table (columns, data types, and constraints) being established already.**

9) You need a development environment with a library of database functions. What type of interface are you using?

   a) **Programmatic access.**

10) How can a client-server application architecture be described if there is the potential for the structure of the application platform to be developed further?

   a) **This could be described as a two-tier application. It could be re-developed as a three-tier application by specifying presentation, application, and data layers.**

Module 3 / Unit 1 / System Components

1) What type of component provides persistent storage?

   a) **A mass storage device such as a Hard Disk Drive (HDD), Solid State Drive (SSD), or flash memory. You could also mention optical discs (CD, DVD, Blu-Ray).**

2) What computer component is most restrictive in terms of determining upgrade potential for a desktop computer?

   a) **The motherboard—it is difficult and expensive to replace.**

3) True or false? A plug-in card is always required to support PC sound.

   a) **False—sound functions are often provided by the motherboard chipset.**

4) What is the main advantage of using a CPU in 64-bit mode?

   a) **Makes more system memory accessible. A 64-bit CPU and OS is also required to run 64-bit applications, but there are not too many of these yet. 64-bit software is more reliable and a bit faster than 32-bit software.**

5) What is a typical speed for a modern CPU to run at?

   a) **Around 2 GHz; budget models might run as low as 1 GHz while the fastest run up to about 3 GHz.**

6) You want to purchase a computer with a fast graphics interface. What type of expansion slot should you look for?

   a) **PCIe x16—this is a type of PCI Express slot that uses 16 'lanes'. Each lane can transfer 250 MBps (or 500 MBps for PCIe 2 and 1 GBps for v3).**

7) What type of component provides a passive cooling solution?

   a) **A heatsink or heat spreader removes heat from the component by convection with no power required. However, it is usually necessary to cool the heatsink or heat spreader itself and this is likely to require active cooling (a fan).**

8) How would you access the system setup program on a PC?

   a) **Historically, by pressing the appropriate key during startup (ESC, DEL, F1, F2, or F10). Modern PCs often use fast boot modes that require some other means of booting to the firmware setup program.**

Module 3 / Unit 2 / Using Device Interfaces

1) True or false? Mice and keyboards must be connected to a computer via PS/2 ports.

   a) **False—they are now much more likely to use USB or wireless (Bluetooth or other RF) interfaces.**

2) True or false? USB cables have the same connectors at either end.

   a) **Partly false—the connectors for the host (PC) and device use different form factors (there are also normal size and mini or micro device connectors). A new reversible Type C connector is starting to be used however.**

3) A user has two USB drives connected to her PC. She complains that when she copies large files to both drives at the same time, it seems to take much longer. Why might this be?

   a) **Bandwidth on the USB bus is shared between all devices.**

4) You want to purchase a flat-panel monitor that can show widescreen movies. You are considering models with native resolutions of 1400x1050 and 1920x1200. Which should you choose?

   a) **1920x1200 as this is a widescreen format.**

5) True or false? HDMI is the only type of display interface that supports High Definition picture resolutions.

   a) **False—there is also DisplayPort and Thunderbolt and some DVI formats also support HD resolutions.**

6) You are considering buying a new display device. The model you are considering accepts digital inputs only. Your computer's graphics adapter has a blue port with 15 holes. Would this flat-panel be a wise purchase?

   a) **Probably not, as this connector is VGA, which supports analog output only. It is possible to buy converters however.**

7) You need to configure settings for an input device. What should be your first step?

   a) **Open the Settings app or Control Panel.**

8) A friend is asking for your help in using her computer. When he presses the key marked @, a different symbol appears. What could be the cause?

   a) **The keyboard is set to use a UK layout—you can correct this using the Language Bar.**

9) What type of mouse would you recommend for someone who uses their computer principally to play computer games and why?

   a) **Laser mouse—this registers cursor movements more quickly and accurately.**

Module 3 / Unit 3 / Using Peripheral Devices

1) Which Windows interface is used for advanced management and troubleshooting of devices?

   a) **Device Manager is used to update drivers and obtain more advanced troubleshooting information. The basic user interface is either Devices and Printers or the device pages in the Settings app, depending on the Windows version.**

2) What do you need to know to connect to a device that is configured over the network?

   a) **Typically the Internet Protocol (IP) address of its management page. Some devices may use a name to locate the page instead. You are also likely to be prompted for a user name and password.**

3) True or false? If you want to configure the DPI of a display device, you would do so via the Personalization app.

   a) **False—Dots Per Inch (DPI) or scaling is configured via Display properties. Personalization is for configuring themes and the appearance of the desktop.**

4) You are configuring dual monitors positioned side-by-side. You want to increase the amount of screen space available. Which multiple display option should you set?

   a) **Extend the displays.**

5) You need to plug a microphone into a computer to make a recording. How would you identify which jack to use?

    a) **The jack should be color-coded (pink). There may be an icon to represent usage though. If neither is present, check the system documentation.**

6) What, if any, type of printer uses a fuser?

    a) **Laser printer—the fuser bonds the toner to the surface of the paper using high heat and pressure.**

7) What are the four inks used to produce color prints?

    a) **Cyan, Magenta, Yellow, and Black (CMYK).**

8) What type of wired interface is a printer MOST likely to use?

    a) **Universal Serial Bus (USB).**

9) You want to configure a printer to use both sides of the paper (duplex) by default. You have alt-clicked the printer object—which command should you select to proceed?

    a) **Printing preferences.**

10) What basic command demonstrates that a printer is connected properly to a computer and that its driver is installed correctly for Windows?

    a) **Print Test Page.**

11) What function of a scanner would you use if you want to convert a letter that someone has mailed to you into a computer-editable document?

    a) **Optical Character Recognition (OCR).**

12) True or false? If your PC does not have a flash memory card reader, you should be able to connect the camera itself to the PC over USB to copy images off the card.

    a) **True—must cameras support USB connections.**

Module 3 / Unit 4 / Using Storage Devices

1) You have a motherboard that is designed for DDR2 memory that works at a bus speed of 533 MHz. You have some DDR3 memory modules that also work at a bus speed of 533 MHz. Are the modules compatible with the motherboard?

    a) **No—DDR3 modules cannot be used in DDR2 slots.**

2) Why can't you use memory modules designed for a desktop computer in a laptop?

    a) **Laptops use a smaller form factor called SO-DIMM while desktops use DIMMs.**

3) A hard drive is rated at 10,000 RPM. What is the significance of this statistic?

    a) **The number of revolutions per minute (RPM) is one of the basic factors determining the speed of the drive. 10,000 rpm represents good performance (15K rpm is the best available).**

4) What type of connector would you use for an external hard drive to connect to a Windows PC?

    a) **USB. Firewire, eSATA, or Thunderbird are also possible but not nearly so popular. Most drives are now USB3 or USB3.1. Note that you can plug a USB3 drive into a USB2 port, so long as you have a USB3 device cable.**

5) Your computer has 4 SATA ports. How many hard drives can be installed?

    a) **Four—each SATA port can be used to connect one drive.**

6) True or false? A single layer Blu-ray Disc has greater capacity than a dual-layer, double-sided DVD.

    a) **True—the capacity of a single layer Blu-ray disc is 25 GB compared to 17 GB for a dual-layer, double-sided DVD.**

7) What sort of device would you need to transfer data from a "Memory Stick?"

    a) **Memory card reader/multi-card reader. Do note that Memory Sticks are no longer in production so you could struggle to locate a suitable reader.**

8) What sort of device could you use to expand the storage capacity of a smartphone?

    a) **Flash memory card.**

Module 3 / Unit 5 / Using File Systems

1) In Windows, you can access data via letter-labeled "drives." Do these correspond exactly to physical disks?

   a) **Not necessarily in the case of hard disks, which can be configured with multiple partitions, each of which can be assigned a drive letter. Optical drives and flash memory cards cannot be partitioned however.**

2) What type of file system must the partition that Windows files are installed on use?

   a) **NTFS.**

3) What default installation folders contain system and application files that should not normally be deleted or modified manually?

   a) **The 'Windows' and 'Program Files' folders.**

4) What is the file path to the Documents folder for a user named "David," assuming Windows is installed to a hard disk with a single partition using the default settings?

   a) **C:\Users\David\Documents**

5) How is a Windows library different from a folder?

   a) **A library acts as a virtual folder by displaying the contents of multiple folders, which could be located on different drives.**

6) If you have made changes to a file and want to keep both the original file and the modified version, what command should you use?

   a) **Save As.**

7) Why should you be more careful about deleting files from a USB flash drive than from the main hard drive?

   a) **The files will not be recycled so there is no possibility of retrieving them if you change your mind (at least, not without using specialist data recovery software).**

8) What view options could you use to show files of a particular type sorted by date?

   a) **Group the files by file type then sort by date.**

9) What kind of data would you expect to find in a file with a TIFF extension?

   a) **This is an image file format.**

10) What is a zip file?

   a) **A file archive containing other files in a compressed format.**

Module 4 / Unit 1 / Networking Concepts

1) What is a WAN?

    a) **A Wide Area Network (WAN) connects sites in different geographic locations. WANs usually make use of telecommunications and service provider networks rather than being directly operated by the network administrators.**

2) What is a packet made up of?

    a) **A packet consists of a number of fields contained within a header section plus a payload. The payload could be a packet from the protocol layer above.**

3) What are the key features of a packet switching network?

    a) **Nodes within the network can perform a forwarding function, allowing a packet to utilize any available path through the network. This makes the network robust against link failures. If is beneficial for the network to use small packets that are easy to re-send.**

4) What protocol is usually used to provide logical addressing on networks?

    a) **Internet Protocol (IP).**

5) What type of address identifies a network interface in the context of the local network segment only?

    a) **A Media Access Control (MAC) address.**

6) What type of device is used to transfer packets between different networks?

    a) **A router.**

7) Which protocol allows people to use names/labels to address network resources rather than numeric addresses?

    a) **Domain Name System (DNS).**

8) Which of the following parts of a web address is usually depends on a name resolution service: protocol type, host location, file path?

    a) **The host location is usually represented by a Fully Qualified Domain Name (FQDN), such as www.comptia.org, resolved to a numeric IP address by DNS.**

9) What does HTTP stand for?

    a) **HyperText Transfer Protocol (HTTP).**

10) Which email protocol(s) are used to download messages from a mail server?

a) **Either Post Office Protocol (POP) or Internet Message Access Protocol (IMAP).**

Module 4 / Unit 2 / Connecting to a Network

1) What device is used to connect computers together in an Ethernet network?

   a) **A switch.**

2) What is the difference between a modem and a router?

   a) **A modem creates a serial link between two computers over some sort of long distance media. It operates at the data link layer. A router makes forwarding decisions between logical networks. It does not need to take account of the framing and transmission details—those are the responsibility of the modem (or of an Ethernet switch or wireless access point). It just needs to know that a particular logical network can be reached over one of its interfaces. Most SOHO devices pack all these functions into a single appliance but it is important to appreciate the differences between the functions.**

3) Can you list at least four Internet access methods?

   a) **Digital Subscriber Line (DSL), cable/Hybrid Fiber Coax, Fiber to the Curb (FTTC), satellite, and cellular radio.**

4) What is the latest Wi-Fi standard and which frequency band(s) does it use?

   a) **IEEE 802.11ac works in the 5 GHz band. Most 802.11ac access points do have 2.4 GHz radios but they use them to support legacy standards.**

5) What information do you need to configure a wireless connection manually?

   a) **Service Set ID (SSID)/network name, encryption type, and authentication information (a preshared key if not using enterprise authentication).**

6) What is the risk of using a free Wi-Fi network to make an order from an online shop?

   a) **Data on an open network may be intercepted by the person running the network or by other computers connected to the network. You need to ensure that the online store uses a secure (HTTPS) connection.**

7) What does attenuation mean?

   a) **Attenuation describes the loss of strength of a signal the farther it has to travel. Attenuation sets the distance limitations on different network media types.**

Module 4 / Unit 3 / Secure Web Browsing

1) If you use an open network, what email configuration setting should you ensure is enabled?

    a) **Enable Secure Sockets Layer/Transport Layer Security (SSL/TLS) encryption to protect the account password.**

2) You have installed a screensaver application. Later, after updating your anti-virus software, a malicious program is found. This appears to have infected your system at the same time as the screensaver was installed. What class of malware is this?

    a) **Trojan Horse.**

3) You want to use a website that hosts training modules in a custom media format. What type of add-on would you need to install to play this media?

    a) **You would need to install a type of browser add-on called a plug-in. Plug-ins should be restricted to interacting with the media object on the web page.**

4) What type of file might a website use to track whether you have visited it before?

    a) **Cookie.**

5) True or false? Browser pop-up windows are definite symptoms of virus infection.

    a) **False—these could be a result of adware or part of the design of a particular site (admittedly, not a site you'd want to visit often).**

6) You are using a computer in an Internet cafe. What should you do at the end of the session?

    a) **Clear the browser cache or use the workstation's browser private/incognito browsing mode.**

7) What identifies a website as using the secure HTTPS protocol with a valid certificate?

    a) **The URL shows the "https://" protocol and the browser shows a padlock icon. For sites that have passed special validation regimes, the address bar will be shown in green. If a site uses https but the certificate is not trusted by the browser, an alert is displayed.**

8) You want to restrict access to a computer on your network to a single Internet host running a particular application. What two things do you need to configure in your firewall's access control list?

    a) **The IP address of the host and the port number of the application.**

Module 4 / Unit 4 / Using Shared Storage

1) True or false? A hard disk connected to a computer via a USB port could be described as "Direct Attached Storage."

    a) **True.**

2) What type of connection would a NAS device use?

    a) **Network Attached Storage (NAS) means using either a cabled (Ethernet) or Wi-Fi link to the network.**

3) Which admin tool or screen would you use to configure a Windows computer to join a domain?

    a) **Via the System applet in Control Panel or via the Settings app (Access work or school).**

4) True or false? Any version or edition of Windows can be used to share files with other users.

    a) **True—non-server editions are restricted in the number of simultaneous clients though.**

5) How could you access a network folder called DATA on a network server called TOWER1 using the Explorer address bar?

    a) **By entering the UNC path: \\TOWER1\DATA**

6) What is a mapped drive?

    a) **A folder shared by a network server that the client connects to via a drive letter that redirects to the network share name (\\Server\Folder).**

7) What protocol would be used to provide encrypted file downloads from a web server?

    a) **HTTPS—HyperText Transfer Protocol with Secure Sockets Layer/Transport Layer Security (SSL/TLS).**

8) You have made a backup of system data using a removable hard disk. What should you do next?

    a) **Store the disk in a secure location—preferably in a different place to the PC.**

Module 4 / Unit 5 / Using Mobile Devices

1) What type of gesture is typically used for zooming on a touchscreen?

    a) **Pinch.**

2) What is the purpose of an accelerometer, as fitted in a mobile device?

    a) **It is one of the components that detects how the user is moving the device around. This is used to set the screen orientation and as an advanced control mechanism.**

3) What feature allows data to be removed from a device if is lost or stolen?

    a) **This is referred to as remote wipe or sometimes as a kill switch.**

4) True or false? A smartphone cannot join a Wi-Fi network if the SSID is not being broadcast.

    a) **False—the SSID (or network name) can be entered manually, as with a computer.**

5) What is "airplane mode?"

    a) **A quick toggle for disabling all wireless functionality (cellular, Wi-Fi, and Bluetooth).**

Module 5 / Unit 1 / Security Concerns

1) Which property of secure information is compromised by snooping?

    a) **Confidentiality—keeping information disclosure restricted to authorized persons only.**

2) An attacker has used a rogue access point to intercept traffic passing between wireless clients and the wired network segment. What type of attack is this?

    a) **This is typical of a Man-in-the-Middle (MitM) attack.**

3) What type of access mechanism is MOST vulnerable to a replay attack?

    a) **Use of a token generated by software. If the token is not authenticated properly by the server, it could be vulnerable to replay, where someone else obtaining the token can masquerade as the original user.**

4) Which specific attack uses a botnet to threaten availability?

    a) **Distributed Denial of Service (DDoS).**

5) In considering availability concerns, what use might a lockable faceplate on a server-class computer be?

    a) **It may prevent the user switching the machine on or off (useful for servers) or accessing removable drives and ports.**

6) What does AAA stand for?

    a) **Authentication, Authorization, Accounting.**

7) Why should a security policy instruct users not to reveal their password to technical support staff?

    a) **It exposes users to social engineering attacks to gather login credentials for malicious use. Any request for a password should be treated by users as suspicious.**

8) How might someone masquerade as someone else when using email or Instant Messaging?

    a) **By accessing their user account—this could be done by stealing their login information, using an unattended computer that was still logged in, or using malware such as a Trojan.**

9) What are the three main areas where redundancy should be provisioned?

    a) **Data/storage (RAID), network links, and power. You might additionally mention site-level redundancy, though this is very expensive to provision.**

10) Why is prioritization a critical task for disaster recovery?

    a) **Services may have dependencies that make restoring them in the wrong order futile. Also, disasters lead to scarce resources so the most critical services must be given priority. These should be identified before the disaster occurs so that staff working to recover systems are properly guided.**

Module 5 / Unit 2 / Using Best Practices

1) Part of host hardening is to reduce the attack surface. What configuration changes does reducing the attack surface involve?

    a) **Removing unwanted and unnecessary software, disabling unused OS features and services, and closing unnecessary network ports. This reduces the ways other hosts or processes can interact with the hardened host.**

2) What is the main difference between virus and worm malware?

    a) **A virus has to infect a file whereas a worm propagates in memory and over computer networks.**

3) How might malware hosted on a website be able to infect your computer simply by your browsing the site?

   a) **By exploiting a vulnerability in software installed on your computer (a fault or "exploit" in the browser, a browser plug-in, or the OS for instance).**

4) How might spyware be able to steal a password?

   a) **Typically by monitoring key strokes (a key logger). It might also be able to steal password databases and decrypt them.**

5) What type of malware is being described? The malware encrypts the user's documents folder and any attached removable disks then extorts the user for money to release the encryption key.

   a) **Ransomware.**

6) True or false? Most anti-virus software can remediate a system by blocking access to an infected file but not actually deleting it.

   a) **True—this is called quarantining the file.**

7) What is the main means by which anti-virus software identifies infected files?

   a) **Using definitions or signatures of known virus code. These definitions must be kept up-to-date.**

8) What are the two main ways that spam might expose recipients to hazardous content?

   a) **Through malware-infected attachments and through links to malicious websites.**

9) Your friend sent you an email link, which you have opened, and now the browser is asking whether you should install a plug-in to view all the content on the page. Should you proceed?

   a) **No—this is a classic phishing attack and your friend's computer could be infected with a virus or Trojan. Check whether they sent the link in good faith first.**

10) True or false? An OEM site is a reputable source of management software and drivers for a particular system.

   a) **True—an Original Equipment Manufacturer (OEM) in the IT industry, such as Dell or HP, assembles systems made from the parts and software of various other suppliers. The components used in their systems may be specific to their brand and so they host their own support files for any system they sell.**

Module 5 / Unit 3 / Using Access Controls

1) What are the four processes of an access control system?

    a) **Identification, Authentication, Authorization, and Accounting.**

2) Users should only be granted the minimum sufficient permissions. What system policy ensures that users do not receive rights unless granted explicitly?

    a) **Implicit deny.**

3) What is the main type of non-discretionary access control?

    a) **Mandatory Access Control—though any rules-based system might restrict discretionary aspects of granting rights.**

4) What type of control prevents a user from denying they performed an action?

    a) **Non-repudiation. Examples of controls providing non-repudiation include logging, video surveillance, biometrics, signatures, and receipts/tokens.**

5) What sort of account allows someone to access a computer without providing a user name or password?

    a) **Guest account.**

6) How does a one-time password work?

    a) **The password is generated by an asymmetric encryption algorithm. This means that the authenticating server can determine that the number was generated by a particular device (fob) at a particular time. When used with a PIN, it also proves that the password was input by a particular user.**

7) What type of system allows a user to authenticate once to access multiple services?

    a) **Single Sign-On (SSO).**

8) What type of cryptographic operation(s) are non-reversible?

    a) **Cryptographic hashing. You might also mention asymmetric encryption and public/private key pairs, where an operation performed with one key can only be reversed by the linked key and NOT by the key that performed the original operation.**

9) What class of data is a transport encryption protocol designed to protect?

    a) **Data in transit (or data in motion).**

10) Why is it important not to use simple words or names as a password?

   a) **Password-cracking software is configured with dictionaries of such names and phrases. Even if the password is encrypted, if it matches a term in the password-cracking dictionary it will be discovered in seconds.**

Module 5 / Unit 4 / Behavioral Security Concepts

1) What is a SOP?

   a) **Standard Operating Procedure.**

2) Apart from passwords and PII, what other type(s) of confidential information should be governed by classification and handling procedures?

   a) **Company confidential information and customer information.**

3) Why might a company ban use of the corporate network and desktop software for personal communications?

   a) **The company might be held responsible for inappropriate content posted by its employees. The issue of privacy is also complex and it is often better for both the company and the employee to use corporate systems for business communications only.**

4) What two main privacy issues arise from using a social networking site?

   a) **Firstly, you need to control how far information you post to the site is distributed. You could make it private, accessible to close friends only, accessible to all your contacts, or accessible to anyone. Secondly, you need to know how the company processes, stores, and transfers or sells any data it collects about you, including information you post and your activity on the site.**

Glossary

32-bit versus 64-bit
Processing modes referring to the size of each instruction processed by the CPU. 32-bit CPUs replaced earlier 16-bit CPUs and were used through the 1990s to the present day, though most CPUs now work in 64-bit mode. The main 64-bit platform is called AMD64 or EM64T (by Intel). This platform is supported by 64-bit versions of Windows as well as various Linux distributions. Software can be compiled as 32-bit or 64-bit. 64-bit CPUs can run most 32-bit software but a 32-bit CPU cannot execute 64-bit software.

8.3 Filenames
The DOS file naming standard—an eight-character ASCII name followed by a three-character file extension (which identifies the file type). Windows supports long file names but can also generate a short file name, based on DOS 8.3 naming rules. This provides backwards compatibility for older applications.

AAA
Authentication, Authorization, and Accounting—the principal stages of security control. A resource should be protected by all three types of controls.

Accelerometer/Gyroscope
Components used in mobile devices to detect motion (accelerometer) and rotation (gyroscope). As well as switching screen orientation, this can be used as a control mechanism (for example, a driving game could allow the tablet itself to function as a steering wheel).

Access Control
Creating one or more barriers around a resource such that only authenticated users can gain access. Each resource has an Access Control List (ACL) specifying what users can do. Resources often have different access levels (for example, being able to read a file or being able to read and edit it).

ACL (Access Control List)
The permissions attached to or configured on a network resource, such as folder, file, or firewall. The ACL specifies which subjects (user accounts, host IP addresses, and so on) are allowed or denied access and the privileges given over the object (read only, read/write, and so on).

Active Partition
The primary partition marked as active; there is only one per system. This becomes the bootable partition. In Microsoft terminology, the partition that the PC boots from is referred to as the system partition.

Adapter Card
Circuit board providing additional functionality to the computer system (video, sound, networking, modem, and so on). An adapter card fits a slot on the PC's expansion bus and often provides ports through slots cut into the back of the PC case. Different cards are designed for different slots (PCI or PCIe).

Addressing (Network)
In order to communicate on a network, each host must have an address. Different protocols use different methods of addressing. For example, IPv4 uses a 32-bit binary number, typically expressed as a 4-part decimal number (dotted decimal notation) while IPv6 uses a 128-bit binary number expressed in hexadecimal. A routable addressing scheme such as IP also provides identification for distinct networks as well as hosts.

Adware
Software that records information about a PC and its user. Adware is used to describe software that the user has acknowledged can record information about their habits. For example, an online store might record past purchases and display prominent advertisements to market new products based on the user's purchase history.

Airplane Mode
A toggle found on mobile devices enabling the user to disable and enable wireless functionality quickly.

Algorithm
Any defined method of performing a process but in encryption, the term specifically refers to the technique used to encrypt a message. The strength of an algorithm depends to a large extent on the size of its key (the code that enables a message to be encrypted or decrypted). A minimum key size of 2048 bits is considered secure by NIST. There are a number of algorithms in use for different types of encryption. Some of the main technologies are SHA-1 and MD5 (hash functions), 3DES, AES, RC (Rivest Cipher), IDEA, Blowfish/Twofish, and CAST (used for symmetric encryption [where the same key is used to encrypt and decrypt]), and Diffie-Hellman, RSA, ElGamal, and ECC (used for asymmetric encryption, where two linked keys are used).

AMD (Advanced Micro Devices)
CPU manufacturer providing healthy competition for Intel. AMD chips such as the K6, Athlon 64, and Opteron have been very popular with computer manufacturers and have often out-performed their Intel equivalents.

Android
Mobile (smartphone and tablet) OS developed by the Open Handset Alliance (primarily sponsored by Google). Android is open source software.

Anti-virus
Software capable of detecting and removing virus infections and (in most cases) other types of malware, such as worms, Trojans, rootkits, adware, spyware, password crackers, network mappers, DoS tools, and so on. Anti-virus software works on the basis of both identifying malware code (signatures) and detecting suspicious behavior (heuristics). Anti-virus software must be kept up to date with the latest malware definitions and protect itself against tampering.

AP (Access Point)
Device that provides connectivity between wireless devices and a cabled network. APs with Internet connectivity located in public buildings (cafes, libraries, airports for instance) are often referred to as hotspots.

Apple
Desktop and portable computer (and latterly smartphone and tablet) manufacturer. Apple computers are built to use OS X which makes them incompatible with IBM PC/Windows-based software.

ARM (Advanced RISC Machines)
Designer of CPU and chipset architectures widely used in mobile devices. RISC stands for Reduced Instruction Set Computing. RISC microarchitectures use simple instructions processed very quickly. This contrasts with Complex (CISC) microarchitectures, which use more powerful instructions but process each one more slowly.

ARP (Address Resolution Protocol)
When two systems communicate using TCP/IP, an IP address is used to identify the destination machine. The IP address must be mapped to a device (the network adapter's MAC address). ARP performs the task of resolving an IP address to a hardware address. Each host caches known mappings in an ARP table for a few minutes. arp is also a utility used to manage the ARP cache.

Array
Identifier for a group of variables of the same type. The number of possible elements in an array is fixed when the array is declared.

ASCII
7-bit code page mapping binary values to character glyphs. Standard ASCII can represent 127 characters, though some values are reserved for non-printing control characters.

Assembly Language
A compiled software program is converted to binary machine code using the instruction set of the CPU platform. Assembly language is this machine code represented in human-readable text.

Attack Surface
Attack surface is the degree of exposure a network or piece of software has to attack. For example, the more ports a server has open or the more features installed under an OS, the greater the likelihood of an attacker finding a vulnerability.

Audio Card
Adapter card providing sound playback and recording functionality.

Audio Port
A number of different audio ports exist on modern computer motherboards or on specialist sound cards. Commonly audio ports may be marked as: audio out, audio in, speaker out, microphone input/mic, and headphones.

Authentication
A means for a user to prove their identity to a computer system. Authentication is implemented as either something you know (a username and password), something you have (a smart card or key fob), or something you are (biometric information). Often, more than one method is employed (2-factor authentication).

Availability
Availability is the principle that something should not be so secure that it is completely inaccessible. A practical example is a password policy that forces users to adopt unsecure practices (such as writing their password on a post-it attached to their monitor). Another example is providing key recovery or escrow so that encrypted data can be recovered if the encryption key is lost or damaged. Availability also involves protecting a resource against loss or damage or DoS attacks.

Backup
Recovery of data can be provided through the use of a backup system. Most backup systems provide support for tape devices. This provides a reasonably reliable and quick mechanism for copying critical data. Different backup types (full, incremental, or differential) balance media capacity, time required to backup, and time required to restore.

Binary
Notational system with 2 values per digit (zero and one). Computers process code in binary because the transistors in its CPU and memory components also have two states (off and on).

Biometric
Identifying features stored as digital data can be used to authenticate a user. Typical features used include facial pattern, iris, retina, or fingerprint pattern, and signature recognition. This requires the relevant scanning device, such as a fingerprint reader, and a database of biometric information (template).

BIOS (Basic Input/Output System)
The BIOS is firmware that contains programs and information relating to the basic operation of PC components such as drives, keyboard, video display, and ports. It also contains specific routines to allow set-up configuration to be viewed and edited and it contains the self-diagnostic Power-On Self-Test (POST) program used to detect fundamental faults in PC components. BIOS can also be used to secure components not protected by the OS by specifying a supervisor password (to prevent tampering with BIOS settings) and a user password (to boot the PC).

Bit/Byte
Units of storage. See: Data Units.

Bluetooth
Short-range radio-based technology, working at up to 10m (30 feet) at up to 1 Mbps used to connect peripherals (such as mice, keyboards, and printers) and for communication between two devices (such as a laptop and smartphone). The advantage of radio-based signals is that devices do not need line-of-sight, though the signals can still be blocked by thick walls and metal and can suffer from interference from other radio sources operating at the same frequency (2.4 GHz). Bluetooth Low Energy (BLE) is designed for small battery-powered devices that transmit small amounts of data infrequently. BLE is not backwards-compatible with "classic" Bluetooth though a device can support both standards simultaneously.

Blu-ray
Latest generation of optical drive technology, with disc capacity of 25 GB per layer. Transfer rates are measured in multiples of 36 MBps.

Boolean
Data type support 1–bit storage, representing FALSE and TRUE. Boolean logic is a statement that resolves to a true or false condition and underpins the branching and looping features of computer code.

Boot Partition
In Microsoft terminology, the partition that contains the operating system (that is, the \WINDOWS folder) is referred to as the boot partition. This is typically a different partition to the system partition (the partition containing the boot files).

bps (Bits per Second)
The term "bits per second" is used to describe data transfer speed—the higher the number, the higher the transmission speed.

Browser
A web browser is software designed to view HTML pages. Browsers must be configured carefully and kept up to date with system patches to make them less vulnerable to Trojans and malicious scripting. As well as the browser itself, plug-in applications that enable use of particular file formats, such as Flash or PDF, may also be vulnerable.

Bus
Buses are the connections between components on the motherboard and peripheral devices attached to the computer. Buses are available in industry standard formats, each with its own advantages and disadvantages. The standard functions of a bus are to provide data sharing, memory addressing, power supply, and timing. Common bus types include PCI, PCI Express, ExpressCard, and USB.

Business Continuity Plan (BCP)/Continuity of Operations Plan (COOP)
A business continuity plan is designed to ensure that critical business functions demonstrate high availability and fault tolerance. Typically, this is achieved by allowing for redundancy in specifying resources. Examples include cluster services, RAID disk arrays, UPS. Business continuity plans should not be limited to technical elements however; they should also consider employees, utilities, suppliers, and customers. Associated with business continuity is the disaster recovery plan, which sets out actions and responsibilities for foreseen and unforeseen critical incidents.

Cable (Hybrid Fiber Coax)
A cable Internet connection is usually available along with a cable telephone/television service (Cable Access TV [CATV]). These networks are often described as Hybrid Fiber Coax (HFC) as they combine a fiber optic core network with coax links to consumer premises equipment but are more simply just described as "cable." Consumers interface with the service via a cable "modem" (actually functioning more like a bridge).

CAD (Computer-Aided Design)
Computer Aided Design (CAD) software makes technical drawings and schematics easier to produce and revise.

Captive Portal
A web page or website to which a client is redirected before being granted full network access. The portal might allow limited network browsing, provide an authentication mechanism, or provide resources such as access to patches or signature updates to allow the device to become compliant with network access policies. I can also function as a secondary authentication mechanism for open access points. On connecting, the user's browser is redirected to a server to enter credentials (and possibly payment for access).

CD-ROM (Compact Disc—Read Only Memory)
CD-ROM disc is an optical storage technology. The discs can normally hold 700 MB of data or 80 minutes of audio data. Recordable and re-writable CDs (and DVDs) are a popular backup solution for home users. They are also useful for archiving material. Unlike magnetic media, the data on the disc cannot be changed (assuming that the disc is closed to prevent further rewriting in the case of RW media). This makes them useful for preserving tamper-proof records.

Celeron Processor Series
Budget processor models produced by Intel alongside their Pentium and Core ranges.

Cell Phone
Mobile telephony works through a series of base station transmitters (cells) that connect to the cellular and telephone networks. This network can be used for voice and data communications. Data communications are divided into 2G (GSM; up to about 14 Kbps), 2.5G (GPRS, HSCSD, and EDGE; up to about 48 Kbps), and 3G (WCDMA; up to about 2 Mbps).

Certificate
A public key that has been certified by some agency, validating that the owner of the key is really who he or she says he or she is. This allows a sender to encrypt a message using the public key in the knowledge that only the recipient will be able to read it (using their linked private key). Certificates can also be used as proof of identity (for authentication or signing documents). Most certificates are based on the X.509 standard though PGP web of trust certificates are also popular.

Char
Data type supporting storage of a single character.

Chipset
The chipset provides communications between different components by implementing various controllers (for memory, graphics, I/O, and so on). The chipset may also provide "integrated" adapters (video, sound, and networking for instance). Historically, "fast" controllers (memory and video) were part of a "northbridge" chipset, placed close to the CPU and system memory. Slower buses were part of a "southbridge" chipset. In modern PC architecture, video and memory controllers are part of the CPU (on-die), the northbridge would mostly handle PCI Express adapters and the southbridge would host SATA, USB, audio and LAN functions, plus PCI/PATA legacy bus support.

Chrome OS
Chrome OS is derived from Linux, via an open source OS called Chromium. Chrome OS itself is proprietary. Chrome OS is developed by Google to run on specific laptop (chromebooks) and PC (chromeboxes) hardware.

CIA Triad
Confidentiality, Integrity, and Availability—the goals for providing a secure information management system.

Client
A network client provides connectivity to file servers. Client-Server is a model for providing network resources from a centrally controlled location. The server computer or application hosts the resource. A client computer or application requests the resource from the server. You will require a client for each type of server to which you have a connection—for example, Windows, NetWare, or Linux.

Cloud Computing
Any environment where software (Software as a Service and Platform as a Service) or computer/network resources (Infrastructure as a Service and Network as a Service) are provided to an end user who has no knowledge of or responsibility for how the service is provided. Cloud services provide elasticity of resources and pay-per-use charging models. Cloud access arrangements can be public, hosted private, or private (this type of cloud could be onsite or offsite relative to the other business units).

Compatibility Mode
Windows can run a program with settings from previous versions of Windows to try to resolve compatibility problems. This is configured from the program's shortcut properties dialog.

Compression Software
To send or store a file it often needs to be compressed in some way, to reduce the amount of space it takes up on the storage media or the bandwidth required to send it over a network. There are a number of compression utilities and formats.

Computer Management Console
The Computer Management provides tools for administering the local computer, including Device Manager, Event Viewer, Disk Management, Services, and Performance Monitor. To access the console, alt-click (My) Computer and select Manage.

Constant
Identifier for a value that is fixed before program execution and does not change.

Control Panel
The primary management interface for Windows.

Cookie
Text file used to store information about a user when they visit a website. Some sites still use cookies to support user sessions. This type of site can be vulnerable to replay attacks, where an attacker obtains a user's cookies and resends the session information.

Cooling Device
A CPU generates a large amount of heat that must be dissipated to prevent damage to the chip. Generally, a CPU will be fitted with a heatsink (a metal block with fins) and fan. Thermal compound is used at the contact point between the chip and the heatsink to ensure good heat transfer. The PSU also incorporates a fan to expel warm air from the system. Modern motherboards have temperature sensors that provide warning of overheating before damage can occur. Very high performance or overclocked systems or systems designed for quiet operation may require more sophisticated cooling systems, such as liquid cooling. Cooling systems that work without electricity are described as passive; those requiring a power source are classed as active.

Core Processor Series
The latest generation of Intel processors. The Core, Core 2, and Core iX CPUs were developed from the Pentium M architecture and have taken on the position of Intel's premium processor for both desktop and mobile platforms, replacing the long-standing Pentium brand.

CPU (Central Processing Unit)
The principal microprocessor in a computer or smartphone responsible for running operating system and applications software.

CRT (Cathode Ray Tube) Monitor
A CRT receives an analog signal from the graphics adapter and forms a color image on the screen by illuminating red, green, and blue dots (triads), The screen size is the diagonal distance across the face of the CRT, though part of this area may be obscured by the case, making the viewable area considerably less than the quoted screen size. CRTs are no longer mass-manufactured and modern systems use LCD panels.

DAC (Discretionary Access Control)
Access control model where each resource is protected by an Access Control List (ACL) managed by the resource's owner (or owners).

Data Rate
Data rate is the speed at which data can be sent or received between two or more computer components. These components may be part of the same computer, or may be connected across a network. The type of link that exists, the bus or port to which it is connected and the rate at which the data can be understood and processed are all factors that influence data rate. The peak (or maximum theoretical) rate needs to be distinguished from actual throughput (or sustained rate).

Data Units
The fundamental unit of data storage is the bit (binary digit) which can represent 1 or 0. A bit can be measured in multiples using Kilobit (Kb) and Megabit (Mb). These units are often used to speak about network data transfer rates. The computer industry abuses the SI system of decimal measurements where kilo=1,000, mega=1,000,000 and giga=1,000,000,000. Kilo is given a binary interpretation (a kilobit is 2^10 = 1024 bits). Different units are used to describe file sizes and memory capacity. 8 bits form a byte (B). 1024 bytes make a kilobyte (that is 2 ^ 10 bytes); 1024 kilobytes (KB) make a Megabyte (MB); 1024 MB makes 1 Gigabyte (GB); 1024 GB makes 1 Terabyte (TB). Other units include the nibble (½byte) and the word (2 bytes).

Database
Most network applications utilize databases. Major database server products include Oracle, Microsoft SQL Server, IBM's DB2 and Informix, and Sybase. Many databases are operated using Structured Query Language (SQL, pronounced "sequel"). The freeware MySQL database is a popular choice to provide database functionality on websites. Database engines are often subject to software exploits, and so should be kept patched. Database design, programming, and administration is complex and security should be considered as a critical requirement.

DDR SDRAM (Double Data Rate SDRAM)
Standard for SDRAM where data is transferred twice per clock cycle (making the maximum data rate 64x the bus speed in bps). DDR2/DDR3 SDRAM uses lower voltage chips and higher bus speeds.

Default Account
Default administrative and guest accounts configured on servers and network devices are possible points of unauthorized access. It is good practice to rename the Windows administrative account and on UNIX/Linux to leave the "root" system owner account unused.

Default Gateway
The default gateway is a TCP/IP address parameter that identifies the location of a router on the local subnet that the host can use to contact other networks.

Desktop
The primary user interface in Windows 7 and earlier is referred to as the desktop. The desktop is at the top of the object hierarchy in Windows Explorer, containing the Computer, Documents, Network, and Recycle Bin objects. The desktop also stores shortcuts to programs, files, and system objects.

Device Driver
A small piece of code that is loaded during the boot sequence of an operating system. This code, usually provided by the hardware vendor, provides access to a device, or hardware, from the OS kernel. Under Windows, a signing system is in place for drivers to ensure that they do not make the OS unstable.

Device Manager
Primary interface for configuring and managing hardware devices in Windows. Device Manager enables the administrator to disable and remove devices, view hardware properties and system resources, and update device drivers.

Digital Camera (Digicam)
A version of a 35mm film camera where the film is replaced by light-sensitive diodes (an array of CCDs [Charge Coupled Devices]) and electronic storage media (typically a flash memory card). The sensitivity of the array determines the maximum resolution of the image, typically 5 megapixels (2560x1920) or better. A digital camera can be connected to a computer via a USB or Firewire port.

Digital Certificate
An X.509 digital certificate is issued by a Certificate Authority (CA) as a guarantee that a public key it has issued to an organization to encrypt messages sent to it genuinely belongs to that organization. Both parties must trust the CA. The public key can be used to encrypt messages but not to decrypt them. A message can only be decrypted by the private key, which is mathematically linked to the public key but not derivable from it. This is referred to as asymmetric encryption. Part of the CA's responsibility is ensuring that this private key is known only to the organization owning the certificate. This arrangement is referred to a Public Key Infrastructure (PKI).

Digital Signaling
Signaling using discrete states to represent simple values, such as 1 or 0.

DIMM (Dual Inline Memory Module)
Dual in-line memory modules are the standard packaging for system memory. There are different pin configurations for different RAM types (SDRAM [168], DDR SDRAM [184], and DDR2/3 SDRAM [240]).

Directory
A file system object used to organize files. Directories can be created on any drive (the directory for the drive itself is called the root) and within other directories (subdirectory). Different file systems put limits on the number of files or directories that can be created on the root or the number of subdirectory levels. In Windows, directories are usually referred to as folders.

Disaster Recovery Plan
A documented and resourced plan showing actions and responsibilities to be used in response to critical incidents. The recovery plan may also provide for practice exercises or drills for testing and to familiarize staff with procedures. As well as facilitating a smooth transition in the event of disaster, plans must stress the importance of maintaining secure systems.

DisplayPort
Digital A/V interface developed by VESA. DisplayPort supports some cross-compatibility with DVI and HDMI devices.

DNS (Domain Name System)
This industry standard name resolution system provides name to IP address mapping services on the Internet and large intranets. DNS is a hierarchical, distributed database. DNS name servers host the database for domains for which they are authoritative. Root servers hold details of the top-level domains. DNS servers also perform queries or lookups to service client requests. The DNS protocol defines the mechanisms by which DNS servers and clients interact. The DNS protocol utilizes TCP/UDP port 53.

DoS (Denial of Service)
A network attack that aims to disrupt a service, usually by overloading it. A Distributed DoS (DDoS) attack uses multiple compromised computers (a "botnet" of "zombies") to launch the attack.

DOS (Disk Operating System)
Single tasking, real-mode operating system developed by Microsoft and widely adopted in the early 1980s. Version 6.3 was released in 1993.

DRAM (Dynamic RAM)
Dynamic RAM is a type of volatile memory that stores data in the form of electronic charges within transistors. Due to the effects of leakage and the subsequent loss of electrical charge, DRAM has to be refreshed at regular intervals. Memory refreshing can be performed when the data bits are accessed regularly, but this periodic access slows down the operation of this memory type. Standard DRAM is the lowest common denominator of the DRAM types. Modern PCs use a DRAM derivative to store data (currently DDR2/3 SDRAM).

DSL (Digital Subscriber Line)
DSL is a technology for transferring data over voice-grade telephone lines. DSL uses the higher frequencies available in a copper telephone line as a communications channel. The use of a filter prevents this from contaminating voice traffic with noise. The use of advanced modulation and echo cancelling techniques enable high bandwidth, full-duplex transmissions. There are various "flavors" of DSL, notably SDSL, G.SHDSL, ADSL, and VDSL.

DTP (Desktop Publishing)
Desktop Publishing (DTP) is similar to word processing but with more emphasis on the formatting and layout of documents than on editing the text.

Dual Core
CPU design that puts two chips onto the same package; a cheap means of providing SMP.

Dumpster Diving
A "social engineering" technique of discovering things about an organization (or person) based on what it throws away.

DVD (Digital Video/Versatile Disk)
DVD discs offer higher capacities (4.7 GB per layer) than the preceding CD-ROM format. As with CDs, recordable and re-writable forms of DVD exist, though there are numerous competing formats (notably ±R and ±RW and DVD-RAM).

DVI (Digital Video Interface)
Video adapter designed to replace the VGA port used by CRT monitors. The DVI interface supports digital only or digital and analog signaling.

Eavesdropping
Some transmission media are susceptible to eavesdropping (listening in to communications sent over the media). To secure transmissions, they must be encrypted.

Email
An electronic store and forward messaging system. Email supports text messages and binary file attachments. For Internet email, an SMTP (Simple Mail Transfer Protocol) server is used to forward mail to a host. A mail client then uses either POP3 (Post Office Protocol) or IMAP (Internet Mail Access Protocol) to access the mailbox on the server and download messages.

Embedded System
A computer system that is designed to perform a specific, dedicated function, such as a microcontroller in a medical drip or components in a control system managing a water treatment plant.

Encryption
Scrambling the characters used in a message so that the message can be seen but not understood or modified unless it can be deciphered. Encryption provides for a secure means of transmitting data and authenticating users. It is also used to store data securely. Encryption systems allow for different levels of security (128-bit encryption is currently considered secure).

Ethernet (802.3)
Popular Local Area Networking technology defining media access and signaling methods. Ethernet has been developed for use with coax (thicknet [10BASE-5] and thinnet [10BASE-T]), UTP cable (10BASE-TX, 100BASE-TX, 1000BASE-T, and 1000BASE-TX), and fiber optic (10BASE-F, 100BASE-FX, 1000BASE-X, and 10G standards). Wireless devices can also connect to Ethernet networks via a Wireless Access Point.

Extranet
A network of semi-trusted hosts, typically representing business partners, suppliers, or customers. Hosts must authenticate to join the extranet.

FAT (File Allocation Table)
When a disk is formatted using the FAT or FAT32 file system a File Allocation Table (FAT) is written in a particular track or sector. The FAT contains information relating to the position of file data chunks on the disk; data is not always written to one area of the disk but may be spread over several tracks. The original 16-bit version (FAT16, but often simply called FAT) was replaced by a 32-bit version that is almost universally supported by different operating systems and devices. A 64-bit version (exFAT) was introduced with Windows 7 and is also supported by XP SP3 and Vista SP1 and some versions of Linux and OS X.

Fault Tolerance (Redundancy)
Protection against system failure by providing extra (redundant) capacity. Generally, fault tolerant systems identify and eliminate single points of failure. For example, data can be made fault tolerant by implementing redundant disks (RAID); a UPS provides for emergency power.

Fax
Transferring an image of a document over a telephone line. Faxing is generally accomplished between two fax modems, often incorporated into Multifunction Devices or PC equipment.

File
Data used by a computer is stored by saving it as a file on a disk. Files store either plain text data or binary data. Binary data must only be modified in a suitable application or the file will be corrupted. A file is created by specifying a name. Naming rules depend on the version of Windows and the file system. Files usually have a three character extension (the last 3 characters in the file named preceded by a period). The file extension is used to associate the file with a particular software application. Files have primary attributes (Read-Only, System, Hidden, and Archive) and other properties (date created or modified for instance). Files stored on an NTFS partition can have extended attributes (access control, compression, and encryption).

File Server
In file server based networks, a central machine(s) provides dedicated file and print services to workstations. Benefits of server-based networks include ease of administration through centralization.

File System
When data is stored on a disk, it is located on that medium in a particular, standardized format. This allows the drive and the computer to be able to extract the information from the disk using similar functions and thus data can be accessed in a predictable manner. Examples of file systems include FAT16, FAT32, and NTFS (all used for hard disks) and CDFS (ISO 9660) and UDF (Universal Disk Format), used for optical media such as CD, DVD, and Blu-ray.

Fingerprint Scanner
Biometric authentication device that can produce a template signature of a user's fingerprint then subsequently compare the template to the digit submitted for authentication.

Firewall
Hardware or software that filters traffic passing into or out of a network (for example, between a private network and the Internet). A basic packet-filtering firewall works at Layers 3 and 4 (Network and Transport) of the OSI model. Packets can be filtered depending on several criteria (inbound or outbound, IP address, and port number). More advanced firewalls (proxy and stateful inspection) can examine higher layer information, to provide enhanced security.

Firewire (IEEE 1394 Standard)
Firewire is the brand name for the IEEE standard 1394. This serial SCSI bus standard supports high data rates (up to 400 Mbps) and this in turn, makes it attractive for applications requiring intensive data transfer (such as video cameras, satellite receivers, and digital media players).

Firmware
This refers to software instructions stored semi-permanently (embedded) on a hardware device (BIOS instructions stored in a ROM chip on the motherboard for instance).

Flash Memory
Flash RAM is similar to a ROM chip in that it retains information even when power is removed, but it adds flexibility in that it can be reprogrammed with new contents quickly. Flash memory has found a popular role in USB thumb drives and memory cards. These tiny cards can provide removable, megabyte or gigabyte storage for devices such as digital cameras. Other evolving uses of flash memory are in Solid State Drives (SSD), designed to replicate the function of hard drives, and hybrid drives (standard hard drives with a multi-gigabyte flash memory cache).

Flatbed Scanner
A type of scanner where the object is placed on a glass faceplate and the scan head moved underneath it.

Float
Data type supporting storage of floating point numbers (decimal fractions).

Fn (Function) Keys
Special command key combos on laptop keyboards for adjusting display output, volume, disabling wireless radio, and so on.

FQDN (Fully Qualified Domain Name)
A name in DNS specifying a particular host within a subdomain within a top-level domain.

Frame
A frame is the basic "unit" of data transmitted at layer 2. Frames contain several components—the source and target MAC (hardware) addresses as well as the data and error checking regions. Start and stop signals signify the beginning and the end of the frame respectively. It is the role of the network interface card to construct and understand frame structures.

FSB (Frontside Bus)
The bus between the CPU and the memory controller (system RAM).

FTP (File Transfer Protocol)
A protocol used to transfer files across the Internet. Variants include S(ecure)FTP, FTP with SSL (FTPS and FTPES) and T(rivial)FTP. FTP utilizes ports 20 and 21.

Fuser
Assembly that fixes toner to media. This is typically a combination of a heat and pressure roller, though non-contact flash fusing using xenon lamps is found on some high-end printers.

Gesture-based Interaction
Modern touchscreen displays support multitouch, meaning that gestures can be interpreted as events and responded to by software in a particular way. Gestures include taps, swipes, pinches, and stretches.

GPS (Global Positioning System)
Means of determining a receiver's position on the Earth based on information received from GPS satellites. The receiver must have line-of-sight to the GPS satellites.

Group Account
A group account is a collection of user accounts. These are useful when establishing file permissions and user rights because when many individuals need the same level of access, a group could be established containing all the relevant users. The group could then be assigned the necessary rights.

GUI (Graphical User Interface)
A GUI provides an easy to use, intuitive interface for a computer operating system. Most GUIs require a pointing device, such as a mouse, to operate efficiently. One of the world's first GUI-based operating systems was the Apple Mac OS, released in 1984. Thereafter, Microsoft produced their Windows family of products based around their GUI. In fact, recognizing that GUI covers a whole range of designs, the Windows interface is better described as a WIMP (Windows, Icons, Menus, Pointing [device]) interface.

HDD (Hard Disk Drive)
High capacity units typically providing persistent mass storage for a PC (saving data when the computer is turned off). Data is stored using platters with a magnetic coating that are spun under disk heads that can read and write to locations on each platter (sectors). A HDD installed within a PC is referred to as the fixed disks. HDDs are often used with enclosures as portable storage or as Network Attached Storage (NAS).

HDMI (High Definition Multimedia Interface)
High-specification digital connector for audio-video equipment.

Hexadecimal
Notational system with 16 values per digit. Values above 9 are represented by the letters A,B,C,D,E,F. Hex is a compact way of referring to long byte values, such as MAC and IPv6 addresses.

Homegroup
Windows networking feature designed to allow Windows 7 home networks to share files and printers easily through a simple password protection mechanism. Earlier versions of Windows are not supported.

Host
In TCP/IP networking terminology, a "host" is a device that can directly communicate on a network. In this sense it is similar to a node.

Hot Swappable
A device that can be added or removed without having to restart the operating system.

HTML
The language (HyperText Markup Language) used to create web pages.

HTTP
The protocol (HyperText Transfer Protocol) used to provide web content to browsers. HTTP uses port 80. HTTPS provides for encrypted transfers, using SSL and port 443.

I/O (Input/Output) Ports
An input-output port essentially describes a device connection through which data can be sent and received.

IEEE (Institute of Electrical and Electronics Engineers)
The Institute of Electrical and Electronics Engineers was formed as a professional body to oversee the development and registration of electronic standards. Examples of IEEE standards include the 802 protocols that describe the function and architecture of different network technologies.

IM (Instant Messaging)
Real-time text communications products. IM also supports file exchange and remote desktop. Like email, communications are generally unencrypted and unauthenticated. IM can be difficult to block on private networks as most applications can work over HTTP.

IMAP (Internet Message Access Protocol)
TCP/IP application protocol providing a means for a client to access email messages stored in a mailbox on a remote server. Unlike POP3, messages persist on the server after the client has downloaded them. IMAP also supports mailbox management functions, such as creating subfolders and access to the same mailbox by more than one client at the same time. IMAP4 utilizes TCP port number 143.

Implicit Deny
Implicit deny is a basic principle of security stating that unless something has explicitly been granted access it should be denied access. An example of this is firewall rule processing, where the last (default) rule is to deny all connections not allowed by a previous rule.

Ink Dispersion Printer
Better known as inkjets, this is a type of printer where colored ink is sprayed onto the paper using microscopic nozzles in the print head. There are two main types of ink dispersion system: thermal shock (heating the ink to form a bubble that bursts through the nozzles) and piezoelectric (using a tiny element that changes shape to act as a pump).

Integer
Data type supporting storage of whole numbers.

Intel
Intel processors were used in the first IBM PCs and the company's CPUs and chipsets continue to dominate the PC and laptop market.

Internet
The Internet is a worldwide network of networks based on the TCP/IP protocol. The Internet is not owned by a single company or organization. At the heart of the Internet are high-speed data communications lines between major host computers, consisting of thousands of commercial, government, educational, and other computer systems that route data and messages.

Internet Appliance
A SOHO device providing Internet routing via a DSL, cable, or satellite link. These appliances also provide a 4-port LAN switch and Wi-Fi plus a firewall.

Internet of Things
The global network of personal devices (such as phones, tablets, and fitness trackers), home appliances, home control systems, vehicles, and other items that have been equipped with sensors, software, and network connectivity.

Intranet
A network designed for information processing within a company or organization. An intranet uses the same technologies as the Internet but is owned and managed by a company or organization.

iOS
Mobile OS developed by Apple for its iPhone and iPad devices.

IP (Internet Protocol)
Network (Internet) layer protocol in the TCP/IP suite providing packet addressing and routing for all higher level protocols in the suite.

IP Address
Each IP host must have a unique IP address. This can be manually assigned or dynamically allocated (using a DHCP server). In IPv4, the 32-bit binary address is expressed in the standard four byte, dotted decimal notation: 10.0.5.1. In IPv6, addresses are 128-bit expressed as hexadecimal (for example, 2001:db8::0bcd:abcd:ef12:1234). IPv6 provides a much larger address space, stateless autoconfiguration (greatly simplifying network administration), and replaces inefficient broadcast transmissions with multicast ones.

ISP (Internet Service Provider)
Provides a connection to the Internet and other web- and email-related services. A connection to the ISP's Internet routing equipment can be made using a variety of methods.

Java
Programming language used to create web server applications (J2EE) and client-side applications (running in the Java VM).

JavaScript
Scripting language used to add interactivity to web pages and HTML-format email. JavaScript can also be used maliciously to exploit software vulnerabilities. It is possible to block scripts from running using browser security settings.

Kernel
All operating systems have a kernel, which is a low-level piece of code responsible for controlling the rest of the operating system. Windows uses a multiprocessor aware, pre-emptive multitasking kernel.

Key (Encryption)
An encryption cipher scrambles a message (plaintext) using an algorithm. The algorithm is given a key so that someone intercepting the message could not just reverse the algorithm to unscramble the message; they must also know the key. In symmetric encryption, the same key is used for encryption and decryption. In asymmetric encryption, different keys are used (one key is linked to but not derivable from the other key).

Keyboard
The oldest PC input device and still fundamental to operating a computer. Desktop keyboards can have PS/2, USB, or wireless (IrDA or Bluetooth) interfaces. There are many different designs and layouts for different countries. Some keyboards feature special keys.

Kinetics
Mobile devices use accelerometers and gyroscopes to detect when the device is moved and this can be the basis of a control system.

Knowledge Base
A searchable database of product FAQs (Frequently Asked Questions), advice, and known troubleshooting issues. The Microsoft KB is found at http://support.microsoft.com/search.

LAN (Local Area Network)
A type of network covering various different sizes but generally considered to be restricted to a single geographic location and owned/managed by a single organization.

Laptop/Notebook
A powerful portable computer offering similar functionality to a desktop computer. Laptops come with built-in LCD screens and input devices (keyboard and touchpad), and can be powered from building power (via an AC Adapter) or by a battery. Peripheral devices are typically connected via USB, PCMCIA, or ExpressCard adapters.

Laser Printer
A type of printer that develops an image on a drum using electrical charges to attract special toner then applying it to paper. The toner is then fixed to the paper using a high-heat and pressure roller (fuser). The process can be used with black toner only or four color toner cartridges (Cyan, Magenta, Yellow, and Black) to create full-color prints. Monochrome laser printers are the "workhorses" of office printing solutions.

LCD (Liquid Crystal Display) Panel
A display technology where the image is made up of liquid crystal cells controlled using electrical charges. Modern active matrix displays produce high quality images. LCD panels are used on portable computers and (as prices have fallen) are popular with desktop systems too, as they take up much less desk space than CRTs. The main problem with LCDs is that they are not good at displaying an image at any resolution other than the native resolution of the display.

Least Privilege
Least privilege is a basic principle of security stating that something should be allocated the minimum necessary rights, privileges, or information to perform its role.

Libraries
Virtual folder feature introduced in Windows 7 as a wrapper for multiple folder locations (which can be local or network) that store files that are part of the same logical "collection." The system is installed with default libraries for documents, pictures, and music and the user can add locations to these or create new libraries.

Licensing
Terms governing the installation and use of operating system and application software. A license may cover use on a single computer or by a number of devices or concurrent users at a site.

Lightning
Proprietary connector and interface for Apple devices.

Linux
An open-source operating system supported by a wide range of hardware and software vendors.

Liquid Cooling System
Using water piped around the PC and heatsinks for cooling. This is more efficient and allows for fewer fans and less noise.

LTE (Long Term Evolution)
LTE is the cellular providers (3GPP) upgrade to 3G technologies such as W-CDMA and HSPA. LTE Advanced is designed to provide 4G standard network access.

MAC (Mandatory Access Control)
Access control model where resources are protected by inflexible, system defined rules. Resources (objects) and users (subjects) are allocated a clearance level (or label). There are a number of privilege models, such as Bell-LaPadula, Biba, and Clark-Wilson providing either confidentiality or integrity.

MAC (Media Access Control) Address
A MAC is a unique hardware address that is hard-coded into a network card by the manufacturer. This is required for directing data frames across a network and for allowing the network card to compare destination addresses (coded into the data frame) and its own unique MAC address. A MAC address is 48 bits long with the first half representing the manufacturer's Organizationally Unique Identifier (OUI).

Mailbox
Part of a message store designed to receive emails for a particular recipient. A mailbox may be associated with more than one email address by creating aliases for the recipient.

Man-in-the-Middle
Where the attacker intercepts communications between two hosts.

MAPI (Message Application Programming Interface)
Windows messaging interface used primarily by the email client software Outlook to communicate with an Exchange mail server.

Mapping
The term used to describe the process of establishing a connection with a file resource on a remote server—for example, mapping a network drive.

Markup Language
System of tags used to structure a document. Examples include HyperText Markup Language (HTML) and eXtensible Markup Language (XML).

Microsoft
The world's foremost supplier of operating system and Office productivity software. Microsoft has dominated the PC market since the development of the first IBM compatible PCs running MS-DOS.

Mobile Device
Portable phones and smart phones can be used to interface with workstations using technologies such as Bluetooth or USB. As such, they are increasingly the focus of viruses and other malware. Portable devices storing valuable information are a considerable security risk when taken offsite.

Mobile Phone
UK English term for a cell phone.

Modem (Modulator/Demodulator)
Modems are devices that are used to convert the digital signals from a computer into the appropriate analog signal that is required for transmission over public phone lines—this is called modulation. The reverse process, demodulation, occurs at the receiving computer. Modems are available in internal and external forms for different computer expansion slots and vary in terms of speed and data handling capabilities.

Motherboard
The computer motherboard, also called the system board, provides the basic foundation for all of the computer's hardware including the processor, RAM, BIOS, and expansion cards. Several motherboard standards are available each with a different layout and associated advantages.

Mouse
The essential device to implement a WIMP GUI, a mouse simply controls the movement of a cursor that can be used to select objects from the screen. All Windows mice feature two click buttons, which are configured to perform different actions. Many mice also feature a scroll wheel. A mouse can be interfaced using a PS/2, USB, or wireless (IrDA or Bluetooth) port.

MPEG
Moving Pictures Expert Group is an ISO standards committee for audio and video compression and playback. There have been numerous MPEG standards over the years. From MPEG-1, the mp3 audio compression format remains very popular. MPEG-2 is widely used for file and broadcast delivery. MPEG-4 (or MP4) extends the MPEG-2 specification, notably providing support for Digital Rights Management (DRM), which enables playback to be tied to particular hardware devices.

Multifactor Authentication
Strong authentication is multi-factor. Authentication schemes work on the basis of something you know, something you have, or something you are. These schemes can be made stronger by combining them (for example, protecting use of a smart card certification [something you have] with a PIN [something you know]).

Multimedia
Multimedia refers to PC components that can playback and record sound and video (or to sound and video files). There are numerous sound and video file formats, including legacy Windows-specific formats such as WAV (for audio) or AVI (for video and audio). The preferred file format for Windows Media Player is ASF (Advanced Systems Format), which is usually compressed (WMA or WMV). Other file formats include those used for Apple's QuickTime player (MOV and QT), Apple's iTunes format (AIFF), and RealNetworks player (RA or RAM). The most popular standards-based format is MPEG.

Multiprocessing
Multiprocessing can be used in systems where two or more processors are used on a single motherboard. This can allow operations to be shared thereby increasing performance. In order to use multiprocessing arrangements, the PC must have a compatible motherboard, an operating system that is able to use multiple processors, and well-written software that does not intensively use one processor above another. Business and professional editions of Windows support a type of multiprocessing called Symmetric Multiprocessing (SMP) with a maximum of 2 CPUs.

NAS (Network Attached Storage)
NAS is a storage device with an embedded OS that supports typical network file access protocols (TCP/IP and SMB for instance). These may be subject to exploit attacks (though using an embedded OS is often thought of as more secure as it exposes a smaller attack "footprint"). The unauthorized connection of such devices to the network is also a concern.

Network
In its most simple form, a network consists of two or more computers connected to each other by an appropriate transmission medium which allows them to share data. More complex networks can be developed from this basic principle—networks can be interconnected in different ways and even dissimilar networks can be linked.

Network Adapter (NIC [Network Interface Card])
The network adapter allows a physical connection between the host and the transmission media. A NIC can address other cards and can recognize data that is destined for it, using a unique address known as the Media Access Control (MAC) address. The card also performs error checking. Network cards are designed for specific types of networks and do not work on different network products. Different adapters may also support different connection speeds and connector types.

NFC (Nearfield Communications)
Standard for peer-to-peer (2-way) radio communications over very short (around 4") distances, facilitating contactless payment and similar technologies. NFC is based on RFID.

Notification Area
Part of the taskbar (on the right-hand side) that displays background applications and status information (such as the date and time, anti-virus software, network connections, and alerts). In early versions of Windows this was managed by a systray process and is sometimes still referred to as the system tray.

NTFS (New Technology Filing System)
The NT File System supports a 64-bit address space and is able to provide extra features such as file-by-file compression and RAID support as well as advanced file attribute management tools, encryption, and disk quotas.

OCR (Optical Character Recognition)
Software that can identify the shapes of characters and digits to convert them from printed images to electronic data files that can be modified in a word processing program. Intelligent Character Recognition (ICR) is an advanced type of OCR, focusing on handwritten text.

OOP (Object-Oriented Programming)
Technique for creating robust code by defining classes of "things" in the code. The objects have attributes, methods, and properties. Code external to the object can only interface with it via its public methods and properties.

Open Source
Open source means that the programming code used to design the software is freely available.

OS X
Operating system designed by Apple for their range of iMac computers, Mac workstations, and MacBook portables. OS X is based on the BSD version of UNIX. OS X is well supported by application vendors, especially in the design industry (Adobe/Macromedia).

P2P (Peer-to-Peer)
File sharing networks where data is distributed around the clients that use the network. Apart from consuming bandwidth and disk space, P2P sites are associated with hosting malware and illegal material.

Partition
A discrete are of storage defined on a hard disk using either the Master Boot Record (MBR) scheme or the GUID Partition Table (GPT) scheme. Each partition can be formatted with a different file system and a partition can be marked as active (made bootable).

Password
A secret text string used as part of a logon. To be secure, a password should be sufficiently complex (so that it cannot be guessed or "cracked" by password-guessing software). A strong password should be over 8 characters and contain a mix of alphanumeric, upper and lower case, and symbol characters. A password is usually stored securely by hashing it (encrypting it so that there is no possibility of deciphering it). When the user enters the password, it should be masked so that no one can discover it by looking over the user's shoulder (users need to take care that they do not let someone watch what they type either!).

Password Cracker
Password guessing software such as John the Ripper or Cain and Abel can attempt to crack user passwords by running through all possible combinations (brute force). This can be made less computationally intensive by using a dictionary of standard words or phrases. If a password is extremely simple or left to a default value, it may also be possible for the attacker to guess it without needing special software.

Password Policy
A weakness of password-based authentication systems is when users demonstrate poor password practice. Examples include choosing a password that is too simple, reusing passwords for different tasks, writing a password down, and not changing a password regularly. Some of these poor practices can be addressed by system policies; others are better approached by education.

Patch Management
Identifying, testing, and deploying OS and application updates. Patches are often classified as critical, security-critical, recommended, and optional.

PCI (Peripheral Component Interconnect) Bus
The PCI bus was introduced in 1995 with the Pentium processor. It connects the CPU, memory, and peripherals to a 32-bit working at 33 MHz. PCI supports bus mastering, IRQ steering, and Plug-and-Play. Later versions defined 64-bit operation and 66 MHz clock but were not widely adopted on desktop PCs.

PCI Express
PCI Express (PCIe) is the latest expansion bus standard. PCI Express is serial with point-to-point connections. Each device on the bus can create a point-to-point link with the I/O controller or another device. The link comprises one or more lanes (x1, x2, x4, x8, x12, x16, or x32). Each lane supports a full-duplex transfer rate of 250 MBps (v1.0), 500 MBps (v2.0), or 1 GBps (v3.0). The standard is software compatible with PCI, allowing for motherboards with both types of connector.

PDF (Portable Document Format)
Adobe's Portable Document Format (PDF) is a file format for distributing documents. PDF was envisaged as a "final" format for the distribution of a published document.

Pentium Processor Series
Previously Intel's premium CPU brand, now re-positioned as a chip for reliable "always-on, always-available" systems.

Permissions
To access files and folders on a volume, the administrator of the computer will need to grant file permissions to the user (or a group to which the user belongs). File permissions are supported by NTFS-based Windows systems.

Phishing
Obtaining user authentication or financial information through a fraudulent request for information. Phishing is specifically associated with emailing users with a link to a faked site (or some other malware that steals the information they use to try to authenticate). Pharming is a related technique where the attacker uses DNS spoofing to redirect the user to the fake site. Vishing refers to phishing attacks conducted over voice channels (VoIP) while spear phishing or whaling refers to attacks specifically directed at managers or senior executives.

PII (Personally Identifiable Information)
PII is data that can be used to identify or contact an individual (or in the case of identity theft, to impersonate them). A Social Security number is a good example of PII. Others include names, Date of Birth, email address, telephone number, street address, biometric data, and so on.

PIM (Personal Information Manager)
Personal Information Manager (PIM) software provides features for storing and organizing information such as contacts and calendar events and appointments.

PIN (Personal Identification Number)
Number used in conjunction with authentication devices such as smart cards; as the PIN should be known only to the user, loss of the smart card should not represent a security risk.

PKI (Public Key Infrastructure)
Asymmetric encryption provides a solution to the problem of secure key distribution for symmetric encryption. The main problem is making a link between a particular public-private key pair and a specific user. One way of solving this problem is through PKI. Under this system, keys are issued as digital certificates by a Certificate Authority (CA). The CA acts as a guarantor that the user is who he or she says he or she is. Under this model, it is necessary to establish trust relationships between users and CAs. In order to build trust, CAs must publish and comply with Certificate Policies and Certificate Practice Statements.

Plug-and-Play (PnP)
A Plug-and-Play system (comprising a compatible BIOS, operating system, and hardware) is self-configuring. When a hardware device is added or removed, the operating system detects the change and automatically installs the appropriate drivers.

POP (Post Office Protocol)
TCP/IP application protocol providing a means for a client to access email messages stored in a mailbox on a remote server. The server usually deletes messages once the client has downloaded them. POP3 utilizes TCP port 110.

Popup Blocker
Pop-ups are browser windows that open automatically using a script in the host page or some sort of adware or spyware installed on the PC. A popup blocker can prevent these windows from being opened. Some pop-ups are now implemented using Flash or Shockwave plug-ins, though blocking software can often deal with these too.

Port
In TCP and UDP applications, a port is a unique number assigned to a particular application protocol (such as HTTP or SMTP). The port number (with the IP address) forms a socket between client and server. A socket is a bi-directional pipe for the exchange of data. For security, it is important to allow only the ports required to be open (ports can be blocked using a firewall).

POST (Power-On Self-Test)
The POST procedure is a hardware checking routine built into the PC firmware. This test sequentially monitors the state of the memory chips, the processor, system clock, display, and firmware itself. Errors that occur within vital components such as these are signified by beep codes emitted by the internal speaker of the computer. Further tests are then performed and any errors displayed as on-screen error codes and messages. Additional interpreter boards can be purchased that can supply information concerning boot failure.

Presentation
Presentation software enables users to create sophisticated business presentations that can be displayed as an on-screen slide show or printed onto overhead projector transparencies.

Pre-shared Key
Symmetric encryption technologies, such as those used for WEP, require both parties to use the same private key. This key must be kept secret, which means that making the key known to both parties securely is a significant security problem. A pre-shared key is normally generated from a passphrase. A passphrase should be longer than a password and contain a mixture of characters.

Printer
"Printer" is often used to mean "print device" but also refers to a term used to describe the software components of a printing solution. The printer is the object that Windows sends output to. It consists of a spool directory, a printer driver, and configuration information.

Privacy Policy
Privacy policy generally covers what monitoring and data collection will be made of an organization's employees. A privacy policy is also important when collecting data from third parties, such as customers and suppliers. Privacy policy may have to be formulated within the bounds of civil rights and data protection legislation, though this is not true of all countries.

Product Key
A product key is often used to authenticate the use of a software package and may be required to activate the software for use.

Program Files
Windows folder providing the default location for installation of application executables and supporting files. Ideally, applications should not write user data back to Program Files but use the appropriate user profile folder. In x64 versions of Windows, "Program Files" stores 64-bit applications while 32-bit applications are installed to "Program Files (x86)."

Projector
Large format display technology. Projectors can use CRT or LCD mechanisms but the market-leading technology is generally considered to be DLP.

Protocol
A set of rules enabling systems to communicate (exchange data). A single network will involve the use of many different protocols. In general terms a protocol defines header fields to describe each packet, a maximum length for the payload, and methods of processing information from the headers.

Proxy Server
A server that mediates the communications between a client and another server. The proxy server can filter and often modify communications as well as providing caching services to improve performance.

PS/2 Connector
A port for attaching a keyboard and mouse to a desktop computer, now largely replaced by USB.

Pseudocode
Writing out a program sequence using code blocks but without using the specific syntax of a particular programming language.

Quarantine
A file infected with a virus that cannot be automatically cleaned can be quarantined, meaning that the anti-virus software blocks any attempt by the user to open it. A PC can also be said to be quarantined by removing it from a network.

RAID (Redundant Array of Independent/Inexpensive Disks/Devices)
Using RAID technology, multiple hard disks can be configured to provide improved performance and/or protection for data (fault tolerance). Several levels of backup are suggested by this system, ranging from level 0 to level 6, each level representing a particular type of fault tolerance (note that RAID 0 provides no fault tolerance).

RAM (Random Access Memory)
Random Access Memory is the principal storage space for computer data and program instructions. RAM is generally described as being volatile in the sense that once power has been removed or the computer has been rebooted, data is lost.

Ransomware
A type of malware that tries to extort money from the victim, by appearing to lock their computer or by encrypting their files for instance.

RCA Connector
Good quality connector with a distinctive collar or ring used for a variety of Audio/Visual (A/V) functions and equipment. The connector is named after its developer (Radio Corporation of America) but the socket is also referred to as a phono plug.

RDP (Remote Desktop Protocol)
Microsoft's protocol for operating remote connections to a Windows machine (Terminal Services), allowing specified users to log onto the Windows computer over the network and work remotely. The protocol sends screen data from the remote host to the client and transfer mouse and keyboard input from the client to the remote host. It uses TCP port 3389.

Recordable CD Drives
CD/DVD writers are now mainstream devices, used for data transfer and archiving. Recordable CDs are available in two general forms: those that can be written to once and read many times (CD-R) and those that can be written to and erased (CD-RW). CD writers use a laser to disrupt the medium of the disk—either by heating a dye, by altering the magnetic properties of the metal disk, or by changing disc structure through phase-change techniques. Media varies in terms of longevity and maximum supported recording speed. DVD also has R and RW formats, both of which feature competing + and - standards. Many drives can write in more than one format and most drives should be able to read from all formats. DVD recorders can also perform CD-R/RW recording. An additional consideration is whether drives and media support dual-layer and/or double-sided recording. Blu-ray has recordable (BD-R) and rewritable (BD-RE) formats and supports dual-layer but not double-sided recording.

Recycle Bin
When files are deleted from a local hard disk, they are stored in the recycle bin. They can be recovered from here if so desired.

Registry
The registry database is the configuration database for Windows. The registry can be directly edited by experienced support personnel using a variety of tools. The registry should be backed up before system changes are made.

Relational Database
Structured database in which information is stored in tables where columns represent typed data fields and rows represent records. Tables can have relationships, established by linking a unique primary key field in one table with the same value in a foreign key field in another table. The overall structure of a particular database and its relations is called a schema.

Remote Wipe
Software that allows deletion of data and settings on a mobile device to be initiated from a remote server.

Removable Media
In order to share files and programs, computers can either be connected to each other (across a direct link or via a network) or must be able store and retrieve files from an interim storage medium. The most common types of removable media are floppy disks and optical discs. However the term "removable media" also covers tape drives, high capacity disks, and removable hard drives.

Resolution
A digital image is made up of many thousands of picture elements (pixels). Resolution describes the number of dots that an imaging device can use to sample or display the image, measured in pixels per inch (ppi); the higher the resolution, the better the quality. On a digital printer, the resolution is the number of toner or ink dots that the print engine can put on paper (measured in dots per inch [dpi]). Note that sometimes dpi is used interchangeably with ppi to describe scanner or monitor resolution, but image pixels and printer dots are not equivalent, as multiple print dots are required to represent a single image pixel accurately.

RF (Radio Frequency)
Radio waves propagate at different frequencies and wavelengths. Wi-Fi network products typically work at 2.4 GHz or 5 GHz.

RFID (Radio Frequency IDentification)
A chip allowing data to be read wirelessly. RFID tags are used in barcodes and smart cards.

RJ (Registered Jack) Connector
Connector used for twisted pair cabling. 4-pair network cabling uses the larger RJ-45 connector. Modem/telephone 2=pair cabling uses the RJ-11 connector.

Role-Based Access Control
Access control model where resources are protected by ACLs. However, management of ACLs is reserved to administrators rather than owners and users are assigned permissions according to job function rather than personally.

Router
Routers are able to link dissimilar networks and can support multiple alternate paths between locations based upon the parameters of speed, traffic loads, and cost. A router works at layer 3 (Network) of the OSI model. Routers form the basic connections of the Internet. They allow data to take multiple paths to reach a destination (reducing the likelihood of transmission failure). Routers can access source and destination addresses within packets and can keep track of multiple active paths within a given source and destination network. TCP/IP routers on a LAN can also be used to divide the network into logical subnets.

Rule-Based Access Control
Any access control model that follows system-enforced rules that cannot be countermanded can be described as rule-based. A firewall is a good example of rule-based access control but the MAC and role-based models can also be described as rule-based. DAC is not rule-based as decisions are made by the resource owner.

SATA (Serial ATA)
Standard IDE/ATA uses parallel data transmission. Serial ATA allows for faster transfer rates and longer, more compact cabling (it features a 7-pin data connector). There are three SATA standards specifying bandwidths of 1.5 Gbps, 3 Gbps, and 6 Gbps respectively. SATA drives also use a new 15-pin power connector, though adapters for the old style 4-pin Molex connectors are available. External drives are also supported via the eSATA interface.

Satellite
System of microwave transmissions where orbital satellites relay signals between terrestrial receivers or other orbital satellites. Satellite Internet connectivity is enabled through a reception antenna connected to the PC or network through a DVB-S modem.

Scanner
A type of photocopier that can convert the image of a physical object into an electronic data file. The two main components of a scanner are the lamp, which illuminates the object, and the recording device, an array of CCDs (Charge Coupled Devices). There are flatbed and sheet-fed versions, with sheet-fed versions typically being incorporated with a printer and fax machine into a multifunction device. Scanners can output images directly to a printer or to a suitable file format (such as JPEG, PNG, or TIFF). Scanners can also interface with applications software using one of several interfaces (TWAIN, WIA, SANE, or ISIS).

Script Support
Many web pages use scripts, ActiveX, Java, or plug-ins to provide "rich" content. Many sites depend on the use of scripts for even their basic navigation tools. Unfortunately, there are scripts can be used to exploit browser or OS vulnerabilities or to perform actions that the user may find annoying (such as opening multiple pop-up windows). Most browsers enable the user to disable scripting and other executable content on a site-by-site basis.

SD (Secure Digital) Card
One of the first types of flash memory card.

SDRAM (Synchronous DRAM)
Synchronous DRAM is a variant on the DRAM chip designed to run at the speed of the system clock thus accelerating the periodic refresh cycle times. SDRAM can run at much higher clock speeds than previous types of DRAM. Basic SDRAM is now obsolete and has been replaced by DDR/DDR2/3 SDRAM.

Security Control
A technology or procedure put in place to mitigate vulnerabilities and risk and to ensure the Confidentiality, Integrity, and Availability (CIA) of information. Control types are often classed in different ways, such as technical, operational, and management.

Server
A server provides shared resources on the network and allows clients to access this information. The advantage of a server-based system is that resources can be administered and secured centrally. Servers must be kept secure by careful configuration (running only necessary services) and maintenance (OS and application updates, malware/intrusion detection, and so on). Where a network is connected to the Internet, servers storing private information or running local network services should be protected by firewalls so as not to be accessible from the Internet.

Service
Windows machines run services to provide functions; for example, Plug-and-Play, the print spooler, DHCP client, and so on. These services can be viewed, configured, and started/stopped via the Services console. You can also configure which services run at startup using msconfig. You can view background services (as well as applications) using the Processes tab in Task Manager.

Share
Any resource, such as a folder or printer device, which needs to be made available on a network must first be shared. For resources to be shared, Windows File and Print Sharing must be installed and enabled.

Shortcut
An item typically placed on the desktop, or in the Start menu, which points to a program or data file. When selected, the referenced program or file loads.

Shoulder Surfing
Social engineering tactic to obtain someone's password or PIN by observing him or her as he or she types it in.

Smart Card
A card with a chip containing data on it. Smart cards are typically used for authentication, with the chip storing authentication data such as a digital certificate.

Smartphone
A mobile device that provides both phone and SMS text messaging functionality and general purpose computing functionality, such as web browsing and email plus running software apps. Smartphones typically have screen sizes of between 4 and 5.5 inches.

SMTP (Simple Mail Transfer Protocol)
The protocol used to send mail between hosts on the Internet. Messages are sent over TCP port 25.

Social Engineering
A hacking technique, widely publicized by Kevin Mitnick in his book "The Art of Deception," whereby the hacker gains useful information about an organization by deceiving its users or by exploiting their unsecure working practices. Typical social engineering methods include impersonation, domination, and charm.

SOHO (Small Office Home Office)
Typically used to refer to network devices designed for small-scale LANs (up to 10 users).

SP (Service Pack)
A collection of software updates and hotfixes released as one installable file. Service packs often add new features to the OS.

Spam
Junk messages sent over email (or instant messaging [SPIM]). Filters and blacklists are available to block spam and know spam servers. It is also important to ensure that any mail servers you operate are not open relays, allowing a spammer to leverage your server to distribute spam and making it likely that it will be blacklisted.

Spoofing
Where the attacker disguises their identity. Some examples include IP spoofing, where the attacker changes their IP address, or phishing, where the attacker sets up a false website.

Spreadsheet
A spreadsheet consists of a table containing rows, columns, and cells. When values are entered into the cells, formulas can be applied to them, enabling complex calculations to be carried out.

Spyware
Software that records information about a PC and its user. Spyware is used to describe malicious software installed without the user's content. Aggressive spyware is used to gather passwords or financial information such as credit card details.

SSID (Service Set ID)
Identifies a particular Wireless LAN (WLAN). This "network name" can be used to connect to the correct network. When multiple APs are configured with the same SSID, this is referred to as an E(xtended)SSID.

SSL (Secure Sockets Layer)
SSL was developed by Netscape to provide privacy and authentication over the Internet. It is application independent (working at layer 5 [Session]) and can be used with a variety of protocols, such as HTTP or FTP. Client and server set up a secure connection through PKI (X.509) certificates (optionally, both client and server can authenticate to one another). The protocol is now being developed as Transport Layer Security (TLS).

SSO (Single Sign-on)
Any authentication technology that allows a user to authenticate once and receive authorizations for multiple services. Kerberos is a typical example of an authentication technology providing SSO.

Start Menu
The standard interface provided to locate and load applications in Windows 7 and earlier, though the layout and features of the Start menu have changed in each version.

Start Screen
User interface introduced with Windows 8 to replace the Start Menu and manage a Windows device using a touchscreen. Windows devices can be set to show the Start Screen or the Desktop at startup.

String
Data type supporting storage of a variable length series of characters.

Stylus
A digitizer usually also employs a stylus as a pointing device (rather than using a finger), often as a drawing tool.

Subnet Mask
An IP address consists of a Network ID and a Host ID. The subnet mask is used to distinguish these two components within a single IP address. It is used to "mask" the host ID portion of the IP address and thereby reveal the network ID portion. The typical format for a mask is 255.255.0.0. Classless network addresses can also be expressed in the format 169.254.0.0/16, where /16 is the number of bits in the mask. IPv6 uses the same /nn notation to indicate the length of the network prefix.

Switch
Ethernet (or LAN) switches perform the functions of a specialized bridge. Switches receive incoming data into a buffer then the destination MAC address is compared with an address table. The data is then only sent out to the port with the corresponding MAC address. In a switched network, each port is in a separate collision domain and, therefore, collisions cannot occur. This is referred to as microsegmentation. Advanced switches perform routing at layers 3 (IP), 4 (TCP), or 7 (Application). Switches routing at layer 4/7 are referred to as load balancers and content switches.

System Requirements
Before installing an OS (or a software application), the installer should check that the system meets the minimum hardware requirements. These are typically for CPU speed, memory, and hard disk capacity. Most software vendors specify minimum and recommended requirements. A system that does not meet the minimum requirements will not be able to run the software; one that does not meet the recommended requirements will run the software slowly.

Tablet
A type of ultra-portable laptop with a touchscreen, widely popularized by Apple's iPad devices running iOS. Tablets are usually based on form factors with either 7" or 10" screens. As well as iOS devices, there are tablets from various vendors running Android plus Microsoft's Surface tablet running Windows and various laptop/tablet hybrid Windows devices. A phablet is a smaller device (like a large smartphone).

Tailgating
Social engineering technique to gain access to a building by following someone else (or persuading them to "hold the door").

Task Manager
Program used to provide recovery of stalled applications. Task Manager also allows for control of running tasks, processes, and CPU/memory utilization. Task Manager can be displayed by pressing Ctrl+Shift+Esc, Ctrl+Alt+Del, or alt-clicking the taskbar.

Task Scheduler
The Task Scheduler enables the user to perform an action (such as running a program or a script) automatically at a pre-set time or in response to some sort of trigger.

Taskbar
The taskbar is a means of locating running programs and also contains the Start menu and system tray/notification area (as well as an optional Quick Launch toolbar). It appears (by default) at the bottom of the desktop.

TCP (Transmission Control Protocol)
Protocol in the TCP/IP suite operating at the transport layer to provide connection-oriented, guaranteed delivery of packets. Hosts establish a session to exchange data and confirm delivery of packets using acknowledgements. This overhead means the system is relatively slow.

TCP/IP
The network protocol suite used by most operating systems and the Internet. It is widely adopted, industry standard, vendor independent and open. It uses a 4-layer network model that corresponds roughly to the OSI model as follows: Network Interface (Physical/Data Link), Internet (Network), Transport (Transport), Application (Session, Presentation, Application).

TFT (Thin Film Transistor) Active Matrix Display
The TFT display provides the best resolution of all of the currently available flat-panel Liquid Crystal Display (LCD) designs, although they are also the most expensive. TFT displays offer very high image clarity, contrast ratios of between 150:1 to 200:1, fast refresh rates, and wide viewing angles.

Thumb Drive
A flash memory card with USB adapter.

Thunderbolt
The Thunderbolt (TB) interface was developed by Intel and is primarily used on Apple workstations and laptops. Thunderbolt can be used as a display interface (like DisplayPort) and as a general peripheral interface (like USB 3).

TKIP (Temporal Key Integrity Protocol)
Mechanism used in the first version of WPA to improve the security of wireless encryption mechanisms, compared to the flawed WEP standard.

Token
A token contains some sort of authentication data. Software tokens are generated by logon systems, such as Kerberos, so that users do not have to authenticate multiple times (Single Sign-on). A hardware token can be a device containing a chip with a digital certificate but is more usually a device that generates a one-time password. This can be used in conjunction with an ordinary user name and password (or PIN) to provide more secure two-factor authentication.

Toner
Specially formulated compound to impart dye to paper through an electrographic process (used by laser printers and photocopiers). The key properties of toner are the colorant (dye), ability to fuse (wax or plastic), and ability to hold a charge. There are three main types of toner, distinguished by the mechanism of applying the toner to the developer roller: dual component (where the toner is mixed with a separate magnetic developer), mono-component (where the toner itself is magnetic), and non-magnetic mono-component (where the toner is transferred using static properties).

Touchpad
Input device used on most laptops to replace the mouse. The touchpad allows the user to control the cursor by moving a finger over the pad's surface. There are usually buttons too but the pad may also recognize "tap" events and have scroll areas.

Touchscreen
A display screen that is responsive to touch input.

Transfer Rate
The amount of data that can be transferred over a network connection in a given amount of time, typically measured in bits or bytes per second (or some more suitable multiple thereof). Transfer rate is also described variously as data rate, bit rate, connection speed, transmission speed, or (sometimes inaccurately) bandwidth or baud. Transfer rates are often quoted as the peak, maximum, theoretical value; sustained, actual throughput is often considerably less.

Trojan Horse
A malicious software program hidden within an innocuous-seeming piece of software. Usually the Trojan is used to try to compromise the security of the target computer.

Troubleshooting
Troubleshooting requires a methodical approach. Having ensured that any data has been backed up, the first step is to gather information (from the user, error messages, diagnostic tools, or inspection). The next is to analyze the problem, again consulting documentation, web resources, or manufacturer's help resources if necessary. When analyzing a problem, it helps to categorize it (for example, between hardware and software). The next step is to choose and apply the most suitable solution. Having applied a solution, the next step is to test the system and related systems to verify functionality. The last step is to document the problem, steps taken, and the outcome. If the problem cannot be solved, it may be necessary to escalate it to another technician or manager.

TWAIN
Standard "driver" model for interfacing scanner hardware with applications software.

UAC (User Account Control)
Security system in Windows designed to restrict abuse of accounts with administrator privileges. Actions such as installing hardware and software can be performed without changing accounts but the user must authorize the use of administrative rights by clicking a prompt or re-entering user credentials.

UDF (Universal Disk Format)
File system used for optical media, replacing CDFS (ISO 9660).

UDP (User Datagram Protocol)
Protocol in the TCP/IP suite operating at the transport layer to provide connectionless, non-guaranteed communication with no sequencing or flow control. Faster than TCP, but does not provide reliability.

UNC (Universal Naming Convention)
Microsoft standard naming convention for local network resources, in the format \\server\share\file, where server is the name of a remote machine, share is the name of a folder on that machine, and file is the file you wish to access.

Unicode
Extensible system of code pages capable of representing millions of character glyphs, allowing for international alphabets.

UNIX Systems
UNIX was originally developed by the telecommunications company AT&T during the late 1960s and early 1970s. UNIX is now a family of more than 20 related operating systems that are produced by various companies. It has become the operating system of choice for many high powered workstations. It is capable of supporting parallel processing and can run on a wide variety of platforms. UNIX offers a multitude of file systems in addition to its native system. UNIX servers are the main types of server that form the Internet and are able to use the TCP/IP protocol suite to provide compatibility between networks.

Updates
Updates are made freely available by the software manufacturer to fix problems in a particular software version, including any security vulnerabilities. Updates can be classified as hotfixes (available only to selected customers and for a limited problem), patches (generally available), and service packs (installable collections of patches and software improvements).

UPS (Uninterruptible Power Supplies)
Uninterruptible power supplies provide an alternative AC power supply in the event of power failure. A UPS requires an array of batteries, a charging circuit, an inverter to convert DC to AC current, a circuit to allow the system to take over from a failing power supply, and some degree of spike, surge, or brownout protection (possibly including a line conditioner).

URL (Uniform Resource Locator/Identifier)
Application-level addressing scheme for TCP/IP, allowing for human-readable resource addressing. For example: protocol://server/file, where "protocol" is the type of resource (HTTP, FTP), "server" is the name of the computer (www.microsoft.com), and "file" is the name of the resource you wish to access. The term URI (Uniform Resource Indicator) is preferred in standards documentation but most people refer to these addresses as URLs.

USB (Universal Serial Bus)
USB permits the connection of up to 127 different peripherals. A larger Type A connector attaches to a port on the host; Type B and Mini- or Micro- Type B connectors are used for devices. USB 1.1 supports 12 Mbps while USB 2.0 supports 480 Mbps and is backward compatible with 1.1 devices (which run at the slower speed). USB devices are hot swappable. A device can draw up to 2.5W power. USB 3.0 defines a 4.8 Gbps SuperSpeed rate and can deliver 4.5W power.

Variable
Identifier for a value that can change during program execution. Variables are usually declared with a particular data type.

Vector
Identifier for a group of variables of the same type. The number of possible elements in a vector can vary during program execution.

VGA (Video Graphics Array) Connector
A 15-pin HD connector has been used to connect the graphics adapter to a monitor since 1987. The use of digital flat-panel displays rather than CRTs means that as an analog connector, it is fast becoming obsolete.

Video Card
Provides the interface between the graphics components of the computer and the display device. A number of connectors may be provided for the display, including VGA, DVI, and HDMI. Graphics adapters receive information from the microprocessor and store this data in video RAM. An adapter may support both analog and digital outputs or analog/digital only (as most LCDs use digital inputs the use of analog outputs is declining). Most adapters come with their own processor (Graphics Processing Unit [GPU]) and onboard memory.

Video Conferencing
Video conferencing or Video Teleconferencing (VTC) software allows users to configure virtual meeting rooms, with options for voice, video, and instant messaging.

Video Standards
Video standards define the resolution and color depth for a graphics adapter and computer display. Early standards defined monochrome, low resolution displays. The VGA standard defined a standard graphics mode of 640x480 in 16 colors. Super VGA (SVGA) standard defines an extensible series of graphics modes, the default being 800x600 in True Color (24-bit). There are also various XGA standards defining resolutions greater than 1024x768 (SXGA, UXGA), some of which are widescreen formats (WSXGA+, WUXGA).

Virtual Memory
Virtual memory (also known as swapping or paging) is an area on the hard disk allocated to contain pages of memory. When the operating system doesn't have sufficient physical memory (RAM) to perform a task (such as load a program) pages of memory are moved to the paging file (also known as a swap file). This frees physical RAM to enable the task to be completed. When the paged RAM is needed again, it is re-read into memory. Understanding and configuring virtual memory settings is critical to optimizing the performance of the operating system.

Virtualization Technology
Software allowing a single computer (the host) to run multiple "guest" operating systems (or Virtual Machines [VM]). The VMs are configured via a hypervisor or VM Monitor (VMM). VMs can be connected using virtual networks (vSwitch) or leverage the host's network interface(s). It is also possible for the VMs to share data with the host (via shared folders or the clipboard for instance). VT is now used as major infrastructure in data centers as well as for testing and training.

Virus
Code designed to infect computer files (or disks) when it is activated. A virus may also be programmed to carry out other malicious actions, such as deleting files or changing system settings.

VM (Virtual Machine)
Operating systems running in Protected Mode can utilize a separate VM for various 32-bit processes. This provides protection so that each program is protected from all other programs. Virtual Machine also (more commonly now) refers to multiple operating systems installed on a single host PC using virtualization software (a hypervisor), such as Microsoft Hyper-V or VMware.

VoIP (Voice over IP)
Voice over IP or Internet telephony refers to carrying voice traffic over data networks. IP telephony provides integration with the fixed and mobile telephone networks. A network carrying both voice and data is said to be converged. Converged networks introduce a whole new class of devices whose security implications need to be considered. There is also a greater vulnerability to DoS (without redundancy the network is a single point of failure for both voice and data traffic) and eavesdropping on voice communications.

VPN (Virtual Private Network)
A secure tunnel created between two endpoints connected via an unsecure network (typically the Internet). VPNs are typically created using SSL/TLS or IPsec. Encryption software is used to ensure privacy of data as messages transit through the public network.

WAN (Wide Area Network)
A Wide Area Network is a network that spans a relatively large geographical area, incorporating more than one site and often a mix of different media types and protocols. Connections are made using methods such as telephone lines, fiber optic cables, or satellite links.

Web Application
Software run from a web server. Clients can access the application using just a web browser.

Web Server
HTTP servers host websites. A basic website consists of static HTML pages but many sites are developed as front-end applications for databases. Web servers are popular targets for attack, particularly DoS, spoofing, and software exploits. Many companies use hosted web servers but if not, the server should be located in a DMZ. Web servers are also commonly used for intranet services, especially on Microsoft networks.

Webcam
A webcam can be used to record video. There are many types, from devices built into laptops to standalone units. While early devices were only capable of low resolutions, most webcams are now HD-capable.

WEP (Wired Equivalent Privacy)
Mechanism for encrypting (protecting) data sent over a wireless connection. WEP is considered flawed (that is, a determined and well-resourced attack could probably break the encryption). WEP uses a 64-bit RC4 cipher. An updated version using longer keys (128-bit) was released but is still considered unsecure. Apart from problems with the cipher, the use and distribution of a pre-shared key (effectively a password) depends on good user practice. WEP has been replaced by WPA.

WIA (Windows Image Acquisition)
Driver model and API (Application Programming Interface) for interfacing scanner hardware with applications software on Windows PCs.

Wi-Fi
IEEE standard for wireless networking based on spread spectrum radio transmission in the 2.4 GHz and 5 GHz bands. The standard has five main iterations (a, b, g, n, and ac), describing different modulation techniques, supported distances, and data rates.

Windows
Ubiquitous operating system from Microsoft. Windows started as version 3.1 for 16-bit computers. A workgroup version provided rudimentary network facilities. Windows NT 4 workstations and servers (introduced in 1993) provided reliable 32-bit operation and secure network facilities, based around domains. The Windows 9x clients (Windows 95, 98, and Me) had far lower reliability and only support for workgroups, but were still hugely popular as home and business machines. Windows 2000 workstations (Windows 2000 Professional) married the hardware flexibility and user interface of Windows 9x to the reliability and security of Windows NT, while the server versions saw the introduction of Active Directory for managing network objects. Windows XP is the mainstream client version (with Home, Professional, Media Center, Tablet PC, and 64-bit editions) while Windows Server 2003/2008/2012/2016 provide the latest generation of servers. The subsequent client releases of Windows (Vista and Windows 7) feature a substantially different interface (Aero) with 3D features as well as security improvements. The latest client versions—Windows 8 and Windows 10—are designed for use with touchscreen devices.

Windows Defender
Anti-spyware tool provided with Windows Vista/7. Defender can detect programs that monitor Internet usage and display pop-up windows but cannot detect other types of malware, such as viruses, worms, or Trojans. In Windows 8, Defender is a complete anti-malware scanner, providing protection against viruses, worms, and Trojans as well as spyware.

Windows Explorer
The standard interface provided for the management of files and folders under Windows. This has been renamed File Explorer in Windows 10 and is often just known as "Explorer."

Windows Firewall
Windows Firewall is enabled by default on every network and dial-up connection. Windows Firewall with Advanced Security also supports filtering outbound ports, but only through an advanced configuration interface.

Windows Update
A website hosting Microsoft Windows patches and security updates. The Automatic Update feature enables Windows to connect to this website and download updates automatically.

Wireless
Network connectivity that uses the electromagnetic broadcast spectrum as the medium. Most wireless transport takes place using spread-spectrum radio, but microwave transmitters and infrared are also used. Wireless connectivity is also used to mean a wireless means of connecting peripheral devices to a computer.

WLAN (Wireless Local Area Network)
A network using wireless radio communications based on some variant of the 802.11 standard series.

Word Processing
Word processing means applications that help users to write and edit documents. A word processor will come with features enabling the user to edit, format, and review text quickly.

Workgroup
A small group of computers on a network that share resources in a peer-to-peer fashion. No one computer provides a centralized directory.

Worm
A type of virus that spreads through memory and network connections rather than infecting files.

WORM (Write Once, Read Many) Drive
A WORM drive is able to write data to a recordable CD disc only once, although the data can be read many times.

WPA (Wi-Fi Protected Access)
An improved encryption scheme for protecting Wi-Fi communications, designed to replace WEP. The original version of WPA was subsequently updated (to WPA2) following the completion of the 802.11i security standard. WPA features an improved method of key distribution and authentication for enterprise networks, though the pre-shared key method is still available for home and small office networks. WPA2 uses the improved AES cipher, replacing TKIP and RC4.

WPS (Wi-Fi Protected Setup)
Mechanism for auto-configuring a WLAN securely for home users. On compatible equipment, users just have to push a button on the access point and connecting adapters to associate them securely. Adapters not supporting push button configuration can use a PIN.

XML (eXtensible Markup Language)
A system for structuring documents so that they are human- and machine-readable. Information within the document is placed within tags, which describe how information within the document is structured.

Zero Day Exploit
An attack that exploits a vulnerability in software that is unknown to the software vendor and users. Most vulnerabilities are discovered by security researchers and the vendor will have time to create a patch and distribute it to users before exploits can be developed so zero day exploits have the potential to be very destructive.

Index

Where a term or phrase is abbreviated, the acronym is the form listed in the index. Note that index references are made to the nearest main heading for the topic in which the term appears.

3

3.5mm Jack 261
32-bit CPU 215

6

64-bit............................48
64-bit CPU 215

8

802.11a/b/g/n/ac.........351

A

Acceptable Use Policy 480
Access Control.............74
Access Denied 305
Access Point 347, 357
Access Time 279
Accessibility Options 56
Accounting 463
ACL....................379, 462
Active Partition 290
Adapter Card 216
Add-on 369, 371
Add-on NIC 211
Address Bar 58, 60, 295
Addressing 331
Administrative Rights ...75, 464
Administrator..............464
Advanced Options 126
Adware.......................368
AGP 216
Airplane Mode............416
Algorithm....................470
AMD...........................213
Android 52
Anti-phishing 378
Anti-spam...................450
Anti-virus Software......444
Apple............................49
Application Architecture Models 188
Application Delivery Models 158, 160
Application Management 127
Application Updates 453
Applications............... 125
Approach Multiple Problems Individually ... 88
Archive Attribute......... 304
ARP........................... 337
Array 152
ASCII......................... 115
Assembly Language... 150
Asymmetric Encryption 471
Attack Surface........... 438
Attenuation 356
Attribute..................... 304
Audio Connector 261
Audio File Types 312
Audio Settings 263
Authentication 465
Authorization 462
AutoComplete 376
Automatic Updates..... 453
Availability 428

B

Back Button................. 60
Backup 187, 397
Backup and Restore... 400
Backup Verification 402
Banner Ads 368
Bare Metal Backup..... 399
Basics of Computing and Processing 4
Batch Files 156
Binary 110
Biometric Device 467
BIOS 44, 94, 220
Bit.............................. 112
Bluetooth................... 239
Blu-ray....................... 282
Boolean 114
Boot Problem 94
bps 113
Branching 153
Breadcrumb............... 295
Browser Cache........... 376
Brute Force Attack 473
Bus Speed................. 215
Business Continuity.... 432
Business-specific 139
Byte 112

C

CA 377, 471
Cable 348
Cable Management 15
Cache 279
CAD...........................138
Cameras....................270
Captive Portal 354
Case Fan...................219
CD/CD-R/CD-RW.......281
CDFS.........................291
Cellular 350
Change Default Password 352
Change SSID 352
Changing Default Passwords.................474
Char...........................114
Chipset 212
Chrome OS 52
Cipher........................470
Clean Installation........128
Clean Uninstallation....128
Clearing Browser Cache 376
Cleartext Credentials..473
CLI...............................73
Client 330
Client-side Scripting....370
Cloud Computing 394, 395
Cloud-based Collaborative Applications 395
Collaboration Software 134
Columns/Fields..........181
Command Line 73
Comments 155
Commercial Software . 130
Company Confidential Information 480
Compatibility Issues....127
Compatible Browser for Applications 368
Compiled Programming Languages.................149
Compression 292
Compression Formats 313
Computer..........15, 19, 54

Computer Management 66
Computer Name 389
Concurrent License 130
Confidentiality 426
Configure and Verify Internet Connection 349
Configuring Peripherals 236
Connecting to New Network 355
Connector Types 226, 261
Consider Multiple Approaches 90
Console 73
Constant Popups 368
Constants 152
Constraints 183
Contact Center 499
Contact Technical Support 97
Containers 152
Contingency Plan 433
Control Panel 55
Cookie 372, 374
Co-ordination of Hardware Components 40
Copying Files 301
Copyright 118
Cores 216
CPU 4, 111, 210, 213, 214
CPU Fan 219
Creating Files 299
Creating Folders 298
Critical Data 398
Critical Error Message 94
CRM 499
Cross-platform Software 158
CSV 180
Customer Confidential Information 480
Cut 301

D

DAC 462
Data Capture/Correlation 122
Data Connections 331, 347
Data Definition Methods 185
Data In-transit/At-rest/In-use 472
Data Management 41
Data Manipulation Methods 185
Data Persistence 179
Data Redundancy 433
Data Representation 115
Data Restoration 435
Data Types 114
Database Access Methods 187
Database Backup 398
Databases 139, 179
Data-driven Business 121
DB15 233
DDR SDRAM 278
Decimal 110
Default Folders 293
Default Gateway 338
Default Passwords/Settings 438
Deleting Files 302
Denial of Service 428
Desktop 21
Desktop PC 6
Desktop Publishing 137
Desktop, Mobile, and Web-based 158
Destruction 428
Determine If Anything Has Changed 88
Device Hardening 438
Device Management 251, 253
Devices and Printers 266
Diagnostic Tools 95
Difference Between Shortcuts and Files 30
Digital Cameras 270
Digital Certificate 377, 466, 471
Digital Products 120
Digital Signature 472
DIMM 277
Direct Attached Storage 387
Direct/Manual Access 187
Directory 41, 294
Disabling AutoFill 376
Disabling Bluetooth 241
Disabling NFC 241
Disabling Plug-ins 371
Disabling Unused Features 438
Disaster Recovery 435
Disinfecting Files 446, 447
Disk Management 72
Display Device 254
Display Settings 257
DisplayPort 231
Distance 356
Divide and Conquer 90
DLP 256
DNS 338
Document Databases 184
Document Findings, Actions, and Outcomes 93
Document Storage/Sharing 134
Documentation 125
Domain 389
Double-click 26
Drag and Drop 26
DRAM 277
Driver 40, 250, 456
Driver Installation 250
DRM 120
DSL 348
Dual Monitors 258
Dual-core 216
Dump 187
Dumpster Diving 430
Duplicate the Problem 88
DVB-S 349
DVD/DVD±R/DVD±RW 282
DVI 232

E

Ease of Access Options 56
Eavesdropping 426
Edit 299
Editions 48
Email 343
Email Client 134
Email Configuration 417
Embedded OS 43
Enabling Passwords 438
Encryption 292, 470
End Task 67
Environment for Software to Function 40
Ergonomic Concepts 17
Escalate the Problem 91
Establish a Plan of Action 91
Establish a Theory of Probable Cause 89
Ethernet Connector 242
EULA 130
Executables 312
Executing Programs 23
Expansion Bus 216
Expectations of Privacy 480, 482
Exploit 442
ext4 291
Extended Partition 290
Extension 298, 371
External Hard Drive 280
External Issues 94

F

Factors (Authentication) 465
Fair Use Policy 480
Fan 219
FAT 291
Fault Tolerance 433
Fiber Optic 348
File 41, 298
File and Print Sharing 390
File Attribute 304
File Backups 398
File Download 393
File Explorer 53, 295
File History 400
File Server 387
File System 290
Financial Software 138
Fingerprint Reader 467
Firewall 378
Firewire 228
Firmware 44, 220
Flash 369
Flash Memory 284
Flat File Systems 180
Flat-panel/Flat-screen 254
Float 114
Flow Chart Concepts 146
Fob 466
Folder 41, 293, 298
Folder and File Permissions 305
Folder and File Size 304
Folder Options 300
Follow Manufacturer Safety Guidelines 15
Foreign Key 182
Forward Button 60
FQDN 339
Free Networks 366
Freeware 131
Frequency 401
FTP 393
Full Device Encryption 413
Function Keys 235
Functions 154

G

Gaming Console 12
Gather Information 89
GB 112
Gbps 113
Gesture-based Interaction 411
GHz 113, 215
GPU 211
Graphic Design 138
Graphics Adapter 229
Group 465
Guest 464
GUI 66

H

Handling Confidential Information 479
Hard Disk 210, 279
Hardware 4, 111
Hardware Compatibility 40, 48
Hardware Failure 428
Hardware Token 466
Hash 472
HDMI 230
Heatsink 218
Help and Support 96
Help Desk 499
Hexadecimal 111
HFS 291
Hidden Attribute 304
History 60
Home Appliances 11
Home Automation 11
Home Page 61
Home Page Redirection 368
Host Firewall 378
Hosted Storage 393
Hot Keys 28
HTML 341, 393
HTTP 341, 393
HTTPS 342, 377
Hyperlink 59
Hypervisor 44

I

I/O Port 226
Icon 30
Identifiers 151
Identify Symptoms 88
Identifying the Problem 87
Identity Fraud 431
Image File Types 138, 311
IMAP 343
Implement the Solution 92
Implicit Deny 462
Information 121
Information as Assets 117
Input 5
Input Device 233
Installing Applications 125
Installing Peripherals 250
Instant Messaging 136
Instant Search 307
Instruction Set 215
Integer 114
Integrity 427
Intel 213
Intellectual Property 118
Interface Between Applications and Hardware 40
Interface Between User and Computer 40
Interfaces 66
Interference 356
Internal Storage Device 279
Internet 332
Internet Cache 376
Internet Explorer 58
Internet of Things 11
Internet Options 61
Internet Search Engine 98
Internet Use 480
Interpreted Languages 149
In-vehicle Computing Systems 12
Investing in Security 117
iOS 50
IP 335
IP Address 335
IP Cameras 11
ISO 9600 291
ISP 330

J

Java 369
JavaScript 369
Journaling 292

K

KB 112
Kbps 113
Kernel 40
Key/Value Pair Databases 184
Keyboard 28, 233, 235, 237
Keyboard Regionalization 237
Keyword 98
Kill Process 67
Kinetics 411

L

LAN 330
Language Options 237
Laptop 9, 16
LCD 254
Least Privilege 75, 462
Legacy Browsers 366

Libraries 296
License 130
Limitations (File System) 292
Linux 51
Liquid Cooling 220
Local Share 296
Local Storage 387
Lock Screen 19
Lock Symbol 377
Locking Workstation 431
Logical Drive 290
Logs 463
Looping 153
Loose Connections 94

M

MAC 462
MAC Address 337
macOS 49
Mail Server 343
Malware 439
Man-in-the-Middle 427
Manufacturer Website/Documentation 95
Markup Languages 150
MB 112
Mbps 113
Meaningful Reporting 122
Medical Devices 12
Memory 277
Memory Card 284
Memory Management 70
MHz 113, 215
Microphone 261
MIDI 261
Minimum Requirements 125
Mobile Applications 414
Mobile Device Encryption 413
Mobile Device OS 42
Mobile Device Synchronization 418
Mobile Media Player 284
Mobile Phone 10
Modern Cars 12
Monitor Level 17
Monitor Types 254
Motherboard 212, 226
Mouse 26, 234, 236
Moving Files 301
MTBF 279
Multifactor Authentication 468
Multimedia 261
Multitouch 411

N

Naming Rules 292
Navigating a File Structure 293, 295
Navigating with Hot Keys 28
Need To Know Policy 462
Network 54, 330
Network Attached Storage 387
Network Drives 391
Network Media 331, 347
Network Prefix 336
Network Printing 388
Network Redundancy 434
NFC 241
NIC 211, 241
Non-repudiation 463
Notational Systems 110
Notification Area 21
NTFS 291
n-Tier 188
Numeric Keypad 233

O

Objects 155
OEM 10, 500
Off-site Backup 397
Onboard NIC 211
One-time Password 466
One-time Purchase 131
Online Workspace 134
Open (File) 299
Open Access Point 351
Open Source 42, 51, 131
Open Wi-FI vs Secure Wi-Fi 366
Open Wireless Authentication 354
Operating System 4, 40, 111
Operating System Updates 453
Operating System Vulnerability 442
Operators 154
Optical Drive 281
Optical Mouse 234
OS Features 129
OS Restore 399
Output 5

P

Packet Transmission 332
Pagefile 71
Partition 290
Passphrase 353
Password 465
Password Best Practices 474
Password Cracking 473
Password Manager 474
Password Reset 475
Passwords 479
Paste 301
Patches 452
Patents 120
PB 112
PC 6
PC Technician 498, 500
PCI 216
PCI Express 216
PDF 310
Peer-to-Peer File Sharing 396
Pen 239
Permissions 186, 292, 305, 462
Personal Email 480
Personal Information Manager 134
Personalization 257
Personally Owned Devices 481
Personnel Management Policies 478
Phishing 378, 449
Physical Damage 94
PII 372, 479
Pinch-to-Zoom 411
Piracy 130
PKI 377, 471
Platform 158
Plug-and-Play 250
Plugging In Cables 15
Plug-in 371
Pointing Device 234
Policies and Procedures 478
POP3 343
Pop-up 373
Pop-up Blocker 374
POST 19, 94
Power 94
Power Outage 428
Power Redundancy 434
Powering On Computer 15
PowerShell 157
Presentation 133, 310
Pre-shared Key 353
Preventive Measures 92
Primary Key 182
Primary Partition 290
Principle of Least Privilege 462

Print Queue.................266
Printer.........................264
Printer Installation 265
Printing Preferences ...267
Prioritization 435
Privacy...............372, 374
Privacy Policy 481
Private Browsing Mode 376
Procedures 154
Process Management...67
Processes.....................67
Processing......................5
Processing Speed.......113
Processor Speed 215
Product ID...................130
Product Key 130
Productivity Software ..132
Profile..........................296
Program Files 293
Programmatic Access.187
Programming 145
Programming Languages 148
Programs and Features 128
Project Management...138
Projector 256
Proper Keyboard and Mouse Placement.........17
Proprietary 131
Protection......................74
Protocol.......................331
Proxy Settings.............381
Pseudocode................147
Public Folder...............296
Public Workstations 366

Q

Quarantining Viruses .446, 447
Query..........................179
Query Languages 150
Query/Report Builder..187
Question the Obvious ...89
Question Users 88
Quick Launch................21

R

Radio Frequency 351
RAM...................210, 277
Ransomware..............442
RBAC..........................462
Reading Agreements ..130
Reading Instructions ...125
Read-only Attribute 304
Recognizing a Secure Connection 377
Recognizing Invalid Certificates 377
Recognizing Suspicious Links.......................... 378
Recognizing Untrusted Source Warnings........ 371
Record 179
Recycle Bin 302
Refresh Button 60
Regional and Language Options...................... 237
Registration................ 131
Registry 66
Regular Anti-virus Scans 445
Reinstallation............. 128
Relational Databases . 181
Relational Methods 185
Relationship of Data to Information 121
Remote Backup.......... 419
Remote Desktop Software 135
Remote Support......... 498
Remote Wipe 412
Removable Storage ... 284
Removal of Malicious Software.................... 446
Renaming Files 300
Replication 434
Report 179
Reporting Problems 97
Research Knowledge Base/Internet................ 89
Resolution 229
Restoring Access 435
Restoring Data 402
RF 241
Right-click.................... 26
Risks of Automatic Updates..................... 453
RJ-11 242
RJ-45 242
Root Cause 91
Rootkit....................... 441
ROSI 117
Router 338, 347, 358
Rows/Records........... 181
RPM 279
RSI 17
RTOS 43
Rules of Behavior....... 480

S

S/PDIF 261
Safe Browsing Practices 366
SATA 280
Satellite.......................349
Save 299
Scanner 268
Scheduled Scans........445
Scheduling..................401
Schema 182
Screen Lock 412
Screen Resolution 257
Screen Saver.............431
Screen Sharing Software 135
Scripted Language 149
Scripting 369
Scripting Languages...156
SD Card......................284
SDRAM 277
Search Engine........98, 99
Search Engine Redirection 368
Search Utility 307
Secret Key.................470
Sector 279
Securing Devices........438
Security 426
Security Certificate 377
Security Control..........117
Security Questions 465
Security Systems..........11
Security Updates 455
Selecting Icons 304
Semi-structured Databases 183
Sequence 145
Serial Number 130
Server....................8, 330
Server OS....................42
Service Outage...........428
Service Pack 452, 453
Services.......................68
Setting WEP vs WPA vs WPA2 353
Settings App 55
Setup 15
SFTP 393
Shake 31
Shareware 131
Shell 40, 73
Shortcuts 30
Shoulder Surfing.........431
Sign In 19
Signal Strength...........356
Silverlight....................369
Single Factor 468
Single Sign-On 469
Single Use License.....130

Single-platform Software ... 158
Sitting Position ... 17
SMART ... 279
Smart Card ... 466
Smartphone ... 10
SMP ... 216
SMTP ... 343
Snap ... 31
Snooping ... 426
Social Engineering ... 429
Social Media ... 480
Software ... 4, 111
Software Compatibility ... 40
Software Exploitation ... 442
Software Installation Best Practices ... 125
Software Registration ... 131
Software Sources ... 452
Software Token ... 466
Software Version Identification ... 127
SOHO ... 347
Solid State Drive ... 280
Somewhere You Are Authentication ... 467
Sound Card ... 261
Spam ... 448
Speakers ... 261
Specialized Software ... 137
Specific Location ... 467
Speech Recognition ... 411
Speed (CPU) ... 215
Speed Limitations ... 356
Spinning Disk ... 279
Spreadsheet ... 132, 310
Spyware ... 368, 441
SSD ... 210, 280
SSID ... 352
SSL ... 342, 377
Standard User ... 74, 76
Start Menu ... 21
Start Screen ... 23, 25
Stop Button ... 60
Storage ... 5
Stores for Mobile Apps ... 414
Streaming Media ... 11
String ... 114
Structured Databases ... 181
Stylus ... 235, 239
Subnet Mask ... 336
Subscription ... 131
Support Concepts ... 86
Surround Sound ... 261
Surveillance ... 481
Suspicious Links ... 378
Swiping ... 411
Switch ... 347, 356
Symmetric Encryption ... 470
System Attribute ... 304
System Board ... 212
System Cooling ... 218
System Folder ... 293
System Health and Functionality ... 41
System Updates ... 452

T

Tables ... 181
Tablet ... 10
Task Manager ... 67
Task Scheduler ... 69
Taskbar ... 21
TB ... 112
Tbps ... 113
TCP/IP ... 332
Technical Community Groups ... 97
Technical Support ... 97
Telephone Connector ... 242
Telepresence ... 137
Temporary Internet Files ... 376
Test a Theory of Probable Cause ... 91
Test Page ... 267
TFT ... 254
Thermal Paste ... 218
Thermostats ... 11
This PC ... 54
Threads ... 67
Thumb Drive ... 284
Thunderbolt ... 231
Time Out ... 431
TLS ... 342
Token ... 466
Touch Interface ... 411
Touchpad ... 26, 235
Touchscreen ... 255, 260
Track ... 279
Tracking ... 463
Trademarks ... 120
Transfer Rate ... 279
Trojan Horse ... 441
Troubleshooting ... 86
Troubleshooting Methodology ... 86
Trust ... 430
Types of OS ... 42

U

UAV ... 12
UDF ... 291
UEFI ... 44
Unauthorized Information Alteration ... 427
Unicode ... 116
Uninstalling Unneeded Software ... 128
Units of Measure ... 112
Unlocking/Security ... 412
Unstructured Databases ... 183
Untrusted Source Warnings ... 371
Update ... 452
Updating Anti-virus Software ... 455
URL ... 59, 340, 343, 378
Usage of Database ... 179
USB ... 227
USB Drive ... 284
User ... 464
User Account 74, 76, 464, 465
User Account Control ... 75
User Account Types ... 464
User Interface/Utility Access ... 187
Users Folder ... 293, 296
Using the PC ... 19, 26
Utility ... 40

V

Variables ... 151
VBScript ... 157
Vector ... 152
Verify Full System Functionality ... 92
Verifying a Wired Connection ... 349
Verifying Internet Connectivity ... 349
Version Identification ... 127
VGA ... 229, 233
Video Card ... 229
Video Conferencing ... 137
Video File Types ... 311
Virtual Memory ... 71
Virtualization ... 44
Virus ... 439
Virus Disinfection 446, 447
Visual Diagramming Software ... 133
VoIP ... 136
Volatile Storage ... 279
Volatile versus Non-volatile Storage ... 277, 279
Volume ... 263
VPN ... 473
VTC ... 137

W

WAN 330
Web Application..........158
Web Browser 58
Web Browser Software
.....................................132
Web Threat.................366
Webcam......................264
WEP............................353
Wi-Fi........................... 351
Window 31
Windows................. 18, 46
Windows Explorer 53, 295
Windows Firewall 379
Windows Folder 293
Windows Phone 48
Windows Settings......... 55
Windows Troubleshooting Tools 95
Windows Update 453
Wired/Wireless NIC 211
Wireless......................351
Wiretapping 426
Word Processing 133, 310
Workgroup..................389
Workstation 6
Workstation OS 42
Worm..........................439
WPA 353

This page left blank intentionally.

ISBN-13 978-164274-089-9
ISBN-10 1-64274-089-6